THE BEST AMERICAN SHORT PLAYS 1992 1994

THE BEST AMERICAN SHORT PLAYS 1992 – 1994

Edited by

Howard Stein and Glenn Young

Best Short Plays Series

GARDEN CITY, NEW YORK

THE BEST AMERICAN SHORT PLAYS 1992–1993

Edited by

Howard Stein and Glenn Young

Best American Short Plays Series

AN APPLAUSE ORIGINAL
THE BEST AMERICAN SHORT PLAYS 1992–1993

ISBN 1-56865-144-9

Manufactured in the United States of America

Applause Theatre Book Publishers

211 West 71st Street
New York, NY 10023
Phone: (212) 595-4735
Fax: (212) 721-2856

406 Vale Road
Tonbridge KENT TN9 1XR
Phone: 0732-357755
Fax: 0732-770219

First Applause Printing, 1993

To Marianne, always

CONTENTS

WRITING AMERICAN DRAMA

For more than half of this century, the playwrights writing for the American theater had models of excellence and form which gave them heart, muscle, courage, and stamina. Those models were Henrik Ibsen, August Strindberg, and Noel Coward. Ibsen and Strindberg, with their emphasis on middle-class people talking in middle-class language about middle-class problems, was easily translatable to the America of the twenties, thirties, forties, and fifties. Noel Coward, with his emphasis on upper-class population and their manners in Britain, was easily translatable into the Main Line of Philip Barry and the Park Avenue set of S.N. Behrman. O'Neill used Strindberg so that his own plays *Before Breakfast, The First Man,* and *Welded,* are absolute replications of works by Strindberg. Miller used Ibsen to the point of literally adapting Ibsen's play, *An Enemy of the People,* for a Broadway production in December of 1950. The available models of both excellence and form provided not only inspiration and security but also considerable uniformity among the plays written during those decades.

Then came the major voices of Samuel Beckett and Eugene Ionesco, heard first in the middle fifties and then building into a low roar by the end of the decade. Those voices, however, were not nearly so accessible to either the playwrights or the audience (including critics). Arthur Miller told a group of students at Yale that he had great difficulty as well as impatience with Samuel Beckett and *Waiting for Godot.* Walter Kerr, critic for *The New York Herald Tribune,* wrote in his review of *Waiting for Godot,* that Beckett had the mind of a child. Can one imagine playwrights such as Paddy Chayefsky, Robert Anderson, Lillian Hellman, William Inge, those playwrights who along with Miller and Tennessee Williams were the major talents of that decade, seeking solace and support from identification with Beckett or Ionesco? Playwrights writing social, psychological, and even poetic realism were certain to find those two radical voices falling on unsympathetic ears. But not so for the new crop emerging: Arthur Kopit, Jack Richardson, Jack Gelber, and Edward Albee.

These young talents forged a meaningful camaraderie with Beckett and Ionesco. Their problem, however, was to Americanize such foreign talents, to incorporate these new sounds into the fabric of their drama the way the earlier writers had managed to naturalize foreign talents such as Ibsen, Strindberg, and Coward. They never quite accomplished this mission, nor did those playwrights who followed—writers such as John Guare, David Rabe, Sam Shepard, David Mamet, Christopher Durang, Ted Talley, and Albert Innaurato. Rather than have models of excellence and form, these playwrights gained other qualities from their predecessors.

What they gained was the audacity to be inventive, imaginative, outrageous, and daring. They did not follow any particular kind of sound or form established by either Beckett or Ionesco. But what did emerge from the music halls of Beckett and the anarchic originality of Ionesco was the license to be wild. The playwrights were free to be as surreal as their fancies dictated. And the prevailing form that came from that marvelous release was the cartoon.

In the seventies, the cartoon became a viable form for the playwright's model. With a semblance of realism still lingering, the cartoon provided the liberty to fly into the surreal wilderness. It was the American departure from realism. All the playwrights mentioned above (Guare, et. al.) as well as Rochelle Owens, Rosalyn Drexler, Maria Irene Fornes, were set free to illuminate what Ionesco has called, "the malaise of being," that which Alexander Pope referred to as "this long disease, my life." The theater was host to practicing cartoonists: Jules Feiffer, Art Buchwald, Al Capp, and Gary Trudeau. The cartoon seemed to provide the most accessible model of form, a surrealistic depiction of the American reality, 1979–1985.

Yet neither the cartoons nor the experiments that tumbled from the imitators of Beckett and Ionesco galvanized the writers under any one convenient banner of excellence and form. Playwrights were essentially now more on their own than ever before. They were forced or freed to create their own individual forms, no holds barred. But form itself was no longer the familiar "arousing and fulfilling of expectation," as posited by Kenneth Burke. A playwright might in fact completely reject the notion of dramatic form as another false promise of order where none can be truthfully sustained. The history of the last third of the twentieth century has not been a primer for the rational order of existence. Instead of making order out of chaos as Burke would have us do, the contemporary playwright might unselfconsciously offer us a chaotic treatment of chaos. Why should the form of a play deliberately mislead the audience? For a playmaker to offer logic and reason in a world informed by accident and chance is to lie to the receiver.

All of this speculation is by way of describing this year's volume of sixteen plays by sixteen playwrights, all of whom had the first public presentation of their plays after 1960. The plays are different from one another in an absolute sense despite some connecting tissue. Susan Miller uses Thornton Wilder's play, *Our Town,* in order to write her own 1990's version, *It's Our Town, Too.* Similarly Regina Taylor uses Langston Hughes' creation, Jess Semple, from *Semple Takes a Wife,* which was adapted into a play (1956) called *Simply Heavenly,* as a means of responding to the present day situation dramatized in *Watermelon Rinds.* Billy Aronson takes the fairy tale that has come down to us through the Brothers Grimm and reworks that earlier story into his own *Little Red Riding Hood,* in order to illuminate the American reality of 1992. Ionesco provides energy and vision to John Ford Noonan for his treatment of modern day society in his play, *The Drowning of Manhattan.* In Stephen Starosta's *The Sausage Eaters* we encounter an American version of Ionesco's powerful humor. Echoes of Ionesco can also be heard in Tony Connor's fantasy *A Couple With a Cat,* as well as in the imaginative game playing of Murray Schisgal's *The Cowboy, The Indian and The Fervent Feminist.*

Cartoon techniques also provide strength and character in those plays of Connor and Schisgal, but the cartoon is even more in evidence in Shel Silverstein's *Dreamers. Show* by Victor Bumbalo owes much of its energy and boldness to Tennessee Williams and Edward Albee, but its vision is closer to that of Beckett and Ionesco than it is to any other playwrights. On the other hand, *The Valentine Fairy,* of Ernest Thompson is much more connected to Tennessee Williams and William Inge and seems quite separate from either Beckett or Ionesco. Mamet's play, *Jolly,* a conventional family scene treated in a totally unconventional dramatic fashion, seems to have taken Beckett to heart more completely than any other script in the volume. By the same token, no playwright in this book has taken Pirandello so much to heart as has David Hwang in his play, *Bondage,* a drama which explores J. Alfred Prufrock's observation that "there will be time, there will be time/ To prepare a face to meet the faces that you meet." Donald Margulies with his play, *Pitching to the Star,* Gabriel Tissian with his play, *Night Baseball,* and Ralph Arzoomanian with his play, *The Tack Room,* all use a recognizable, representational, even somewhat conventional population to dramatize their stories. But they also have plays with grim conclusions, with what Toby Zinman has recognized as sit-trag. "A sit-trag," says Zinman, "is a fine play about the triumph of sleaze, presenting life as an empty formula without moral or aesthetic possibilities." Such a vision might equally apply to Elizabeth Page's *Aryan Birth.*

And yet, despite all this diversity, there is indeed one unifying feature of all sixteen plays: laughter. All of the plays are constructed with humor as a major element in the drama, and that humor for the most part is ironic. Dick, the producer in *Pitching to the Star* says over and over again, "funny is money." But money is not the only reason for the playwright's being funny. Duerenmatt said as early as 1954 that a playwright could not write tragedy in this day and age without writing it comedically. He objected to a grim treatment of his play, *The Visit,* and demanded that the production be funny. Humor plays a special role in the drama of the latter part of this century. It seems to be our single source of salvation, and the playwrights included in this volume are no exception to their time. They all feel and express their uncertain romance with the universe with the help of laughter, echoing what Beckett refers to in *Happy Days,* as "laughing wild amidst severest woe." The playwrights collected here know what they are talking and laughing about.

HOWARD STEIN
Columbia University
September, 1993

LITTLE RED RIDING HOOD

Billy Aronson

Billy Aronson

Billy Aronson's theatrical life has considerable energy and variety to it, an energy and variety that is matched by his personal life as well. Having graduated from Princeton and then been accepted in playwriting at the Yale School of Drama, Aronson took a leave of absence at the end of his first year at Yale in order to join Vista, the domestic version of the Peace Corps. He was assigned to rural North Carolina where he functioned as a community educator for legal services, and where he created a newspaper item titled, "Plain Talk". He returned to Yale after that service and completed his MFA in playwriting.

Aronson is interested in plain talk, as his plays demonstrate. His plays have been featured at Home (Lunatic Fringe Festival), the Public (No Shame Festival), the American Place (Women's Project), Ensemble Studio Theater (New Voices), Alice's Fourth Floor, The Edinburgh Festival, Manhattan Class Company, Manhattan Punch Line, The National Theater Workshop of the Handicapped and others. His play at the American Place was a cabaret piece titled, *The Snicker Factor,* an appropriate piece for a political cabaret. Directed by Liz Diamond, that piece is a representative reflection of Aronson's preoccupation with political, social and aesthetic concerns.

His latest project, *Twisted Tales,* includes *Little Red Riding Hood* (published here for the first time), *Jack and the Beanstalk* (a version informed by economics), and *The Sleeping Beauty* (a version informed by the Nine Blessings devoted to Art). He also writes comic material for television, magazines and funny science books. Much of Aronson's inspiration comes from opera as well as a healthy habit of reading. He lives in Brooklyn, New York with his wife, Lisa Vogel, and their son, Jake.

Characters:

LITTLE RED RIDING HOOD

MOTHER

BIG BAD WOLF

HUNTER

GRANDMOTHER

Scene 1

Little Red Riding Hood and her Mother.

MOTHER: This fresh fruit pie should help make Grandmom strong again, don't you think, Red?

RED: Yes, Mother.

MOTHER: Let's add a warm muffin for the woman who made my bed and kissed me goodnight.

RED: Yes, Mother.

MOTHER: Let's stuff the muffin with a stone so she'll choke.

RED: Yes, Mother.

MOTHER: That woman said I was worthless, Red.

RED: I understand, Mother.

MOTHER: When she chokes force this wine between her lips 'til she gags.

RED: Yes, Mother.

MOTHER: She banged my head against a cupboard.

RED: I understand.

MOTHER: But she sure could soothe me to sleep with a bedtime story. So lean Grandmom forward and pat her back 'til she coughs up the stone.

RED: Yes, Mother.

MOTHER: Apologize to the woman who gave birth to your Mother.

RED: Yes, Mother.

MOTHER: Then smash her head with a chair.

RED: Yes, Mother.

MOTHER: On second thought, it would be a shame to smash Grandmom when she's already suffering so. Let's wait 'til she's feeling better to choke her and smash her. For now just bring her the goodies.

RED: Yes, Mother.

MOTHER: Stay on the open path the whole way, don't wander into the woods.

RED: I won't, Mother.

MOTHER: If a stranger pokes his head out ignore him.

RED: I will, Mother.

MOTHER: Move in a smooth steady step and he won't even notice you.

RED: I will.

MOTHER: Eyes ahead. Face down. What's that ugly frown? We're talking about keeping the stranger at a distance, not disgusting him.

RED: All right, Mother.

MOTHER: If he smells like a toad he's a king. Kiss his lips.

RED: I will, Mother.

MOTHER: Don't suck his tongue or he'll turn into a dwarf who'll haul you to his hovel and you'll never be heard from again.

RED: I understand.

MOTHER: If he tries to touch you scream.

RED: I will.

MOTHER: If he doesn't try to touch you put his hand on your breast.

RED: I will.

MOTHER: If he enjoys touching you he's a hideous gnome. Run like crazy.

RED: I will.

MOTHER: If he charms you he's a prince. Stab him to death.

RED: I will, Mother.

MOTHER: Stab him right to death or he'll carry you to his castle and you'll never be heard from again.

RED: I will, Mother.

MOTHER: Unless he's a handsome prince.

RED: Okay.

MOTHER: In that case ignore him completely so he'll follow you forever.

RED: I will.

MOTHER: What are we saying. You're too young to talk to strangers. Go straight to Grandmom's.

RED: Bye bye.

MOTHER: You're going?

RED: To Grandmom's.

MOTHER: How dare you desert me.

RED: Sorry, Mother.

MOTHER: You'll stay? Oh wonderful. Help me with my chores?

RED: All right, Mother.

MOTHER: First, take these goodies to your Grandmother's.

RED: All right, Mother.

MOTHER: Wait. There are dangers out there. Not if she stays on the path. But if she strays from the path. She won't stray. She might stray. Stay.

RED: All right.

MOTHER: You're sitting? Don't cling to your Mother.

RED: All right.

MOTHER: Sit down, I'm talking to you.

RED: All right, Mother.

MOTHER: It's a beautiful day. Get some sunshine.

RED: Okay.

MOTHER: Better yet, run these goodies over to your Grandmother's.

RED: I will. (*Red exits*)

MOTHER: I knew one day she'd leave.

Scene 2

Little Red Riding Hood and the Big Bad Wolf.

WOLF: Nice hat. You from around here?

RED: Yeah.

WOLF: It's a pretty area.

RED: Your woods seem nice.

WOLF: Much cooler.

RED: Don't get much light I guess.

WOLF: Less light. Lots of space. Good location.

RED: It is.

WOLF: Fine view.

RED: You call it woods or wood?

WOLF: Woods, wood, forest . . .

RED: Both.

WOLF: Don't ask me what a thicket is. Come sit in the shade.

RED: No thanks.

WOLF: I like your basket.

RED: It's my Mom's.

WOLF: Can I see?

RED: I have to get to my Grandmother's.

WOLF: That's your Grandmother?

RED: You know her?

WOLF: Down at the end of the road, right at the fork—

RED: Left—

WOLF: Yeah, left, 'til you pass the lake—

RED: Right before the lake.

WOLF: What's the number on her door . . . ?

RED: Four.

WOLF: Right. Sweet woman.

RED: She's been sick.

WOLF: She has seemed kind of . . . unwell.

RED: Does your face sweat a lot?

WOLF: No more than yours.

RED: How far out do your claws come?

WOLF: Tah dah.

RED: Gleaming needles.

WOLF: I keep them clean.

RED: They're so long.

WOLF: Thank you.

RED: I've never seen such big teeth.

WOLF: I've never seen such smooth bare hands. How do you make them glow like that?

RED: I don't know. (*Red slaps her ankle*)

RED: Mosquito.

WOLF: I'll scratch it for you.

RED: No thanks.

WOLF: It's the least I can do. You wouldn't have been bitten if you hadn't stopped to talk with me.

RED: Somebody scratching somebody else's bite?

WOLF: When you scratch yourself you can't fully enjoy the relief. Let me have your leg. Come on. Pull up the cape. Up, I don't want to tear it. Slide down the sock. Relax.

RED: Ow. Ee.

WOLF: Now with the teeth.

RED: Ooo—Stop. Someone could see. What would . . .

WOLF: You're right.

RED: So.

WOLF: The itch is gone, right?

RED: Just a little dot of blood.

WOLF: Are you blushing?

RED: No.

WOLF: Your face is as red as your hood.

RED: That's the way it goes.

WOLF: So how about a tour of the woods?

RED: Oh no.

WOLF: You're sure?

RED: I have to get to Grandmom's house.

WOLF: I should be going too. But let me give you some advice. You walk too fast. Take some time to admire all the beautiful flowers along the path. Pick your Grandmother a bouquet.

(*Wolf goes. Red plucks flowers*)

RED: Staring at the sun. Sobbing little drops. Pluck. Gripping the dirt. Soft little stem. Pluck. Whispering? Shh. Pluck. Pluck. Blue. Pluck. Purple. Pluck. Pink. Pluck. Pluck. Pluck. Pluck.

Scene 3

The Hunter sits, is served by the Mother.

HUNTER: Where's my slab o' steak?

MOTHER: Coming dear.

HUNTER: If a hunter doesn't have his slab o' steak he can't grab his gun and if he can't grab his gun he can't blast the beasts and if he can't blast the beasts how's he gonna market their meats if he can't market their meats there's no way he can house his spouse and if he can't house his spouse then where's he supposed to eat his slab o' steak, in the gosh darn mud crap slop?

MOTHER: You didn't get one of your arms into your shirt, dear.

HUNTER: Sure you miss a sleeve now and then or sometimes you forget to button a few buttons, but what about the sleeve you did get into the shirt, what about the buttons you did button. I'm sick and tired of people who always focus on the empty sleeve or the unbuttoned button—

MOTHER: Your fly's open.

HUNTER: —or the opened fly, when the fact is if the truth be known when push comes to shove it's the people with the unbuttoned buttons and unsleeved arms who are out there not looking at the lookers who are looking at them but just plain out there being out there. I'm out there.

MOTHER: I know you're out there, dear.

HUNTER: I'm the one who faces the heat and the snow and the dirt—and let me tell you it gets dirty—so I can brave the hills and the lakes and the pebbles—which inevitably get in your boots—to grapple with the branches and the ragweed and the pollen—'til I'm sneezin' my head off—don't make me remind you about the time I got poison oak all across the cheeks o' my butt—do you have any idea how filthy my toenails get by the end of the day?—and why? So I can shoot the beasts that make the coats that coat the backs of the very people who stand there staring at my empty sleeve when they should have been paying more attention to the arm in their own back yard in the first place.

MOTHER: There's grease on your nose and steak on your forehead, and your fork is lodged behind your ear.

HUNTER: What's a drop o' grease on a hunter's nose for the sake of his home, or a fork in his ear for his family? I love this fork and I love this family and let me tell you something, sister, I may have a slab of greasy beef suspended from my brow but that won't stop me from pumping ten ounces of lead into a fat-assed quadruped at close range because it's a dog eat dog jungle in that forest.

MOTHER: You're tangled up in the chair, dear.

HUNTER: Of course there'll be a few tangled chairs along the way. A night in hell is no picnic.

MOTHER: You've put your head through the table.

HUNTER: You're darn straight there are gonna be a few heads stuck in a handful of tables, but you can rest assured that when I feel the fresh air in my lungs I'll be thanking God I live in a house where I have the right to shove my foot through a chair and bash my head through a table and ram a fork in my ear—

MOTHER: It's in your eye now.

HUNTER: —in my eye if I want so I can go out and fetch my family a sack of juicy shanks.

MOTHER: And a new table.

HUNTER: And a new table.

MOTHER: And a chair.

HUNTER: And a chair.

MOTHER: And some eggs.

HUNTER: Did you make a list?

MOTHER: See you at supper.

(*Hunter's rifle goes off as he struggles to get through the door with the chair on his leg. Mother shakes her head and smiles*)

Scene 4

Grandmother in her bed.

GRANDMOTHER: Yecch. (*Spits*) I'm spitting up my rotten guts. Where's my lousy bowl. Have to crawl to the cupboard on my throbbing knees. Can't open the latch with my cracked-up knuckles. Back to the bed for that worthless ointment. Can't grip the cap in my rotten wrecked-up teeth, where's my busted tweezers. Lousy bowl was right here the whole time. Useless eyes. Yecch. (*Spits*) Missed.

(*A knock at the door*)

GRANDMOTHER: Knock knock yourself.

WOLF: It's Little Red Riding Hood with a snack from Mother.

GRANDMOTHER: Couldn't keep down a snack if I wanted to.

WOLF: There's a pie and a muffin . . .

GRANDMOTHER: Leave me alone.

WOLF: and some wine . . .

GRANDMOTHER: Get in here. 'Snot locked.

(*Wolf enters*)

WOLF: Into the closet. I'm here to eat your Granddaughter.

GRANDMOTHER: You discriminate against the aged?

WOLF: I'll eat you later.

GRANDMOTHER: Right now, or I don't budge.

WOLF: Sorry but I'm going to relax now, to get ready for Little Red.

GRANDMOTHER: You could put an end to every ache in my body in an instant and I demand you do it.

WOLF: I'm a wolf, not a charity worker. I'll get to you when I feel like it.

GRANDMOTHER: You'll never eat me, I know it. I'll keep getting more dumb and decrepit 'til there isn't a tooth left in my—ocean? teaspoon? and I can't even get myself up out of the—soldier? celery? —Oh stitch. I'm losing my ability to think of the right word to plant. I can hardly pair. Please shove me into your three and cloud me. Chew my worthless green and my aching born and my throbbing hilltop into a thousand tiny candle. This is knit. Look at my tree. Are you glorious? Blades are streaming down my sun and it's all because you won't open up your jolly is. I'm begging on my bended how.

WOLF: Old ladies are a pain in my ass. Okay, I'll eat you if—

GRANDMOTHER: Huh?

WOLF: I'll eat you—

GRANDMOTHER: What?

WOLF: I'll—

GRANDMOTHER: Now I can hardly hear a word you flay. There's just this loud table. I'm losing my powder. I'm going as.

WOLF (*into her ear*): I'll eat you if you hand me your shawl.

GRANDMOTHER: Greetings.

(*She hands him her shawl, crawls under the sheets. Wolf crawls under, eats her, emerges in her shawl*)

Scene 5

Red and the Wolf.

RED: Grandmom?

WOLF: Come on in, honey. Shut the door. Get comfy. Surprise.

RED: Hi.

WOLF: Hi.

RED: How've you been?

WOLF: Thinking about you. How have you been?

RED: Since Grandmom's gone we can have a muffin.

WOLF: I would love a muffin.

RED: Okay.

WOLF: How'd it get smushed?

RED: My Mother put a stone in and took it out again.

WOLF: Why'd she do that? Anyway, it's a delicious muffin.

RED: You looked weird in Grandmom's shawl.

WOLF: Did I surprise you?

RED: Uh, no.

WOLF: I was afraid if you saw me right when you walked in you might run. You seemed so bashful before.

RED: I picked flowers like you said.

WOLF: Very pretty.

RED: You like this place?

WOLF: Nice light. I live in a hole. What?

RED: Huh?

WOLF: I thought you were going to say something.

RED: Oh no. When I'm in your stomach will I be alive?

WOLF: You'll be unconscious.

RED: For how long?

WOLF: A few minutes. Then you run out of air. But you won't feel anything at that point.

RED: No one's woken up and couldn't breathe?

WOLF: Not that I know of.

RED: Couldn't you kill me with your teeth on the way in?

WOLF: It's better for me if I swallow you whole. And for you too. Less mess.

RED: Should I get undressed?

WOLF: Just take off your shoes.

RED: How was Grandmom?

WOLF: I prefer kids.

RED: On the bed?

WOLF: Sure.

(*They go to the bed*)

WOLF: I really do like that hat.

RED: I'm now scared.

WOLF: Don't be.

(*He eats her, falls asleep*)

Scene 6

The Hunter enters followed by the Mother.

MOTHER: She always comes straight home.

HUNTER: Would you pipe the heck down with your pointless panic before you work yourself up—See? There's her basket and her shoes and the Wolf—into a dizzy freakin' frenzy. Help Wolf help Wolf.

MOTHER: You've got a gun, he doesn't have a gun. And besides he's fast asleep.

HUNTER: Right. I'm in the perfect position to blast the biggest beast in the forest with the flick of a finger.

MOTHER: Let me cut Little Red from his belly first.

HUNTER: The Big Bad Wolf is mine. Oh yes. Oh good. Oh very good.

(*Hunter sings, as Mother pulls Red and Grandmother from the Wolf's belly and embraces them*)

Oh hooray for my land
And hooray for my clothes
And hooray for my hand
And hooray for my nose

GRANDMOTHER: Eyelid melon Friday.

MOTHER: She's lost her mind, Red. Should we weep? Should we scream? Should we hug her with all our might?

RED: I don't know, Mother.

MOTHER: Should we press her with flowers?

RED: Uhh . . .

MOTHER: Should we bring her the usual goodies?

RED: Uhhh . . .

GRANDMOTHER (*spits*)

MOTHER: Should we make our hands into claws?

RED: I don't know, Mother.

GRANDMOTHER: Screaming hailstones.

HUNTER: C'mon, Wolf. Arise and be blasted.

MOTHER: Should we whip ourselves with belts?

RED: Uhhh . . .

MOTHER: Should we sink in silent horror?

RED: Uhhh . . .

HUNTER: That does it. You leave me no choice but to count backwards from ten.

MOTHER: There's nothing we can do.

HUNTER: Nine.

MOTHER: But it happens to everyone.

HUNTER: Eight.

MOTHER: And the sun still shines for us.

HUNTER: Seven.

MOTHER: And the birds still sing for us.

HUNTER: Six.

RED: I want . . .

HUNTER: Five.

RED: . . . the Wolf.

HUNTER: Four.

MOTHER: But the Wolf will eat you . . .

HUNTER: Three.

MOTHER: . . . to death.

HUNTER: Two.

MOTHER: She wants to be dead.

HUNTER: She wants to be dead?

MOTHER: Talk to her.

HUNTER: I'm about to blast the Wolf.

MOTHER: You can't blast the Wolf 'til you've talked to her.

HUNTER: Listen, young lady. You are a piece of God.

MOTHER: There is no God, dear.

HUNTER: I know that. Listen, young lady. You are a piece of fish.

MOTHER: What he means is—

HUNTER: No one knows what you are.

MOTHER: So it's important to—

HUNTER: A life unlived is a terrible thing to lack.

MOTHER: He means—

HUNTER: You have what you are, but you get what you make.

MOTHER: Although now you feel ugly and stupid—

HUNTER: Your Mother's right.

MOTHER: —rest assured that I've been there, dear.

HUNTER: Your Mother's right.

MOTHER: And I know tomorrow's going to be better.

HUNTER: Your Mother's right.

MOTHER: The day after tomorrow won't be quite as good, but the day after that will be just fine.

HUNTER: She's right.

MOTHER: The weekend will stink.

HUNTER: She's right.

MOTHER: But by the end of the month—

GRANDMOTHER (*silent scream*)

MOTHER: Please, Mother.

HUNTER: What your Mother's trying to say is life's filled with hills but every pitfall has a silver lining.

MOTHER: You see someday—

HUNTER: She's trying to tell you every stormy sea strengthens your spirit.

MOTHER: Because before long—

HUNTER: She's trying to say that with each roadblock your spirit grows stronger and stronger and stronger and stronger—

MOTHER: And then one day you'll look up to see someone walking towards you on the horizon and he'll—

HUNTER: How can this guy walk on a horizon?

MOTHER: —along the horizon and he'll—

HUNTER: If he were walking along the horizon how could he also be walking towards her?

MOTHER: —against the horizon and he'll take you in his—

HUNTER: Oh I get it are you saying that you're here and she's here so the guy's walking towards her along your horizon?

MOTHER: Listen, Red: Life is good, death is bad.

HUNTER: Right. Now hold your ears, ladies.

(*The Hunter shoots several times until the entire room is blasted to bits and the stage is filled with smoke*)

Got him. Probably.

Epilogue

Red pursues the Wolf.

RED: Please eat me again, Mister Wolf. I'll just curl into a little ball and slide right down. Let me in, please please?

WOLF: I can't eat you. I'm dead. So I've really got to be moving on.

RED: Eat me first?

WOLF: No time. Sorry.

RED: It's not fair.

WOLF: Tell me about it.

RED: My heart wants you and my bones want you and my toes want you and my everything wants you.

WOLF: I wanted you, too. Very much. But I can't help you now. Let go.

RED: So what do I do.

WOLF: Live happily ever after, I guess.

RED: Huh.

THE TACK ROOM

Ralph Arzoomanian

To Howard Stein,
in so many more ways than this.

Ralph Arzoomanian

Ralph Arzoomanian was among the first group of O'Neill playwrights back in 1965, a group which included Sam Shepard, John Guare and Lanford Wilson. The next year he was awarded an ABC Fellowship at the Yale School of Drama, and soon after had two of his plays produced off-Broadway, *The Coop* and *The Moths.* Much of his work was subsequently produced at both the Washington Theater Club and the Mark Taper Forum. Four of his plays were published under the title of *Four Plays by Ralph Arzoomanian.* All of his plays reflect that other than real quality of Armenians like William Saroyan, without the sentimentality frequently associated with that group.

Arzoomanian, a native of Rhode Island, now lives in Roxbury, Connecticut. Since 1966, he has been a Professor in the Department of Speech and Theatre of Herbert Lehman College of the City University of New York. He attended Boston University and the University of Iowa, where he received his Ph.D. in 1965. A fan of horse racing for most of his life, he has every intention of underlining Runyon's observation that all horse-players die broke.

Characters:

MEL, *a man in his early seventies. Burly and ethnic*

PAUL, *His nephew. An attorney around forty*

FRENCHY, *A neighborhood "fool". Gaunt in appearance, preferably without teeth, wearing a highly decorated hat, cowboy or straw. He speaks with something of a tinny staccato and carries a message board that hangs from his neck*

Scene

A tavern with the walls covered with photographs, caricatures and newspaper clippings. There is a large display case housing an array of horse racing paraphernalia including trophies.

Time:

The present.

Mel is behind the bar as Frenchy comes through the front entrance. Throughout the 1st half of the play Mel occupies himself doing set-up work around the bar.

MEL: Where's the cranberry juice?

FRENCHY: Couldn't get it, Mister Mel.

MEL: How come?

FRENCHY: That lady knows why.

MEL: That lady—what lady?

FRENCHY: That lady who chased me out of the store.

MEL: Now, why would she do that, Frenchy?

FRENCHY: I don't know that much.

MEL: Come here, closer. (*Mel checks over Frenchy's message board*) Who wrote this garbage on here?

FRENCHY: Miguel.

MEL: And you let him?

FRENCHY: He gave me a buck, Mister Mel.

MEL: Course he did. And what's more, it makes perfect sense. But Frenchy, had you been a good boy in school you would've learned that this word "love" is spelled with an "O" and not a "u". And "eat" here has an "a" in the middle and not two "ees". This one, Frenchy's a mockery of justice. Frenchy, "pussy" doesn't have two "o"s, and it doesn't have one but *two* esses. Got that straight? Well?

FRENCHY (*snappily in his fashion*): Oh-oh, think I'm gonna get a headache!

MEL: Fat chance. There's gotta be an occupant in the penthouse for that to happen. (*There's a rap at the door*) Tell whoever it is we open at three.

(*Frenchy opens the door and Paul enters with a brief salutation to Frenchy. He's nattily dressed in a tennis outfit*)

PAUL: Don't start.

MEL: Who said anything?

PAUL (*posing*): So do you like the look?

MEL: I'd like the look a lot better if I got to look at it more often. Where the hell have you been?

PAUL: Just this once, no complaints. (*Pause, as he cases the tavern*) You're not open for a while?

MEL: Around three, *if* the bartender shows.

PAUL: Good. No one has to know I'm here.

MEL: What's up?

PAUL: I think Frenchy's drawn a blank.

MEL: Well, Frenchy, remember who this is? Mister Very Big-Shot Lawyer himself. Come on, Frenchy, my nephew Paul, you remember him.

FRENCHY: I don't think so, Mister Mel.

MEL: How could you forget? You were his principal in high school.

FRENCHY: I don't know about that.

MEL: What *do* you know about, Frenchy?

FRENCHY: Not much of that, either.

PAUL: My last time through he remembered. Frenchy, I'm crushed.

MEL: Maybe if you showed your face more often—*next* time he would. But Frenchy ain't the whiz kid he used to be so everything goes on the board. Come here, Frenchy. (*Mel writes something on the board*) Directly to the store, no wise guys going or coming. Kabeesh?

(*Frenchy nods*)

PAUL: Frenchy, you fifty yet? Gotta be that.

MEL: He can't remember what hemisphere he's in and you're asking him his age? I thought you were smarter than that.

PAUL: Well take a peek at him!

MEL: Take a peek at him? He's been sporting that puss since his tenth birthday party. It took me sixty years to get mine. Him? The human race should have half his racket.

FRENCHY: It's post time, Mister Mel, time to scoot!

MEL: You just missed the fun, Paul. Wait up, Frenchy. One of the exercise boys just got Frenchy's ass thrown out of the supermarket. It figured. A while back I kept sending him out for bar fruit and he kept bringing back those female tampons. Over and over again. Got so bad the place was climbing the walls with them. So one day I decided to exchange them, get some of my money back. But not so fast. "We don't know they haven't been tampered with," they told me. "Tampered with," I said, "what can you do with those God-damn things—make'm into firecrackers? Do I look like the kind of sicko that would do that to a woman?" No dice. Back all the boxes came. However, I did a little investigating on my own and discovered that the tampon kibitzer was a consistently accurate speller. Every t-a-m-p-o-n, beautiful. Miguel, that guy's life and death to get his name lined up the same way twice. *You,* I've got more when you get back so make it pronto.

FRENCHY: Mister Mel, that lady scared me. She said some meanest things.

MEL: So? If it happens again let her do her bitching on the board. Get out of here.

(*Exit Frenchy*)

PAUL: So you're big brother now.

MEL: Who's gonna do it? None of the old bunch are around. This God, he keeps a very immaculate blackboard.

PAUL: When Mom called me—

MEL: Eight days ago why don't you mention that? Once upon a time next day delivery. (*Sing-songs*) Not anymore. So you're making a buck. Good. But I've got a small problem. I'm all family and you're the only one I got left. Eight days? In eight days I could be picked up for child molesting some old lady, get tried and canned. You want that on your conscience?

PAUL: Conscience? Moi, Uncle Mel? What ever would I do in this line of work with one of those?

MEL: I was getting anxious. Even Frenchy picked up on it.

PAUL: This feeling I've had that Frenchy was history. He's one of those you half expect to get the call about.

MEL: As long as there's a buck to be made on the street? Not my Frenchy. And like Fifth Avenue, the money with him only goes in one direction. Unless it's for a slice of apple pie, no one's ever seen him pop a dime. When it comes to money management he's a genius.

PAUL: You're not suggesting he's an idiot savant.

MEL: No, no, he's no savant anything. Scientifically speaking, he's strictly an idiot type idiot.

(*Paul begins to tour the tavern, handling things as he gets around*)

PAUL: What a joint. Nothing in here ever changes. Frozen in time, space. Every photograph, every poster, clipping, exact spot it's ever been. This stuff in the case . . . my father's stopwatch, forgot about that.

MEL: Take it with you if you like.

PAUL: Naah, leave it where it is.

MEL: If time froze he'd still be training those can't-run-a-lick-horses of his.

PAUL: Could swear he still does when I'm in this mausoleum.

MEL: Mausoleum my foot. And by the way do I look the same as I did thirty five years ago? Aah, they're just pictures. The owners, the trainers, every horse for sure, dead. Anyway, how's your mother?

PAUL: Rita's Rita. She's not mellowing the way I had in mind.

MEL: Still playing house with that Irish beercan?

PAUL: Since when was she a day at the beach? He pays his dues.

MEL: Don't ask me where she finds them. And that includes my brother Joey. It takes a rare individual to transform a perfectly good racehorse into a donkey in just three days, but he could do it. He had a real knack, my brother did.

PAUL: He had a collection of pikers for owners and you know it. If he kissed more rich ass, who knows?

MEL: Trainers can't afford to be proud. He had a barn full of Timexes and he ran them against Rolexes. I've got a closet full of empty bank books to prove it.

PAUL: Except for Bum Rap.

MEL: So you remember Bum Rap.

PAUL (*wryly*): *Do* I?

MEL: Then there's hope for you yet, kid. The day that horse won the Discovery he gave your father the gift of a lifetime. And when they walked him over here that night this joint was like Christmas, New Year's, and VJ Day rolled into one. All of them were here. Arcaro was here, one of the Vanderbilts, Cab Calloway, Willie Pep, Gimpy McAdams, even the mayor. You were too young. You don't remember.

PAUL: Oh, I remember.

MEL: Your father was shitfaced, the owners double shitfaced, the mayor himself. Anyway, they brought along this horse bucket and filled it with top-of-the-line-thirty bottles of beer. And when that bucket was dry the horse was as shitfaced as the rest of them. And when he started singing, that was it, the whole place went up for grabs! Thirty five years later I still get stories about that night.

PAUL: The horse wasn't singing.

MEL: I'm telling you Bum Rap was singing.

PAUL: And there's a shitface you left off your list.

MEL: Who?

PAUL: You.

MEL: The horse was definitely singing and not only that, but as horses go he sang very well. I was impressed, I won't lie.

PAUL: Spare me, come on . . .

MEL: It's understandable why a little twerp like you didn't pick it up. You weren't shitfaced. It was explained to me by Louie the Clocker that you had to be half cocked to zero in on the horse's musical frequency.

PAUL: No kidding? High or low?

MEL: Low, wise guy, very low. Dogs sing, why can't a horse two hours after he won a stakes race. Can you think of a better time?

PAUL: Come on, give it a rest.

MEL: And in the middle of all that we mounted you on Bum Rap. No saddle, no nothing. Up you went. You couldn't been more than six or seven.

PAUL: Five, barely.

MEL: Remember what Arcaro said about the way you sat a horse? And he *wasn't* shitfaced. A natural, that's what he called you, a natural from the master himself. What a party! It nearly made up for the stiffs your father gave me over the years.

PAUL: Do you have a clue as to what you guys put me through?

MEL: What're you getting at?

PAUL: Bad dreams. Two reelers. Nightly, ten years maybe more.

MEL: You're kidding.

PAUL: You Bozos toss a five year old kid on the back of a hopped up race horse in a bar with a low ceiling and you wonder that the kid started having nightmares? Can you count the times that horse bolted out of here and through the streets of Manhattan? And he didn't stop for red lights, Uncle Mel. And he didn't stop for tractor trailers, either.

MEL: No way I would've figured that one.

PAUL: No need to, now.

MEL: You're not having them anymore?

PAUL: Get the picture. We're coming from different places when it comes to horses. If you recall, one in particular drop-kicked my old man and sent him to an early grave.

MEL: Your father had a bum ticker, a *very* bum ticker. That horse only helped him along.

PAUL: Helped him along? You saying the horse was my father's cardiologist?

MEL: That's not what I said. But if you're saying he died young, yes, he did.

PAUL: I spent more time with you and Aunt Marge when he was alive than I did with him. Four-thirty mornings he was at the barn and by the time he passed through here coming home I was already rolling down Bleecker with Bum Rap. An absentee father doesn't figure in the equation. Not like Aunt Marge did, the way she pushed and pushed on me about school.

MEL: She took you for her own. You know that.

PAUL: None of that was lost on me, Uncle Mel. Wherever I've gotten I owe to her.

MEL: Too bad she's not around to hear you say that.

(*Pause*)

PAUL: I never understood why no kids—the two of you.

MEL: Aah, she was up to here with female problems. Name it she had it . . . anyway I didn't call you in here to write my life story.

PAUL: So. Why did you?

MEL: How old do I look to you?

PAUL: I'm here to guess your age? Twenty miles to guess your age?

MEL: So what if you are?

PAUL: You still look like you could knock over a building, Uncle Mel.

MEL: I'm seventy-one. What I've accumulated goes to you whether you need it or not.

PAUL: Money? I don't want to discuss money.

MEL: Money? That's a laugh. One sentence summarizes the good and bad news in my life. That sentence begins with, "I own a tavern" and it ends, "next to a race track." Unquote. Life and playing the ponies have a lot in common but primarily they are one and the same losing games. Nothing else even comes close. So forget about the money, there isn't any.

PAUL: Then what's the story?

MEL: This place, that's what. The Tack Room bughouse and sanctuary for all the shoulda-woulda-couldas of the world. Did you know that in that showcase I've got the shoes that Ruffian wore the day she died? That same night her groom was so broken up that he came in here to get out of his grief. The next day he made us a gift of those. Would you believe some of these degenerates were crying over a pair of horsehoes?

PAUL: Were you?

MEL: You bet I was. Over there's Seabiscuit's old bridle, Secretariat's oat bucket, one of jockey Cordero's favorite whips, the blanket Whirlaway used the day he won the Belmont. So what if some of it's stolen? Can I help it if the stable help are a bunch of thieves? I've seen men in their eighties and nineties stand before that case like a newsreel of their lives was playing in front of them.

PAUL: So what's the gimmick?

MEL: I don't want The Tack Room down the tubes after I'm gone. Why should it? Business is still brisk. For some reason a bomb went off in this family and you're the only one still standing, the only one I can count on.

PAUL: Uh, huh.

MEL: Did your father ever tell you we were gonna change the name of this place that night? "Goodbye Tack Room, hello Bum Rap." Great idea or so it seemed. But the next day wiser heads prevailed. The combination of bum and tavern do not a public relations marriage make.

PAUL: What you're suggesting is that I keep this place going.

MEL: Yes, Paul. I would be very grateful and relieved if you would do that for me. And a check-on-it once a week would do the trick.

PAUL: Uncle Mel, I appreciate what you're trying to do, don't read me wrong. But there are questions that have to be asked.

MEL: So shoot.

PAUL: How long has it been since Tiger Malletto was killed in here?

MEL: It wasn't in here, Paul, it was out there on the sidewalk.

PAUL: But he died inside. The police pictures were taken *in* here not *out* there.

MEL: Because he was a blowhard loudmouth who didn't have the common sense or consideration to croak where he was supposed to. No, he had to stagger back in here and give out a horse that was running the next day. "And you can bet your lungs on this one," he said. Then . . . (*Mel gives the thumbs down*)

PAUL: Speaking of public relations Malletto didn't do yours any favors.

MEL: What could I do? "Sorry, Pal, we have strict rules. Shirts, shoes, and a house limit maximum three bullet holes. Oh, what a shame! You just missed by one." Malletto was a loser. So was his horse.

PAUL: Suppose you auctioned this stuff. You don't think you'd make a killing?

MEL: Who'd want it?

PAUL: You're not serious.

MEL: Ninety percent of it's junk the minute it goes out that door.

PAUL: Not necessarily. Why not look into it?

MEL: And what's this sudden interest in Malletto?

PAUL: Because I'm not comfortable about how it's going to look if I'm hooked up with an establishment where hoods get murdered. Some courthouse barracuda would tee off on that one. I know.

MEL: But I'm saying it had nothing to do with this place! If they didn't get him here they would've gotten him down the block.

PAUL: But it wasn't the drycleaners that made the newspapers, it was you! Now, we're just having a conversation, Uncle Mel. I've concerns of my own, if that's okay by you.

MEL: I can't pretend to be in your shoes.

PAUL: Want a for instance?

MEL: Sure.

PAUL: These shoes you mention are walking into court on Monday and the guy inside them is representing one Mister Chooch. Aha, got you that time!

MEL: Johnny the Chooch?

PAUL: Himself.

MEL: That sonofabitch is the one who squashed Malletto.

PAUL: Hearsay, and I doubt it very much.

MEL: You're defending that guy and you're concerned about your reputation in this place?

PAUL: That's not the point.

MEL: You telling me you *like* him?

PAUL: I'm not marrying the guy, I'm representing him.

MEL (*cynically*): Money so good?

PAUL: No, as a matter of fact. I'd do better with a big shot matrimonial or some bungled tit job. But believe it or not, his case intrigues me. And *he* called me. I don't call anybody.

MEL: You've got that one right.

PAUL: Chooch deserves a fair shake and I can get him one. Uncle Mel, don't get him mixed up with Malletto. Malletto was a criminal, criminals take. A gangster like Chooch, he operates by *giving* people what they want. Malletto never gave anything to anyone but himself. And if a Malletto kills somebody it's always some innocent civilian. As funny as it sounds, gangsters take great pains to only kill one another.

MEL: Sounds like you're making a saint out of him.

PAUL: No, I'm not. He's a pompous ignoramous and he smells like a rosebush. But he's been shafted by the government and it's my intention to get him off so he can run home to his mommy.

MEL: You saying it's illegal if I put The Tack Room in your name?

PAUL: No, no I didn't say that.

MEL: Then what are you saying? There's ways around the other stuff and we both know it.

PAUL: All right, there's been talk of the state buying out the track and extending the runways at the airport.

MEL: Everybody's heard that. You know anything I don't know?

PAUL: Nothing. And I don't think it's going to happen. But it doesn't exactly enhance the value of this property. And just suppose it was a done deal? This place would be a dinosaur. A few years down the line, kaput.

MEL: My regulars are my regulars. They're not going anywhere.

PAUL: Your regulars are going the way of Malletto. Not from bullets maybe but they are going, and definitely not in the direction of Nova Scotia.

MEL: I'm getting a strange intuition here.

PAUL: I don't want to make promises I can't keep and I can't promise anything until we barf it all out. You have a problem with that?

MEL: Not when you put it that way.

PAUL: That's all I'm trying to do. So relax.

(*Frenchy enters*)

FRENCHY: I've got what you sent me for, Mister Mel.

MEL: You didn't stop by Miguel's?

FRENCHY: Oh no, Mister Mel, but when I do I'm telling him everything you said.

MEL: What's that?

FRENCHY: What you said.

MEL: What did I say, you banana?

FRENCHY: Oh-oh . . .

MEL: Go put the juice in the back, then go next door and take that shower you owe me.

FRENCHY: Okie-dokie. (*Exit Frenchy*)

MEL (*in Frenchy's direction*): And there's something I need you for when you get back.

PAUL: What now?

MEL: I'll think of something. If the genius isn't going or coming his wheels fall off.

PAUL: Why not a television? That's his speed.

MEL: Aah, it's been tried. He gets agitated with the yelling and violence. And don't ask me why but that Bugs Bunny individual rattles his cage. Maybe it reminds him of his mommy. How am I supposed to know? You think it's easy seven days a week coming up with things for Einstein to do?

FRENCHY (*out*): Did you call me, Mister Mel?

MEL: "Wheels" reminds me. Get in here, Frenchy.

(*Frenchy appears*)

What about that bike I got you. Why don't you tell my nephew about that little caper.

FRENCHY: Oh-oh, headache for sure now.

MEL: A few years back I noticed it was taking him longer and longer to run his errands so I got him a bike with all kinds of flags and streamers and decorations. You loved that bike, didn't you, Frenchy?

FRENCHY: That was my favorite bike, Mister Mel.

MEL: THEN WHY DID YOU SELL THE GODDAMN THING?

FRENCHY: Oh-oh . . .

PAUL: Sold it?

MEL: And considering he never paid for it he realized a neat little profit. Ten dollars to be exact.

PAUL: Ten dollars, why Frenchy . . .

MEL: But let's not be too hard on him. He obviously had inside information that the rest of us didn't about bicycle depreciation. But to go from two hundred and fifty smackers to ten in just one afternoon is a bit steep, wouldn't you say? Like falling off the Empire State (*then, to Frenchy*) or getting thrown off. I bet you sure miss that bike, Frenchy.

FRENCHY: Um, I don't know much about that.

MEL: Some people might say you took me for a sucker, Frenchy.

FRENCHY: Not me, Mister Mel, I never said that.

MEL: Get out of here and take that shower and make sure you get behind those floppy ears.

FRENCHY: Gabye, Mister.

PAUL: Goodbye, Frenchy.

FRENCHY: Post time! (*Frenchy exits*)

MEL: Like a little puppy. He gets a rush every time he leaves and every time he gets back. You know, Paul, I've never had a clue on what gets your blood up.

PAUL: Come on, Uncle Mel . . .

MEL: Take a crummy morning in February. What gets you out of bed? I really would like to know.

PAUL: The job . . . prestige . . . (*pause*) clout.

MEL: Clout of what?

PAUL: What else? No one knocks on my door unless he's in very deep shit. With a setup like that you can't help but play a little God. *And* when it's a Johnny Chooch you get beaucoup media. We all love the showbiz. I'm no exception.

MEL: Okay, but where's the . . . fun?

PAUL: Fun I don't know about. When you spend all your time with wife beaters, bloodsuckers and weasels? They pay, but fun?

MEL: That's not saying much.

PAUL: To you maybe not. But the payback's soup to nuts and back—you name it. And that one you *can* bet your lungs on.

MEL: But what is it that gives you a sense of well-being?

PAUL: Well being? I just told you—

MEL: No. I mean when you're by yourself and *no one's* peeking in. That kind of well-being.

PAUL: Well-being can mean a lot of things. I'm in a position to pick my way through the garbage and leave the dreck for others. I just wish it happened a lot sooner.

MEL: And that's it?

PAUL: That's a lot.

MEL: I suppose it is.

PAUL: Would you prefer a nephew-to-uncle con job?

MEL: You got a girlfriend?

PAUL: Got to have one of those.

MEL: You going to marry her?

PAUL: No, I'm not. I wouldn't do that to her. I did a lot of matrimonial once. That cured me. But you can be sure that if things change you'll be the first to know.

MEL: Some of your talk reminds me of this new breed of horseplayers we're starting to get in here with their computer print outs, speed sheets and pisswater light beer. They don't do much better than the rest of us, but when they lose they don't behave like they lost. Instead they use these special words that make it seem as though the race was a distortion and shouldn't have turned out the way it did. Very convincing, too. And they're bum tippers, not friendly, and talk like a bunch of funeral directors. Hey, if that's what America's coming to it's gonna be a long sleep for everybody. Maybe they'll wise up to what the score is. That in this game winning's what's the distortion and that's the straight dope.

PAUL: Straight dope-losing mentality, Uncle Mel.

MEL: Guilty as charged. But if you ask me half the fun around these parts is listening to the miserable belly aching that goes on ten seconds after a race is over. Do you act any different when you lose a case? You do lose one once in a while, I hope.

PAUL: I don't belly-ache.

MEL: You don't. Why not?

PAUL: Because I don't take it personally.

MEL: But wouldn't that be better? To take it personally?

PAUL: No. Not at all.

MEL: But there has to be something that burns your toast.

PAUL: Sure. Getting a bad shake does.

MEL: What's a good shake? Getting some guilty party off? Has that ever happened to you?

PAUL (*ingenuously*): Me? Never . . .

MEL: So what burns you more? Getting a guilty party off or losing a case for a guilty one?

PAUL: Only schlocks indict their own.

MEL: You're talking in circles.

PAUL: The law *is* in circles.

MEL: What a coincidence! So's horse racing.

PAUL: I'm referring to the legal and philosophical circles, not the mindless.

MEL: S'not so mindless when you win, Paul.

PAUL: Shit luck and you know it.

MEL: The lucky ones in this racket do their homework.

PAUL: And you don't win in mine unless you charm the pants off a jury of getmeoutaheres. And it ain't easy. It takes guts, it takes information, and it's more creative, I think, than doping out a race. And it can be fun.

MEL: And it can be bullshit.

PAUL: That, too.

MEL: I'll stick to my brand anyday, pal.

PAUL: I'm really curious. What's so special about this *clientele* you cater to? Do they have any idea that there's a misinhabited planet screaming for help on the other side of that door?

MEL: They're in from there, aren't they?

PAUL: But all that's left to the rest of us saps to muddle through. Do you believe for a second that I get my jollies being the white magician in everyone else's nightmare?

MEL: So who put the gun to your head?

PAUL: No one.

MEL: Then why do it?

PAUL: Because I don't want to dance on my toes, can't draw a naked bimbo, and I'm tone deaf. But I am pretty good at what I do and I'm getting the impression you don't give a damn.

MEL: I do give a damn.

PAUL: Well, show it.

MEL: Look who's taking things personally.

PAUL: Where you're concerned? (*Pause*) Why glorify a race track that's a depository for lost souls? Desperate, no nothing else to piss away the time. I suppose it's okay if they're getting what they want. But there are some of us who don't get it, don't want it.

(*Pause*)

MEL: Finished?

PAUL: No. I've got some advice to give you if you'll take it. All I ask is a fair hearing. Will I get it?

MEL: Seems to me you've been getting one right along.

PAUL: You say you're seventy-one. There's still time on your clock to enjoy. Knock on wood your health isn't a factor and your mind's still sharp. When's the last time you took a vacation?

MEL: Vacation? Don't make me laugh.

PAUL: I'm not laughing. I think this rut you're in is pitiful. Why don't you travel? What're you afraid of missing? Go chase some rich widows around. Smoke some Cubans instead of those cheap stogies. See some humanity, for crissakes, not just these regulars and Frenchy. There's a whole other world, get in it while you can. The track'll be here when you get back. Those guys are not going anywhere. They never do.

MEL: What are you driving at?

PAUL: Burn the place down.

(*Pause*)

MEL: Burn it down . . .

PAUL: To the ground. That's my advice. You say you've no savings but you do have insurance on this place. It's a good policy. Burn it and cash it in.

MEL: Cash—

PAUL: You'll get over it, Uncle Mel, this joint's a few years from being an endangered species. Do you want it to go belly up? Do you have any idea of what that would do to you?

MEL: That burning it wouldn't?

PAUL: One day, like any other, you simply take a walk out that door. Leave everything as is, everything down to the most insignificant mousetrap or a jacket that's been hanging a while from the same hook. We don't want to arouse any suspicion. And your attachment to this place definitely works in your favor. Keep playing it up. Just say the word, I'll flip all the switches. It's as simple as that. And I know Rita would be thrilled to see more of you.

MEL: How about you? You want to see more of me?

PAUL: Dumb question.

MEL: You know I won't do it.

PAUL: Think about it.

MEL (*with irony*): Sure. I'll think about it.

PAUL: For two years I watched Aunt Marge die. She was twice the woman, had twice the class my mother does. And to see her go from what she was to what she became was unspeakable. More than once the smell of what was coming out of her made me want to puke.

MEL: Jesus, cut it out! I called this meeting. Who called who anyway?

PAUL: What difference does it make?

MEL: To me it does. I feel as though I'm being hacked up for stew meat.

PAUL: I don't know what else to do! Time's not your friend, Uncle Mel. You've got to be objective.

MEL: When you were a kid you'd come in here, sandwiches and candy, toys . . .

PAUL: Even then I never felt a part of this place. I don't think your wife did, either. But in your home it was . . . not everyone hears the singing horse, Uncle Mel. And all this seems just a bit passe to me now. (*Suddenly*) I did love you all, but love is a bit overdone, don't you think? It can't provide a place, a focus. If it could—I'd have never left. And people press some grotesque buttons, don't they, in the name of love.

MEL: That's not love.

PAUL: Oh, but it is to them. Absolutely.

MEL: Tell me honestly. Right now, in here. What do you feel?

PAUL: Honestly?

MEL: No, lie like a sonofabitch.

PAUL: I feel . . . like I'm confined in my father's crypt. (*Pause*) And I don't think I'm ever coming back, Uncle Mel.

MEL: Listen to me, Paul. Give it a shot. Six months, what's to lose? You're not even forty. What's the big deal? I mean, who's to say, some night you might be in here schmoozing and some macaroni in that corner might come out with something that makes you laugh so hard you go numb. Maybe you'll surprise yourself, kid. Don't write your life in granite. You're too young for that.

PAUL: Mel, if you will me this place I'll dump it ten minutes after it goes through probate. I will take whatever I can get and vanish. And if I were in a position to burn it for myself I would. But I can't. You can. Don't ever forget that.

MEL (*to himself*): How cockamamey did I have this figured? Jesus . . .

(*Enter Frenchy*)

FRENCHY: I just heard a funny joke, Mister Mel.

MEL: That makes two of us.

FRENCHY: Don't you want me to tell it?

MEL: Not right now Frenchy, if it's all right with you.

PAUL: Let him, Uncle Mel, we both could use it.

MEL: Then spit it out, come on.

FRENCHY: Here I go! Okay then, what's the difference between a moose and a front porch?

MEL (*mutters to self*): Fouled it up. Okay what is it.

FRENCHY: A moose has goofy antlers, that's what!

MEL: THAT'S NOT THE GODDAMN JOKE!

FRENCHY: It isn't?

MEL: The joke goes what's the difference between a hippo and a *Porsche automobile?*

PAUL: And the answer is . . .

MEL: With a Porsche the asshole's *inside.*

FRENCHY: Oh . . . oh.

(*Pause*)

PAUL: Ready for the bonus punch line? There's a Porsche parked right outside that door. Anybody up for a quick game of "where's the asshole?"

(*Short pause*)

MEL: Go in the back, Frenchy, 'til I call you. Please, do as I ask.

FRENCHY: Sorry about the joke, Mister Mel. (*Frenchy exits into the back room*)

PAUL: Uncle Mel, both my numbers are on this card. I'd like us to stay in touch, whatever you decide, okay? I don't have those special words right now for how I feel about that.

MEL: What will you say to Rita? What special words you got for her?

PAUL: No, no words. Rita's not the entity you are. You, Uncle Mel, you're a . . . (*uses hands to illustrate*) you're a world, a population. And I'm not so sure you can pass that on. You can see that for yourself.

MEL: See? See what?

PAUL: Me. I'm living proof.

(*Pause*)

MEL: I lied to you about something.

PAUL: You did.

MEL: I'm seventy-four.

PAUL: I knew that. You know your secrets are safe with me. (*Pause*) All those tampons. What ever happened to them?

MEL (*a bit resigned*): The ladies with the trumpets . . .

(*Slight pause*)

PAUL: Well goodbye, Uncle Mel. (*They shake hands*) 'Bye, Frenchy.

(*Exit Paul*)

FRENCHY (*out*): Can I come out now, Mister Mel? (*Mel shakes his head "no". Out*) There's nothing for me to do back here, Mister Mel. (*Pause*) Is there something you need? Something you need me to get?

MEL: Just give me a second. Can you do that for me, Frenchy?

(*After a couple of seconds Frenchy partially emerges from the back room. Mel senses his presence*)

FRENCHY: Is it time to come out now, Mister Mel? (*Pause*) Mister Mel? (*Pause*) Should I come out right now?

(*Slow fade. Curtain*)

SHOW

Victor Bumbalo

for Stephen Greco

Victor Bumbalo

Victor Bumbalo was the 1987 winner of an Ingram Merrill Award for writing. In 1979 his one-act play, *Kitchen Duty,* was produced by The Glines. This play has had productions across the country and usually appears on a bill with *After Eleven,* a one-act comedy written for EEGO's 1983 Playwrights Gala. His award-winning play, *Niagara Falls,* was produced by Barry Laine and Candida Scott Piel for The Glines and followed its Off-Broadway run with subsequent openings in cities throughout the United States, England and Australia. *Niagara Falls* and *Other Plays,* a collection of comedies, is published by Calamus Books.

Victor is also the recipient of two MacDowell Fellowships and residencies at Yaddo and the Helene Wurlitzer Foundation. Other works include, *628 Blandina Street, Tell, Some of Us,* and his latest play *What Are Tuesdays Like.* Most recently, his play, *Adam and the Experts* was performed at the Apple Core Theatre.

From 1982 to 1987 he worked as a volunteer with GMHC, first as a crisis counselor and then as a team leader. As an actor, he was last seen in Martin Scorsese's *After Hours.*

Characters:

MICHAEL, *a Catholic priest*

JOEY, *an orderly*

Scene

An institution.

Time:

Present.

Note: Between the scenes, instead of a blackout, music—short fragments from one continuous piece—designates the passage of time.

The lights come up on a bare setting—a bed, a table, a chair, and a crucifix. Joey, an attractive and confident young man, is standing and has his back to the audience. Kneeling in front of him is Michael. Michael is dressed as a priest. He is a nervous man who speaks rapidly and at moments with desperation. He peeks around Joey.

1.

MICHAEL (*to the audience*): I'm looking for God. (*To Joey*) Thank you Joey. You can leave if you want. I know you have chores to do. Here's the twenty.

(*Joey, his back still to the audience, zips up*)

I can't afford twenty again this week. Maybe I can give you ten. What can I get for ten?

(*Joey, back to the audience, strokes his crotch*)

I get to rub it?

(*Joey nods*)

I don't think I'll find God that way. Not by rubbing. But hell, let me give it a try.

(*Music*)

2.

MICHAEL: I'm waiting for Joey. He's late. Maybe he's not coming. I wish I had more money. They pay him so little here and work him so hard. If he doesn't get here before I have to go to chapel, I won't get to see him until tomorrow. I hope he's all right. They don't treat him so good here. They should. But they don't. That's because they're all jealous. Beauty intimidates. Youth frightens. It's all that tight skin. It makes them evil around here. Someday, after I fool them, they'll let me leave. When I'm out of here, then I know I can find God. I just know it. All I have to do is fool them. Where is he? If I don't get to see him, how will I get through the night?

(*Music*)

3.

MICHAEL: This is a bed. This is a chair. This is a cross. This is Michael. This is a crazy house. I know it. That makes me not crazy. It's a crazy house for priests. They call it a rest home. Isn't that a fabulous euphemism? A rest home. Nobody rests here. A rest home for the lunatics working in the profession. I'm the youngest loony in this joint. They better start collecting more during mass. They're going to have to build more of these places. There are so many of us out there. So many loonies. Excuse me. I mean priests under duress. I mean under stress. I mean in distress. I mean bonkers. Joey just left. I only had five dollars this week. He only let me feel it. It wasn't God. I know that. But it was fun. As he was leaving, I wanted to be held. Snuggled like a little puppy. Joey held me. He kissed me on the neck. He did it for free. I didn't even have to beg. Do you think Joey comes from God?

(*Music*)

4.

MICHAEL: I want to get out of here. I hate it here. I'm so alone. But I have to fool Father Mancuso. If they ever let me out, I have to fool him. He's like so many of them. He doesn't know God. I'm beginning to think he comes from the devil. He's one of those cheery types. You know the kind of guy. The God he talks about is the instant gratification, fast food kind of God. Father Mancuso is so butch. Too bad he's so ugly. He believes we all wouldn't be crazy if we played sports. He has this poor old priest, Father Crowe—who's here recovering from too much booze—doing high impact walking. Well, the poor old guy nearly dropped dead the first week. He actually cried when Father Mancuso gave him his walking sneakers. Now the dear geezer loves it. He does it six days a week. Not on Sunday. Father Mancuso is so proud. Our dear Father Crowe found a liquor store down the road with a very understanding salesman. Father Mancuso's assistant is Father Burns. He's—let's just say—a client of Joey's. I know this because Joey told me. Father Burns is round. He looks like a bowling ball. That's what I call him and Joey laughs. He doesn't appreciate Joey like I do. He treats him like help. But I'm going to tell you something, Joey makes a bundle from that ass. Excuse me, I don't like using words like that. But that's what he is. An ass. The type that thinks that when he goes to the bathroom he makes Faberge eggs. For the "bowling ball" to taste it, it's a hundred bucks. I only pay twenty. For a rub, it's fifty. I give my ten and I can rub until the fabric on his jeans qualifies as museum quality. I know about the "bowling ball" because Joey told me. The "bowling ball" doesn't know about me, because Joey has principles. I advise Joey on his prices. Can you imagine? It's fifty—just to rub it. (*He laughs. Music*)

5.

MICHAEL: I only had two dollars this week. Joey took off his shoes and socks. I kissed his toes. Joey is so generous.

(*Music*)

6.

(*Joey has his back to the audience. He is naked to the waist. Michael has been licking his chest. Michael stops*)

JOEY: Smile more.

MICHAEL: Now.

JOEY: No. When you go to chapel. When you meet Father Mancuso. When Father Burns asks you how's it hanging.

MICHAEL: Going. He says, "How's it going?"

JOEY: Right. Going. Smile. Say, "Fine." That's what they say here. Fine. Enough "fines" and you'll be out.

MICHAEL: I only have a dollar left this week. A dollar. Will you come back for a dollar?

JOEY: Can you say, "Fine"?

MICHAEL: I just want to see you. I won't touch you. Will you come?

JOEY: For a dollar you can kiss my face. Say, "Fine."

MICHAEL: Fine. That's too cheap. You're letting me get away with murder.

JOEY: Times are rough.

(*Music*)

7.

MICHAEL: I guess I should clue you in. Isn't that a manly expression? "Clue you in." Men all over this universe are using that expression —right now—at this moment. Determining our fates and cluing each other in. But they're not really cluing anybody in. They're doing what they do best. Lying. That's what I'm trying to learn how to do. But I'm not going to lie to you. So I'll clue you in—

(*Joey enters*)

Well, I can't. Not right now. I have company.

(*Joey stands in front of Michael and unzips*)

I got my disability check today. I don't need new shoes. And there's God I'm looking for. (*Michael buries his head in Joey's crotch. Music*)

8.

MICHAEL: I'm sorry I was so rude. I was supposed to clue you in. But I almost saw God. Isn't that the best excuse for bad manners? How I got here? I was on my search. I believe in God the Father Almighty. And I'm human. Young. I love God. I love life. I love people. And Our Lord always knew I love men. I have a spot. A small purple spot. (*Michael begins to undress*) I'll show you. Here under my robes. With all its powerful meaning. It was there then. It's there now. I wore it under my cassock. Thought about the love of God. The Crucifixion. And wondered if my spot would lead me to any wisdom. But I'm weak. Sometimes I cursed. Scream—Jesus H. Christ. Do you know what the "H" stands for? (*Michael stops undressing. Music*)

9.

MICHAEL (*without his cassock. In a t-shirt and pants*) I'm cluing you in, right? I'm a young priest. I believe in and look for God, the Father Almighty everywhere I go. I work in a hospital. I see so many men with spots. I'm their priest. Their brother. I hold their hands. When they need breath, I breathe into them. If they need a kiss, I brush their lips with mine. And I wonder? Where is He? Where is our God? Maybe He's in the spots. I kiss as many as I can. I lick them. Maybe I'm tasting God. Are you getting clued in?

(*Music*)

10.

(*Joey has his back to the audience. Michael is still only wearing his t-shirt and pants*)

JOEY: Fifty cents. You can brush my lips for fifty cents. I need to make two phone calls.

MICHAEL: I only have a quarter.

JOEY: Make it a quick brush. I'm such a push-over.

MICHAEL: Oh dear Lord, I love you. I love you, I love you, I love . . . .

(*Music*)

11.

MICHAEL: . . . you. I love you. Oh my God, where are you? (*Noticing the audience*) I was saying Mass. I held up the Eucharist—the body—the blood of Christ—and I felt it. My spot burning. Wanting air. Wanting to be free of my robes. So . . . I freed it. I freed my spot. I tore my robes off. Ripped them from my body. "Wait," I said. "Wait." "Look." "Let me show you. Please. Let me show you something." (*Michael suddenly rips off his t-shirt, lowers his pants a bit, turns his back to the audience, and points to a lesion on his lower left hip*)
I said, "See the spot. Help me. Help me see God in it."

(*Music. Michael puts on his cassock*)

12.

MICHAEL: Where is he? He hasn't been here for a while. I need to see him. Touch him. Oh God, I wish I had more money. My spot. I was talking about my spot. I said, "See my spot." Well, Mrs. Fazio passed out. Mrs. Cunnings also fainted. But the lucky bitch hit her head on the pew, landed in the hospital, and sued St. Agnes. No one saw any meaning in my lesson. They only saw it as "show and tell." And I interrupted the Mass. Perhaps, I should have showed my spot during the coffee hour. Then maybe I wouldn't be here. (*After a moment*) It's been a while. I haven't seen him. Do you know where he is?

(*Music*)

13.

MICHAEL (*on his knees*): Oh dear Jesus, help me. Where is he? I need . . . (*suddenly spotting the audience*) Mrs. Cunnings . . . I was talking about Mrs. Cunnings. She was awarded $10,000 out of court.

The scar on her forehead is smaller than my spot. Is there any justice? Mrs. Fazio is furious she didn't hit her head. I don't blame the sweet thing. I was interviewed. Well, questioned. Did I know my name? The date? Where I lived? Never a question about God. They brainwashed my family. Had them sign papers. Now I have to stay here until the authorities agree I'm sane. So I have to pretend this is God's house. That the Devil doesn't exist here. Pretend until I get out of here. Then I can begin my daily search. I have to pretend real fast and real good. Before my spots double, triple. Before they devour me. I'm not afraid anymore. I'm seeing the Devil. So there has to be a God. I have a dime. One dime. Joey's late. He was supposed be here already. He says he needs my dime. So he'll let me touch his skin. Trace that skin with these hands. Just for one dime. (*Michael mimes tracing Joey's face. Music*)

14.

JOEY: I need your dime to flip into a wishing well.

MICHAEL (*feeling Joey's face*): And what will you wish for?

JOEY: You don't have enough money to know. I told you, you have to learn to smile.

MICHAEL: Why?

JOEY: It will make the lying you have to do easier. Learn to say—"I'm fine thank you." Say—"It's good to be here." Say—"I'm getting stronger." Forget about your spot. And tell them you've found God. In them. In their kitchens. In their TV's. In their Weight Watchers Chicken Kiev.

MICHAEL: But I'm still looking.

JOEY: Lie.

MICHAEL: That's right. I'm supposed to lie. Will you come every day and teach me?

(*Music*)

15.

MICHAEL: Father Mancuso said I talk too loud. He said it after dinner. He took me aside and said, "Father Mike . . ." He calls me Father Mike. Do you believe it? "Father Mike, you probably don't realize it, but you have a strong voice and it carries." What he was really saying was you'll never get out of here. You're one of those permanent crazies like Father Lupa who sings instead of talks. But I wasn't talking loud. I was trying to act animated. You know, interested and jovial. And I thought I was doing a good job. They don't like me here. They pretend they do, but they don't. It's because of my spot. I've got to act calm tonight. Father Mancuso will be watching. I can't fidget during chapel. I can't act nervous. I can't act sad. You know, I haven't seen Joey in two whole days. I feel like I'm dead.

(*Music*)

16.

MICHAEL: They fired him. Let him go. I'm never going to see him again. I'll never get out. I'll never know God. I know I shouldn't have asked why. Shouldn't have appeared interested. But I couldn't help it. Father Mancuso wouldn't give me any reason. He said, "Was there a special friendship there, Father Mike?" "I loved him." "Oh Father Mike, let's pray together." I'm so stupid. I shouldn't have said I loved him. You can't admit to love in this place. There can be no love here.

(*Music*)

17.

MICHAEL: I've two spots now. And there's no Joey. I wish I had a gun.

(*Music*)

18.

MICHAEL: They've got me on medication now. But I saw *One Flew Over the Cuckoo's Nest.* You hold the pill under your tongue and let them think you swallowed it. God bless Jack Nicholson. The "bowling ball" looks depressed. Father Mancuso must have discussed Joey and me with him. I wonder what the "bowling ball" is going to do. Try and increase my medication? He frightens me.

(*Music*)

19.

MICHAEL: The "bowling ball" asked me "How's it going?" I said, "Fine." Just like Joey taught me. "Fine." He didn't believe me. I could tell. He just looked at me. But it wasn't with devil eyes. It was with sad eyes. Maybe he dreams of Joey too. Maybe he hugs his pillow at night. Maybe he hurts. Maybe the "bowling ball" cries. "How you doing?" Could he have meant it?

(*Music*)

20.

MICHAEL: If it weren't a sin, I'd take all the pills I've been hiding and eat them. But God doesn't like cowards. What am I supposed to do here alone? If Joey were here, I'd know how I'm supposed to act. He'd tell me. I'm a little bit more nervous, but I'm not crazy. But every time I'm near that bastard, I mean Father Mancuso, I do something screwy. He brings out the loon in me. Like today, I was trying to act calm. Father Mancuso said, "Father Mike would you like to talk to me today?" I said, "Only if you give me candy." It was a stupid joke. Because he's a health freak. Never in the vicinity of sugar. But I should have known how he'd take my lame bit of humor. "Did some man once give you candy?" I tried to explain I was kidding, but he just looked at me. Crazy queer is what he was thinking. Well, maybe I should have fed his cliches. Maybe I should have sent his head spinning. Maybe I should have told him I sucked dick for Tootsie Rolls, ate ass for Mars Bars, got fucked for Snickers.

Because I'm never getting out of here. Oh dear Jesus, oh dear Joey, help me, help me. (*Kneeling*) Our Father who art in Heaven . . . .

(*Music*)

21.

MICHAEL: "I've seen him." That's what the "bowling ball" told me. He's seen him. "Is he all right?" "We'll talk later." "Tell me now." I grabbed him, but I quickly let go and said, "I'm sorry, I'm sorry." Then he said, "It's okay." "You're not going to report me." Then he took his little fat hand and touched my cheek—the way a friend would. "Forgive me," I said. "There is nothing to forgive." As he walked away I thought—oh yes, there is. I called you names. I thought ill of you. Thought like Father Mancuso does—in cliches. Oh my God, I helped Joey with his prices. I've hurt this man. Do you think he's going to try to get even and do something mean? No. I'm going to open my heart and believe that Father Burns will tell me about Joey. Dear God, please let him tell me about Joey. Please.

(*Music*)

22.

MICHAEL: God. The Devil. They are not entities. They are not what they tell you here. They are only pieces. Fragments. Chips. Moments. I'm beginning to know God. Father Burns is a piece of God. He's helping me to look better. He held my hand and said, "Joey's fine. He asks about you." "And what did you tell him?" "I told him you were having a difficult time. Father Mike, he's worried about you." Oh dear Jesus, oh dear Joey, I love you.

(*Music*)

23.

MICHAEL: I dream. I'm acting calmer. The "prick"—Father Mancuso—thinks this reversal has to do with him. Father Burns—as I pass him in chapel, in the corridors, says, "Let him. Let him think anything that makes you look better." My little "bowling ball," my angel, I love you. This morning, during Mass, when Father Mancuso turned his back to us, Father Burns whispered, "I was with him last night." "And," the anguish in my voice made poor Father Burns frightened. He said, "Be quiet. Just listen." "Yes. I'm sorry. I'm listening." Father Mancuso still had his back to us. He was holding up the Eucharist. "This is for you. He gave me this to give to you." Then my new friend slipped me this envelope. I am not going to die here. (*Holding up an envelope*) From Joey. A fragment from God. (*Michael rips the envelope open. Showing it to the audience*) Look. Look what my love says. "Smile."

(*Blackout*)

A COUPLE WITH A CAT

Tony Connor

Tony Connor

Tony Connor is the author of a number of celebrated plays including *The Last of the Feinsteins.* His dramatic work has appeared throughout the world including such major venues as London's Old Vic and National Theatres.

Born in Manchester, England, he became a naturalized U.S. citizen in 1984. His poetry has appeared in five volumes published by Oxford University Press.

Mr. Connor is Professor of English at Wesleyan University in Middletown, Connecticut, where he is also the founder of Captain Partridge's Home for Wayward Playwrights.

Characters:

JOE TRISKIN, *a middle-aged man*
MARY TRISKIN, *his wife*
DALE TRISKIN, *his son*

Scene

A lower middle-class living room. Door leading off to the kitchen. Joe Triskin is reading the newspaper. His wife is sewing something.

JOE (*without looking up*): I use ta know this married couple. Guy an his wife. They spoke only through the cat. (*Pause*) Lawrence, his name was.

MARY (*without looking up*): What was his wife's name?

JOE: Huh?

MARY: What was his wife's name, I said.

JOE: I'm talkin' about the cat. The cat's name was Lawrence.

MARY: Well, what was the *husband's* name. What was the *wife's* name?

JOE: What does it matter. You didn't know 'em. It was before I met you.

MARY: How do you know I didn't know them? You're presumptious. You're jumping to conclusions.

JOE: Now that's a bit of Dale! University talk. "Presumptious"—I'll give him "presumptious" when I see him!

MARY: Aw, leave it alone will ya? You'd think our son was my . . . my . . . Cavalier Servante, to hear you talkin'.

JOE: "Cavalier" . . . now that's university talk, too. What other garbage has he been fillin' ya head with?

MARY: I'm just waiting to hear you say, "He's no son of mine."

JOE: He's no son of . . . be careful. I'm not made of stone.

(*Pause. They read and sew*)

MARY: This cat: what was it's name?

JOE: Lawrence.

MARY: After Lawrence Welk?

JOE: No. (*Pause*) After Lawrence of Arabia. The guy's mother came from Syria or somewhere.

MARY: That band, with all the players in Tuxedos, and Lawrence Welk lookin' so masterful. And the dancing—walzes, fox-trots, quick-steps. Remember how we used to enjoy it?

JOE: No.

MARY: Oh, Welk went a long way back. Those little TVs with a small screen. Black and white. He started out on the radio. (*Pause*) It made you *imagine* things, the radio did. Like Dale says, it induced mental evocations.

JOE: How does he know? He wasn't born.

MARY: Have you never heard of records, and and CDs?

JOE: He wasn't thought of.

MARY: Or NPR. They did an item on Welk in "All Things Considered."

JOE: Jesus, I'd never thought of *you,* never mind *him!*

MARY: Data is very available nowadays. Information is big business. You don't have to have been sitting there with your ear glued to the set to have heard Truman announcing that the atom bomb had been dropped on Japan.

JOE: That was years ago. I was only ten, or nine. Come to think of it, you was only five. *You* don't know. And Dale knows less than you.

MARY: Or MacArthur making his famous speech of farewell. "Old soldiers never . . ."

JOE (*interrupting*): I heard it, I heard it!

MARY (*pausing to think*): Now, I don't think you did. I seem to recall that General MacArthur made that speech to a closed session of Congress. It shows how memory can deceive you.

JOE: I heard it and saw it, I'm tellin' ya! I was visitin' my Gramma in Maine. Gifford. I can picture it like it was yesterday. (*Pause*) She used ta have a kinda velvet cover she draped over the TV at night—like it wus a parrot or sumthin'. I even remember what Gram said ta me afterwards.

MARY: What did she say?

JOE: "Joe," she said, "You've just heard General MacArthur's last public speech."

MARY: That's what you remember her saying? Anybody could've said that.

JOE: I have a photographic memory for some things. Phot-o-graphic!

MARY: You're wrong. That speech was never broadcast and never televised.

JOE: I saw it and heard it, goddammit.

MARY: Oh! . . . Well, that's my point. If you've heard it, so's our Dale heard it. Archives. Information retrieval. Any kid growing up today can hear exactly what you heard. *And* he's got the advantage of historical perspective, which you never had.

(*Pause*)

JOE: Do ya want ta hear about this cat, or dontcha. (*Flexing newspaper*) If you're not interested I'd just as soon read about yesterday's launch at Cape Carnival.

MARY: They gave the place a new name.

JOE: If NASA wants to call it Cape Kennedy, that's *their* business. *I* call it Cape Carnival.

MARY: "Carnaveral", you pronounce it.

JOE: I pronounce it the Navy way. Carnival. (*He opens the paper. Pause*)

MARY: Must have been an educated couple? I mean, naming the cat after Lawrence of Arabia. Is that what they called it—"Lawrence of Arabia"?

JOE: No; "Lawrence".

MARY: The diminutive.

JOE: It *was* diminutive. A kitten when I knew it. I didn't know it. When I heard of it. No; I mean when the guy an his wife spoke through it, or when they began to. I heard about it later from Pat Cooney.

MARY: Who used to do landscaping.

JOE: The man.

MARY: He owned a rotorooter—whatever that might be. He used to bitch about the blades—how much it cost to have them sharpened. He worked all over Connecticut in that old *Chevy* van of his. Turning old turf under. Didn't he used to re-seed yards afterwards as part of his service? His wife left him, didn't she?

JOE: Goddam right she did! Poor old Pat. If ever a man deserved better from life it was Pat. Workin' his butt off thirteen, fourteen hours a day with a friggin' rotorooter, an his wife leaves him. (*Shakes head*) Shameful!

MARY: Did she get fed up of communicating through the cat?

JOE: Poor old Pat. Mind you, the guy's soldierin' on; still at it . . . *Chester* . . . *Roxbury* . . . *Hebron* . . . *Granby* . . . all over the place. It'd take more than his wife leavin' to stop Pat!

MARY: Sounds like reasonable grounds for divorce to me: a cat as an intermediary.

JOE: Now that's another of those university words, another bit of Dale. One of these nights I'll . . .

MARY (*rushing on*): Now this *is* getting interesting! I never even knew Lawrence of Arabia came into it!

JOE: Lawrence, OK? Not "Lawrence of Arabia".

MARY: This gives me an entirely new view of Pat Cooney and his rotorooter.

JOE: Well, ya can forget it, because it wasn't his cat. Ya don't listen ta what I say. Your head's so full of Dale and the crap he brings back from the university you don't understand simple common sense any longer. I said I *heard* it from Pat Cooney. Heard it; right?

MARY (*patiently*): You started off by saying: "I used to know this couple that spoke only through the cat." That's what you said. You're contradicting yourself. First you say you *knew* the couple, then you say Pat Cooney told you about them.

JOE: Where's he gone tonight. Some party at one of those fraternities, I shouldn't wonder, mixing with all sorts of . . . of . . . perverts an' smokin' mar-i-juana, sniffin' coke. Those students have never heard of the War on Drugs—I read about it. And free sex. Teenagers, huh!

MARY: You want to lay off the booze. That damn Polish Club is debauching you.

JOE: Now lay off my friends! Nothin's sacred to you when ya start squabblin'.

MARY: Dale's graduating this year. He isn't a teenager.

JOE: They're all teenagers to me.

MARY: Who?

JOE: Kids at college. Guys who look like gals. They've not got two balls between 'em, as far as I'm concerned!

MARY: Y'know, Joe, you're the limit! One minute you're on about free sex, the next minute you're complaining about the same people having no balls—and you should keep such talk for the bar of the Polish Club, where it belongs.

JOE: I know, alright? I know.

MARY: Save it for your drinking buddies. Ed, and Dave, and whats-his-face?

JOE: Mike Pazutto.

MARY: I don't mean that sex maniac.

JOE: Well, I don't know who ya mean. *Who* you have taken a sudden an' secret dislike to.

MARY: Come on! I have *not* taken a sudden and secret dislike to Mike Pazutto. You know very well, I've hated him for years.

JOE: It's news ta me!

MARY: What about the night of Rita's party?—when he got me in the bathroom with him. It's three years ago if it's a day. You don't imagine I *like* him after that.

JOE: Errr, let bygones be bygones. The guy was drunk.

MARY: And so were you, or I hope you'd have done something about it there and then.

JOE: I did, didn't I?

MARY: If you call *speaking* to him the next day "doing something". And I've not noticed any rift in your friendship.

JOE: Say what ya like; Mike is genuine. Ya know where you are with Mike.

MARY: Oh yeh, he's genuine alright. What he exposed to *me* was genuine, I'll tell you that. *And* I knew where I was with him—in the bathroom with the door locked!

JOE: Can it will ya! You were hysterical. Ya gettin' hysterical now.

MARY: My god! Well, if the attempted rape of your wife doesn't deserve a rift in the friendship between you and Mike Pazutto, I don't know what does!

JOE: Ya made a damn' quick recovery, as I remember. You were down gigglin' with Rita about it two minutes later, an' poor Mike throwin' his guts up down the lavatory pan. He only went in there fer a piss—he still had his pecker out when I went to see how he was.

MARY: And of course, you're satisfied that's all he had it out for.

JOE: Yep. He was so drunk an' desperate fer a piss he unzipped before he got there. He was inter the bathroom at the ready—he never even saw you. Ya flatter yourself. An' what wus the bathroom door doin' open, anyway? An invitation to all comers, perhaps?

MARY: You and your stupid friends! I'll tell you this: Dale's friends are infinitely preferable, as far as I'm concerned. Long hair and all!

JOE: Maybe, have it your way. I'd just like ta see 'em called upon ta defend their country.

MARY: What does that mean?

JOE: Never mind.

(*Pause*)

I wus goin' ta tell ya a very interesting story.

MARY: Go on then.

JOE: Interestin' an' instructive.

MARY: I'm listening.

JOE (*coughs*): I used ter know this couple who spoke only through the cat.

MARY: The cat could speak, could it?

JOE: Uh?

MARY: Was it a talking cat?

JOE: Nooo!

MARY: Well, explain what you mean.

JOE: I'm goin' to. But it's difficult.

MARY: You introduced the subject. Surely you know what you want to say?

JOE: I do. I know exactly what I wanna say. But why should I, eh? Why should I? Your mind's not on me—it's on Dale, wherever *he* is.

MARY: Fer cryin' out loud, you're like a kid: jealous. Jealous of your own son. Afraid he's alienating your wife's affections.

JOE: Now that's him. I recognize the language. He put that idea in ya head—go on; deny it.

MARY: *I* put ideas in *his* head, if you want to know. And they're different to those of you and your cronies, I can tell you.

JOE: One of these nights there's gonna be a bust-up between me an' that son of yours. He's gettin' too big fer his boots.

MARY: What's got into your head? Don't you provoke him. He's done Judo, and Karate, *and* Kendo. Don't go starting any trouble.

JOE: Huh! I thought he was at university to study, not ta fritter away his time on oriental boxin' an such.

MARY: He *is* studying, he's working his brain harder than you ever worked yours—that's certain.

JOE: An' what good's it doin' him, that's what I'd like ta know. Philosophy of Religion; Jac-o-bean drama; Feminist Theory. What job's that kinda stuff gonna get him, huh?

MARY: You're very interested for somebody who thinks it's all garbage. You've been looking at his essays, haven't you?

JOE: I consider it my duty as a father to know what kinda crap the university is fillin' my son's head with.

MARY: Well, now you know.

JOE: It's the old capitalist game. Keep the blue-collars down by milkin' them of their best brains.

MARY: Don't be stupid! He's going on to graduate school. He'll finish up as a teacher.

JOE: You can't see further than the end of ya nose. He's bein' trained as a lackey—a tool with which ta educate the rulin' class. The big guys.

MARY: My God! When you get into politics its the limit. *Yours* come frothing out of a can of Bud!

JOE: I am not gonna argue. I started ta tell ya a story. D'ya wanna hear it?

MARY: I used ta know this guy an' his wife who spoke only through the cat. Lawrence, his name was.

JOE: Yeh? What was his wife's name?

MARY: Oh, come on! That's the beginning; I'm reminding you.

JOE: What? Oh yeh . . . well . . .

MARY: Listen! That's Dale's car. What time is it? I wonder if he's got somebody with him? (*To Joe*) Make yourself tidy. I'll put some coffee on.

(*She exits*)

JOE (*to nobody*): I'm always tidy. Navy training. (*Mimics*) "Fine turn-out, Sailor, a credit to the ship." (*Own voice*) "Thank you, sir." (*Mimics*) "You're a credit to the Third Fleet." (*Own voice*) "Yessir!" (*He salutes, and is still at attention when Dale enters*)

DALE: Hi, Dad! Where's Mom? It's really gettin' cold out there. I have ta get that heater fixed.

(*In his son's presence Joe is forthright and kindly. Quietly self-confident, with hardly an edge of micky-taking humour*)

JOE: Ya Mom's makin' coffee—she heard ya comin'. I was rememberin' my time in the Navy. Hair-cut every week, then son. Crew cut. You'd have bin fer the high-jump with that mop!

DALE (*sitting down*): Yeh, lot ta be said fer short hair. This is startin' ta bug me. I'm thinkin' of havin' it cut.

JOE: Wouldn't be a bad idea, son. (*Confidentially*) Ya Mom doesn't like it, ya know. She holds her tongue but she ain't as free-thinkin' as I am on the length of hair and morals, an such. Women are natural conservatives—take it from me.

DALE: I've seen a terrific movie tonight—in the Film Series. Ingmar Bergman: *The Silence.*

JOE: Yep, a lovely actress. We watched her on video last week . . . leading a crowd of Chinese kids somewhere.

DALE: That's Ingrid Bergman, Dad—similar name. No; this is a man. Makes movies, well films. Very serious. Perhaps the greatest living director.

JOE: Oh, is that right?

MARY (*bustling in with coffee*): Hello, hon. Are you by yourself? I thought you'd have had somebody with you. That young woman you introduced me to.

DALE: Hi, Mom. Tania?—no, she went to some meeting or other. I was just telling Dad. I was at the Film Society: Ingmar Bergman, *The Silence.*

MARY: Right—that's one of his trilogy, isn't it? About man's alienation from God, you were telling me.

DALE: Only this one's more to do with people being cut off from one another, I reckon.

JOE: If I'd known that I might've come with ya, son. It's a subject in which I'm interested. *Deeply* interested. I was talkin' ta your mother about it, matter o'fact, before you came in.

MARY: Were you? *I* never noticed.

JOE (*mildly*): Ya weren't listenin'. Ya were chatterin' on about this 'n' that, and ya stopped me from gettin' started.

MARY (*to Joe*): I'm sorry. (*To Dale*) It's freezing out there. Have you had that heater fixed yet? (*Giving him mug*) Here, this'll warm you up.

DALE: Thanks, Mom.

MARY: How about something to eat?

DALE: Crackers and cheese'd be great.

MARY: A burger? It'd only take a minute.

DALE: Crackers and cheese'll do.

MARY: OK, hon. Take those boots off, get your feet warm. (*She exits to the kitchen*)

DALE (*removing boots*): Umm, that's better. (*Pause*) How are things at the yard, Dad? Anything dramatic happening in the lumber business?

JOE: We're kinda slack at the moment. It'll pick up around September —always does.

DALE: Uhhu.

JOE: Old man Epstein's retirin' next month, y'know. That'll make a difference. Jason won't let things slide the way his dad's done. *He's* gotta degree—Economics. Course, the old man's been past it fer years. I've been carryin' him, strictly speakin'. Come in one day—Epstein's always askin' about ya?

DALE: Yeh, well, I'd like to . . .

MARY (*interrupting from the kitchen. Offstage*): Did it have sub-titles or was it dubbed—the picture?

DALE (*shouting back*): Subtitles.

MARY (*offstage*): Dubbing ruins the rhythms, I always think.

DALE (*to Joe*): I will, Dad. After exams—or in Reading Week, maybe. I'm really pushed at present.

MARY (*returning with crackers, etc.*): I liked that other Bergman you took me to—*Through a Glass Darkly.*

JOE: I Corinthians, 13—"For now we see through a glass darkly; but then face to face: now I know in part; but then shall I know even as also I am known . . ."

MARY: Listen to your Dad!

JOE: "And now abideth faith, hope, charity, these three; but the greatest of these is charity."

DALE: Hey! (*Amused but impressed*)

JOE: I was brought up on it. Dinned inter me at Church an' Sunday School when I was a kid.

MARY (*to Dale*): He's not been inside a church since the day we were married.

JOE: Well; Church is one thing, th'bible's another. Like my old pa used ta say: "Ya can't expect ta reap if yer . . .

MARY (*interrupting*): You're not comfortable there, Dale. Put your feet up. That's right.

DALE: Go on, Dad. What did Grandpa used to say?

JOE: It doesn't matter. (*Pause*) He had a fine collection of pipes, y'know—well, you won't remember. Meerschaums, churchwardens with lids on. Some with animal heads carved on 'em . . .

MARY: Of course he won't remember. Your Dad died when Dale was five or six.

JOE: Yep, it was quite a while back. (*Pause*) His cat died the same day. *With* him, you might say.

DALE: I've not heard that part of it before, Dad!

MARY: Neither have I and I was there! (*To Dale*) His Mom and Dad never *had* a cat. (*To Joe*) Your Dad couldn't abide the creatures. (*To Dale*) They did have two or three dogs, though I remember helping to bury a German shepherd of theirs in the backyard. (*To Joe*) Your Ezra scraped R.I.P. into a stone. (*To Dale*) How did your class go today, hon? Are the discussions still boring?

DALE: OK, but I've decided Psych's not my bag. Nope. (*To Joe*) Y'know, Dad; I wish I'd met Grandpa. I think I'd've got on with him.

JOE: His cat did, I'll tell ya that! Worshipped the ground he walked on —well, dyin' the same day, it's obvious.

MARY: Your Dad's going bananas. He knows as well as I do his parents never had a cat.

JOE: Whose parents were they? Who's likely to know best?

MARY: You're getting it all confused in your mind. (*To Dale*) First he starts telling me a story about a couple who spoke only through their cat. Then he drags Pat Cooney in, then . . .

DALE (*interrupting*): Pat with the rotorooter, y'mean?

JOE: Right, son; but that has nothin' ta do with it. Ya mother has imagined it.

MARY (*continuing*): —then he drags Pat Cooney in, and *now* he's switching to his parents!

JOE (*patiently*): I'm not switchin' at all, if ya'd listen.

MARY: Anyway, it's often struck me that I knew your Mom and Dad better than you ever did.

JOE: Nothin' of the kind.

MARY: Who was with your Mother when she died? I was!

JOE: I was off the coast of 'Nam, that's why. People dyin' all around me. How could I have been with Mom?

MARY: It *means* something to be with a person when they die—you can't deny that.

JOE: I'm not doin'.

MARY: And *I* was with your Mother.

(*Pause*)

JOE: As a matter of fact—so was I.

DALE (*laughing*): Hey, Dad: You were off the coast of 'Nam with the third fleet. You've just said so!

JOE: *So was I,* I said.

MARY (*turning away*): I don't know what's up with your father. I don't know what he's talkin' about.

JOE: Metempsychosis. Familiar with the word, Dale?

DALE: Transmigration of souls, or something, isn't it?

JOE: It is. That's what it is.

(*Pause*)

MARY: Well?

JOE: I was *in* the cat. A livin' witness, an *eye* witness of my mother's death.

(*Joe leans back. He takes his pipe out and starts to light up during the pause that follows his revelation*)

MARY: I've never heard anything like it. (*To Dale*) How about some more coffee, hon?

DALE: No thanks, Mom. (*To Joe*) Is this cat the same one that died with Grandpa?

JOE (*puffing. Quietly in command*): No, no, son. That was a different cat altogether. The two animals were alike in only one respect.

DALE: How's that, Dad?

JOE: Neither of 'em was called Lawrence—and you've got things out of their right order, anyway. Ya Grandpa died before, some years before, ya Grandma. They *had* ta be different cats. It stan's ta reason.

MARY (*incensed. To Dale*): There's nothing reasonable about anything your Dad's saying. (*To Joe*) You've got goddamn cats on the brain. And as for that lovely old couple your Mother and Father—jeeze, I just don't know what's got inta ya!

DALE: Come on, Mom! Where's ya sense of humour? Dad's puttin' you on, aren't you, Dad?

JOE: Right, Dale. I'm kiddin' her. Metempsychosis—now that's not my language, is it?

MARY: He's getting at me. I don't know how, but he is.

JOE: In her own way, your Mother has a subtle sense of humour.

MARY: I like a joke. But not about the dead.

JOE (*still to Dale*): However, there are some places into which she cannot follow me.

DALE: "Men only", eh, like the bar at the Polish Club!

JOE (*gravely*): I'm talkin' about the recesses of the human mind, son.

DALE (*bewildered*): Oh!?

JOE: Yep. (*Pause*) Now your Mother sometimes talks to me as if I'm retarded.

MARY (*to Dale*): That's not true.

JOE: Oh yes it is. (*To Dale*) And I must admit I encourage her to. There's no one easier to get the better of than someone who's convinced she's cleverer than you.

MARY: What are you on about?

DALE: Yeh, Dad; what are you gettin' at?

JOE: Well. (*Pause*) Now, Mary; I'm askin' ya to remember back ta the night my mother was dyin'. It wasn't a bad death, she was old 'n' tired, so there's nothin' nasty ta picture. She died in her sleep.

MARY: Yes; about half past two in the morning. Me an' your Ezra were taking shifts sitting with her—she always wanted someone to talk to when she woke up. She talked a lot more *after* she was bedridden than she ever did before.

JOE: She was a silent kind o' woman. Dad was the talker.

MARY: She went back over her whole life in that room. I can see her now. She had a pink bed-jacket—but she wore it like a shawl; never used the arms. Sometimes she'd rock backwards and forwards with laughing at some joke till she nearly fell out of bed.

JOE: But the moment of her death: what about that?

MARY: I'd been having a snooze. I woke up and the room was quiet. At first I thought nothing of it—then I remembered how heavy her breathing usually was. "She's gone," I thought—and she had. Lying there peaceful as if she was asleep.

DALE: What did you do, Mom?

MARY: Well; something about death—even the death of someone you love—always frightens you. (*To Joe*) I ran out of the room and shouted for your Ezra—he was sleeping on the couch downstairs. He came rushing up . . . (*coming to herself, as it were*) Anyway, what are you asking me all this for? I wrote you a long letter at the time telling you all about it. You know all this very well!

JOE: But you've omitted ta say *what* frightened you most.

MARY (*to Dale*): Oh yes. It seemed really weird, although it was nothing. As I came back into the room I saw two eyes staring in through the window. They were glistening in the light from the streetlamp. It was a big, black tomcat. It gave me a fright, for a minute.

DALE: I'll bet it did, Mom!

JOE: That big tomcat was *me* I saw everything. (*This is spoken with flat authority*)

MARY (*flabbergasted*): Are you crazy! I told you all about the cat in a letter I wrote to 'Nam. (*To Dale*) That's how he knows so much about it!

JOE: I saw you remove from my Mother's chest of drawers the pearl clip you've still got. You knew Mom wanted you to have it, so you took it before our Bonnie could get her greedy hands on it.

MARY (*to Dale*): I told him all this! I wrote it all to him when he was in the Navy. I've never heard anything like it! (*To Joe*) And the cat belonged to a couple up the street—lived at 56. He was a big guy, worked for the city. His wife was anemic. I don't think they had any kids.

JOE: They hadn't.

MARY (*to Dale*): This is something I know very well . . . Just let me recollect . . . Now I *knew* this cat. It was 'round all the time—

that's why I wasn't scared after the first shock—y'know, the surprise of it. (*Concentrating*) It was black. One of its paws was white—a front one. It had a tattered ear, it was always fighting. (*She pauses to remember hard*) Its name was . . . Lawrence.

JOE: Perfectly correct: Lawrence. (*To Dale*) And it wasn't named after Lawrence Welk, son.

DALE (*laughing*): I should hope not. Lawrence of Arabia? More likely!

JOE: Right. (*To Mary*) Now where does *that* leave you? (*Pause*) Do ya remember how keenly the cat's eyes flashed? How pre-ter-naturally intelligent its stare was?

MARY: It was on heat probably; how do I know!

JOE: Male cats do not go on heat.

MARY: Course they do! Their sexual cycles are seasonal, like those of females.

JOE: No; you've got it wrong.

MARY: I haven't.

JOE: Dale: as a Senior at a prestigious university, would you like to tell your Mother that she knows nothing about cats and their physiology.

DALE (*laughing*): Hey, I'm studyin' literature, y'know.

JOE: And Kendo, I hear. "The Way Of The Sword."

DALE: Yeh, but neither of 'em's the way of cats!

MARY (*with irrelevant grimness*): Did I ever tell you about our wedding day. (*To Dale*)

DALE: The cars turning up late, and so on?

MARY (*heavily*): Remind me to, one of these days.

JOE: Well, I'm making a simple statement. I saw my Mom's death, an' I saw it through the eyes of a big, black tomcat called Lawrence. (*To Dale*) Your Mother won't believe me because she doesn't *want* to believe me—as in the case of Mike Pizzuto.

DALE: Mike Pazutto? What d'y'mean, Dad?

MARY (*to Dale*): He doesn't know *what* he means.

JOE (*to Dale, ignoring Mary*): Mike Pazutto is a sex maniac, in your Mother's eyes.

DALE: Mike? Mike at the Polish Club?

MARY: Shut up, Joe. There's no need to drag that up again.

JOE (*to a mystified Dale*): Excuse me; I'm draggin' somethin' up.

MARY: You've been talking nonsense all night.

JOE: As you wish. (*He pauses, ruminating, and then addresses Dale*) I was with Pat Cooney one day. In Chester. Or was it East Haddam—it doesn't matter. It was just after his wife left him an' he wasn't his usual self.

DALE: How d'y'mean, Dad?

JOE: He was *normally* a man of few words.

MARY: Pat Cooney? Never! He's always on about B'Hai, Theosophy, Scientology, Yoga, or some other religion he's trying. You can't get a word in edgeways. (*To Dale*) *You* know what Pat's like. Loves the sound of his own voice.

JOE: As I was sayin', he wasn't his usual self, an' he started philosophisin'. He'd turned the rotorooter off—somethun' had jammed the blades—an' he wus bendin' down when he said it. (*Pause*) "Joe," he said, "In this job ya gotta plough a lotta good stuff under if ya wanna show a profit." An' you know Pat: he wasn't talkin' about money!

DALE: Right, Pat never bothered about money. That's why his wife left him, I heard.

JOE: From ya Mother.

DALE (*standing, stretching*): Well, I've got an early class in the morning.

MARY: Take the alarm, hon. Your Dad wakes anyway. Is it tomorrow, that Senior picnic?

DALE: Yeh, five o'clock. Are you coming?

MARY: I thought you were going with Tania?

DALE: Well, you come too. There aren't many seniors who live at home—you'll be among the very few parents.

MARY: I'll tell you in the morning. Goodnight, hon. (*Kisses him*) Your razor's behind that foam shaving stuff on the top shelf.

DALE: Goodnight, Dad. I'll fix-up to come to the yard about the week after next, OK?

JOE: OK. Sweet dreams, son.

(*Dale exits*)

MARY: I'm going up, Joe. Don't forget to lock the back door. And put the cat out.

JOE: We haven't got a cat.

MARY (*imperviously*): And turn the lights out. (*Mary exits, but puts her head back to say*) Mike Pazutto *is* a sex maniac, whatever you say.

JOE: Goodnight. (*Joe remains on stage alone, smoking his pipe. After a while he leans forward in his chair, and starts making persuasive noises towards an imaginary cat, which is at the other side of the room*) Cluc, cluc, cluc, cluc, come on, come on . . . . come here to your dad . . . that's it. Ah, you love a tickle, dontcha—roll over at the touch of a finger . . . go on . . . how's that then? (*Tickling cat's belly. He pauses, and then mimics his earlier self*) "Metempsychosis—are you familiar with that word, Dale?" (*He laughs. Addressing cat*) Are *you* familiar with that word, Lawrence? (*Pauses to listen*) Well, I'm not surprised! What would a good-fearin' cat like you be doin' with such pagan ideas? (*He laughs. To nobody in particular*) Oh, what th'hell! (*Pause. Patting his knee*) Come on, l'l buddy; come up here. (*Cat jumps on his lap*) Give'm somethun' ta think about, huh? (*Strokes cat*) Ow, ya l'l bastard! (*Sucks hand*) What ya doin'? Have I ever shown you anything but kindness? No need to friggin' bite me! Now lie still, an' let us enjoy a few moments of peace an' understanding. (*Lies back, stroking cat*) Did you know I played second trumpet in the Navy Band, Lawrence? (*Pause*) Yep, for about four months. First trumpet was Duane Marsalis—I sat next to him. Proud of that, I am! . . . What? . . . You've heard of *Winston* Marsalis, well Duane's his dad, yep. A great musician. (*Pause*) Curl up nicely . . . there's a good cat. (*Pause*) Yep. (*Pause*) Duane Marsalis . . . But there are folks to whom such honours mean nothin'. (*Pause*) I am not jokin', no sir. That's the way the world goes, Lawrence. Education's the thing nowadays, y'know. Take Mike Pazutto: even *he's* goin' ta night school. Community College . . . Huh? . . . (*In answer*) Nav-i-gation. Dreams of ownin' a boat, does Mike—when he wins the lottery, that is! (*Laughs. Business with tie*) Hey! Gettoff, stop foolin' around! Leave m'tie alone, or I'll put you out, like the wife said. Now lie still. (*Pause*) Huh? Was it true? How can you ask such a question after all these years! You know me better than that, Lawrence. (*Pause*) Course it was true. (*Pause*) Like I said, I was inhabitin' the body of a big, black tomcat. Yep, I saw my mother die. (*Pause*) Well, *I've* never heard anything like it, either—believe it or not, as you wish. (*Pause*) Course, I may have dreamt it; anyway, it threw the wife into a loop for a minute. (*Laughs and shakes his head*) Huh? (*Pauses, listening to cat*) Now don't *you* start moralizing, Lawrence—that's the last straw. (*Pause*) I'm not insultin' ya colleagues and co-cats at all. (*Rising angrily*) Geddoff my lap! Ya friggin crazy—ya never knew that big, black tomcat, anyway! (*Moving across room*) Geddout! (*Pointing off*) Come on: out—I've had enough. L'l basterd, who d'y' think you are? Geddout, I said. (*Pause*) It's not my business where ya gonna sleep. (*He is poised, pointing. He relents*) Oh, all right, stop there—but mind that tongue of yours. You've too much ta say for such a l'l' cat. (*Bending and stroking cat*) I *know* it's ya only home. I'm sorry. (*Pause*) I've *said* I'm sorry, let it drop, huh? (*Confidentially*) Tell ya what: Next time I drive to Chester, I'll take you with me. See Pat Cooney, huh? Ya like Pat, dontcha? (*Pause*) Good enough. All forgiven. (*Standing up*) OK. (*Pause*) Metempsychosis?—you're a clever cat, look it up for yaself. Good night, Lawrence, Goodnight puss. Goodnight. (*He exits to bed, switching light off as he goes*)

BONDAGE

David Henry Hwang

David Henry Hwang

David Henry Hwang won his first major award, an OBIE for Best New Play with the production of *F.O.B.,* when Mr. Hwang was only twenty-four years old. Born in Los Angeles and educated at Stamford and at the Yale School of Drama, Hwang has won a host of awards and inspired a number of productions. He is the author of *The Dance and the Railroad* (Drama Desk nomination, Guernsey's Best Plays of 1981–82), *Family Devotions* (Drama Desk nomination), *The House of Sleeping Beauties* and *The Sound of a Voice,* all of which were produced at the New York Shakespeare Festival. *Rich Relations* premiered in 1986 at The Second Stage.

Then in 1988 with his play *M. Butterfly,* Hwang made the giant leap into Broadway stardom. His play won the 1988 Tony, Drama Desk, Outer Critics Circle, and John Gassner awards as well as the 1991 L.A. Drama Critics Circle Award, and has subsequently been produced in some three dozen countries around the world. His one-act play, *Bondage,* premiered in 1992 at the Humana Theatre Festival.

He wrote the libretto for Philip Glass' opera *The Voyage,* which premiered at the Metropolitan Opera House (October 1992). He previously collaborated with Glass and designer Jerome Sirlin on *1000 Airplanes on the Roof.* Mr. Hwang's screenplay of *M. Butterfly,* starring Jeremy Irons and John Lone, is scheduled to be released by Warner Brothers in the fall of 1993. Another film, *Golden Gate,* starring Matt Dillon and Joan Chen, will be released in October, 1993.

For many years a volume of Hwang's plays was published by Avon under the title *Broken Blossoms.* A new volume of plays is being prepared for publication. A force in the theater world for the last dozen years, David Hwang is a young, powerful dramatist for whom the theater can be especially grateful.

Characters:
TERRI, *late-twenties, female*
MARK, *early-thirties, male*

Scene
A room in a fantasy bondage parlor. Terri, a dominatrix, paces with her whip in hand before Mark, who is chained to the wall. Both their faces are covered by full face masks and hoods to disguise their identities.

MARK: What am I today?

TERRI: Today—you're a man. A Chinese man. But don't bother with that accent crap. I find it demeaning.

MARK: A Chinese man. All right. And who are you?

TERRI: Me? I'm—I'm a blonde woman. Can you remember that?

MARK: I feel . . . very vulnerable.

TERRI: You should. I pick these roles for a reason, you know. (*She unchains him*) We'll call you Wong. Mark Wong. And me—I'm Tifanny Walker. (*Pause*) I've seen you looking at me. From behind the windows of your—engineering laboratory. Behind your—horn rimmed glasses. Why don't you come right out and try to pick me up? Whisper something offensive into my ear. Or aren't you man enough?

MARK: I've been trying to approach you. In my own fashion.

TERRI: How do you expect to get anywhere at that rate? Don't you see the jocks, the football stars, the cowboys who come 'round every day with their tongues hanging out? This is America, you know. If you don't assert yourself, you'll end up at sixty-five worshiping a Polaroid you happened to snap of me at a high school picnic.

MARK: But—you're a blonde. I'm—Chinese. It's not so easy to know whether it's OK for me to love you.

TERRI: C'mon, this is the 1990's! I'm no figment of the past. For a Chinese man to love a white woman—what could be wrong about that?

MARK: That's . . . great! You really feel that way? Then, let me just declare it to your face. I—

TERRI: Of course—

MARK: —love—

TERRI: It's not real likely I'm gonna love you.

(*Pause*)

MARK: But . . . you said—

TERRI: I said I'm not a figment of the past. But I'm also not some crusading figure from the future. It's only 1992, you know. I'm a normal girl. With regular ideas. Regular for a blonde, of course.

MARK: What's that supposed to mean?

TERRI: It means I'm not prejudiced—in principle. Of course I don't notice the color of a man's skin. Except—I can't help but notice. I've got eyes, don't I? (*Pause*) I'm sure you're a very nice person . . . Mark. And I really appreciate your helping me study for the . . . physics midterm. But I'm just not—what can I say? I'm just not attracted to you.

MARK: Because I'm Chinese.

TERRI: Oh no, oh heavens, no. I would never be prejudiced against an Oriental. They have such . . . strong family structures . . . hard working . . . they hit the books with real gusto . . . makes my mother green with envy. But, I guess . . . how excited can I get about a boy who fulfills my mother's fantasies? The reason most mothers admire boys like you is 'cause they didn't bother to marry someone like that themselves. No, I'm looking for a man more like my father—someone I can regret in later life.

MARK: So you're not attracted to me because I'm Chinese. Like I said before.

TERRI: Why are you Orientals so relentlessly logical?

(*She backs him up around the room*)

MARK: Well, for your information . . . it doesn't—it doesn't hurt that you're not in love with me.

TERRI: Why not?

MARK: Because I never said that I loved you, either!

(*They stop in their tracks*)

TERRI: You didn't?

MARK: Nope, nope, nope.

TERRI: That's bullshit. I was here, you know. I heard you open yourself up to ridicule and humiliation. I have a very good ear for that kind of thing. (*Cracks her whip*) So goddamn it—admit it—you said you love me!

MARK: I did not! If I don't tell the truth, you'll be angry with me.

TERRI: I'm already angry with you now for lying! Is this some nasty scheme to maneuver yourself into a no-win situation? God, you masochists make life confusing.

MARK: I came close. I said, "I love—," but then you cut me off.

TERRI: That's my prerogative. I'm the dominatrix.

MARK: I never finished the sentence. Maybe I was going to say, "I love . . . the smell of fresh-baked apple pie in the afternoon."

TERRI: That's a goddamn lie!

MARK: Can you prove it? You cut me off. In mid-sentence.

TERRI: It does . . . sound like something I would do. Damn. I'm always too eager to assert my superiority. It's one of the occupational hazards of my profession. (*Pause*) So I fucked up. I turned total victory into personal embarrassment. God, I'm having a rotten day.

MARK: Terri—

TERRI: Mistress Terri!

MARK: Mistress Terri, I—I didn't mean to upset you. It's OK. I wasn't really going to say I loved apple pie. Now—you can whip me for lying to you. How's that?

TERRI: I'm not about to start taking charity from my submissives, thank you. That's one good way to get laughed out of the profession. (*Pause*) Sorry, I just—need a moment. Wouldn't it be nice if they'd put coffeemakers in here?

MARK: Look—do what you want. I'm a Mexican man, and you're an Indonesian—whatever.

TERRI: What went wrong—was I just going through the motions?

(*Mark kneels behind her, places his hands gently on her shoulders*)

MARK: You feeling OK today?

TERRI: Of course I am! It just . . . hurts a girl's confidence to stumble like that when I was in my strongest position, with you at your weakest.

MARK: Why were you in such a strong position?

TERRI: Well, I was—a blonde!

MARK: And why was I in such a weak one?

TERRI: Oh, c'mon—you were . . . an Oriental man. Easy target. It's the kind of role I choose when I feel like phoning in the performance. Shit! Now, look—I'm giving away trade secrets.

MARK: Asian. An Asian man.

TERRI: Sorry. I didn't know political correctness had suddenly arrived at S & M parlors.

MARK: It never hurts to practice good manners. You're saying I wasn't sexy?

TERRI: Well . . . I mean . . . a girl likes a little excitement sometimes.

MARK: OK, OK . . . look, let's just pretend . . . pretend that I did say "I love you." You know, to get us over this hump.

TERRI: Now, we're pretending something happened in a fantasy when it actually didn't? I think this is getting a little esoteric.

MARK: Terri, look at us! Everything we do is pretend! That's exactly the point! We play out these roles until one of us gets the upper hand!

TERRI: You mean, until I get the upper hand.

MARK: Well, in practice, that's how it's always—

TERRI: I like power.

MARK: So do I.

TERRI: You'll never win.

MARK: There's a first time for everything.

TERRI: You're the exception that proves the rule.

MARK: So prove it. C'mon! And—oh—try not break down again in the middle of the fantasy.

TERRI: Fuck you!

MARK: It sort of—you know—breaks the mood?

TERRI: I'm sorry! I had a very bad morning. I've been working long hours—

MARK: Don't! Don't start talking about your life on my time!

TERRI: OK, you don't need to keep—

MARK: Sometimes, I really wonder why I have to be the one reminding you of the house rules at this late date.

TERRI: I didn't mean to, all right? These aren't the easiest relationships in the world, you know!

MARK: A man comes in, he plops down good money . . .

TERRI: I'm not in the mood to hear about your financial problems.

MARK: Nor I your personal ones! This is a fantasy palace, so goddamn it, start fantasizing!

TERRI: I have a good mind to take off my mask and show you who I really am.

MARK: You do that, and you know I'll never come here again.

TERRI: Ooooh—scary! What—do you imagine I might actually have some real feelings for you?

MARK: I don't imagine anything but what I pay you to make me imagine! Now, pick up that whip, start barking orders, and let's get back to investigating the burning social issues of our day!

TERRI (*practically in tears*): You little maggot! You said you loved me . . . Mark Wong!

MARK: Maybe. Why aren't I sexy enough for you?

TERRI: I told you—a girl likes a little excitement.

MARK: Maybe I'm—someone completely different from who you imagine. Someone . . . with a touch of evil. Who doesn't study for exams.

TERRI: Oh—like you get "A" 's regardless? 'Cuz you're such a brain?

MARK: I have a terrible average in school. D-minus.

TERRI: I thought all you people were genetically programmed to score in the high-90's. What are you—a mutant?

MARK: I hang out with a very dangerous element. We smoke in spite of the surgeon general's warning. I own a cheap little motorcycle that I keep tuned in perfect condition. Why don't I take you up to the lake at midnight and show you some tricks with a switchblade? (*He plays with the handle of her whip*) Don't you find this all . . . a lot more interesting?

TERRI: I . . . I'm not sure.

MARK: I'm used to getting what I want.

TERRI: I mean . . . I wasn't planning on getting involved with someone this greasy.

MARK: I'm not greasy. I'm dangerous! And right now, I've got my eye set on you.

TERRI: You sound like some old movie from the 50's.

MARK: I'm classic. What's so bad about—?

TERRI: Oh, wait! I almost forgot! You're Chinese, aren't you?

MARK: Well, my name *is* Mark Wong, but—

TERRI: Oh, well . . . I'm certainly not going to go out with a member of the Chinese mafia!

MARK: The Chinese—what? Wait!

TERRI: Of course! Those pathetic imitations of B-movie delinquents, that cheap Hong Kong swagger.

MARK: Did I say anything about the Chinese mafia?

TERRI: You don't have to—you're Chinese, aren't you? What are you going to do now? Rape me? With your friends? 'Cuz I've seen movies, and you Chinatown pipsqueaks never seem to be able to get a white woman of her own free will. And even when you take her by force, it still requires more than one of you to get the job done. Personally, I think it's all just an excuse to feel up your buddies.

MARK: Wait! Stop! Cut! I said I was vaguely bad—

TERRI: Yeah, corrupting the moral fiber of this nation with evil foreign influences—

MARK: "Vaguely bad" does not make me a hitman for the Tong!

TERRI: Then what are you? A Viet Cong? Mmmm—big improvement. I'm really gonna wanna sleep with you now!

MARK: No—that's even more evil!

TERRI: Imprison our hometown boys neck-high in leech-filled waters—

MARK: No, no! Less evil! Less—

TERRI: Will you make up your goddamn mind? Indecision in a sado-masochist is a sign of poor mental health.

MARK: I'm not a Chinese gangster, not a Viet Cong . . .

TERRI: Then you're a nerd. Like I said—

MARK: No! I'm . . .

TERRI: . . . we're waiting . . .

MARK: I'm . . . I'm neither!

(*Pause*)

TERRI: You know, buddy, I can't create a fantasy session solely out of negative imagines.

MARK: Isn't there something in between? Just delinquent enough to be sexy without also being responsible for the deaths of a few hundred thousand U.S. servicemen?

(*Terri paces about, dragging her whip behind her*)

TERRI: Look, this is a nice American fantasy parlor. We deal in basic, mainstream images. You want something kinky, maybe you should try one of those specialty houses catering to wealthy European degenerates.

MARK: How about Bruce Lee? Would you find me sexy if I was Bruce Lee?

TERRI: You mean, like, "Hiiii-ya! I wuv you." (*Pause*) Any other ideas? Or do you admit no woman could love you, Mark Wong?

(*Mark assumes a doggy-position*)

MARK: I'm defeated. I'm humiliated. I'm whipped to the bone.

TERRI: Well, don't complain you didn't get your money's worth. Perhaps now I'll mount you—little pony—you'd like that wouldn't you?

MARK: Wait! You haven't humiliated me completely.

TERRI: I'll be happy to finish the job—just open that zipper.

MARK: I still never said that I loved you, remember?

(*Pause*)

TERRI: I think that's an incredibly technical objection this late in the game.

MARK: All's fair in love and bondage! I did you a favor—I ignored your mistake—well, now I'm taking back the loan.

TERRI: You are really asking for it, buddy . . .

MARK: After all, I'm not a masochist—no matter how this looks. Sure, I let you beat me, treat me as less than a man—

TERRI: When you're lucky . . .

MARK: But I do not say "I love you!" Not without a fight! To say "I love you" is the ultimate humiliation. A woman like you looks on a declaration of love as an invitation to loot and pillage.

TERRI: I always pry those words from your lips sooner or later and you know it.

MARK: Not today—you won't today!

TERRI: Oh, look—he's putting up his widdle fight. Sometimes I've asked myself, "Why is it so easy to get Mark to say he loves me? Could it be . . . because deep inside—he actually does?"

MARK: Love you? That's—slanderous!

TERRI: Just trying to make sense of your behavior.

MARK: Well, stop it! I refuse to be made sense of—by you or anyone else! Maybe . . . maybe you *wish* I was really in love with you, could that be it?

TERRI: Oh, eat me!

MARK: 'Cuz the idea certainly never entered *my* head.

TERRI: Oh—even when you scream out your love for me?

MARK: That's what we call—a fantasy . . . Mistress.

TERRI: Yeah—*your* fantasy.

MARK: The point is, you haven't beaten me down. Not yet. You may even be surprised sometime to see that I've humiliated you. I'll reject *you* for loving me. And maybe, then, I'll mount *you*—pony.

TERRI (*bursts out laughing*): You can't dominate me. I'm a trained professional.

MARK: So? I've been your client more than a year now. Maybe I've picked up a trick or two.

TERRI: I'm at this six hours a day, six days a week. Your time is probably squandered in some less rewarding profession.

MARK: Maybe I've been practicing in my spare time.

TERRI: With your employees at some pathetic office? Tsst! They're paid to humiliate themselves before you. But me, I'm paid to humiliate you. And I still believe in the American work ethic. (*She cracks her whip*) So—enough talking everything to death! I may love power, but I haven't yet stooped to practicing psychiatry, thank you. OK, you're a—a white man and me—I'm a Black woman!

MARK: African American.

TERRI: Excuse me—are you telling me what I should call myself? Is this another of our rights you're dying to take away?

MARK: Not me. The Rev. Jesse Jackson—He thinks African American is the proper—

TERRI: Who?

MARK: Jesse—I'm sorry, is this a joke?

TERRI: You're not laughing, so I guess it's not. Tell me—the way you talk . . . could you be . . . a liberal?

MARK: Uh, yes, if you speak in categories, but—

TERRI: Um. Well, then that explains it.

MARK: Explains what?

TERRI: Why I notice you eyeing me up every time I wander towards the bar.

MARK: Let me be frank. I . . . saw you standing here, and thought to myself, "That looks like a very intelligent woman."

(*She laughs*)

Sorry. Did I—say something?

TERRI: What do they do? Issue you boys a handbook?

MARK: What?

TERRI: You know, for all you white liberals who do your hunting a little off the beaten track?

MARK: Now, look here—

TERRI: 'Cuz you've all got the same line. You always start talking about our "minds," then give us this *look* like we're supposed to be grateful—"Aren't you surprised?" "Ain't I sensitive?" "Wouldn't you like to oil up your body and dance naked to James Brown?"

MARK: I can't believe . . . you're accusing *me* of—

TERRI: Then again, what else should I have expected at a PLO fundraiser? So many white liberals, a girl can't leave the room without one or two sticking to her backside.

MARK: Listen—all I said was I find you attractive. If you can't deal with that, then maybe . . . maybe *you're* the one who's prejudiced.

TERRI: White people—whenever they don't get what they want, they always start screaming "reverse racism."

MARK: Would you be so . . . derisive if I was a Black man?

TERRI: You mean, an African American?

MARK: Your African American brothers aren't afraid to date white women, are they? No, in fact, I hear they treat them better than they do their own sisters, doesn't that bother you even a bit?

TERRI: And what makes you such an expert on Black men? Read a book by some other whitey?

MARK: Hey—I saw "Jungle Fever."

TERRI: For your urban anthropology class?

MARK: Don't get off the subject. Of you and me. And the dilemma I know you're facing. Your own men, they take you for granted, don't they? I think you should be a little more open-minded, unless you wanna end up like the 40% of Black women over 30 who're never even gonna get married in their lifetimes.

(*Silence*)

TERRI: Who the fuck do you think you are? Trying to intimidate me into holding your pasty-white hand? Trying to drive a wedge through our community?

MARK: No, I'm just saying, look at the plain, basic—

TERRI: You say you're attracted to my intelligence? I saw you checking out a lot more than my mind.

MARK: Well, you do seem . . . sensuous.

TERRI: Ah. Sensuous. I can respect a man who tells the truth.

MARK: That's a . . . very tight outfit you've got on.

TERRI: Slinky, perhaps?

MARK: And when you talk to me, your lips . . .

TERRI: They're full and round—without the aid of collagen.

MARK: And—the way you walked across the room . . .

TERRI: Like a panther? Sleek and sassy. Prowling—

MARK: Through the wild.

TERRI: Don't you mean, the jungle?

MARK: Yes, the . . . Wait, no! I see where you're going!

TERRI: Big deal, I was sniffing your tracks ten miles back. I'm so wild, right? The hot sun blazing. Drums beating in the distance. Pounding, pounding . . .

MARK: That's not fair—!

TERRI: Pounding that Zulu beat.

MARK: You're putting words into my mouth . . .

TERRI: No, I'm just pulling them out, liberal.

(*She cracks the whip, driving him back*)

What good is that handbook now? Did you forget? Forget you're only supposed to talk about my mind? Forget that a liberal must never ever reveal what's really on his?

MARK: I'm sorry. I'm sorry . . . Mistress!

TERRI: On your knees, Liberal! (*She runs the heel of her boot over the length of his body*) You wanted to have a little fun, didn't you? With a wild dark woman whose passions drown out all her inhibitions. (*She pushes him onto his back, puts the heel to his lips*) I'll give you passion. Here's your passion.

MARK: I didn't mean to offend you.

TERRI: No, you just couldn't help it. C'mon—suck it. Like the lily-white baby boy you are.

(*He fellates her heel*)

That statistic about Black women never getting married? What'd you do—study up for today's session? You thought you could get the best of me—admit it, naughty man, or I'll have to spank your little butt purple.

MARK: I didn't study—honest!

TERRI: You hold to that story? Then Mama has no choice but to give you what you want—roll over!

(*He rolls onto his stomach*)

You actually thought you could get ahead of me on current events!

(*She whips his rear over the next sequence*)

MARK: No, I mean—that statistic—it was just—

TERRI: Just what?

MARK: Just street knowledge!

TERRI: Street knowledge? Where do you hang out—the Census Bureau? Liar! (*She pokes at his body with the butt of her whip*) Don't you know you'll never defeat me? This is your game—to play all the races—but me—I've already become all races. You came to the wrong place, sucker. Inside this costume live the intimate experiences of ethnic groups that haven't even been born. (*Pause*) Get up. I'm left sickened by that little attempt to assert your will. We'll have to come up with something really good for such an infraction.

MARK: Can I—can I become Chinese again?

TERRI: What is your problem? It's not our practice to take requests from the customers.

MARK: I—don't want you to make things easy on me. I want to go back to what you call a position of weakness. I want you to pull the ropes tight!

TERRI (*laughs*): It's a terrible problem with masochists, really. You don't know whether being cruel is actually the ultimate kindness. You wanna be the lowest of the low? Then beg for it.

(*He remains in a supplicant position for this ritual, as she casually tends to her chores*)

MARK: I desire to be the lowest of men.

TERRI: Why?

MARK: Because my existence is an embarrassment to all women.

TERRI: And why is that?

MARK: Because my mind is dirty, filled with hateful thoughts against them. Threats my weakling body can never make good on—but I give away my intentions at every turn—my lustful gaze can't help but give offense.

TERRI: Is that why you desire punishment?

MARK: Yes. I desire punishment.

TERRI: But you'll never dominate your mistress, will you? (*Pause*) Will you?! (*She cracks her whip*) All right. Have it your way. I think there's an idea brewing in that tiny brain of yours. You saw me stumble earlier tonight—then, you felt a thrill of exhilaration—however short-lived—with your 40% statistic. All of a sudden, your hopes are raised, aren't they? God, it pisses me off more than anything to see hope in a man's eyes. It's always the final step before rape. (*Pause*) It's time to nip hope in the bud. You'll be your Chinese man, and me—I'll be an Asian woman, too. (*Pause*) Have you been staring at me across the office—Mark Wong?

MARK: Who? Me?

TERRI: I don't see anyone else in the room.

MARK: I have to admit—

TERRI: What?

MARK: You are . . . very attractive.

TERRI: It's good to admit these things. Don't you feel a lot better already? You've been staring at me, haven't you?

MARK: Maybe . . .

TERRI: No, you don't mean "maybe."

MARK: My eyes can't help but notice . . .

TERRI: You mean, "Yes, sir, that's my baby." The only other Asian American in this office.

MARK: It does seem like we might have something in common.

TERRI: Like what?

MARK: Like—where'd your parents come from?

TERRI: Mom's from Chicago, Dad's from Stockton.

MARK: Oh.

TERRI: You didn't expect me to say "Hong Kong" or "Hiroshima," did you?

MARK: No, I mean—

TERRI: Because that would be a stereotype. Why—are *you* a foreigner?

MARK: No.

TERRI: I didn't necessarily think so—

MARK: I was born right here in Los Angeles!

TERRI: But when you ask a question like that, I'm not sure.

MARK: Queen of Angels Hospital!

TERRI: Mmmm. What else do you imagine we might have in common?

MARK: Well, do you ever . . . feel like people are pigeonholing you? Like they assume things?

TERRI: What kinds of things?

MARK: Like you're probably a whiz at math and science? Or else a Viet Cong?

TERRI: No! I was editor of the paper in high school, and the literary journal in college.

MARK: Look, maybe we're getting off on the wrong foot, here.

TERRI: Actually, there *is* one group of people that does categorize me, now that you mention it.

MARK: So you *do* understand.

TERRI: Asian men. (*Pause*) Asian men who just assume because we shared space in a genetic pond millions of years ago that I'm suddenly their property when I walk into a room. Or an office. (*Pause*) Now get this straight. I'm not interested in you, OK? In fact, I'm generally not attracted to Asian men. I don't have anything against them personally, I just don't date them as a species.

MARK: Don't you think that's a little prejudiced? That you're not interested in me because of my race? And it's even your own? I met this Black girl a few minutes ago—she seemed to support *her* brothers.

TERRI: Well, her brothers are probably a lot cuter than mine. Look, it's a free country. Why don't you do the same? Date a Caucasian woman.

MARK: I tried that too . . . a couple of women back.

TERRI: I'll tell you why you don't. Because you Asian men are all alike —you're looking for someone who reminds you of your mothers. Who'll smile at the lousiest jokes and spoon rice into your bowl while you just sit and grunt. Well, I'm not about to date any man who reminds me even slightly of my father.

MARK: But a blonde rejected me because I *didn't* remind her of her father.

TERRI: Of course you didn't! You're Asian!

MARK: And now, you won't date me because I *do* remind you of yours?

TERRI: Of course you do! You're Asian!

(*Pause*)

MARK: How—how can I win here?

TERRI: It's simple. You can't. Have you ever heard of historical karma? That's the notion that cultures have pasts that eventually catch up with them. For instance, white Americans were evil enough to bring Africans here in chains—now, they should pay for that legacy. Similarly, Asian men have oppressed their women for centuries. Now, they're paying for their crime by being passed over for dates in favor of white men. It's a beautiful way to look at history, when you think about it.

MARK: Why should my love life suffer for crimes I didn't even commit? I'm an American!

TERRI: C'mon—you don't expect me to buck the wheel of destiny, do you? This is the 1990's—every successful Asian woman walks in on the arm of a white man.

MARK: But—but what about Italian men? Or Latinos? Do you like them?

TERRI: I find them attractive enough, yes.

MARK: Well, what about their cultures? Aren't they sexist?

TERRI: Why do you stereotype people like that? If pressed, I would characterize them as macho.

MARK: Macho? And Asian men aren't?

TERRI: No—you're just sexist.

MARK: What's the difference?

TERRI: The—I dunno. Macho is . . . sexier, that's all. You've never been known as the most assertive of men.

MARK: How can we be not assertive enough and too oppressive all at the same time?

TERRI: It's one of the miracles of your psychology. Is it any wonder no one wants to date you?

MARK: Aaargh! You can't reject me on such faulty reasoning!

TERRI: I can reject you for any reason I want. That's one of the things which makes courtship so exciting. (*Pause*) It seems obvious now, the way you feel about me, doesn't it?

MARK: It does not!

TERRI: C'mon—whether Black, Blonde, or Asian—I think the answer is the same. You . . . what?

MARK: I . . . find you attractive . . .

TERRI: Give it up! You feel something—something that's driving you crazy.

MARK: All right! You win! I love you!

TERRI: Really? You do? Why, young man—I had no idea! (*Pause*) I'm sorry . . . but I could never return your affections, you being so very unlovable and all. In fact, your feelings offend me. And so I have no choice but to punish you.

MARK: I understand. You win again. (*He heads for the shackles*)

TERRI: Say it again. Like you mean it.

MARK: You win! I admit it!

TERRI: Not that—the other part!

MARK: You mean, I love you? Mistress Terri, I love you.

TERRI: No! More believable! The last thing anyone wants is an apathetic slave!

MARK: But I *do* love you! More than any woman—

TERRI: Or man?

MARK: Or anything—any creature—any impulse . . . in my own body —more than any part of my body . . . that's how much I love you.

(*Pause*)

TERRI: You're still not doing it right, damn it!

MARK: I'm screaming it like I always do—I was almost getting poetic, there . . .

TERRI: Shut up! It's just not good enough. *You're* not good enough. I won't be left unsatisfied. Come here.

MARK: But—

TERRI: You wanna know a secret? It doesn't matter what you say—there's one thing that always makes your words ring false—one thing that lets me know you're itching to oppress me.

MARK: Wha— what do you mean?

TERRI: I don't think you want to hear it. But maybe . . . maybe I want to tell you anyway.

MARK: Tell me! I can take the punishment.

TERRI: What sickens me most . . . is that you feel compelled to play these kinds of parlor games with me.

MARK: What—what the hell are you—?!

TERRI: I mean, how can you even talk about love? When you can't approach me like a normal human being? When you have to hide behind masks and take on these ridiculous roles?

MARK: You're patronizing me! Don't! Get those ropes on me!

TERRI: Patronizing? No, I've *been* patronizing you. Today, I can't even keep up the charade! I mean, your entire approach here—it lets me know—

MARK: I don't have to stand for this!

TERRI: That you're afraid of any woman unless you're sure you've got her under control!

MARK: This is totally against all the rules of the house!

TERRI: Rules, schmules! The rules say I'm supposed to grind you under my heel! They leave the details to me—sadism is an art, not a science. So—beg for more! Beg me to tell you about yourself!

(*Panicked, Mark heads for the wall, tries to insert his own wrists into the shackles*)

MARK: No! If I'm—If I'm defeated, I must accept my punishment fair and square.

TERRI: You're square all right. Get your arms out of there! Stand like a man! Beg me to tell you who you are.

MARK: If I obey, will you reward me by denying my request?

TERRI: Who knows? Out of generosity, I might suddenly decide to grant it.

MARK: If you're determined to tell me either way, why should I bother to beg?

TERRI: For your own enjoyment.

MARK: I refuse! You've never done something like this before!

TERRI: That's why I'm so good at my job. I don't allow cruelty to drift into routine. Now, beg!

MARK: Please, Mistress Terri . . . will you . . . will you tell me who I really am?

TERRI: You want to know—you wanna know bad, don't you?

MARK: No!

TERRI: In the language of sadomasochism, "no" almost always means "yes."

MARK: No, no, no!

TERRI: You are an eager one, aren't you?

MARK: I just don't like you making assumptions about me! Do you think I'm some kind of emotional weakling, coming in here because I can't face the real world of women?

TERRI: That would be a fairly good description of all our clients.

MARK: Maybe I'm a lot more clever than you think! Do you ever go out there? Do you know the opportunities for pain and humiliation that lurk outside these walls?

TERRI: Well, I . . . I *do* buy groceries, you know.

MARK: The rules out there are set up so we're all bound to lose.

TERRI: And the rules in here are so much better?

MARK: The rules here . . . protect me from harm. Out there—I walk around with my face exposed. In here, when I'm rejected, beaten down, humiliated—it's not me. I have no identifying features, and so . . . I'm no longer human. (*Pause*) And that's why I'm not pathetic to come here. Because someday, I'm going to beat you. And on that day, my skin will have become so thick, I'll be impenetrable to harm. I won't need a mask to keep my face hidden. I'll have lost myself in the armor. (*He places his wrists into the wall shackles*) OK—I bent to your will. You defeated me again. So strap me up. Punish me.

TERRI: But why . . . why all these fantasies about race?

MARK: Please, enough!

TERRI: I mean, what race *are* you, anyway?

MARK: You know, maybe we should just talk about *your* real life, how would you like that?

(*Pause*)

TERRI: Is that what you want?

MARK: No . . .

TERRI: Is that a "no" no, or a "yes" no?

MARK: Yes. No. Goddamn it, I paid for my punishment, just give it to me!

(*She tosses away her whip, begins to strap him up*)

What are you doing?

TERRI: Punishment is, by definition, something the victim does not appreciate. The fact that you express such a strong preference for the whip practically compels me not to use it. (*Pause*) I think I'd prefer . . . to kill you with kindness. (*She begins kissing the length of his body*)

MARK: Please! This isn't . . . what I want!

TERRI: Are you certain? Maybe . . . I feel something for you. After all, you've made me so very angry. Maybe . . . you're a white man, I'm a white woman—there's nothing mysterious—no racial considerations whatsoever.

MARK: That's . . . too easy! There's no reason you wouldn't love me under those conditions.

TERRI: Are you crazy? I can think of a couple dozen off the top of my head. You don't have to be an ethnic minority to have a sucky love life.

MARK: But there's no . . . natural barrier between us!

TERRI: Baby, you haven't dated many white women as a white man lately. I think it's time to change all that. (*Pause; Terri steps away*) So —Mark . . . Walker. Mark Walker—how long has it been? Since anyone's given you a rubdown like that?

MARK (*after a pause*): I usually . . . avoid these kinds of situations . . .

TERRI: Why are you so afraid?

MARK: My fright is reasonable. Given the conditions out there.

TERRI: What conditions? Do you have, for instance, problems with . . . inter-racial love?

MARK: Whatever gave you that idea?

TERRI: Well, you . . . remind me of a man I see sometimes . . . who belongs to all races . . . and none at all. I've never met anyone like him before.

MARK: I'm a white man! Why wouldn't I have problems? The world is changing so fast around me—you can't even tell whose country it is any more. I can't hardly open my mouth without wondering if I'm offending, if I'm secretly revealing to everyone but myself . . . some hatred, some hidden desire to strike back . . . breeding within my body. (*Pause*) If only there were some certainty—whatever it might be—OK, let the feminists rule the place! We'll call it the United States of Amazonia! Or the Japanese! Or the gays! If I could only figure out who's in charge, then I'd know where I stand. But this constant flux—who can endure it? I'd rather crawl into a protected room where I know what to expect—painful though that place may be. (*Pause*) I mean . . . we're heading towards the millennium. Last time, people ran fearing the end of the world. They hid their bodies from the storms that would inevitably follow. Casual gestures were taken as signs of betrayal and accusation. Most sensed that the righteous would somehow be separated from the wicked. But no one knew on which side of such a division they themselves might fall.

(*Silence*)

TERRI: You want to hear about yourself. You've been begging for it so long—in so many ways.

MARK: How do you know I just said anything truthful? What makes you so sure I'm really a white man?

TERRI: Oh, I'm not. After all these months, I wouldn't even care to guess. When you say you're Egyptian, Italian, Spanish, Mayan—you seem to be the real thing. So what if we just say . . . (*pause; she releases him*) You're a man, and you're frightened, and you've been ill-used in love. You've come to doubt any trace of your own judgment. You cling to the hope that power over a woman will blunt her ability to harm you, while all the time you're tormented by the growing fear that your hunger will never be satisfied with the milk of cruelty. (*Pause*) I know. I've been in your place.

MARK: You . . . you've been a man? What are you saying?

TERRI: You tell me. Fight back. Tell me about me. And make me love every second of it.

MARK: All right. Yes.

TERRI: Yes . . . WHO?

MARK: Yes, Mistress Terri!

TERRI: Yes—who?

MARK: Yes . . . whoever you are . . . a woman who's tried hard to hate men for what they've done to her but who . . . can't quite convince herself.

(*She pushes him to the ground*)

TERRI: Is that what you think? (*Beat*) Tell me more . . .

MARK: You went out—into the world . . . I dunno, after college maybe—I think you went to college . . .

TERRI: Doesn't matter.

MARK: But the world—it didn't turn out the way you planned . . . rejection hung in the air all around you—in the workplace, in movies, in the casual joking of the population. The painful struggle . . . to be accepted as a spirit among others . . . only to find yourself constantly weighed and measured by those outward bits of yourself so easily grasped, too easily understood. Maybe you were harassed at work—maybe even raped—I don't know.

TERRI: It doesn't matter. The specifics never matter.

MARK: So you found your way here—somehow—back of the Hollywood Star—something—roomfuls of men begging to be punished for the way they act out there—wanting you to even the score—and you decided—that this was a world you could call your own.

TERRI: And so, I learned what it feels like to be a man. To labor breathlessly accumulating power while all the time it's dawning how tiring, what a burden, how utterly numbing—it is actually to possess. The touch of power is cold like metal. It chafes the skin, but you know nothing better to hold to your breast. So you travel down this blind road of hunger—constantly victimizing yourself in the person of others—until you despair of ever again feeling warm or safe—until you forget such possibilities exist. Until they become sentimental relics of a weaker man's delusions. And driven by your need, you slowly destroy yourself. (*She starts to remove her gloves*) Unless, one day, you choose to try something completely different.

MARK: What are you doing? Wait!

TERRI: It's a new game, Mark. A new ethnic game. The kind you like.

MARK: We can't play—without costumes.

TERRI: Oh, but it's the wildest inter-racial fantasy of all. It's called . . . two hearts meeting in a bondage parlor on the outskirts of Encino. With skins—more alike than not.

(*She tosses her gloves away*)

Haven't we met before? I'm certain we have. You were the one who came into my chamber wanting to play all the races.

MARK: Why are you doing this to me? I'm the customer here!

TERRI: No, your time is up. Or haven't you kept your eyes on the clock? At least I know I'm not leaving you bored.

MARK: Then . . . shouldn't I be going?

TERRI: If you like. But I'm certain we've met before. I found it so interesting, so different your fantasy. And I've always been a good student, a diligent employee. My Daddy raised me to take pride in all of America's service professions. So I started to . . . try and understand all the races I never thought of as my own. Then, what happened?

MARK: You're asking me?

TERRI: C'mon—let me start you off. I have a box in my closet—

(*She runs her bare hands up and down his body as he speaks*)

MARK: In which you keep all the research you've done . . . for me. Every clipping, magazine article, ethnic journals, transcripts from Phil Donahue. Blacks against Jews in Crown Heights—your eyes went straight to the headlines. The rise of neo-Naziism in Marseille and Orange County. And then, further—the mass-murderer in Canada who said "The feminists made me do it." You became a collector of all the rejection and rage in this world. (*Pause*) Am I on the right track?

TERRI: Is that what you've been doing?

MARK: And that box—that box is overflowing now. Books are piled high to the hems of your dresses, clippings slide out from beneath the door. And you . . . you looked at it . . . maybe this morning . . . and you realized your box was . . . full. And so you began to stumble. You started to feel there was nothing more here for you.

TERRI: If you say it, it must be true.

MARK: Is it?

TERRI (*she starts to unlace her thigh-high boots*): I'm prepared to turn in my uniform and start again from here.

MARK: You're quitting your job?

TERRI: The masks don't work. The leather is pointless. I'm giving notice as we speak.

MARK: But—what if I'm wrong?

TERRI: I'm afraid I'll have to take that chance.

MARK: No, you can't just—what about your hatred of men? Are you really going to just throw it all away when it's served you so well?

TERRI: I've been a man. I've been a woman. I've been colorful and colorless. And now, I'm tired of hating myself.

(*Pause*)

MARK: And what about me?

TERRI: That's something you'll have to decide.

MARK: I'm not sure I can leave you. Not after all this time.

TERRI: Then stay. And strip. As lovers often do.

(*As Terri removes her costume, Mark turns and looks away*)

MARK: I worry when I think about the coming millennium. Because it feels like all labels have to be re-written, all assumptions re-examined, all associations re-defined. The rules that governed behavior in the last era are crumbling, but those of the time to come have yet to be written. And there is a struggle brewing over the shape of these changing words, a struggle that begins here now, in our hearts, in our shuttered rooms, in the lightning decisions that appear from nowhere.

(*Terri has stripped off everything but her hood. Beneath her costume she wears a simple bra and panties. Mark turns to look at her*)

MARK: I think you're very beautiful.

TERRI: Even without the metal and leather?

MARK: You look . . . soft and warm and gentle to the touch.

TERRI: I'm about to remove my hood. I'm giving you fair warning.

MARK: There's . . . only one thing I never managed to achieve here. I never managed to defeat you.

TERRI: You understand me. Shouldn't I be a lot more frightened? But —the customer is always right. So come over here. This is my final command to you.

MARK: Yes, Mistress Terri.

TERRI: Take off my hood. You want to—admit it.

MARK: Yes. I want to.

TERRI: The moment you remove this hood, I'll be completely exposed, while you remain fully covered. And you'll have your victory by the rules of our engagement, while I—I'll fly off over the combat zone.

(*Terri places Mark's left hand on her hood*)

So congratulations. And goodbye.

(*With his right hand, Mark undoes his own hood instead. It comes off. He is an Asian man*)

TERRI: You disobeyed me.

MARK: I love you.

(*She removes her own hood. She's a Caucasian woman*)

TERRI: I think you're very beautiful, too.

(*Mark starts to remove the rest of his costume*)

TERRI: At a moment like this, I can't help but wonder, was it all so terribly necessary? Did we have to wander so far afield to reach a point which comes, when it does at last, so naturally?

MARK: I was afraid. I was an Asian man.

TERRI: And I was a woman, of any description.

MARK: Why are we talking as if those facts were behind us?

TERRI: Well, we have determined to move beyond the world of fantasy . . . haven't we?

(*Mark's costume is off. He stands in simple boxer shorts. They cross the stage towards one another*)

MARK: But tell the truth—would you have dated me? If I'd come to you first like this?

TERRI: Who knows? Anything's possible. This is the 1990's.

(*Mark touches her hair. They gaze at each other's faces, as lights fade to black. Curtain)*

JOLLY

David Mamet

David Mamet

David Mamet's play *Glengarry Glen Ross* won the Pulitzer prize for drama in 1984. Other plays by Mr. Mamet include *American Buffalo, A Life in the Theatre, Edmond, Lakeboat, Reunion, Sexual Perversity in Chicago, The Water Engine* and *The Woods.* His plays *The Shawl* and *Prairie Du Chien* inaugurated the new Lincoln Center Theatre Company in New York City. His play, *Speed-the-Plow,* enjoyed a successful run on Broadway at the Royale Theatre in 1988 and his play, *Bobby Gould in Hell,* was produced (with Shel Silverstein's play, *The Devil and Billy Markham* under the title, *Oh! Hell*) at Lincoln Center in the fall of 1989. Mr. Mamet's adaptation of Chekhov's *Three Sisters* is planned for production at the Philadelphia Festival Theatre for New Plays in association with The Atlantic Theatre Company.

Mr. Mamet is the author of two books of essays, *Writing in Restaurants* and *Some Freaks.* He wrote the screenplays for *The Postman Always Rings Twice, The Verdict* and Paramount's *The Untouchables,* as well as Orion's *House of Games,* which marked his directorial debut. Mr. Mamet directed his second film, *Things Change* (co-written with Shel Silverstein), in the fall of 1989 which was released to critical acclaim. His feature screenplay, *We're No Angles,* was released by Paramount in December of 1989. Mr. Mamet wrote the screenplays *Ace in the Hole* and *Deerslayer* for Paramount, *High and Low* for Universal and *Hoffa* for 20th Century Fox. Recently, he directed his screenplay, *Homocide* for Cinehaus/Bison Films in Baltimore.

Most recently he wrote *Oleanna* for the stage, a play that has enjoyed not only a successful run in New York City, but has aroused considerable if not significant controversy everywhere that it has played.

Mr. Mamet has taught acting and directing at New York University, The University of Chicago, The Yale Drama School, as well as being a founding member of The Atlantic Theatre Company and Chicago's St. Nicholas Theatre, of which he was also the first Artistic Director.

Characters:
JOLLY, *a woman in her thirties*
BOB, *her brother*
CARL, *her husband*

Scene
Jolly's home.

One:
Evening. Jolly, Bob and Carl.

JOLLY: . . . and he said, "I disapprove of you." "Of what?" I said. "Of, well, I don't know if I want to go into it . . ." "Of something I've done . . . ?" I said. "Yes." "To you?" "No." "To *whom?*" I said. He said he would much rather not take it up. "Well, I wish you *would* take it up," I said, "because it's important to me." "It's the way," he said, "It's the way that you are with your children."

BOB (*pause*): What? (*Pause*)

JOLLY: "It's the way that you are with your children."

BOB: Oh, Lord . . .

JOLLY: I . . .

BOB: . . . how long can this go . . .

JOLLY: I . . .

BOB: . . . how long can this go *on?*

JOLLY: I wanted to, you know, I stayed on the pho . . .

BOB: How long can this go on? *Wait a* minute. *Wait* a minute: you should call all . . .

JOLLY: . . . I know . . .

BOB: . . . you should cease . . .

JOLLY: . . . I know.

BOB: . . . all *anything,* all *meetings, dialogue, thoughts* of them . . . *fuck* them. *Fuck* them. And fuck their whole family. *Fuck* them. The *swine,* the way they treated us . . . you, you should *never* . . .

JOLLY: . . . but the children . . .

BOB: You should never . . . listen to me, Jolly.

JOLLY: I'm . . .

BOB: You sh . . .

JOLLY: Yes, I know.

BOB: You should take an oath never to *talk* to, *meet* with, *mention* . . .

JOLLY: . . . but the children . . .

BOB: And the children most especially. How can this, are we going to expose another generation to this . . . this *bile,* this . . .

JOLLY: And the thing of it is, is . . .

BOB: He said *what? What* did he say . . . ?

JOLLY: He . . .

BOB: He didn't like the way you raise your children . . .

JOLLY: . . . he said that he'd been in *therapy* . . .

BOB: . . . yes.

JOLLY: . . . and he'd, he'd come to . . . *what* was it . . . ?

CARL: "See."

JOLLY: . . . he was a different *man.* From the man we knew.

CARL: He'd come to "realize" that he had "changed."

JOLLY: . . . to realize that he had changed, yes, and the things which, in a prior life, he might have "suppressed" . . .

BOB: . . . that's their way. That's their way. That's their swinish, selfish, *goddam* them. What *treachery* have they not done, in the name of . . .

JOLLY: . . . I know . . .

BOB: . . . of "honesty". God *damn* them. And, always "telling" us we . . .

JOLLY: . . . yes.

BOB: . . . we were the bad ones . . .

JOLLY: Well, we were.

BOB: . . . *we* were the bad ones. *We* were the . . . the "wanting" . . .

JOLLY: And when he said it, I heard his father's voice.

BOB: Well, *fuck* him . . .

JOLLY: And I saw. He'd turned into his father.

BOB: . . . he didn't like the way you raise your kids . . .

JOLLY: And so, you know, I knew, I *remembered.* Way back. They were . . .

BOB: . . . they were sweet kids.

JOLLY: *He* was a sweet kid, Buub. You weren't there . . .

BOB: I was there for part of it.

JOLLY: NO. You weren't there, you know. I see where it all comes from. Both of the, the traits . . .

BOB: . . . Yes.

JOLLY: . . . and they . . . I don't mean to excuse them. I don't want to *excuse* them.

BOB: . . . there's no excuse for them.

JOLLY: NO. I believe that. And I am not a vindictive person.

BOB: No.

JOLLY: I'm not, Buub. I've been thinking of this.

BOB: I know that you're not.

JOLLY: And I think about all those years . . .

BOB: They treated you like filth. (*Pause*) Are you alright?

JOLLY: Yes. I'm fine. They did. They treated me like filth. Do you know, you don't know, cause you weren't there—when they first came. *Mother* told me, I was ten. So she was, what eight; she was going to sleep in my bed. She took up the bed, as she was a "creeper", you know. I'm a rock. You put me in bed. And unmoving. Morning. She was all over the place. And I went in and told Mom that I couldn't sleep. She said, "she is my daughter, and this is the case. If you can't sleep, sleep on the floor."

BOB: No.

JOLLY: . . . and . . . yes. And she wouldn't let me take the covers. My life is a charade.

CARL: . . . and she wanted to call him back.

BOB: Call him back. And say *what?*

JOLLY: I was so . . . *astonished.* By the phone call . . .

BOB: Someone calls me up, says "I don't like the way you raise your kids . . ."

JOLLY: I was, you know, like sometimes when you are in *shock* . . . ?

BOB: . . . yes.

JOLLY: The most bizarre events seem "commonplace."

BOB: . . . yes.

JOLLY: I was . . . because you know, I called HIM. *This was the thing of it:* The kids. They were *close* to him. When he and Susan first got married . . .

BOB: . . . yes . . .

JOLLY: They used to, they'd say: "What are a list of their favorite . . ."

CARL: . . . activities.

JOLLY: . . . and we would write them *down* . . . and they would come over and take the kids, and take the *list* and do all of them.

BOB: Hm.

JOLLY: . . . and *loved* the kids, and "this" . . . and the kids grew quite *close* to them. So. Since we've moved. And we had not *heard* from them. For six months. So I picked up the phone . . .

BOB: . . . that was your big mistake.

JOLLY: I picked up the phone. And I called them. "How are you? Sorry we haven't . . . 'called' you" . . . and the stress of *moving* . . . "pause". Is there something *wrong?* Is something the *matter?* No. He doesn't want to talk about it. "What is it?" and then . . .

BOB: And then you have to wrench it from him . . . "Please *tell* me . . ."

JOLLY: The "counseling." He's *"changed"* . . . He's come to see.

BOB: . . . uh huh . . .

JOLLY: How he was re . . .

BOB: He was repressing his feelings. About the way that you raise your kids?

JOLLY: Well, you know, and the *counselling,* and *she* is in the counselling and all this psychobabble, and they see *they'd never lived their lives.* And they never took "responsibility" for any aspect of the things, you know, the things that they were "feeling" . . . For, for the people *around* them . . . It's all . . . "I." "Me." "What I Feel." "What was *Done* to mmm . . ." Oh, oh, he said he's learning —you're going to love this: he's learning to live "facing his past."

BOB: Facing his past.

JOLLY: Facing his past.

BOB: Well, of course. Of course. That's how they *all* live. Past. Facing the past. Facing the past. Looking at the past. Facing backwards. *Fuck* him. AND fuck "counselling," is the thing I'm saying . . .

JOLLY: . . . I'm with you.

BOB: Fucking leeches. "Weakness." "Weakness." the Defense Budget of Weakness. the Defense of weakness. I thought. It's, it's like a "Roofing" counsellor. Huh?

JOLLY: Yes.

BOB: Hey? Y'don't need a *roofing* counsellor. You need, you may need a *roofer,* tell you "get a new roof," or not. You don't need, *sit* there, five years, five hours a week, *talking* about "Do we need a roof," the *roof* caves. Fuck the . . . And fuck the lot of em, and this excuse to *act badly*—to go around, and *their whole family.* Their attitude. "I hold you responsible. For all things. Not to my . . ."

JOLLY: . . . liking.

BOB: But *I—I* had my reasons.

JOLLY: You know, he told me, when he did Mom's estate . . .

BOB: Her estate? She never had a thing of her own, her whole life.

JOLLY: Hold on. I went to him, you know, all the antiques . . . ?

BOB: . . . he's selling them, you know.

JOLLY: He *sold* them.

BOB: . . . he sold them . . . ?

JOLLY: HE *sold* them. He kept saying, "anything you want. Just *tell* me . . . ?"

BOB: Uh huh.

JOLLY: So I told him. *Everything I said* . . .

BOB: . . . Of course . . . .

JOLLY: He said, "Waaallll . . . that's a very special *piece* . . . uh . . . huh huh." *Susan* goes in there . . . HE goes . . . anything they want . . . The the, the *dress* THAT SHE SAID I COULD HAVE . . . and I was the only one. Related to her by blood. What do I get? NOTHING. NOTHING. Nothing. Some cheap . . . and it doesn't *matter.* The money is not the thing. But she—was my mother. (*Pause*) She was my mother. And I was there while she was dying. *I* was there. *I* was there. He'd drop her off, when he went to the Coast, he'd drop her off, and I was left, an infirm woman. I was left with her. Twelve, fourteen hours a day. And when she'd wake up at night, and my two kids, and no "Nurse," no. And he could afford it . . . *I* couldn't . . .

BOB: . . . no . . .

JOLLY: *He* could. And just drop her off. And sonofabitch that *cunt* that *cunt* that *Carol.* DIDN'T EVEN COME TO THE . . .

BOB: . . . I know . . .

JOLLY: . . . the *funeral.* And who gets the armoire?

BOB: Which?

JOLLY: In the Hallway. And the, who gets the Mink Coat? Couldn't get her *hands* dirty. *SHE* DON'T GOT KIDS. And does *she* come up to . . .

BOB: . . . I know . . .

JOLLY: Who couldn't spare the time, from her . . .

BOB: . . . yes . . .

JOLLY: . . . from her *counsellors* . . . who are, what, going to teach her how to Lead a Good Life . . . ? Fuck HER. And all the married *men* she's screwing. As her way. Of expressing herself, and could not even come to Mom's *funeral.* Who *loved* her. And he gives *her* the armoire. And Bill and *Susan* come, and Susan hardly *knew* her, and who gets the Dresses, and who gets the little *Tchatchkes,* and the, the, you know, the *toys,* and the *hobo* art . . . and the "memorabilia" . . . And he says "What do you want, Jolly . . . ?" And I *tell* him. And it's like I *always do.* And *"couching"* it, as if it's going to offend some *GOD* if I come right out and I say "several pieces" . . .

BOB: . . . yes . . .

JOLLY: Nothing very valuable, God forbid, except that it had a meaning for me. AND EVERY PIECE, Buuby, that I say . . .

BOB: . . . I know . . .

JOLLY: He tells me *why I can not have it.* Until . . .

BOB: . . . of course . . .

JOLLY: I stop asking.

BOB: . . . I know . . .

JOLLY: . . . because . . .

BOB: . . . I know, Jol . . .

JOLLY: . . . because, because, why get my *heart* broke, on the, just like always, things I can never *have* and feel like a *schmuck* ASKING for them. When I know . . . (*pause*) So . . . so . . . he sold them. (*Pause*) What's the alternative?

BOB: You know what I . . .

JOLLY: Yes. I do. Yes. I do. (*Sighs*)

BOB: I think we should have a *lawyer,* and . . .

JOLLY: I know, but . . .

BOB: And I respect you . . . You know. I, yes . . .

JOLLY: . . . my what?

BOB: Yes. I think it's foolish. Your opinion. I do. But I respect it. As "compassion." I don't know. As "fellow feeling." You always, always. You, always treating them so much better than they treated you.

JOLLY: Well.

BOB: Then, so tell me.

JOLLY: Anyway (*sighs*) *I* don't know.

CARL: Tell him.

JOLLY (*sighs*): So he says. So he says . . . .

CARL: He's "sold" the stuff . . .

JOLLY: So he says the money is in an "estate."

CARL: A trust.

BOB: A trust, I know.

JOLLY: So he says . . . *I* say, you know, we are having some tight times, we we could really *use* some of the money . . .

BOB: . . . uh huh . . .

JOLLY: "It's in a trust." Uh huh. Round and round. I suppose. Then he says, "I could, you know, I could *invade* the trust . . ."

BOB: . . . invade the trust . . .

JOLLY: Yes. "If it's . . . if it's truly . . ."

BOB: . . . why did it have to be "truly" . . . ?

JOLLY: "I . . ."

BOB: . . . wasn't it enough that you *asked* for it . . . ?

JOLLY: Wait. It gets worse. (*Sighs*) So. Round and round. I call. You know. This and that. The *Kids.* "I really could *use* the money. We are really—you know . . . *moving* . . ."

BOB: . . . yes . . .

JOLLY: "We're really *tight,* and we could use" . . . I, taking my heart in my hand . . .

BOB: . . . no, baby. I know what it cost. To ask him.

JOLLY: "Ten thousand dollars" . . . (*pause*) the way he lives.

BOB: The way they *both* live. But that isn't the *point* . . . the money's *yours* . . .

JOLLY: "Ten thousand dollars" . . . Long long pause. "Waal . . ." I jump in. "Whatever it took, that it took, out of the 'will'," I don't mean the will, what do I mean, the . . . ?

BOB: . . . Estate.

JOLLY: The "estate". "Whatever it took, out of the estate. From . . ."

BOB: . . . God Damn him.

JOLLY: ". . . from Bill and Carol . . ."

BOB (*softly*): God damn him . . .

JOLLY: "Whatever it took, just, if I have to *sign* something, I'll sign whatever . . ."

BOB: . . . yes.

JOLLY: ". . . and subtract . . ."

BOB: . . . of course . . .

JOLLY: "And just give me my 'portion' *now.*" (*Pause*) And we really *need* it. (*Pause*) Because we did.

BOB: . . . I know you did.

JOLLY: And he says "no." (*Pause*) Just "no." (*Pause*) Just "no." And this bullshit "entreating" he felt . . .

BOB: . . . I know . . .

JOLLY: . . . right after Mom's death. This bullshit "I know what a bad 'Man' I've been, and, I just want to *apologize*" . . .

BOB (*pause*): I know.

JOLLY: . . . that he said. (*Pause*)

BOB: . . . and you were so good to him.

JOLLY: . . . I don't know . . .

BOB: . . . you *were* . . .

JOLLY: . . . I don't know . . .

BOB: To a man who, hey, you know what, he treated you cruelly twenty-five, *thirty* years, and you turned around and said "I forgive you." And . . .

JOLLY: . . . I don't know . . .

BOB: I do. You took him in. (*Pause*)

CARL: She asked him to invade the trust and he said "no." (*Pause*)

JOLLY: That was the answer. (*Pause*)

BOB: "No."

JOLLY: Well . . . Oh. Oh. And it gets better. He didn't say "No." He said, he said "I am not convinced I would invade the trust if I *could.*" (*Pause*)

BOB: What does that mean?

JOLLY: Well, *That's* what it means. (*Pause*)

BOB: How are you doing, Carl?

CARL: I'm fine.

BOB: You ever get tired of this. (*Pause*) You must. (*Pause*) It's the same. Isn't it? Every year. It's the same.

CARL: Yes. It's the same.

BOB: Don't you get tired of it?

CARL: Well, I *tell* you . . .

JOLLY: . . . they made fun of us. You know that.

BOB: They?

JOLLY: You know they did. Carl and me. *"Jolly . . ."*

BOB: Uh huh . . .

JOLLY: "I'm sure he's a fine '*man*' . . ."

BOB: Uh huh . . .

JOLLY: "But 'we want to say' . . ."

BOB (*to self*): "We want to say . . ."

JOLLY: "Your mother and I want to say . . ."

BOB: Well, that was how they were . . .

JOLLY: *Wasn't* it . . .

BOB: Yes.

JOLLY: *Wasn't* it?

BOB: Yes.

JOLLY: . . . the shit at Christmas. You know, you know, Marshall Fields . . . ? She would take me to Fields. "What do you think?" Some dress. If I *wanted* the dress, I would have to say "naaaaah". She would take me back. "*I* think it rather suits you." "No, uh . . . it's . . . it's 'pretty,' *but* . . ." And of course, she would *buy* it for me. If I said, "God, what a gorgeous dress." Hey. You know what? Hey, you know what I'm going to *tell* you something: "fuck her, though she's dead." (*Pause*) Fuck *her,* and fuck the *lot* of 'em.

BOB: . . . they never loved us.

JOLLY: No no no. They "loved" us, they despised *themselves.*

BOB: Jol . . .

JOLLY: They, no, Buub, in their "way" . . .

BOB: Jo, Jo, That's, that's your *problem* . . .

JOLLY: What is? (*Pause*) What is?

BOB: I say I'm gonna sue the guy. You say "no." I mean. What in the hell *possesses* a man. To *treat* you like that; he's going to tell you how to raise . . . not *even* tell you. To *withhold* this information, how he's never going to *call* you anymore. Because he doesn't like the way you raise your kids . . . ??? It's monstrous. It's, whatever is the next thing beyond cruel. Do you see? It's *cruel.* Jol. *They're cruel.*

They were *cruel* toward us, and if there's such a thing as "abuse," we got it. And *your* problem is . . .

JOLLY: I know what my problem is . . .

BOB: . . . your problem . . .

JOLLY: I know what my problem is . . .

BOB: *Your* problem is: you could not face the fact. They didn't love you. (*Pause*) And that's your problem. (*Pause*) That they did not love us. (*Pause*)

JOLLY: They loved *you,* Buub.

Two

Jolly's home. Middle of the night. Bob and Jolly.

JOLLY: "If you don't like it . . ."

BOB: "No, no, no, I *like* it."

JOLLY: "Waal, if you *don't* like it, you can take it back."

BOB: "I like it."

JOLLY: "Waaal. If you *don't.* If you find . . ."

BOB: "No. I *like* it. I *do.* I think that it's . . ."

JOLLY: "Waal, your mother and I, only want to *say* . . ."

BOB: "I think that it's . . ."

JOLLY: "You take it back. We 'saved the slip' . . . and . . ."

BOB: . . . fucking *right* I'm going to take it back. Because what would I *do* with it?

JOLLY: You remember the skis?

BOB: The skis.

JOLLY: I remember the skis. I wanted the skis. (*Pause*) I wanted skis that year.

BOB: You don't ski, Jol.

JOLLY: *Why* don't I ski? I wanted to have skis. I don't know. In some magazine. I saw it. I . . . I broke the, as we know, cardinal rule, and I said "Mom," I really would like . . .

BOB: . . . uh huh . . .

JOLLY: Every moment that it seemed appropriate. Or inappropriate. You know. "Yes. I know that I am transgressing . . ."

BOB: . . . as you were . . .

JOLLY: The . . .

BOB: Oh yeah. Oh yeah. As *abasing* yourself always helped.

JOLLY: *So* much.

BOB: It helped sooooooooo much.

JOLLY: Nothing helped.

BOB: . . . nothing helped.

JOLLY: . . . *death* did not help. *Sickness* did not help. The . . .

BOB: . . . nothing helped.

JOLLY: I said "Mom: . . ."

BOB: Uh huh . . .

JOLLY: Oh shit. (*Sighs. Pause*)

BOB: . . . well?

JOLLY: Christmas *day.* (*Pause*) Christmas *day.*

BOB: I know.

JOLLY: She . . .

BOB: Wait. Wait. I remember.

JOLLY: Uh huh.

BOB: A plaid . . . something . . . plaid.

JOLLY: A reversible *raincoat.*

BOB: That's right.

JOLLY: A reversible raincoat.

BOB: . . . what did I do . . . ?

JOLLY: Monday morning, back to Fields.

BOB: I took it back to Fields.

JOLLY: And . . . what?

BOB: For a . . . year?

JOLLY: Easily . . . easily . . .

BOB: Oh yeah. "Where is the *raincoat* . . . ?" Oh, I left it at . . . Oh. Ah. Ah. Wait Wait Wait Wait Wait wait wait. I Went Back To Fields to See, Could I . . .

JOLLY: Um hum . . .

BOB: COULD I BUY BACK THE COAT.

JOLLY: . . . that's right.

BOB: Could I buy back the raincoat.

JOLLY: That's right, Buuby.

BOB: Oh, what a pathetic fucking thing. (*Pause*) My plaid. My Reversible Raincoat. (*Pause*)

JOLLY: And, you know, I'm thinking, twenty years, after the fact, all of this *bullshit* . . . all of this "If you don't *like* it, you can Take it Back . . ." If they had *loved* us. Mighten't they have *known* what we might want? I know what *my* kids want. It's not that goddamned difficult. It's Just Not. I'm sorry. Carl says . . . Carl, say what you will. I'm sorry, every weekend, Every weekend. You know what we *did* last weekend? They had friends sleep over. We made *Popcorn.* We made *fudge.* Next morning we made *pancakes.* You know, you know, I turned into a fine cook.

BOB: I know you did.

JOLLY: No, I mean, you ain't seen *nothing* here . . .

BOB: It was fantastic . . .

JOLLY: I mean a *fine* cook.

BOB: Jol, I had the dinner . . .

JOLLY: That was nothing.

BOB: No. It was fantastic.

JOLLY: No, I mean, Carl, I make, Carl, you know, Carl never *had* it. He never *had* it. I wanted to do it, to *do* it for him, to do it . . .

BOB: . . . uh huh . . .

JOLLY: Because before *Carl* you know . . .

BOB: Uh huh . . .

JOLLY: Before *Carl* . . . I . . .

BOB: I remember, Quiche Soup . . .

JOLLY: . . . I couldn't Drop an Egg.

BOB: Uh huh . . .

JOLLY: Why *Should* I . . . ? Hummm? *She* never taught me . . . She never taught me a *thing* . . . I'm in there, the girls. *Every night* . . . Every Night I'm in there . . .

BOB: I saw them.

JOLLY: *And they're learning to cook.*

BOB: I know.

JOLLY: You see, Bob? Do you see? This is a *family.* (*Pause*) *And some day.* Bob. I'm going to be dead. Some day. *They* are going, they are going to be in a Kitchen. And they're going to say. To their girls . . . *"My* mom . . ." (*Pause*) Because this IS a Family. And every weekend. We had a four-hour session. We played Monopoly. We, God Forgive us, we went bowling . . . we . . .

BOB: . . . the kids seem so . . .

JOLLY: We rented a *film* we thought they and their friends would enjoy. And I say God Bless That Man . . . do you hear?

BOB: Yes.

JOLLY: "Your *Mother,* and I 'just don't feel', that *Carl* is the 'right sort'."

BOB: Mm.

JOLLY: The Right Sort. The Right Fucking Sort. The right sort for . . . huh? Bob. Huh? For *who?* For a Piece of Shit Like *Me?* For a piece of shit they *despised.* Like ME? For us special, special . . .

BOB: . . . mmm.

JOLLY: Am I wrong? And the *finest* . . . (*pause*) The *finest,* the Best Man . . . And he *loved* me, you understand, and that, God Damn Them. That was thing, you see, that *disqualified* him. "We Just Don't Feel . . ." WHOSE MARRIAGE WORKED? WHOSE

MARRIAGE WORKED? Out of the *Pack* of them. Three generations. And I don't mean you, Buub . . .

BOB: No, I . . .

JOLLY: No, I don't mean you. I mean of them. Who Had The Marriage That Worked? And it's been what has it been, "easy"?

BOB: No.

JOLLY: You are Fucking In Hell *Right* it hasn't. And, You know. When we were in *Seattle.* Out of *Work.* And she'd come, "Mom . . ." (*Pause*) "Mom . . ." (*Pause*)

BOB: It's okay, Jol. (*Pause*) It's okay. (*Pause*) It's okay, Jol.

JOLLY: Gimme a cigarette. (*Pause. He gives her one*) I can't smoke these.

BOB: Break the filter.

JOLLY: I can't smoke these.

BOB: Yes, you can. (*She smokes*)

JOLLY: When we were in Seattle. We Had No Cash, Buub.

BOB: I know. (*Pause*)

JOLLY: And she would come. (*Pause*) And I'd say, "Mom . . . you know . . ." she'd first, she'd say, "What do the kids need?" "And I'd say Shoes. They need shoes." (*Pause*) Well, *you* know how kids . . .

BOB: I know . . .

JOLLY: . . . grow out of shoes.

BOB: I know.

JOLLY: *You* know what they cost . . .

BOB: Yes.

JOLLY: Uh huh. "The Kids Need Shoes." The end of her stay, she would give them, God Bless her, these, two, *incredibly* expensive, what are they, "vanity" sets. A desk. A desk to put on makeup . . . A "vanity set"?

BOB: . . . I don't know . . .

JOLLY: And I would say . . . *Carl* would say "forget about it." I . . . I'd say . . . No. "Mom . . . Mom . . ." (*Pause*) Mom . . . And the fucking *skis* . . . (*pause*) The Big Present.

BOB: I remember.

JOLLY: I'm sure that you do.

BOB: The Big Present.

JOLLY: "Waal, we've opened *everything* . . ."

BOB: "Oh, *Wait* a second . . . 'What Is That Behind The Door.' "

JOLLY: And the fucking skis year it was this expensive Red Leather Briefcase. And I was "Behaving Badly." I was behaving. Oh *So* badly. I got Sent to My Room. And why must I ruin these occasions.

BOB: Why did you ruin those occasions, Jol?

JOLLY: Well, that's right, because I was a Rotten Swine. Why did *you* ruin those occasions?

BOB: I was a Rotten Swine.

JOLLY: I know that you were.

BOB: I was an ungrateful swine.

JOLLY: I know that you were. You know, and I *carried,* I had to *carry* that fucking red briefcase for three, or four years, all day, every day, full of books, These Are Your Skis. Did I tell you . . .

BOB: What?

JOLLY: I had a dream about her.

BOB: About Mom . . .

JOLLY: Uh huh. (*Pause*) I'll tell you later. Can I tell you later. You know, because, what was I saying? (*Pause*) Hm . . .

BOB: The Red Briefcase.

JOLLY: Yes. (*Pause*) You know, the girls. So adore having you here.

BOB: It's good to be here.

JOLLY: You . . . it's good of you to come.

BOB: Jol . . .

JOLLY: No, I know that . . .

BOB: Jol, I've been, well *fuck* "remiss" . . . it's been criminal of me not to . . .

JOLLY: I know. You've got a Busy Life . . .

BOB: No, I've just . . .

JOLLY: Buub . . .

BOB: Hey, I've been *lazy.* I'm sorry. I *owe it* to you. I've been . . .

JOLLY: . . . and I know it's been a difficult time for you, Buub . . . (*pause*)

BOB: And so I come here to get Comfort.

JOLLY: Times of stress, you . . .

BOB: Isn't that "selfish" of me . . . ?

JOLLY: . . . times of stress, you, No. It isn't selfish. Yes. It is. We need comfort. You think that you can do without it? You can't. I know you can't. You deserve it. I love you. I love you, Buub . . . I love you.

BOB: I love you, too.

JOLLY: And you are the only one who was there. (*Pause*) You are my best friend. (*Pause*) You are the person I am closest to On Earth.

BOB: I love you, too, Jol. (*Pause*)

JOLLY: Carl and I . . . you know, many times . . . (*pause*)

BOB: How are you getting on?

JOLLY: We're . . . (*pause*) Hey, what the fuck are you going to expect. From the Sort of a Background That We Come From. It's a miracle that we can Wind our Watch. It is a wonder we can walk down the mother fucking Esplanade, huh? To the Corner *Store.* (*Pause*) That's what Carl said about you. And, you know . . . how *good* you're doing.

BOB: He said . . .

JOLLY: He said that he knows. How incredible *difficult* this has been for you, and he thinks that you are doing, that he thinks that you are doing well. And *that's* the man, you understand . . . that's the man they made *fun* of. That they said "wasn't good enough for me." Enough for me. This person. Not worthy the Pure Consideration to Listen, the simplest requests. To This DAY. I cannot ask for what I need. To this day. How could I? Cause I wasn't going to get it. Was I? Were we? No. (*Pause*) And I don't *blame* you. For *whatever* happened in your life. And *fuck* them. Fuck the *lot* of them. (*Pause*) *Fuck* 'em. And I'll *stay* here. With my girls. (*Pause*) With my "life." My husband, say what you will, who *cares* about me. And Who I Can Really Rely On. Who I can Rely On. And anybody I can NOT, they can kiss my ass. (*Pause*) What are you gonna do?

BOB: About?

JOLLY: About your life. (*Pause*)

BOB: I don't know.

JOLLY: You don't know. Tell me. You gonna go back to her?

BOB: I don't know.

JOLLY: Cause I wanted to tell you. If you *do.* No one's going to think you foolish. I swear to you.

BOB: I'm not going back to her.

JOLLY: If you *do.* (*Pause*) I'm not saying you *should* . . .

BOB: I un . . .

JOLLY: Or you should *not.* But if you *do,* always . . .

BOB: . . . I know . . .

JOLLY: You remember, Bob. Carl, Carl said it: He said it, baby. You, you can *Kill the Pope,* and you are wel . . .

BOB: I'm not going to go bbb . . .

JOLLY: . . . if you *should.* And I am not "plumping" for it.

BOB: I know.

JOLLY: I WANT ONE THING. And that is: the thing that is best for you. Period. Paragraph. And the rest of the world can go to hell. I don't give a fuck. I'm too old. (*Pause*) I see. Every day. More of Rivka in me.

BOB: Uh huh . . .

JOLLY: Isn't that something . . .

BOB: Nana Rivka.

JOLLY: Yes.

BOB: Mm. Tell me.

JOLLY: The way I *look* . . . I look at *photos.* Carl tells me, too.

BOB: I always told you you looked like her.

JOLLY: Yes. You did. I never saw it. I look back . . . she loved you so, Buub.

BOB: She loved you, too.

JOLLY: No, she didn't. I don't think she did.

BOB: She did, Jol.

JOLLY: Well, I don't know. I don't know if *any* of 'em. (*Pause*) I was going to say, if any of them liked women. Yes. That is what I mean. The Europeans. The whole thing. Do you know. Separate galleries in this Shul. Do the *Worsch,* lie down, shut up.

BOB: . . . I don't think it was all like that.

JOLLY: All of them I know. Were. Look at Mom. And Papa Jake.

BOB: Um hm.

JOLLY: Now, you're talking, you were talking about "love" . . . *He* never loved her. Never loved her one day. And she knew it.

BOB: Um hm.

JOLLY: Spent Her Whole Life. Looking for. That love she never got. And she could not admit it. "Yes. I'm bad. I'm so bad. I'm Bad. Yes. Mistreat me . . ." With *Dad* . . . with that *swine* . . . "Mistreat me . . ." her whole life. And at the end. You know, Even at the end. Who was there? (*Pause*) Who was there for her? Who was there?

BOB: You were, Jol.

JOLLY: Who was there for her?

BOB: You were, Jol.

JOLLY: "He" was alone on business . . . what do I . . . ?

BOB: "Away."

JOLLY: He was away on business. Eh? No Ceremony. "Take Care of Your Mother." Two kids. No money. And he . . .

BOB: . . . and never a thank you.

JOLLY: I didn't want thanks.

BOB: Of course not.

JOLLY: I . . . Fella comes up to me, I'm driving, fella comes up to me I'm drivin, the girls, somewhere, "don't you know," No. "Did you know. This is a One Way Street . . ." I'm . . . never in my life, Bob. I'm sick. I'm a sick woman. I know that. I'm aware of that, how could I not be, my mind is racing "Did you know," "Didn't you know . . ." Did I drive down On PURPOSE? I did *not* know . . . IS YOUR QUESTION . . . what? The proper, I would say, response, is "One Way Street!" Smiles. One way. You, we would *assume,* did not know that you are, why *would* I, and even, I HAD, how *terrible* is that, some SHIT. Some piece of shit JUST LIKE ME, who was RAISED IN HELL and has either to mourn or to *mistreat* the . . ."DON'T YOU KNOW," "Didn't You Know" . . . no. I *didn't* know, and FURTHER, Whether or not I know, your . . . your "rights" end with "this is a one-way street," and what I MAY HAVE KNOWN is none of your *concern,* and FUCK YOU, and I'm SEETHING at this fat, short, this emasculated piece of . . . has to take out his *aggression* on some haggard, sexless, unattractive *housewife,* with her *kids* in the car . . . who is going to . . . bear him in her memory . . . the hate, and this is my fantasy life. (*Pause*) A rich, "full" life. (*Pause*)

BOB: You should go to bed.

JOLLY: Why should I go to bed?

BOB: Because you have a husband up there. (*Pause*)

JOLLY: Yes. (*Pause*) I thought you gave up smoking.

BOB: You remember. The Nickel.

JOLLY: The Nickel.

BOB: The story of the Nickel.

JOLLY: The . . . the Movie Theatre.

BOB: That's right. She . . .

JOLLY: She had to Go Back to Return the Nickel.

BOB: That's right.

JOLLY: She had to Give the Nickel Back.

BOB: Mmm.

JOLLY: They gave her an extra nickel.

BOB: She . . .

JOLLY: They gave her a nickel too much. In what? In *change.* She took the change back. To Poppa Jake. "I've got a nickel." She must have felt guilty. Why would she *tell* him? It occurs to me. Why did she, she could have *spent it.* She could have Thrown It Away. She *knew* what he was going to do. WHY DID SHE BRING IT BACK. Ah. Bob, Ah. Bob, why did she bring it back? Because. They gave it to her Because She Was Bad. "Daddy. I've got a nickel." (*Pause*)

BOB: You know, some times I can't. I can't, it seems I can't . . . (*pause*) Oh, god, I get so *sad* sometimes, Jol. I can't, it seems, getting up from the *table.* I can't seem . . . or I look at the *wall,* you know, and I . . . I suppose that it's *grief.*

JOLLY: . . . I know.

BOB: . . . but I can't . . . I can't seem to . . . (*pause*) I wake up in the night. "Where am I?" Three times a night. And I saw that I was waking up.

JOLLY: To go pee the kids.

BOB: To pee the kids. You get a Red apple.

JOLLY: "And Where Were They . . . ?"

BOB: Oh, It's all so fuckin' *sordid.* It's some . . .

JOLLY: . . . it's a machine . . .

BOB: It's some . . .

JOLLY: Some self-replicating virus.

BOB: I go back. Eighty years. How many years? Eighty years. Seventy years. *Her* mother. Her grandmother, excuse me, was abandoned. By her husband. Not her husband, her *father. Not* her father, her . . . "husband". Her Husband. Abandoned her.

JOLLY: Her . . . ?

BOB: . . . grandmother grew up. "Men are Swine. Don't like them . . ."

JOLLY: . . . uh huh . . .

BOB: ". . . don't trust them."

JOLLY: Hm.

BOB: And . . .

JOLLY: Raised her daughter . . .

BOB: *So* on, and a *hundred years,* you see? *Those* kids: "men are swine. Don't *like* them." One hundred years. It's like some well "river." Some Alluvial Plain. All of these *rivers.* Flowing in. All this. (*Pause*) All.

JOLLY: Your kids are going to be okay.

BOB: No, they won't. Of *course* they won't. *We're* not okay . . .

Three
Morning. Carl. Bob comes in.

CARL: How did you sleep?

BOB: Like a rock or like a baby.

CARL: You know, he *dumped* this stuff here.

BOB: Jolly said something.

CARL: Mm.

BOB: What was it?

CARL: It was . . . "trash", you'd say. It was . . .

BOB: . . . *my* stuff . . .

CARL: Your stuff. Stuff you couldn't want. Cancelled *checks,* twenty years old. It was nothing anyone would ever want to keep. Just some . . . "trash", really . . . (*Pause*) So much stuff Jolly wanted. When he sold the house. (*Pause*) Well.

BOB: How can you put up with it?

CARL: What "it," then . . . ?

BOB: The misfortune of our family. Do I overstate the case . . . ?

CARL: Oh, I don't . . . (*Pause*) That's a very personal question. Isn't it? (*Pause*)

BOB: Yes. It is.

CARL: Well. (*Pause*) You know. I love Jol.

(*Jolly enters*)

JOLLY: Sleep well?

BOB: Yes.

JOLLY: How well?

BOB: Very well.

JOLLY: Why?

BOB: Cause I feel "safe" here.

JOLLY: How safe?

BOB: Very safe.

JOLLY: Safer than Other Places . . . ?

BOB: Yes.

JOLLY: Good, Then. The girls say goodbye.

BOB: Goodbye to *them.* (*Pause*)

JOLLY: You okay?

BOB: Yeah.

JOLLY: Thanks for coming.

BOB: Oh, hell.

JOLLY: No, no. Thank you. We . . .

CARL: Jol, he wanted to come.

JOLLY: Was I talking to you . . . ?

CARL: No. Goodbye, Bob.

BOB: Goodbye, Carl.

JOLLY: Did you know, this stupid schmuck. Drove to Hillcrest to Pick Up three boxes of, turned out to be, drafts of your *term* papers, something, Junior High. (*Pause*) Carl . . . ?

CARL: Bye, Hon.

JOLLY: See you at Six?

CARL: Yes.

JOLLY: The Girls at Gymnastics.

CARL: Yes, I know. Bye, Buub.

BOB: I'll see you, Carl.

CARL: You Hang On.

JOLLY: Bye, Sweetheart.

CARL: Bye, Jol. (*He exits*)

JOLLY: How did you sleep, oh CHRIST, I'm tired. (*Yawns*)

BOB (*to himself*): ". . . how did you sleep . . . ?"

JOLLY: You, oh, shit, Buub—an the goddamn times that we'd get on the goddamn *train* to go to some, "home," where we didn't . . . where they didn't "want" us . . . But we "went" there. Didn't we . . . ?

BOB: We did.

JOLLY: Smiling through.

BOB: I know we did.

JOLLY: And I'm having this dream. How's *this* for dreams . . . ? They're knocking on my door. All of us. "Let me in," and I know that they want to kill me. *Mother: Mother's* voice, from just beyond the door: "Julia, Let Me In." "I will not let them hurt you . . ." the sweetest voice. "You are my *child* . . ." and it goes on. "I won't let them hurt you, darling . . . you are my *child.* You are my *child.* I *adore* you. Open the door. Oh. *Julia.* I love you so. I will not let them Hurt You. My *dear.* OH. My Dear . . ." I know they're out there. I know they're out there. I open the door, this sweetest voice, and there is *Mom,* with this *expression* on her face . . . (*Pause*)

BOB: Well.

JOLLY: "Thank god it was only a dream . . ."

BOB: "Isn't that a mercy . . . ?" (*Pause*)

JOLLY: Well, Don't go. (*Pause*) Or we could go back to Seventy First Street is where we could go. To the Jeffrey Theatre. And Saturday Kiddie Shows. Twenty Five Cartoons. And a Western. For a quarter. And the Chocolate Phosphate at J. Leslie Rosemblum's "Every Inch a Drugstore." Do you remember, Dad, he used to take us there?

BOB: Yes. I do.

JOLLY: Do you remember how it smelled?

BOB: Yes.

JOLLY: And we'd go to the Peter Pan Restaurant on the corner of Jeffrey, and get a Francheezie, and the french fries, and a cherry coke. And we would go to the South Shore Country Club, where they wouldn't let us in. And we would sit in the window in the den, and Dad would come home every night, and we would light the candles on Friday, and we would do all those things, and all those things would be true and that's how we would grow up, Bobby. With such love, and the old men, who said that they remembered Nana. Back in Poland. And, Oh. Fuck it. Oh the hell with it. Oh, Goddamn every thing that I have touched or felt in this shithole of a life. Goddamn it, and every one I ever knew.

BOB: And goddamn me, too.

JOLLY: *No.*

BOB: I never came to see you.

JOLLY: *I don't care,* Oh, Bobby . . .

BOB: I . . .

JOLLY: No, No. I don't care . . . (*pause*) I don't care . . . (*pause*) Oh, Bobby. (*Pause*) Oh, God . . . (*Carl re-enters. Pause. Picks up sheet of paper*) The address of the Gymnastics.

CARL: Mm.

JOLLY: What a good man.

CARL: What are you doing?

JOLLY: We're being bad. We've been bad. We're being punished. And we're going to go to our rooms. And cannot come out until we're prepared to make, a . . . what is it . . . ?

BOB: A Complete and Contrite . . .

JOLLY: A Complete and a Contrite Apology.

CARL: Are you alright, Jol?

JOLLY: Of course.

CARL: Do you want me to stay home?

JOLLY: No. Thank you. *Bobby* will be here a while, you see. And he's the only one who knows. (*Pause*) Cause he was *there* . . .

(*End*)

PITCHING TO THE STAR

Donald Margulies

Pitching to the Star was first presented at the West Bank Cafe Downstairs Theatre Bar in New York City on March 20, 1990, with Lewis Black as Dick, Robert Sean Leonard as Peter, Mary Kane as Lauri, Kathryn Rossetter as Dena, and Lynn Chausow as the voices of Jennifer and Tyne. Rand Foerster was the director.

Donald Margulies

With the recent huge success of his play *Sight Unseen* (OBIE awards for both Playwriting and Performance) at the Manhattan Theater Club and then Off-Broadway at The Orpheum, Donald Margulies has become one of the major talents now writing for the theater. That play, first commissioned by the South Coast Rep, was his eighth full-length play.

His first efforts at playwriting came as a result of his exposure to Julia Novick, former *Village Voice* critic, who tutored Margulies while the playwright was a student in graphic arts at SUNY Purchase. From 1982–1984 he had the following plays produced: *Luna Park* and *Gifted Children* at the Jewish Repertory Theater, *Resting Place* at Theater for the New City, and *Found a Peanut* at the New York Shakespeare Festival. He began his association with the Manhattan Theater Club in 1985. They produced *What's Wrong With This Picture?* in 1985, and in 1989 produced *The Loman Family Picnic,* which was published as one of the ten best plays in the annual *Burns Mantle Theater Yearbook 1989–1990.*

He was the writer in residence at The Jewish Repertory Theater in 1990, where he enjoyed a critical and popular success once again with *What's Wrong With This Picture?* Margulies has traveled the modern playwright's journey in the realizing of this play: first developed at New York Writers Bloc and the Sundance Institute Playwrights's Lab, then produced by Manhattan Theater Club in 1985 and then given a new production while writer in residence at The Jewish Repertory. He is currently working on two screen plays. He is a frequent contributor to the 52nd Street Project and is a member of both New Dramatists and The Dramatists Guild.

Characters:

PETER ROSENTHAL, *32, the writer*
DICK FELDMAN, *40s, the producer*
DENA STRAWBRIDGE, *40s, the star*
LAURI RICHARDS, *28, the D-Girl*
VOICE OF JENNIFER, *30s, Dick's secretary*
VOICE OF TYNE, *10, Dick's daughter*

Scene

The office of Dick Feldman at his home in Sherman Oaks, California. The present.

Primarily, the office furnishings are white. Cans of Diet Coke are on the Santa Fe-style coffee table. A voice-activated intercom/speaker is prominently placed on the rear wall.

DICK: It's a courtesy thing.

PETER: Uh huh.

DICK: No big deal. What, you're scared?

PETER: No.

DICK: You're *nervous?* (*To Lauri*) Look at him.

(*Lauri laughs; to Peter*)

Dena *Straw*bridge, you're *nervous?*

PETER: No, I just didn't expect . . .

DICK: She's the *star.* So *what?* Big fucking deal. People *know* her? She's well-known? So?

PETER: I didn't think (*today*) I'd . . .

DICK: People know her *face?* So? She's a has-been. A druggie. Her tits sag. Boy, this celebrity shit really impresses you, doesn't it?

PETER (*a little p.o.'ed*): No, it's just—

DICK: You're *really* new in town, aren't you?

PETER: —I didn't think I'd have to *pitch* . . .

DICK: I'm *teasing* you. Hey. We want to *include* her a little bit, that's all. Make her feel, *you* know, like a star. Important. So you pitch her the pilot. Nothing to it. She likes the pitch?, she doesn't like it?: Same difference. You don't have to sell *her,* you sold *us.* Get it?

PETER: Uh huh.

DICK: You're *ours,* not *hers.* Remember that. You don't have to *deal* with her, let *me* deal with her. You just be nice. Be pleasant. Be cute. You *are* cute. She'll like you. Just be cute, you'll see. Be yourself. She'll love you. It's not what you *say* (you understand?), it's not what you *pitch.* Let her think we care what she thinks. She says something? Go: "Uh *huh,* let me think about that." She'll love you for life. Don't write it *down* even, just: "Uh *huh."* Like: "What an interesting idea. Gee, I must give that some thought, Dena, thank you." Guarantee she won't remember what she said thirty seconds later but you made a friend for life. You were pleasant. You didn't show an attitude. You don't *want* to be her friend. Remember that. I'm talking purposes of the show solely. She's the star. You don't fuck with a star, so to speak. She, in her mind, is apart from the rest of the world. She's a star. Stars don't know *how* to be a friend. They don't *have* friends. They're suspicious of everyone. They don't *like* people. They're ambivalent about their success. They don't know what they did to *deserve* it, which makes them very suspicious of people. With good reason when you think about it: People *want* things from stars. So, consequently, as a result, they're suspicious, lonely, deeply fucked-up people. Remember: you don't *want* to be her friend. You don't need *her.* She needs you. *Fuck* her. (*Calls*) Jennifer? Jen?

JENNIFER'S VOICE: Yes, Dick?

DICK: What time is it?

JENNIFER'S VOICE: Twelve-twenty, Dick.

DICK: *What* time?

JENNIFER'S VOICE: Twenty after twelve.

(*Lauri shows Dick her watch*)

DICK: She's late. *Star* shit. Already it's starting. I'm telling you, she pulls that shit with *me* . . .

PETER: So she knows about the style of the show? She knows how we want to shoot it?

DICK: Bubbie, what did I just finish saying? She doesn't know shit.

LAURI: I think what Peter's asking—

DICK: It's not like we have to *consult* with her. We're not looking for her *approval.*

PETER: I mean, she knows we're talking about a one-camera film show?

DICK: We'll get you as many cameras as you want.

PETER: I only want one.

DICK: So we'll get you one. Jesus Christ. What are you so worried about? (*To Lauri*) You ever see such a worrier? (*Lauri laughs*)

PETER: I'm not worried. I just want to make sure—

DICK: What, what's the problem here?

PETER: Nothing. I just want to make sure . . . Remember the very first conversation we had? I told you I wasn't interested in writing a three-camera sitcom? I'm only interested in writing a half-hour film.

LAURI: Yes, Peter feels very strongly about this, Dick.

DICK: Huh?

LAURI: Peter feels—

DICK (*to Peter*): What are you suggesting?

PETER: I'm not suggesting anything. I just want your assurance that—

DICK: And you have it. Period. The End. I don't understand the problem here.

PETER: Dick, there's no problem. Don't misconstrue my concern.

DICK: Nobody's misconstruing anybody.

LAURI: I think what Peter is saying—

PETER: What if—just listen to me a second—indulge me, okay?—What if we pitch the show to Dena Strawbridge and she loves it, and then we say, "By the way, this is a film show," and she says, "Oh, sorry, I don't want to do a film show." What do we do?

DICK: We dump her.

PETER: Really?

DICK: She doesn't want to do it our way? Absolutely. We dump her. "Sorry, Dena," whatever. "Ah, that's too bad, we want to go for something else." That's all there is to it.

PETER: Yeah?

DICK: You worried about getting this on the air? Write it good, bubbie, it'll get on the air, Dena Strawbridge or no Dena Strawbridge. There are hundreds of has-been Dena Strawbridges out there. We can always find a new star. This is Los Angeles.

PETER: Okay.

DICK: Hundreds. Are you fucking kidding me? Look through the Players Guide. People you thought died horribly long ago are in there, waiting for a shot like this, are you kidding?

PETER: Okay. Good.

DICK: Alright? You feel better now?

PETER: Yeah.

DICK: Good. Thank God. (*To Lauri*) New York playwrights, I'm telling *you* . . .

(*She laughs; Dick claps his hands together: to Peter*)

Alright, boychick, let's hear it.

PETER: You mean *now?*

DICK: Yeah, run it by me.

PETER: Oh, okay.

DICK: What, you don't wanna?

PETER: No, I didn't know we were gonna . . .

DICK: We're going in to the network tomorrow, bubbie, we're not gonna walk in *cold.* You didn't think we were just gonna walk in . . .

PETER: No. I don't know . . . (*making light of it*) I just got here from the *airport,* Dick. I mean, I haven't even had a chance to take a *shower.*

DICK (*kibitzing, sort of*): What, you're gonna be *sensitive?*

PETER: No, I'm kidding . . .

DICK: You can't pitch if you smell? Huh? You're worried you smell?

PETER: I'm *kidding* . . .

DICK: We're *friends* here. (*To Lauri*) Right?

LAURI: Absolutely.

DICK: We're *friends.* We don't care you smell. I'm *teasing* you. (*To Lauri*) Look at him, look how sensitive . . .

PETER: Who's sensi— Okay. So . . . You mind if I refer to my notes?

DICK: Go head.

PETER: I promise tomorrow I'll be more "up." I'll be rested, I'll be bathed . . .

DICK (*to Lauri*): Boy, this guy is a real (whatayacallit?) a cleanliness freak or something.

(*Lauri laughs*)

A shower fetishist.

PETER: I'm kidding . . .

DICK: I *know* you're kidding, bubbie, I *know. I'm* kidding. (*To Lauri*) He's stalling. Look at how he's stalling.

PETER (*launching into the pitch*): Okay. *Working Mom.*

DICK: What is this, a *book* report? (*To Lauri, who laughs*) He's doing a book report. (*To Peter*) Only *kidding.* Go head. Great so far, I love it. I love that title. (*To Lauri*) Don't you?

LAURI: Great title.

DICK (*to Peter*): Go head. Sorry. No more interruptions.

PETER: Okay. So—

DICK (*calls*): Jen?

JENNIFER'S VOICE: Yes, Dick?

DICK (*calls*): Hold all calls.

JENNIFER'S VOICE: I am, Dick.

DICK (*to Peter*): All yours, pal.

PETER: Okay, here we go. (*Clears throat*) What we hope to do with *Working Mom,* what we hope to *accomplish,* is to explore, in very real terms, what it means to be a single, working-class working mother today.

(*Dick takes the notes out of Peter's hands, looks them over*)

DICK: What *is* this?

PETER: These are the notes I sent you.

DICK: What notes?

PETER: I FedExed them to you two weeks ago. I don't have a FAX, remember? You wanted them as quickly as possible.

DICK: How come *I* never saw these notes?

LAURI: I gave them to you, Dick. Remember?

DICK: All I can say is I never saw these notes.

LAURI: I *gave* them to you.

DICK: And I'm telling you I never saw them.

LAURI: They were right on your desk. I *put* them on your desk.

DICK: And I never *saw* them, okay? I never *saw* them. (*Hands them back to Peter*) You should've gotten feedback on this.

PETER: When I didn't hear from you, I assumed they were okay.

DICK: Never assume. I'm saying I'm sorry. The error occurred in this office.

LAURI: I put them on your desk, Dick.

DICK (*to Peter*): Go on.

PETER: Um . . . to explore, in very real terms—

DICK: I'm not sure about this "explore" shit . . .

PETER: No?

DICK: Sounds so . . . surgical. This is *comedy,* man.

PETER: I know. I'm just trying to . . .

DICK: You do this at the network (I'll be perfectly honest with you) . . . You do this at the network tomorrow, you might as well hand out pillows and blankies and tuck everybody in.

PETER: I said I'll have more energy tomorrow.

DICK: Fuck energy. Excuse me. I'm not talking energy or no energy. *The pitch has got to entertain.* Believe me. I've been doing this a lot longer than you have.

PETER: I know . . .

DICK: If you don't grab them from the word go . . .

LAURI: It's true.

DICK (*to Lauri*): Am I right?

LAURI: Absolutely. It has to—

DICK: This is key. *You have to make it sound like fun.* These guys don't know. You think they know shit? You have to show them *the potential for fun.* They need to know it's okay to enjoy themselves. You need to smile.

PETER: Smile?

DICK: Yeah. You look like you're sitting shiva.

PETER: I do? I'm sorry.

DICK: Hey. That's okay. That's what I'm here for. That's what today is about. These are things to keep in mind. Go on.

PETER (*continuing*): Dena Flanders was a junior at Atlantic City High when she got pregnant for the first time. Her boyfriend, Paulie

Vanzetti, married her and, even though they had two more kids, Paulie never could stop gambling and chasing cocktail waitresses. Well, Dena's finally had it. She moves herself and her kids into her mother's house. All she wants is to get her life back on track. So, with the help of her tart-tongued mother (Olympia Dukakis), Dena takes night classes to finish her high school degree. In the pilot, she gets a job as a paralegal in the storefront office of a crusty old leftie attorney named Al Sapirstein (Jerry Stiller).

DICK: Wait a second.

PETER: Yeah?

DICK: Pete. Hold it. (*Pause*) You know that *play* of yours?

PETER: Which one?

DICK: The one I flipped over. The Jewish guy?

PETER: *Shabbos Goy?*

DICK: *Shabbos Boy,* that's right.

PETER: *Goy.*

LAURI: *Goy,* Dick.

DICK (*smiling*): Funny play. You had some scenes in there . . .

PETER: Thank you.

DICK: You're a funny guy.

PETER: Thanks.

DICK (*to Lauri*): Isn't he a funny guy?

LAURI: Oh, God, are you kidding?

DICK: Very funny guy. And funny is money. (*To Lauri*) No?

LAURI: Definitely.

DICK (*to Peter*): Let me tell *you:* Funny is money, my friend, and you are funny.

PETER: Well, thanks.

DICK: When I discovered that script of yours . . . Howling! I was howling!

PETER: Really?

DICK: Uh! Funny funny stuff.

PETER: Thanks.

DICK: *Now:* you know how you wrote in your play?

PETER: Yeah . . . ? What.

DICK: You know how *funny* you wrote?

PETER: Yeah . . . ?

DICK: Do that here.

PETER: What?

DICK: Do that here. Be *funny.* Write funny. This isn't funny.

PETER: It may not *sound* funny . . .

DICK: No. This is not funny.

PETER: When I *write* it . . .

DICK (*to Lauri*): You think this is funny?

LAURI: Well I understand what he's—

DICK: No. It's not. Pete. Listen to me. You don't understand. Make this funny. What you've got *here* (believe me, I know what I'm talking about) it isn't funny. Plain and simple. No matter how you cut it.

When you write it (believe me) it's gonna suck. Just think of your play. I read it. I know what you can do. Do what you did there.

TYNE'S VOICE: Daddy?

DICK: You can do it, Pete. (*Calls*) Yes, baby.

TYNE'S VOICE: Daddy, Consuelo says I can't have Mrs. Fields. She says it's for supper.

DICK: It *is* for supper, Tyney. For coffee after.

(*A beat*)

Tyne?

(*He listens; she's gone; he takes off shoes, lays down on sofa*)

So, *good* so far. Let's hear the pilot. Pitch me the pilot.

PETER: Okay. So. The opening. I thought it would be fun if we opened with sort of a parody of that great sweeping pan of the Statue of Liberty that opens *Working Girl?* Remember the opening of *Working Girl?*

LAURI: Uh huh.

PETER: Well, I thought what we could do for *Working Mom* is the camera swoops really dramatically around the statue and then, instead of heading over to the Manhattan skyline, it ends up in New Jersey.

LAURI: Ooo. Nice. Isn't that nice, Dick?

PETER: You know, kind of working-class, industrial New Jersey. Refineries, highways, smog sunset. So there's a kind of irony there, from the word go, that tells us that this isn't gonna be another glossy single-working-mother kind of show. The irony is you think—

DICK: Wait wait wait. "Irony"? (*To Lauri*) He's an intellectual.

(*She laughs*)

Intellectuals (what can I tell you?) they love "irony."

(*She laughs even more*)

I don't give a *shit* "irony."

PETER: I was just—

DICK: Excuse me. You pushed a button. I'm very emotional about this. You pushed a—there it goes . . . You will learn this about me, Peter. Ask anybody who's worked with me. They will tell you the same: I do not bullshit. (*To Lauri; meaning, True?*)
Huh?

LAURI: It's true.

DICK (*to Peter*): Hey, I don't mean to blow you away.

PETER: No, I'm alright . . .

DICK (*to Lauri*): He's looking at me like God knows . . . (*to Peter*) I'm your *friend* for telling you this. I know you're just off the plane so to speak. You're new in this town. Save your "irony" for the *stage.* Okay? (I'm about to save you a lot of grief.) Save it for the *theater.* That's all I have to say on the subject. Period, end quote. I don't bullshit people I like, I have *respect* for. (*To Lauri*) Am I right?

LAURI: Oh, absolutely.

DICK: I don't have time for irony. Give me a story. Tell me a good story, I'm happy. That's all I ask. Whatever happened to stories? Hm? Remember stories? Bubbeleh, this is what I'm telling you. We gotta clear your brain of that shit. We gotta vacuum it out. Simple stories, Peter. Where a cow is a cow for a change. Boy meets girl. Yeah. No symbols. No irony. One thing doesn't mean another. Who wants to sit there (no really now) who wants to have to *sit* there and *work* and figure it out? "Oh, I get it: the so-and-so really means the *Holocaust.*" "Child abuse." Fill in the blank. Fuck it. Life is too short for irony. Please. Tell me the fucking story. *This* happens, then *this* happens, then *this* happens, so-on and so-forth. People after a hard day, they do not want to have to put on their thinking caps. (*Getting up, unzipping his fly*) These are important lessons in this town, pal . . . I swear one day you're gonna thank me. (*To Lauri*) Look at him, he hates me. (*Lauri laughs*) Fucking Diet Cokes . . .

(*While reaching into his fly, Dick exits to the bathroom. Pause*)

LAURI: You know Dick's never done TV before.

PETER: What do you mean?

LAURI: He's done *movies.*

PETER: Oh, yeah, I know.

LAURI: He had that one Tom Cruise thing, he got this deal as a result.

PETER: Uh huh.

LAURI: Sure, he was kicking around for years (who hasn't).

PETER: Uh huh.

LAURI: But the truth is . . . when it comes to television . . . ?

PETER: Yeah . . . ?

LAURI: He doesn't know the first thing.

PETER: Oh, really.

LAURI: Not a thing. It's embarrassing. I *work* for this guy. I *work* for him. We go into these meetings at the network?

PETER: Yeah . . . ?

LAURI: And it's like *unbelievable.*

PETER: Huh.

LAURI: The guy. Doesn't. Know. The business. Television, I mean. Okay, so he had a hit movie. A lot of people have hit movies, doesn't make them experts in *television.* He thinks he knows how to put together a *series?* It's a joke. I'm saving his ass all over town. I'm covering for him. I have to call the network after we meet with them?

PETER: Yeah . . . ?

LAURI: To like patch-up for all the schmucky things he said? It's a joke. I was instrumental in *Charles in Charge*—before it went into syndication! I was *there,* learning, paying my dues, seeing how it's done. What does *Dick* know? Do you think he knows good material when he sees it? I have to *tell* him what's good. I have to *find* what's good (but that's not enough) *I have to get him to read it.* A writer doesn't exist out here until he's read. They don't know New York theater. I really had to fight for you, you know.

PETER: Oh, yeah? How do you mean?

LAURI: *I'm* the one who kept on pushing your play on him.

PETER: Well, thank you.

LAURI: These people don't read. They do *not* read. I was in Theater, you know.

PETER: Oh, yeah? Where'd you go to school?

LAURI: B.U.?

PETER: Uh huh.

LAURI: I always felt that we could really break ground with *Working Mom,* we could really do some important television—*if* we found the right writer for the pilot. Someone who's fresh and doesn't know all the sitcom tricks. We wanted you because you *don't* know the formula. You *don't* know the tricks. We wanted *grit* and humor *and* ethnicity, *authenticity.* You've got it all.

PETER: Thanks.

LAURI: You *do.* "Peter Rosenthal is who we want for *Working Mom,"* I said. No, "Peter Rosenthal is who we *need.* If we don't get Peter Rosenthal—and he's very hot right now—(this is what I told him) if we don't *nab* him (and if we don't, we're idiots), if we don't fly him out here *right* away, then I ask you: My God, what are we all doing here?" (*Grasps his wrist; confidentially*) Peter?

PETER: Yes, Lauri?

LAURI: Feel free to call me any time. You have my home number?

PETER: Yeah, I think you . . .

LAURI: Any time.

PETER: You wrote it on your card.

LAURI: You're gonna need someone to talk to out here.

PETER: I appreciate that, Lauri, but I have friends . . .

LAURI: No, I mean, these things can get pretty intense. Development, I mean. It can get dirty. You can get hurt if you don't watch out.

PETER: Thanks, Lauri.

LAURI: Hey, I feel responsible. I'm the one who got you out here. We have to protect writers like you. Do you know how *rare* it is to find a writer like you? I *cherish* writers. Writers are all we have. Really, when you think about it. Promise you'll call me.

PETER: I promise.

LAURI: Peter, you have *such* a unique comic *voice,* I can't tell you.

PETER: Thank you.

LAURI: No, thank *you.* You have no idea how many scripts I read. And it's all shit. Then to discover someone like you?! It's like: "Oh, yeah, right, *this* is why I want to produce. *This* is why I came out here."

(*The toilet flushes. Dick returns*)

DICK: What's this?

LAURI: Nothing. I was just telling Peter what a unique voice we think he has.

DICK: Oh, yeah. Really unique. So, where are we?

JENNIFER'S VOICE: Dena's here, Dick.

DICK: In the house or on her way?

JENNIFER'S VOICE: *Here.*

DICK: Shit.

LAURI (*to Peter*): Don't worry.

(*Dena Strawbridge, early 40s, brittle, nervous, enters*)

DENA: Hi. Sorry. I was at Pritikin.

DICK: Hey. Dena. There's my girl. (*He hugs her*) Oh, man, so good to see you.

DENA: Good to see you, too.

DICK: You're looking sensational.

DENA: Yeah? Oh . . .

DICK (*to Lauri*): Doesn't she look—?

LAURI: Mm, yes!

DENA: Thank you. Do I know you?

DICK: My development exec, Lauri Richards?

DENA: Oh, hi.

LAURI: Hello. Really nice to meet you finally.

DENA: Thank you.

DICK: And, Dena? Remember that *terrific* young writer we told you about? From New York?

DENA: Yes!

DICK: This is Peter Rosenthal. From New York.

PETER: Hi. Nice to meet you.

DENA: Thank you. Wow. Really really nice to meet you, too . . .

DICK: So! We were just pitching, the three of us.

DENA: Oh, yeah?

DICK: Sounds great.

DENA: Yeah?

DICK: Uh! You're gonna love it.

DENA: Oo! I can't wait. (*Grasping Dick's hand*) *God,* am I glad we're working together . . .

(*He hugs her again*)

DICK: Me, too. Didn't I tell you we *would* one day?

DENA: I am so so excited about this project. You mind if I eat?

DICK: No. Eat. What is that?

DENA: Oh, I'm on macro. It's great. You ever do it?

DICK: No.

DENA: Oh, it's great. I'm keeping my weight down, I'm more regular than I've ever been in my entire life . . . It's great. Really. You should try it. I'll give you my nutritionist's number. He's fabulous. Oh! I have regards for you!

DICK: Oh, yeah? From who?

DENA: Joel Kaplan?

DICK: Joel Kaplan, no shit! How do you know Joel?

DENA: He produced my miniseries.

DICK: No kidding, is that so?

DENA: Yeah, and he's looking really good. Have you seen him lately?

DICK: He's had a hell of a time.

DENA: I know, but he's looking great. I just ran into him at Pritikin. He lost something like fifty pounds.

DICK: No kidding. Good for him. (*To Peter and Lauri*) This guy was a fucking fat pig.

DENA: He's seeing Leonard, too. My nutritionist. Remind me to give you his number, you will love him.

DICK: Gee, I really should give Joel a call . . . Where *is* he now?

DENA: Warners.

DICK: I thought he was at Universal.

DENA: That deal ran out. He got an even better deal at Warners. An *incredible* deal. And he looks really really great.

DICK (*calls*): Jennifer?

JENNIFER'S VOICE: Yes, Dick?

DICK (*calls*): Put Joel Kaplan on my call list? (*To Dena*) Warners?

DENA: Uh huh.

DICK (*calls*): He's at Warners. (*To Dena*) Is he clean now, Joel?

DENA: Oh, yeah. You should see him.

DICK: I heard he had his nose redone.

DENA: Oh, yeah, he was in big big trouble. He was killing himself.

DICK: I didn't know it got so bad.

DENA: The man was killing himself.

DICK: Jeez . . . (*to Peter*) Joel Kaplan? You know him?

PETER: No.

DICK: Biggest asshole alive.

DENA: Well, he did a great job on my miniseries.

DICK: Good.

DENA: A super super job. Considering what he was going through.

DICK: I'm glad he came through for you, Dena. I'm truly glad to hear that.

DENA: Absolutely terrific.

DICK: I'm an asshole: Tell me the name again?

DENA: *The Deadly Weekend of Marilyn Monroe?*

DICK: Oh, of course!

LAURI: Oh, yes!

DICK: I am an asshole! That was supposed to be . . .

DENA: I know.

DICK (*to Lauri*): Did you see that?

LAURI: No, I was in the hospital for my lumpectomy.

DICK: We heard that was terrific! (*To Lauri*) Didn't we hear that was terrific?

LAURI: Oh, yes! Everybody was—

DENA: It won me my Emmy nomination so I guess it must've been pretty—

DICK: Yeah, congratulations on that!

LAURI *and* PETER: Congratulations.

DENA: *Thank* you.

DICK: Did you win it? I forget.

DENA: No, no. Katharine Hepburn got it that year. But, I tell you, I was so honored just to be *nominated* with that lady.

LAURI: Hm, yeah.

DICK: Wow. Now I want to see it.

DENA: I was so frigging proud. A role like that doesn't come along very often for a woman, let's face it. I got to do everything. The Bobby Kennedy scenes? I mean, between takes Marty Sheen had to *hold* me, that's how much I was shaking . . .

LAURI: Wow.

DICK: Shit, I really want to see this . . . (*calls*) Jen?

JENNIFER'S VOICE: Yes, Dick.

DICK: Call the agency, see if they can get us a copy—

DENA: No, you don't have to do that . . .

DICK: —of Dena's miniseries, *Deadly* . . .

DENA: *Weekend of Marilyn Monroe.*

DICK: The Marilyn Monroe thing.

DENA: You really don't—

DICK: Tell them to messenger it over—

DENA: Dick, you really don't have to do that . . . (*To Lauri*) What a crazy nut.

(*Lauri nods*)

DICK (*overlap*): —I want to look at it tonight.

DENA: You *don't* have to do this on my account.

DICK: I *want* to. Are you kidding? It'll be fun.

DENA: Well, good.

JENNIFER'S VOICE: Dick?

DICK (*calls*): Yeah, Jen.

JENNIFER'S VOICE: I've got Joel Kaplan for you.

DICK (*calls*): Joel Ka—? Who called who? (*To others*) Isn't this freaky?

JENNIFER'S VOICE: You told me to get him.

DICK (*calls*): I said put him on my *list,* Jennifer.

JENNIFER'S VOICE: Oh, I thought . . .

DICK (*calls*): Uh, look . . . I said on my list . . .

JENNIFER'S VOICE: Sorry, Dick . . . I've *got* him . . . (*a beat*) What do you want me to do with him?

DICK: Tell him I'll have to get back to him. I'm in a meeting.

JENNIFER'S VOICE: Okay. Sorry, Dick.

DICK (*calls*): Yeah. (*To others*) Jesus. Do you believe her? She can be such a flake sometimes. —*Now.* This *guy* . . . Are we lucky! This *boy* . . . *How* old are you?

PETER: 32.

DICK: Nah. You are not . . .

PETER: Yes, I am.

DICK: You look 25, 26.

PETER: I'm 32, though, believe me.

DICK: Doesn't he look 25?

DENA: Yeah, he does.

DICK: 25, 27 *maybe* . . .

PETER: No, I'm 32.

DICK: You could pass. Easy. Lie. Fib. Tell people you're 25, they'll eat it up.

PETER: But I'm not.

DICK: Fib, I said. People out here, everybody's very impressed with how young you are. Everybody loves a prodigy. Say you're 25, mark my words. —*Anyhow* . . . this *guy* . . . this *boy* . . . wrote a *play* . . . ran in New York . . . Joe *Papp* produced this play.

DENA (*with interest*): Uh huh?

DICK: This play . . . *Shabbos Boy* . . . I'm telling you . . . had me peeing in my pants. (*To Lauri*) Right?

LAURI: It did.

DICK: Peeing! On the floor!

DENA: Really?

DICK: In my pants! (*To Lauri*) Tell her.

LAURI: It's true.

DENA: Oh, how great!

DICK: Funny, funny play.

PETER: Thanks, Dick.

DICK: Funny is money. I keep telling him that, he doesn't believe me.

PETER: I believe you.

DICK: He doesn't believe me. He thinks I'm *lying* he can be a gold mine out here.

PETER: I believe you.

DICK: There's a scene he's got in this play, Dena . . .

DENA: Yeah?

DICK: Dena, this *scene* . . . with the mother?

PETER: The grandmother, actually.

DICK: Huh?

PETER: You mean with the grandmother? You told me . . .

DICK: The mother, the grandmother, whatever . . . Anyhow, he's yelling at her about his bris? (*To Dena*) Circumcision. You know, when they *perform* it, the people, they throw a party . . .

DENA: Oh, yeah, I know some people who did that . . .

DICK: Anyhow, he's yelling, "How could you do something like that to me!"

DENA: Oh, how funny.

DICK: And she *sits* there. She *sits* there, the mother, the grandmother, and she doesn't say a word!

PETER: Oh, you mean the stroke scene?

DICK: What?

PETER: The stroke scene. The grandmother's had a stroke. That's why she doesn't say anything.

DICK (*thinks he's kidding*): Nahhh . . .

PETER: Yes! She's had a stroke and he doesn't realize it. That's what the scene is about.

DICK: Oh, you mean the *stroke* scene! Sure! Oh, yeah, of course. Well, the point is (whatever): a riot. The *play* is a riot.

DENA: What's the name of it again?

PETER: *Shabbos Goy.*

DICK: *Shabbos Boy.*

PETER: *Shabbos Goy.*

DICK: *Goy?* I thought *Boy.*

PETER: No.

DENA: What does it mean? I mean, I don't know Jewish.

PETER: A shabbos goy is a non-Jew hired by Orthodox Jews to do little chores . . . like lighting the stove, turning on the electricity . . . Orthodox Jews aren't allowed to do certain things on the sabbath. Saturday. That's what "shabbos" means: Saturday.

DENA: Oh! I get it.

DICK: That's a good title.

PETER: Thanks.

DICK: I mean, you should've called it that: *Shabbos Goy* not *Boy.*

PETER: I did.

DICK: Wait . . . you did or you didn't?

LAURI: Dick? The name of the play is *Shabbos Goy.*

DICK: *Shabbos Goy* has irony—I mean, it, uh, has more *meaning.*

PETER: I agree. That's why I called it that.

DICK: The copy we read . . . I could swear it said "Boy." (*Calls*) Jen? Jennifer?

JENNIFER'S VOICE: Yes, Dick.

DICK: Bring in a copy of Peter's play?

JENNIFER'S VOICE: *Shabbos Goy?*

DICK: Uh, never mind.

DENA: So, what's it about, your play?

PETER: It's a comedy, I guess. About assimilation.

DENA: Uh huh. Neat. A comedy, huh? Isn't that kind of a tough subject?

PETER: Well . . .

DENA: I mean, considering what's going on?

PETER (*a beat*): What do you mean exactly?

DENA: I mean, you know, South Africa.

PETER: South Africa?

DENA: You know, what's going on over there with that?

PETER (*a beat*): Oh. Apartheid?

DENA: *That's* it. *That's* the word . . .

PETER: No, my play's about Jews who have assimilated into a gentile society.

DENA: Wow. Oh. I getcha.

DICK: The Public Theater did it.

DENA: Hm.

DICK: The Public Theater in New York? Joe Papp?

DENA: Oh, yeah. I know him. Wasn't he at Fox?

DICK: Joe Papp?

DENA: Yeah, I think he was. Short guy, right?

DICK: Yeah . . .

DENA: Yeah, he was at Fox. I'm positive.

DICK: Joe Papp?

DENA: Jewish guy, right?

DICK: Yeah . . .

DENA: I did meet him. At Fox.

PETER: I really don't think so.

DICK (*over "think so"*): Yeah? Maybe. Whataya know? Yeah, I think you're right. Leave it to Dena. Anyhow . . . Let's hear this pitch . . .

(*All eyes are on Peter*)

TYNE'S VOICE: Daddy, Consuelo ate a Mrs. Fields.

DICK (*calls*): Tyne? Daddy's in a meeting, honey.

TYNE'S VOICE: Daddy, I want a cookie, too. I want *two* cookies.

DICK (*overlap; to others*): Sorry, my kid.

DENA (*overlap*): Perfectly alright.

DICK (*calls*): Tyne? Tyney honey? You can have *one.*

TYNE'S VOICE: I want macadamia with dark chocolate *and* milk chocolate.

DICK: No, Tyney. One. Pick one.

TYNE'S VOICE: I want both. Consuelo had one or two, I'm not sure, and she wasn't supposed to have *any.*

DICK (*calls*): You can have one chocolate and one—

TYNE'S VOICE: What kind of chocolate? There's dark chocolate and milk chocolate.

DICK (*overlap; calls*): Daddy's in a meeting, sweetheart, this isn't a good time for this.

TYNE'S VOICE: Daddy, it's not fair Consuelo should have.

DICK: Consuelo *shouldn't've* had, okay?! (*To others*) These fucking . . . (*calls*) Take a chocolate chip and an oatmeal raisin and—

TYNE'S VOICE: I don't like oatmeal.

DICK: Oatmeal is healthier.

TYNE'S VOICE: I want one macadamia with dark chocolate . . .

DICK: Tyne . . .

TYNE'S VOICE: . . . and one milk chocolate chip.

DICK: Okay! Now leave Daddy alone! So what do you say? Tyne? What do you say, honey? Tyne? Tyney? (*A beat. To others*) Anyhow . . . (*to Peter*) Let's hear the pitch.

PETER: Okay. Um . . . *Working Mom* . . .

DICK (*to Dena*): Don't you love that title?

DENA: Oh, yeah, I do.

LAURI: So do I.

DICK: I love it. *Working Mom:* it just *says* it.

DENA: It really does.

DICK (*to Peter*): Go head.

PETER: Okay, and I see the opening . . . The opening's this sweeping pan of the Statue of Liberty? You know, the camera will sweep around it—

DICK (*sort of discreetly*): Skip it.

PETER: Hm?

DICK: Skip it. Cut to the chase.

DENA: No, I'm with you.

DICK: I want you to hear the story. This stuff, it's trimming.

PETER: I just thought I'd give you a sense of the—

DICK: Don't worry about it. Tell the story. Like you did before. Just tell it.

DENA: Yeah, tell me who she is. I'm dying to know who she is.

PETER: Alright. Um . . . Dena Flanders—

DENA (*laughing*): —"Flanders"?

PETER: Yeah—was a junior at Atlantic City High when—

DENA: Atlantic City? Where is that again?

PETER: New Jersey.

DENA: Oh, right.

PETER: So, when she was a junior in high school—

DENA: Excuse me. Can I say something?

DICK: Sure. Go head. Feel free. That's what you're here for. Jump right in whenever you like.

DENA: Thanks. I was just wondering . . .

DICK: I got some Evian for you. Want some?

DENA: No, thanks. Now: Why does she have to be from New Jersey?

PETER: Well . . .

DENA: I mean, like, take *me* for instance.

PETER: Uh huh.

DENA: I'm from Wisconsin.

PETER: Yeah . . .

DENA: I mean, couldn't she be from Wisconsin?

(*A beat*)

LAURI: Huh. Interesting.

PETER: But this *character* is *from* New Jersey. Where she's from has a lot to do with who she is.

DICK: I think Peter would have to think about that, wouldn't you, Peter?

PETER: Um . . . Yeah. I'd have to think about that a lot.

DENA: You see, let me just say something—do you mind?

PETER: Not at all.

DENA: The thing about Wisconsin . . . I'm *from* Wisconsin, okay? I grew up there. I *know* it. I *lived* it. I know the *people.* I know what Wisconsin *smells* like.

PETER: Well, gee, that's interesting, I'll have to—

DENA: There's something about really really knowing a place . . . You know what I mean? You don't have to act. I mean from an acting standpoint. You do not have to *act,* it's there, it's in your skin, it's in your soul, it's *just there.*

DICK (*taking to the idea*): Uh huh, uh huh. I don't hate that.

PETER: But the story revolves around—

DICK: I don't hate that at all. I like it, in fact.

PETER: Wait, but the story . . .

DICK: The story you can always fix. I do not hate this, there's something to it.

DENA (*to Dick*): You know what I mean?

DICK: I do. I absolutely do. (*To Lauri*) You know?

LAURI: Oh, yeah.

PETER: Wait a second . . .

DICK: Just go on.

PETER: But where she's from affects everything *about* the story.

DICK: It's a small fix. A tiny thing, just like that. Believe me, bubbie, it's nothing. Just go on.

PETER: I don't know . . .

DICK: Go *on.* Don't worry about it. Let *us* worry about it.

PETER: Well, I had her getting pregnant when she was a junior in high school.

DENA: Oh, how awful.

PETER: Hm?

DENA: Pregnant in high school? Isn't that like setting a really bad role model?

PETER: Well, no, I mean, realistically . . .

DENA: None of the girls at *my* high school ever would've *dreamed* . . .

DICK: Where'd you go to high school?

DENA: Holy Trinity in Green Bay. I mean, that is like a completely far-fetched idea where I come from, that a girl would get herself *pregnant* . . .

PETER: Yeah, but this is Atlantic City, New Jersey in the sixties.

DENA (*after a beat*): Not the sixties.

PETER: Hm?

DENA: I can't say I was in high school in the sixties. Are you kidding?

PETER: No?

DENA: That would put me close to forty.

PETER: Oh. Yes.

DENA: I can't play close to forty. Next you'll have me playing mothers.

(*Peter looks at Dick. A beat*)

DICK: We'll fix it.

DENA: Something wrong?

PETER: No. I'm just a little confused. The name of the show, the title of the show is *Working Mom.*

DENA: I know. And by the way, did I tell you how much I love that title?

PETER: Yes. You did.

DENA: Well, I'm only saying: one kid, alright, I can do that. That's like an accident. Okay, I can accept that. We all make mistakes. But more than one (two or three?), I just can't see it. How many did you give her?

PETER: Well, three.

DENA: No. Now that's a stretch. We're talking about the public now, too, Peter. I have fans. They're used to seeing me on *Molly's Marauders.* I mean, that's who they think I am. There's an obligation I have. And this is very very important to me. (*To Lauri*) You're a woman, you know what I mean.

LAURI: I do absolutely.

DENA: It's very important.

LAURI: Tell me about it.

DICK: These are all points for discussion. Let's hear what David here has to say first.

PETER: Hm?

DICK: Go head.

PETER: Peter.

DICK: What?

LAURI: You said "David," Dick.

DICK: No, I didn't.

DENA: Yeah, you did. I heard that, too.

(*She laughs, the others join her*)

DICK: I did? Jesus, who'm I thinking of? Oh, *I* know: *Him,* the schmuck. Never mind. Anyway, let's just hear what the guy has.

DENA: Yes. Let's. And by the way, I think what you've done so far is just great.

LAURI: Oh, yes.

DICK: Didn't I tell you he was something?

PETER: Anyhow . . .

DICK: He can't take a compliment. Look at him.

PETER: Well, what I had was: her high school boyfriend marries her because she's pregnant. Paulie Vanzetti his name is, or, that's what I called him. You can call him anything you like, it doesn't matter. Anyway, he never really treated her very well, so finally, (this is where the pilot starts), she decides to leave him. She takes her kids —or kid or whatever—and she moves in with her mother, a kind of tart-tongued Olympia Dukakis type and—

DENA: Oh, I love that! Didn't you love her in *Moonstruck?*

LAURI: Oh, yes!

DENA: Now if this could be a kind of *Moonstruck-Fried Green Tomatoes*-fish-out-of-water-*Beverly Hills Cop* kind of thing . . .

LAURI: That's interesting. We were thinking of it more in terms of a *Moonstruck-Working Girl-Parenthood*-Tracy Chapman urban grit kind of thing.

DICK: Just think of her as a female *Rocky.*

LAURI: Yes!

DENA: I like that.

DICK: A female *Rocky.* That's all you have to say. Someone you really root for. What more is there to a good story besides rooting for someone?

DENA: I think so, too. You know, that's it, isn't it: really really caring. God, that's so true. (*To Peter*) Please. Continue.

PETER: What's the point? I mean, we seem to be all over the place.

DICK: Uh-oh. Somebody's attitude is showing . . .

(*Dena and Lauri laugh*)

Look at him. He hates me. (*To Peter*) Bubbie, you gotta let go. It's the collaborative process. Everybody gets to speak his or her mind, writer or no. It's not New York theater anymore. Now go head. Tell us what happens in the pilot.

PETER: Nothing. She gets a job.

DICK: Peter . . .

PETER: Okay, she gets a job working in, you know, a kind of storefront law office (they have them back East) and her boss is this old leftie attorney.

LAURI: A crusty Ed Asner-*Lou Grant*-Jerry Stiller type.

DENA: Hm.

DICK: What?

DENA: Nothing. Well . . . What if . . . What if . . . You know what would be fun? What if she went to beauty school?

PETER: No, I don't see how that fits our idea of—

DICK: Shh.

LAURI: Sort of an urban *Steel Magnolias.*

DENA: Yes! Didn't you just love that movie?

LAURI: Oh, yes.

PETER: But I thought we were going for something gritty and socially relevant.

DICK: Who said?

DENA: Well, this way you'd get to bring in a whole lot of interesting characters. You know, the gay guy, the black manicurist, the fat make-up girl? I mean, this really says something about our culture.

LAURI: You know, maybe we don't need all that backstory at all.

DENA: See, I don't think we do.

LAURI: We can get rid of the kids. We don't need the kids.

PETER: *Working Mom* without kids! Interesting!

DENA: If she's this repressed Catholic woman from Wisconsin who comes to L.A. to go to beauty school . . .

DICK: I don't hate that. I don't hate that at all.

DENA: I mean, wow, think of the possibilities, this repressed person in the middle of L.A. with all these freaks?! Talk about fish-out-of-water!

LAURI (*to Dick*): It's a classic *MTM-Cheers-Murphy Brown* ensemble show. We could do three-camera, one-set (the beauty school)—

DICK: I have no problem with that.

LAURI: —and we could get it set up at NBC like that.

DENA: Oh, yes!

DICK (*to Peter*): Maybe you should write some of this down.

PETER: Maybe you should go fuck yourself.

DICK: There goes that attitude again.

PETER: You know, Dick? I'm sitting here thinking, "What am I doing here? I don't need this." And then I realize, "Well, yeah, I do, I do need this, I need the money." And I think, "That's a lousy reason to subject yourself to something like this." But *then* I think, "Well, tough, you've got to survive; hell, even *Faulkner* did this, this is what a writer has to do, just take the money and run." Okay, well *then* I ask myself: "Shit, is it really worth the humiliation? Is it really worth feeling so scuzzy? Is it worth this constant burning sensation in my stomach?" And the answer comes back: "Yeah. It is. Just do it and stop caring about it so much. Stop thinking so much." But I *can't* stop thinking. I can't stop thinking how I could get by for two months on what it cost you guys to fly me out here. And I can't stop thinking, What is this "unique voice" shit when you can't even bear to let me finish a sentence?

LAURI: Peter. Please. Sit down. We can still make a go of this.

PETER (*a lover's farewell*): No, Lauri. I'm leaving you. We're through.

(*He starts to go*)

DICK: Hey.

(*Peter stops. A beat*)

It's development, bubbie.

(*Peter goes. Pause*)

DENA: What just happened?

DICK (*shrugs, then*): Typical New York writer shit.

(*Dena and Lauri nod and murmur in agreement. Blackout*)

Alternate Ending

PETER: You know, Dick? I'm sitting here thinking, "What am I doing here? I don't need this." And then I realize, "Well, yeah, I do, I do need this, I need the money." And I think, "That's a lousy reason to subject yourself to something like this." But *then* I think, "Well, tough, you've got to survive; hell, even *Faulkner* did this, this is what a writer has to do, just take the money and run." Okay, well *then* I ask myself: "Shit, is it really worth the humiliation? Is it really worth feeling so scuzzy? Is it worth this constant burning sensation in my stomach?" And the answer comes back: "Yeah. It is. Just do it and stop caring about it so much. Stop thinking so much." But I *can't* stop thinking. I can't stop thinking how I could get by for two months on what it cost you guys to fly me out here. And I can't stop thinking, What is this "unique voice" shit when you can't even bear to let me finish a sentence?

LAURI: Peter. Please. Sit down. We can still make a go of this.

PETER (*a lover's farewell*): No, Lauri. I'm leaving you. We're through.

(*He starts to go*)

DICK: Hey.

(*Peter stops. A beat*)

It's development, bubbie.

(*Peter goes. Pause. Calls*)

Jen? Jennifer?

JENNIFER'S VOICE: Yes, Dick?

DICK: Get me Peter's agent. Now, Jen. (*To Lauri*) I want him. Exclusively. Money's no object. We can't let him get on that plane.

(*Dena and Lauri nod and murmur in agreement. Blackout*)

IT'S OUR TOWN, TOO

Susan Miller

Susan Miller

Although her play, *Confessions of a Female Disorder,* received an O'Neill award and made her an O'Neill playwright in 1973, it wasn't until her play *Flux* traveled to London and won considerable praise that Susan Miller became a significant playwright for the American theater. *Flux* had been presented Off-Broadway at the Phoenix theater in New York in 1975, but it was the London production which inspired Joseph Papp to offer the play at his Public Theater in 1976. *Flux* was then subsequently produced at The Second Stage. The New York Shakespeare Company also produced her play, *For Dear Life,* as well as *Nasty Rumors and Final Remarks.* Ms. Miller won an OBIE for the writing of *Nasty Rumors and Final Remarks.* Her plays *Cross Country* and *Confessions of a Female Disorder* were produced at the Mark Taper Forum in Los Angeles, and she has also worked with Home for Contemporary Theatre in New York as well as The Cast Theatre in Los Angeles.

She has received, in addition to the O'Neill award, NEA awards, and a Rockefeller grant in playwriting. She has twice been a finalist for the Susan Blackburn Prize in playwriting, once for *Nasty Rumors and Final Remarks* and again for *For Dear Life.* She is also a Yaddo fellow and a part time faculty member of the NYU Dramatic Writing program. Her work is published in Avon's *Gay Plays, Vol. 1,* ed. William Hoffman; the forthcoming anthology, *Facing Forward,* ed. Leah Frank, for Broadway Publishing, and *One on One, The Best Women's Monologues for the Nineties,* ed. Jack Temchin for Applause. The play published here, *It's Our Town, Too,* was first staged by the Fountainhead Theater Company in Los Angeles in November, 1992.

Characters:

STAGE MANAGER, *to be played by a woman, if possible*
EMILY, *same actress plays both young and older Emily*
ELIZABETH, *same actress plays both young and older Elizabeth*
GEORGE, *Louis's lover and Molly's Dad*
LOUIS, *George's lover and Molly's other Dad*
MOLLY, *the daughter of George and Louis*
CHANCE, *the son of Emily and Elizabeth*
DOC MCADOO, *the family doctor, older*
ANGRY RIGHTEOUS CITIZEN, *man or woman, any age*

Scene

No curtain. No scenery. The Stage Manager walks on and as she talks, begins placing the minimal boxes or chairs that will suggest a sense of place. House lights remain on until she begins to speak.

STAGE MANAGER: This play is called *It's Our Town, Too* and all you need to know about who wrote it is she's still here and constantly wondering. (*Beat*) This first scene is called "An Ordinary Afternoon" and you'll see two of our main characters, Emily and Elizabeth.

(*A train whistle is heard*)

It's 4 P.M. in our town. Last night the stars were out like a promise and someone kissed someone they'd never thought of kissing before. Teachers doubted their lessons and Mrs. Kim could be heard singing the overture to "Carousel". If you were passing through our town, and you happened to stop at the general store for some of Terese Rivera's peach pie, you might be lulled into thinking that people here were small and narrow and wouldn't give a rightful place to the world's concerns. But we're no different from anyone else, trying to grasp the meaning of things. We're mean and lost and fragile and shrewd. We're lonely and aiming too high, bitter and good. We come up thinking the world is sweet but it's every human's experience to meet disappointment.

(*Sound of a bird*)

Sometimes there's a commotion that sets in over a new possibility. Like the summer three entire families swore they spotted a UFO, when it turned out to be Emily Rosen's hopes making themselves known in a burst of light. (*Beat*) Which brings me to Emily and

Elizabeth. I suppose there aren't any two people on the planet put together in one place for very long, who don't have their disagreements, who don't feel sometimes like maybe they made the worst mistake of their lives or wish the person they thought was so sweet just a few hours before, would pack up and leave. There isn't anybody who hasn't looked across the dinner table and thought, I don't know if I love you anymore. And it can drive good people to saying cold words. But it's not really the fact. It's no more true than the first day when you looked at somebody and thought, "She's the one." Thought, "I'm saved." We're just scared is all, everyone of us.

(*School bell, sound of young people*)

Now we're going to go back to the day two of our kind really saw each other for the first time. And knew that there was some future in it. (*Beat*) Oh, this is high school and well, you all remember what that was like. In your heart of hearts aren't you still standing by your locker waiting for that certain one to walk by and maybe, just maybe stop to say your name?

(*Stage Manager backs away as Emily and Elizabeth walk on, as if carrying books. They are seventeen and breathless*)

EMILY: I liked what you said in class today.

ELIZABETH: Did you? God, 'cause I was looking at you the whole time. Trying not to. I wasn't too—well, too, full of myself was I?

EMILY: Oh, no. Not at all. You were just talking like . . . like you. I mean, it was very smart and everything but sweet, too. It was like, you were saying, okay, there are some things I know pretty well but then you wanted us to see that there are lots of things you don't know, either, and it's okay not to know them. In fact, maybe it's important not to know them to be a real human being. I was just so proud of you for that.

ELIZABETH: You're something, Emily. You know that. You're just about the best person I ever met.

EMILY: Did you ever think that maybe it's someone else who puts us up there? I mean, just by being near to something good and true, brings out our real nature?

ELIZABETH: You have a great way about you, Emily.

EMILY: Well, I don't know about that.

ELIZABETH: I hope when we graduate we'll still be friends.

EMILY: I wouldn't want to live without talking to you everyday.

ELIZABETH: I guess that's just about how I feel.

(*We hear parents calls out: Emily! Elizabeth!*)

EMILY: So, it's good we had this talk, then.

ELIZABETH: Sometimes I think the earth is just gonna spin me off and I'll fly by night and keep you safe, Emily.

EMILY: I'd rather if you stayed here on the ground with me. If you could, I mean. If you didn't think it was holding you back, that is.

(*Elizabeth suddenly kisses her. They are both stunned*)

ELIZABETH: I had to, that's all.

EMILY: Oh, my.

(*Lights dim on the girls, as they leave, and the Stage Manager speaks from the corner of the stage*)

STAGE MANAGER: Well, that's how these things get started. Somebody fastens inside of you, and you're lost. Of course it's always pleasing to watch two such fresh ones as Emily and Elizabeth. If we didn't know so much about the terrible turn the heart takes, we could be happier for them. (*Beat*) Anyhow, twenty years have passed. A wedding's about to take place. Emily and Elizabeth set up house over on Taft Street. And you remember Georgie, the newspaper boy, well he lives across the way with his life partner—that'd be Louis. And today all these fine friends are preparing to send their offspring out into the world together. (*Calling out*) Chance! This is Emily and Elizabeth's son and the bridegroom in today's event.

(*Chance enters*)

Chance, I thought the audience might like to know how it's been growing up with two mothers.

CHANCE: Well, I don't think of it like that, exactly. They're my parents is all. Oh, sometimes we fight about if I leave my clothes all over the floor. We laugh pretty much too, like, about—well you had to be there. Mom, that's Emily—she kind of spurs me on, you know. Won't let me quit when I'm down low. Being the son of a doctor, you see how people have it a lot harder than you. Mama—she's more moody, sorta like me. But she's a poet and you know how they are. I'm working as a stringer for the Times. I think I'd like to write about medicine.

STAGE MANAGER: Okay, Chance. Thank you for—

CHANCE: One more thing. The day my Mom and Mama were arrested. The day the very same country I call home, broke up ours—saying we weren't a real family—that was a hard day. Nearly broke my faith. Molly and I, that's my bride to be, we were thinking rash thoughts. It was our parents pulled us through it.

STAGE MANAGER: How's that?

CHANCE: Sat us down and said, "You know what's true. You know what's right." And same as always they wouldn't stop talking until everyone came around to their way.

(*An intense young woman approaches*)

STAGE MANAGER: Well, now here's young Molly. And she'll be wanting to say something too.

MOLLY (*to audience*): Hi. Uhm. I guess you probably want to know how I turned out and all. Okay, sure, sometimes I wished I had Eleanor Jones' parents, but who doesn't. I mean, when one of your fathers is being overprotective or a real pain in the butt about doing your homework. Still, when we have our children, if one of them wants to climb Mt. Everest or fix machines or stay at home and tend the next generation, well, as long as she's a friend you can count on and gives something back to the world in her own particular way, I'll be proud to call her mine. And if her heart opens up to someone decent—woman or man—I'll be glad my whole life for them to pair off and meet the world together.

STAGE MANAGER: Well, kids, that was fine. Just fine. Now you better run off. Got a wedding to get ready for.

(*Lights up in area of Emily and Elizabeth's house*)

CHANCE (*presenting himself*): Is my tie straight?

EMILY (*moving to adjust it*): Here, you never could do that right— (*She fights back tears*)

CHANCE: Mom! You're not going to start again?

EMILY: I'm not. Really, I'm not.

ELIZABETH: Well, a mother's got a right to cry at her son's wedding.

CHANCE: Did Nana cry at yours?

EMILY: We didn't have an official wedding. No one would perform it. (*Beat*) But we took vows.

ELIZABETH: A person takes vows every day. Really. Over the first cup of coffee. When she looks up at you from reading the newspaper.

EMILY (*to Chance*): There. You're gorgeous.

CHANCE: I don't feel so good.

EMILY: I know. It'll pass.

ELIZABETH (*launching into a game they used to play—this time to calm his nerves*): Okay, Bauer steps up to the plate, Jerhovic gets his sign, throws it. Bauer swings, it's a—

CHANCE (*very animated*): Strike! Jerhovic tosses a curve, Bauer goes for it misses. Strike two. Another one fired down the pike and—

ELIZABETH: Bauer connects! It's going going—

CHANCE: Caught. He's out. We win!

(*Lights up on the area of George and Louis' house*)

MOLLY: Daddy, how did you and Dad do it? I mean, all these years with the same person, day after day, night after night. Doesn't it get terribly predictable? The same face and how he smells and what he's going to say next?

GEORGE: Yes!

LOUIS: I never know what he's going to say next.

MOLLY: But, isn't it awfully terribly monotonous?

GEORGE: Moll, you and Chance, you're going to have afternoons when it seems everything is just the way it was the day before. Days when the pipes go bad and that sofa you ordered doesn't arrive and— Bless those days, Molly.

MOLLY: I'm going to miss you guys.

LOUIS: What do you mean? We're not going anywhere.

MOLLY: Well, I know that. But you won't be shouting up to me to wake up, lazy bones or forcing me to listen to some article that makes you crazy mad.

GEORGE: Don't worry, we're gonna call you up on the telephone and make you listen to some article that makes us crazy mad.

(*We hear "The Wedding March"*)

MOLLY: I'm scared.

LOUIS: Perfectly reasonable response.

GEORGE: We're holding you up, sweet girl. We're on your side.

(*Stage Manager steps forward*)

STAGE MANAGER: Maybe before the wedding Doc McAdoo can fill you in a little on some history.

(*Doc McAdoo comes on*)

DOC MCADOO: I guess you want to know how they did it. Had their babies. Well, I guess you know where babies come from. I don't have to tell you that. But where children come from—how they survive—well that's a mother's explanation, a father's humor, a thousand sleepless nights and constant arms of welcome. (*Beat*) But for you more technically minded, Emily and Elizabeth adopted Chance when he was two days old. George and Louis, well they got Molly when she was a few weeks. Now I've delivered lots of human beings. And it doesn't matter how they get delivered. Some arrive the old fashioned way and still find sorrow, even get beat up by their own flesh and blood. No, it's not about where a person comes from—it's who they come home to that gives them the odds in this life. And for what it's worth, Chance here and Molly, they lucked out.

(*There is an audible cacophony of sounds from the parents in question. Doc McAdoo looks over in their direction*)

Excuse me, Em, Elizabeth, George, Louis—I stand corrected. (*To audience*) They hate when anyone puts it like that. See, they figure they're the ones who got lucky. Anyhow, that's the story.

(*He leaves the stage. The two fathers stand with their daughter. And the two mothers, with their son. Their children remain still, while the parents speak to one another*)

EMILY: Well, did you ever think we'd be seeing this day?

GEORGE: They're the most beautiful creatures I ever saw.

ELIZABETH: Louis, I thought we put you in charge of him.

LOUIS: Sorry. He's out of control.

ELIZABETH: Now if you keep this kind of thing up, Georgie Warren, we won't make it through the ceremony.

EMILY: I wasn't sure we'd make it to this day.

ELIZABETH: We're okay now. We're fine.

EMILY: Oh, I hope it lasts!

LOUIS: Can't guarantee anything.

ELIZABETH: So when the time comes do you want to be called Granpa or Zada or—

EMILY: Stop!

GEORGE: Do you think we did all right by them?

EMILY: We did the best we could, Georgie.

GEORGE: I don't know.

LOUIS: Gotta let them blame us for one thing or another. It's a tradition.

ELIZABETH: Don't they just stop your heart?

(*Louis puts his arm around George, Emily touches Elizabeth*)

EMILY: You know what I think? I think we did good.

(*Suddenly an eruption, as a citizen steps forward*)

ANGRY RIGHTEOUS CITIZEN: Just hold everything. Doesn't anybody care that this is a play celebrating sodomizers! There's known felons in our community and some of you turn your heads the other way. People wake up. This isn't right! Not before God, not under the—

STAGE MANAGER: Excuse me, you're interrupting a wedding. (*To audience*) There's never any lack of trouble for what ought be a person's own business. George's father never spoke to him again after he found out. Emily's mother, well she kept in touch but wouldn't look Elizabeth in the eye. It's a hard thing when your own turn away. It's a powerful hold they've got on our hearts and minds—Mother. Father. The world is unforgiving enough without the people who brought us up in it, taking the other side. So, let's not allow that part of the world in today. Just for a little while, let's give these families a break. (*Beat*) It seems to me we'd all sleep better at night knowing our children had someone decent to worry over them each and every day, each and every time they laid their head down to rest from the day's struggle. What does it matter, all the rest of it?

(*Music starts again. Stage Manager turns her back to the audience and toward the couples*)

I now pronounce you part of the human race that has the good fortune and the daily struggle of being married. (*Turns her head back to the audience*) We wish them all the best, don't we?

(*The lights shift, as the couples move out. The Stage Manager rearranges the boxes or chairs on stage*)

Well now, this is the hard part. This last scene, if you haven't already figured it out—is called "The End of Things". Of course, that's only one way of seeing it. Once you've known someone, they never stop being a part of how you look at the world. That goes for the living as well as the dead. And who knows but that we're being watched over somehow or carried out into the eternal universe, by every soul we ever mattered to or mattered to us. (*Beat*) But, our sad friends don't know any of this today. So bear with them.

(*There are chairs or boxes now arranged with "The Dead" seated and staring ahead. Among them, Elizabeth and Louis. Nearby laying flowers at a fresh gravesite, are Emily, George, and Molly*)

This is a funeral for young Chance. Who was walking down the street one chilly day bringing home the newspaper with a story he was proud to write and caught someone's anger in a stray bullet.

MOLLY: Why? Why him?

GEORGE: I don't know.

EMILY: What are we going to do now?

GEORGE: Go on.

MOLLY: I don't think I can.

GEORGE: Emily—help us.

(*Emily gathers them up in her arms. Chance walks among the dead*)

ELIZABETH: Over here, Chance. Next to me.

CHANCE (*overcome*): Mama!

ELIZABETH: It's all right, it's all right.

CHANCE: We missed you so!

ELIZABETH: Yes.

CHANCE: Look at them! What can I do for them?

ELIZABETH: Let them go.

CHANCE: But they're burning in my throat. I see them behind my eyelids.

ELIZABETH: And you always will. But in a while it won't hurt as much.

(*George moves over to put flowers on Louis' grave*)

LOUIS: I'm here, honey. I'm right here.

STAGE MANAGER: Louis died of a disease that took too many too young. And Elizabeth, from breast cancer. Too many, too young.

CHANCE: The last moment I spent on earth, was so . . . small. So normal. I never got to tell anyone what I really felt. What did I ever give anyone?

ELIZABETH: You were loved. And you loved in return. That's about all anyone can ask of the days we have. And don't you for a minute regret one casual morning or nights there wasn't some deep thought in the air. Even if you just sat near someone watching television—why even then, dear boy, you were a comfort. Someone was thinking: he means the world to me. And I mean the world to him. And we don't have to speak of it.

(*Emily moves in front of Elizabeth and Chance and falls to her knees*)

EMILY: Do you know how much? How very much?

ELIZABETH: We know. Don't we Chance?

STAGE MANAGER: The human heart has a way of making itself large again, even after it's broken itself into a million pieces. Once a person knows a kiss and a kind word, you can't blame him for never wanting to live without them again. Our friends here will go on a long time past their partners and they'll make room again for kisses and kind words, but the heart never forgets, never gives up the territory marked off for the ones who came before. They'll always have a place. And their kisses and kind words, beat on.

(*Emily gathers up George and Molly*)

EMILY: Come home now. Come home with me.

(*They walk off*)

CHANCE: Mama?

ELIZABETH: What is it, honey?

CHANCE: Remember that game we used to play?

ELIZABETH: I remember.

CHANCE: Can we?

ELIZABETH: Of course. Of course we can.

(*Lights dim on the dead*)

STAGE MANAGER: Well, it's turning into the next day. People are picking up their mail, making plans. Having opinions. This is who we are, I guess. This is us. It's a mystery isn't it?

(*Sound of a train whistle. A bird. A conversation. As lights dim*)

THE DROWNING OF MANHATTAN

John Ford Noonan

John Ford Noonan

John Ford Noonan is a 1989 inductee into the French Society of Composers and Authors. He first came to prominence in 1969 with the highly-acclaimed Lincoln Center production of *The Year Boston Won the Pennant,* starring Roy Scheider. It won Mr. Noonan an Obie, a Theatre World and a Pulitzer Prize nomination.

From 1972 to 1977 at Joe Papp's New York Shakespeare Festival, Noonan wrote *Older People* (a Drama Desk Award winner), *Rainbows For Sale* (an Obie Award Winner), *Concerning the Effects of Trimethylchloride, Where Do We Go From Here?, All the Sad Protestants* and *Getting Through the Night.* In 1978 his play *The Club Champion's Widow,* with Maureen Stapleton, opened the premiere season of the Robert Lewis Acting Company.

In the 1980's he wrote *A Coupla White Chicks Sitting Around Talking,* which ran for more than 800 performances at the Astor Place Theatre, and *Some Men Need Help* (three months on Broadway). In 1987 Mr. Noonan's *Spanish Confusion, Mom Sells Twins For Two Beers, Green Mountain Fever* and *Recent Developments in Southern Connecticut* all ran simultaneously in Los Angeles (three of which won Drama-Logue Awards). The Asolo State Theatre presented Noonan's *Why Can't You Be Him?* during the 1987–1988 season.

Noonan has twice been nominated for Emmys—in 1984 for an episode of *St. Elsewhere* called "The Women" (for which he won) and in 1985 for the television adaptation of *Some Men Need Help.* On screen he has acted in such movies as *Brown Wolf; Next Stop, Greenwich Village; Heaven Help Us* and *Adventures in Babysitting.* Twice he has been acclaimed in Andrew Sarris's favorite film performances of the year.

Mr. Noonan's proudest accomplishments to date are: (1) his children: Jesse Sage Noonan, Chris Noonan Howell, Olivia Noonan Howell, and Tracy Noonan Howell; and (2) his acclaim by *Rolling Stone* magazine as "the greatest white boogie dancer in the world."

Characters:

SGT. ROCK

TOTALITY BROWN

TRACY JO KEROUAC

J.J. KILBOURNE

CHARLEY THE LIZARD

Time:

More than a few years from now.

Place:

NYC. Midtown Manhattan. EMOTION CENTER 2000 (a huge building that occupies the area where Manhattan Plaza once stood). 46th floor. Over the door hangs a sign reading: PAIN CAGE 46. Upstage left: a door offstage. Upstage right, against back wall: what looks like a gas pump with a huge meter with markings from 0 to 1000. Hanging down from the side of the pump is a nozzle with a mouth bit. A sign over the pump reads PAIN PUMP 200-1000. Next to the pump are several "off" and "on" buttons plus a large intercom speaker. To one side is a glass-enclosed case filled with immense Pain-Clips (clothespin-like clips) to wear on the nose against smells.

Lights up. Downstage center two large men looking down at midtown Manhattan from 46 stories above. One a black man, Totality Brown. Next to him a white man, Paul Michael Muldoon, also known as Sergeant Rock.

ROCK: We'll stay here by the window. We'll look out and pretend.

TOTALITY: Pretend what?

ROCK: That it isn't the last day.

TOTALITY: Rock, stop.

ROCK: I smelled it. The stink woke me. Today, today, today they're doing it.

TOTALITY: Doing what?

ROCK: Look down at midtown and tell me there's nothing wrong. Look at the bags of babies. Why aren't they in the dumpsters?

Where are the smell volunteers? Why aren't they patrolling the Port Authority?

TOTALITY: It's still early. Maybe—

ROCK: In twenty two minutes, tops twenty five, and it'll be all over. Smell, Man, smell, can't you smell the smell within the smell.

TOTALITY: It's why I brought you here. You smell the smell inside the smell.

ROCK: They're on the way. We'll all be drowned within an hour.

(*Totality takes out huge muffler size earplugs and puts them on his ears*)

TOTALITY: It was in your dreams. It's not real.

ROCK (*trying to remove earplugs*): I didn't dream it, I smelled it.

TOTALITY: I taped you last night in the pain cage. Want me to replay it for you? (*Totality goes to tape machine on wall and presses play button. Rock's voice on tape:* "I WANT TO DIE. I CAN'T TAKE THIS PAIN ANYMORE. ANOTHER DAY OF SMELLING THE SMELL WITHIN THE SMELL AND MY HEAD WILL EXPLODE." *Rock races to tape machine and turns it off. Totality grabs HIM and pulls HIM to the pain pump, and putting nozzle in Rock's mouth, needle leaps into red danger zone. Needle stops at 655*) No one can live over 400.

ROCK: I can.

TOTALITY: If we get through today, will you promise to work on it.

ROCK: Work on what?

TOTALITY: The pain, the puke and the stink.

ROCK: We're not going to make it through today.

TOTALITY: That's what you're always saying. Is it a deal?

ROCK: What?

TOTALITY: If we get through, will you?

(*Rock takes a huge breath, as only he can smell the smell within the smell, and lets out a howl*)

ROCK: If you look out over Bayonne, you'll see the flood zeppelins within sixteen minutes. What have we done that they want to drown us all?

(*Suddenly, upstage door flies open, and enters Tracy Jo Kerouac. In one hand she carries a huge boom box and in the other a suitcase*)

TRACY: Boys, I'm heading home to Maine. Crawling home to Portland. I came here to be a poet but I can't take this.

TOTALITY: Baby, what's the matter?

TRACY: Listen to Greasy George on WVBD. (*Tracy presses "ON" button and turns up volume very loud*)

VOICE (*from radio*): "NEWS FLASH FROM MID-TOWN. TO REPEAT: NEWS FLASH FROM MID-TOWN. TO UPDATE ONCE AGAIN THE MONUMENTAL DECISION OF THE MORNING. CONGRESS, IN AN EMERGENCY JOINT SESSION CALLED BY THE PRESIDENT, HAS VOTED 566 TO 3 TO DROWN MANHATTAN. TO REPEAT: AMERICA HAS VOTED TO DROWN MANHATTAN. THE DROWNING OF MANHATTAN WILL COMMENCE IN SOME 22 MINUTES. EIGHT HUNDRED AND TWENTY TWO FLOOD ZEPPELINS HAVE JUST LEFT JERSEY CITY AND WILL BE VISIBLE FROM MANHATTAN WITHIN TEN MINUTES. TO REPEAT: THE DROWNING OF MANHATTAN WILL COMMENCE IN 22 MINUTES." (*NEWS ANNOUNCER suddenly laughing*) "FIND A LIFE JACKET, RENT A BOAT, SAY A PRAYER, WE'RE FUCKED . . . TAKE IT AWAY CINDY LAUPER."

TOTALITY: Honkey paranoia. Turn on WBLS.

(*Tracy quickly changes station. Barry White-like voice comes on*)

VOICE (*from radio*): "WBLS NEWS FLASH FROM MID-TOWN. TO REPEAT: NEWS FLASH FROM MID-TOWN. TO UPDATE ONCE AGAIN THE MONUMENTAL DECISION OF THE MORNING. CONGRESS, IN AN EMERGENCY JOINT SESSION CALLED BY THE PRESIDENT, HAS VOTED 566 TO 3 TO DROWN MANHATTAN. TO REPEAT: AMERICA HAS VOTED TO DROWN MANHATTAN. THE DROWNING OF MANHATTAN WILL COMMENCE IN SOME 22 MINUTES. EIGHT HUNDRED AND TWENTY TWO FLOOD ZEPPELINS HAVE JUST LEFT JERSEY CITY AND WILL BE VISIBLE FROM MANHATTAN WITHIN TEN MINUTES. TO REPEAT: THE DROWNING OF MANHATTAN WILL COMMENCE IN 22 MINUTES."

TOTALITY: What the hell are we going to do?

TRACY: I want to read from my uncle. When I'm afraid to die I always read Jack Kerouac.

TOTALITY: He's not your uncle, Tracy.

TRACY: When I read him, he is.

ROCK: Listen, Kid—

TRACY: Shut the fuck up and give me my Kerouac book. (*Suddenly Tracy moans*) I lent it to J.J. last night.

TOTALITY: He hasn't gotten back yet. He's been up working on Columbus.

TRACY: Fuck it. I'll do some Ginsberg from memory. (*Sitting on floor and quoting Ginsberg from memory, having to yell loudly to be heard over a loud rock song*)

AMERICA, by Allen Ginsberg.
AMERICA I'VE GIVEN YOU ALL AND NOW I'M NOTHING.
AMERICA TWO DOLLARS AND TWENTYSEVEN CENTS
JANUARY 17, 1956.
I CAN'T STAND MY OWN MIND.
AMERICA WHEN WILL WE END THE HUMAN WAR?
GO FUCK YOURSELF WITH YOUR ATOM BOMB.

I DON'T FEEL GOOD DON'T BOTHER ME.
I WON'T WRITE MY POEM TILL I'M IN MY RIGHT MIND.
AMERICA WHEN WILL YOU BE ANGELIC?
WHEN WILL YOU TAKE OFF YOUR CLOTHES?
WHEN WILL YOU LOOK AT YOURSELF THROUGH THE GRAVE?
WHEN WILL YOU BE WORTHY OF YOUR MILLION TROTSKYITES?
AMERICA WHY ARE YOUR LIBRARIES FULL OF TEARS?
AMERICA WHEN WILL YOU SEND YOUR EGGS TO INDIA?
I'M SICK OF YOUR INSANE DEMANDS.

(*As Tracy finishes poem, RADIO resumes news flash*)

VOICE (*from radio*): NEWS FLASH FROM MID-TOWN. TO UPDATE ONCE AGAIN THE MONUMENTAL DECISION OF THE MORNING. CONGRESS, IN AN EMERGENCY JOINT SESSION . . ."

(*Totality in rage, turns boom box off*)

TOTALITY: Rock, what the hell are we going to do?

(*SUDDENLY, a huge red light next to PAIN PUMP begins blinking*)

It's the Emergency Pain Intercom.

(*Rock races upstage and presses "ON" button*)

VOICE (*Spanish accent from intercom*): Boss, I'm going to patch you in to the Spanish station. They're the only ones delivering a direct report from the floor of the Senate.

WARREN TAFFITER (*voice from intercom*): LADIES AND GENTLEMEN, THIS IS MINORITY WHIP WARREN TAFFITER SPEAKING TO YOU FROM THE FLOOR OF THE SENATE. THIS IS ONE OF THE SADDEST, MOST TRAGIC MOMENTS IN THE HISTORY OF AMERICA. FELLOW AMERICANS, WE MUST CUT OFF OUR FAVORITE FINGER TO SAVE THE REST OF OUR BODY. WE DO NOT WANT TO DROWN MANHATTAN. WE MUST, MUST BECAUSE THE PAIN EMA-

NATING FROM THE MOST FAMOUS ISLAND IN AMERICA IS DESTROYING US ALL. I AM CRYING. I HATE MY TEARS. I GIVE YOU SENATOR GEORGE J. JOHNSON FROM THE GREAT STATE OF ARKANSAS.

GEORGE JOHNSON (*voice from intercom*): MY FELLOW AMERICANS. THIS DECISION HAS COME ABOUT BECAUSE OF A REPORT MADE BY A BLUE RIBBON PANEL ABOUT THE STATE OF AMERICAN PAIN. AFTER THOROUGH AND PAINSTAKING RESEARCH IT HAS COME TO OUR ATTENTION THAT ALL THE PAIN STARTED IN THAT GREENWICH VILLAGE PLACE BACK IN THE FIFTIES. THAT DRUNKEN KEROUAC AND THAT JEWISH GINSBERG WERE THE REAL CULPRITS.

TRACY: They can't shit on my uncle.

ROCK: He's not your uncle, shut up.

GEORGE JOHNSON (*voice from intercom*): WE SHOULD HAVE DONE SOMETHING ABOUT IT THEN, BUT BACK THEN WE DIDN'T HAVE BLUE RIBBON REPORTS. IF WE HAD, THE HORROR WE NOW KNOW THAT MAKES THE ENTIRE ISLAND OF MANHATTAN STINK TO THE HEAVENS COULD HAVE BEEN AVERTED. I PERSONALLY LOVE MANHATTAN, BUT I SEE THE TEARS IN THE EYES OF MY CONSTITUENTS AND THEIR CHILDREN. TEARS CAUSED NOT ONLY BY THE GREENWICH VILLAGE FIFTIES, BUT WHAT ABOUT THE BEATLES! DIDN'T THEY LAND IN MANHATTAN AND START MAKING US FEEL THINGS WE WEREN'T READY FOR? AND WHAT ABOUT THAT EAST VILLAGE JUNGLE THAT'S SO FULL OF BLOOD AND HURT IT DESERVES TO BE FENCED IN. JUST THE OTHER MORNING I HEARD MY DAUGHTER AND HER FRIENDS LISTENING TO A PUNK SONG FROM MANHATTAN CALLED "KILL YOUR PARENTS, THEN WE'LL TALK." AND LAUGHING LIKE THEY MIGHT ACTUALLY DO IT. BEFORE I BEGIN TO CRY LET ME TURN THINGS OVER TO THE JUNIOR SENATOR FROM MINNESOTA.

CONRAD ST. CLOUD (*voice from intercom*): I AM SO ANGRY I CAN BARELY TALK. I WILL SHARE A SIMPLE EXPERIENCE

ABOUT WHY I VOTED YEA FOR THE DROWNING OF MANHATTAN. LAST WEDNESDAY, UNDER THE COVER OF DARK, WE HAD A MANHATTAN POET SNUCK IN TO WASHINGTON. IN READING TO US FROM HER WORK SHE MADE EVERY SENATOR WEEP AND CRY. WE CAN'T HAVE THE LEADERS OF OUR COUNTRY WEEPING AND CRYING.

CARL BELZER (*voice from intercom*): FELLOW AMERICANS, I'LL TELL YOU HOW ANGRY I AM. IF THIS DROWNING DOESN'T WORK, I AM OFFERING SEVERAL ANTARCTIC GLACIERS TO BE SENT DOWN THE HUDSON TO WIPE THAT AWFUL PLACE OFF THE MAP. NEW YORKERS, YOU MAY NOT KNOW IT YET, BUT LAST NIGHT THE FRENCH GOVERNMENT AIRLIFTED THE STATUE OF LIBERTY OUT OF NEW YORK HARBOR AND BACK TO FRANCE.

TRACY (*looking out window down Hudson*): They've taken her away. Our harbor's empty.

(Before Senators can continue their report, Totality presses "OFF" button on the Emergency Pain Intercom. Tracy starts to turn on boom box, but Totality stops her)

If I'm going to die, I want to hear some LED ZEP.

TOTALITY: This can not be happening. I have worked so hard for Manhattan. I had the death bars on 8th Avenue closed. I was responsible for installing Rage Booths on every corner in Midtown. I started the Midtown Smell Volunteers. Why just yesterday the Mayor told me I might be picked as Manhattan Man-of-the-Year. I don't even know how to swim. I don't want to drown. It's not fair. None of us deserve this.

ROCK (*howling with laughter*): Fair?! Deserve?! Don't you understand? The harder we work to face the pain, the more they are going to want to get rid of us.

TOTALITY: So what do we do?

ROCK: Let's turn it into a baptism. (*Rock races to wall, presses button. Microphone descends center of room. Rock grabs microphone and races with it to Totality*)

TOTALITY: What do I do?

ROCK: Give them a short speech about baptism. Pretend it's Sunday in Harlem.

(*Totality, about to give speech, door flies open and enters J.J. Kilbourne, short, blonde and very cute. He is dressed in a Midtown Smell Volunteer uniform*)

J.J.: My smell wagon's caught in the elevator. Rock, please go get it in here.

TRACY (*grabbing Rock*): Come on, I'll help you.

(*EXIT Rock and Tracy*)

J.J.: Wait till you hear what's happening up on Columbus Avenue. At 69th Street Columbus Cafe is completely covered in foam. I break through the foam wall. All these movie stars are frozen at the tables. No one can move. I say to myself, "STARS NEVER DIE. FUCK 'EM." I take a deep breath and smell the human pain downstairs. I crawl past the stars. Several pretty waitresses are frozen dead next to the kitchen. I feel my way to the narrow back stairs. I crawl down. Hear screams and moans. I come to a door. It says: PAULIE'S PIT CELEBRITIES ONLY. I move on. I come to a second door. It says: CHARLIE'S CHURCH CRIPPLES ONLY. I hear moaning and groaning. I knock. No one answers. I burst through the door. Inside is a miniature church with statues of all the girls Charlie the Lizard death-pimped. Charlie's dressed as a priest and he's standing at the altar.

(*Door flies open and enter Rock and Tracy pushing smell wagon covered by huge, white sheet stained by several, large splotches of blood*)

TRACY: Someone's under there. I can hear them moaning.

(*J.J. tears off the sheet. In the middle of pain wagon sits Charlie the Lizard, head swollen and disfigured, a dead rat on each side of his neck and stuck in his mouth a book of Kerouac poetry*)

What's my Kerouac doing in his mouth?

J.J.: It was the only way to stop the rats.

CHARLIE (*speaking in babble*): RUTKA . . . IMUSCH . . . SICK DICK LICK SLICK.

TRACY: What's he saying?

CHARLIE (*continuing to babble through book*): IKZA . . . AIELLO . . . BLAH-POO . . . WALKEN . . . P.P. NO DICK.

TOTALITY: Get him to the pain pump.

(*J.J. and Tracy push cart upstage to pain pump*)

Rock, remove the Kerouac from his mouth.

ROCK: But—

TOTALITY: Remove it!

(*Tracy pulls book from Charlie's mouth, horrendous scream is heard*)

TRACY (*examining book*): He ate through my uncle's best work.

TOTALITY: Get the nozzle in his mouth.

(*Rock does as instructed. Needle on meter shoots to the sky*)

ROCK: He's at 781.

TRACY: He can't live.

CHARLIE (*Charlie uttering more incoherent babble*): SORRY . . . SICK . . . DRIP . . . MY MOTHER DIED LAT WEEK. (*Repeating final line three more times*) IKZA . . . AIELLO . . . BLAH-POO . . . WALKEN . . . P.P. NO DICK.

TOTALITY: I'll make the incisions on both sides of his neck and you start sucking the puss.

ROCK: Why me?

TOTALITY: 'Cause no one in the world can suck pain like you.

ROCK: I'm not saving the guy who sat me at the bar the night of the Midtown Policeman's Ball. (*Suddenly turning on Charlie*) Remember that night you promised me Table 19? I walked in with all my fellow sergeants. Remember what you said? (*Quoting*) "YOU GUYS ARE GOING TO HAVE TO SIT AT THE BAR. WE'RE FULL UP." Full up! Who is the guy who covered up when Madonna beat the lesbian to death in the men's room? Who is the guy who made the cocaine disappear when Bobby, Harvey, Sean and Chris got caught snorting with their pants down in the ladies room? Who is the guy who made the dead girls disappear behind Port Authority? And I come in Columbus and you tell me, "YOU GUYS ARE GOING TO HAVE TO SIT AT THE BAR. WE'RE FULL UP." I'm no have-not. Never been a have-not. And so I say I don't suck. I don't suck your puss for anything.

(*Totality makes first cut on Charlie's neck*)

TOTALITY: Suck!

ROCK: No!

J.J.: I'll do it.

ROCK: You can't. You'll die.

CHARLIE (*speaking through all his pain*): If you let me live, I'll always give you Table 19 at Columbus.

ROCK: What did you say?

CHARLIE: Table 19 at Columbus day and night.

TOTALITY: Suck.

ROCK: Table 19. Day and night for a year?

CHARLIE: Save me please. I'm a live human with rights.

(*Rock begins sucking the poison out of Charlie's neck as Tracy and J.J. get huge pain buckets hanging from wall*)

ROCK: I had no idea the pain this man lived in. I've never known a stink like this.

TOTALITY: That's cause you haven't tasted yours yet. Now suck good.

(*Rock keeps sucking*)

Put the nozzle in his mouth.

TRACY: He's down to 391.

TOTALITY: Rock, you saved the day.

CHARLIE (*half dazed, looking about room, recognizing Tracy. Suddenly hugging Tracy*): I guess we didn't get to the really deep stuff in our last session.

ROCK: What the fuck's going on here?

TRACY: I've been sneaking north of the Midtown line to help Charlie work on his stink.

ROCK: What about my stink? Isn't mine bad too?

TRACY: Charlie was willing, you weren't.

(*Suddenly a loud buzz which sounds like thousands of bees buzzing*)

TOTALITY: Oh God, the Zeppelins are here.

(*They all reach down stage center and look out over audience as though viewing the Hudson River heading south*)

TRACY: What are those big hoses hanging out of the tails?

TOTALITY: They're stuck into the North Jersey swamps.

ROCK: They're flooding Midtown Manhattan with North Jersey shit?

TRACY: They must really want us dead.

ROCK: These mother fuckers have fucked with the wrong fuck. (*Rock takes deep breaths and begins smelling deeply. Sputters in spasms of pain and agony*) Don't get scared. I've got to stretch out my smelling. Here comes my first all the way down. (*Takes huge gulp of air and smells*) I smell the pain in the alleyway. In Scranton, Pennsylvania. A garbage man named Jason. Jason Royalton. I smell the smell inside of Dr. George Sheehan. Smell, down in Redback, New Jersey, as he ties his sneakers to go for his morning jog and breathes in terror of the cancer he knows is returning as the little carcinogenic rats nibble towards his prostate. My nose flies south. Oh God . . . Little baby Mary Carolli, screaming out her three-year-old hurt. (*Lets out one last horrendous howl*) I'm fuckin' ready.

CHARLIE (*whispering to Totality*): What's he going to do?

TOTALITY (*whispering back to Charlie*): Smell the smell inside the smell of the Captains piloting the Zeppelins and turn them around.

ROCK: Everyone out of the way. First off, I need my boots.

(*Tracy runs and gets his boots*)

I need to plug up my ears against the oozing.

(*Tracy produces earplugs*)

I need someone to hold my hand.

(*Charlie takes his hand*)

Totality, I need someone to write down the zeppelin numbers and the captain I smell.

TOTALITY (*taking out small pad and pencil*): Go, YOU WHITE MONSTER.

ROCK: Zeppelin 331. Captain Lorenzo Lawrence.

(*Totality copies down*)

Zeppelin 66. Admiral Martha Pfloog.

(*Totality copies down*)

Zeppelin 111. Captain Peter Loffredo.

(*Totality copies down*)

Zeppelin 696. Lieutenant Pavel Pavelovich.

(*Totality copies down*)

Zeppelin 274. Captain Melinda Markovich.

(*Totality copies down*)

Tracy, put a nose plug on me.

(*Tracy goes to wall, removes nose plug, and puts it on him*)

Charlie, the ultra sonic bull horn on the wall.

(*Charlie gets bull horn and hands it to Rock*)

Totality, please repeat the zeppelin number and the captain.

(*Totality does as instructed*)

TOTALITY: Zeppelin 331. Captain Lorenzo Lawrence.

ROCK: LORENZO, I KNOW YOUR SON HAS AIDS. I KNOW IT'S ALL YOU CAN THINK ABOUT. BUT PLEASE REMEMBER WHAT WILLIAM FAULKNER SAID IN GREENWICH VILLAGE IN 1937. (*Quoting Faulkner*) "BETWEEN PAIN AND NOTHING, GIVE ME PAIN EVERY TIME." Give me the next one, Totality.

TOTALITY: Zeppelin 66. Admiral Martha Pfloog.

ROCK: ADMIRAL, YOU KNOW THIS IS THE WRONG THING. YOUR STOMACH IS SCREAMING NOT TO PRESS THE

FLOOD BUTTON. JUST REMEMBER WHAT KEROUAC TOLD GINSBERG ON MACDOUGAL STREET IN 1953. (*Quoting Kerouac*) "DON'T PISS ON THAT TRANSVESTITE'S PAIN, ALLEN. FACE YOUR OWN."

TRACY (*whispering to Totality*) How does he know so much about Manhattan poetry?

TOTALITY (*whispering back*): Rock's the resident poet of modern pain.

ROCK: NEXT!

TOTALITY: Zeppelin 111. Captain Peter Loffredo.

ROCK: PETER, I KNOW YOU HATE BEING ITALIAN AND CONFUSED ABOUT YOUR SEXUALITY AT THE SAME TIME. I KNOW HOW MUCH PAIN YOUR WIFE'S AFFAIR WITH THAT NEW YORK KNICK IS CAUSING YOU. BUT I QUOTE YOU PABLO NARUDA FROM HIS FABULOUS INTRODUCTION. (*Quoting Naruda*) "FORGET THE FACTS, FACE THE PAIN."

TOTALITY: Zeppelin 696. Lieutenant Pavel Pavelovich.

ROCK: LIEUTENANT. I KNOW WHAT HAPPENED THAT SATURDAY AFTERNOON WITH YOU AND YOUR WIFE IN FRONT OF THE PLAZA, BUT THAT HOMELESS PERSON COULDN'T HELP IT. JUST REMEMBER THE LIE THAT E.E. CUMMINGS TOLD GARCIA LORCA. (*Quoting E.E. Cummings*) "NOTHING HAPPENS HERE IN MANHATTAN THAT DOESN'T HAPPEN IN YOUR HOME TOWN."

TOTALITY: Zeppelin 274. Captain Melinda Markovich.

ROCK: MELINDA, YOU KNOW—

(*Tracy and Charlie suddenly scream out*)

TRACY: It's working. The zeppelins are turning around.

TOTALITY: You pain dog, you. You did it again.

CHARLIE: Not only Table 19 any time you want it for a year, but a free meal once a week.

ROCK: (*taking off nose plug. Continues to take deep smells and yell through bull horn*): GENE TEROUSO, I SMELL YOU DOWN THERE IN BRIGANTINE. I KNOW YOU WANT TO THROW YOUR YOUNG BABY OUT THE WINDOW. PUT HER DOWN AND GO FOR A WALK. (*Taking another breath*) PEGGY JO PALATIN, GET YOUR HAND OUT OF YOUR MOTHER'S POCKETBOOK. COCAINE WILL ONLY SWALLOW YOUR SOUL. PUT THE MONEY BACK OR I'LL COME DOWN TO RED BANK AND SPANK YOUR ASS. (*As nose begins to bleed. Continues to yell through bull horn*) LOUIS ANTIFIRMO, I KNOW HOW MUCH YOUR COLON HURTS. CRY, IF YOU WANT TO CRY. SCREAM. SPIT IT ALL UP. MY ARMS ARE IN THE AIR, REACH OUT. (*Rock now spitting up blood*)

TOTALITY: Stop, or you'll die.

ROCK: I'm going to save everyone in Jersey from their pain. (*Again smelling deeply, yelling through bull horn*) FRANKIE QUINN, YOU FUCKIN' WIMP. YOUR SPIRIT HANGS LIKE PERFUME OVER HOBOKEN. UNDIE, COME BACK FROM HELL. WE NEED YOU. (*Suddenly Rock collapses to floor*)

TOTALITY: Tracy, you and Charlie get some pain buckets ready.

(*Totality putting clip back on Rock's nose and lifting him into chair*)

ROCK: (*coming to*): I'm in enough pain to smell all the way to Washington.

TOTALITY: But—

ROCK: Give me my bull horn back, so I can address the Senate. (*Rock, taking bull horn from Totality, and taking the biggest smell of his life*) SENATORS, CONGRESSMEN, I SMELL YOUR PAIN. IT HAS NOTHING TO DO WITH OURS. LEAVE US ALONE AND FACE YOUR OWN. I FORGIVE YOU YOUR MISTAKE, BUT DON'T EVER AGAIN FUCK WITH MANHATTAN. NOW GO HOME AND HAVE A GOOD LOOK IN THE MIRROR.

TRACY: J.J., I thought I loved you, but I love Rock.

ROCK: I'm not worth loving. I'm not worth saving. I'm not worth caring about.

TOTALITY: What about tomorrow? If you don't face some of your stink right now, you're going to explode all over these walls and we'll have no one to help us against tomorrow's attack.

J.J.: Totality's right. Those government people are crazy. Tomorrow they may try and bomb us.

ROCK: No one can stop bombs.

TOTALITY: You can do anything if you get to work on your stink. J.J. give me a bucket.

ROCK: No.

TOTALITY: Blow.

ROCK: I can't face all 91.

TOTALITY: Blow me your blow. One at a time. (*Taking bucket from J.J.*) Blow me your blow now. (*Rock finally blows breath at Totality. Totality interprets Rock's stink*) "STOP HITTING MY HEAD. STOP HITTING MY HEAD." Go on, say it, Rock.

ROCK: IT . . . IT . . . IT . . .

TOTALITY: "STOP HITTING MY HEAD. STOP HITTING MY HEAD."

ROCK (*in howling agony*): "STOP HITTING MY HEAD. STOP HITTING MY HEAD." (*Repeating it over and over as Rock vomits into pain bucket*)

TOTALITY: One down and 90 to go. Blow me your next breath.

ROCK: Can I read you my latest poem while I puke?

TOTALITY (*shaking head "NO"*): Blow me your next breath.

(*Tracy lets out a scream and points out window down Tenth Avenue*)

TRACY: Look!

J.J.: Everyone's coming out onto Tenth Avenue.

CHARLIE: It's a parade.

TRACY: Look at all those floats. Oh God. There's a Filmore East Float. All the dead greats: Hendrix, Joplin, Morrison, Bill Graham.

CHARLIE (*pointing*): My fuckin' childhood hero. Iron Man Lou Gehrig.

TRACY: Hey asshole, that's Babe Ruth next to him.

ROCK (*jumping up from chair*): That's the 1970 Knicks. I saw them play 31 home games.

TOTALITY: All the ones who made Midtown famous are floating back.

TRACY (*suddenly laughing*): Rock, look at that little kid with the poster.

ROCK: Say what it says.

TOTALITY (*reading poster*): "SERGEANT ROCK, CLEAN OUT THE CRAP AND GIVE YOUR ASSHOLE TIME TO HEAL."

(*Everyone starts laughing as chant floats up from street. As chanting is heard, actors on stage pick it up*)

ALL: MIDTOWN CANNOT DIE. MIDTOWN IS A DREAM. MIDTOWN IS THE MAGNET. MIDTOWN DOESN'T HAVE TO BE CLEAN. GO, MIDTOWN, GO.

(*Repeating three times, in the ensuing silence, everyone smiles warmly*)

TRACY: If my Uncle Jack were here, he'd love to write about this.

ROCK: Jack who?

(*Lights descend. END OF PLAY*)

ARYAN BIRTH

Elizabeth Page

Aryan Birth is the first of *The Nazi Plays. The Nazi Plays—Aryan Birth, Stop, Grethel und Hansel* and *Blue Egg*—are designed to be performed together and run approximately ninety minutes. They were first read as part of the Ensemble Studio Theatre's Octoberfest and later developed at the Denver Center Theatre Company's US West Theatrefest. *The Nazi Plays* are dedicated to Ziva Kwitney.

Elizabeth Page

Elizabeth Page's *Spare Parts* was produced at Circle in the Square Downtown where it was nominated for the John Gassner Award for Playwriting by the Outer Critics Circle. *Spare Parts* was originally produced at Whole Theatre by Olympia Dukakis and is published by Samuel French. Ms. Page's other plays include *The Job,* presented at Theatre for the New City's Anti-Nuke Festival; *Tomorrow Mornings Lasts All Night,* presented at the Nat Horne Theatre's Directors' Festival; and *Beside the Still Waters,* developed at the American Place Theatre by the Women's Project, of which she's a member. Ms. Page is also a member of the International Women Playwrights Conference, for whom she edits a newsletter, *Boomerang.*

Characters:
DAVID, *30s, Jewish, contemporary American*

Scene
A bare stage. A wallet, several press clippings.

Time:
The present.
Lights up on David. He addresses the audience.

DAVID: You can't help who your parents are, right? I mean even if you buy the Hindu thing—that the soul is out there looking to get reborn. Waiting for, say, two child abusers to get pregnant. Not that I'm blaming the kids on the wrong end of a cigarette, I'm not.

And not that I'm blaming her parents. Necessarily. Y'see that's the thing about the Hindu trip—if the soul wants to come back, you're stuck. This is your life. Too bad if you don't like it.

So why blame her, right? She's stuck. "Fraulein Mueller, in ziss lifetime you vill vork on your anger, if you please. And you vill take it out on David Cohen. You'll know him. He's a nice boy viss a bullseye on his heart."

Is there anything worse than whining? Besides, if you pick your parents, you damn sure pick your lover. So we're both to blame.

You want to see her picture?

(*He takes out his wallet and stares at her picture for a moment. He gets lost in the picture, forgets to show us, shuts the wallet, puts it back in his pocket*)

The first thing I saw was her soul. Scene: I'm in the islands, in a temple, on my ass, meditating. The sun's coming up—you can hear it, the wind picks up, the trees start to move, the birds sing. I open my eyes . . .

She's so deep in the meditation it's like she isn't there. I can't even make out her face. Just this hum—energy. Hummm . . . She hummed me in and that was it.

Yeah, she was beautiful. And perfect legs. She'd grown up in Austria in the mountains—Badgastein. Anybody? Basically they ski to the drugstore. The back of her knees. There were times I'd turn her over and bury my face right there where the leg breaks . . .

We chose each other. We couldn't help it.

She was working at this ashram—actually working her way

around the world. The Germans—Austrians, Germans, same thing basically—they travel more than the Japanese if you can believe it. Anyway she was there, I'd dropped in to recharge, we started sneaking out to the beach at night, sleeping in her tent.

Yogis are supposed to practice celibacy. You didn't know that? Every religion, forget about it, you want to hang out with god, you've got to get your mind out of your body. And we were definitely into our bodies. So they've got a point.

But I didn't care, I was sleeping. Falling asleep with her. That's not a problem for you? My whole life, the sex could be galactic but the moment we settle in, Bing! I'm beyond awake. I mean I'm counting the breaths till dawn, afraid to move, trapped in legs and long hair and matching sheets and lemme outa here.

But with Maria the bell would ring for morning meditation and I'd wake up, we hadn't moved, I was sometimes still inside her.

I knew it wasn't going anywhere, I was going home. She was going back to Austria.

I went home. And she came with me.

New York to somebody who's never been here before.

We didn't much leave the apartment.

The only problem—actually there were two problems. The visa and the TV. The visa meant she had to leave the country. Soon. Actually I guess it's tied in—borders, nationalism, the World War II thing. I live in this country, she lives in that country. And in this country we hate that country. Which is where the TV comes in. We were in the apartment a lot so the TV was on. "Nazis und communists. Nazis und communists. Das ist all you people know." This on a night when the choices were *Night and Fog, Hogan's Heroes, The Rise and Fall of the Third Reich, Sophie's Choice*—you get the idea. She wouldn't watch any of it. She said it was theatrical and untrue. She's right. She is, it's an easy out. You make the bad guy a Nazi, you don't even have to give him a character, just put him in a uniform. Or her.

Where we got into trouble was when I'd try to defend the programming—which meant, of course, defending the obsession in this country with Nazis. Because I'd have to get into, y'know, what they did. And then she'd get all defensive and think I was attacking her family. And I'd get all defensive and say that her family would have gassed my family. And you can imagine what that did to our sex life.

I don't know what I expected. I guess, well, remorse. Not that she did anything but y'know, sort of collective remorse. I mean I could understand why she was defensive. If my father were a Nazi . . .

When I saw her meditating I didn't pick up that her father was a Nazi. It didn't occur to me, all right? They were all Nazis. It was a political party. People were starving, there weren't any jobs, it was politics. They lived in the mountains, her father'd never even seen a Jew.

So fine, I wasn't shtupping her father. He used to beat her. And lock her in a closet. Now this was interesting. She didn't think there was anything particularly wrong with that. Not that she enjoyed it, she hated him. But that's how kids were brought up there. If they misbehaved, they were hit. Or locked up.

Do you read the Times? The New York Times? Did you see that article on the op-ed page, when, right when they were talking about unifying the German currency? Okay, this psychiatrist gets this hunch—he's been travelling around Europe, noticing how kids in different countries are different, play differently, and he gets this hunch. This is in the early 70s. He gets a bunch of kid shrinks—it's all strictly scientifically statistical—and guess what?

(*He takes a newspaper article out of his pocket*)

I carry this around. It makes me feel like less of a jerk. Okay . . .

"The result was that the Danish and Italian adults committed no acts of aggression against children as compared with 73 aggressive acts by German adults against children. The German children committed 258 acts of aggression against other children, as compared with 48 aggressive acts by Italian children and 20 by Danish children. The tentative moral of the story is that Germans mistreat their children more often than Danish or Italian adults, and that the children take it out on other children. One would suppose that aggressive children grow up into aggressive adults—adults whom I don't trust . . ."

It goes on. Anyway. Now obviously the point is not that the Fascists had troubled childhoods and we should like overturn Nuremburg. But he used to beat her up. And that does something to a person. I mean you can understand how they might not be as sensitive maybe as they could be. People like that need a lot of love.

So I've got this wounded bird. And she doesn't even know she's wounded. She thinks she's this invincible Rhine maiden Brunhilde, running around the world, having an affair with a Jewish man. She doesn't even realize she should be terrified.

Okay so she decides she wants to go to this peace conference being held at another ashram up in Canada. A lot of people she knows are gonna be there. This is, what, '87, before the wall came down and I'm thinking, okay, maybe we can break through some of the denial going on here. An international peace conference has to deal with Fascism. Doesn't it?

So we go.

You ever been on the Freedom Trail? You follow the yellow brick road around Boston from one old thing to another? Since she moved in I'd gotten real patriotic. I couldn't help it, she criticized everything she saw and it pissed me off. In fact we'd just had another screaming match about Reagan—trust me, I wasn't defending him, I was trying to make her understand that most of this country doesn't vote.

Anyway we're driving and we hit Boston—and she's heard of it—so I take her on the Freedom Trail and we get to I guess it was the state house and talk about kharma. I'm expecting, what, some Betsy Ross diorama or maybe a 3-D shot of a case of tea being dumped in the harbor. "Images of the Holocaust." Don't ask. There it was, these floor to ceiling blow-ups of emaciated—skeletal—children, mounds of corpses. You've seen 'em. She's very quiet. I ask her if she wants to leave—she's always dismissed this stuff before—but she says no and so we walk through the exhibit. It was pretty good. I've seen more gruesome stuff—y'know the documentation of some of the medical—and I use the term loosely—experiments. Where they filled women's wombs with cement, froze people alive. In the name of science. But they had a jar full of hair, piles of baby shoes, memos describing transport and "disinfection" and of course the photographs.

One of our main arguments was about the nature of the camps. Really of the "final solution" itself. She claimed it was wartime and that the camps were prisoner of war camps. I know, but I'm telling you, she actually believed that. I found that out in Boston. Until that day she'd say, okay, there were maybe individual sadists who got carried away, that the Japanese had camps, that the Brazilians slaughter their Indians. I kept screaming about the decision coming from the top, that it was planned, that it started in someone's heart and mind, that it wasn't just separate, impulsive acts of sadism, that the act of deciding to annihilate a people—that's what made it such an abomination.

More patriotic . . . and more Jewish.

We leave the exhibit. She says, "They don't teach this in the schools. Our parents don't talk about it. It is taboo. Verboten."

She's quiet the rest of the day. And when we lie down that night in this dump motel outside of Boston, she's different. I don't know, it was like she'd taken off more than her clothes.

I changed her. Whatever you can say about what happened, she was changed.

Okay so we get to this peace conference. I don't know what I expected. I guess . . . "Us and Them." Y'know, what you get when you take the bus to Washington to do a march. Placards, cameras, people with hangers on their heads screaming at people with pictures of butchered fetuses. A "we shall overcome" kinda thing.

Well this was all "Us". I mean it makes sense that none of "Them" are gonna pack a sleeping bag and catch a cab to the mountains so "Us" could have a target. But it was weird. It was like whatta you do when the enemy isn't there.

You mill around a bunch of the shabbiest people since Rip Van Winkle. I swear it's a Winkle convention—they haven't been out since '68. And then, because this is an ashram don't forget, you eat Indian food. Bad Indian food. And then there's the main event.

Okay, picture this. Some guy, an Indian, so he's sort of bluish-brown. Which only figures in terms of the total visual impact because he's in this loin cloth affair and he's smeared with dust. Sacred dust but dust all the same. And he's got weird squiggly marks all over him. And he's been meditating for hours and hasn't eaten and is generally in some Beta state you never even heard of. And get this—they're poking spears in him. I kid you not. He's standing there and his little gaggle of sacred guys are sticking these needles and spears through his lips, through his cheeks—and leaving them there so he looks like something off the cover of National Geographic. And he's just counting star specks offa some planet—I mean not a whimper. And these Eastern European scientist types are running around confirming everything and giving us moment by moment reports in Czechoslovakian about how his brain waves are doing. And the guy starts to dance. They've got him rigged up in this headdress and harness that support all these spears sticking outa him so he looks like some giant filthy porcupine. And he starts to dance. And believe me, you get outa the way. And he dances and he's waving his hands and he starts off down the hill to town. So fine, we follow him.

Now, much as this ashram would like to believe it's on its own planet, it's not. So after a couple of hundred yards or so we start hitting, like, houses and sidewalks and Jacque's Auto Repair and

Madeleine's All You Can Eat. And the porcupine is dancing and the Winkles have pulled out their tambourines and the swamis are Hari Omming and it's the National Enquirer on Parade.

And then suddenly this guy comes outa his split level with his kid —they're taking out the trash. And he stops at the end of his driveway with his kid and his trash and his mouth open. And I'm waiting —I'm thinking, y'know, finally, one of Them. But he just starts laughing and then his kid starts laughing and I start laughing and I get it, it all makes sense, I couldn't explain it to you but I got it and it was funny, all of it, life, death, suffering, joy, porcupines, trash, east, west, up, down—funny. It's funny. And I look around for Maria, I have to share this—and she's gone, I can't find her. And I go from being the whole cosmic thing to being a speck surrounded by weirdness.

And the weirdness turns around and we go back to the ashram where they've hacked down about 200 trees in the forest to make a road to a little shrine so the porcupine can do his thing. And the sacred guys take out the spears and the porcupine lies down on the ground and the swamis lie down on the ground and everybody lies down on the ground and then it's over.

About an hour later I'm sitting at dinner next to this clean cut guy with a bad case of razor burn and I realize it's him. It's the porcupine after a shower. He's a noodle maker from Kuala Lumpur and he does this on weekends. Kinda like playing in a bar mitzvah band.

That's not what brought me down—the man behind the curtain. If Oz gets you there, fine, it doesn't matter how you bridge it. But you can't look back. And you can't bring her with you. Especially if she's gone, getting a back rub, excuse me, a massage from Jean Michel who's the most spiritual man she ever met. And I can't even object because hey, this is a peace conference and we love everybody, right? And it's an ashram and you're supposed to detach even if it kills you. And I don't own her.

There was an article in Vanity Fair awhile back about how the children of the Nazi superstars are getting together for group therapy. This blew my mind—having been through every kind of therapy, self-help, analysis, primal scream, tonka bats—you name it. I'd practically written the article in my head before I paged back to where it started—middle-aged Nazi kinder holding hands and sobbing. Let me just read you this one little bit.

(*He takes the article out of his pocket*)

This is Martin Borman, Jr., about age 14, who's been taken for tea with his little sister at Frau Pothast's—Himmler's mistress. Okay, they've had chocolates, a little turn around the garden, now it's time for a special treat. She takes the kids up to the attic.

"When she opened the door and we flocked in, we didn't understand at first what the objects in that room were—until she explained, quite scientifically, you know. Tables, and chairs, made of parts of human bodies. There was a chair . . . The seat was a human pelvis, the legs human legs—on human feet. And then she picked up one of a stack of copies of Mein Kampf—all I could think of was that my father had told me not to bother to read it, as it had been outdated by events. She showed us the cover, made of human skin, and explained that the Dachau prisoners who produced it used the Ruckenhaut—the skin of the back—to make it."

(*David takes several long breaths and then looks around the audience for a moment*)

Be glad it hurts. That's the point. It should hurt. It must hurt.

Borman, Jr.—who after all was showing up for therapy, I mean, he's at least acknowledging there's a problem—Borman Jr.'s described as relating this incident with a "toneless voice." He later says that to call the people who did this swine is an insult to swine but other than getting red in the face, that's it.

Am I the only crier here? No. Something's missing—maybe it was never there or maybe they bred it out of them but that inclination to pity, compassion, emotional identification, tears . . .

Anyway, I'm having a wonderful time in the mountains . . . enjoying simultaneous translations of scintillating speeches by obscure Nato attaches, taking Kirlian photographs of my chakras and learning how to manipulate my aura so as to create a peaceful personality, grading an airstrip behind the tents and meditating nightly so as to attract peaceful extraterrestrials, learning everyone's rising sign, eating soggy samosas, smiling at Jean Michel and chanting in the rain. Let me tell you, peace is hard work.

And Maria? Well, we're fucking our brains out every night in the tent. But during the day, she might as well be in Berlin. She won't connect. And I'm not making her. Hey, I've read as many self help books as the next American. If the fraulein needs her space, fine. I know Boston wigged her out. I saw something and she's scrambling for cover. So let her scramble, we're going home. Bye bye, Jean Michel, may you get carpal tunnel.

We took a train back from Montreal. She wasn't feeling well and slept against me for an hour. You remember the dumbest things, y'know. The way that felt, the weight of her head against my shoulder. Like a baby's head, heavy.

We get back to New York and I don't know. Maybe it was being around a lot of people at the ashram but suddenly the silence in the apartment was sonic. I mean I could hear her breathing. And since she wasn't doing much talking, I started reading her breaths. A short one—she just thought of something. She's holding her breath—she knows I'm listening. A long one—how long till I get out of here.

Fine. I go see my sister for a couple of days. She wants space, I'll give her some space. Sixteen hours and she wants me to come back. I don't know. Are you any better at this stuff? Could you meet me later, maybe write it down? Anyway I go home—she's still not feeling good. And I start thinking . . . What the hell. You can get your suspense someplace else. She's pregnant.

Okay, so what do we have here. This woman who I really, y'know, care about. And she's pregnant. And I really always thought that someday, y'know, when it was right—meaning I have no idea what that means. Oh and she's Austrian and the clock's ticking, she's got, what, a couple weeks and her visa runs out which means if I even want to talk to her without paying Ma Bell we have to get married. So.

Jews don't have reincarnation. Not that they don't take the long view but you only get one chance with them. Hindus get all the second chances they want only they don't enjoy them. Basically Vishnu says okay, you want it, you got it—the punchline being that someday you'll realize you don't need it and then you get the door prize—bliss divine. But until then, you're coming back.

Which puts a certain spin on parenthood. I mean your kid isn't new—he's coming back. Which makes it less intimidating—you're just one in a long line of fathers—and more intimidating—why me? What does this kid need? What are we going to teach each other? I was really curious. I was ready.

She wasn't. I had my life, my career—I used to play a little, now I do sound editing, it's not like it's my fucking life—but she hadn't found herself yet. Couldn't I understand that she needed to do that? Didn't I realize . . .

Did you notice half the women stopped looking at me? I'm not a right-to-lifer, okay? I mean I let it happen. I realize it's more on you, I'm not a macho asshole. I've marched, I send money, I let it happen. But that doesn't mean I have to be happy about it. This wasn't just a tablespoon of cells to me, okay? This was her, this was our relationship, this was me, my son, my daughter, my genes, my history. Fuck reincarnation.

(*He takes a deep breath. He's rattled. He starts searching in his pockets . . .*)

They kept correspondence . . . .

(*He finds a Xerox, spreads it out. Touching it seems to steady him. He reads . . .*)

"To the Central Construction Office of the SS and Police, Auschwitz.

Subject: Crematoria Two and Three for the camp.

We acknowledge receipt of your order for five triple furnaces, including two electric elevators for raising the corpses and one emergency elevator . . ."

It's that cleaning up thing, y'know? (*Singing*) "The party's over . . ." You think I'm sick? They were competing for these gigs. (*He searches his pockets . . .*) And the competition suggested . . . (*He finds another Xerox*) . . . what . . .

"For putting the bodies into the furnaces, we suggest simply a metal fork moving on cylinders. For transporting the corpses . . ."

(*He trails off. He's rattled and takes a deep breath, speaks quite calmly . . .*)

Look, I'm glad I live where it's legal. But you have to admit it's not like filling a tooth or getting a mole cut off. I mean if you choose to "not continue" a life for the sake of your own life, you pay the price. Life is expensive.

But Maria, she was impervious. She'd made the decision and that was it. Who cares. At first I thought she was just reacting to me, y'know because I was really upset. So, y'know, she'd be cool. But no. It wasn't that. And it wasn't just that she was selfish although I think she is. It really honestly didn't mean anything to her. And I don't mean me or the relationship. She claimed she still cared about me, wanted the relationship. But the baby—it might as well have been a hangnail.

And that scared me. She called it "the procedure"—I thought she didn't like the word abortion but to her that's what it was. A "procedure." (*In a German accent*) "For putting ze bodies into ze furnace, ve suggest simply a metal fork moving on cylinders."

As soon as she made her decision she started drinking again—I mean she's not an alcoholic but y'know pregnant women aren't supposed to drink. And she started having wine with dinner again. And I thought of that poor kid being drowned in Beaujolais. Even if it was gonna die in a couple of days. She said I was sentimental. And I called her a fascist bitch. And that was the end of that.

Ever since the wall came down, the Berlin Wall, I've been having a dream. I hear knocking at the window and I turn to see what it is—a branch maybe. But it's a little child, a little girl, hanging out there in the darkness, knocking on the window, wanting to come in.

I know what I'm about to say is not spiritual. But I feel like I was allowed to experience something. She was cold. Maybe I'm sentimental but she was ruthless. Without Ruth. Who, if you remember the story, was a very compassionate woman. Maria had no compassion and I don't think any of them do. That was always my trouble thinking about the holocaust. I could never imagine how a human being could do that to another human being. But now I can. And maybe that makes me a racist and just as bad as they are but I don't trust them. And I never will.

(*Blackout. End of play*)

THE COWBOY, THE INDIAN AND THE FERVENT FEMINIST

Murray Schisgal

Murray Schisgal

Murray Schisgal was born in New York City in 1926, attended Thomas Jefferson High School and then continued his education at the Brooklyn Conservatory of Music, Long Island University, Brooklyn Law School and the New School for Social Research. He served in the United States Navy, played saxophone and clarinet in a small jazz band in New York City, practiced law from 1953 to 1956 and taught English in private and public schools. His initial experience in the professional theater came in 1960 when three of his one-act plays were presented abroad, soon followed by the very successful off-Broadway production in 1963 of *The Typists* and *The Tiger.* This production won for Schisgal considerable recognition with both the Vernon Rice and the Outer Critics Circle Awards, but the next production won for him everlasting fame. In November, 1964, *Luv,* directed by Mike Nichols and starring Anne Jackson, Eli Wallach and Alan Arkin, opened at the Booth Theater on Broadway. His subsequent Broadway productions have been: *Twice Around the Park, Jimmy Shine,* (starring Dustin Hoffman), *All Over Town* (directed by Dustin Hoffman), *An American Millionaire, The Chinese* and *Dr. Fish.* Off-Broadway he also had produced *Fragments and the Basement* (starring Gene Hackman), the musical of *Luv* and *Road Show.* Off-Off-Broadway a number of his plays were produced, including *The Pushcart Peddlers, The Flatulist, Walter* and *The Old Jew.*

Mr. Schisgal was nominated for an Academy Award and won the N.Y. Film Critics Award, the L.A. Film Critics Award, and the Writers Guild Award for his screenplay of *Tootsie,* starring Dustin Hoffman. His novel *Days and Nights of a French Horn Player* was optioned by Marvin Worth Production for a feature film. His teleplay *The Love Song of Barney Kempiniski* was nominated for Outstanding Dramatic Program by the National Academy of television Arts and Sciences. Recently his musical play *The Songs of War* was produced at the Gem Theatre in Garden Grove, California and at the National Jewish Theater in Illinois; his play *Popkins* was presented in Paris and Rome; *74 Georgia Avenue* at the Jewish Ensemble Theatre in Michigan; and staged readings around the country of *Play Time, The Japanese Foreign Trade Minister* and *Circus Life.* Eight of his short plays have appeared in Best Play anthologies over the years. The latest was *Extensions* which was published last year.

Mr. Schisgal lives with his wife, Reene, and his two children, Jane and Zachary, in New York City and Easthampton.

Characters:

ALICIA GERARD

STANFORD GERARD

DOCTOR BIBBERMAN

Scene:

Glendale, Long Island, a middle-class suburban community within fifty miles of New York City.

Time:

The present; late autumn; early evening.

Sound:

A drum beating, softly.

At rise:

A symmetrically furnished contemporary dining-room: at rear right and rear left, two long, narrow, pine buffet tables. Center, down-stage, a fairly large, rectangular, pine table with two ladder-back, pine chairs, cushioned, at either end. The table is set for dinner: glasses, silverware, napkins, a bottle of mineral water; a small vase of freshly-cut flowers. One is asked to imagine doors, windows and walls. A TV set and stereo unit are in view.

Alicia Gerard enters from left, carrying a tray on which there are two bowls of chicken broth, an oval sourdough bread and condiments. She hears the drum beat and is puzzled by it. What is that noise? A drum? Who would be beating a drum? Is someone playing a radio too loudly? The drum beat fades to silence.

Relieved, Alicia continues to the dining table; she transfers everything from the tray to the table; puts empty tray on buffet table. It's apparent Alicia is under great stress. We see it in her behavior and facial expression. She's an attractive woman, in her late thirties, normally willful and self-confident. She wears a too short, too tight, black skirt; black stockings; black, mid-heeled shoes; a white, rayon, long-sleeved blouse. There's been an effort on her part to look "sexy." She takes a beat or two to steel herself. Then she moves to rear, far right.

ALICIA (*calls to outside*): Stanford? (*Clears her throat; a bit louder*) Stanford, sweetheart, dinner is ready! Will you come in, please? (*Hesitates a beat*) I . . . I don't want the soup getting cold. And I have a roast chicken with baked potatoes in the oven. I made everything myself. And . . . And it wasn't my turn for cooking tonight . . . darling. (*Hesitates a beat*) Please, Stanford. Do come in now.

(*Evidently he's starting towards the entrance door. She quickly moves to sit at left end of dining table; pulls down her skirt, fluffs her hair, etc. Stanford Gerard enters. He is fifty-plus years of age, dressd in full cowboy regalia: boots, spurs, chaps, flannel shirt, bandana, leather vest with sack of Bull Durham visible in one of its pockets, Stetson, all purchased second-hand or "bruised" by Ralph Laurent. He slaps at his pants, raising puffs of dust around him. He gives the impression of having been on horseback for several hours if not several days*)

STANFORD (*with Texas twang as he imagines it*): Whew, Goddamn! It's like a dustbowl out there! You can't go ten feet without gettin' the breath knocked outta you! Whew, I was up on the north range, bringin' in this here stray heifer that got itself separated from the herd. I never seen anything like it. The sand was blowin' right up into my nostrils. (*He pulls out farmer's handkerchief from rear pants pocket and blows his nose*) Damn, it's more work than I bargained for. I been thinkin' a puttin' on another hired hand. Oh, I know your objection, girl: it's more outta pocket expense. But it's the only way we're gonna get that herd to market come spring.

ALICIA (*repressing her impulsive anger*): Stanford, would you . . . would you like to wash before you sit down . . . ?

STANFORD: Can't be doin' that, girl. Ain't you heard? The water's frozen in the well. Thick as an iceberg down there. I'm gonna have to start chippin' at it in the mornin' to get us a couple a buckets a drinkin' water. (*He moves to buffet table, looks through tapes next to cassette player*) I tell you, this winter's gonna be a real humdinger. We got a heap a preparation to be doin' if we're gonna survive the next couple a months.

ALICIA (*forcing a smile*): The soup is getting cold . . . dear. Will you please sit down and . . . .

STANFORD: I bought us some new-fangled tunes at the general store. I'd like you to be hearin' one of 'em. It's a real amusin' piece a music. Now you jus' listen. See if it don't get your tootsies knockin' on the floor.

(*He pushes tape into cassette. We hear "I'm An Old Cowhand," or some such Western song. Stanford mimes the lyrics, lip-synching with the singer on the tape, moving and gesturing like a television cowboy*)

I'm an old cowhand
From the Rio Grande
But my legs ain't bowed
And my cheeks ain't tanned,
I'm a cowboy who never saw a cow,
Never roped a steer
'Cause I don't know how,
And I sho' ain't fixin'
To start in now,
Yippy-I-O-Ki-Ay,
Yippy-I-O-Ki-Ay . . .

(*Stanford shuts the cassette player. He moves to dining table, throws his leg over back of chair and sits down*) Hot-diggity-dog. Nothin' like country music to get your juices flowin'. What you be thinkin' a that, girl? Ain't she a humdinger? I'm gonna be rehearsin' it over an' over until I get it plum right. I'm hopin' to be doin' it for our New Year's Eve bash down at the Silver Dollar Saloon.

ALICIA: Stanford, today I saw . . .

STANFORD (*raises his hand*): Hold it. Hold it right there. You forgettin' what we do when we sit down at the dinner table?

ALICIA (*with effort*): I . . . I'm sorry. I apologize.

(*Stanford takes off his Stetson, presses it to his heart, staring downward. Alicia also stares downward, her hands clasped on edge of table. She is very unhappy with all of this*)

STANFORD: Lord, we thank you for your blessings and for givin' us the strength to do our daily chores. I'm offerin' a special prayer this evenin' for my neighbor Ezra Slocum's wife, Annabelle Slocum, and ask you in your mercy to relieve her of child-bearin' fever. I also be offerin' a special prayer for my friend Bald Eagle who I hear was bit by a grizzly up on Mount Morgan. We do humbly thank, dear Lord, for the bounty on our table. Amen. (*He stares fixedly at Alicia*)

ALICIA (*with effort*): Amen.

STANFORD: Now we can eat. (*He tears a handful of bread and bites into it*)

ALICIA (*anxiously*): Stanford, I saw Doctor Bibberman today. We had a truly rewarding conversation. I asked him innumerable questions and he was very forthcoming and . . . (*a breath*) I want to apologize to you, my sweetheart. I was so involved with what *I* was feeling that I was totally blind to what *you* were feeling. Doctor Bibberman pointed out that you've been under enormous stress and you have *not* been having an easy time of it since you were let go by our mutual employers. It was as if Doctor Bibberman had removed a blindfold from my eyes and I saw you, myself and our precious daughter in a new and healthier and more optimistic light.

(*Stanford picks up bowl of soup between his hands and drinks quietly from it. Alicia swallows several spoonfuls of soup*)

I admit, I admit, I was wrong, I was insensitive, I was cruel even. But not nearly as cruel and insensitive as Benton, Berber and Pollock. And I say this knowing full well that I started working there myself as a lowly secretary, your secretary, my sweetheart, my darling. You gave me my first opportunity, my first chance, my first introduction into the fascinating world of advertising, and today I'm proud to say, I'm second in line for Chief Merchandising Officer. But what they did to you, darling, discharging you so summarily after having served them faithfully for twenty-four years, half of that time as Executive Vice President of Creative Copy . . . To discharge you without reprieve or redress during this awful recession we're having . . . That was unforgiveable of them. And even though I fought on your behalf, my darling, my dearest, fought with Ray Pollock until my own job was in imminent jeopardy . . . I don't have to go into that. But I do want you to know how ashamed I am. I had no right these past few weeks, no right whatsoever to dispute or ridicule you about your desire to . . . to have a new life for yourself, whether that life be based in reality or fantasy. Doctor Bibberman pointed all that out to me today. He even brought up the subject of your deeply unhappy relationship with your father, how removed you were from each other, how your father never took you to a baseball game or on camping trips or passed on to you values that would help you achieve maturity. It may sound far-fetched but Doctor Bibberman also spoke of your childhood games of Wagon Train and Gunsmoke and how they affected your decision to become a cowboy after you suffered the trauma of sudden unemployment.

STANFORD: You jus' reminded me, girl. Did you chop the firewood like I tol' you?

ALICIA (*with effort*): No. No. But I will. Tomorrow. Do let me finish, please.

(*Stanford tears off another handful of bread*)

When you left your first wife and your three young children to marry me, your secretary, an unsophisticated, callow, somewhat slovenly woman seventeen years your junior, a woman without prospect or resources, and when you took on the burden of supporting two families, sending our own precious Lucinda and your three children from your former marriage to private schools and then on to universities at great expense and obligation on your part, you proved beyond a measure of a doubt that you were a man of rare principle and generosity. And now that you're practically penniless, my darling, my love, my dear, dear husband, now that you're getting on in years so that future employment is highly problematic for you, I want you to know that I will do *every, every, everything* humanly possible to make your burden lighter and less suffocatingly oppressive.

STANFORD (*stares at her a beat*): You soap an' brush down the horses like I tol' you?

ALICIA: I will. Tomorrow. I promise. I'll finish my little speech to you by saying that it's my wholehearted intention to love you, love you, love you to death, and be supportive of whatever dream it is that gets you through the day. Doctor Bibberman feels that with time and with your continued visits to his office, you'll eventually discard this . . . this fantasy of yours and return to a reality that we both can share and enjoy and build a happy, happy future on. In other words, my sweetheart, my dearest, you're not going to have any more quarrels or arguments with me, no matter what demands you make or how improbable your suggestions are. As an active feminist this is all very difficult for me, but my love for you is so complete, so enormous a part of my life that I will do whatever has to be done to make you healthy again, so help me God.

STANFORD (*stares at her a beat*): You feed the hogs this mornin'?

ALICIA: I . . . I couldn't find the hogs.

STANFORD: They were in the barn! I seen 'em myself on the way out to pasture! Ten beautiful-lookin', prize-winnin' hogs! (*Rises*) I best go an' find 'em. We can't be affordin' to lose . . .

ALICIA: No, no, no, don't . . . (*With effort*) I . . . I forgot. I did see them. And I fed them. I did. I've been so busy, it slipped my mind.

STANFORD: Whew, you scared the bejeebers outta me. I'm plannin' to sell those hogs for us to be gettin' through the winter.

ALICIA: Stanford, I deposited a thousand dollars in our joint account. You're free to withdraw any of that money for whatever . . .

STANFORD (*leans across table*): What I tell you, girl?

ALICIA: Tell me?

STANFORD: 'Bout callin' me Stanford. Didn't I tell you that when we came out to Tombstone the boys gave me the nickname a Sonny?

ALICIA: Sonny?

STANFORD: You heard right, girl.

ALICIA (*forcing it out*): Yes. You did.

STANFORD: An' didn't I say I prefer bein' called Sonny over my Eastern name a Stanford?

ALICIA: Yes. You did.

STANFORD: You know why the boys come to call me the nickname a Sonny?

ALICIA: No. I don't.

STANFORD: They gave me the nickname a Sonny 'cause I got the disposition of a man much younger than my years. I can ride, I can shoot an' I can lasso like a nineteen year old. That's why they call me Sonny.

ALICIA: Then I will definitely call you Sonny. From now on. I promise. And darling . . . dearest . . . since you brought up the subject of names, would you be terribly offended if I asked you not to call me girl?

STANFORD: You don' like me callin' you girl?

ALICIA (*vehemently*): I *loooath* it! I find it so demeaning and . . . (*Controlling herself*) Sonny, I . . . I would appreciate it, greatly, greatly, if you called me "Alicia" or "Alish" or "Allie" or even "Al," but I beg you, from the bottom of my heart, do not call me girl.

STANFORD: I meant you no offense.

ALICIA: Oh, I know that, sweetheart.

STANFORD: I jus' figured my bein' seventeen years your senior it's only natural for me to be callin' you girl.

ALICIA: Forgive me but . . . No, it's not natural. And it's not right. I am a woman . . . Sonny. A woman is not a girl. Would you like it if I called you boy?

STANFORD: I wouldn't be objectin'. I done ask the boys to call me Sonny-boy insteada jus' plain Sonny. But they kinda objected to it. Would you be again' me callin' you woman?

ALICIA: No, no, not at all. I like that. So long as it's said with respect.

STANFORD (*raises hand*): Okay. We got us a deal, woman. Now how about that there roast chicken an' baked potatoes? My gut is jus' about ready to start in barkin'. (*He moves to cassette player as Alicia exits to kitchen*) An' while you're doin' your chores, I'll be rehearsin' that there tune for the New Year's bash. I gotta be gettin' it right if I'm not gonna be embarrassin' the Lazy Bones ranch. (*He presses start button. And at once he mimes along with tape, refining his movements and gestures*)

I'm an old cowhand
From the Rio Grande
And I learned to ride
'Fore I learned to shoot,
I'm a ridin' fool who is up to date,
I know every trail
In the Lone Star State,
'Cause I ride the range
In a Ford V-Eight,
Yippy-I-O-Ki-Ay,
Yippy-I-O-Ki-Ay . . .

(*During the above, Alicia enters with a platter of roast chicken and baked potatoes. She puts it at Stanford's end of the table so that he can carve the chicken. She then sits at her end of the table*)

STANFORD (*shuts cassette player*): So whatta you be thinkin' a my performance? Gettin' any better?

ALICIA (*with effort*): You're doing . . . well. It's entertaining and . . . You seem to enjoy it.

STANFORD: You again' me doin' it? (*Picks up carving utensils*)

ALICIA: No, no, if that's what you want to do . . . Stan . . . Sonny, I want you to be happy. I want us both to be happy and have a full, productive, emotionally rich life together. I know you love me and you must know I love you and if we allow anything to separate us . . .

STANFORD (*points at chicken with knife*): What's that on top there, woman?

ALICIA (*rises; leans over to look at chicken*): On top of what, dear?

STANFORD: On top a that chicken! That brown stuff layin' on it!

ALICIA: Oh, I see, I see it. It burned a little. I can scrape it off . . .

STANFORD (*on his feet; indignant*): Scrape it off? Whatta we talkin' about here, woman! That's a roast chicken. That ain't a piece a linoleum. If you burn a chicken, you don' scrape it off 'cause that there burnin' goes straight to the middle a the chicken! An' I can't be eatin' no burn' chicken!

ALICIA (*rises*): Stan . . . Sonny, I . . . I am sorry. It's unfortunate but . . . I have not had an easy time of it these past few weeks either. As I told you, tonight was not my night for cooking and yet I went ahead and tried to cook you a very special meal . . .

STANFORD (*knocks his chair to the floor*): I don't wanna hear any more a that! Your night a cookin'! My night a cookin'! I been out there workin' my butt off since sunup, woman! I been fixin' fences, herdin' strays, brandin' calves, helpin' Ezra Slocum nail down a new roof on his shed. Now I been doin' all a this so come winter there'll be food on this here table and heat in this here house and maybe some pretty ribbons an' bows for Lucinda when she comes visitin' us for the holidays.

ALICIA: I don't want us to quarrel, darling. That's the last thing I want. But you have to realize that I work, too. I get up every morning at six A.M. and I travel over an hour to get to the . . .

STANFORD (*picks up chair*): Now that's somethin' I been meanin' to talk to you about. Your goin' to town an clerkin' for Ray Pollock. That's got to come to an end.

ALICIA (*tightening*): Are *you* suggesting that I quit my . . . ? (*Cools it; with effort*) Darling . . . Dearest, I've worked very, very hard to get where I am in business. I can't throw all that away to . . . to cook and clean and bake and sweep. It's . . . retrograde. You're not asking me to do that, are you, sweetheart?

STANFORD: Yeup. That's what I be askin'.

ALICIA: But I . . . I can . . . I can bring in money to help you through the winter! I told you I deposited a thousand dollars. I'll deposit . . . five, ten, twenty thousand dollars! More if necessary! I can support you and the Lazy Bones ranch! We can buy all the hogs and horses and chickens you . . .

STANFORD (*knocks his chair to the floor*): I don't wanna be hearin' that kinda talk, woman! How many times I tell you I got the responsibility a providin' for this here family! Don't you be takin' away *my* job! An' if none a this here suits you, you can jus' pack your bags an' take the next stage to your folks in Yuma county!

ALICIA (*moves away; wrings her hands; to herself*): It's hard. It's so hard. Why is it so hard to live with . . . someone? (*Turns to him*) Stan . . . Son . . . Would you like me to call you Sonny-boy?

STANFORD (*picks up chair*): I sure enough would. Sonny-boy was my choice but the boys wouldn't go for it.

ALICIA (*a brave smile*): Then Sonny-boy it is, darling. I made a promise to Doctor Bibberman and I will try with all my heart to keep my promise. Let me . . . think about giving up my job and staying home to be a . . . (*swallows*) . . . housewife. But I would like you to know that in the Old West there was a feminist movement, the suffragettes; they fought for women's rights a hundred years ago and today their descendants are still fighting for women's rights.

STANFORD (*sits in chair; puts potatoes on his plate*): I don't recall seein' any of 'em in Tombstone.

ALICIA (*sits in chair; invents story she tells him*): Don't you remember seeing Abigail Gibson carry that sign down Main Street?

STANFORD (*perplexed*): What sign you talkin' about?

ALICIA: On it was printed, "Our bodies. Our choice." She walked right into the Silver Dollar Saloon carrying that sign and spoke out clearly and powerfully for women's rights. Weren't you there that day, Sonny-boy? It was sometime last week, I believe.

STANFORD (*inventing his own story*): Oh, yeah. You bet I was there. I was playin' poker with Ezra, Big Sam Cooper an' Doc Halaway. Abigail come in an' she made that there little speech a hers an' then Big Sam Cooper gets up, stands on his chair . . . (*stands on his chair*) . . . an' he says, "That there was a mighty pretty speech, Abigail, but I gotta be remindin' you that you can't be changin' the natural order a things. You go out to the barnyard an' you'll see the bull get up on top a the cow; you'll see the stallion get up on top a the mare; an' you see the rooster get up on top a the hen. That there be the natural order a things an' you can't be changin' God's work!"

ALICIA: Yes, yes. Big Sam Cooper did say that standin' on his chair, but then Abigail Gibson's sister, Felicity, she stood up on her chair . . . (*stands on her chair*) . . . and she said, "Big Sam, I hate contradicting you, but God's work is man and woman living together fruitfully, with mutual love and mutual respect. God's work is not confrontation, is not sexual aggression, is not who's on top and who's on bottom! Women will no longer tolerate second-class citizenship in politics, in business, or in the home! So you better change your ways, Big Sam, or consider yourself doomed to bachelorhood for the remaining days of your life!"

STANFORD: Yeup, I recall Felicity Gibson sayin' all a that 'cause it was right then an' there that I stood up on the table . . . (*steps from chair to table*) . . . an' in a thunderin' voice I said, "Ladies an' gentlemen a Tombstone, I regret to inform you that the institution a marriage is dead as a doorknob. For thousands a year it was the basis for Christian civilization. For thousands a years Pop went off to work in the fields six days a the week, an' Mom stayed home an', after sendin' the kids off to school, she'd be fillin' the kitchen with the smells a baked bread an' boilin' potatoes an' roast chicken that didn't get itself burned 'cause a inattention an' neglect. (*With reverance; removes hat*) An' then it'd be that on the seventh day a the week, there'd be no workin' the field, no washin' an' cookin', no sendin' the kids off to school. There'd be the Sabbath, a day put aside so's the family could go off to church, scrubbed an' polished an' filled with gratitude for the Lord's blessins an' the Lord's bounty. (*Harshly; puts on hat*) But all a that is gone now," I declared in a righteous voice. "It's gone 'cause the womenfolk were dissatisfied, like in the days a the Garden a Eden when they took from the tree a Knowledge a crabapple an' condemned all a us to the aches an' pains a mortal life. This time the womenfolk were dissatisfied at the way the family was arranged an' they started in rearrangin' it. No more Pop goin' off to the fields, no more Mom fillin' the kitchen with smells a good cookin', nobody home anymore to see the kids off to school, that's iffen they're goin' off to school at all. (*Sadly*) The womenfolk have won their battle, ladies an' gentlemen a Tombstone," I said. "Nowadays there's divorce an' there's separation an' broken homes an' broken hearts an' no more family to be speakin' of. We are all equal an' we are all livin' our separate lives, cold and lonely like Ol' Mount Morgan in the middle of a winter frost."

ALICIA (*embittered*): Yes, you said all of that to the people in the Silver Dollar Saloon, Sonny-boy. And that's when I decided to take things into my own hands. (*Steps from chair to table*) "My dear friends, my dear neighbors," I began my speech in a firm, reverberating voice. "I do thank the Gibson sisters, Abigail and Felicity, for expressing their opinions to you, but it's time I spoke with my own tongue and my own mind. What my husband, Sonny-boy Gerard, failed to tell you is that family life as practised since biblical times is far from the rosy picture he painted for you. Physical and emotional abuse, sexual degradation and a life of servitude and exploitation were the inevitable consequences for a woman entering into the state of holy —forgive me for laughing—matrimony. Of necessity, out of pain and humiliation, women were forced to open their eyes, recognize the barrenness of their lives and cry out, 'Enough! Enough! I am no beast in the field! I am no rib, no handmaiden, no receptacle for a man's feeble excesses!' Women fought back, my friends, fought ferociously for their lives. And at last, at long last, in the second half of the twentieth century, women succeeded, women *were* victorious. And for the first time in all of recorded history, a woman could look a man straight in the face and shout out jubilantly, joyously, triumphantly . . . !"

STANFORD (*interrupts; he's heard enough of her fantasy*): You didn't say any a that, woman! You're makin' it up!

ALICIA: I did so say it! We were in the Silver Dollar Saloon . . .

STANFORD (*gets down from table*): You were in no Silver Dollar Saloon! I was in there, playin' poker . . .

ALICIA (*gets down from table*): I saw you! I know you were in there! Don't you remember we got into an argument, the two of us, about how men and women have changed over the years?

STANFORD (*a chance to even the score*): Oh, yeah. Ohhh, yeah. I remember us arguin'. I said to you, I said, "Ain't it strange how women ain't women anymore? You notice how they be changin', how their skin's gettin' all chapped an' rough, how their breasts are gettin' smaller an' how they're growin' whiskers on their chins?"

ALICIA (*grimly*): Yes, you said that. And I said, I said, "You notice how men can't do a day's work anymore; how lazy they've become; you notice how they talk less and less, move less and less, and how in bed, at night, with their wives . . ."

STANFORD: I don't remember you sayin' any a that.

ALICIA: I did say it. You made me so angry that I . . . I couldn't restrain myself. I told them everything.

STANFORD (*incredulously*): You tol' my friends . . . ?

ALICIA (*nods*): Everything. I told them about you losing your job back East, about your visits to Doctor Bibberman, about your . . . sexual . . . disabilities.

(*Wow! That hurts. Taking a deep breath, pulling back his shoulders, Stanford walks with a deliberate swagger to the stereo, presses start button. And at once he mimes along with the tape, giving his best, upbeat performance*)

STANFORD:

I'm an old cowhand
From the Rio Grande
And I come to town
Just to hear the band,
I know all the songs that the cowboys know,
'Bout the big corral
Where the doggies go,
'Cause I learned them all
On the radio,
Yippy-I-O-Ki-Ay,
Yippy-I-O-Ki-Ay . . .

(*Stanford shuts the stereo, moves to table, pleased with his performance. He sits in his chair and starts mashing the potatoes on his plate with his fork. He totally ignores Alicia. Alicia sits in her chair and watches him. She wishes she hadn't offended him. Sound: a drum beat; softly. Alicia leans forward in her chair to listen*)

ALICIA: Stan . . . Sonny-boy?

(*No response from Stanford*)

Are those drums I'm hearing?

(*No response from Stanford*)

It's . . . inordinately difficult for me to surrender, not to fight back when I'm assaulted. It goes against my nature. (*A short beat*) If it's an apology you want, I . . . apologize. I didn't tell your friends or . . . anyone about . . . your problems. I wanted to hurt you, that's why I said all of that. I'm sorry. You must know that Doctor Bibberman believes your . . . impotence is a stage and it will pass and it's nothing for us to be overly concerned with. (*Irritatedly*) Where are those noises coming from?

STANFORD: Injuns.

ALICIA: Are you trying to frighten me now?

STANFORD (*rises*): Nope. There's been trouble between the Comanche an' the Sioux. Bald Eagle's callin' for a meetin'.

ALICIA: Darling, is there no hope for us? Can't you just stop it? Can't you come back to those who love you?

STANFORD (*moves to the buffet, right*): I don't know what you're carryin'-on about, woman. We might be havin' a war an' you're still talkin' nonsense.

(*Sound: drums grow louder, more insistent*)

ALICIA: Who is that? Who's making that noise? Why doesn't . . . ? ("*. . . someone stop them?*")

STANFORD: Shhh!

(*He listens. Sound: drums a bit softer now*)

The ranchers are gonna have to choose between joinin' the Comanche or the Sioux. Ezra an' Sam Cooper are votin' for the Sioux. I'm votin' for the Comanche 'cause a my friendship with Bald Eagle.

(*He pulls a shotgun out of buffet drawer. He breaks it open to make certain it's loaded, then snaps it shut*)

ALICIA: Where . . . Where did you get that gun?

STANFORD: Don't be askin' silly questions. I advise you to keep your voice low an' when I say get down on the floor, you get down on the floor.

ALICIA: Did you . . . ?

STANFORD: Shhh. (*He moves to rear, crouched over; he peeks out of an imaginary window*)

ALICIA (*whispers*): Did you pay someone to beat a drum out there? Are you trying to deliberately frighten me?

STANFORD (*whispers*): There's somebody near the barn. I don't see more 'an one. Douse some a the lights.

ALICIA (*moves to buffet, right; determined*): I'm telephoning the police. This has gone far enough. I'm not playing any more of your games, Stanford. Where . . .? Where is the phone? Did you take the phone?

STANFORD (*shuts a light or two; crouching low; he peeks out of "window"*): You gonna get us both killed if you don't stop your yappin'! (*Moves to second "window"; peeks out*) He's comin' closer. He's down by the gate now.

(*Sound: Along with the beating drum, an Indian chant is heard*)

ALICIA (*clutching chest; frightened*): What is that, Stanford?

STANFORD (*waves her toward him; whispers*): Come here. Over here. Stay down low.

(*Crouched over, Alicia moves towards him. They both lean against an imaginary rear wall. The chanting and drum-beating fades to silence*)

ALICIA: What is he doing now?

STANFORD (*peeks out*): I . . . I can't see him. I don't know where he is.

ALICIA: Stanford, this isn't real! There's no one out there! You've arranged for someone to pretend . . .

(*Suddenly an ear-splitting scream as an Indian flies into the room, after, presumably, smashing open the entrance door. In warrior paint and fairly authentic costume, with a single feather taped to his bald head, the Indian chants as he beats the drum and dances about in a circle. His knowledge of Indian culture is gleaned from television re-runs of old westerns*)

Bald Eagle!

ALICIA: Bald Eagle? That . . . That's Doctor Bibberman!

(*The Indian stops chanting and dancing*)

BIBBERMAN: When sun high in sky, me Doctor Bibberman. When sun fall under sky, me Bald Eagle, Comanche Chief!

ALICIA (*to Stanford*): What is this? What is he doing here? Has he gone crazy, too?

STANFORD: Don't you be interferin', woman. This here's man's work. (*To Bibberman*) Did you get to speak to the Sioux?

BIBBERMAN: I speak to Chief Gray Wolf. I say, "Before brother kill brother, we talk. I bring ranchers. We all meet at campfire on banks of Iron Horse Creek." You come now. They wait.

STANFORD: Is Ezra Slocum . . . ?

BIBBERMAN: He be there. Sam Cooper be there. And I ask Senator Monahan to be there.

STANFORD: Good. (*Turns to Alicia*) Woman, you lock that there door after we go an' you don't open it for anybody. It's gonna be a long night. (*Suddenly a bit shy*) I . . . I think you should be knowin', if it ain't in the cards for me to be comin' back, I did the best for you an' Lucinda I could. But you ladies had no use for a workin' cowpoke. Once you got yourselves a college education an' your equal rights an' your banks a frozen spermatozoa, you had no need for the like a me. I bear you no animosity. It's been a rewardin' experience. (*To Bald Eagle*) We better get movin'. (*He moves to rear, right*)

BIBBERMAN: I watch your husband, Mrs. Gerard. You have promise of Bald Eagle. (*He moves to rear; turns to Alicia*) And Doctor Bibberman, too.

(*And he continues to rear, softly beating on drum, chanting. Stanford joins him in chant. They exit. We can still hear the chanting and drumbeat, faintly. Alicia moves downstage. She stares upwards, her fists clenched in front of her; in a fierce voice*)

ALICIA: I swear by all that's sacred in this world, I will *never, never* trust a man again . . . as long as there's a breath of life in me . . . *so help me God!*

(*A loud, insistent beating of the drum, a screeching chant from Stanford and Bibberman, and, simultaneously, silence, and . . . Blackout.*)

DREAMERS

Shel Silverstein

Shel Silverstein

Shel Silverstein was last represented on the New York stage with his play *The Devil and Billy Markham,* which played a double bill with David Mamet's *Bobby Gould in Hell,* collectively titled *Oh! Hell,* at the Mitzi Newhouse Theatre at Lincoln Center. With Mr. Mamet, he co-wrote the screenplay *Things Change* for Columbia Pictures which starred Don Ameche and Joe Mantegna. This last spring his play, *Hamlet,* was performed at the Ensemble Studio Theatre in New York.

Mr. Silverstein has written and illustrated several children's classics, including *Where the Sidewalk Ends, A Light in the Attic,* and *The Giving Tree.* His plays include *The Crate, Lady or the Tiger, Gorilla* and *Little Feet.* He is also a noted cartoonist and the author of many songs and poems. Most recently, his song *I'm Checking Out of the Heartbreak Hotel* from the film, *Postcards from the Edge,* was nominated for an Academy Award.

Characters:

RITCHIE

NICK

Scene:

A bathroom.

Nick works on sink drain. Ritchie sits on edge of tub.

RITCHIE: I'll tell you something—that son of a bitch gives me nervous stomach.

NICK: You let him get to you. I wouldn't give him the satisfaction.

RITCHIE: How do you not let him get to you when he pulls that arbitration compensation shit? How does he expect me to work after that?

NICK: He don't give a damn if you work or not. He hopes you fuck off and get fired and starve to death.

RITCHIE: Then he'd hear from me about some compensation.

NICK: He wouldn't hear nothin' from you—you'd be dead. Gimme that bucket. (*Ritchie hands it to him*) Gimme that crescent wrench. (*Ritchie hands it to him—Nick begins to unscrew plug*)

RITCHIE: It's that fuckin' Sorenson—he gives me nervous stomach.

NICK: It's that fuckin' Sorenson and it's the fuckin' union, it's the fuckin' weather, it's the fuckin' wrench, it's the fuckin' everything—You got a wild hair up your ass or somethin'? (*Nick takes plug out and examines it*)

RITCHIE: I don't know, maybe it's the pressures of the work—(*He goes to medicine cabinet—opens it and begins to examine pills*)

NICK: The pressures of the work? The pressures of the profession? The stress associated with—

RITCHIE: I don't sleep. I don't know what it is.

NICK: I sleep too much. Carole says it ain't normal. Come home—eat supper—a little TV—and *out.* She says to me, "Is this all there is?"

Like the song—(*He sings*) Is this all there is? Jesus—look at this—(*He begins to pull various items out of sink trap—hairpins, toothpaste caps, a hair curler, four bobby pins, a tampax, a toothbrush, a rubber, and a great blob of matted hair—he finds a ring which he wipes off and casually puts into his pocket*)

RITCHIE: At least you sleep—I don't sleep. I keep havin' weird dreams.

NICK: If you don't sleep how can you have dreams?

RITCHIE: When I do sleep—for a minute I have these strange dreams.

NICK: What kind of strange?

RITCHIE: You know—strange.

NICK: There are lots of kinds of strange—you mean—scary or sick or what?

RITCHIE: I'm embarrassed to discuss it.

NICK: What's to be embarrassed about? It's just a dream. (*Wiping out plug and examining it*) These threads are shot.

RITCHIE: A weird dream.

NICK: What? Did you screw a cow? (*He laughs*)

RITCHIE: *Worse.*

NICK: You screwed a bull.

RITCHIE: You're gettin' closer.

NICK: Well what? Did you screw a dead rat? Gimme a piece of that teflon tape. (*Ritchie tears off tape and hands it to him—Nick wraps tape around threads of plug and screws plug back in*)

RITCHIE: I fucked a guy.

NICK: What guy?

RITCHIE: I don't know.

NICK: You don't know—hey, Ritchie, you first oughtta ask a guy's name before you fuck him. (*He giggles*)

RITCHIE: Y'see, you son of a bitch, that's why I didn't want to tell you —I *knew* you'd do this shit.

NICK: OK—I'm sorry—what's he look like.

RITCHIE: Forget it—I shouldn't of said a fuckin' word.

NICK: I was kiddin'—I shouldn't have kidded you—bad taste—I'm sorry. How did it happen?—I mean, where were you?—where were you?

RITCHIE: I don't know—I think out in the country or somewhere.

NICK: And what happened? He just walked up to you and—

RITCHIE: He didn't walk up to me—we were just—shit, it was only a dream.

NICK: That's right—so what are you gettin' so pissed off? You were just what?

RITCHIE: What?

NICK: You said you were just—

RITCHIE: We were just talkin'—I think he was holding a book or something.

NICK: And then he grabbed your cock—

RITCHIE: No, it was just sort of vague—You know, like a dream. One minute we're talkin' and the next minute we're—

NICK: Fuckin'.

RITCHIE: We're naked—sort of wrestlin' around on the ground.

NICK: Naked.

RITCHIE: Yeah.

NICK: And then you started fuckin'.

RITCHIE: No, we just rolled around on the grass and hugged each other and laughed a lot—

NICK: Well, when did you start fuckin'?

RITCHIE: We never really started fuckin'.

NICK (*impatiently*): You said you started fuckin'. You said you fucked a guy—

RITCHIE: Well, it was like we were gonna—I was gonna—but I didn't quite do it. You know in dreams—how you're almost about to do somethin' and you never quite—

NICK: But did you *want* to do it?

RITCHIE: I guess so—maybe not—I don't know—Maybe I didn't want to do it—

NICK: So what's the big deal? If you didn't want to do it and you didn't do it, what's the big damn deal? Turn on the water. (*Ritchie turns on water*)

RITCHIE: I didn't say I didn't want to do it—in the dream—I don't know if I wanted to do it—I woke up.

NICK: Before anything happened.

RITCHIE: I told you, nothing happened.

NICK: Did you have a hard on? (*Nick stands up and examines faucets*)

RITCHIE: When?

NICK: When you woke up—or *in* the dream—did you have a hard on?

RITCHIE: When—In the dream?—I don't know.

NICK: What about when you woke up?

RITCHIE: I don't know. I think maybe.

NICK: Maybe? You either wake up with a hard on or you wake up without a hard on.

RITCHIE: Sometimes it's sort of—in between.

NICK: So you woke up with a hard on—semi-hard—

RITCHIE: Yeah, I guess so.

NICK: But you didn't come.

RITCHIE: No, I didn't come—what the hell difference does that make?

NICK: It makes a lot of difference—if you come or don't come—

RITCHIE: Well, I didn't.

NICK: I mean like sometimes you wake up and there's a little drop of come at the end of your dick?

RITCHIE: What the fuck is the difference if I came or not? We rolled around on the grass and we hugged. That was enough.

NICK: And you were laughin'.

RITCHIE: Yeah.

NICK: What were you laughin' about?

RITCHIE: I don't know. How the hell do I know what we were laughin' about? What are you, some kind of psychologist? I told you what happened—it was just a fuckin' dream.

NICK: Correction—it was a non-fuckin' dream.

RITCHIE: Right—it was a non-fuckin' dream.

NICK: Did he look like anybody you know? Shut off that cold water.

RITCHIE (*under sink turning shutoff*): It won't shut off.

NICK: Shit. (*He gets back under sink and tries to turn the shutoff. He mutters obscenities*)

RITCHIE: I don't remember what he looked like. What's the difference what he looked like?

NICK: Well, it could be symbolic—you know, like the guy represents the union—or Sorenson—and—

RITCHIE: It wasn't Sorenson—that's for sure.

NICK: Or the guy just represents the union—and it's symbolic because you think the union's fuckin' you—so it's not like the guy is a real guy—it's like he's the union.

RITCHIE: I said the union is fuckin' me. That's not the same as me fuckin' the union.

NICK: It could be you gettin' back at the union for fuckin' you—by fuckin' the union—it's symbolic.

RITCHIE: You know what I read in a magazine? I read that *all* dreams you dream it cause you want to do it but you're afraid to really do it so you just dream it.

NICK: That's a crock a shit.

RITCHIE: That's what I read.

NICK: That's what you read—so you have one dream where you're not even fuckin' some guy and you scare yourself into thinkin' you're a faggot—

RITCHIE: It's just what I read.

NICK: And you think you're a faggot.

RITCHIE: I just don't want it to be wish fulfillment, for chrissake.

NICK: It ain't wish fulfillment, Ritchie—it's a dream—it symbolizes somethin'. It could symbolize you fuckin' the government on your income tax—

RITCHIE: And the guy is the government?

NICK: He could be.

RITCHIE: OK, then answer me this—Why wasn't the government a girl?—In the dream—why was it a guy? Why wasn't it a girl—like the Statue of Liberty—she symbolizes the government—Why was it a guy?

NICK: Hey, Uncle Sam symbolizes the government—eh? eh?

RITCHIE: Uncle Sam?

NICK: It could be. He could be the guy you sold your Chevy to last year —you knew the transmission was all messed up but you sold it to him without tellin' him so maybe it's you're guilty about fuckin' him on the deal, so you dream about it.

RITCHIE: It wasn't the guy I sold my Chevy to—It was just some guy who—never mind.

NICK: You think you're a faggot? You do. You have one dumb dream and you're ready to go have a sex change operation. I'm gonna have to break the fuckin' riser to get to the shutoff—Shit—gimme that hammer—(*Ritchie hands it to him*) Gimme the chisel—(*Ritchie hands it to him—he begins to knock hole in wall tile*)

RITCHIE: Hey, it's just that it seemed so damn real—and when I—

NICK: Here—(*He unzips his fly and takes out his dick*) Here, look at this.

RITCHIE: What the hell are you doin', Nick?

NICK: I'm showin' you my dick—if you're a faggot you're gonna wanna grab it or suck it—do you wanna grab it or suck it?

RITCHIE: Nicky—they see you doin' that, they're gonna think you—

NICK: *Do you wanna grab it or suck it?*

RITCHIE: No, for God's sake.

NICK: OK—now feel your own dick. Feel your own dick—see if it gave you a hard on.

RITCHIE: Nick, the lady walks in here and sees you with your dick out —and me feelin' my own dick. She's gonna—have a—

NICK: After what we just pulled outta her sink she's not gonna say nothin'—now feel your own dick—or do I have to feel it for you?

RITCHIE: Jesus—(*He feels his dick*)

NICK: Is it hard?

RITCHIE: No.

NICK: OK—Subject closed. (*Reaches through hole*) Damn. This shutoff is stripped—Mother of God—(*He keeps trying to turn it—muttering*) Hey—that would of been good, if Sorenson seen us grabbin' each other's dicks in here—he'd of really been on your case. Eh? eh? I'll tell you what—I'll bet I just saved you a fuckin' fortune in psychiatrist's bills—seriously, you let those things fester inside your mind, they can grow like a cancer and the next thing you know you *are* a faggot. It's no good—you're gonna have to go down and shut off the riser in the basement—wait a minute—I *got* it—Ha ha—(*He turns it*) Jesus, just because you dream something that doesn't mean you want to do it, for God's sake. You know what I dreamt about last week? You know what I dreamt about? I dreamt about fuckin' my daughter—my own daughter—Gimme the big Stillson—(*Ritchie hands him wrench—he turns wrench*)

RITCHIE: Karen?

NICK: Francie—

RITCHIE: The younger one?

NICK: What if it was the older one? It was a dream. You think I wanna fuck my own daughter? Even the older one? I'd kill anybody who fucked my daughter. It was symbolic—

RITCHIE: Of what?

NICK: How the hell do I know that? I'm no fuckin' psychiatrist. Maybe it was that she was my youth—escaping me—maybe she was like something I was striving for.

RITCHIE: Striving for.

NICK: Like say—she's the dispatcher's job that I been tryin' to get.

RITCHIE: The dispatcher's job?

NICK: Or Sorenson's job—or whatever. You don't think I wanna fuck my own daughter, do you?

RITCHIE: No.

NICK: You're damn right "no." I can't get no leverage—gimme that piece of inch and a half pipe—(*He slips pipe over wrench handle and tries to turn it*) Come on, you son-of-a-bitch—She symbolizes somethin'—I don't know what—so I don't worry about it—I don't wake up in a sweat every time I dream it.

RITCHIE: You dream about it a lot?

NICK: Sometimes—Other times I dream I'm flyin'—sometimes I dream my brother is dead—You think I want my own brother dead? Sometimes I dream I'm back in the army. Sometimes I dream my father is alive and we're sittin' around havin' dinner.

RITCHIE: What does that symbolize?

NICK: What?

RITCHIE: Your father—what do you suppose he symbolizes?

NICK: I don't suppose—(*To pipe*) You rotten motherfuckin'—(*Nipple breaks loose*) Aha! (*He sticks his finger into riser and feels around*) I don't suppose because I don't have the qualifications to suppose anything and neither do you—but we do have the qualifications to make ourselves into nervous wrecks by *supposing*—

RITCHIE: I suppose you're right.

NICK: Now you're supposing right—Don't suppose. Look at that rust buildup—It's a miracle any water got through at all—(*He begins to scrape out rust*) Hey, you wanna hear another one? A couple of times I dreamt of fuckin' my mother—my own mother—Is that somethin' or is that somethin'?—She's always sittin' on the back porch and it's late at night and I'm a kid and I come home—and we do it—right there on the porch and she always says, "Quiet or you'll wake up your father." You think I wanna fuck my own mother?—come on—

RITCHIE: Does your father ever wake up?

NICK: I don't know. It never goes on that long—but the point is I dream about it—and so what? Gimme that new valve—(*Ritchie hands it to him*) Gimme the teflon—(*Ritchie hands it to him—he puts teflon on and screws valve in*) I'll tell you another one—sometimes I dream my wife's dead—you think I want my wife to die? Anyway, in this dream she dies and I come home and she's layin' on the couch dead—but instead of screamin' or cryin' or anything I go right to the fridge and I start to fix myself a sandwich and—

RITCHIE: What kind of sandwich?

NICK: How do I know what kind of sandwich? It was a fuckin' dream.

RITCHIE: Well, I thought it might symbolize somethin'.

NICK: What the hell's the difference?—a cheese sandwich—a ham and cheese—what the hell's the difference?—The point is I was fuckin' Carolyn and she was dead—what does *that* mean.

RITCHIE: I don't know.

NICK: *Nobody* knows—that's the point—it symbolizes something—It's a dream—did you save the pieces of those tiles?

RITCHIE: They're all busted up.

NICK: Mix up a little plaster and stick 'em back on—(*Ritchie mixes plaster and replaces tiles while Nick examines medicine cabinet*) You dream a lot of things, Ritchie—you dream about fuckin' your daughters, you dream about fuckin' guys, you dream about fuckin' your pets, you dream about—

RITCHIE: Pets?

NICK: Everything—what's the difference?—It's all fuckin' symbolic.

RITCHIE: I suppose so.

NICK: I know so—you can't worry about every little dream—(*Nick turns on faucet and washes hands*)

RITCHIE: I suppose not.

NICK: You can't let the little things bother you.

RITCHIE: I guess you're right.

NICK: I'll tell you one thing—I bet I saved you a fuckin' fortune in psychologist bills.

RITCHIE: It's still drippin'—I think we cracked the porcelain—

NICK: Gimme that putty—(*Ritchie extends can—Nick takes a fingerful and runs it under crack in sink*) It was cracked when we got here. You can't let every little thing bother you—

(*They exit. Curtain.*)

THE SAUSAGE EATERS

Stephen Starosta

To The Elichalts
For making Laughter a sand dune.
This play's for you.

Stephen Starosta

Stephen Starosta is one of those rare playwrights who came to that profession from his passion for film. As a student at Bowdoin College, he may have majored in Government and Legal Studies with a considerable interest in Literature and Art, but his predominant activity was the making of films. That activity justified an acceptance at the Yale School of Art where for three years he made films under the supervision of Michael Roemer and where he earned his MFA. For Mr. Starosta, the happy journey to California was immediate upon graduation. While there, he wrote *I Am A Fish,* a film about incest and ghosts set on the rocky coast of Nova Scotia, and *The Hat Trick,* where a hat, legendary for its powers, surfaces in Los Angeles, and two crime buddies rekindle the magic of their relationship for one last job. This writing eventually took him to acting class in Los Angeles, a class which kindled his desire for stage writing. And from that first inspiration, Starosta has developed a passion for stage writing which has resulted in five plays, none of which have as yet been professionally produced, but all of which have been given staged readings and workshop development at New Playwrights Reading Series in Los Angeles, Naked Angels in New York, Tribeca Film Center in New York, and the Padua Hills Playwrights Festival in Los Angeles. This Festival is comprised of a group of playwrights headed by David Hwang, John O'Keefe, Sam Shepard and Maria Irene Fornes. The Festival supports the passion of young playwrights and sees that their work gets attention. Starosta was born in Newfoundland and raised on Cape Cod, where he now makes his home when he is not in Los Angeles.

Characters:

FELICITY, *a near-sighted upper cruster*
NORMAN, *her pathological husband*
GABRIELLA, *their gypsy maid*
NILLY, *a hungry half-wit*
MARY, *a job seeker*

Scene:

An out-dated apartment that once knew better days.

Time:

Present day.
Nilly sits on the living room couch. He's dressed shabbily, poor..
Felicity, an older woman, paces the room. She's dressed simply but with a refined elegance. She wears strong prescription glasses.
Norman, her husband, reads the paper. He wears a ratty bathrobe. Stacks of newspapers lie at his chair's side.
Their apartment is a mess.

FELICITY: He took it. (*To Nilly*) Tell Norman. You can't just loiter in, take whatever you want. That's against the law. Bad boy, Bad, bad boy.

NORMAN: You saw it in his hand.

FELICITY: Standing right there.

NORMAN: That doesn't mean he took it. The hallway's full of riff-raff.

FELICITY: There's no riff-raff in that hall, Norman. That's the neighborhood.

NORMAN: That's what I mean, dear. Anyone could've walked in, walked out.

FELICITY: Anyone? Who is anyone?

NORMAN: The mailman.

FELICITY: No mail up here.

NORMAN: Plumber.

FELICITY: Don't be ridiculous. My pipes flush perfectly well.

NORMAN: OK. I give up.

FELICITY: He took my sausage!

NORMAN: Slap me, Poo.

FELICITY: Did you take my sausage?

NORMAN: I just thought you might get a thrill out of spanking me.

FELICITY: Don't mock me, Norman. I want to get to the bottom of this. I'm sick of things disappearing.

NORMAN: A missing weenie is not the end of the world.

FELICITY: And stop trivializing me! I'm in a state. I want satisfaction. Give me satisfaction.

NORMAN: What sort of sausage is it?

FELICITY: A Bratwurst.

NORMAN: Mmm, too bad. I like my Bratwurst.

FELICITY: And I'm practically catatonic without one.

(*Nilly reaches for peanuts in the silver nut dish on the coffee table. Felicity slaps his hand*)

No! See that! As if I don't exist!

NORMAN: Where's his mother?

FELICITY: How should I know where his mother is.

NORMAN: The boy needs his mother. The boy's helpless without her.

FELICITY: She's probably on that street corner with all the rest of the unemployed. Honestly, I feel I'm living in some stone age. All these marauding tribes roaming the streets. And now this, in the sanctuary of my own home . . . rape. Did you hear that, Norman? He rapes me and you sit there like some stooge.

NORMAN: Who.

FELICITY: I ought to report all of you. I'm a victim and nobody does a thing about it.

(*Nilly grabs some peanuts*)

Give me those!

(*Nilly attacks Felicity . . . strangling her with his hands*)

NORMAN: Poo, dear, I think it's time you let the boy go. Enough of this folly. Mmm? No sense arousing hostility in the young man. World's full of that. Don't need that sort of thing at home. Do we?

(*Felicity breaks away*)

FELICITY (*gasping*): Norman.

NORMAN: Mmmm.

FELICITY: He attacked me. (*Showing marks on her neck*) NORMAN, LOOK AT ME!

NORMAN: I hear you, dear. I'm not deaf yet.

FELICITY: Him! (*Demonstrating*) Did this.

NORMAN: Why didn't you just let him do the job, dear. Gets me off the hook.

FELICITY: Very funny, Norman.

NORMAN: That boy couldn't hurt a fly. He can't even button his shirt correctly.

(*She destroys his newspaper*)

FELICITY: Stop making me disappear!

(*Norman picks up another newspaper from the pile next to his chair*)

NORMAN (*calmly*): And what would you like me to do about that?

FELICITY: I want truth!

NORMAN: And what makes you think you're not getting truth.

FELICITY: Where's my sausage? Can you answer that?

(*No response*)

Norman!

NORMAN (*angrily*): For crying out loud, Felicity! You sure you even bought the damn thing?

(*Felicity burps. Lights out*)

(*Lights up. An hour later. Felicity looks at her magazines . . . flipping madly through the pages. Norman reads his newspaper. Nilly stands at the desk by the window. He turns on and off the desk lamp. He's making a signal to someone on the street below*)

NORMAN (*to Felicity*): Tell him stop playing with that lamp!

FELICITY: You tell him. Nobody listens to me.

(*Norman turns to reprimand Nilly. Nilly growls at him. Norman returns to reading his newspaper*)

NORMAN: They'll arrest you for kidnapping, dear.

FELICITY: I get the truth, he goes.

NORMAN: Stiff penalties for kidnappers these days.

FELICITY: Stiff? I'd like to see anything stiff. I don't know what stiff means any more.

(*Knock on door. A sneeze outside that door. Nilly stops playing with the lamp*)

NORMAN: Someone's at the door.

FELICITY: Well . . . it's about time. Now we'll get to the bottom of this. (*Felicity rings silver bell*) Don't pretend you're hiding, Norman . . . we have a guest. (*Felicity takes off her glasses to look more presentable*)

NORMAN: I suspect that's nothing more than a solicitor or some petition seeker.

FELICITY: Oh, is that who it is? The girl scout?

NORMAN: If it's that girl scout, let her in.

FELICITY: Believe me, Woo, Poo never deprives you of pleasure. I don't stand in the way of that.

(*Door knock. Sneeze outside door*)

NORMAN: Someone's at the door.

(*Felicity rings bell*)

FELICITY: Gabriella!

(*Gabriella, a maid, enters*)

GABRIELLA: What?

FELICITY: The door.

GABRIELLA: I'm stuffin' a chicken!

(*Gabriella exits. Nilly follows her through the swinging kitchen doors*)

FELICITY: Never mind the bird, get the door.

NORMAN: Mashed potatoes with my chicken?

FELICITY: Norman, please. Mashed potatoes every night is a ridiculous notion.

NORMAN: Then don't ask me, Felicity. I don't know anything anymore.

(*Nilly is pushed out of the kitchen. He eats, practically ravishes, a celery stalk. Door knock. A sneeze outside door*)

NORMAN: Someone's at the door.

FELICITY: That refugee's incompetent and a tart! (*Felicity rings bell*)

(*Gabriella enters and crosses behind them. She carries a sign that reads:* UNFAIR WORK LOAD. Door knock. A sneeze outside door)

NORMAN *and* GABRIELLA: Someone's at the door.

(*The other side of Gabriella's sign reads:* FELICITY EATS CROW)

FELICITY: DO YOUR JOB!

(*Nilly rings bell. Felicity grabs the bell from him. Door knock. A sneeze outside door*)

NORMAN *and* GABRIELLA: Someone's at the door.

FELICITY: THAT'S ENOUGH!

GABRIELLA: Oh don't get a heart attack. OK, so I'll get the door.

FELICITY: NO! Stay away from my door!

GABRIELLA: Now you don't want me to get it?

FELICITY: Go to kitchen now! And stay there till I've made up my mind whether you're worth the tax evasion.

(*Gabriella threatens Felicity with a large carving knife*)

GABRIELLA: In my country . . . (*demonstrates throat slashes and stabbings*) . . . like this! And so! And that! This person, she takes no more.

FELICITY: Norman!

GABRIELLA: So you want me get door or not? Make up your head, you selfish dried prune.

FELICITY: Parasite!

GABRIELLA: Blood sucker!

NORMAN (*standing*): Wait!

FELICITY: Oh, thank God. You tell her, Norman.

(*Nilly opens the door. Mary enters*)

NORMAN: I'm not wearing underwear!

(*Mary is dressed in a woman's business suit that is worn and tattered. Her stockings are torn and her shoes are badly scuffed. She wears torn gloves that expose her fingers. She looks like a street beggar. Nilly is hidden behind the door*)

MARY: I'm sorry. I don't mean to barge in like this but I'm looking for . . .

(*Door swings shut, exposing Nilly behind it. Nilly gyrates his hips*)

NILLY: Hey, baby.

MARY: There you are. My son. (*Mary embraces Nilly*) Didn't I say don't leave the apartment without telling me where you go.

NILLY: Uh?

MARY: He loves to roam the building. All the tenants have been so accommodating. I just can't tell you what that means to me. It's not easy having a child (well, he's not really a child anymore) . . . Still, it's difficult. I appreciate your understanding.

FELICITY: Care for some tea? Gabriella, steep us a pot of tea. And I don't mean the roots and bark concoction you chant over. Just ordinary tea please.

GABRIELLA: No. That's not my job description today. (*Gabriella lounges on the couch*)

MARY: Maybe some other time. (*Mary grabs Nilly's hand and starts for the door*)

FELICITY: Hold it! Nobody leaves this room till I get my truth!

(*Mary shoves Nilly outside the door and closes it shut*)

MARY: Oh, I would love to talk your truth. But I have a job interview in fifteen minutes.

NORMAN: What did she say?

FELICITY: She's unemployed.

GABRIELLA: You want my daily grind? I'm sick a waiting for the idle rich to drop dead.

FELICITY: Go stuff bird, Gabriella!

(*Door knock. Mary sneezes*)

NORMAN: Someone's at the door.

(*Nilly opens the door. He rings the silver bell. Felicity grabs the bell from him and closes the door in his face*)

FELICITY: Now go do job, Gabriella. And I'll ring if I need more of your half-baked services.

(*Felicity leads Mary by the arm to the couch. Gabriella pulls out her knife and stalks Felicity*)

FELICITY (*to Mary*): So tell me, who's this employer you're hoping to entice this afternoon?

MARY: Ray's Dry Cleaners.

FELICITY: Oh, Ray. Of-course Ray. The Ray, Norman.

(*Door knock*)

Don't you dare! Any of you!

NORMAN: What if it's that girl scout?

FELICITY: I don't care if it's Chinese food! I'm not answering it. No one does. That's the law.

GABRIELLA: Oh, I'll get it.

FELICITY: NO!

GABRIELLA: Alright! (*Gabriella exits into kitchen*)

MARY: I don't mean to sneeze. I'm not a Sneezer. But lately, and it only happens when I enter a home, someone else's home, I sneeze. Some say, the pollen. Others say a germ. A feather under the nose? And a few say, psychological.

FELICITY: Every time my husband tells me one of his lies, he hiccups! Not only is that psychological, it's pathological as well.

NORMAN: I'm not pathological, dear. I'm too stupid for that. Remember?

FELICITY: A hiccup can't lie, Norman. (*To Mary*) Does it?

MARY: I know that a sneeze won't.

FELICITY: Tell that to the Liar and what do I get . . . another hiccup. Just like all the other hiccups before it. Your hiccups tell the truth, Norman, don't tell me they don't!

NORMAN: I'm always honest (*hiccup*) with you, Felicity. I've never (*hiccup*) been anything but that.

FELICITY: You don't see me a Hiccuper! I don't hiccup! Not like him! And I don't sneeze either! Not like you! And the People today who use their hiccups and sneezes as fronts to hide behind, is a disgrace! This country was founded on truth! Not some bearded hiccup or some reactionary sneeze!

(*Door knock. Felicity sneezes then hiccups*)

NORMAN: Someone's at the door.

(*Mary rings the bell. Gabriella enters*)

GABRIELLA: WHAT?

FELICITY: Would you please get the door, Gabriella.

GABRIELLA: But your own law prohibits me, Madam.

FELICITY: I take back the law!

GABRIELLA: What're you a Supreme Court Judge now?

(*Mary stands*)

MARY: I should go.

(*Felicity pulls her back down*)

FELICITY: And get that Dry Cleaner, the Ray, on the phone. Tell him I'm detaining his candidate.

MARY: Oh, please don't do that.

FELICITY: Oh, no problem at all. The Ray and I go way back. He's been scrubbing all my unmentionables since . . . when, Norman . . . how long have we been sending our soiled ones to the Ray?

GABRIELLA: I do all the stinkin' wash 'round here. Who's the Ray?

(*Door knock. Mary is about to sneeze but Felicity holds a finger under Mary's nose to stop her. Norman is about to speak but Felicity motions he better not. She does the same to Gabriella. Felicity and Mary walk to the door*)

FELICITY: Who's there?

NILLY (*outside door*): Telegram.

FELICITY: Telegram who?

NILLY (*outside door*): Your sausage! You find it yet?

(*Felicity opens the door. Nilly comes flying into the room. He flips over the couch and lands sitting upright as if he never left the room*)

FELICITY (*to the empty hallway*): Hooligans! (*Felicity slams the door shut*) Now bring the tea, Gabriella.

(*Gabriella opens the window*)

GABRIELLA: Eh, do us all a favor, jump out this window!

(*They laugh at Felicity. Nilly knocks on the table. They all sneeze*)

ALL OF THEM: Someone's at the door.

(*Nilly rings bell*)

FELICITY (*stomping her feet*): Tea! Tea! Tea!

MARY: Can I have a rain check?

GABRIELLA: Ask the prune. She writes all the checks.

FELICITY: Boil water!

GABRIELLA: Sit face!

NORMAN: STRING BEANS! With mashed potatoes! And chicken. I'm hungry.

MARY: We should go.

(*Mary stands. Felicity sits her down*)

FELICITY: Peel potatoes, Gabriella, and if you can manage two tasks at once, bring us the tea. Now.

GABRIELLA (*mocking Felicity*): In my country, mashed potatoes every night is a ridiculous notion.

(*Norman hides his laughter. Gabriella laughs and exits into the kitchen*)

FELICITY: Norman!

(*Norman hiccups. Nilly follows Gabriella into the kitchen*)

MARY: I'm afraid I don't have time for tea. The truth is . . . first impressions are so important. And if I'm late on the first date, how will that make me rate? With Ray. But I'd love to come back some other time. Maybe we could plan a game of Bridge?

FELICITY: Did you hear, Norman. She plays Bridge.

MARY: I played all the time in our last building . . . before we were evicted that is. I lost my income.

NORMAN: What did she say?

FELICITY: She's poor.

NORMAN (*returning to his paper*): Oh.

MARY: Hard times these days. Not easy staying above water.

FELICITY: And I'm shocked! . . . every time I set foot outside that door. Something wrong in a neighborhood when a tax payer can't even walk to the grocery store without being accosted by one of those street lepers. That's the disease. The ones who don't give a rip, who'd rather beg their dimes than work an honest day's pay. In my day, no one got away with such laziness. Right, Norman? Tell her what we think.

NORMAN: Who.

FELICITY: And you? What is your opinion?

MARY: I didn't eat yesterday.

NORMAN: What did she say?

MARY: But I'm not complaining. Nilly doesn't understand it though.

FELICITY: Have a nut. (*Felicity can't find her silver nut dish*)

MARY: We don't want to impose nor do we expect charity. But we do like it here and we would very much like to stay, if that's OK. And as soon as I'm able . . . I'll commit to any lease. I promise you that.

FELICITY: Which apartment are you?

MARY: The basement.

FELICITY: In this building? I had no idea an apartment is down there. Did you, Norman?

MARY: I wouldn't call it an apartment. More like, a refuge. If it wasn't for that back door, we'd be on the streets.

FELICITY: You're transient?

MARY: No, no. Not that. More like a Temporary without a permanent position.

(*Felicity stands*)

FELICITY: Have you by any chance put your hands on my wiener.

MARY: Your wiener?

FELICITY: My sausage!

MARY: No I can't say I have. But did you look in the laundry room? Just yesterday, I found a very large, adult size Girl Scout frock.

(*Norman hiccups. Gabriella screams. She runs out . . . chicken in hand. Nilly behind her*)

GABRIELLA: He's got the knife!

MARY: He sees the food.

FELICITY: Look, Norman! She provoked him!

GABRIELLA: He poked at me!

FELICITY: He's poking because she provoked him!

GABRIELLA: I'm stuffin' the chicken. He grabs his tool and insists to stick it inside me.

FELICITY: I'm not surprised.

MARY: I'm so sorry. He gets this way around dinner time.

NORMAN: Dinner? What time?

GABRIELLA: I want compensation for this.

FELICITY: I suppose she'll want a health plan next.

GABRIELLA (*to Norman*): Stuff your own chicken! (*Gabriella throws the chicken at Norman*)

FELICITY: Norman!

(*Norman flings the chicken over his shoulder. Felicity catches it. Gabriella exits the front door*)

MARY: LOOK AT ME!

NORMAN: I can't, dear. I'm reading.

MARY: No God. Don't let him surrender just because he's hungry.

FELICITY: Oh, take the damn chicken. I can't uphold principles when I'm being cheated on by an ungrateful husband!

(*The front door opens. Gabriella enters. She smokes a cigar*)

GABRIELLA: Mutant turtles, spray painting halls again.

FELICITY: Where?

(*Felicity, chicken still in her hands, enters the outside hall to have a look. Gabriella shuts the door*)

GABRIELLA: What're you starin' at? You never seen Worker take break before?

MARY: I've never seen Woman toke cigar.

(*The front door opens*)

FELICITY: I don't see anyone.

(*Felicity has spray paint all over her dress. Nilly laughs first. Then one by one they all laugh, including Felicity*)

NORMAN: My wife's blind without her glasses.

(*They laugh*)

FELICITY: I'm blind with them.

(*Nilly laughs so hard he rolls on the floor*)

GABRIELLA: You Americans. One minute, Psychos, the next, Happy Go Luckys.

(*They all laugh*)

I stay this country, I get schizophrenia like everyone else.

(*Gabriella exits to the kitchen, laughing*)

MARY: We should go.

FELICITY: Oh, take the chicken! Gorge yourselves. Go on. Get fat.

(*They laugh*)

NORMAN: Have an orgy.

(*They laugh*)

MARY: Thank you. That's so kind. But we can't. We couldn't.

FELICITY: Oh, what's the matter with you. This no ordinary chicken, this here Hen's a Perdue.

MARY: Wouldn't be right. Would it, Nilly.

(*Nilly lunges for the chicken*)

Nilly, no! That food is not ours! Remember we were not invited here, properly. Nor have we earned that chicken, honestly. And we certainly don't have the money to pay for it. No matter how hungry we are, just can't take that chicken.

(*Nilly strangles Mary*)

FELICITY: Did you hear that, Norman. She won't accept our offer because she feels she hasn't earned our respect. I applaud your sense of decency, young lady. We don't see much of that these days. (*Mary pulls away from Nilly. She's gasping for breath. Nilly pursues the chicken in Felicity's hands. To Mary*) Tell me, what's he paying that Ray. I bet I could match his offer. I'll fire that she-wolf and hire you right here on the spot.

MARY: Oh, but I couldn't replace a woman who needs this job just as much as I do. I wouldn't be able to sleep my nights.

FELICITY: You say you're looking for a job. I'm offering you one and you turn me down?

MARY: Unfortunately, my conscience says I must do that, yes.

FELICITY: And what does your conscience have to do with you getting a paycheck? If your conscience is like any conscience I know, it will soon forget that Gypsy even breathes. Isn't that so, Norman.

NORMAN: You make all the decisions, dear. That's fine with me.

(*Norman hiccups*)

FELICITY: So if you're as hungry as you say you are, don't let your conscience get in the way. Take my offer. Forget that Ray.

MARY: Nilly, no! (*Mary grabs Nilly from behind and drags him toward the door*)

FELICITY: And besides, I haven't even told you about our tax free bonuses. Then you'll see your conscience has no conscience when you're stiffing the IRS and liking it.

MARY: My conscience has a conscience, and He is my guide. No matter how hungry we are, I won't let that Spirit go.

(*Felicity drops the chicken in Norman's lap and goes toward Mary and Nilly at the door*)

FELICITY: Not so fast. I'm owed an explanation.

(*Nilly's shirt tears off and he goes toward the chicken in Norman's lap. Norman flings the chicken over his shoulder and it goes out the window*)

FELICITY: That boy . . . he was in this apartment. Standing there. Why?

MARY: I hope he didn't damage anything.

FELICITY: Well, he fondled that lamp for one.

(*Nilly knocks over the lamp. He's angry that he lost the chicken*)

MARY: I'm sorry. He just can't leave those light switches alone.

FELICITY: So the lamp's his fetish!

NORMAN: I put my fingers in Vaseline.

FELICITY: Norman!

NORMAN: I like wet.

(*Nilly knocks over a chair. Mary hooks a leash to Nilly's belt loop and pulls him toward the door*)

MARY (*at the door*): Thank you. We must go now.

FELICITY: No one leaves this room till I get my truth!

(*Gabriella enters. She holds a pole with a Sausage dangling from it. She hovers the Sausage over Felicity's head*)

FELICITY: Who took my sausage?

(*Nilly, on his leash, tries very hard to grab at that food*)

NORMAN: How do you know someone took it and you didn't just forget to buy it. You do that. You spend your money then you forget you even bought the damn things.

FELICITY: Someone took it! This morning, yesterday, day before and the day before that! I save my receipts, Norman. I have food files that date back to '62. So don't tell me I didn't buy that sausage, I did. I know I did. (*To Mary*) Tell him!

MARY: I'm sure you did if you say so. I'd certainly know it if I was missing my sausage. I think every woman does.

FELICITY: Of-course we do! What do you think—we just rant for no reason at all! I'll find that sausage if it kills me. Did you hear that, Norman? I'll drop dead!

(*Mary yanks at Nilly's leash and his pants tear off. Mary's released like a slingshot through the swinging kitchen doors. We hears the sounds of pots and pans crashing on top of her. Norman lowers the newspaper. He's smiling*)

NORMAN: Now that would be a shame. That you'd expire because you mislaid your sausage. I can't think of a more senseless way to go.

FELICITY: I'll jump out that window! I'll slash my own throat! Turn red and blue all over. Won't that be a lovely sight before dinner, Norman.

(*Nilly, in his underwear, pursues that Sausage on the pole*)

NORMAN: Totally up to you, Poo. Do whatever your heart makes you do.

FELICITY: And when they come to bury me, they'll ask you questions. They'll want to know why I'm dead. And you'll have to tell them the truth. And they'll put you in jail. Because you lie to me. All these years. One big, fat liar.

NORMAN: I'll tell them you croaked for a weiner. How's that?

(*Mary enters from the kitchen. She holds the carving knife to Gabriella's throat and covers Gabriella's mouth with her other hand. She drags Gabriella into the kitchen. Nilly follows the Sausage*)

FELICITY: Very funny, Norman. I'm glad you think I'm such a joke. WELL I WON'T DROP DEAD FOR YOUR CONVENIENCE! I'll butcher everyone in this apartment first! I'll be the last to go! (*Just before the Sausage is about to disappear into the kitchen, Nilly grabs it. To Nilly*) You! Don't you move. I know right where that wiener is. And don't tell me you don't. Every man I know, knows his wiener can't stay hidden for very long. Cough it up! (*Mary enters. Nilly throws the Sausage to her. To Mary*) And you! I may be blind but I'm not that blind. He's not your son. You're his partner. You share the wiener together. Say it. Say what you do.

MARY (*pointing*): Look! (*Mary throws Sausage to Norman*)

FELICITY: What's there? I don't see anything. That's a wall.

(*Norman flings the Sausage out the window. Nilly runs to the window*)

NORMAN: Poo, I think it's time for your nap.

FELICITY (*stomping her feet*): Truth, truth, truth!

NORMAN: Truth is everywhere. You just don't want to see it.

FELICITY: WHERE'S MY WEENIE?

(*Nilly charges toward Felicity. He'll kill her. Gabriella enters with a tray. She's dressed in a Girl Scout uniform*)

GABRIELLA: Hors d'oeuvres!

(*Mary grabs the tray from Gabriella*)

MARY: Food, Nilly!

(*Nilly beelines for the food tray. He eats ferociously. Mary joins him*)

FELICITY: Hors d'oeuvres? I didn't say hors d'oeuvres.

GABRIELLA: This the tea. Like you said. Now you don't want it?

FELICITY: That's not tea! That's my Bratwurst! Norman!

NORMAN: Dear, I want gravy tonight. String beans, mashed potatoes and gravy, lots of gravy, with my chicken.

GABRIELLA: Oh, I do gravy alright. Lots of gravy. Then we pour it all over the dead Hen. (*Gabriella clucks like a chicken and sits on Norman's lap*)

FELICITY: SAUSAGE EATERS! ALL OF YOU! SAUSAGE EATERS!

(*They laugh at Felicity. Gabriella tickles Norman. Norman chases after her*)

Norman!

NORMAN: I told you, Felicity . . . I get hungry my nights.

(*Norman and Gabriella exit to the kitchen. Nilly follows them but Mary grabs him by the hair on the back of his head and yanks him back*)

MARY: We may be hungry but we are not thieves.

(*Mary and Nilly exit. Felicity staggers toward the couch. Nilly returns with a cigar in his mouth. Felicity is surprised by him. She steps back, expecting he'll harm her. Instead Nilly returns the silver bell and the silver nut dish. He walks toward the door but then stops. He returns to drop a handful of peanuts into the silver dish*)

FELICITY: Wait! (*Felicity puts on her glasses. She offers Nilly the peanuts in the silver nut dish*) You take them. I can't see a Man starve.

NILLY: No thanks. I'm stuffed. (*Nilly exits*)

(*Felicity slams the front door so hard the window falls shut*)

FELICITY: Liars! (*Felicity sneezes. Hiccups. Then burps. Lights out*)

WATERMELON RINDS

Regina Taylor

Regina Taylor

Regina Taylor is an actress turned playwright. She appeared on Broadway as Juliet in *Romeo and Juliet,* won a Dramalogue Award as Ariel in *The Tempest,* and was featured in the film *Lean On Me,* as well as television's *Crisis at Central High,* and *The Howard Beach Story.* For her role as Lilly Harper in *I'll Fly Away,* Ms. Taylor won a Viewers for Quality TV Award, was nominated for an Emmy and won the Golden Globe Award for best leading actress. In addition to her work as an actress, she is a writer of children's books, poems, and stories.

With the publication of *Watermelon Rinds,* she joins the profession of playwriting. Readings of that play were done at both The McCarter Theater and The Women's Project. The play was produced in the 1993 Louisville, Kentucky Humana Festival. Her adaptations of two one-acts by Franz Xavier Kroetz were performed in a workshop at Joseph Papp's New York Public Theater. With this writing work behind her, Ms. Taylor has now been commissioned to write the book for a musical based on *The Fisk Jubilee Singers* for the Alliance Theater's 1994 season. She has also been hard at work on a new full-length play for the Humana Festival's 1994 season. The playwriting profession welcomes one of its newest members, Regina Taylor.

Characters:
JES SEMPLE
WILLY SEMPLE
LOTTIE SEMPLE
LIZA SEMPLE
PINKIE SEMPLE
MAMA PEARL SEMPLE
PAPA TOMMY SEMPLE
MARVA SEMPLE-WEISSE

Scene 1

Jes stands in a spotlight DSR.

JES: I don't like to go to plays. I'd rather sit on the corner and play poker, a little dominoes, talk loud at passing women, watch cats copulating on the side walk, turn up the volume and do the loose goose . . . or do the nasty with a lady who's butt costs less than the price of a gd theater ticket.

I bought a theater ticket once. The paper said it was a black comedy. I went inside. I sat there for hours. I didn't see one black. And it sure wasn't a comedy. Just a bunch of white people talking about throwing babies out with their bathwater and putting hedgehogs up their you-know-what's. (Excuse me ladies.) But and I said, this ain't no black comedy. This is absurd. Then I got up and walked out.

(*Blackout*)

Scene 2

Lights come up on livingroom stacked high with articles of living . . . clothes, books, furniture, a candelabra, old toy baby carriage . . . everything including the kitchen sink. Boxes are scattered. Some empty, half full, and full, taped and labeled. Labels read—POTTERY, LOTTIE'S CLOTHES, BAR-B-QUE GRILL, SAM . . . etc. . . . There is a clearing that leads off right to the kitchen. Another path leads to a door USL to the other parts of the house. Off left is the door to the outside. DSL is a window.

Lottie, fourteen-years-old, wearing a white slip that shows her newly-budding form, is standing on a table doing a barefoot softshoe.

LOTTIE (*singing cheerfully*): YANG YANG YANG YANG. YANG YANG YANG.

(*There is a knocking on the door*)

I'll get it.

WILLY (*voice off stage*): Don't touch that door. Nobody lives here. We're moving.

LIZA (*voice off stage*): Are they here already? Everything isn't prepared yet.

WILLY (*voice off stage*): You never know who's on the other side—

LIZA (*voice off stage*): Lottie, are you dressed yet?

WILLY (*voice off stage*): Damn BEAN EATERS.

LIZA (*voice off stage*): If they're here and you're not dressed yet . . .

(*More knocking*)

LOTTIE: Who's there?

JES (*voice off stage*): Jes.

LOTTIE: Jes who?

JES (*voice off stage*): Jes me and my shadow . . . Let me in.

(*Lottie opens the door. His best Groucho imitation*)

This country club once refused me entrance. I said—Fine, I don't want to join any club that would have me for a member. They said—their swimming pool was for whites only—I said my great-great-grandmother was raped by her slave master—I'm part white—can I go in up to my knees?

LIZA (*voice off stage*): Is anyone here yet?

LOTTIE: No, ma'am.

JES: I'm hungry. When we were growing up we were so po'—our parents had to sleep in the same bed. We were so po' . . .

(*Willy enters from upstage right carrying a bundle and a box. He begins sorting*)

WILLY: They'll all come, they'll eat, they'll leave, we'll move. Get off the table Lottie.

LOTTIE: Guess who I am. (*Tapping and singing*) YANG YANG YANG YANG. YANG YANG YANG.

WILLY: You're my daughter is who.

JES: Though a man can never tell for sure—

LOTTIE: No. Not you're daughter.

JES: A woman can tell a man anything.

LOTTIE: Shirley Temple. Get it?

JES: Shirly Temple Black.

LOTTIE: Shirley Temple in *The Blue Bird of Happiness.*

WILLY: Shirley-going-to-get-her-butt-beat-for-dancing-on-the-table-when-I-told-her-to-get-off-Temple.

(*Lottie gets off the table*)

JES: You may be Shirley but your hips are Monroe. Girl, you are getting as big as your mama.

LIZA (*voice off stage*): I know I'm not known for my cooking but this is a special occasion. I can feel it. (*Then*) Lottie, are you dressed yet? You're getting too big to run around with nothing on.

(*Lottie takes two nickels and drops them down the front of her slip and sticks out her chest*)

LOTTIE: TADA! They didn't fall down. Get it?

JES: Do you know another one?

LIZA (*voice off stage*): They'll be here any minute and if you're not dressed yet . . .

(*Jes takes a glass, puts it to Lottie's elbow, pumps her arm and the glass fills with milk*)

LOTTIE: How did you do that?

LIZA (*voice off stage*): Heard of a girl abducted, half naked from her own house . . .

(*Jes drinks the milk*)

LOTTIE: How?

LIZA (*voice off stage*): . . . never seen again.

JES: I'll tell you the secret when you get older.

LIZA (*voice off stage*): Found out later that it was a member of her own family.

LOTTIE: I don't want to ever grow up. Do you remember Shirley Temple in *The Blue Bird Of Happiness?*

JES: *The Blue Bird Of Happiness?* That's the one with Bill "Bojangles" Robinson. She used to do a lot of films with old Bojangles. He was one of the best tap dancers in the world. They attributed it to his big feet. What else can you do with feet that big? I heard he taught little Miss Shirley everything she knew about dancing. And how she loved to dance with her Bojangles. Sweet, black, big-footed Bojangles. Always smiling, both of them together—dancing and smiling—That's why they took him away.

LOTTIE: Who did?

JES: When they found out why they were always grinning—they dragged him away, kicking and cut off his—

WILLY: JES!

JES: His feet. Nigger with all that rhythm and no feet—what's he going to do?

LOTTIE: That's not funny, Uncle Jes.

JES: Bojangles didn't think it was funny either. Can't tap with your hands—though some have tried—just can't get the same kind of satisfaction.

(*We hear a round of firecrackers. Lottie runs to the window*)

WILLY: Damn Bean Eaters!

JES: Blow your hands off—Don't come crying to me.

WILLY: That's why we're moving.

JES: "Don't come crying to me." That's what they used to say.

WILLY: Lottie, get away from that window.

LOTTIE: It was so pretty. It shot straight up—a bright red ball and exploded in mid-air. It sprinkled down like rain. Red rain . . .

JES: "Blow you hands off . . ."

WILLY: I don't want you going out of this house today, Lottie.

LOTTIE: You never want me to go out.

WILLY: Damn neighborhood. BEAN EATERS—try to find any excuse for disturbing my peace of mind. (*To Lottie*) I don't want you to talk to them, touch them, look at them directly. (*Then*) That's why we're moving.

LOTTIE: When are we moving?

WILLY: Soon. Very soon. Leave everything behind. It's just going to be good things for my little blue bird. (*Tying up the box he has been filling*) Boxes. Everything I own, memories, conversations—in these boxes. S-h-i-t. Tombs. I've been sitting in the same spot, the exact same spot for the last twenty years and steadily progressing backwards. How can that be? This used to be my favorite shirt. What's left of it . . . rags . . . pieces of something else . . .

JES: Heard you got King Tut's tiara stashed away up in there.

WILLY: Maybe . . . but damn if I can remember which box.

JES: Ain't that the way it goes?

WILLY: One day real soon we're going to move—move forward—move out and get us a big mansion for my little blue bird. Sacrifices have been made and it's any moment now.

JES: People can't move forward without some sacrifices.

WILLY: Mortgages, loans, scraping, saving, hard work.

JES: Man knew from the beginning. While beating on their drums, and getting high on moo-loo juice—they dipped their bodies in monkey fat and danced—danced until the earth gave way to valleys. While praying to their gods they burned sacred offerings . . .

LIZA (*voice off stage*): Fried chicken . . . bar-b-que ribs . . . smoked ham . . .

JES: . . . the fatted calf, the lamb, the first born male, the virgin.

LOTTIE: Everybody is coming today. YANG YANG YANG YANG.

LIZA (*voice off stage*): . . . pickled pig's feet . . . ox tail stew . . . cow brain cheese . . . I know I'm not known for my cooking but I've really outdone myself today.

WILLY: She used to be able to cook.

LIZA (*voice off stage*): MMMMM. It smells good in here.

WILLY: That's why I married her.

LIZA (*voice off stage*): I don't want anyone peeping into my kitchen until I'm ready. You're going to be so proud.

WILLY: Every Friday and Saturday, this was before I proposed, she would lure me into her kitchen with a promise of a taste from her pot.

LIZA (*voice off stage*): Remember the things I used to fix for you, Willy? I'm feeling it again.

WILLY: Yes, Liza.

LIZA (*voice off stage*): You don't believe me, do you? Man doesn't believe anything until it's rolling around on his tongue. You'll see.

WILLY (*hopeful*): It is beginning to smell . . .

LOTTIE: I smell something.

JES: I'm hungry enough.

(*Willy picks up another bundle and exits*)

When we were growing up, we were so po'—our termites reported us to the better housing bureau. We were so po'—we'd wait until the lights went out and stole the left-overs from our rat's pantry. We were so po'—No, po' ain't funny, there is nothing funny about being po'—We were so po' that fourteen of us had to sleep in one bed while the rest slept on the floor—which was pretty difficult considering that we were so po'—we couldn't afford a house with indoor plumbing—so po' we lived in the outhouse. We lived in an outhouse so small that those sleeping on the floor were likely to fall into that hole if they weren't careful. Those sleeping on the floor learned to hold on to each other and the walls. But every once in awhile you would awaken in the middle of the night by a surprised echoing scream and you'd know another brother or sister had let go or was pushed and was lost in that bottomless stinky pit. They said that if you were lucky that you would fall straight to China. If you were lucky.—We were so po'—we had a dog once. We named him Lucky. He starved to death. Lucky—we ate him. I did keep a pet cockroach. He was as big as a dog. Named him Rex. Walked him on a leash. Ever try to teach a cockroach to roll over and play dead? Ever try to curb a roach? Which leg does he raise? Listen, Lottie—we were so Po'—we had to devour our own in order to survive. Do you know what c-a-n-n-i-b-u-l-l spells?

(*We hear firecrackers. Jes falls to the floor and convulses as if he were repeatedly shot. Willy re-enters, carrying another box*)

WILLY: Damn bean eaters.

LOTTIE (*watching Jes convulse*): Are you dead yet? Uncle Jes is such a riot.

JES (*finally*): Hear that?—'NAM.

LOTTIE: Were you in 'nam, Uncle Jes.

WILLY: That's why we're moving.

JES: The summer of '68. Hot, white beach. Beirut.

WILLY: You were never in Beirut. Shooting, killing, raping.

LOTTIE: That's what it's like in Beirut?

WILLY: This neighborhood. Bean eaters with their ghetto blasters and UZI's.

JES: If I wasn't in El Salvador—then—What happened to my hands?

(*Jes loses his hands up his sleeves and chases Lottie around the room—screaming*)

WILLY: The real-estate man said that we were buying into a good solid middle-class neighborhood. We moved in. The first on the block. Fine. A couple of families moved out. Fine. Next thing you know—another black family wants to move in. White flight. They flew. Mass Exodus. The next thing you know—any kind of nigger and his pit bull is moving in. Drug dealers, bean eaters and their pet cockroaches big enough to walk on leashes. If I wanted to buy into a ghetto—I would have never moved. This is not what was promised. Sacrifices have been made.

JES: When we were growing up, we were so po'—

WILLY: We were never poor. Yes, we had to struggle, but we were never poor. Anything worth anything is worth some sacrifice. Remember that, Lottie.

JES: We weren't poor. We were so po' we couldn't afford the extra o and r. Ever been to a all white beach in Alabama with a sign on it "No dogs or coloreds allowed."?

WILLY: . . . can he go in up to his knees . . .

LOTTIE: That's how it was in the old days?

WILLY: They don't have beaches in Alabama.

JES: 1968. Hot white beach. Alabama. He said, "Boy, what you doing on this here beach?" I said, "Boy? Who are you talking to?" And he and his friends took out these knives, long enough for shishkebobin' and he says, "I'm talking to you, nigger." And that is how I lost my hands down a white woman's bikini in Alabamy.

(*Jes loses his hands up his sleeves and chases Lottie—screaming—around the room*)

WILLY: First on the block.

JES: No, I've never been to Iraq.

WILLY: Should have been the last.

JES: But I know how it feels.

LIZA (*voice off stage—singing*):
There is a fountain filled with blood
Drawn from Emanuel's veins . . .

WILLY (*hopeful*): It's been a long time since I heard her singing in the kitchen.

(*We hear a knocking on the door*)

LOTTIE: Who's there?

PINKIE (*voice off stage*): The big bad wolf. Let me in.

LOTTIE: Not by the hair on my chinny, chin, chin.

PINKIE: Your chin, my ass. Girl, open this door.

(*Lottie opens the door and Pinkie enters. She is very pregnant*)

WILLY: Well look what the cat dragged in.

PINKIE: Boy, don't get started with me. I came here to celebrate, to have a good time. This time I'm going to have a nice time with my family. (*To Lottie*) Look at this girl, getting so healthy and fat. I see the bees done bit.

JES: You can't talk about getting fat . . .

PINKIE (*rubbing her belly*): . . . any minute now.

WILLY: What's the count up to now. Everytime I see you, you're pregnant. What do you do, Pinkie?

PINKIE: Well if you don't know—I'm not going to tell you.

JES: Where are the rest of them?

PINKIE: Left them at home. You know my kids . . .

WILLY: Wild and untamed.

PINKIE: I see you redecorated the place.

WILLY: We're moving any day.

PINKIE: I heard that before. When are we going to eat?

LOTTIE: You know how slow Mama is.

PINKIE: Ain't you fast. Why aren't you in there helping?

LOTTIE: She said that she didn't want any help.

(*We hear a crash of pots and dishes*)

PINKIE: Liza, are you alright in there?

LIZA (*voice off stage*): Pinkie!—I'm just fine. Everything is fine in here. Never mind me. Any minute, and we'll be feasting at a banquet.

PINKIE: Alright, then . . . (*Lower*) I hope you got a MacDonalds nearby. I'm hungry. My feet hurt and my back. (*She rubs her stomach*) I might name this one—Jessee.

WILLY: I don't want to hear it.

PINKIE: I didn't say nothing. Let me hush. But this one is going to turn out.

WILLY: Just like your other ones.

PINKIE: They just weren't inspired. They had it in them but they just weren't inspired.

WILLY: Where's little Lumumba?

PINKIE: Big Lumumba. He hasn't written to me in a long time.

WILLY: And coke-head Marion? Heard Eldridge went crazy—

PINKIE: He was a hyperactive child . . .

WILLY: Carmichael fled the country . . . George was in a shoot-out in prison.

PINKIE: He's dead. They were just born in the wrong time, is all. That's what I figure. The time wasn't right. Not for them. But this one by the time he gets through puberty . . . (*She notices Lottie staring at her belly*) You never seen a pregnant woman before? Do you want to rub my belly?

(*Lottie places her hands on Pinkie's stomach. Then, startled—Lottie jerks away*)

Don't be scared. That's just him saying hello. (*To her belly*) What's that? You saying, "Who's that rubbing on mama's belly?" That's your cousin, Lottie . . . no, you haven't met her before.

LOTTIE: He can hear you?

PINKIE: Of course he can. Talk to you too—if you want to get to know him better. He'll talk your ear off.

LOTTIE (*her head on Pinkie's belly*): I can hear him breathing.

WILLY: Unborn babies don't breath, Lottie.

PINKIE: Who are you—Dr. Spock? The girl knows what she hears.

LOTTIE: I think I can make out . . . . he's saying something . . . but it's too low.

PINKIE: He can be a bit soft-spoken.

WILLY: I may not be a pediatrician but most fetuses don't speak.

PINKIE: That's brilliant, Sherlock. Most don't. I think I'll name him X.

JES: X. I like that.

WILLY: First, Jessee and now—X. As far as I know Malcolm X died a long time ago. Just who are you claiming this child is by?

PINKIE: Do you really want to know? I didn't think so.

JES: X Semple. I like that.

PINKIE: Thank you.

WILLY: And how do you know it's going to be a boy.

PINKIE: How does every mother know?

WILLY: Oh, he told you.

PINKIE: He didn't have to—He isn't just kicking up in there . . . I can feel him. Three inch erections pounding against my womb, four or five times a day. That's how I know.

WILLY: Three inches! . . . four or five . . . PINKIE!

PINKIE: I suppose you're going to tell me that it's not possible. How would you know. You've never been pregnant.

WILLY: Why wife has and she never told me . . .

PINKIE: How would she know? The only child she had was a girl. X Semple. Finally, a manchild to do credit to this family.

WILLY: And what does that mean?

PINKIE: I mean, that not since our brother Sam, as stupid as he was, has there been a Semple man in this family worth the salt he pees.

WILLY: Wait a minute . . .

PINKIE: Let me hush. I came here to celebrate and have a good time with my family.

LOTTIE: I can feel it. It is a boy . . . daddy . . . it IS a boy!

WILLY: Lottie, take your hands off this second.

PINKIE: Yeah, that's him. Just humping away.

LOTTIE: I felt him!

WILLY: Didn't your mother tell you to go get dressed? Go get dressed, Lottie.

PINKIE (*rocking*): Um-um . . . that's my boy . . . mm-hmm.

(*Lottie relunctantly exits*)

Why do you want to send Lottie out, Willy. She's a woman now. There are things she needs to know. You always have been overprotective.

WILLY: She's still a child.

(*Lottie is in her room, dressing*)

LOTTIE: When the hens come home . . .

Sometimes the voices come from outside. My parents. At night I can hear them through the walls. Sometimes I hear the walls quaking, banging. Their voices rise and fall in arias. On the other side. Of the wall. The sheets flapping. Flapping above them. And the beating of bird wings against its bars.

In those mornings I sneak into their room. After they've risen. And search the room. The closets, between the bedcovers . . . searching for signs . . . feathers of the slaughtered birds. Sometimes I find a spot of blood and always the fresh smell of death.

Yang, yang, yang, yang, yang, yang, yang.

When the roosters come home? When the chickens . . . —What Pinkie's baby whispered in my ear . . .

Sometimes the voices come from outside. On the other side. Out there. Like low flying helicopters, their voices. One day—looking out. Three boys talking loud and throwing bottles against the wall. One was black as midnight. One with coiled snakes hissing all over his head. And the third tall and sinewy like a swaying palm. The first one saw me spying and smiled at me. His teeth glistened with gold.

Repunzel, Repunzel, let down your golden hair. And he climbed up to her ivory tower . . .

Sometimes the voices come from inside me. Clear as a bell.

She was a poor peasant girl and barely thirteen when she saw the visions and heard the voices that told her to pick up the shield and sword and march to . . . New Orleans?

One day my voices will tell me what and when. My voices will explode. The walls will be knocked down. And you'll see freedom flapping its wings and crowing. When the morning comes.

WILLY: Some things she doesn't need to know. Not now.

PINKIE: Then when?

WILLY: Some things she doesn't ever have to know about. Not like we knew them. No need. Some things she never needs to hear, see or touch.

PINKIE: No pain, no gain.

WILLY: The things we went through—I went through so she would never have to. I cherish her, protect her, fight for my destiny.

PINKIE: One day she'll have to learn to fight for herself. Locking her in her room isn't going to help. It's just going to make the lessons she's going to have to learn just that much harder.

WILLY: Yeah, you know all about it.

PINKIE: That's right. I have the proof of my life experience written all over my body. From stretch marks, to razor scars from a drunken lover . . . I still have the whelps on my back which were the gifts from our dear parents.

WILLY: Our parents never beat us.

PINKIE: That's how bad they beat you—BRAIN DAMAGE. You can't even remember. I remember—Mama tried to break my neck, one time.

WILLY: If only she had broken your tongue.

PINKIE: You know it's true.

WILLY: The only time our parents laid hand on us was in love.

PINKIE: They loved to lay hand on me, fist on me, extension cord . . . frying pan.

WILLY: It wasn't so bad. Though, there was this time when Daddy chased Jes with a baseball bat.

JES (*to audience*): Yeah, yeah . . . I gave him a good run. He was fast back then. I ran into the park and lost him around the lake.

WILLY: You had to come back home sometime.

PINKIE: Daddy sat patiently on the porch.

JES (*to audience*): For three days.

PINKIE: Three hours. Dinnertime, you came home.

WILLY: Slunk home with your tail tucked between your legs.

JES (*to audience*): He said, "Boy, are you ready?" "Yes, sir." "Then, get on in the house and let down the shades and then let down your pants."

PINKIE (*sarcastic*): They only laid hands on us in love.

JES (*to audience*): "This is going to hurt me more than you. I'm only starting what the MAN is going to finish."

WILLY (*to audience*): He always said that we couldn't afford to be lazy and undisciplined. That's what they expected from us. And he came down harder on us for living up to their expectations. That was the world. That's what I learned from the whuppings.

PINKIE (*to audience*): Your own will treat you as bad or worse than anyone else. That's what I learned.

WILLY: Pinkie . . .

PINKIE: Sam never got any licks.

JES: I sure do miss Sam.

WILLY: He was always the favorite.

PINKIE: He should have been. He was a saint, as stupid as he was.

WILLY: Like the time he fell out of the treehouse.

JES (*to audience*): . . . Some got lost down the hole . . .

PINKIE: Jes pushed him.

JES (*to audience*): He jumped.

PINKIE: I was in the house cleaning up after you lazy lunkheads, as usual, when I heard his scream. I never will forget it.

WILLY: I had gone to the candy shop and left Jes up in the tree house with little Sammy. I heard him five blocks away . . .

PINKIE: I ran to the back yard, yelling, "What's going on?," and there was little Sam lying flat on the ground.

JES: He just jumped.

PINKIE: And Jes was up in the tree house, looking down, laughing.

JES: I told him not to.

PINKIE: Just laughing your head off.

JES (*to audience*): We were playing—TARZAN—and he was cheetah. I lost my balance and the next thing I knew—he had flung himself off. He said something about wanting to cushion my fall. I told him not to.

PINKIE: Just laughing your head off.

WILLY: That was just like little Sam.

JES: Saigon.

PINKIE: He volunteered.

JES (*to audience*): I was a conscientious objector.

PINKIE: How was Canada?

JES: 1968. Hot, white beach. The Bahamas.

WILLY: One of my legs is longer than the other.

PINKIE: He was a real hero. Worth his salt. Stupid as mud, but a hero, just the same. Should have died for his country. What'd he die for? Should have been blown to bits on some land mine, fighting someone else's battle. Instead of . . . What did he die for? (*Silence*) Don't look at me like that. You're the one with all this stuff. (*Indicates box marked "SAM"*) Look at this. What's in here?

WILLY: Don't start stirring things up, Pinkie. Everything's packed down and ordered . . .

PINKIE (*in Sam's box*): His football trophy, basketball trophy, baseball . . . track . . . varsity jacket, honor roll pin, medals of honor, dog tags, pieces of a uniform . . . (*Cradling the rag*) Wasn't enough of him to piece together for a decent funeral.

WILLY: This isn't the time, Pinkie.

PINKIE: When? When, then? What did our brother die for?

WILLY: Too late now to look back. Time now to look to the future.

PINKIE: Keep your eyes on the prize . . . And what a sweet cracker jack prize you got. Big old house, two car garage, a fence for them junkies outside to lean up on . . . and now your moving to a bigger, brighter, whiter neighborhood. Leave all us po' dunk Negroes behind. You and Marva. Especially Marva, living fat.

WILLY: Everyone got theirs. You grabbed your share with both hands.

PINKIE: My children were hungry—

WILLY: Weren't we all. Enough said.

PINKIE: Let me hush.

JES: All of that is past and done. Let it go. Spit it out like a old woman's dried up tiddy. No use sucking on that. Set your teeth on the futures firm sweet breast.

(*We hear a clear sweet bell. A light comes up on Lottie in her room. Then*)

Look at this—Aunt Celine's iron, Great-grandma Semple's quilt . . .

PINKIE: My first baby carriage . . .

JES: Uncle Matt's lucky horse shoe . . . Lola Ann's straightening comb . . . Shaka Zulu's spear, I expect. And these . . . (*Holding up shackles*) You're taking these?

WILLY: I'll sort things out once we get there.

(*Lottie enters in a white dress*)

LOTTIE: We are gathered here today, though everyone isn't here yet . . .

PINKIE: I hope that Marva, heifer, doesn't show.

LOTTIE: . . . to celebrate the death of—

PINKIE: BIRTH.

LOTTIE: . . . to celebrate the birth of the King. "His life was the manna that fed the soul weary masses." I read that in a book.

JES (*overlapping*): K-A-N-I-B- . . . I may not be able to spell it—but I know what it means.

LOTTIE: I don't remember the King, I wasn't born back then, but from the films in schools. I saw the marches and the people in dashikis and 'fros, carrying signs and singing those old negro spirituals. Those were the days of the King, of Camelot, when legendary heroes arose. Women like Angela . . . Angela . . . something . . . Angela and her brothers in prison . . . Soledad. Angela Soledad.

PINKIE: Angela DAVIS.

LOTTIE: Angela Davis? Angela Davis and her sister, Patricia Lumumba.

PINKIE (*remembering, longingly*): PATRICE Lumumba was a man.

LOTTIE: It reminds me of when we studied that French woman who fought alongside her brothers and she heard voices and bells and was burned at the stake for her beliefs.

JES: A steak sounds good. I'm hungry.

LIZA (*voice off stage*): Any minute now we'll be sitting at the table. The day of feasting has arrived.

LOTTIE: And the King and his knights sat around the table . . .

PINKIE: What knights?

JES: Ku, Klux and Klan.

LOTTIE: Jackson, and Bond, and Young Andrew the lion-hearted . . .

PINKIE: And Toto and Dorothy flew over the cuckoo's nest . . . Willy, I told you to let this girl grow up.

LOTTIE: In the days of Camelot there came forth a king whose holy quest took him to the mountaintop. And he looked over to the other side and heard the voices and visions which he brought back to his people. He brought to them a dream. But before he could lead them to the promised land, he died. But "his life was the manna that fed the soul weary masses."

(*Blackout*)

Scene 3

We hear voices in the BLACKOUT.

VOICES (*overlapping and repeating*): YANG YANG YANG YANG. YANG YANG YANG.

It is a far, far better thing I do than I have ever done before.
All for one and one for all . . .
Ungawa!
Kings are not born: they are made of universal hallucination.
Fight the power.
Free Mandela.
Viva Zapata.
Remember the Soledad Seven.
I have a dream.

(*Voices are drowned out by bells. Spotlight comes up on Jes*)

JES: I'm not bitter. I'm not hostile, I'm not angry. I'm not going to sneak into your house at night and slit your throat.

I'm Jes Semple. I like white people. There are two kinds of white people. The kind-hearted liberals who subscribe to the Village Voice, Jet Magazine, and Town and Country. And then there are those that still believe that Gerry Cooney is the Great White Hope. Not that white folk can't fight. But you put a black man who's either consciously or unconsciously aware of his over one-hundred years of oppression, in the ring with a white man and he's going to beat the shit out of that white man. And he's getting paid for it, too. Just as if you put a Latino male in the ring, he's going to beat the shit out of that white man and depending on what oppressed dictatorial regime he might have come from—he'll give that black man a good whupping too. You take an American Indian—and this is the fight I personally want to see—he'll beat the shit out of all of them . . . with his hands tied behind his back . . . blind folded.

I'm not bitter, I'm not hostile, I'm not angry. Call me Jes Semple.

(*Lottie enters the spotlight, laughing*)

LOTTIE: You're so funny, Uncle Jes.

JES: Come here, my sweet naive. Let Uncle Jes whisper in your ear.

(*Lottie goes over to Jes and he begins whispering in her ear. She laughs and laughs and laughs*)

LOTTIE: Oh, stop Uncle . . . oh, don't, stop . . . oh . . . oh . . . (*Lottie laughs until she cries . . . Blackout*)

Scene 4

Lights come up on living room. Mama Pearl has entered and takes center stage. Lottie is at the window watching Papa Tommy. Everyone else is in their usual positions.

PEARL: I started out as a singer. Most of my first engagements were in the cotton fields. I was a healthy alto. I could sing. I can't anymore. (*Tries singing*) Brighten the corner where you are . . .

You could hear me a mile away. They used to call me Big Mouth.

LOTTIE: He's wearing a bow-tie! He just got into the gate.

PEARL: Then I started sneaking to Bubba's at night—singing the blues, yeah. I was my mama's only child and this man says to me "Girl, you sound good. Let me take you to Louisiana with me." I was sixteen at the time or was I fifteen . . . . His name was Floyd. A piano player. He said, "Girl, you can be a great singer. Come on with me." And I said that I would first have to ask my mama.

LOTTIE: He's up to the garden.

PEARL: That morning I told mama that I could become a great singer if she would just let me go with Floyd to Louisiana. Don't you know that woman played those evil blues upside my head, that I will never forget. First, for sneaking out at night. Second, for wanting to sing that nasty, evil, low-down blues. Thirdly, for hanging around shiftless lazy musicians—My daddy was a musician and had run out on mama and me for some no account, hulley-gulley gal. And lastly, for wanting to leave her alone—me, being her only child. She beat me for seven days and seven nights.

LOTTIE: He's past the zinnias.

PEARL: After she finished beating me, she was so tired, she went to sleep. While she slept, I packed my things and took the next bus to Louisiana. I caught up with Floyd and we teamed up. We called ourselves—Big Mouth and Ivory. We toured Mississippi, Virginia, Florida and all the way up to Chicago. That's where I met your Daddy. A tap dancing fool. Talk about some quick pepper feet! As big-footed as that man is, it's amazing how fast he could move them. I met him in this club and I said, "Hey, fool, where you learn to dance like that?" He said that he knew how to tap before he learned to walk. Shoot, people remember Bojangles, The Hines Brothers, Sammy Davis . . . Sandman . . . your Daddy was the best.

LOTTIE: He's stopped.

PEARL: I quit Floyd and teamed up with your Daddy. Big Mouth Pearl and Mr. Pepper Feet. We went to New York in '41 or '42.

LOTTIE: He's taking off his hat and pulling out a handkerchief.

PEARL: '41. We were in love. He said that he loved me more than anything in the world and that was good enough for me. So we got married and the same night we debuted at the Apollo.

LOTTIE: He's wiping his head and looking around.

PEARL: Mama wrote to tell me that she was coming up to see the fool I had married.

LOTTIE: He's at the foot of the steps.

WILLY: Maybe I should help him up.

PEARL: Let him be. He said he didn't need any help, the fool. (*Continuing*) I met her at the train station and she beat me over the head with her suitcase. "When I woke up that morning you were gone." She moved in with us and prayed for our souls every night we went on stage.

LOTTIE: He's on the second step.

PEARL: I got pregnant with Marva, swell up so bad, I was laid up in bed. Tommy was tapping at the Cotton Club and packing them in. Mr. Pepper Feet.

LOTTIE: He's still on the second step.

PEARL: He felt it would help the act if he had a partner. I was laid up in bed. So he hired this stringy-haired skinny gal by the name of Lola.

(*There is knocking on the door. Lottie opens the door and an ancient, shuffling, Tommy enters*)

WILLY: Come on in. How are you, pop?

TOMMY: Umm-hmmm. Ummm-hmm.

JES: Let me rub your head for luck, old man.

TOMMY: Rub my butt.

PINKIE (*offering a seat*): Sit over here.

TOMMY: Naw.

(*He continues his slow shuffle, flapping walk past Pinkie and sits on the box labeled—SAM*)

PEARL: She thought she was cute—that skinny hulley-gulley child.

(*Tommy wheezes and laughs*)

Yeah, you know who I'm talking about. Lola. And she sure was LOW, wasn't she? Mr. Pepper Feet.

TOMMY (*enjoying himself*): Dem was de days.

PEARL: Yes they were. Living in a two-room, heatless apartment with a evil mother, laid up in bed swollen to the size of a cow, and you tap dancing at the Cotton Club with LOW-LA.

TOMMY: Yowsah, yowsah, yowsah.

PEARL: I was singing them Saint Louis Blues . . . Blue as I can be . . .

TOMMY: Dat de way. Yo' Moms was a sanging fool. Bi' Mouf . . .

PEARL: Big Mouth and Mr. Pepper feet.

TOMMY: De Apollo—19 and 40-somethin' . . .

PEARL: I told them already.

TOMMY: '41. And de Cot-tone Club.

PEARL: And LOW-LA.

TOMMY: Yowsah, yowsah, dem was de days. (*Then*) I gots to pee.

PEARL: Who's stopping you?

TOMMY: Woman, I's tie-ud.

PEARL: And I's a bony-backed mule.

WILLY: I'll take him, Ma.

PEARL: When did he become *your* husband?

(*She stands, wide-legged in front of him and squats so that he can climb on her back*)

PINKIE: Mama, you're going to break your back.

PEARL: It'd take more than this fool to break my back.

TOMMY (*as they exit UR*): Can't you go no fast-uh?

PEARL: Man, don't you pee on me.

WILLY: Mama, I'll take him.

PEARL: I can take him.

WILLY: I'll take him.

TOMMY: Bony back 'oman, let he take me. You too slow.

PEARL: Gone, take him. The fool.

(*Willy and Tommy exit*)

Calling somebody a bony-backed woman. That's the second time. We couldn't find a parking spot in front of the house. Too many people out front running back and forth. I parked a block away. Started walking with him on my back. His feet ain't any good anymore. He know. He called me a bony-backed woman. Said I was too slow. You talk about somebody bony . . . Lola was bony. She was the skinniest thing I'd ever seen. The only thing big on her was her knees. She was so skinny you could thread her through the eye of a needle except for them knees. She was as skinny as a tooth pick. Looked like somebody has used her to clean the junk from between their teeth. She wasn't that clean. Always smelled of that toilet of Paris. She smelled like she poured that stuff all over herself to hide the fact that she didn't bathe regular. It must have gotten pretty funky up there on stage with her. Especially doing them highkicks. They must have smelled her all the way in the back row balcony. She was a skinny, musty-smelling hulley-gulley gal. That was a long time ago. I don't know why I'm thinking about her now for. Haven't thought of her in a long time.

PINKIE: Didn't Marva buy dad a motorized wheelchair, Mama?

PEARL: You know your Father. He doesn't go for them new fangled electicized contraptions. He didn't want to sit in it. He didn't want to sit comfortable in somebody's electric chair and then get fried and served up with mashed potatoes and cornbread. He said—What did God make strong backed womens for? I have lost a few extra pounds but my back is still strong. We all have our crosses to bear. And as long as I'm able . . .

PINKIE: All I'm saying is that you shouldn't have to carry a grown man on your back.

PEARL: I didn't have to bear five big-headed children and raise them up. But I did. I didn't have to buy you new clothes and shoes while I wore the same Sears and Roebuck dress that I patched for twelve years and stuff my shoes with newspaper. But I did. I didn't have to take an extra job scrubbing floors at the Sheridan Hotel at night scraping knees on the tiles so you could get your teeth fixed and get you that saxophone you begged me for and then played it once, deciding that you'd rather take up bongos. But I did. Who stayed up with you all night wiping your snotty nose and giving you mustard compresses to ease the fever when you had the flu? Changed your diaper and gave you my tiddy when you were a bawling baby girl. Not that I'm complaining. You do what you are able, to provide the best for your family. Your Daddy ain't heavy. Compared to the burdens I've had to shoulder in my lifetime—He's light. When are you getting married?

PINKIE: Who said anything about getting married?

PEARL: That baby sitting in your belly. I swear, Pinkie, you should give at least one of your children a name.

PINKIE: All mine have names.

PEARL: Your Daddy told me that he loved me more than anything in the world and that was good enough for me. None of my children had to wonder where they came from.

PINKIE: Nobody has to wonder about mine. The truth is . . .

WILLY: Hush now, Pinkie.

PINKIE: Let me hush. I came here to have a nice time. Let me close my mouth. My child will speak for me, one day. I'm quiet, now.

PEARL: I've been with one man for over fifty years. Promised to love only me to the day he died. None of mine had to wonder.

PINKIE: Let me hush.

(We hear a clamor of voices outside: "hungry"—"I'm hungry," "Spare some change . . . ," "I want a VCR, a porsche, and chicken in every pot . . . ," "I feel hungry . . ." "My children need food." . . . Then a rapid knocking at the door)

MARVA *(voice off stage)*: Let me in . . . please, open the door.

(Willy grabs a baseball bat and opens the door. Marva rushes in. She looks like a white woman with heavy makeup and disheveled but expensive clothes)

PEARL: Marva, what happened?

MARVA: They tried to kill me . . . they were going to kill me. Three black boys. They surrounded me at my car. Pulling at my purse . . . my hair . . . my hair . . . my suit. Calling me names. They don't know me. They don't know who I am. Calling me out of my name. Who the hell are they. Who do they think they are. No count, worthless . . . my hair . . . my suit . . . my car.

WILLY *(re-enters)*: Scattered like rats. That's why we're moving. This isn't what was promised.

MARVA: They tried to kill me. They shot at me.

LOTTIE: Fire-crackers.

PINKIE: No one bothered me when I came up.

MARVA: Well, I guess they wouldn't bother you.

PINKIE: And what do you mean by that?

PEARL: Marva didn't mean anything by that. You've always been so high strung, Pinkie.

MARVA: I didn't mean anything by that, surely.

PINKIE: Surely, let me close my mouth.

PEARL: Let me look at you. What'd they do to my baby, my bright morning star . . . oh . . . (*Surveying and smoothing out the damage*)

MARVA: It was terrible, Mama. And I wanted to look especially nice for this occasion—my nails . . .

PEARL: Mama kiss it. All well again—see.

(*Pearl kisses her hands and face. Marva laughs. They hug*)

MARVA: Jonathan couldn't make it today—he was on call. He sends his regards.

JES: How is Dr. Hatchet?

PEARL: Now, Jes . . . Never mind him. One child crazier than the other. But he's crazy that's for sure. Always has been, always will be. But the lord never gives you more than you can handle and sometimes he sweetens the pot. (*To Marva*)—My chocolate drop, on the cover of Essence Magazine this month, and once again voted Black Woman of the Year. I save the articles, put them in the scrapbook . . .

WILLY: I was voted manager of the month . . . gave me a plaque with my name on it.

PEARL: And your eyes—hazel?

MARVA: Blue.

PEARL: You looked so beautiful on the cover of Jet Magazine.

MARVA: That was the first cover I did.

PEARL: That was back when you looked like Dianne Carol. Then for Ebony you looked more like Diana Ross.

MARVA: Before Diana Ross looked like Diana Ross.

PEARL: By the time she did Vogue she looked like a young Lena Horne.

MARVA: That was around my sixth operation. And I had just started the chemical peels. They burn away the darker outer layers . . . the nerve endings become so sensitive that you can't touch or be touched. They wrap you in a cocoon until you heal.

PINKIE: When you were little, they used to call you tar-baby. Big lipped, flat nosed, tar-baby, remember?

MARVA: I remember.

PEARL: My daughter was named "The Black Woman of the Year," three years in a row.

MARVA: I take pride in setting a standard.

PEARL: And married herself a doctor.

PINKIE: Who burned, tucked, cut and sucked all the black out of you years ago.

UNISON: HUSH PINKIE.

PINKIE: Let me hush.

TOMMY (*voice off stage*): Gits me off dis shit house.

WILLY: I'll get him. (*Willy exits*)

MARVA: And how is Father?

PEARL: You know your Father . . .

TOMMY (*voice off stage*): OOOHHH, Lordy . . . de pain, de pain, de pain o' him-roids.

MARVA: Have you thought of a home?

PEARL: He's got a home.

LOTTIE (*she's been looking out the window*): Sometimes I sneak out and give them things. The homeless. I give them handouts. Leftovers . . . bread, rice, beans . . . fruit to their children. Dried fruit keeps longer. Raisins.

JES: Next thing you know—they'll want a seat at the table.

LOTTIE: It makes me sad to see them. We can spare a little.

(*Willy enters carrying Tommy*)

WILLY: We don't have enough to feed the whole damn neighborhood . . .

MARVA (*adjusting her face*): Of course we do contribute to various charities . . . SAVE THE POOR . . . UNICEF . . .

WILLY: The whole crippled, mangy-assed breed. They're no kin to me.

MARVA: . . . The Negro College Fund . . . NAACP . . .

WILLY: They're no kin to me.

MARVA: I'm a life member of the NAACP.

LOTTIE: Some live in subway tunnels . . . the children . . . I give them raisins . . . they give me smiles . . .

WILLY: I pay taxes so welfare mothers can sit at home watching the VCR . . .

MARVA: Just last year we adopted a boy from Honduras and a girl from Ethiopia. They're in the finest boarding schools in Europe. The question is "What is to be done?" and "When have we done enough?"

TOMMY (*looking at Marva*): Who is you?

MARVA: Who am I? I'm your daughter, Father.

TOMMY: Youse ain't mine.

MARVA: I'm not yours? I'm your daughter, Marva, Father.

PEARL: Your eldest girl.

TOMMY: Eldest? Cain't be mine. Naw, uh-uh, cain't be mine.

LIZA (*voice off stage*): All that's left is the garnish and then I'm done. Set the table everyone . . . the day of feasting has arrived.

UNISON: HALLELUJAH!

(*Everyone begins to set the table, finding table cloth, dishes and silverware amoung the rubble*)

LOTTIE: We are gathered here today to celebrate the birthday of Rev. Martin Luther King.

MARVA: I was there. 1963. The march on Washington.

WILLY: I had to work that day.

MARVA: Thousands of us walking hand in hand to the great lawn. Reverend Martin Luther King uttered his famous speech. He was a beautiful orator. Black as coals. In the heat of the revolution. America had lost its innocence—our sons were in a foreign land fighting strange battles for causes we couldn't understand. This was before the assassinations. Before LBJ threw up his hands and wept. Before the fall of Nixon, the peanut farmer, the movie star, and the lessons of Bush tactics. Back when America lost its first blush, King spoke of a vision, a dream. In the midst of the bombings and fires he spoke of his vision of the future. They killed the man but his memory burns on in an eternal flame. His dream burns on in the minds of the survivors. In those frightful days, America lost its innocence in the jaws of the revolution. (And with that thought some might argue that it was our innocence that fed the revolution.) Point taken. And with the devouring of that innocence came hope. Reverend Martin Luther King Jr. had a dream. And he passed that dream on in a voice that rang out to us all on that fateful day. And on that day we were all brothers and sisters . . . in that moment in time we were all family and holding hands. White man, Black man, Gentile, Jew, Arab, Indian . . . I remember sitting on that great lawn and listening to a man, a king as he cast bread upon the waters. And we sang WE SHALL OVERCOME . . .

UNISON:

WE SHALL OVERCOME
WE SHALL OVERCOME SOME DAY
DEEP IN MY HEART
I DO BELIEVE
WE SHALL OVERCOME SOME DAY.

(*Humming as . . .*)

PINKIE: Yes, I remember that day. I was there. I can still hear his voice. Our dream was one. It was as if he was speaking only to me, looking only at me. He knew he was going to die. The death threats were common knowledge. Who would carry on his dream? Rev. Abernathy had told me to come to the motel (*humming stops*) that night and I could meet him, speak with him . . .

UNISON: Hush, now, Pinkie.

PINKIE: It had always been my dream to conceive a child that would lead his people . . .

UNISON: Lies . . . that's enough . . . Hush!

PINKIE: And that night with the revolution burning in my thighs . . . (*H/*)* you know it's the truth . . . (*H/*) I laid down . . . (*H/*) the truth will set you free . . . (*H/*) when I laid down . . .

UNISON (*overlapping*): HUSH! HUSH! HUSH!

(*They sing again WE SHALL OVERCOME—with fervor as Willy, Marva, and Pearl tie Pinkie up and tape her mouth. Willy places her in a box. Song stops at . . . I DO BELIEVE*)

PEARL: She always was high-strung.

* (*H/*) indicates UNISON: HUSH!

MARVA: Fantasies . . . .

PEARL: I always told her to settle down. No telling who all those children of hers are by.

(*Willy tapes up the box and labels it*)

No telling.

TOMMY: I's just regusted.

PEARL: I cried when Kennedy died. I don't pay any attention to all that sluttish gossip. I don't care what anybody says . . . I cried when King died. (*At Tommy*) Lord, seems like he takes the good ones early.

TOMMY: Where's Sambo.

MARVA: Who?

TOMMY: Li'l black Sambo. Now he could dance. Only one of my chirren who could feel it. Feel where he come from.

PEARL: You know he's dead, Tommy. Been dead for a while now.

MARVA: Sam.

TOMMY: That's right. Mmm-hmmm—he was good. Mmm-hm. Lip-smacking good seved up with them pancakes.

MARVA: What?

TOMMY: Pancakes. With pancakes. That's how we ate 'im.

LOTTIE (*laughing*): Pancakes and Aunt Jemimah's syrup.

WILLY: Shut up.

LOTTIE: But, Dad, it's just a joke—get it?

WILLY: Go to your room.

LOTTIE: You can't send me to my room for the rest of my life—

WILLY: Shut up. Shut him up.

MARVA: He's just an old man, talking out of his head. Sam had a proper funeral. Just close your ears child.

JES: Though there wasn't enough of him to piece together for a decent funeral.

PEARL: He was the one that wanted to be cremated.

LOTTIE: SAMBO! PANCAKES—FRIED . . .

WILLY: SHUT UP. This is not the time to get into this. This is not the time.

PEARL: It was an accident. He's the one that bought the insurance.

JES: Blow your hands off. Don't come crying to me.

MARVA: It was declared by the authorities as an accidental death.

JES: Don't come crying to me.

WILLY: Not murder. Not suicide.

JES: We each got a piece.

TOMMY: Leg, thigh, wings . . .

PEARL: He was a saint.

LOTTIE: You're joking, right? Aren't you?

JES: Some got more than others.

MARVA: We all got the same inheritance. Some used it more wisely than others.

JES: Life insurance.

WILLY: For the lives of our children.

TOMMY: Paid in blood. Still gnawing on his bones.

MARVA: He was cremated.

JES: What was left of him.

TOMMY: Burnt offerings.

LOTTIE (*covering her ears and singing loud*): Yang yang yang yang yang yang yang yang . . .

(*Pause*)

MARVA (*pulls up her face*): How do you put up with it, Mother.

PEARL: Put up with what?

MARVA (*at Tommy*): Him.

PEARL: That's your pa, Marva.

WILLY: He's our Father.

MARVA: I'm the one that's called to pay the bills when he needed the new kidney, the bladder operation . . . the hip joint . . . the gallstone operation . . . the bypass . . . the new teeth . . . You're trying to tell me that what's left of him is my father . . . this babbling, illiterate, incoherent, shuffling, head-scratching, dinosaur used to be my father but ceased to exist with Amos and Andy reruns. Yet he attaches himself to our hems as we drag him into the next century and we're supposed to continue to pay tribute by calling him Father. (*Breaking*) You can't be my . . . oh . . . Daddy . . . (*Sits on his lap*) Dad . . .

TOMMY (*low*): Bastid. (*Pushes her out of his lap*) And ya'll BASTIDS. Cain't be mine. (*Getting up*) No ridim. No ridim. Cain't be mine. Uh-uh . . .

PEARL: Calm yourself.

TOMMY: Damn Bastids. Git outta my way. Yeah, I feel it. Feelin' it. (*Begins to tap*) Dat de way. Uh-huh. Dat de way. Dem was de days. (*His whole body comes to life*) Yowsah. Dem was de days. All uh God's niggah chirren had ridim. Yeah. Dat de way, yowsah. Day knew where it come from. Day could feel it. Don't feel nothin', now. But I ain't dead . . . I ain't dead . . . naw suh . . . (*He taps faster and faster then drops*)

PEARL: Tommy . . . Tommy . . .

TOMMY (*whispering*): Dem . . . was . . . de . . . days . . . Pepper Feet . . . and (*clutches his heart*) Lo . . . la.

PEARL: Lola? Lola? (*Shaking his lifeless body*) I'll kill him . . . I'll kill him.

MARVA (*trying to keep her face from falling apart*): He's dead. He's dead . . .

(*Willy gently places Tommy in a box, tapes the box and labels it. Lottie covers her eyes*)

JES (*to Lottie*):

What happens to a dream deferred?
Does it fester like a sore and then run
Does it stink like rotten meat
Or sugar over like a syrupy sweet
Does it sag like a heavy load—

LOTTIE (*uncovering eyes*):

JES: Or does it explode?

(*We see smoke coming from the kitchen*)

LIZA (*voice off stage, hysterically repeating*): Everything is fine. I don't need any help. Soups on.

(*Smoke billows from the kitchen as everyone runs in . . .*)

EVERYONE: Water, more water . . . Save that turkey . . . etc. . . .

PINKIE (*voice from box*): What's going on out there. Somebody let me out. I came to celebrate.

(*Lottie hearing Joan of Arc bells, she runs out the front door to the clamoring masses*)

LOTTIE (*as she exits, singing—*): YANG YANG YANG YANG . . .

(*Marva enters from kitchen trying to fix her face which has melted to one side*)

MARVA: I don't know what else I can do here.

PINKIE (*voice from box*): OH! I feel him . . . OH . . .

MARVA: Lottie! Lottie!

(*Outside, we hear gunshots. Pearl enters from the kitchen and lays herself across Tommy's box. A huge bone is thrown through the window shattering the glass, as* . . .)

PINKIE (*voice from box*): He's coming . . . Jesus . . . Jesus . . . Jesus . . . HE'S COMING!

(*Blackout.*)

Scene 5

Spot light up on Jes.

JES (*he's eating a whole pie*): You can only slice an apple pie so many times. Somebody is always going to go home hungry.

Scene 6

The room is cleared except for a few boxes—including those labeled LINEN, STEREO, PINKIE, MA, PA, AND MARVA. Liza sits in the living room wrapped in gauze from head to toe. Lottie sits, her white dress ragged, soiled and bloodstained.

WILLY: Signed the papers. Ha. Ha. Highland Hills. This is the open door we've been waiting for. That step into the future. My little blue bird's future. We're moving.

(*Willy picks up a box and exits outside. Lottie gets up on the table and begins to do a lewd grind-dance*)

LOTTIE (*singing, bitterly*): YANG YANG YANG YANG. YANG YANG YANG.

(*Willy re-enters*)

LIZA (*voice in bandages*): Don't forget my good china.

WILLY: Yes, Liza.

(*Willy picks up a small box next to Pinkie's box—As he exits—he stops, measures its weight and then curiously shakes it. Sound of baby crying comes from within. Spotlight up on Jes—he puts on a record—and watches Lottie's dance. We hear a recording of MLK*)

MLK: Today I want to tell the city of Selma, today I want to say to the state of Alabama, today I want to say to the people of America and the nations of the world: We are not about to turn around. We are on the move now. Yes, we are on the move and no wave of racism can stop us. The burning of our churches will not deter us. The bombing of our homes will not dissuade us. The beating of our clergymen and young people will not divert us. The arrest and the release of known murderers will not discourage us. We are on the move now. Like an idea whose time has come, not even the marching of mighty armies can halt us. We are moving to the land of freedom.

(*Lottie's dance becomes a stomp shuffle stomp. She picks up spear and continues her warrior dance which evolves into a summation out of space and time evoking spirits past and present from child to woman*)

MLK: . . . However difficult the moment, however frustrating the hour, it will not be long because the truth crushed to the earth will rise again.

LOTTIE: HOW LONG?

MLK: Not long because the arc of the moral universe is long but it bends towards justice.

LOTTIE: HOW LONG?

MLK: Not long, because mine eyes have seen the glory of the coming of the Lord.

LOTTIE: HOW LONG?

(*Blackout. End of play.*)

THE VALENTINE FAIRY

Ernest Thompson

Ernest Thompson

The Valentine Fairy was first performed at Alice's Fourth Floor, in New York City on February 13, 1993, and was directed by Suzanne Brinkley with Rudyard played by Steve Foster and Ingrid by Coco McPherson. Most of us know Ernest Thompson, however, because of his earlier work, especially *On Golden Pond.* That play which was voted Best Play by the Broadway Drama Guild, was made into a hugely successful movie which won The Academy Award for the Best Screenplay Adaptation. Other plays by Mr. Thompson include *The West Side Waltz* (produced on Broadway starring Katherine Hepburn), *A Sense of Humor* (starring Jack Lemmon), *The One About the Guy in the Bar, Human Beings, The Playwright's Dog, Amazons in August* and *Murdering Mother.*

Mr. Thompson has shared his playwriting talent with screen writing and screen directing. He directed in 1969 *Sweet Hearts Dance,* and his upcoming projects include *The Lies Boys Tell* (adapting and directing), *The West Side Waltz* (starring Olympia Dukakis), *The Love Line* and *Rip Your Heart Out.*

Mr. Thompson resides in New Hampshire with his wife, architect Kristie Lanier, and their three children: Heather, Danielle, and August.

Characters:

INGRID

RUDYARD

Scene:

In a New York apartment, defined mostly by its over-eager effort to conform to too many fashions, sits Rudyard, a curious man of 40 dressed in a blue leotard and red slippers and white gloves and lacy skirt, and a rumpled red hat and several days' growth of beard. He thumbs through a worn notebook, checks a slide projector at his feet, checks his appearance. Ingrid bursts in, raging in a New York accent. 30, hard, lovely, furious, weepy. She throws a box of chocolates on the table, yanks off her coat and boots.

INGRID: Fucking men. Fucking men! Who thought them up anyway? The experiment's over, it didn't work! (*She opens a window, climbs up, looking as if she's going to jump*)
Misogynist! Misanthrope! Mis . . . representer. Mister Potato Head! God, I wish I could piss out the window. That's the one thing they've got over us. (*She turns away, picks up the box*) Candy. 10 years of Jane Be Like Me Be Like Me, I'm Anorexic Fonda . . . (*She throws it down, kicks it*) . . . half my life on the Somalian Rice Diet and he gives me candy! Let's just send Betty Ford a bottle of Jack Daniels. (*She sits by it*) I should eat it, I should *eat* the candy and weigh a thousand pounds. (*Shouting*) Is that what you would like, a female manatee for a girlfriend? (*She pokes in the box*) It's a good way to pick out the peanut ones anyway. (*She tries one*) I suppose that's supposed to taste good. Oh, God, that tastes good. (*She spits it out*) Ecch, puke, Alien! What am I doing? (*Squeezing her stomach*) I'm already Roseanne Arnold! I've got Barbara Bush Disease. (*She starts to cry*)

RUDYARD (*singing softly*): You are so beautiful . . . to me.

INGRID (*she screams*): Acch! Who are you? Don't hurt me!

RUDYARD: I'm the Valentine Fairy.

INGRID: Go away! I'm warning you. I have my period! And I'm pregnant, so forget it! I couldn't let you even if I wanted to . . . who?

RUDYARD: The Valentine Fairy. (*He smiles*)

INGRID: Oh? I'm Princess Di. Haven't seen old Big Ears, have you?

RUDYARD: You're Ingrid Paloma, you're 31 years old and you work for Fat Cat Advertising. And you're lonely and you're blue.

INGRID: You don't know that. You don't know anything about me.

RUDYARD (*checking his notes*): You gave your boss a hand job, that was dumb.

INGRID: Get out of here! Go! I have a gun!

RUDYARD (*again the notes*): It's not registered. That's illegal.

INGRID: Who cares if it's registered? I'll get it, I swear to God, and I'll shoot your face off.

RUDYARD: Oh, boy, I wish you wouldn't. It's so not me. You could try one of the Veterans' Day fairies, they love guns.

INGRID (*a new tack*): Look. You just go and I won't tell anybody you were here, I won't report you or anything. I'll even lend you my coat so you don't get arrested for impersonating Elton John.

RUDYARD: Well, that's very pleasant of you, but I have a job to do.

INGRID: What job?

RUDYARD: To bring a little love into your heart. To make you believe once again in the power and the glory and the beauty of Ingrid.

INGRID (*scowling at him*): My mother put you up to this. She's not normal. She has used like *tankers* of hair dye in her life, nobody knew. Magenta, tangerine, aqua. And now she tends to . . . tangentalize. In addition to being almost completely bald.

RUDYARD (*he smiles, setting up the projector*): I thought about being a Mother's Day fairy, but I wasn't cut out for it. I like to be able to win a few rounds now and then.

INGRID: Excuse me. Do you mind? Was I evicted or is this still my apartment? What is that?

RUDYARD: This is a slide projector. You're young, aren't you? Earlier generations were required to sit still for hours and watch one another's slides of the Grand Canyon and graduation and disturbing photographs of people they did not know looking uncomfortable. It was a blip in the evolutionary process.

INGRID: You're going to show me slides?

RUDYARD: Yes, sorry. All the young guys have gone computer. VCRs, laser discs, all very impressive. But it's not me. I'm a Bell and Howell man and proud of it. Could you get the lights?

INGRID: You're not listening to me. Hello? You know why? Because even though—and I'm not asking questions—you're wearing a tutu, you're still one more major big dumb dick of a man.

RUDYARD: Well, aren't you kind? What I really am is in something of a hurry, I don't mean to be rude. This is my night, you know. I don't think you'd sit around arguing with Santa Claus.

INGRID (*dubious, facetious, but softening*): What's wrong with Cupid? I thought Valentines was like his . . . bailiwick.

RUDYARD: Cupid is a naughty little boy who likes to fly around shooting arrows at people and showing his penis! He's not a professional. We can't go tossing our affections to the first taker with a cute butt and a je ne sais quoi. You could at least show me the courtesy of listening to my presentation. If it doesn't work for you, fine, the Easter fairies don't always bat a thousand either. (*Calming*) I'm sorry. This is a very stressful night, Valentines is not what it used to be.

(*Ingrid looks at him warily. She turns off the light and sits*)

Thank you. (*He pulls himself together, hums "Love's Serenade"*) God, I hate Petula Clark. (*He puts up the first slide, a heart with the word LOVE*) Love! (*Unfortunately it's backwards, reading EVOL*) Oh, Goddammit! (*He corrects it*) Sorry, technical difficulties, stay tuned. (*He puts it up again*) Love. A Journey Into Your Heart.

INGRID (*she raises her hand, skeptical*): Um. Is this going to be a long journey? Because I do have places to go.

RUDYARD: Oh, really? Well, thank you, Pinnocchio. The heart is a tough nut to crack. Sometimes it's buried under a lifetime of fatty tissue and cynicism. Do you eat a lot of triglycerides, Ingrid?

INGRID (*cool*): Are you familiar with the Pritikin Diet? That's what I reward myself with on Holidays.

RUDYARD: Well, let's not bog ourselves down in Nutritional Review, this is not health class. Let's talk about the three Rs! Rage, Resentment, self-Recrimination. They'll work wonders in turning the heart into another appendix. Is that what you want to do, you want to spend my valuable time and the rest of your life in the eat-shit line at a pity party?

INGRID: Huh? No. I don't believe I do, actually.

RUDYARD: All right then. Good. (*He puts up a slide—a bird feeding its young*) Let's go back to the beginning, when we were young, let's focus for a moment on what our dear old mother gave us.

INGRID: Worms.

RUDYARD (*he laughs*): Well, that's very funny, Ingrid. (*He makes a note*) Humor still functioning. Now. (*He changes slides—a middle-aged man*) Dad. Daddy. Papa. Pops. Pete. Petey.

INGRID: Pervert. Where did you get that? You know my old man? What, did you meet him in Sex Rehab at Bellevue?

RUDYARD: We had a problem with father, did we?

INGRID (*quietly*): He did not respect me.

RUDYARD: I'm sorry. (*He pauses, affected. Puts up a new slide—a man of 25*) And what about this person?

INGRID: That's my husband! Where'd you get that? I'm dead, right? I got hit by a cross town bus when I jumped out of the cab. And you're really an angel. And I'm an atheist and I'm fucked.

RUDYARD: Was it moving? The cab.

INGRID: The cab was parked at the red light in front of Papaya King, where my most recent boyfriend—I'm surprised you don't have his picture, too, you're not very up to date . . .

(*Rudyard put up a rapid succession of slides, young men, older, a sexy woman, and, finally, a pompous man. Ingrid watches, distracted*)

My most recent boyfriend decided to inform me it was time to reevaluate our relationship. I think that's a very romantic spot, don't you, the Papaya King, to have your heart broken? (*She stares at the passing photos, troubled, fascinated*)

RUDYARD (*making a note*): And now . . . he doesn't love you . . . any more.

INGRID: He doesn't love me any less. Ha ha. He told me he has so much love it was only fair to share the surplus with girls who don't have any. I think sometimes that's the only language men know, the mixed message. A kiss goodbye and a box of candy. "I just need a little outside pussy, but I'll always love you, fatso." (*His picture comes up*) That's him, the motherfucker. Ovary breaker! Mouse prick! (*She shows Rudyard her little finger*)

RUDYARD: You're angry, aren't you? (*He makes a note*)

INGRID: No. Is that how it seems?

(*She lights a cigarette, puts it out. Rudyard watches, concerned*)

RUDYARD: Well, you're probably better off without him. Forge your own trail through the wilderness, who needs the abuse?

INGRID: Am I going to get a bill at the end of the 50 minutes? Because you are not the first know-it-all in a skirt to point out the obvious. You're not even the first one in a skirt and beard.

RUDYARD: Really? I'm sorry, we're not supposed to do that. We're supposed to be impartial, which is usually very easy for me, usually the transactions and transgressions and transferences between consenting adults I find frankly a little tedious.

INGRID: Yeah? What is not tedious to you—transvestites?

RUDYARD: What?! Is that what you think? Oh, dear. Is it the outfit?

INGRID: Ummm. The outfit, the outfit could suggest any . . . number of possibilities. It's a lovely outfit.

RUDYARD (*strained*): Thank you.

INGRID: I'm sorry. If I hurt your feelings. I didn't mean any harm.

RUDYARD: Doesn't matter. I'm used to it. Being a fairy is not something that immediately commands respect. (*He smiles bravely*) But this is not about me and my poor trod upon feelings. This is about Ingrid. What are we going to do about Ingrid?

INGRID (*affected*): You're very kind, aren't you? That's nice. That's an unusual commodity for a man. Or for anybody for that matter. You're an unusual person. Or whatever you are.

RUDYARD: Well. I think you're unusual, too. Whatever you are.

(*They share a look, a moment*)

INGRID: What's your name? Since you know everything about me. You have a name or are you just . . . a fairy?

RUDYARD: I'm a fairy with a name. My name is Rudyard. As in Kipling. We're allowed to choose. I find him so romantic. (*Dramatic*) "Ship me somewhere East of Suez, where the best is like the worst, Where there aren't no Ten Commandments, an' a man can raise a thirst." (*Embarrassed*) I'm sorry, I get worked up.

INGRID: Well. That's OK. I get worked up sometimes, too. Big surprise, huh? Glad to meet you. Rudyard.

(*She shakes his hand shyly. He smiles, also shy. A moment passes*)

Are you really a fairy?

RUDYARD: Yes.

INGRID: What . . . what are you doing here?

RUDYARD: Wherever there's a need, that's where we go. If it's an emergency, we stay till the danger passes. We're just like the Marines, except we don't beat up gay people. (*He salutes*)

INGRID: And what, I'm an emergency, is that the idea?

RUDYARD: Oh, that's not up to me to say. That's your decision. But. I'm here, I've got my Bell and Howell, shall we press on? Anything else we want to say about the candyman or shall we put him where he belongs?

(*She shakes her head, troubled. He pulls out the slide, drops it in a waste basket. Goes back through, discarding each slide in turn. Puts up the penultimate, a man in denim*)

Good enough. What about this character? Were we going through our lumber jack period?

INGRID: Um. That was Austin. He had a charge account at Ralph Lauren. Bought a lot of outdoor things he never used. Why would someone buy a jet ski in Manhattan? He couldn't handle intimacy.

RUDYARD (*next slide, a man in black*): This one? Have Gun Will Travel.

INGRID: Zack. Major Tom Waits fan. We listened to an inordinate amount of Tom Waits. He couldn't handle intimacy either.

RUDYARD (*next, a father type*): Did we put ourselves up for adoption?

INGRID: Mr. Jannislaw, my Human Development teacher at night school. Not a course he was qualified to teach. Also couldn't handle intimacy.

RUDYARD (*next, a very young man, cute*): Ah ha. Ingrid's revenge.

INGRID: He was 19. Delivers groceries for Gristedes. Hadn't heard of intimacy.

RUDYARD (*next, a handsome black guy*): Uh oh. This is a picture we should send to Dad.

INGRID: That was Willy. He was OK. He just hated white girls.

(*Next slide, a gentle-faced man*)

He hated all girls, as it turned out. He was standing on the brink of homosexuality and I pushed him over.

RUDYARD (*next, a beefy jock*): Not this one, too? The gay community's going to nominate you for sainthood.

INGRID: No. That was Rick. He loves girls. Loves to beat the shit out of them.

RUDYARD (*next, a bookworm type*): This person never beat the shit out of anybody. I could take this person on.

INGRID: Alden. Very smart boy. Did the Times crossword puzzle on the typewriter. He broke the news to me that I'm stupid.

(*Next slide, the sexy woman. Rudyard gives her a look*)

Um. That was an experiment. She couldn't handle intimacy either. In addition to having no penis.

(*Next slide, male, 40 and glum*)

My boss. No comment.

(*Next slide, a young guy*)

Ronnie, couldn't handle intimacy.

(*Another slide, another guy*)

Couldn't handle intimacy.

(*Another*)

Couldn't handle intimacy.

(*Another*)

Couldn't handle me.

(*Another*)

Couldn't handle my mother. Him I liked okay.

(*Another*)

He died. Not of AIDS. He died of jumping in front of the IRT Uptown express, I try not to personalize.

(*Another, a teenager*)

That's Chip. Good old Chipper. We loved each other, until I got pregnant.

(*Another teenager*)

Tommy. We couldn't figure out how to get pregnant.

(*Another teenager*)

Lou. First blow job. That was a shock.

(*Another teenager*)

Rocky. First hand job.

(*Another teenager*)

Bobby. First premature ejaculator.

(*Another, younger*)

Morgan. First base.

(*Another, very young*)

Ben. There was no first base.

(*A ten year old boy*)

Oh. Christopher. Sweet little Christopher. First kiss.

(*Donny Osmond*)

Donny. The only boy who never broke my heart.

(*Rudyard turns on the lights. Ingrid looks, dazed, upset*)

That's it? That's my whole resume? That makes the guys in the post office look interesting. What is the point of this? I fucked up every single relationship I've been in and I should have my license revoked? Is that going to put you in the Fairy Hall of Fame? You're a genius fairy, big fucking deal.

RUDYARD: It's not part of my job description to draw conclusions, sorry. At least you've got something to work with here. Some of my clients think life is a Judith Krantz novel. I would merely point out, once upon a time you loved every one of those boys and men—and woman—and had faith and multiple orgasms and a very nice ride at 90 miles an hour, till you smashed your face into the hard brick wall of disappointment and almost bled to death. It's time to get back behind the wheel, Ingrid, and go find your innocence again before it's too late . . .

INGRID (*interrupting*): Is this Rudyard Kipling, cuz it sounds more like Tom Waits, I'm telling you.

RUDYARD: You know what's going to happen to you, you're going to turn into a pissed off old broad, it's not an attractive image.

INGRID: Well let's not be cheery, I hate that. So what if I'm pissed off? I like being pissed off, it's something to feel anyway. I hate men, I hate women, I hate myself, I'm starting to look like Elizabeth Taylor in her John Warner phase. I've had a very hard time! OK?

RUDYARD: I'm sorry.

INGRID: You don't know what you're talking about, you're just a fairy.

RUDYARD: Right. (*He waits patiently*) I have another slide for you, if you're interested.

INGRID: Oh, we forgot someone? Who is it, Quasimodo? I passed through a brief slutty phase. I thought it was character building.

RUDYARD: Well. We don't judge. (*He puts up a slide of a little girl*)

INGRID: Who's that? That's me. That's me. You could at least've found a picture with teeth. That's embarrassing. (*But she stares at the picture*)

RUDYARD: You used to love her. Didn't you?

INGRID (*for a moment it looks as if she'll give in to it, but then turns*): Let me guess, you're really John Bradshaw and I'm supposed to go kiss her. I always wondered about that guy, nobody can be that enthusiastic. Why are you showing me this?

RUDYARD: Because. Because you weren't mad yet. You were filling out all those little wispy Valentines children inexplicably give one another. "I love you, Ingrid." "Your friend forever, Ingrid." Because every time your heart breaks it's harder to put it back together. Because half my clients have died from love, or are dead inside. Because you still have a fighting chance; look at the little girl.

INGRID: Could you turn that off, please? You were on a roll there for a minute, but this is not inspired, I'm telling you.

(*He keeps the slide up, waiting*)

Get away, go on! Leave a person in peace to jump out the window, maybe that's what I'm gonna do. No, first I'm gonna eat the chocolates, then I'm gonna jump out the window. Would you please leave now? I don't need help, thank you just the same. And if I did, I wouldn't be seeking it out from some bad joke in red toe shoes. OK? Go away! This is not a Frank Capra movie. This is the Ingrid Paloma Story and it ain't gonna have a happy ending, I can tell you that right now. Go! (*She pushes him*) There's the door. Or are you gonna fly like Tinkerbell? Where's the magic, incidentally? You're a fuckin phony, did you know that?

(*Rudyard looks at her grimly. He nods, packs up his slide projector, the image of the little girl staying on the wall. He seems darker now, stronger than before*)

RUDYARD: You're right. I'm too old for this. Should've been a Thanksgiving fairy when I had the chance. They've got it made. A few family squabbles and all you can eat. And a little clinical depression, sounds good to me. But I'll tell you this, Ingrid: you're a big fat spoiled brat. Sorry, I didn't mean fat. (*Checking his notebook*) I've got a 78 year old woman in the Bronx, and a priest downtown—they're the worst, want love, can't have love, get love anyway, get in trouble—but at least they still have hope. There are plenty of people out there who could use a good fairy. (*He glances at the audience*) But you—you be careful. You're only as stupid and worthless as you want to believe. Who cares if all the scumbags in the world love you or not, if you don't love yourself, you big baby? Don't you read the goddam Valentines? (*He's ready to go*) "If you can dream—and not make dreams your master . . ." Ah, forget it. That's Kipling, by the way. (*He starts out*) Usually I go in a poof of smoke, but, you know—budget cuts.

INGRID (*picking up the waste basket*): What about the slides?

RUDYARD: They're your problem, you sort 'em out.

INGRID: What about her? How'd you do that anyway?

RUDYARD: Well, there's got to be a little magic, even in a recession.

(*He salutes, gives the audience a knowing look, and walks out. Ingrid watches him go, anxious*)

INGRID: Well, wait a minute. What if I decide I'm an emergency? (*No response, he's gone*) Emergency, emergency! (*She starts to cry, drops the waste basket behind a chair, sits*) Everybody hates me, nobody loves me, I'm goin' out and eat chocolates. (*She opens the box*) Big fat juicy ones, long yucky buttercreams . . . (*She cries. Traipses to the window like a child. Barking at the slide*) Oh, shut up. (*She climbs up. It looks as if she's going to jump. But she tosses a piece of candy, calling*) Candy for the homeless. Valentines for the loveless. Free Valentines. From Ingrid, with love. (*She dumps out the box. Starts to throw it. Steps in, crumpling it. Drags out the waste basket, sits on the floor, drying her eyes. She turns the basket over. Instead of slides, hundreds of Valentines tumble out, covering her lap. She stares in wonder. Picks one up*) "To Ingrid. When you grow up, I'm gonna marry you. Love, Christopher." Well, I'll let you know, Christopher, if that ever transpires. (*She tucks the card in her blouse, pulls a pillow off the couch and an afghan and curls up on the bed of Valentines. Too tired to get up, she yanks the lamp cord out of the wall. The room is dark except for the slide. Ingrid gazes up at it*) Good night, little girl.

(*She closes her eyes. Pause*)

RUDYARD (*somewhere in the dark.*): Goodnight, Ingrid.

(*She looks about. Closes her eyes. A distant smile*)

INGRID: Goodnight, Rudyard.

(*A scratchy recording of Petula Clark singing "Love's Serenade" fills the air as the stage goes dark.*)

NIGHT BASEBALL

Gabriel Tissian

Gabriel Tissian

Gabriel Tissian was born in Ames, Iowa, on February 16, 1973, and has lived practically since that day in Center City Philadelphia. He is currently a sophomore at Stanford University, majoring in creative writing. Though originally a poet and short story writer, he has focused entirely on drama in the last four years and has written six plays to date, two full-lengths and four one-acts. His one-act play, *Smoker's Paradise,* was a Finalist in the 1991 New York Young Playwrights Festival, where it received a staged reading at Playwrights Horizons. His one-act *Night Baseball* was a Finalist in the 1992 New York Young Playwrights Festival and also received a staged reading at Playwrights Horizons. *Night Baseball* was originally produced by Stanford University as part of their Original Winter One-Acts Festival, and it was entered by Stanford in the American College Theater Festival, where it was one of three Regional winners for Best One-Act Play (Region Eight: California, Arizona, Nevada, and Hawaii) and was re-produced (with the original Stanford production) in Las Vegas at UNLV's Black Box Theater. Mister Tissian has just completed the screen adaptation of *Night Baseball* and is currently attempting to return to prose fiction, dedicating most of his time to writing short stories and drafting plans for his first novel.

Characters:

JOE

LOU

PETE

OLD PETE

MICK

SAL

Scene:

Place:

The living room of a rowhouse in the Fairmount section of Philadelphia.

Time:

The present.

Lights up on Mick, seated at the poker table with a beer.

MICK: It's like this . . . hands down, baseball is the greatest sport in the world . . . (*Sounds of incredulous laughter from the other men*) And Pete Rose is without a doubt one of the greatest ball players that ever lived . . . (*More laughter*) Ergo . . . Pete Rose is one of the greatest athletes the world has ever seen.

(*Lights up on the poker table. Pete, Old Pete, and Sal laugh together at Mick's expense*)

PETE: You gotta be kidding me, Mick. Ain't you seen the gut on this guy?

OLD PETE (*pouring himself a shot of whiskey*): Deal the cards . . .

SAL: I don't know, Petey, they didn't call him Charlie Hustle for nothing. This guy could run some serious bases.

PETE: Oh, come on, Sal, the only reason they called him Charlie Hustle's 'cause he used to slide head first. That don't make him an athlete—that just makes him stupid.

MICK: Let me ask you this, then: you think we ever woulda won the series in eighty if it wasn't for Pete Rose?

OLD PETE: Peter, deal the cards . . .

PETE: No—look, you're not listening to me. I ain't saying he ain't a great ball player. He is, no argument. I'll even give you he's a great athlete, of a sort, but . . .

MICK: Of a sort?! What the hell is that supposed to mean?

PETE: It means . . . he's like a pro golfer, you know? Great hand-eye, lousy conditioning.

MICK: Wait a minute . . . just one goddamn minute . . . you're comparing Pete Rose to Fuzzy Zoeller?

SAL: Now Fuzzy Zoeller, there's one of the greatest strokes I ever seen . . .

MICK: I mean, give me a break, you're comparing apples and . . . Sal, you don't know a fucking thing about golf.

SAL: I know enough.

MICK: You do, huh? You ever played it?

SAL: Yeah, I played it. Sure I played it.

MICK: I'm not talking about the kind with windmills and astroturf now. I'm talking about the real thing.

SAL: Yeah, the whole bit. I done it.

MICK: How many times?

(*Pause*)

SAL: Once or twice.

MICK: You're full of shit.

OLD PETE: Peter, will you tell your moron friends to shut up and deal the cards . . . ?

PETE: Hold on, Pop, just a second. Look, Mick, give it a rest, will ya?

SAL: Hey, Pete, you got anything else to drink around here . . . ?

MICK: What's a double bogey?

(*Pause*)

SAL: What?

MICK: What's a double bogey? Anyone who's played golf knows that. So what's a double bogey?

PETE: For crying out loud . . .

MICK: You don't know, do you? He don't know.

SAL: Yeah, sure I do.

MICK: So what is it? Explain it to me.

(*Pause*)

SAL: What is what?

MICK: A double bogey, Sal. Double bogey. Am I stuttering here? Am I failing to annunciate myself? A DUH-BLE BO-GEY.

SAL: A double bogey.

MICK: Yeah, Sal, a double bogey. What is a double bogey? (*Pause*) You don't know, do you?

SAL: I just told you I knew.

MICK: So . . . enlighten me. Pretend I don't know.

(*Pause*)

SAL: But you do know.

MICK: I know I know what it is, Sal, I want to know if you know what it is. I'm saying pretend I don't—all right, listen, Sal. Say you're walking along the street one day, some guy comes up behind you, you never met him before in your life, he puts a gun to your head and says, "Hey, moron, what's a double bogey?" Now what do you tell him?

SAL: He black or white?

MICK: It don't make any difference, Sal. The point is, the guy's gonna blow your brains out if you don't answer his question. He says, "What's a double bogey?" and you say, "It's a . . . ?" (*Pause*) "It's a . . ."

SAL: It's a hole in two.

MICK: A hole in two?! (*Mick and Pete explode in laughter*)

SAL: What? Ain't that right?

OLD PETE (*smashing his fists on the table*): STOP MAKING FUN OF THAT STUPID GUINEA AND DEAL THE CARDS!

(*Pause*)

PETE: You know we can't deal the cards, Pop. Lou ain't here yet.

OLD PETE: Why the hell we always gotta wait for Lou? Who the fuck is Lou?!

PETE: He's my best friend, Pop.

OLD PETE: He's a thug—

PETE: Lou's a good man, Pop, and he's always shown you respect.

OLD PETE: He was always getting you into trouble. Seventeen years old, I gotta go bail my own son outta jail. Tell me, huh? What kind of friend is that?

PETE: Pop, how many times we gotta go over this? It wasn't Lou's fault. He was protecting me.

OLD PETE: He was protecting himself. He didn't have to turn around. You think them two nigs woulda chased you past twenty-third street? Not too fucking likely, Peter. I'm telling you, the guy don't think.

PETE: Pop, those two nigs were from Hunting Park, they had records a mile long. What were we supposed to do? We didn't have no money to give them. Who knew if they were gonna cut us? Lou did what he felt he had to do.

MICK: Lou's a good man, Mister McGuire.

SAL: Yeah, he looked out for all of—

OLD PETE: I don't want to hear it.

PETE: Look, Pop, Lou gave up a lot that day. He took everything, remember? You think that's easy? An eighteen year-old kid? He did two and a half years, Pop. Christ, the state pen makes the Nam bush look like fucking Candyland—you know the kind of filth we send there. But Lou, he survives—only to get out and find he lost his job and no one'll hire him. So what does he do—an ex-con? He's forced —not by choice—he's forced to go chop meat for his old man. You of all people, Pop, should appreciate Lou, show him some respect, because that man gave up his future to protect your son.

OLD PETE: That's exactly what I'm talking about.

PETE: What?!

OLD PETE: If he was smart, he wouldn'ta had to give up nothing.

PETE: Pop, what are you talking about?

OLD PETE: If Lou was smart, he wouldn'ta had to go to the joint.

MICK (*stands*): Sal, you want another beer?

PETE: Pop, it's the law. You beat two guys half to death, you gotta do time. You been a cop thirty-five years you don't know that—?

SAL: Yeah. Get me another Rock, will ya—? (*Mick exits through the stage left door*)

OLD PETE: Of course I know that, and don't get smart, boy, I been a cop twenty years longer than you. All I'm saying is, if he was smart, he wouldn't have done time.

PETE: Yeah? How?!

OLD PETE: By finishing what he started. If he'd a killed them two black bastards, he never woulda been picked up. You think anyone's gonna ask questions in this neighborhood? Two dead moulies lying on the sidewalk with switchblades in their hands? Come on.

PETE: Pop, you weren't there. You don't know what it was like. I mean, he was a kid, for Chrissake. He was scared. He wasn't even thinking that way—

OLD PETE: Aha! See, see, you admit he wasn't thinking—

PETE: Pop, all I'm saying is, Lou's a friend. He saved my ass more times than I can remember. I owe Lou.

OLD PETE: And all I'm saying is, he worries me. He's a hothead. He don't think about what he's doing. I don't like him playing baseball with us.

PETE: First of all, Pop, you don't play baseball with us, you sit in the car, remember? Second, we wouldn't even be able to play in the first place if it hadn't been for Lou. None of us have his size, you know that.

SAL: Yeah, Lou's the anchor, Mister McGuire. Without him we'd never . . .

OLD PETE: All right, all right, enough. (*Old Pete pours himself another shot*) When the hell's he gonna get here? I want to play some cards.

PETE: He'll be here soon. He's picking up Joey at Community first.

SAL: Joey?! Tonight's the night?

(*Mick re-enters with two beers*)

PETE: Yeah, we're bringing him in tonight.

SAL: Mick, you hear this?

(*Mick tosses a beer to Sal*)

Lou's bringing Joey tonight.

MICK (*to Pete*): You think he's ready?

PETE: Well, he bat three fifty-seven for Roman last year . . .

MICK: Sounds like a ball player to me.

PETE: Well, we'll see. But me . . . I think he's ready. He's a good kid. And he loved Mikey as much as any of us.

MICK: Hell, if the kid survived eighteen years with Lou as a father, he's gotta be tough.

SAL: And let's not forget . . . Frannie's been dead—what? Five years? Can you imagine living alone with Lou for five whole years? The kid's gotta have balls of steel.

PETE: Well, we'll find out if he does tonight. Joey's had it rough, no question. But Lou and I, we been watching him for a while, and we both think he's got what it takes.

OLD PETE: Bullshit!

PETE: Pop, what's the matter?

OLD PETE: What am I, an idiot, Peter? You think I don't know what's going on here?

PETE: What are you talking about?

OLD PETE: You're trying to retire me, aren't you? You and Lou, you're bringing in the kid to replace me.

PETE: We're not trying to replace you, Pop . . .

OLD PETE: You think I'm too old to see the writing on the wall, Pete? Well let me tell you something. I may be retired, but I can still—

PETE: Look, Pop, you're an important part of the team. We couldn't play without you—

OLD PETE: You don't even let me play. I'm the goddamn chauffeur. Part of the team . . .

PETE: Pop, you know you can't play.

OLD PETE: Oh no? Why the hell not?!

PETE: You're too old. You'd hurt yourself.

OLD PETE: See that? Now that's what I'm talking about. You think I lost the edge, don't you? Arthritis of the brain, eh? Well let me tell you all something . . . I can still swing that bat just as hard as any one of you, and if you think you're gonna replace me with that little pimple-faced prick—

PETE: We're not looking to replace you, all right?! We just need some more muscle at the plate, that's all. Gotta bring in some youth, start planning for the future, you know?

SAL: Don't you worry, Mister McGuire. Joey's a good kid. Don't forget, he was your grandson's best friend—

OLD PETE: Yeah? Well if they were so fucking tight, where the hell was Joey when my poor little grandson got his head—

PETE: POP!!

(*Pause*)

OLD PETE (*to Sal, grabbing his empty beer bottle*): You using that bottle?

SAL: No. Take it. It's yours. (*Old Pete takes out a cigar and lights it, using Sal's bottle for an ashtray*)

PETE: Why, Pop? Why you gotta smoke in here? You know I hate that.

OLD PETE: Yeah, I know. That's why I'm doing it.

(*Pete gets up, annoyed, and goes to the window by the fireplace. He opens the window, fanning out the smoke, and looks up at the portrait of Mikey over the fireplace*)

MICK: Christ, Petey, you imagine what a year Roman woulda had if Joey and Mikey played together?

SAL: They never woulda lost a game! With Joey's bat and Mikey's glove—I tell you, Petey, that boy of yours was headed for the show. He had golden hands if I ever saw 'em.

(*Pause*)

PETE: Well, he wasn't no Pete Rose.

MICK: Oh no, Petey, we ain't gonna start this again . . .

PETE (*returning to the table, smiling*): So you're gonna tell me that some pot-bellied, pug-nosed felon with a bad haircut is a better athlete than Larry Bird?

MICK: Oh, yeah, like bouncing a big fucking orange ball takes half the co-ordination you need to hit a pro slider . . .

PETE: Oh, yeah, like running around a couple a bases takes half the stamina you need to run up and down the court for an hour . . .

MICK: Look, ya fucking communist, you keep talking like that about our national pastime, you're gonna get hurt . . .

PETE: Come on, give me your best shot, you dumb, ugly, cabbage-eating Irish son of a bitch!

MICK: Kiss my Blarney stone, you fucking dirty mick . . .

SAL (*stepping between Pete and Mick*): Fellas, fellas, come on, we're all friends here. Besides, we all know Fuzzy Zoeller's the greatest athlete that ever lived . . .

MICK: Shut up, you fucking wop . . .

PETE (*to Mick*): Who do these fucking guineas think they are?

(*The three men chuckle together, returning to their seats*)

MICK: Well, I don't know about you, Petey, but I had a bitch of a time getting Katey to take Peg bowling again.

PETE: No, no, don't even talk about it, Mick, I get the same thing. It's getting to be like pulling teeth with Peggy. Every month, it's the same thing. 'Why can't we come watch you play baseball? Why's it always gotta be just the guys' night out? I hate bowling, Peter.'

MICK: Jesus, Pete, I get the same fuckin' thing. I swear they must get together and rehearse this shit when we're not looking . . .

SAL: Christ, do I gotta listen to you two bitch about your wives again?! I can't even get laid, and I gotta sit here—

(*A loud knock comes at the door*)

PETE: Gee, I wonder who that could be?

MICK: Forty-three years old, you'd think the guy woulda learned how to knock on a door by now.

(*The door receives a second pounding*)

OLD PETE: Peter, answer the door. Your pet gorilla's getting anxious.

(*Pete goes to the door. More pounding*)

PETE: Take it easy, take it easy . . . I'm coming!

(*Pete opens the door. Lou and Joe enter. Both men carry baseball bats; Joe also carries a glove*)

PETE: So these are the two bums who were trying to knock down my door.

LOU: How you doing, Petey?

PETE: Not bad, Lou. Not bad. Good to see you. (*Pete and Lou hug*) Do me a favor though, will ya? Take it easy on the door. It's gonna collapse you keep pounding on it like that.

LOU: Sure, Petey.

PETE: You gonna remember this time?

LOU: Yeah, I got it.

PETE: All right, enough said. Now who is this big fucking slugger you brought with you? Hey, fellas, look's like Lou's got himself a ringer.

MICK: Well the way he hits, he needs one.

JOE: How are you, Uncle Pete?

PETE: Jesus, will you look at this kid? Didn't I tell you, fellas? Joey, you get any bigger you're gonna be able to kick your father's ass one of these days.

LOU: Don't count on it.

PETE: Good to see you, Joe. (*Pete and Joe hug*) What's with all the equipment? Lou, why you tell him to bring a glove?

LOU: I didn't. He just brought it.

JOE: What are you talking about? Of course I brought my glove. We're playing ball tonight.

PETE: You think we actually play baseball? Bunch a old men like us?

SAL: Jesus, Lou, what have you been teaching this kid?

JOE: You're kidding me, right?

PETE: Joey, would I lie to you? (*Pause. Pete looks sternly at Joe, then suddenly smiles and ruffles Joe's hair affectionately*) Come on, sit down. And remember—don't ever trust an Irishman. They're worse than the fucking Arabs. Now put your bat by the door, take a seat.

(*Lou and Joe place their bats in the umbrella stand with the others. Joe hangs his glove on the coat rack. The three men go over to the table, Joe and Lou nodding hellos at the other men as Pete pulls out two chairs. Sal and Mick stand; Old Pete remains seated, ignoring the other men*)

Lou, we got you next to Mick, and Joey can sit between the two of us, all right? (*Lou and Joe take their seats*) We okay here?

LOU: Whatever.

MICK: How you doing, Lou? (*Mick and Lou shake hands*)

LOU: Same as last month, Mick. Meat's meat, you know? No one eats it no more.

MICK: It's the goddamn yuppies. All they eat is rabbit food. Christ, I walk down Parish these days, I never seen so many assholes without socks in my entire life.

LOU: How you doing, Sal?

SAL: Same old shit, Lou. You know how it goes. Good to see you. (*Sal and Lou shake hands*)

LOU: Hey, Old Pete, how's it hanging?

OLD PETE: It ain't hangin'. When you're sixty-eight years old, all it's good for is keeping your hands warm.

LOU: Sorry to hear that.

OLD PETE: Well, it could be worse. (*Pours himself another shot*) I could be chopping meat for a living.

PETE: Dad, behave yourself, will ya? This is Lou you're talking to, for Chrissake.

OLD PETE: Oh, Jes—I'm sorry, Lou. What was I thinking? I'd bend down and kiss your ass, too, but my back ain't what it used to be.

PETE: Pop, what is your problem?

LOU: Forget it, Petey . . .

OLD PETE: That's right, Peter, forget it. I'm just a dumb old man, right? You got your young stud over here, you don't need me, right?

PETE: Pop, for the last time, we're not replacing you with Joe! (*To Lou and Joe*) Don't listen to him. He just looking for attention.

SAL: Jesus, Joe, how many feet you grow since last month?

JOE: Just a couple, Sal. One or two at most. (*Joe and Sal shake hands*)

MICK (*pointing at Joe*): Rollie Fingers.

JOE: What fingers?

MICK: No, no, you look just like Rollie Fingers.

JOE: Uh, thanks, Mick . . .

SAL: Not that I want to know, but who the hell is Rollie Fingers?

MICK: Who is Rollie Fingers?! Sal, come on, even you gotta know who Rollie Fingers is. The man just happens to be one of the greatest pitchers to ever play the game. Holds the record for career saves.

PETE: Oh yeah? How many is that, Mick?

MICK: Three hundred and forty-one. And you can look that one up.

PETE: That's all right, Mick. We trust you.

MICK (*extending his hand*): Put 'er there, Joe. (*Mick and Joe shake hands*)

JOE: How are you, Mick?

MICK: Ehh, the ulcer's killing me and the lumbago starts up when it rains, but all in all, life's shit and then you die.

JOE: Same old Mick.

MICK: Yeah, well, some things never change. Talk to me after I win the lottery tomorrow, I'll be a new man.

JOE (*to Old Pete*): How are you, Mister McGuire?

(*Joe extends his hand. Old Pete ignores the gesture, taking a puff on his cigar and blowing the smoke into Joe's face*)

OLD PETE: You call that a beard?

JOE: What?

OLD PETE: That shit on your face. You trying to grow a beard or what?

JOE: No, sir, I just ain't shaved for a couple a days . . .

OLD PETE: How old are you? Sixteen?

JOE: No, sir. I'm gonna be nineteen in a few weeks.

OLD PETE: Jesus, Peter, nineteen and the kid can't grow a beard . . .

PETE: Pop, he ain't trying to grow a beard. Didn't you just hear what he said—

OLD PETE: I grew my first beard when I was fifteen years old. Fifteen! At Eighteen I worked sixty hours a week, supported a sick father and three younger sisters. This kid's nineteen years old, can't even show whiskers. Christ, this is humiliation . . .

PETE: For the absolute last time, Pop, we ain't getting rid of you . . . !

OLD PETE (*to Joe*): You got hair on your balls, kid?

JOE: What is this . . . ?!

PETE: Pop, you apologize to Joe . . .

OLD PETE: How 'bout your armpits? You got hair in your armpits . . . ?

PETE: Dammit, Pop, you apologize to Joe now, or so help me . . .

OLD PETE: You ever fucked a girl, kid? You do like girls, don't you?

LOU (*smashing the table with his fist*) HEY!!

(*Pause*)

Old Pete, you're lucky you're an old man, 'cause you ain't got no fucking manners. Now apologize before I rip your goddamn arms off.

(*Pause*)

OLD PETE: Sorry, son. Maybe I am getting a little funny in the head.

JOE: Forget it, Mister McGuire. No harm done.

PETE (*standing*): Lou, Joey . . . what can I get you?

LOU: Get us a couple a beers, Petey.

PETE (*heading for the kitchen*): Coming up . . .

JOE: Uh, you better make mine a Coke, okay, Pete?

PETE: A Coke?! (*The older men join in a chuckle*)

SAL: Joe, you can't drink Coke when you're playing with the big boys.

JOE: I just . . . uh . . . I don't like beer, you know? The taste . . . it just doesn't do nothing for me.

MICK: You're Lou's son and you don't like beer?

LOU: Two beers, Petey . . .

JOE: No, look, I just don't got a taste for—

LOU: Two beers.

(*Pause*)

PETE: Two beers it is. (*Pete exits into the kitchen*)

JOE: Sal, help me out here. What's with the cards? I thought we were playing baseball.

SAL: We will, we will, but we gotta play some cards first.

JOE: Why?

SAL: We always play cards first. It's sort of a tradition.

JOE: Yeah, but come on—I mean, it's gonna be dark in an hour. We're wasting time here—

MICK: Be patient, Joe.

(*Pete re-enters from the kitchen with two beers, hands them to Lou and Joe*)

PETE (*returning to his seat*): All right, gents, let's get down to business. (*Pete picks up the deck and shuffles during the following speech*) The game is poker, dealer's choice. Ante is one chip. Deal starts with me. No time is called. We each start with twenty-five chips—which you each see sitting before you, and we play 'til there's only one of us left. No loans allowed—if you're busted, you're out. Whoever's got all the chips in front of him at the end is the winner . . . unless it's my Pop, in which case whoever comes in second is the winner. But he never wins, so . . .

OLD PETE: You're goddamn right I don't. Why the hell should I? I still gotta be the fucking chauffeur.

PETE: . . . so don't worry about it. Any questions?

JOE: Look, Pete . . . I ain't got any cash to pay for these chips.

PETE: Don't worry about it, Joe. We ain't playing for money.

JOE: We're playing poker, but we're not playing for money?

PETE: Nope.

JOE: Then what are we playing for?

MICK: We're playing to win, Joe.

JOE: Win what?

PETE: You'll know soon enough, Joe. Don't worry about it. Just know that you want to be the guy with all the chips at the end.

SAL: So what's the game, Petey?

PETE: I'm thinking maybe warm up with a little five-card draw. Objections? (*Each man shakes his head*) All right. Ante is one chip. (*Each man throws a chip in the center of the table*) Sal, pick a number between one and ten.

SAL: Uhhhh . . .

MICK: Christ, Sal, you gotta count on your fingers? Just give him a number.

SAL: Six.

PETE: Sixes wild, gents. (*Places the deck before Old Pete*) Cut 'em, Pop. (*Old Pete cuts the deck. Pete scoops up the cards and begins the deal*) Coming around, fellas. Sixes wild. Trade in up to three, 'less you got an ace. Trade in four if you got one, but you gotta show it.

(*Joe reaches for his cards*)

LOU: Don't pick 'em up.

JOE (*drawing his hand back*): Why?

LOU: 'Cause I said so.

MICK (*to Joe*): You ain't supposed to look at your cards until they're all dealt. Poker etiquette, you know?

PETE (*stopping the deal*): How many is that?

MICK: Four. Keep it coming.

PETE (*resuming the deal*): Five . . .

(*Everyone picks up their cards, arranges them in their hands*)

Betting starts with you, Pop.

OLD PETE: Check.

SAL: Check.

MICK: Check.

LOU: Three. (*Lou bets three*)

(*Pause*)

PETE: You in or out, Joe?

JOE: Uh, check.

LOU: You can't check after a bet's been made. Either call, raise or fold.

JOE: I'm in.

(*Pause*)

PETE: Throw your chips in, Joe.

JOE: What?

LOU: Put three chips in the pot.

(*Joe throws his chips in*)

PETE: I'm in. (*Pete calls*) Pop? Back to you.

OLD PETE: I'll see three, raise two. (*Old Pete bets five*)

PETE: Five to you, Sal.

SAL (*throwing his cards down*): I'm out. Hey, Lou, Mick tell you the news?

LOU: What news is that, Sal?

MICK: Couple of Girard niggers broke into my shop.

LOU: When was this?

MICK: Saturday night. I locked up about eleven, got a call from Petey about four.

PETE: The store alarm went off about three thirty. Ed and Jimmy got there first, but they were long gone.

LOU: What they get?

MICK: What else? Sneakers. They bust my front window for six lousy pairs of Pumps. They're like the fucking gypsies.

PETE: It's to you, Mick.

MICK: Yeah, what the hell. (*Mick calls*)

PETE: Two more for you, Lou.

LOU: I'm in. (*Lou calls*)

PETE: Two more for you, too, Joe. Less you want to fold.

JOE: No, I'm in. (*Joe calls*)

PETE: Dealer decides to ride. (*Pete calls*) How many you want, Pop?

OLD PETE: Three.

(*Pete deals out three*)

LOU: You pick 'em up, Petey?

PETE: Who's that?

LOU: The junglebunnies who busted Mick's window.

PETE: Yeah, we got 'em the morning after.

LOU: How'd you manage to bring 'em in?

PETE: Christ, listen to this, Lou. Jimmy Fitz's patrolling around Brewerytown Sunday morning and all the nigs are walking to church, right? So he's cruising slow up Poplar and he passes a family of 'em, walking in their Sunday best—you know, suits, ties, dresses, the whole bit—but get this: they're all wearin' brand new pairs of Reeboks. Can you imagine this? They're dressed in suits and ties, going to church, and they're all wearing hightops! So Jimmy stops the whole group, gets their names and tells them all to take off their shoes. Well, surprise surprise—off come six shiny white brand new pairs of Pumps.

SAL: Can you believe that shit, Lou? The whole fucking family's wearing stolen hightops to church. If that ain't blasphemy, I don't know what is.

LOU: So who were they?

PETE: Christ, I don't know—Washington, Jefferson—what difference does it make? Just another pack of moulies. How many, Mick?

MICK: Three.

(*Pete deals out three*)

How funny is that, Lou? Junior steals some sneakers, brings 'em home, and Mom and Dad are so proud they wear 'em to church the next morning. We're supposed to believe these people got morals? Ain't they ever heard of the eighth commandment?

SAL: Know it?! How could they know it?! You gotta be able to read to know it, am I right? I'll tell you one thing they do know, though—"be fruitful and multiply"—that's what they know. Right, Joe?

JOE: Yeah, fuckin' A, Sal.

MICK: But it ain't just that they're stupid . . . it's more than that. They're pissed. I mean, they're getting dangerous. And worse, they're all working together these days . . . the niggers, the spics, the Orientals. They're going right for us—our jobs, our stores, our neighborhoods. Hell, you already gotta speak wonton to buy your fucking groceries . . .

SAL: Will someone tell me what the hell that little chink is saying? Every morning I go in there to buy the paper, he's smiling at me and going like 'chin chow chin chow' over and over again. (*Laughs from the other men*) What the hell is that? 'Chin chow'?

MICK: Sal, didn't you just see me talking?

SAL: Yeah, but look, I been wondering about this for months now. I mean, is he making fun of me?

MICK: He's probably saying he does dry cleaning, too . . . who the hell knows?! Do any of us look like we speak fucking Saskatchewan . . . ?

SAL: Saskatchewan?! I didn't say nothing about Saskatchewan. What the hell is Saskatchewan?

JOE: He means Szechuan.

MICK: Whatever. The point is—

SAL: The point is, I don't know what either of you are talking about. All I'm saying is, I get my paper and—

MICK: You wanna know what the point is, Sal? The point is, shut the fuck up! Don't interrupt me when I'm making a point.

PETE: Lou, what can I get you?

LOU: One.

(*Pete deals out one card*)

PETE: What point is that, Mick?

MICK: I'm thinking . . . okay. What I was trying to say before I was so rudely interrupted was, we gotta defend ourselves, right, Joe?

JOE: Right, Mick.

MICK: We laugh about it now, but pretty soon they be across the street, on the block, next door . . . hell, if we ain't careful, the nigs'll be fucking our women and selling crack to our kids. Don't think I'm kidding about this, Joe . . .

JOE: I hear you, Mick. I know what you're saying . . .

MICK: . . . 'cause I am dead fucking serious about this . . .

JOE: I know you are, Mick. What can I say? The truth's the truth . . .

MICK: You bet your ass it's the truth.

PETE: How many you want, Joe?

JOE: One.

(*Pete deals out one*)

PETE: You listen to your Uncle Mick, Joe. He's a wise man.

JOE: I know it, Pete.

MICK: I mean it, Joe. You gotta watch your ass these days. Don't you ever trust 'em . . . always remember that they hate you. They think we don't hear their ghettoblasters, they think we don't hear 'Down with the man' and 'Fight the power' and all the rest of that get whitey shit, but we do. We know what they're thinking. You know, Joe, I was just about your age when King got shot. We got three bricks through the window that day . . . one hit my Pop in the back of the head . . . eighteen stitches. What the hell did me and my Pop have to do with killing King?! You understand?

JOE: Yeah, sure I do.

PETE: Dealer's taking three. (*Pete deals himself three*)

MICK: Why they put bricks through our window?! We didn't do a fucking thing. For crying out loud, I never even met the poor bastard who wacked King . . . understand?

(*Pause*)

JOE: Sure, Mick.

PETE: What I can't figure out, Joe, is how you survived for eighteen years in this jungle they call a neighborhood. I mean, it was rough when we were growing up, but at least we knew we were safe once we crossed twenty-first street.

JOE: It wasn't easy, Pete, you know? We used to get jumped by the nigs and the spics from nineteenth all the time. And why? No reason. They just liked fucking with us.

SAL: You really musta mixed it up, Joe. Seemed to me like you had a black eye or a bloody nose every week.

JOE: Yeah, well, it was tough. Me and Mikey, we used to get the shit kicked out of us all the time till Lou taught us how to fight. One thing I'll say about the nigs, though . . . one on one, they can't fight. Mikey used to say to me, he said, "You only gotta remember one thing when you fight a nigger: go for their balls and they'll never bother you again. No one cares more about their cocks than the niggers . . ." (*All laugh except Pete and Lou. All eyes turn to Pete, who is visibly upset*) Jesus, Pete, I'm sorry. I didn't mean to—

PETE: It's all right, Joe. It's all right. (*Pause*) I know you loved Mikey. And he loved you. You just . . . these memories . . . I can't control 'em . . . you know?

JOE: Sure, Pete. Sure.

(*Pause*)

PETE: How could they do it, Joe? You tell me, how could they do it? He didn't do a fucking thing to them.

JOE: I don't know, Pete. Word is they thought he was one of Frankie's boys.

PETE: That's right, Joe. Now why would they think something like that? Mikey never hung out with Frank.

JOE: Well, I guess 'cause they figured he was—

PETE: 'Cause he was white, Joe. 'Cause he was white. (*Pause*) Five on one. Nothing to defend himself with. He never even had a chance.

SAL: Mikey was a good kid, Pete.

(*Pause. Pete looks over soberly at Sal, then suddenly chuckles*)

PETE: Sal, you really are a fucking moron.

(*All join in a tension-releasing laugh*)

SAL: Yeah, but you love me anyway. Now let's give a toast for Mikey. Come on . . . (*Sal raises his glass. The rest of the table follows suit*) To Mikey.

ALL: To Mikey! (*All drink*)

MICK: Now let's play some cards, for Chrissake . . .

PETE: Bet starts with Pop.

OLD PETE: I'm in for two. (*Throws in two*)

PETE: Mick?

MICK: I don't think so. Out. (*Throws in his cards*)

PETE: Lou?

LOU: I'll pay two to see his cards. (*Lou calls*)

PETE: What do you say, Joe?

JOE: Uh, yeah, I'm in. (*Joe calls*)

PETE (*throwing in his cards*): Dealer folds. What do you got, Pop?

OLD PETE (*laying down his cards*): Pair of aces.

LOU: What's your high card, old man?

OLD PETE: King.

LOU (*tossing his cards in*): Take it.

PETE: What you got, Joe?

JOE (*laying down*): Uh, all I got's a couple a eights, a seven, a six, and a two.

(*General groans and chuckles from the older men*)

MICK: That's three eights, Joe. Sixes are wild, remember? Take it.

OLD PETE: Christ, not only do I gotta lose to a fucking kid, I gotta lose to one who don't even know what he has.

JOE: Wait a second . . . I win?

LOU: Yeah. Pot's yours.

PETE: Cards in.

(*Everyone throws their hands in to Pete. He starts to shuffle as Joe rakes in the pot*)

Joe . . . you know how to play poker, right?

JOE: Yeah . . . sort of.

PETE: Sort of?

JOE: Well, I'm a little fuzzy on the rankings, you know?

SAL: Look, Joey, it's easy. It goes high card, one pair—you listening to me?—two pair, three of a kind, straight, flush, full house—you know what that is, don't you?

JOE: Yeah.

SAL: All right . . . full house—

LOU: Hold it, Sal. What is it, Joe?

JOE: What?

LOU: A full house. What's a full house?

JOE: It's, uh, three of a kind and two of a kind, right?

LOU: Two of a kind?!

JOE: Yeah, two of a kind and three of a kind. That's right, isn't it?

LOU: It's called a pair. Not two of a kind . . . a pair.

JOE: Yeah, a pair, right . . . that's what I meant . . . a pair.

(*Pause*)

SAL: That's right. Now after full house is four of a kind, then straight flush, then royal flush. You think you got it now?

JOE: Yeah. I think so. Thanks, Sal.

PETE: Deal goes to you, Pop. Your choice. (*Pete slides the deck to Old Pete*)

OLD PETE: The game is seven card. Follow the queen.

SAL: You know how to play seven card, right, Joe?

JOE: Yeah, I think so. It's just like with five cards, but now you got seven and you pick the best five, right?

SAL: You got it. Now this is how it goes: you get two cards down, four cards up, and one last card down. After the first three cards are dealt, we all bet—that's called third street—then we each get another card and bet—that's fourth street—and it goes like that 'til we get to seventh street, okay?

JOE: Yeah, no sweat.

LOU: When do you trade in your cards, Joe?

(*Pause*)

JOE: After seventh street?

LOU: Uh uh. Try again.

JOE: After fourth street?

LOU: Fourth street?! What are you, a fucking idiot? Think, for Chrissake. SEVEN-CARD STUD . . .

JOE: Look, Lou, I don't know. I . . . I ain't never played poker before.

LOU: You ain't gotta know how to play poker. All you gotta do is use that fucking brain (*Lou starts smacking Joe in the head*) you're always wavin' in my face. Now when do you trade your cards in, smart guy? Huh . . . ?

JOE (*desperate as Lou continues to deck him*): Christ, Lou, I . . . I don't know. I told ya . . . I . . . ain't ever played . . .

LOU: Come on, college boy, all that education an' you can't answer a simple question like that . . . ?

PETE: Lou . . . that's enough!!

(*Lou's hand stops just inches short of Joe's face. Pause*)

LOU: They call it stud because you don't get no more fucking cards.

(*Lou gives Joe's head a final push on the word "get." Pause*)

PETE: Deal, Pop. Seven-card . . . (*Old Pete begins the deal*) Ante-up, fellas . . . (*everyone antes*) Listen, Joe, this is how you play follow the queen. In normal seven card, you don't play with wilds, but in this game you do. Whenever a queen is dealt face-up, the queen and the next card dealt is wild. So let's say I deal Sal a queen face-up and then deal Mick a three. That means that threes are wild. Now if I deal Mick a queen the next round and then deal your father a seven, then sevens are wild and threes are back to being just normal threes. Queens are always wild, whether they're showing or not. You think you got all of that?

JOE: Yeah, I think so. Thanks, Pete.

OLD PETE: Comin' up . . . (*As Old Pete deals each face-up card, starting with Sal, he announces the rank*) Ace . . . jack . . . two . . . eight . . . five . . . seven. Bet goes to the ace.

SAL: Ace bets one. (*Throws down a chip*)

MICK: I'll bump it one. (*Raises a chip*) By the way, Joe, was I dreamin' or was that you working in the Gulf station on Spring Garden?

LOU: Call. (*Lou calls*)

JOE: Yeah, Mick, that was me. (*Pause*) How much is the bet?

LOU: Two chips.

JOE (*throwing his two chips in*): Call.

SAL: Ain't you a full-time student at Community, Joe?

JOE: Yeah.

SAL: What are you studying?

JOE: Building Design. I want to maybe be an architect . . . you know, construction. Two to you, Pete.

PETE: For two chips I'll ride it. (*Pete calls*)

SAL: Well, that's great, Joe. Lot a money in construction these days. I got a cousin—

MICK (*to Joe*): Wait a minute. You're going to Community full-time and working at the gas station?

JOE: Yeah.

PETE: Pop?

OLD PETE: Yeah, I'm in, I'm in. (*Old Pete calls*)

MICK: Help me understand this, Joe. If you're going to Community full-time, why the hell are you pumping gas?

JOE: Well, you know, I got expenses.

MICK: Expenses?! What kind of expenses?! You're eighteen years old, you live at home.

PETE: Back to you for one, Sal.

SAL: Yeah, what the hell. (*Sal calls*)

JOE (*to Mick*): Well, you know, I gotta pay for my classes.

MICK: You mean you're footing the bill for Community?

JOE (*slowly*): Yeah.

OLD PETE: Fourth street . . . (*Deals the next round*) King . . . queen . . . ace—aces wild . . . queen . . . queen . . . nine to the dealer. Three queens out. Nines are wild, aces null. Bet goes to the pair of jacks.

MICK: Check. (*Mick taps the table with his knuckles*) I can't believe that, Lou.

LOU: One. (*Lou bets a chip*) What's that, Mick?

MICK: You ain't payin' for Joey's college?

LOU: That's right.

MICK: I don't get it. A kid's got as much brains as Joe and you won't even pay to send him to Community?

LOU: Yeah, Mick. You got a problem with that?

MICK: Well, no, I just thought, you know, the kid's talented. I mean, don't you want him to be somebody? Don't you want him to be successful, for Chrissake?

PETE: Mick, can we change the subject please—

LOU: Joe knows what I want.

MICK: What does that mean? (*Pause*) Joe, what's he talking about?

JOE: Lou wants me to go to work for him.

MICK: Come on . . . in the butcher shop?! Lou, you gotta be shittin' me.

LOU: What are you tryin' to say, Mick?

MICK: Nothing, nothing . . . I just think the kid's talented, that's all.

PETE: To you for one, Joe.

JOE: Call. (*He calls*)

PETE: I'm with you. (*Pete calls*)

LOU: Something wrong with being a butcher, Mick?

MICK: No, Lou, of course not . . . no. I'm just saying, you know—I mean, Christ, Lou, look at him . . . he's beautiful . . . you got a fucking race horse for a son. I just, I think it'd be a waste if—

LOU: So what you're saying is I'm a bad father . . .

PETE: Over to you, Pop.

OLD PETE: Uhh, dealer's in. (*Old Pete calls*)

MICK: No, no, no—look, Lou, don't get pissed, okay? I'm not trying to upset you here.

PETE: Sal, bet is two.

MICK: I'm just saying that Joey, he's the only one in this room ever even went to college, you know?

SAL: Uhh, I'll stick around. (*Sal calls*)

MICK: If he's got a shot at getting out a this filthy fucking neighborhood, well . . . that's all I'm saying. All right?

LOU: Sure, Mick.

MICK: What's the bet? Two lousy chips? Call. (*Mick calls*) You're not pissed, are you, Lou?

LOU: No, Mick. I understand what you're trying to say.

MICK: Good, 'cause you know I just want what's best for Joe—

(*Lou slams Mick's head down on the table and wraps his hands around Mick's neck, strangling him. All rush to restrain Lou except for Old Pete, who remains seated and pours himself another shot*)

SAL: Pin his other arm, Joe . . . !!!

(*The other men manage after a struggle to pry Lou's hands from Mick's throat. Mick rolls immediately out of harm's way, coughing severely and his mouth bleeding slightly. As Lou continues to struggle, Pete grabs his head with both hands*)

PETE: Look at me, Lou!! Who am I?! What's my name, Lou?!!

LOU: Pete . . . Peter . . . (*Lou's grip on Pete's hands begins to relax*)

PETE: Peter who?! Come on, Lou, Peter who?!

LOU: Peter . . . Peter McGuire . . .

PETE: That's right, Lou. This is Peter McGuire. Peter McGuire.

(*Lou has now fully calmed. Mick angrily strokes his neck as he warily returns to his seat. Pete walks Lou back to his chair and Lou sits back down without a word, staring down coldly at the table. Joe, Sal, and Pete slowly return to their seats when they are convinced that the danger has passed. Silence. Lou rises suddenly and enters the kitchen. A moment later he reappears with three beers. He places one before Joe, the second before Mick, and the third he keeps for himself, returning to his seat without a word. After a long moment of silence, Mick accepts the beer and opens it*)

OLD PETE (*resuming the deal*): Fifth street. Six . . . two . . . seven . . . six . . . six . . . two. Betting stays with the pair of jacks.

MICK: Three. (*Bets three*)

LOU: Out. (*Lou folds*)

JOE: I'm in. (*Joe calls*)

PETE: Yeah, what the hell. (*Pete calls*)

OLD PETE: Dealer's in. (*Old Pete calls*)

SAL: Can't do it. Out. (*Sal folds*)

MICK: You know, Sal, I really admire your balls.

SAL: Yeah? Well then you can lick 'em. I'm getting another beer. Petey, there any more beer in the fridge?

PETE: Yeah, Sal, Peggy shoulda picked up a case a Rocks this morning. Help yourself.

(*Sal exits into the kitchen*)

OLD PETE (*dealing the next round*): Sixth street. King . . . king . . . four . . . three. Bet goes to pair of kings, jack high.

MICK: Let's keep it light till seventh. I'm in for one. (*Mick bets one*)

JOE: Call. (*He calls*)

PETE: Chump change. (*Pete calls*)

OLD PETE: Call. (*Old Pete calls*) All right, seventh street. This one's down . . . (*Old Pete deals out the final cards face down*) Bet to the kings, jack high.

MICK: What do you say to three, Joe? (*Mick bets three*)

JOE: I'd say no sweat. (*Joe calls*)

MICK: You think I'm bluffing?

JOE: I think either way you're gonna lose.

MICK: Tough talk, tough talk . . .

PETE: Christ Almighty, Lou, half an hour and this kid's already a pro. Out. (*Pete folds*)

OLD PETE: Can't do it. (*Old Pete folds, then lights another cigar*) Don't you give this kid any more chips, Mick.

MICK: I ain't worried. What do you got, Joe?

LOU: He called you, Mick.

(*Pause*)

MICK: That's right . . . he called me. (*Turns over his cards*) Three jacks.

JOE (*laying down*): Four sixes.

MICK (*banging the table with his fist*): Christ! Who the hell invited this kid?!

JOE: Sorry, Mick. (*Joe starts to collect the pot as Sal re-enters*)

MICK: It's all right, Joe. You know I'm just kidding around.

SAL: What happened? Mick lose?

MICK: He was holding four sixes. Can you believe that shit?

SAL: Luck of the Irish, eh, Mick?

MICK: Ain't that the fucking truth.

SAL: That a boy, Joe. (*Sal sits*) Nothing we like better than seeing your Uncle Mick get his clock cleaned.

PETE: You learn fast, Joe. I like that. We like that.

JOE: Look, Pete, I got almost all the chips in front of me . . . you think you can tell me what we're playing for now?

PETE: When the game's over . . . and you ain't won it yet, so don't get cocky. Deal's to you, Sal.

SAL: Pass. I got a beer to drink. (*Sal slides the deck to Mick*)

PETE: All right. What's the game, Mick?

MICK: I don't know, Petey. I'm getting a little tired of this pussy poker.

PETE: What do you think, fellas? Time for a little night baseball?

(*General nods of agreement. Joe stands, stretches, then walks over to the door*)

JOE: It's about fucking time. (*Picks up his bat and glove and turns to the other men*) So where we playing? Taney? Star Garden? Taney park ain't got no lights, so I guess we . . . (*Joe pauses. All the men are seated and staring at him*)

PETE: Sit down, Joe.

JOE: I thought we're going to play . . . didn't you just say it's time for—

LOU: Sit down, Joe. When Pete tells you to do something, you do it. Got it?

(*Pause*)

JOE: Yeah, yeah, I got it . . . (*Joe reluctantly walks back to his seat*) But I thought—didn't you just say we were gonna go play some night baseball?

PETE: Yeah, I did. And we are. Tell 'em the rules, Mick.

MICK: Night baseball is seven-card stud, Joe. All your cards are face down and you can't look at them . . .

JOE: You gotta be shitting me—another card game?!

MICK: Threes and nines are wild, and if you show a four, you get an extra card . . .

JOE: Just tell me this. Are we actually gonna play baseball—and I'm talking about the real thing now—sometime tonight?

PETE: Yes.

JOE: When?

PETE: When the game's over. Now sit down and relax.

(*Pause. Joe sinks back down into his seat*)

MICK: Now the first guy to bat, Joe—that's your Pop—turns over his top card and makes a bet. If you wanna keep playing for the pot, you gotta call. The second guy then starts turning over his cards till he beats what the first guy's got showing with what he's got showing, and he makes another bet. Then the next guy has to beat what the last guy has showing, and it keeps on going around until somebody wins.

JOE: What if I can't beat what the last guy has showing?

MICK: Then you're out of the pot. Whoever's still in and has the highest hand at the end wins.

JOE: All right, I'll figure it out as we play.

PETE: Deal the cards, Mick. Night baseball. (*Mick begins the deal*) You know what I love about night baseball, Joe? You can look like you ain't got shit, and then with one card, two cards, find out you got the winning hand. This is the toughest game in poker, Joe, 'cause things may be looking one way one minute, and then all of a sudden—one card—you got a whole new ball game.

MICK: Ante up. Lou starts. (*All throw in one. Lou draws his top card*) Nine—wild card, ace of hearts.

LOU: One. (*Lou bets one. Everyone calls*)

MICK: All in. Joe's gotta beat an ace of hearts. (*Joe turns over his first two cards*) Ten . . . nine—pair of tens.

JOE: I'll go one. (*Joe bets one. Everyone calls*)

MICK: To you, Petey. Pair of tens. (*Pete turns over his first three cards*) King . . . five . . . king—pair of kings. Kings bet.

PETE: I'm in for my two last chips. (*Pete bets two*)

OLD PETE: I'm out. (*Old Pete folds. Sal, Lou, and Joe call*)

MICK: Go ahead, Sal. High pair.

SAL: Two kings? No problem. (*Sal turns over his first two cards*)

MICK: Three—wild . . . four—extra card . . . (*Mick deals the extra card*) Queen—pair of queens . . . (*Sal turns over his next card*) Three—three queens. Trip queens bets.

SAL: Sorry, Petey.

PETE: Don't sweat it, Sal. Someone's gotta lose. (*Pete throws his cards in and sits back*)

SAL: I'll go in for two. (*Sal bets two. Lou and Joe call*)

MICK: All right . . . I'm out, Petey's out, Pete Senior is out. Just Sal, Lou, and Joe left. Lou is up to bat. Gotta beat three queens. (*Lou turns over three cards*) Six . . . three—three sixes . . . eight—three eights . . . four—extra card . . . (*Mick deals Lou an extra card*) Deuce—five diamonds. Bet goes to the flush.

LOU: Three. (*Lou bets three. Sal and Joe call*)

MICK: Back to Joe. Gotta beat an ace high flush to bet. (*Joe turns over his next four cards*) Six . . . king—pair of kings . . . six—three sixes . . . king—full house, kings over sixes. Full house bets.

JOE: Four. (*Joe bets four. Lou and Sal call*)

MICK: And Sal is out of chips. Last chance, Sally.

SAL: Well, here goes nothing . . . (*Sal turns over his four remaining cards*)

MICK: Seven . . . eight . . . . five . . . ace—five hearts. Heart flush, ace high. Not good enough. Sal's out. Lou's gotta beat a full house. (*Lou turns over his two remaining cards*) Seven . . . eight—four eights! Lou's still alive. Your bet, Lou.

(*Pause*)

LOU: I'm in for everything I got in front of me. (*Lou counts his chips*) Eighteen. (*Lou slides his chips into the pot. Pause*)

JOE: I'm in. (*Joe grabs two large handfuls of chips and drops them cooly into the pot. General murmurs of excitement and approval from around the table*)

SAL: This kid's got some balls, Petey.

PETE: Did I tell ya?

MICK: This is it, fellas. The moment of truth. Joe, you gotta beat four eights with one last card.

(*Joe slowly turns over his last card*)

Four—extra card. This is the game . . . . (*Mick deals the extra card*) Three!! Four kings!!

(*Cheers and groans from around the table*)

Christ, this fucking kid's got some luck!! Joe takes the pot . . . and the game!

(*Joe rakes in the pot as everyone except Lou and Old Pete congratulates him. Pete pats him on the back*)

SAL: The boy's a shark, Petey!

OLD PETE: Beginner's luck . . .

PETE: You did good, Joe. I'm proud of you. All of us . . . . we're very impressed.

JOE (*standing suddenly*): I, uh . . . thanks very much, Pete, but . . . look, I don't know what you all want from me, but it's pretty clear we ain't playing baseball tonight, and I'm getting pretty tired of the third degree. I won your stupid little game, I listened to all your bullshit, and now I want whatever I get for these chips in front of me and then I'm gonna go home. All right?

(*Pause*)

PETE: You are tough, Joe. We seen and heard enough tonight to know you're ready.

JOE: Look, if it's all the same to you fellas, I'm going home. I'm tired, I got floor plans due tomorrow . . .

PETE: We're not keeping you here, Joe. You can leave if you want . . . but if you do, you can't collect your prize.

JOE: Oh, yeah? What the hell is that?

PETE (*smiling warmly*): You get to bat first.

JOE: You gotta be shitting me. All this crap with the cards . . . that was to decide who bats first?!

SAL: It's a great honor to bat first, Joe.

JOE: Why? What the hell's the difference?

MICK: That's the only way you get to see the expression.

JOE: What expression?

SAL: Can I tell him, Petey?

PETE: Go ahead, Sal.

SAL: You know, the expression . . . the look on that nigger's face when you bash his head in with the bat.

JOE: Bash whose head in?!

SAL: The nigger . . . whichever jig from the Mount Vernon Crew we pick up.

(*Pause*)

JOE: Hold on . . . what . . . what are we talking about here?

PETE: We're talking about night baseball, Joe. We're letting you in.

OLD PETE: This is a big mistake, Peter . . .

PETE: It's done, Pop. (*Pause*) Tell him the rules, Mick.

MICK: It goes like this, Joe . . . very simple. You're up to bat . . . let's say Lou and Sal are holding up the nigger . . . you take one swing as hard as you can. If his eyes are open and he can still talk after you hit him, that's a single. To be perfectly honest, though, Joe, singles are garbage . . . only Sal hits singles. Now if you draw blood, maybe knock out a few teeth, that's a double . . . which is a little more respectable. Now if you knock him out cold, that's a triple . . . and that ain't easy, let me tell you. But the grand-daddy of all, the name of the game, Joe, and where your father is a master . . . is when you break that nigger's neck with one swing. That is what we call a home run. Got it?

(*Pause as Joe, stunned, looks away in shock*)

Joe . . . ?

(*Pause*)

Petey, what's a matter with him?

JOE: How many times have you done this?

PETE: You're a smart guy, Joe; figure it out. What's today?

JOE: It's . . . uh . . . it's the twenty-third.

PETE: That mean anything to you?

JOE: The twenty-third? No, I don't . . . March twenty-third.

PETE: That's right. March twenty-third. The night my fucking heart died. How many months ago was that, Joe?

JOE: That's seven . . . seven months ago.

PETE: There's your answer.

JOE: You . . . you done this to seven people?!

PETE: Well, six . . . we ain't gone out tonight yet.

JOE: So you—all of you—you killed six people—

PETE: Listen to me, Joe, 'cause I feel like I'm losing you here. We get together every month on the twenty-third—the same night that five pieces of fucking dog shit from the Mount Vernon Crew murdered my Mikey. We play some cards, then when it gets dark we climb into Sal's van and head down to Mount Vernon. We drive around a little, wait till we find a Crew member alone, then one of us—usually it's Mick—goes out and tells him we're looking to score some rock. We get him to come to the van, we pull open the side door, wack him a few times, and we're off nice and quiet. We take him out to Taney park, we stand him up on home plate, and then we get some payback. It's quiet, it's clean, and it's simple . . . and a lot of fucking fun, too, eh? (*The older men chuckle. Pause*) What's on your mind, Joe? You look upset. You worried about getting caught?

JOE: No, no . . . I just don't understand how—

SAL: Don't you worry about getting caught, Joe. We got this down to a science, you understand? See, the cards determine the order. You won, so you bat first. Lou came in second, so if it comes to that, Lou bats second. Then I go third, Petey fourth, and Mick was first out, so he's clean-up . . . and clean-up never bats; he just holds the gun.

JOE: The gun?!

SAL: Yeah, the gun . . . in case he tries to get away. We use Petey's .38 . . . we figure a cop's piece is about as clean as they come.

MICK: Really, Joe, the whole thing . . . it's beautiful. We got Pete Senior driving the van, so right there, you know we're in the clear no matter what. Even if someone sees something suspicious, what are they going to do? As soon as they see whose driving the van, they know it won't mean nothing but grief if they say something. I mean, who they going to believe? A respected cop or some fucking crackhead felon? And no one's missing anyone, either. We're performing a public service, Joe. Cleaning up the scum.

PETE: I know it sounds like a lot of risk, but trust me when I tell you there's nothing to it. We use new bats every time—courtesy of Mick's Sporting Goods, of course. After each game, we take all the bats and burn 'em. We take the body down to Penn's Landing, pier 38, tie a couple of cinder blocks around its ankles and sink it—probably feeds the fishes for weeks, which is nice, 'cause . . . you know . . . we care about the environment just as much as the next guy. (*Chuckles from around the table*) So what's there to worry about? No witnesses, no weapon, no body . . . in other words, no worries. And you got two cops to boot, making sure our private business stays private. No risk, Joe, I promise you.

JOE (*exploding*): Christ, Pete, it ain't the risk! Don't you understand?! I mean, you . . . how do you even know they're the ones?! No one could I.D. the five who did it, right?

PETE: That's right, Joe, none of the witnesses could I.D. the five nigs in the dark. My son was murdered and we couldn't do a fucking thing about it. You think that's justice?

JOE: No, but that's not the point! When is it gonna stop, Pete?!

PETE: Well, we gotta be systematic about this. Since we don't know which ones did it, we gotta wack the whole Crew.

JOE: Christ, that's twenty guys!! You're gonna wack twenty—

PETE: Look, Joe, what is the problem?! I'm getting the impression you're not behind this.

OLD PETE: Course he ain't behind this, Peter. Any idiot can see that. He's a little boy. He ain't ready to grow up yet.

JOE (*to Old Pete*): What?! You're killing innocent people and I'm supposed to pat all of you on the fucking back?! That what I gotta do to be a man?!

PETE (*standing*): Innocent?! Who the fuck are you calling innocent?! They had to mop my son's brains off the goddamn sidewalk, and we have these animals to thank for it. They're all guilty, Joe . . . even the ones who didn't wack Mikey. These people will shoot you on a dare, Joe, for the ten dollar gold chain around your fucking neck. How many people you think each of these punks has killed? With their crack and their MAC-10s? They're all killers, Joe . . . and if we don't get them, you can bet your ass they'll get us.

JOE: But when's it gonna end, Pete? The nigs that jumped Mikey, they didn't do it for kicks . . . they were looking for some payback, too. Three Crew members got the shit kicked out of them that morning by Frank Connelly and his boys. Word got back to Seventeenth Street, and the Crew went looking for a little justice. They found a white boy about the right age, right neighborhood, alone . . . and they wacked him. Simple as that. We wack them, they wack us, we wack them back . . . on and on and on. When's that gonna end, Pete?

PETE: It ends, Joe, when they respect us . . . when they fear us . . . when they have no doubt in what little minds they got that for each thing they do to us, twice as much will be done to them . . . that's when it ends. These people ain't got morals, Joe, they can't be reasoned with. They think of Christ, they think of weakness. They see a peaceful neighborhood, they see a happy hunting ground. You can't reason with the wolves, Joe.

JOE: I just . . . I don't understand how you can do it. How, Sal? How can you kill an eighteen year old kid? How 'bout you, Mick? How can you—

PETE: How?! How could those fucking moulies do that to my Mikey, eh?! That's all you gotta ask yourself, Joe. One simple question. Your best friend is gone, Joe, and you ain't ever gonna see him again, do you understand me? Never. And why? 'Cause the niggers hate our guts, Joe. And that's never gonna change. It's the way things are, Joe. You can either deal with it, or die by it. It's your choice.

JOE: There's gotta be another way, Pete. There's gotta be something—

(*Lou suddenly stands and walks to the door. The other men fall silent. Lou takes a bat and walks over to Joe*)

LOU: It's time to go play some baseball. (*Lou extends the bat to Joe*) Here's your bat, Joe.

(*Joe freezes, tense and suspicious. Pause*)

Take it.

(*Joe remains frozen. Lou slams the bat down on the table. Chips fall and bottles overturn. Lou shoves the bat in Joe's face*)

TAKE IT!

(*Pause*)

JOE: I don't want it, Lou.

LOU (*controlled, but threatening*): Take the bat, Joe.

JOE: I'm not playing baseball with you, Lou.

LOU: I'm gonna tell you one more time. Take the fucking bat! (*Joe remains frozen*) What are you, a nigger-lover?

JOE: No, Lou, I ain't got no love for the niggers. I just ain't a killer.

LOU (*behind Joe*): Oh, I see, you ain't a killer. Hey, fellas, Joe here, he ain't a killer. Course, he ain't a nigger-lover, either, so I guess that leaves . . . (*Whispering in Joe's ear*) PUSSY.

JOE: Get away from me, Lou . . .

LOU: You're blind, Joe. Blind and stupid. You ain't gonna last long.

JOE: I ain't stupid, Lou. And I ain't gonna be a part of this.

SAL: Joe, be reasonable, will ya . . . ?

MICK: Please, Joe, think about what you're doing—

LOU: Shut up!! (*Pause. To Joe*) Who the fuck do you think you are?

JOE: I don't know, Lou . . . I just know I ain't a murderer.

LOU: I'll tell you who you are. You're a filthy fucking wop, just like your old man, and all you know how to do is chop meat. That's who you are, Joe.

JOE: No, Lou, that's who you are . . . and I don't want no part of it—

LOU: YOU'RE A FUCKING DISGRACE, JOE!! You're a disgrace to your own kind . . . to me, to your mother, to Mikey. You are nothing without your family, do you understand?! And your family is nothing without the neighborhood. They come first, you little fuck, capeche?! Now take the bat!

JOE (*pushing the bat away*): NO!!

(*Pause*)

LOU: All right, Joe. I understand. You ain't a killer, is that right? Well, you know what . . . I don't believe you.

(*Lou gives Joe a sudden shove. Joe staggers back. Lou advances*)

I think you're nothing but a pussy. Are you a pussy, Joe?

MICK: Jesus, Lou, take it easy . . .!

LOU: Come on, you little pussy . . .

(*Lou jabs Joe in the stomach with the bat. Joe doubles over*)

SAL: Christ, Lou! He's just a kid . . .

LOU: I'll tell you what I think, Joe. I think you're a pussy and a nigger-lover. How can you do it, Joe? How can you stand those fucking junglemonkeys? You seen what they done to me, you seen what they done to your friend, and you, you just couldn't give a fuck.

JOE (*backing away*): You trapped yourself, Lou.

(*Lou makes another jab with the baseball bat, but Joe smacks it away just in time*)

PETE: That's enough, Lou . . . !

LOU: I'm tired of you, Joe. You don't respect me. You don't respect the family, the neighborhood, your friends and loved ones . . . you think you're just too good for all of us. (*Lou advances, raising up the bat*)

PETE: Lou, put the bat down . . . !

JOE: You don't scare me, you dumb fucking bully . . .

LOU: Oooooh, tough guy, eh? Well we both know words don't mean shit, don't we, Joe? Action talks, and bullshit walks, am I right? (*Takes another step toward Joe*) I mean, you say you're tough, but you ain't exactly shown you're tough, now have you . . . ?

JOE: Don't you come any closer, Lou, or so help me . . .

LOU: This is your lucky day, boy. Now you get a chance to show us what you're made of. (*Takes another step toward Joe*)

PETE: Lou, look at me . . . !

LOU: We're gonna see if the nigger-lover is full of shit or not, 'cause you know what, Joe? (*Raising the bat in one mighty fist*) I'm gonna fucking kill you.

PETE: LOU . . . !

(*Lou rushes at Joe as all the men at the table except Old Pete jump to their feet. Joe grabs hold of Lou's wrist before he can bring the bat down and knees Lou full-force in the groin. Lou doubles over, paralyzed with pain. There is an amazed pause as Joe punches Lou savagely in the side and pulls him down to the floor*)

JOE: Who you fuckin' kidding?! Who you kidding, old man?

(*Joe pins Lou's arm around his back and pushes his face against the floor*)

PETE: All right, Joe, that's enough. This has gone too far already—

LOU: Don't you ever forget who's boss here, you little fuck!

JOE: You think you're the boss, Lou?! Jesus, you are a dumb fuck. Pete, he's the boss. He's the brains . . . you're just the fucking muscle. You're too fucking dumb to be the boss.

PETE: Take it easy, Joe. It's over, son. Just let your father up and walk away. It's over.

JOE (*lifting Lou's head by the scalp*): Is that right, Lou? Is this over?

LOU: I'm gonna break every fuckin' bone in your body, boy . . .

JOE (*chuckling bitterly*): No, no, Pete, it ain't over. Not by a longshot. (*To Lou*) Is it . . . Pop?

LOU (*wheezing*): Don't you let me up, boy, 'cause if you do I'll rip you to fucking—

JOE (*punching Lou in the side*): That's ENOUGH! (*Joe strips the bat from Lou's hand*) Think I'm scared of you, old man?! Think I'm scared of you?! I ain't scared of you, Lou. You ain't so tough . . . (*Joe suddenly jumps to his feet, bat in hand*)
Get up, Lou.

(*Lou slowly rises to his feet*)

Get up, YOU PUSSY!

(*As soon as he is fully up, Lou growls and makes a feeble lunge at Joe. Joe steps in and hauls off with the bat, smashing Lou across the face. Lou flies back and sprawls out across the table. Pete, Sal, and Mick check his condition: Pete slaps his cheek; Mick listens to his heart; Sal checks his pulse. Old Pete nonchalantly lights another cigar. Joe paces around, clearly a bit deranged*)

What was that, Mick? Single? Double? It's gotta be at least a double, right?

MICK: Jesus Christ, Joe . . .

PETE: Lou?! Lou, if you can hear me, do something . . . move something so we know you're okay . . .

JOE: He's . . . he's all right, isn't he?! I mean, he's breathin' and everything, right, Petey?

PETE: I don't know, Joe. I just . . . I don't know. Come on, Mick, let's get him sitting up. Count of three. One . . . two . . . three . . .

(*Pete and Mick pull Lou up into a sitting position on the table, his back supported by Pete's shoulder. Lou groans, his mouth bleeding. Pete again slaps his face lightly*)

Wake up, Lou. Come on, we know you ain't out, you faker.

(*Joe stares at the bat in his hands and walks away from the table in a daze. He walks over to the mantelpiece and stares up at Mikey's portrait in a fog*)

Pop, go get some ice from the kitchen.

(*Old Pete remains seated*)

Pop, what are you doing?! Go get us some ice.

OLD PETE: Hey, Peter . . . fuck you! I'm smoking.

PETE: Great, Pop. Thanks for the help.

(*Lou's chest starts to heave up and down*)

MICK: Jesus, Petey, what's wrong? Is he dying or something?

PETE: I don't know . . . I think he's . . . crying . . . or something . . .

(*Lou starts to chuckle out loud. In a moment, Pete joins in*)

I knew you were faking, you son of a bitch.

LOU: Hey . . . Pete . . . Petey . . . ?

PETE: Yeah, Lou, I'm here, I'm here.

(*Pete takes out a handkerchief and wipes the blood from Lou's mouth*)

LOU: You see that?

PETE: Yeah, I saw it, Lou.

LOU: That was something, wasn't it, Petey?

PETE: It was something, Lou.

LOU: Hey, Petey?

PETE: Yeah, Lou?

LOU: That Joe . . . he's my boy.

PETE: That he is, Lou. That he is.

(*Joe turns and stares at Lou. Pause*)

JOE: What did he just say?

PETE: Come on over here, Joe. Your father . . . he needs you.

(*Lou feebly extends his hand to Joe*)

LOU: Come here, Joe. Gimme your hand.

(*Joe doesn't move*)

JOE: I can't.

LOU: Gimme your hand, Joe.

JOE: I won't let you do it!

PETE: Joe, what is the matter with you?! Your father, he's calling for you . . .

JOE: What's a matter with me?! What's a matter with you, Pete?! Mikey is dead . . . your son is gone . . . and you killed him! Don't you fucking understand that?!

PETE: You're upset, Joe. Just calm down and think about . . .

JOE: All a you . . . Sal, Mick, Old Pete . . . you all had a hand. And now, now you're trying to kill me . . . !

PETE: What?! What are you . . . Mick, what's he talking about . . . ?

MICK: I don't know, Petey. He ain't making any sense . . .

PETE: Joe, put down the fucking bat . . .

SAL: Look, Joe, take a deep breath and . . .

JOE: None of you . . . none of you understand . . .

PETE: Yes we do, Joe. We understand. Mikey's death hit you hard, we all know that, and it's only natural that you . . .

(*Joe turns around and smashes the portrait of Mikey with the baseball bat*)

Jesus Christ, Joe, are you fucking nuts . . . ?!

(*Joe begins to smash all of the memorabilia that lines the mantle. Pete protects Lou's head as Sal and Mick jump up and move on Joe. Joe turns on the two men, bat at the ready. Sal and Mick circle at a safe distance*)

MICK: Don't do anything stupid, son . . .

SAL: Joe, you're not thinking clear. We're your family, for Chrissake. Now just put the bat down . . .

JOE: You ain't getting me, you fucking animals. I'll bash all a your fucking brains in . . .

SAL: Joe, what are you saying? I watched you grow up . . . we all did . . .

PETE: Come on, Joseph, you're doing things the hard way. If you fight us, you know you can't win . . .

JOE: Sal, get away from that door . . .

(*Joe starts to move toward the door, his back to the wall, as Sal and Mick back away*)

OLD PETE: Where you going, son?!

(*Joe stops*)

Where? The police? We are the fucking police. Or maybe you just figured you'd run away? But you know we'll find you, and even if we don't, what's the difference? You can't go nowhere. You're as much a part a us as we're a part a you. This neighborhood, the men in this room . . . we're all you know. You can't do a fucking thing without us, and without our protection you wouldn't last ten goddamn seconds on the street. We're all you got, son. Now put the bat down. Come sit, join your family.

(*Pause*)

JOE: Please . . . just let me go . . . Jesus, I gotta . . . you gotta let me go . . .

SAL (*stepping forward*): Gimme the bat, Joe.

(*Pause. Joe hands the bat to Sal, then leans back against the wall and slowly sinks down, defeated*)

JOE: Please . . . just let me out . . . I can't do this . . . I ain't a . . . killer . . .

LOU: The hell you're not!

(*Pause*)

PETE: Take Lou a second, will ya, Mick?

MICK: Sure, Petey.

(*Mick returns to the table and positions himself behind Lou's right shoulder. Pete shifts Lou's weight to Mick. Lou groans. Pete walks over to Sal, who hands him the baseball bat*)

PETE: I know it hurts, Joe. I know you're thinking things like it ain't right, it ain't fair, and you're right. It ain't fair at all, Joe . . . but it's the way things are. Hell, the first few days in Nam, I was puking all the time, crying . . . I saw these people doing these horrible things and I . . . I thought to myself, this is insanity . . . this is . . . murder. But then one day, Joe, I woke up . . . the day I shoved my bayonet in the throat of a V.C. scout . . . knowing that that poor bastard wanted to do the same to me . . . so I got him first. Once I saw what these hands could do, Joe, I knew that this is what I am, and all my ideas of truth and fairness . . . bullshit. Morals are only . . . weakness. But you know what I'm talking about . . . you're scared, angry, confused, 'cause tonight you saw the animal within you. Yeah, I know it hurts . . . it's tearing you up inside, and you're trying to fight it, but you can't win, Joe . . . to be a man is to accept that animal . . . accept it in you . . . and accept it in everybody else. Now . . .

(*Pete offers the bat*)

You ready to be a man, Joe? (*Pause*) We need you, Joe. We need you and you need us. Together we got a fighting chance, but alone . . . you're naked . . . they'll tear you apart. Just ask Mikey.

(*Pause*)

Stand up, Joe.

(*Joe slowly rises to his feet*)

You can bullshit us, but don't bullshit yourself.

(*Pete again offers the bat*)

Take the bat, son. The fear and the pain . . . they don't last.

(*Pause*)

Take the bat.

(*Pause. The two men stand together in silence, neither one moving a muscle. Blackout. Curtain.*)

THE BEST AMERICAN SHORT PLAYS 1993–1994

Edited by

Howard Stein and Glenn Young

Best American Short Plays Series

AN APPLAUSE ORIGINAL
THE BEST AMERICAN SHORT PLAYS 1993–1994

Applause Theatre Book Publishers

211 West 71st Street
New York, NY 10023
Phone: (212) 595-4735
Fax: (212) 721-2856

406 Vale Road
Tonbridge KENT TN91XR
Phone: 0732-357755
Fax: 0732-770219

First Applause Printing, 1995

To Marianne, always

CONTENTS

INTRODUCTION

To make a long story short is not the function of American short play writing; the size and shape which the form generates is of infinite variety. At Louisville each year, The Actor's Theatre presents a series of "ten-minute shorts"; during the 1993 festival, the company produced *Slavs* by Tony Kushner, which is described by the playwright as "A Short Play in a Prologue, Three Acts, and an Epilogue," extending over seventy-five pages. In our present volume, we have chosen some short plays that are part and parcel of longer pieces: *Tall Tales* is one of nine short plays that comprise a unified history of *The Kentucky Cycle; Barry, Betty and Bill* is one of twenty-three short plays on a single subject unified under the title *Love Allways; Window of Opportunity* is one of fourteen short plays which comprise John Augustine's depiction of *Generation X; The Universal Language* is one of six completely disparate pieces produced collectively as *All In the Timing.* We have also included here *The Midlife Crisis of Dionysus,* first heard as a radio play on *The Prairie Home Companion,* and then converted to a short play suitable for this volume. There is a parody of a classic American full length play, Christopher Durang's *For Whom the Southern Belle Tolls,* and a dynamic monologue aimed directly at the audience, Susan Miller's *My Left Breast.* The diversity of forms which the short American play takes seems to be without limit.

What is common to all of these "short" plays, however, is the quality crucial to all dramatic forms: the experience of a character, or characters, being tested. What separates drama from other literary adventures is the relentless nature of the test. We refer to a dramatic condition in our daily lives, as in literature, in terms of a challenge to a person's presumed mettle. This challenge may threaten the spectator and reader as well. Can we blame Hazlitt and Lamb for wanting to steer away from the theater where the likes of Hamlet, Lear, Othello, and Macbeth in the throes of their terrible struggles barged into their complacent drawing-room lives?

Although the essence of drama is testing, decision-making is an equally critical component. Hegel tells us that tragedy involves a choice between rights, two tenable rights in untenable conflict, rather than the clear-cut right and wrong of melodrama. The tragedy, according to Hegel, is in the inexorable wanton waste of a rightful force. The test *demands* a choice whose result generates the drama. Tests and their concomitant choices arise out of various states of being, at times a result of deliberation, at others of impulse, even of fatigue. Hedda Gabler justifies her marriage to Tessman by the fact that "she danced herself out." In Carol K. Mack's *The Magenta Shift,* Jane walks into the subway at three in the morning, and discovers the greatest test of her life in the form of Rhea. What she does surprises them both. Inside the urgency of time and space, a playwright invents situations or incidents which test the mettle (the ethical habit of action) of the story's major characters. What we do in times of challenge, rather than what we say in times of tranquility (remember *Lord Jim*), reveals our character, not our personality. The revelation of personality makes for very limited drama; character revelation makes for very exhilarating drama. It teaches us to see with our own eyes.

Among the plays you are about to read is a story of a marriage gone sour in which Betty, after considerable bickering with her husband Barry, finally succumbs to Barry's rational test. Tee, in *Come Down Burning,* has gotten where she is because of the choices she has made like a bad habit. Tee flunks her tests and Skoolie is forced to repair the failures as best she can. Each of the plays grapples with this kind of event and condition, sometimes with levity (*The Midlife Crisis of Dionysus*), sometimes with grim reality (*My Left Breast*). The tests confronted in *The Interview,* in *An Act of Devotion,* and in *Date With a Stranger,* are distinctly different from the tests which confront Emma Thorn in *Blue Stars* or Marianne, Tommy, Jed, and JT in *Tall Tales.*

The nature of our dramatic condition may be encapsulated in one sentence by Robert Frost: "The trouble with living a human life is that you have to act on insufficient evidence." We are obliged to choose during the time of a test when we do not yet know enough. And alas, we can never know enough to act with complete conviction. When we choose, we sometimes resort to chance, sometimes to intelligence, sometimes to intuition. But no matter what instrument we trust or employ, we are left with the nagging uncertainty as to the rightness of that choice.

The dramatist for our stage takes her or his cue from the divine playwright in the sky, whose testing is constant and by which we mortals are revealed, discovered, and developed.

HOWARD STEIN
Columbia University
January, 1995

WINDOW OF OPPORTUNITY

John Augustine

John Augustine

John Augustine's first two plays, *Mrs. Smith Plays The Piano* and *Back To Canton,* were presented at Ensemble Studio Theatre's Octoberfest. *Urban Blight,* a musical evening of sketches at Manhattan Theatre Club, included his playlet *Subway.* His plays *Insatiable!, Temporary People,* and *Scab Writes A Song* (in which he played the title role), all premiered at Contemporary Theatre in Soho.

As part of *Generation X,* an evening of one-acts, *Window Of Opportunity* premiered at HOME for Contemporary Theatre in December, 1993. Bill Russell directed Gerit Quealy as Sally and Sherry Anderson as Leslie. In a production directed by the author in 1994, at Ensemble Studio Theatre, Ms. Anderson reprised her role, with Allison Janney as Sally.

As an actor, John has appeared in Christopher Durang's *Naomi In The Living Room,* Bill Russell's *Elegies, A Walk On The Lake* by Heather McCutcheon, and *Seven Blowjobs* by Mac Wellman (a title which has played havoc with his resume!) at Soho Rep.

Augustine sang and danced the role of Dawne in the satirical night-club act *Chris Durang And Dawne* at the Criterion Center and Caroline's Comedy Club. Augustine is a member of the Dramatists Guild and recently received a Revson Fellowship from Playwrights Horizon commissioning a new play.

Characters:

SALLY, *late 30s, strong, sexy, intelligent*
LESLIE, *her friend, supportive, friendly.*

Scene:

Sally's bedroom. DSL is a small chair and table with Sally's makeup. USR is a bed or chaise for Leslie to sit on. Sally begins the play in her lingerie, with a robe, looking at herself in the full-length mirror on the fourth wall. During the play, she is dressing to meet her husband for dinner. She puts on garterless stockings and a sexy outfit. By the end of the scene she has transformed herself. Aside from getting dressed, she and Leslie are perhaps having a glass of wine.

Acting note: Sally is in breakTHROUGH, not breakDOWN. This means she is excited by analyzing and articulating her problems. She is not meant to be lethargic.

SALLY: Who am I? I just woke up one day and I was in this body, in this house, in this life. Next to that man and I thought, "I don't know who that is." No, I really don't. I'm so afraid to admit the truth to myself. I'm so afraid to admit that I'm not in love.

LESLIE: You're not in love?

SALLY: No. I think I was in love with the idea of a nice life. An uneventful . . .

LESLIE (*trying to encourage her to go on*): Uneventful . . .

SALLY: I don't mean uneventful. I mean un-dramatic. Is that a word?

LESLIE: I know what you mean.

SALLY: I find lately that I'm dead inside. Really dead.

LESLIE: Are you seeing a therapist?

SALLY: Well no. But it seems the more self-help books I read, the more meetings I go to, the more I realize what a lie my life is.

LESLIE: Wow.

SALLY: No, it's true. It's like I'm living some idea of something. I don't know. My mind is so cluttered I can't even articulate it. Is that a word?

LESLIE: Yeah. I think so. Sure. Articulate. Well yeah.

SALLY: And then it's like, here I am admitting to you, my friend, another human being that I am not in love with my husband but the idea of him with somebody else, it makes me want to kill him.

LESLIE: I get jealous.

SALLY: No, but you see it's not about jealousy exactly. I think I want to be *adored* by him. But I don't want to love him back. I don't want to make love to *him,* but I also don't want him to make love with anyone else.

LESLIE: I understand that. I haven't had sex in two years.

SALLY: But shouldn't I want him to find somebody? Have an affair or whatever. Why do I care?

LESLIE: I think that's normal.

SALLY: See. If he had an affair, maybe he'd leave me alone in the bedroom. So. Theoretically, shouldn't I want him to be fooling around?

LESLIE: I don't think men can be faithful. It's not even their fault. It's something about, something primal. About hunting—or like, the male energy thing. That pounding drums thing in the woods.

SALLY: I married him because he could take care of me. I didn't really know that at the time, but I wanted to be rescued. I wanted him to rescue me from my life. He was older and I used what I had. I used my youth. My hair, my young hands, my breasts. I did. I consciously dressed them up.

LESLIE: You dressed up your breasts?

SALLY: Yes. I did. I really did. Because I knew what he wanted. I acted like I was interested in what he liked. I became like a chameleon, is that the right word?

LESLIE: Yeah. You changed a lot.

SALLY: Yeah. I adapted so well, that I don't know who I am. And now I'm old.

LESLIE: You're not old.

SALLY: I am! I used what I had. I used my youth. I used it up. I just gave it all away. I see how he looks at a waitress say, when we're out at a restaurant. I see that waitress flirt the way I used to flirt. I see him brighten up when a new secretary comes into his office. He gets that *playfulness* he had when we were dating. He doesn't have that with me now.

LESLIE: Oh. No. That's. Well you're just. I mean, my husband.

SALLY: I hate myself. I really do. I'm not trained in anything. I have no money without him. I don't earn enough to leave. I'm like a live-in prostitute without ever getting paid.

LESLIE: Most of the women in America.

SALLY: NO. It's different. I sold out because I was afraid. I saw a train come through and I hopped on in a hurry. I was afraid I couldn't do it alone. I saw this tiny window of opportunity and I went through it.

LESLIE: Wow. This seems really bad.

SALLY: Thank you for letting me ramble.

LESLIE: No. It's fine. It makes me actually feel better.

SALLY: Oh?

LESLIE: Well, yes. I was depressed too. You know. I feel all used up too. You know. The feeling of missed opportunity—never having really achieved anything—I thought my life was a mess. But now that I hear you talk, I realize—my life is actually pretty good. I don't feel so bad anymore.

SALLY: I'm sure you didn't mean that to sound the way it did.

LESLIE: Well, I don't know. How did it sound? Maybe I did.

SALLY: No. I'm sure you didn't. You're too nice.

LESLIE: I'm not too nice. (*Sally smiles*) Sally. I think you love your husband. I think you made a very good marriage. I just think you're going through your mid-life crisis. (*Sally snaps her a look*) Early. Society doesn't treat women like us well. They eat us up and spit us out. I read that somewhere.

SALLY: I just feel really hopeless.

LESLIE: Well, don't feel that way.

SALLY: Oh. Okay! (*She smiles*)

LESLIE: Here. I brought you a crystal. It unblocks something or other and it'll make you feel better. I think it's meant to improve self-esteem.

SALLY: That is so thoughtful of you. You see. It is that kind of a gesture that gives me hope.

LESLIE: I don't think they actually work. I've stopped using them.

SALLY: Oh? So you don't feel they help?

LESLIE: Well, they didn't help me. But you're different. And more desperate. I think it's all in the mind anyway.

(*Sally holds the crystal hoping it will work*)

SALLY: Were you ever at home, trying to decide what to do? And you can like—see a friend, or you can go to a movie, you can look for a job, or return something to the store, and you can't decide what to do—so you don't do anything?

LESLIE: I do that every day.

SALLY: So I make a list. And the list is either blank or there are so many things on the list that I decide I can't do anything because there's no time.

LESLIE: The list is blank?

SALLY: That's not . . . that doesn't make sense, does it. There's no such thing as a blank list. Isn't there a word for that? In grammar? Blank list, blank list.

LESLIE: Oxymoron. People said I was charming.

SALLY: They said that about me too.

LESLIE: Yeah, but they really meant it about me. No they really did. And I was charming.

SALLY: But—past a certain point—It's gone. It goes away. It dries up. It's how the world is meant to work, I'm afraid. It's only right that new young people come along. Now it is *their* chance. Their turn to be charming and young and attractive. Mine's over.

LESLIE: It doesn't have to be over. Why do you feel that way?

SALLY: The order was, questions went like this. What are you going to do with your life. Then it was—What *do* you do? Soon it will be—What did you do? And I never did anything. But oh. Once. I had so much potential.

LESLIE: At least you *had* potential. I didn't even have that.

SALLY: That's true. About me I mean.

LESLIE: Maybe it's not too late. Can you say "Nam myoho renge keyo?"

SALLY: No.

LESLIE: I know. I tried that too. But it seemed to work for Tina Turner.

SALLY: I know. You see. And we love her. We think she is so powerful. And look what she had to go through.

LESLIE: This mood we're in can't possibly serve us.

SALLY: Let's change our mood.

LESLIE: Okay.

SALLY: Let's act happy.

LESLIE: Okay. You start.

SALLY: Weeee! Weee.

LESLIE: Weee. Weee!

SALLY: Oh Boy. I am so happy. Wee . . . Wee.

LESLIE: I am happy too. Weeee.

SALLY: I didn't make a bad marriage to a sex addict and a bisexual who can't be faithful and doesn't love me. Weeee . . .

LESLIE: Weeee . . . And I didn't have an affair with your husband who has sex with lots of strangers as well as friends who use Ivory soap, so they *look* clean. Weeee.

SALLY (*stops; stares*): You had sex with my husband?

LESLIE: I'm sorry. I thought we were purging. Weeeeeeee. (*Sally looks out*)

(*FADE OUT.*)

BARRY, BETTY AND BILL

Renée Taylor
Joseph Bologna

Renee Taylor and Joseph Bologna

Renee Taylor and Joseph Bologna's first collaboration was *Lovers And Other Strangers,* in which they co-starred on Broadway in 1968. The play became a hit motion picture and earned them an Academy Award nomination for Best Screenplay in 1970.

Ms. Taylor is a native New Yorker, a graduate of the American Academy of Dramatic Arts, and the star of many off- and on-Broadway plays. Her film appearances are legion, including roles in *The Last Of The Red Hot Lovers* and *White Palace.* She was Brian BenBen's mother in the HBO television series *Dream On.*

Mr. Bologna was born in Brooklyn and received his B.A. from Brown University. A stint in the Marines was followed by a career in the theatre and films, with roles in *My Favorite Year, Blame It On Rio,* and *Chapter Two.*

Together, Ms. Taylor and Mr. Bologna have authored a series of one-act plays under the heading *Love Allways* (which includes the present play and was presented on PBS) and the Broadway hit *It Had To Be You,* which was also a successful feature film. Husband and wife since 1965, they have a son, Gabriel, who is also an actor and playwright. They have homes in New Jersey, California and Vermont, which they share with various pets.

Characters:

BILL

BETTY

BARRY

The lights are out in the sleeping alcove. The sitting room is lit romantically. Sitting at the table are Bill and Betty, a couple in their late thirties or early forties. They have obviously just had dinner. They are sipping champagne, romantic music is heard from offstage. There is a lit candle on the table. As the scene opens, Bill and Betty are laughing heartily.

BILL: You think this is fun? This is nothing. Think of the ball you're gonna have when I do my Lorne Greene impersonation.

BETTY: You do a Lorne Greene impersonation?

BILL: Sure . . . Hey, you get those cows over there . . . how's that?

BETTY: Your talent is overwhelming. (*She laughs*)

BILL: How about you? Don't you do impressions?

BETTY: Sure, I can do Martha Washington.

BILL: Let me hear.

BETTY: Hey, George, come over here and have your soup.

(*They both laugh. The laughter dies down. They look at each other lovingly*)

BILL: You're really terrific, Betty.

BETTY: Never mind terrific. Am I sexy?

BILL: Can you keep a secret?

BETTY: Pinky swear.

BILL (*reaches across the table and touches her hand*): I got a feeling that if you stick by me, you're gonna have yourself some wild affair.

BETTY: You think so?

BILL: It's gonna be worth every penny we each paid to come here. They may even put us in their brochure.

BETTY: If not, don't worry. I'll advertise you when we get back, because I've got a very big mouth.

(*They stare at each other. He leans over the table. She closes her eyes. He's about to kiss her tenderly on the lips when there's a knock on the upstage door*)

BILL: Perfect timing. Must be the hot hors d'oeuvres. (*He gets up*) Who is it?

MAN'S VOICE (*O.S.*): Is Betty Lombard in there?

BETTY: Oh, my God, I don't believe it.

BILL: What's the matter?

BETTY: It's my husband.

MAN'S VOICE (*O.S.*): Is Betty Lombard in there?

BILL (*shocked*): Your husband? I thought you said you were separated.

BETTY: I am.

BILL: What's he doing here?

BETTY: I don't know.

(*We hear a frantic knock on the door*)

MAN'S VOICE (*O.S.*): Betty? Betty, are you in there?

BILL: No, she's not.

(*The banging on the door becomes louder*)

BILL: You better climb out the back window.

BETTY: I will not. He has no right to be here.

MAN'S VOICE (*O.S., knocking again*): I know you're in there, Betty. The babysitter told me.

BETTY: Go away, Barry. I don't want to see you. (*To Bill*) Don't let him in.

MAN'S VOICE (*O.S.*): Open the door, or I'll put my foot through it.

BILL: Maybe I better climb out the back window.

BETTY: No, Bill, I want him to know about the wild affair we're going to have.

(*Betty goes to the door and opens it. Barry enters. There's a long pause, as they stare at each other*)

BARRY (*curtly*): Hello.

BETTY (*curtly*): Hello.

BARRY: How are you?

BETTY: Fine.

BARRY: How are the kids?

BETTY: Fine.

BARRY: Who's this guy?

BETTY: Bill Travis, Barry Lombard.

BILL: Hello.

BARRY: What do you say? (*To Betty*) Are you sleeping with him?

(*In unison*)

BETTY:	BILL:
That's none of your business.	No.

BETTY: Are you crazy? How dare you follow me here? I told you I want a divorce. Now, you get right back on a plane and go home.

BARRY: Look, I traveled four thousand miles to talk this out with you. After fifteen years of marriage to me, the least you could do is be decent.

BETTY: You want me to be decent? You want me to talk to you? Fine. What would you like to talk about?

BARRY: You and me.

BETTY: I see, you and me. Very well, first me. I feel fine. I never looked better. I never felt better. I'm beautiful, I'm entitled, I'm secure, and I'm living and laughing it up. Now you. I feel absolutely nothing for you. No pain, no anger, no remorse, no guilt, no pity, no anything. It's all over and I hate your guts. Now, what else shall we talk about? The weather? Hot, isn't it?

BARRY: Go on, I'm the only man you could ever love and you know it. (*Turns to Bill*) I met her when she was fifteen. I was her first boyfriend.

BETTY: Don't make a fool of yourself, Barry. It's so typical of you to do something like this. We've been separated for two months. You had plenty of time to contact me and say whatever you had to say to me. But, you, with your incredible sense of jerkiness, had to wait until I came to the most romantic place on earth and fell madly in love. (*She puts her arm through Bill's*) Yes, Bill, I have fallen madly in love with you.

BARRY: Well, I figured you needed time to get all your bad feelings toward me out of your system, but I didn't expect you'd do something potentially lewd like this. I mean, this isn't like you, Betty.

BETTY: Oh, yes it is. This is the real me. I'm no longer the woman you impressed in high school only because you were two years older than me. Nor am I the woman who was married to you. Alice-sit-by-the-fire, wash the floors, clean the closets, darn the socks and get a kick in the backside for it. She died along with her need for security from the big bad bread winner. I'm finally selfish, unsacrificing, and who-needs-you.

BARRY: Have you been seeing a psychiatrist?

BETTY: No, I've been seeing Bill. He's quite a wonderful man, Barry. He's witty, he's kind, he's exciting, he's extremely handsome, he's newly widowered, he's a pediatrician and he's sexy.

BARRY (*tenderly*): Betty, why don't you admit it. You're hurt by what the private detective told you about the woman I had in Washington.

BILL: Why don't I leave you two alone?

BETTY: No, stay, Bill. I don't want us to have any secrets from each other.

BARRY: You didn't know I knew you hired a detective, did you?

BETTY: Don't be silly. I wanted you to know. That's why I had him send you the bill. I didn't want to have secrets from you either.

BARRY: Look, Betty, you've got to believe me. That woman meant nothing to me. I was at a party. I just lost a big account . . . I was drunk . . . she was old . . . I felt sorry for her. I don't remember any of it. I blacked out. When I came to, she told me what happened. I couldn't believe it. She was very old. I was very drunk.

BETTY: She was blonde, twenty-three years old, a fashion model, 38-22-36. You took her to the Top of the Statler, and the Château Caprice. You bought her a fox muff, a red nightgown and a stuffed monkey on a stick.

BARRY: Gee, Betty, what can I say? I'm sorry. I really didn't mean anything by it. It was just one of those crazy things. Like the song says, a trip to the moon on gossamer wings. Nothing. (*He turns to Bill*) You know what I mean. (*Bill shrugs*) Betty, I didn't even enjoy it, because all I thought about was you and I felt guilty. I love you, Betty, only you.

BETTY: But I hate you, Barry. I really hate you.

BARRY: I thought you said you felt nothing. Hate is the biggest feeling there is next to love.

BETTY: Hate is the opposite of love.

BARRY: No, Betty, despise is the opposite of love.

BETTY: Alright, I despise you . . . feel better?

BARRY: I can't believe you feel that way because of one crazy affair I had in fifteen years of marriage.

BETTY: Three. Your old secretary and a call girl in Chicago.

BARRY: Betty, I never would have told you about those other two if you hadn't forced me to come clean. When you found out about the other one, I figured honesty was the best policy. You can't fault me for that. (*To Bill*) Right, Bill? (*Bill shrugs*) How can you stand there and tell me you're going to end fifteen years of marriage because I indulged myself with just three other women in fifteen years. That's only one every five years. If you thought for one minute about the tremendous tensions and business pressure I was under, you'd want to give me a medal for my restraint.

BETTY: I was under just as much tension and pressure raising the kids and running the house, but I never did once.

BARRY: Because you were a good wife and wonderful mother.

BETTY: Because I was a jerk.

BARRY: Alright, Betty, it is unfair. There's no doubt about it. There is a double standard here, but I didn't invent it. But, when you compare me to every other married man I know, I look like Mr. Clean. Only four women in fifteen years of marriage. That's nothing.

BETTY: Four? You had four?

BARRY: Four. Did I say four? I meant three. I must have added wrong.

BETTY: You had four extra-marital affairs?

BARRY: I'm sorry, Betty, I'm really sorry, but four in fifteen years is still a pretty good average. Let's see, that's one every 3.75 years.

BETTY: You don't have to apologize. I don't care if you had as many as five or six. I told you whatever feelings I had for you are dead, so who cares how many? . . . Who was she?

BARRY: I thought you said it didn't bother you.

BETTY: I don't. Just curious.

BARRY: Look, I don't want to upset you more than you already are.

BETTY: Don't be silly. Nothing you could say or do could upset me. Who was she?

BARRY: Susan Midlin.

BETTY: I see. Susan Midlin. My best friend, Susan Midlin.

BARRY: That's right.

BETTY: I see. (*There's a pause. She goes crazy*) I could kill you, you bum! You no good bum! You betrayed me, you bum betrayer. I could stab you a hundred times and string you up and pull you apart by wild horses and poison you slowly and that wouldn't be enough, you rat bum, bum!

(*She sits down and stares at the floor*)

BILL: I really think I should go.

BETTY: Please, Bill, I need you with me to see me through this.

BARRY (*softly*): You see, honey, you still do have feelings for me.

(*Suddenly she jumps up and hits him with an ashtray*)

BARRY: You hit me with an ashtray. I'm bleeding. What did you do that for? I told you I didn't want to hurt your feelings. You made me tell you, honey.

(*Betty sits down again and starts crying. Bill moves to comfort her. Betty turns slowly to Bill*)

BETTY: If you ever cheat on me, Bill, I will hire somebody to break both your legs. Do you understand? Do I make myself clear?

(*Bill nods. Betty gets up again and walks toward Barry*)

BETTY: And, as for you, you're lower than low, meaner than mean and creepier than creepy, and don't flatter yourself. This pain I feel isn't because I love you, but because I didn't leave you years ago.

BARRY: Look, honey, I had an affair with Susan Midlin after you kicked me out of the house and told me you were leaving me, and I wouldn't even have done it then if you were still speaking to her. I knew you had never forgiven her for the remark she made about your hair at the Braxton's party. So, why don't we just forget that one, huh? What do you say?

BETTY: Please leave. Bill, please get him to leave.

(*Bill starts to open his mouth*)

BARRY: You touch me, Bill, I break your nose. (*Bill shrugs*) Now look, Betty, you can't just write off fifteen years of marriage like this. We owe it to ourselves to give it another chance.

BETTY: Alright, you really want to give it another chance? Well, I'll tell you what. Come back and talk to me after I've had four affairs because then we'll be even and I'll be able to discuss the problem with you more objectively.

BARRY: You mean you want to deliberately hurt me?

BETTY: Both physically and emotionally.

BARRY: Alright, Betty, here's the bottom line. I've come crawling back on my hands and knees but, if you willfully let another man touch you, just to get even with me, you'll never see me again.

BETTY (*shrugging*): C'est la vie.

(*There's a long pause*)

BARRY: Look, Betty, please don't do it. Think of the kids. Don't tarnish the image they have of you. And my family. They think you're a saint, Betty. Don't hurt them. You'll never be able to look my mother in the eye again.

BETTY: Into every life a little rain must fall.

BARRY: Alright, look, maybe you're right. You got married young and I'm the only man you ever had and you think you missed out on something terrific. Okay, you want tit for tat and then we'll start fresh? I'll show you what a big person I am. You go have an affair with this man. You see what it's like. I won't tell anybody, you won't tell anybody. It'll just be between the three of us . . . you, me, and . . . uh . . . Bill, right? (*Bill nods*) And then we'll be even, okay? I'll wait for you at the bar, okay?

BETTY: Fine.

(*There's a pause*)

BARRY: You mean you would still do it even after I was big enough to offer my permission?

BETTY: That's right.

BARRY: I see. (*There's a pause. Suddenly Barry turns to Bill and starts screaming out of control*) I could strangle her. With my bare hands. I could pick her up and throw her in the ocean and hold her head under water till her ears turn green and she screams for help. I could kill her, Bill, I could really kill her!

BETTY: I just had a terrific insight, Barry. All the years we were married I felt like your dishrag. Now I realize you were as helpless as me, and it's a very unattractive quality, Barry.

BARRY: Alright, you want me to apologize, is that it? You want me to say I'm sorry? You want me to admit I was wrong, that I messed up this marriage? Okay, I'll say it, I'll admit it. I was wrong. I was the bad one. I shouldn't have cheated, and I'm sorry, okay? Now, pack your things and let's go back to Cleveland. (*She just sits there without looking at him*) What the hell's the matter with you? What do you want from me? You want me to tell you I love you, and I thought I could make it without you but I can't? Alright, I love you and I can't make it without you, okay?

BETTY: Will you please leave.

BARRY (*to Bill*): What's the matter with her? Is she crazy? Is she abnormal? (*To Betty*) Look, Betty, I was really wrong. I swear on my mother that I'll never cheat again and, if I ever do, you can leave me and take everything I own and I'll put it in writing. Okay? (*Betty continues to stare at the floor*) Betty, I'm humbling myself to you. I never did that before in my life. Look at me, Betty. Look at my eyes. You decide if I'm sincere.

BETTY (*she looks into his eyes*): You're definitely lying.

BARRY (*to Bill*): Look at my eyes, Bill, am I lying?

(*Bill looks closely and shakes his head*)

BETTY: Even if you're telling the truth, it's not as simple as you make it. Your cheating was only the tip of the iceberg. You did an awful lot of things to hurt me, Barry.

BARRY: What things?

BETTY: I don't want to tell you.

BARRY (*screaming*): What things?

BETTY (*blurting it out, almost stream of consciousness*): How dare you keep me waiting three hours for you on a night you said you were taking me out while you were with Ralph Pastor looking at real estate, when you knew whatever money we had we needed to renovate our house first. But you went ahead and bought that stupid lot instead of fixing the kitchen. And, when you finally did do the kitchen, you made me wait for two hours at the decorator's. You knew how much I hated to be kept waiting, and you did it a million times. You kept me waiting at the hospital when Emily was born, on our honeymoon, when you were working, and at Joan's wedding when you stopped for a few drinks with the ushers. My brother told you how he needed money for his second mortgage. You never sent it, but you bought your sister a new breakfront. And then, when your father insulted me that Thanksgiving, you laughed; and when I just turned thirty, and I told you how needing I was, for a present, you gave me pots.

BARRY: The pots cost over a hundred dollars.

BETTY: I don't care what they cost. They were still pots. You don't give pots on a tenth anniversary to someone who's needing.

BARRY: Okay, you want to hear my motive? I had a very good motive. I was mad at you. Where do you come off telling Walter Dunderman that we couldn't afford a concrete pool. What business was it of his? (*To Bill*) Am I right, Bill? (*Bill shrugs*) That's why I laughed when my father told you you talked too much on Thanksgiving, because you sided with your family when I bought that Chinese aluminum stock.

BETTY: Well, that's no excuse for cheating. You shouldn't have cheated.

BARRY: You're right. I should have come right out and told you our sex life was lousy. (*To Bill*) The sex life was really lousy, Bill, really lousy.

BETTY: What are you talking about?

BARRY: We haven't had good sex for the last five years.

BETTY: You mean you haven't been enjoying our love making?

BARRY: Have you?

BETTY: I never thought about it.

BARRY: Well, think about it.

BETTY (*she thinks about it*): You're right. It was lousy.

BARRY: El stinko. N.G. Thumbs down on our sex. You turned yourself off.

BETTY: I didn't turn myself off, you did. When your business became so successful, you were getting enough pleasure from your work, so you didn't need me, because all you cared about was making more money.

BARRY: What are you talking about? You wanted a bigger house, you wanted better furniture, you wanted to put the twins in private school.

BETTY: Those things were a substitute for the attention you weren't giving me.

BARRY: Why couldn't you share my success? We struggled for ten years. You helped put me through college. We had to live in the back room of your parents' apartment. We hung in there when my reserve unit was called up to active duty. We lived in that miserable fourth floor walkup with two kids who were sick all the time and then, when I finally made it, you couldn't appreciate it with me. Why couldn't you enjoy my success with me. Godammit, why couldn't you enjoy it?! (*He starts crying*) That's all I wanted. I wanted you to enjoy it with me.

BETTY (*she starts crying*): Oh, Barry, why didn't you tell me that? Why did you act like you didn't need me?

BARRY: Because it hurt too much.

(*There's a long pause*)

BETTY (*matter of factly*): Gina learned how to snorkel yesterday.

BARRY: No kidding.

BETTY: You should have seen her expression when she saw a fish under water for the first time. I'm sorry I didn't take Billy out of school. He would have loved it here. This is the most beautiful place I've ever seen. Wait until you see it in the daytime.

(*Bill tiptoes out the door*)

BARRY: I hope you brought the camera. It'll be nice to show the kids pictures when we get back.

(*Slow fade to BLACK.*)

COME DOWN BURNING

Kia Corthron

Kia Corthron

Kia Corthron's *Come Down Burning* premiered at the American Place Theatre in 1993 under the Artistic Direction of Wynn Handman. A previous workshop production at the Long Wharf Theatre was presented by Arvin Brown, Artistic Director, and M. Edgar Rosenblum, Executive Director. The companion piece, *Cage Rhythm,* was workshopped at Crossroads Theatre Company's Genesis Festival and won the 1993 New Professional Theatre Playwriting Contest.

Ms. Corthron's *Wake Up Lou Riser,* which was workshopped at Circle Rep's LAB, won the Delaware Theatre Company's first Connections contest in 1994. Her plays have received widespread public readings at Playwrights Horizons in New York, the Hartford Stage in Connecticut, the McCarter in Princeton, the Philadelphia Theatre Company, and the North Carolina Playwrights Festival.

Kia was awarded Manhattan Theatre Club's first Van Lier Fellowship and, under its commission, wrote *Catnap Allegiance.* Other commissions have come from the Goodman Theatre in Chicago and the Second Stage Theatre.

Ms. Corthron received her M.F.A. from Columbia University, and is a member of the Dramatists Guild.

Characters:

SKOOLIE, *32*

TEE, *28*

BINK, *32*

EVIE, *9*

WILL-JOE, *6*

Skoolie has legs that don't work. She gets around very ably on her cart, a flat wooden steerable board with wheels. She lives in a shack that she has renovated; the set is the living room/kitchen, and off are the bedrooms. All appliances, cupboards are floor level—a hot plate rather than a range, floor refrigerator, etc. From a standing person's waist-level to the ceiling is completely bare.

In the mountains, Skoolie lives on a hill, making moreso the difficult task of getting around outside of her own walls, although she does make periodic rolls to the general store which is just across the path.

At the moment, her sister Tee and Tee's children are staying with Skoolie.

Scene 1

Skoolie on the couch, Evie close to her.

SKOOLIE: Skoolie take care a ya.

EVIE: My mama take care a me.

SKOOLIE: Skoolie. And your mama. Who done your hair for ya, huh? Pretty plaits, thick, pretty, who done that, run the comb make it pretty make it don't hurt?

EVIE: Snap went them teeth, my mama yankin' it and fling go them comb teeth, fly 'cross the room. Me cryin', my mama say Why? then see why: us here on the bed, comb teeth there on the dresser. Okay, baby, Don't cry, Don't cry, baby, Sorry, Mama sorry, Mama sorry, baby. Then I don't get nothin' but the brush nine days straight.

(*Tee enters, fumble-searches through several drawers of a cabinet*)

SKOOLIE: No tears I see. Today.

EVIE: You make it pretty and don't even hurt. Not even the comb.

SKOOLIE: How school? (*Pause*) Teacher tell your mama Two times two on the board, but you don't care: your eyes out the winda, your mind on wadin' in the crick, tree climbin'.

EVIE (*pause*): She don't like me, Skoolie.

SKOOLIE: Why? (*To Tee*) Middle drawer.

(*Having now glanced at Tee for the first time, Skoolie is startled. Tee, oblivious, opens middle drawer and retrieves a jar, pours change out of it*)

SKOOLIE (*to Evie*): What she say? (*No answer*) School's cruel. Make ya sit, hours. Write. Listen. But put ya next to the winda, you ain't got nothin' to do but stare out at empty seesaw, slidin' board, basketball hoop. So maybe she likes ya but you don't like her, putcha near that temptation.

EVIE: No. (*Pause*) Likes the other kids.

TEE: She say somethin' to ya, baby? (*Evie shakes her head*) She say somethin' tell me. Hear? (*Evie nods*) Want peanut butter?

SKOOLIE: I fixed 'em. (*Refers to packed lunches*)

TEE (*calls to other room*): Will-Joe.

EVIE: How come we keep our milk money in a jar?

TEE: Gotcher numbers? (*Pause*) Go on get 'em, keep me up half the night countin' on my fingers not so forget cher homework next day. (*Evie has already run off into other room*) Bring your brother.

SKOOLIE: Tee. What did you do to your mane?

TEE: Trim.

SKOOLIE: O my God lemme get my scissors—

TEE: It okay. I like it, Skoolie.

SKOOLIE: I don't, and your boss gonna faint when she see it.

TEE: It okay.

(*Children enter. Will-Joe with very short hair and thumb in mouth*)

SKOOLIE: Well good mornin', Mr. Will-Joe, how're— (*To Tee*) Went crazy with them shears last night, didn't ya?

TEE: Grow too fast.

EVIE: See, Mama? See, Skoolie done my hair, make it pretty it don't even hurt, not even the comb.

TEE: I see.

EVIE: How come we keep our lunch milk money in a jar?

TEE: Don't set aside lunch milk money Friday when I get paid, by Thursday ain't be no lunch milk money.

SKOOLIE: Set aside my customer money too.

EVIE: How come?

TEE: Goes, Evie. Money goes, in eggs, butter. In hair ribbons. (*Opens door*)

SKOOLIE: 'Fore you walk 'em I need a word with ya.

TEE: Ain't walked 'em two days, Ricky's daddy take 'em all in his truck since he got laid off. I jus' watch 'em to the road, down the hill to the other kids 'til he come. What word? (*Skoolie looks at her*) When they's gone. (*Tee opens door*)

SKOOLIE: Wait. (*She motions for Will-Joe to come to her. He does*) Uneven, Tee, some places on that boy's head longer than the rest, lemme fix it.

TEE: Can't, Skoolie, twenty to nine, gotta be ready when the pick-up come. Skoolie. Jazzman wouldn't take my milk last night. Give him half a ounce he spit it right back up.

SKOOLIE: All the kiddies gonna laugh at him, he go in lookin' like a clown. Like that.

TEE (*pause*): Can't. Twenty to nine.

SKOOLIE: Bottle neither? (*Tee shakes her head*) I'll check. (*Hops down onto her cart and rolls off into other room*)

TEE: Wait down there, don't cross the road. (*Children exit*) Don't run, ya slip! (*Tee closes the door, looks out the window*) I don't stink too much, huh, Skoolie? Not run you out the room. Last night I playin' with Will-Joe, kissin' on him, he pull away. God watchin', though. I say. Gimme this job, eleven to two-thirty lunch shiff, five to seven-thirty dinner, I see my kids off in the mornin', pick 'em up between shiffs, three. Perfeck. And not too far a walk to the junior college, bye bye. (*Waves*) Just a couple miles to the two-year college, what I do . . . dirty but . . . only food, I jus' scrape off sucked-on meat, I use rubber gloves, no need touch it even. But damn college kids, damn college kids sometime send through cigarette butt stick up outa mash tatas, jus' dirty. They dirty, no respeck somebody else gotta look at it, wipe it off, they know it, why they do it, think they better can do somethin' like that to me, think I used to it, think I like it. My baby okay?

SKOOLIE (*rolls in with baby and bottle*): Vacuum cleaner suckin', I put the nipple in, he whip the milk up. Third bottle in last two minutes.

TEE: Liar. Takin' it though, ain't he?

SKOOLIE: Belly cramps.

TEE: Sure, could see it painin' him soon that milk hit his tummy. Why?

SKOOLIE: Who knows why, why ain't nothin'. What to do about it's somethin', which is rub in the right place, his belly, but also back, his back just above his tushy, on the side. Work for you too, your bad day out the month. Tried it?

TEE: Uh uh.

SKOOLIE: Guess when you're pregnant much as you, them days you don't got to worry 'bout comin' 'roun' s'much.

TEE: I got kids nine, six, three months, Skoolie. Plenty a periods in between, plenty a pain.

SKOOLIE: Been pregnant more 'n three times . . . (*Pause*)

TEE: Maybe he wanna drink from me.

SKOOLIE: What about our tête à tête.

TEE: Maybe he wanna little drink. You talk, I listen.

SKOOLIE: He ain't gonna take it, Tee, he's full.

TEE: Little bit.

SKOOLIE (*hands over baby*): Don't cry, he don't take it. Babies as moody as anybody else. (*Pause*) See, his belly full let him sleep.

TEE: Took a sip.

SKOOLIE: Don't give him no more, make his belly thumpin' worse—

TEE: I ain't! I ain't. He jus' took a sip. Went to sleep. Skoolie. I the one pay for the lunch milk.

SKOOLIE: You stay here, I charge nothin', you stay free, wanna make a point cuz you pay for the milk.

TEE: Not a point! Not a big point. Little point. Skoolie. Evie say every time she raise her hand, teacher pretend she don't see her, call on somebody else. Or look right at her, call on somebody else.

SKOOLIE: Bad week, teacher got one comin' to her. 'Member you comin' in, baseball cap and coat wide open in the snow, tears, "How come Teacher don't like me no more?" Couple days, yaw's kissin' again. Give her couple days. (*Pause*)

TEE: Won't stay long.

SKOOLIE: Four months already.

TEE: But out soon. I'm savin'. Get our own place. Me/Evie/Will-Joe/ Jazzman place.

SKOOLIE: Hmm.

TEE: Gonna do it, maybe next week.

SKOOLIE: You ain't never stayed here less 'n six months at a time.

TEE: Do it.

SKOOLIE: 'Til your landlord tell ya three-months-no-rent is plenty enough. 'Til the sheriff knock knock Get out or I get you out. (*Pause*) You know I count them things. (*Tee looks at her*) Pads. I been through two rounds now, ain't had to share with nobody. Not one you took since your last time. Fifty-two days back. (*Pause. Skoolie rolls to a drawer, pulls out a comb, brush, scissors*) Come here.

TEE: That all our talk?

SKOOLIE: What been said all needs be said. For now. We do some thinkin' to ourself. Later we resume the conversation. (*Indicates for Tee to sit*)

TEE: Cut it? (*Skoolie looks at her*) I got work eleven, what it don't go right? I'm stuck.

SKOOLIE: When I done it it ain't go right?

(*Tee is still hesitant. Skoolie "surrenders": tosses scissors back in drawer, shoves it shut*)

SKOOLIE: Come on. I make it pretty.

(*Tee sits in front of Skoolie. Skoolie begins brushing Tee's hair*)

Scene 2:

Skoolie cornrowing Bink's hair, frequently rolling across floor with ease to retrieve a special comb from this drawer, a towel way over there, etc.

BINK: What's 'em two humps out back?

SKOOLIE: Two girlies, Markie-Ann was fifteen months toddlin' and J.B. a week and a half, then Markie-Ann down and died and J.B. eight days behind her.

BINK: O moni O moni Kai Lhita Extridi—(*Skoolie bonks Bink on the head with the brush*)

SKOOLIE: Toldja: No tongues.

BINK: I can't help it, Skoolie, somethin' like that, like buryin' babies, somethin' like that I hear and the Holy Spirit just come down overtake me. They's Tee's?

SKOOLIE: Wa'n't mine.

BINK: Now she pregnant again.

SKOOLIE: Evie then Will-Joe then Markie-Ann then little baby J.B. Then them youngests died, three years later come Jazzman.

BINK: Five months old that baby is, now she pregnant again.

SKOOLIE: I didn't tell ya so's ya tell the town.

BINK: Ain't tellin nobody.

SKOOLIE: Just tell ya cuz you was here. We's ole friends. Yeah.

BINK: And who's the daddy? I ain't heard 'bout no one 'round Tee.

SKOOLIE: Don't ask here, I don't see 'em. I could be a right hand swear the nothin' but the truth witness for immaculate conception, that's how much I know. (*Pause*)

BINK: Bored, bored, bored, I sure would like to move back. (*Bonked again*) Ow!

SKOOLIE: Don't wanna hear no Oh-hi-oh neither.

BINK: Just the convenience of it, Skoolie, nice to go shoppin' on Sunday.

SKOOLIE: You know how I feel, I feel Well, guess it wa'n't too important, six days out the week and you forget to buy it all them days. I feel you didn't need it too bad if you couldn't think to buy it on Monday, on Tuesday, on Wednesday, on—

BINK: And wheelchair access, everywhere, you'd like it, Skoolie.

SKOOLIE: I 'on't own no wheelchair, Bink.

BINK: Ramps and stuff, your cart'd work.

SKOOLIE: My cart rolls 'cross the path to the store and back, I got access thereby to my eggs, to my shampoo, to my relaxer kits, to my toothpaste, to my large roller clips, don't need no more access.

BINK: What if ya wanted to go visit somebody sometime?

SKOOLIE: I don't.

BINK: 'Steada make 'em trek up this ole hill all the time.

SKOOLIE: I do the kinda hair job, customers trek up: no complaints.

BINK: Hm. Well I'm complainin'.

SKOOLIE: Then go back to Oh-hi-oh. Why didn't you just stay out there in the city, anyway? I'll tell ya why, money.

BINK: Obligation, Skoolie, Gary's daddy wanted us to come back, take over the hardware store, so we done it. Shoot, coulda done lots better in the city if we wanted to, everything we got here ain't ours, it's the credit card's. But Toledo. Toledo ain't like here, Toledo ain't dependent on no factories, close ya down, lay ya off soon's they find a country got enough protrudin' rib cages to take a dime a day with a smile.

SKOOLIE: Do your own hair! I'm tired a "City's better, City's better."

BINK: Aw come on, Skoolie. (*Pause*) Please? (*Pause*) I can't cornrow. (*Pause*) No one done hair good as you in the city, that's for sure.

SKOOLIE (*pause*): Wouldn't want cher half-baked head walkin' aroun' discouragin' future business. (*Resumes*)

BINK: How long you livin' on the hill, this shack? Ow, Skoolie, dammit, ya pullin' too hard.

SKOOLIE: Wannit to fall right out? Just what's gonna happen soon's you march out that door, you don't lemme pull it tight. Course what's it matter with you, you gonna pull 'em out in a hour, soon's ya get home.

BINK: I ain't. My head be too sore anyhow.

SKOOLIE: Maybe lived in the city awhile, but you always be too country for the cornrow. Twelve years, I moved up here right after you married and left when we was twenty.

BINK: Done it up right. Wouldn'ta even recognized it was our playshack. Musta bought it cheap, huh? Never used to have a floor, just dirt, soda cans. And no ceilin', nothin' but a few boards on top, half a them missin'. Now it's pretty, now it's warm. Still, (*shudders*) I couldn't live next to that tree.

SKOOLIE: You want beads?

BINK: They cost extra?

SKOOLIE: Whatchu think?

BINK: No thanks, I think I got me some barrettes at home. How long Tee, the kids with ya?

SKOOLIE: Why ya so damn nosy?

BINK: Nothin' else to do. Back three months bored out my mind already.

SKOOLIE: Don't remember ya bein' so bored when we was kids. Always found somethin' when we was kids.

BINK: Always *is* somethin' when ya kids.

SKOOLIE: Out and in, out and in. Started when she's twenty-three, me twenty-seven, Evie four, Will-Joe one plus a month, one a them suckers, Will-Joe's daddy I think, cuts outa town. Wasn't livin' with 'em but did help with the rent 'til he gone. Didn't know 'til the rent due. Three of 'em on my doorstep. She'll stay awhile, leave, get evicted come back, leave, come back.

BINK: Well that's Skoolie and Tee, when yer daddy die?

SKOOLIE: I was thirteen, Tee nine.

BINK: Well that's Skoolie and Tee, Tee fall down, Skoolie pick her up ever since thirteen and nine, Mr. Jim at the mill catch his arm in that machinery it pull him in, and yaw find out what that mill care 'bout its employees.

SKOOLIE: Thin back here. I got hair pieces, only need two a buck each, fill it in.

BINK: Mr. Jim work twenty years, die and not enough pension to feed a flea.

SKOOLIE: Twenty-three.

BINK: Then here's Skoolie, thirteen, full-time mama to her baby sister cuz suddenly their mama out cleanin' this house seven to three, that house four to ten.

SKOOLIE: Twenty-three years my daddy work for 'em twenty-three years.

BINK: Me in a fancy pink ruffled thing, and you got me on a pilla on the floor cuz you know the latest curls to set off my prom look. But a forty-five minute 'do hits a hour and a half cuz every five minutes you rollin' next door to check on Tee's junior high fractions and decimals.

SKOOLIE: My daddy start work when he's fifteen. (*Pause*)

BINK: Them babies get fever? Or born sick.

SKOOLIE: Hungry. Markie-Ann was doin' okay, three babies was in the budget. But we tried four. Not enough for the last one and put a strain on the other three. Oldest two could take it. Youngest two couldn't. (*Finishes hair*) Fourteen.

BINK (*pays*): Skoolie. Help me with somethin' else? (*Pause*)

SKOOLIE: I helped ya with that just 'fore ya left, now back in town and first thing ya need it again?

BINK: Charged me forty then. Got fifty on me now.

SKOOLIE (*pause*): Sixty-five.

BINK: Okay. I gotta go home, get it.

SKOOLIE: How many you had since the one I give ya?

BINK: None.

SKOOLIE: Whatchu got at home?

BINK: Sarah's ten, Jay's eight. That's enough.

SKOOLIE: How you know I still did it?

BINK: Do ya?

SKOOLIE: Not for a couple years, ain't lost my touch though.

BINK: What I thought.

SKOOLIE: Mind if Tee come? I like the help.

BINK: Okay. Confidential though.

SKOOLIE: Well I guess so, Bink, I think I like to stay outa jail.

BINK: Tonight?

SKOOLIE: Naw. Gotta find somebody watch Evie and Will-Joe.

BINK: My Gary watch 'em. He knows it got to be done.

SKOOLIE: Okay, but tomorrow. Need ta talk to Tee.

BINK: Okay. Okay. And I'll make yaw some lemon meringue pie, know ya like that.

SKOOLIE: Bink. Don't eat nothin' tomorrow.

Scene 3:

TEE: C'mere, Evie. (*Tee takes Evie's arm, shows Skoolie who groans*) How you get that big scratch?

EVIE: Went down to lunch and forgot my milk money, Mrs. Shay grab me, say "How many times?" then march me back to my desk, get my nickel and dime.

TEE (*to Skoolie*): She don't haveta pull that hard.

SKOOLIE: She don't haveta pull at all.

TEE: Mrs. Shay do the white kids like that?

EVIE: Do it to Charlie Wilt, but he cusses.

TEE: She a good girl, Skoolie, no reason do her like that.

SKOOLIE: I know.

TEE: All the teachers before kiss her love her, this 'n mean, nasty, no reason. (*To Evie*) Hurt? (*Evie shakes her head*) Go play with Will-Joe 'til they come. (*Evie exits*) What I gonna do?

SKOOLIE (*going to cabinet*): Cut ain't deep, but p'roxide on it get ridda the sting, keep it don't get infected.

TEE: Done it. What I gonna do 'bout the teacher?

SKOOLIE: Wamme call her? (*Tee shakes her head*) Whatchu want?

TEE: Want . . . I do somethin'.

SKOOLIE: Wamme talk to her? Ya ain't s'good at talkin', Tee. I'll call, straighten it out. Think it better I ask Evie first?

TEE: Face-to-face, Skoolie. Oughta be.

SKOOLIE: Uh huh. Well I can't help ya on that, my cart ain't built so to take that hill, plus tomorra my market day, cart will scoot cross the path, get my body soap, hair grease, all I need.

TEE: I know.

SKOOLIE (*pause*): You gon' do it? (*Tee nods*) Go down there, your face 'gainst hers, that teacher? (*Tee nods*) Okay. Okay.

TEE: I do alright, Skoolie. I be fine.

SKOOLIE: Need a babysitter. You requestin' I reschedule my Wednesday market outin'?

TEE: Bink and Gary be here few minutes, maybe I ask she watch Jazzman tomorra. My check come Friday, think she watch my baby I promise her little somethin' enda the week?

SKOOLIE: Keep your pennies, I'll knock five off her fee tonight. (*Pause*) Tee. You been thinkin'? Boutcher decision?

TEE: Ain't none.

SKOOLIE: Tee, ya can't . . . not think about it. Jus' can't . . . jus' can't have another baby, not think 'bout no options. We's hungry.

TEE: I know, Skoolie, I ain't thinkin' 'bout it cuz I know, cuz I know not much choice. I gonna pull it out.

SKOOLIE: Sure?

TEE: I love my babies, Skoolie, I can't let it incubate, bring it on in here, nothin' happen but it die, it die take another with it, I can't kill my babies, Skoolie. No more. (*Knock at the door. Evie and Will-Joe rush on*)

EVIE and WILL-JOE: I'll get it! I'll get it! (*Children open door. Bink, hair straightened and styled, enters. Children step back, shy*)

BINK: Yaw's sure Tee's. (*Pause*)

TEE (*pulling coins from pocket*): Here's some ice cream money, maybe Mr. Gary take ya . . . (*Realizes it isn't enough*)

BINK: Go on. Think we got some ice cream at home. Yaw like chocolate? (*They stare at her*) Wanna get a movie?

EVIE: You got a VCR?

BINK: Maybe Mr. Gary swing ya 'round the video store. Pick out whatcha want, one apiece. (*Children look at Tee*)

TEE: Go on. (*Children exit*)

SKOOLIE: I'll get it ready. (*Rolls off into other room. Bink starts slowly moving toward the window, stares out, mumbles indiscernibly except for an occasional "Jesus"*)

TEE: Tonguin', Bink?

BINK (*stops*): Sorry. Know yaw hate it.

TEE: Skoolie hate it, I don't. Go on.

BINK: Can't now. Know that tree?

TEE: Oak.

BINK: June. Skoolie and me six, and swingin', swingin'. Then we think we'll race to the top. We almost make it, but get caught up in each other's legs, fall side-by-side. I get up. Skoolie don't. Week later I come back here, by myself, think: We fall the same way, right next to each other, I ain't got a scratch. Skoolie ain't walkin' no more. Then my mouth start movin' in tongues. Ain't been able to stop it since. (*Skoolie rolls on*)

SKOOLIE: Okay. (*Bink hesitantly moves toward the other room. Skoolie and Tee follow. Bink suddenly turns around*)

BINK: So much bleedin', Skoolie, so much bleedin' and pain, pain the last time, I don't know if I can . . . take it, Skoolie, don't know if I can . . . take it, I jus', I jus' . . . If all the sudden, if all the sudden I start speakin' in tongues, if all the sudden the Holy Spirit come down burnin' me, come down burnin' me, I start speakin' in tongues—

SKOOLIE: Do whatcha have to, Bink. (*They exit*)

Scene 4:

Tee sits cross-legged, stapling all over a single piece of paper. Skoolie rolls on, pulls herself onto couch. Tee continues stapling, then suddenly stops. Looks up.

TEE: Appointment at eleven, bad for me, I miss mornin' work, good for Mrs. Shay, kids got the music teacher then, she free, so we do it. Meet at the secretary's office, I'm there ten 'til eleven. Wait. Wait, "Ten after, sure she comin'?" "She'll be here," secretary say, nice but fast. Wait. "Eleven-thirty, she be here soon?" Secretary nod, secretary say "Eleven-thirty!" call her over the loudspeaker, no answer. Quarter to twelve. Noon. I teary cuz I know music's over now. Secretary check her schedule. "She takin 'em to lunch now," say she, "Catch her twelve-thirty. She send the kids out for playground break, go back to solitude classroom half a hour." I outside Mrs. Shay door, five after noon, what she lock it for anyhow? I wait, belly growlin', smell cafeteria grill cheese, tomato soup, wait. Eight minutes to one she come, say, "Mrs. Edwards or Mrs. Beck?" cuz she know just two little black kids in fourth grade. I say Beck, she unlock door, I follow her in, she on and on "Evie a sweet little girl but limited attention span Kids watch too much unsupervise TV Parents always let 'em watch TV Won't tell 'em Read a book Won't tell 'em Do their homework Then come to school, no TV, they's bored." (*Pause*)

SKOOLIE: Whatchu say? (*Tee shrugs*) How long she go on?

TEE: Long.

SKOOLIE: How come you don't say nothin'—?

TEE: She got three piles. Papers, she pick up left sheet pick up middle sheet pick up right sheet one staple, clamp, upper left corner, make a fourth pile. She take next one next one next one clamp, fourth pile. Talk all the time clamp talkin' clamp clamp I stare at the stapler clamp She talkin' clamp She talkin' clamp clamp clamp clamp She talkin' clamp She not talkin'. Suddenly she quiet. Wait for me, say somethin'.

SKOOLIE: Whatchu say?

TEE: "Our TV been broke three years."

SKOOLIE: What she say? (*Pause*) What she say?

TEE: "Oh."

SKOOLIE: Then—

TEE: Then kids clamorin' in and . . . Evie come, Evie see me, run, grab me—

SKOOLIE: Hug ya?

TEE: Uh uh! Uh uh! "Don't tell her, Mama! Don't tell her, Mama, I fibbed! Don't tell her, I fibbed!" She tryin' to whisper, but too panicked, so loud enough Mrs. Shay can hear. Then Mrs. Shay tell her Sit down, take me out in the hall, shut the door and lean on it. She say . . . She say . . . "Somethin' a matter with Evie?" I say . . . "Well . . ." I say, "Well . . . got this big scratch on her arm." My head look down. Don't know what should say now. Hope she do.

SKOOLIE: Well? (*Tee nods*) What?

TEE: Pause. Then she say . . . Then she say, "Somebody else at home?"

SKOOLIE: *Huh?*

TEE: I say, *"Huh?"* She say, "Evie's daddy or . . . somebody else? Come back to live with ya?"

SKOOLIE: Aw . . .

TEE: I say, "Uh uh! Jus' me, my sister."

SKOOLIE: Tee, I hope ya told her she done 'at scratch.

TEE: I say, uh, I say, "Mrs. Shay, I gotta ask you how come that scratch on her arm." She look at me: I nuts. I say, "I think . . . I think maybe one time you pull her too hard." (*Pause*)

SKOOLIE: She say what?

TEE: She say, "Oh. I'm sorry."

SKOOLIE: What else?

TEE: That all, she look at me, her eyes talk: "What else?" I say "That all, well, I guess that all."

SKOOLIE: That wa'n't all, Tee, she been mean to Evie.

TEE: I didn't cry! She never see me cry. She go back in the class, ten after one, I walkin' fast up and down up and down. Slower. Slow. I halt by the trashbasket sittin' in the hall. It full, I wanna pour it all out, fronta her door, but she gonna know I done it. I stoop by the trashbasket, by the door. If I wait 'til two she ain't gonna figure it's me I think, I think she gonna figure I left figure this done by someone else. So I stay stooped, still. But after 'bout ten minutes this little boy walks by, looks at me, wonderin'. I find the door says "Girls," go in a little stall, sit, my feet up won't no one know I'm here. Quiet 'til two, I wait ten extra, make sure. Tiptoe back, pour real easy, keep my face down case someone walk by. Only thing that make a noise is this stapler tumble out. Surprise. Perfeck condition this stapler and Miss Shay gonna toss it in the trashbasket. I grab it. I run. (*Pause*)

SKOOLIE: The end?

TEE: We need a stapler, Skoolie. Never had one before.

SKOOLIE: I'll call.

TEE: No! no, whatchu callin' for? I talked to her.

SKOOLIE: Did no good. I'll call. (*Tee staples viciously at Skoolie's face*) You crazy?

TEE: I talk to her! She know I don't take it lyin' down.

SKOOLIE: Took it worse 'n lyin' down, girl, ya started somethin', not finish it. Just make her mad.

TEE: No!

SKOOLIE: Just make her mad, take it out on Evie.

TEE: NO, that a lie, Skoolie! (*Skoolie picks up receiver*) *That a lie, Skoolie!* (*Tee slaps receiver out of Skoolie's hand*)

SKOOLIE: What'sa matter with you?

TEE: I done it myself! I done it myself!

SKOOLIE: What?

TEE: I can take care a my own kids, Skoolie!

SKOOLIE: Well who said you couldn't, Tee—?

TEE: I can take care a myself, Skoolie, don't need you, I can take care a my own kids, take care a myself! myself!

SKOOLIE: Okay . . .

TEE: Don't need you!

SKOOLIE: Okay!

(*Pause. Sound of the operator recording from the receiver. Tee hangs it up*)

TEE: Gonna hurt, Skoolie?

SKOOLIE: Tomorra? (*Tee nods*) Maybe.

TEE: Bink say she got that pain again, blood again, all night, but now pain gone. She think it worked.

SKOOLIE: Uh huh.

TEE: Wish we could do it in a hospital, Skoolie. Make sure it done right.

SKOOLIE: Uh huh. (*Pause*) Maybe we call the principal?

TEE (*sits down and staples. Doesn't look up*): Said she sorry, Skoolie.

SKOOLIE: I know. Good thing you was there, make her say that. But. She didn't say wouldn't happen again. Did she.

TEE (*continues stapling*): Uh uh.

SKOOLIE: So. Maybe we oughta call her boss. Principal.

TEE: He gonna say we gotta come down though. In person. (*Stops stapling*) I could carry ya, Skoolie.

SKOOLIE (*pause*): You can't liff me.

TEE: Yes I can. (*Starts to*)

SKOOLIE: No! Carry me? Mile and a half? Naw, Tee, we can't. (*Pause*) Long time I been in school.

TEE: You ain't never been in school. I carry ya.

SKOOLIE: No! I'm heavy, Tee.

TEE: You ain't fat.

SKOOLIE: I'm a big person, I'm a grown woman, I ain't light.

TEE: Easy for me.

SKOOLIE: Naw, Tee, I ain't used to that.

TEE: I can holdja.

SKOOLIE: I'm grown!

TEE: I can holdja. (*Pause*)

SKOOLIE: Okay. (*Tee starts to lift*) Careful. Now— Careful, Tee, now— Now watch— Watch my leg, watch my leg!

TEE: Got it.

SKOOLIE: Don't raise me too high now, jus' . . . All right. All right, this all right, this all right. Walk slow, hear? uh . . . Don't let no one see.

TEE: Okay.

SKOOLIE: Don't jostle too much, make me dizzy. Watch . . . Watch goin' down to the road, hear? Pretty bumpy on that hill. Now watch —Watch, Tee. Tee, ya drop me, I'm crawlin' right back, hear?

TEE: I hear. You can't crawl.

SKOOLIE: I can pull myself for sure, I sure will pull myself, you . . . you drop me . . . Okay. That's right. (*They are in the doorway*)

TEE: Skoolie. Pretend like . . . Pretend like all along I plan on bringin' you, tell 'em that. Pretend like we's doin' this together, pretend like you ain't no bigger 'n me.

SKOOLIE: Set me in a chair before any of 'em come, teacher, principal. Make sure my feet pointed in the right direction: heels in the back.

Scene 5:

Skoolie holds a flashlight

SKOOLIE: 'S open. (*Bink enters*)

BINK: Where them kiddies?

SKOOLIE: Tree skippin'. Tee always could separate the spruces from the pines, likes to share them smarts with the babes.

BINK: Tee, Tee, Tee, this I remember 'bout Tee, starin' at a matchbox waitin' for it to flip.

SKOOLIE: 'S go.

BINK: Off? (*Skoolie nods*) How come? (*Pause*) My dress too tight, how come? (*Skoolie nods. Bink undresses*) Why you cancelled three o'clock?

SKOOLIE: School. (*Pause*) Went to school.

BINK (*pause*): How? (*Bink stands in bra, ragged from use, half-slip, stockings*)

SKOOLIE: Off.

(*Bink removes stockings and panties, lies supine on couch, knees bent, feet spread. Trembles. Skoolie rolls to her, clicks on flashlight under Bink's slip. Sudden laughter offstage, then Tee and Children enter through outside door*)

BINK: Skoolie, them babies! them babies!

SKOOLIE: OUT!

(*Tee and children rush out, never seeing Bink who is blocked by the back of the couch. Skoolie briefly concludes examination*)

SKOOLIE: You's clean.

(*Bink quickly dresses except shoes, sits on couch, hides face in hands, begins rocking upper body*)

SKOOLIE: Stop.

BINK (*not stopping*): I needta go out the back door, Skoolie. Aintcha got a back door?

SKOOLIE: They ain't seen ya, Bink.

BINK: Too much coffee, I gotta pee. I gotta pee, I gotta go out the back door.

SKOOLIE: They ain't seen ya. When I call 'em back in they gonna look atcha funny cuz they know somethin' funny's goin' on, but they ain't seen ya. (*To door*) Come on. (*They re-enter. Children run through to other room without stopping*)

TEE: Wait for me, I run the bath. (*To Skoolie*) Sorry.

SKOOLIE: Toldja wait 'til eight-thirty, toldja keep 'em half-hour just in case.

TEE: Sorry, Skoolie.

BINK: Skoolie pull the magic again, everything clean, everything fine. I knowed it.

SKOOLIE: Hope you and Gary be wearin' the proper equipment in the future.

BINK: We was always careful, Skoolie, nothin' a hundred percent. How you got to school? (*Tee looks at Skoolie. Skoolie glances at Tee*)

SKOOLIE: In the principal's office, three-thirty, I sittin' comfy and in come Shay with her wristwatch. (*Jazzman starts crying, Tee exits*) With her wristwatch, she glance at her wristwatch, then say I must be Evie's aunt, principal told her I was waitin'. "That I am," say I, tall sittin', erect. Quiet, contest to see who gonna break the quiet. (*Long pause, quiet except for Jazzman's cries*) "You wanted to speak to me?" Hah! blew it! (*Tee enters with bawling Jazzman*)

TEE: Won't take my milk, Skoolie, I don't know, won't take my milk.

SKOOLIE: Dummy blew it cuz she showed she was the weaker, showed me, showed her. Leaves me to fight confident. Leaves her to fight compensatin'.

TEE: Skoolie, won't take my milk, he gonna be sick.

SKOOLIE: "Yes, I did," said I, "I wanted to talk to you. You put that scratch on Evie's arm." She all over the room—

TEE: Skoolie, he sick! My baby Jazzman sick! (*Skoolie rolls to refrigerator, retrieves bottle of milk, rolls back and slams it down in front of Tee*)

SKOOLIE: She all over the room! pacin' back and forth. I in chair, don't move. If ever a nervous moment come for me, she don't see it. She see me calm, still. I see her all over the room.

TEE: Won't drink me.

SKOOLIE: "Evie forgot her milk money, Evie always forgettin' her milk money, why go to the lunch room without milk money? I know she's only fourth grade but—. Well I know I mighta pulled too rough but—. Well I got twenty-four kids I gotta look after I try to be patient but—." I say "Chicken butt, I lay it down, you lick it up."

BINK: Naw . . .

SKOOLIE: Naw. I just sit. All I gotta do. My whole body smilin' but she won't never see it.

TEE: Won't drink me!

SKOOLIE: In come principal: Why she so loud? He don't even hear me, I so soft, relaxed. She hysterical. Give that baby some milk!

TEE: Won't take it.

SKOOLIE: He'll take the bottle, Tee! he's hungry, give him some. (*Pause, then Tee tries again to give him her breast*) Give that baby his bottle, Tee, ya wanna starve him?

TEE: Take mine. (*Skoolie grabs bottle and baby and begins to feed him*)

SKOOLIE: Casual I say, "Nothin', Mr. Principal, nothin' goin' on, just me and her havin' a little chitty chat, just me wonderin' how come she gonna scratch our little girl, then lie 'bout it, then claim scratch come from our men, claim we bringin' men in the house claim one of 'em scratch our little girl."

TEE: My little girl.

BINK: What principal say?

SKOOLIE: Blew up.

TEE: My little girl.

SKOOLIE: Notice this, Tee, notice I'm ignorin' your crybaby mood, Tee. Like Shay wa'n't hysterical enough, now the principal's face a hundred ten degrees red. "You said what to her? You said what to her? Don't you never again—I sure am sorry, Miz Beck, sorry 'bout cher little girl please accept my humblest apologies—" (*Tee grabs Skoolie's cart and begins violently shaking it. Jazzman starts bawling again. Tee backs off*)

TEE: Sorry. I sorry.

SKOOLIE: Ya say that too much, Tee. (*Skoolie rocks baby. He quiets*)

TEE: I hold him?

SKOOLIE: Then she apologize. Don't wanna, but the pupils in the principal's eyes say she better. (*To Tee*) No. (*To Bink*) Then I leave.

BINK: What Tee do? Say?

SKOOLIE (*pause*): Nothin'.

BINK: Nothin'?

SKOOLIE: Nothin', in the bathroom with Evie so Evie don't get upset, seein' my tongue smackin' her teacher around.

TEE: Proteck Evie. She scared. (*Pause*)

BINK: Aw, let her hold her baby, Skoolie, don't be so mean.

SKOOLIE: Better keep your mind on your business, Bink. (*Pause. Offers baby to Tee*) Careful, he's sleep.

TEE (*taking baby*): Aw, see 'at little grin on his face. He know his mama come.

BINK: How you leave, Skoolie, how you got there?

TEE: I carry her. (*Pause*) I carry her. (*Pause*)

BINK: All that way?

TEE: Set her down 'fore them people come: principal, teacher. Pick her up after they's gone.

BINK (*to Skoolie*): All that way? (*Pause*) Huh. (*Pause*) Huh. (*Pause*) I gotta pee, Skoolie.

SKOOLIE: We ain't moved the bathroom.

(*Bink exits. Skoolie looks at Tee. Tee looks at Jazzman whom she has laid on the floor and is rocking. She gradually rocks harder until finally roughly enough that he again starts crying, and she cradles him*)

SKOOLIE: Tee, stop that! what're you doin' to that baby?

TEE: He take my milk.

SKOOLIE: He don't want it! (*Grabs Jazzman. Now both sisters clutch baby*)

TEE: Gon' take it.

SKOOLIE: He don't wantcher damn milk, Tee!

TEE: Yes—

SKOOLIE: No! he don't wantcher damn milk, Tee!

TEE: Gon' take it, gon' take it, Skoolie, somethin' wrong! cuz somethin' wrong with baby don't want his mama's milk.

SKOOLIE: No—

TEE: Somethin' wrong—

SKOOLIE: Not with him! Gimme that baby 'fore ya kill him!

EVIE: Mommy! (*She is onstage; stillness*)
Mommy.
Mommy.
Mommy, can I give Jazzman a haircut? He need one.

TEE (*pause*): Tomorra maybe. You remind me, we see. (*Evie exits. Skoolie sets Jazzman on couch, rocks*) I carry you, Skoolie.

SKOOLIE: Why don't you go to the center a town and paint it on the billboard, Tee.

TEE: I could do it again, ya need me. (*No answer*) Ya need me. (*No answer*) I could do it, ya want me to or not. You in my way, I could pick you up, move. Nothin' you could do. You bother me, I pick you up, carry you, I carry you someplace else, carry you where you don't bother me.

SKOOLIE: You ever do, Tee, I'll pray God Gimme back my legs jus' long enough to kick you. Hard. (*Bink enters*)

BINK: Gettin' late.

SKOOLIE: You ain't been here ten minutes.

BINK: Gettin' late. Too dark on this hill, Skoolie, how I gonna walk twenty feet down to the road, down to the car not kill myself.

TEE (*with Jazzman*): See, Skoolie! he took a little. Couple drops, now he sleep good. (*Bink looks at her*) It ain't nothin', Bink. Sometime he want my milk, sometime he full. (*Pause*) Whatchu lookin' for? jus' normal.

SKOOLIE: Tee. You hold the flashlight for Bink? (*Moving toward the other room*) I better go kiss them babies, let 'em know I ain't sore no more. (*Stops*) Let him sleep, Tee. (*Exits*)

BINK (*putting on shoes*): Yaw tree skippin', huh.

TEE: I was a girl scout, Bink, one year, fifth grade. Leader take us a all-day hike, name this tree, name that plant, hundreds. I remember all, no one else hardly remember one. Easy for me.

BINK: Tee. I come in your house, you sittin' starin' at a matchbox. Skoolie and I be in your mama's bedroom gettin' in real trouble, try on a gown, try on high heels, pinch earrings, come out two hours you still starin' at the matchbox. Skoolie say you waitin' for it to flip. How?

TEE: My mind make it.

BINK: Your mind didn't. (*Pause*) Hold the light steady at my feet. Move it a inch to the left or the right leaves me in the dark, I miss one step fall in one a them groundhog ditches, you know I'm laid up six weeks.

Scene 6:

Tee, Evie and Will-Joe outside on the stoop.

TEE: The whole sky move. Unison. (*Points*) Big Dipper? Watch it. It stand on its handle now, but wait. Slow slow it flip back, a circle. Couple months, May, it upside down, pour its soup out. Then September, upright again, flat on the burner. Everything shift, everything move together, I see it, I know the map. 'Cept a few lights, they not interested in the rhythm a the rest, got they own mind, never know where they end up. We call them this: (*Points*) Mars, Venus, Jupiter. I like lookin' up. I like watchin' the change.

EVIE: I wake up to pee, Mama, you whisper us out here, make sure Skoolie don't wake. Why?

TEE: News: We movin'.

EVIE and WILL-JOE: Aw . . .

TEE: Lug our suitcase up the slope, 'member I say don't get too comfy? Temporary arrangement.

WILL-JOE: I like the hill. (*No answer*) Why?

TEE: Cuz we can. Money I make now, and Jane, scrape plates next to me, she say other half her place empty enda the month. Cheap, and two bedrooms: me, Jazzman in one, the second you share. Your own bed. Twins.

WILL-JOE: I like sharin' with you.

EVIE: I like sharin' with Skoolie.

TEE: Gettin' big.

WILL-JOE: Skoolie mad at us?

TEE: You think that the reason? (*Will-Joe nods*) We not done nothin' make her mad. Have we?

WILL-JOE (*meaning Evie*): Her. She been swingin' on the bad tree. (*Pause. Then Evie swings at him*)

EVIE: Squeal-mouth! (*Tee intercepts her aim*)

TEE: That the truth?

EVIE: Tattletale, it ain't nice!

TEE (*pause*): Skoolie and me nasty to that tree, huh. I change my mind. That tree ain't got the evil eye, it not the devil. Skoolie's thing was a freak, that white oak not housin' the spirits. It old. Earn some respeck. Don't let her catch ya near it though. (*Pause*)

EVIE: You and Skoolie mad?

TEE: Naw. But two different people. Grownups. Everything Skoolie do not necessarily my business. Everything I do not necessarily hers.

WILL-JOE: We come back to visit?

TEE: Sure.

WILL-JOE: And her visit us? (*Tee looks at him*) She call, wanna watch our TV, you come pick her up? Carry her down the hill, cross the bridge, cross the traffic light? Like today?

TEE (*considers this*): Yeah. I travel her. (*Sky*) Funny thing: Uruguay, Australia, Zimbabwe—they ain't got the same map. Their stars ain't ours, down there they got a different sky. I wanna see that. You wanna see that? (*They nod*) One day, we gonna.

Scene 7:

Tee sits up on couch. She is slicing an apple. Skoolie rolls in. As she chatters she makes preparations: water, towels, etc.

SKOOLIE: Warm like spring, smell like spring. The babies feel it, they get the giggles whilst we wait on the truck. He just pullin' off, I'm still wavin' and here Irene Halloway come. "Skoolie! Heardja told that Shay off." She had trouble too, said Shay thought both her oldests was dumb, now she worried: her youngest got her in the fall. Well I always thought Irene's boy was dumb, but that big girl was smart enough. I nod, say nothin'. Roll to the store, a hullabaloo . . . seven at me, grinnin', already got the Bink word. I'm brief: we let her have it. "Dontchu never no more try sayin' they hurt that girl," says principal, "Dontchu never no more lay a hand on that girl." Well, we get the principal to say it, we done the best thing: he signs her paycheck. Tee and me get him to say it, I tell them store people, just shut her up, embarrass her a bit. Make her think. Whatchu doin'! (*Runs to Tee. Blood all over Tee's hand and the apple*)

TEE: Stomach hurts.

SKOOLIE (*wiping hand*): Nervous. Normal.

TEE: Salt. My mouth.

SKOOLIE: Better not, toldja not ta eat. And why your hands s'clammy? No draft in here.

TEE: Not eat, my belly clean.

SKOOLIE: Then whatchu got this apple for?

TEE: Ain't hungry, just peel it for you. Know ya love 'em, I like to peel.

SKOOLIE: Where's the cut, Tee?

TEE: Peel it, then I wanna cut it, fours. Then cut again. Again, sixteen. Again—

SKOOLIE: I don't see the cut, all this blood can't be from your hangnail-suckin'.

TEE: Wish I slice it off, whole hand. Then I be better. Like you.

SKOOLIE (*back to preparations*): Nasty talk, Tee. But you got stuff to go through today, so no dwellin' on it. (*Pause*)

TEE: Skoolie. I think . . . time to go.

SKOOLIE: Where we goin'?

TEE: Us. Me, my kids. I found a place. It in the budget, my new money.

SKOOLIE: Well. I won't be rushin' in no new boarders. Just in case your budget don't hold up two months down the road. When we's done, remind me to dunk your hand in alcohol. Not now, I don't like no chemicals in the vicinity 'til things all patched up.

TEE: You like my place, Skoolie. It got a basement.

SKOOLIE: Here? Or the other room? (*Pause*) You better not mess up my couch. (*Skoolie exits into the other room*)

TEE: You know that video store jus' open? My new house right round the corner. You gon' come visit, Skoolie. And I make a pot a spaghetti. Hot bread. (*Pause*) Skoolie. (*Pause*) Skoolie, I think I made a mistake, sorry.

(*Skoolie rolls in, her back to Tee. She has a wire hanger, and proceeds to untwist it*)

TEE: I sorry, Skoolie, I think . . . I think I yanked the wrong thing.

(*Tee will pull from under the blanket another straightened—and bloodied —hanger. Eventually Skoolie, absorbed in her task and ignoring Tee, turns around. Stillness. Then Skoolie rushes to lift blanket. Blood all over Tee's groin, legs, the couch*)

SKOOLIE: NO! (*Rushes to phone*) Tee! Tee, what'dju do? Need the clinic, need the emergency room. S'pose ta wait for me, toldja wait for me! This a emergency, we live on the hill, my sister, my sister got blood, my baby sister got a lotta blood, come from her vagina. We live on the hill, shack on the hill, right cross from the general store, know it? Fast, please, cuz, lotta blood, lotta, big . . . pool . . . (*Hangs up. Rushes back toward Tee but falls off cart*) Dammit! wher-esa goddam clean towels?

TEE: Belly hurt . . .

(*Skoolie finds towels, rushes back to Tee, positions towel between Tee's legs. Tee shivers*)

SKOOLIE: Cold?

(*Skoolie puts a towel over Tee, rolls, falls off cart again. Screams in frustration. Gets back on cart, goes to cabinet and retrieves blanket. Starts to go back to Tee but cart gets stuck*)

SKOOLIE: I hate this thing!

(*Skoolie gets off cart, pulls herself to Tee, covers her. Quiet*)

SKOOLIE: Don't go to sleep! Don't go to sleep!

TEE: Will-Joe do his readin' last night, he come ask for help. I say better if he get Evie. Or you. (*Pause*)

SKOOLIE: Say somethin'!

TEE: Nothin' else.

SKOOLIE: There is, you gonna talk to me. (*Pause*) *Hear?* Tell me 'bout . . . uh . . . Tell me 'bout that time ya steal my cart, Mama catch ya, fan yer heiny. How come ya done it?
How come ya done it?

TEE: Don't know—

SKOOLIE: Say!

TEE: Jus' mean . . .

SKOOLIE: How come ya steal that cart, Tee?

TEE: Because. It was you.

SKOOLIE (*pause*): Talk!
Aw. Aw, don't cry, don't cry, honey. Just talk for me, please? Jus' say somethin', Tee.

TEE: How come "Skoolie"?

SKOOLIE: How come, ya think?

TEE: Cuz ya never went to school.

SKOOLIE: Uh uh. Uh uh, probably toldja that cuz I like ya to believe it, was a lie. Me and Bink . . . Me and Bink fall outa that tree June before first grade. All summer I bein' carried. To the bed. To the couch. Out the door. *Hate* it. September Daddy carry me to his truck, drive me, set me at my desk, leave. Everyone see it. No one play with me. Not come near, but watch all the time, point. One day, I start pullin' out. Teacher turn her head, I pull myself out the door. I rollin' you over, hear? (*Starts to*)

TEE: Hurts . . . Skoolie, hurts . . .

SKOOLIE: Okay, just yer face. Needta see yer face. Ambulance here soon. (*Pause*) Kids giggle, they like I get away, won't tell. She find me in the hall, or the playground, carry me back, tell Daddy, he gimme a beatin', take me back next day, I do the same. Just too many kids, always could find a time to make my break, she couldn't watch all us and she couldn't tie me up and she wanted to. Year over, beatin' every day, Daddy say he gonna give 'em to me harder I start doin' it in second grade. Well I start doin' it in second grade, but guess what? 'Steada harder, they gettin' softer. Finally, Thanksgivin', Daddy say, "You done the effort, girl, guess it ain't your pleasure. You ain't gotta go back to school no more." Round then I get my name. And he build me a cart, no more bloody cut legs from pullin' 'em, ugly for everybody else, I didn't care, I couldn't feel 'em nohow. Now I go where I please, no more carryin', I go where I want. So "Skoolie" ain't cuza no school. Cuz I did taste school. Spit it out. (*Pause*)

TEE: Skoolie, when you fall out that tree . . . it hurt?

SKOOLIE (*pause*): Me and Bink fall out. I hear a big funny crack. From me. Felt somethin'. If it hurt I never knowed it . . . over too quick. Then we start to gigglin'. Cuz the crack noise was so weird, cuz the whole thing's so funny, us flip out the tree. Then we push our palms down, gonna pull ourselves up. Bink's up the first try, not me. I push again . . . nothin' movin'. Look up at her. Push a third. Nothin'. Look up at her. I start to get scared. (*Looks at Tee. Tee is dead. Skoolie rolls to cabinet and gets a brush, rolls back and starts stroking*

Tee's hair) Not so bad a haircut you give. Just stroke it right. (*Pause*) Shoulda got a pitcher a us yesterday, Tee, both us, you takin' me down the hill, not bump me once. Smooth ride. I ain't been carried in a long time, Tee.

End.

FOR WHOM THE SOUTHERN BELLE TOLLS

(or "The Further Adventures of Amanda and Her Children")

Christopher Durang

Christopher Durang

Christopher Durang grew up in New Jersey. He attended Harvard, and received an MFA in play writing from Yale School of Drama.

His on- and off-Broadway plays include *The Nature And Purpose Of The Universe, Titanic, A History Of The American Film* (Tony nomination for Best Book of a Musical), *Sister Mary Ignatius Explains It All For You* (Obie Award), *The Marriage Of Bette And Boo* (Obie Award), *Baby With The Bathwater, Laughing Wild,* and *Beyond Therapy.*

His most recent play, *Media Amok,* premiered at American Repertory Theatre in Cambridge, MA, in 1992. *For Whom The Southern Belle Tolls* was presented in the Ensemble Studio Theatre's one-act festival in June, and was part of *Durang Durang,* an evening of one-acts which premiered at Manhattan Theatre Club in November, 1994.

Christopher's screenplays include *The Nun Who Shot Liberty Valance, The Adventures Of Lola,* and *The House Of Husbands,* which he co-authored with Wendy Wasserstein.

As an actor, Durang won an Ensemble acting Obie for *The Marriage Of Bette And Boo,* and appeared in both the New York and Los Angeles productions of *Laughing Wild.*

Several of Durang's works are published by Grove House, and a collection of short plays is forthcoming from Smith and Krauss. He is a member of the Dramatists Guild Council.

Characters:

AMANDA, *the mother*

LAWRENCE, *the son*

TOM, *the other son*

GINNY

Lights up on a fussy living room setting. Enter Amanda, the Southern belle mother.

AMANDA: Rise and shine! Rise and shine! (*Calls off*) Lawrence, honey, come on out here and let me have a look at you!

(*Enter Lawrence, who limps across the room. He is very sensitive, and is wearing what are clearly his dress clothes. Amanda fiddles with his bow tie and stands back to admire him*)

AMANDA: Lawrence, honey, you look lovely.

LAWRENCE: No, I don't mama. I have a pimple on the back of my neck.

AMANDA: Don't say the word "pimple," honey, it's common. Now your brother Tom is bringing home a girl from the warehouse for you to meet, and I want you to make a good impression, honey.

LAWRENCE: It upsets my stomach to meet people, mama.

AMANDA: Oh, Lawrence honey, you're so sensitive it makes me want to hit you.

LAWRENCE: I don't need to meet people, mama. I'm happy just by myself, playing with my collection of glass cocktail stirrers.

(*Lawrence limps over to a table on top of which sits a glass jar filled with glass swizzle sticks*)

AMANDA: Lawrence, you are a caution. Only retarded people and alcoholics are interested in glass cocktail stirrers.

LAWRENCE (*picking up some of them*): Each one of them has a special name, mama. This one is called Stringbean because it's long and thin; and this one is called Blue because it's blue.

AMANDA: All my children have such imagination, why was I so blessed? Oh, Lawrence honey, how are you going to get on in the world if you just stay home all day, year after year, playing with your collection of glass cocktail stirrers?

LAWRENCE: I don't like the world, mama, I like it here in this room.

AMANDA: I know you do, Lawrence honey, that's part of your charm. Some days. But, honey, what about making a living?

LAWRENCE: I can't work, mama. I'm crippled. (*He limps over to the couch and sits*)

AMANDA: There is nothing wrong with your leg, Lawrence honey, all the doctors have told you that. This limping thing is an affectation.

LAWRENCE: I only know how I feel, mama.

AMANDA: Oh if only I had connections in the Mafia, I'd have someone come and break both your legs.

LAWRENCE: Don't try to make me laugh, mama. You know I have asthma.

AMANDA: Your asthma, your leg, your eczema. You're just a mess, Lawrence.

LAWRENCE: I have scabs from the itching, mama.

AMANDA: That's lovely, Lawrence. You must tell us more over dinner.

LAWRENCE: Alright.

AMANDA: That was a joke, Lawrence.

LAWRENCE: Don't try to make me laugh, mama. My asthma.

AMANDA: Now, Lawrence, I don't want you talking about your ailments to the feminine caller your brother Tom is bringing home from the warehouse, honey. No nice-bred young lady likes to hear a young man discussing his eczema, Lawrence.

LAWRENCE: What else can I talk about, mama?

AMANDA: Talk about the weather. Or Red China.

LAWRENCE: Or my collection of glass cocktail stirrers?

AMANDA: I suppose so, honey, if the conversation comes to some godawful standstill. Otherwise, I'd shut up about it. Conversation is an art, Lawrence. Back at Blue Mountain, when I had seventeen gentlemen callers, I was able to converse with charm and vivacity for six hours without stop and never once mention eczema or bone cancer or vivisection. Try to emulate me, Lawrence, honey. Charm and vivacity. And charm. And vivacity. And charm.

LAWRENCE: Well, I'll try, but I doubt it.

AMANDA: Me too, honey. But we'll go through the motions anyway, won't we?

LAWRENCE: I don't know if I want to meet some girl who works in a warehouse, mama.

AMANDA: Your brother Tom says she's a lovely girl with a nice personality. And where else does he meet girls except the few who work at the warehouse? He only seems to meet men at the movies. Your brother goes to the movies entirely too much. I must speak to him about it.

LAWRENCE: It's unfeminine for a girl to work at a warehouse.

AMANDA: Lawrence, honey, if you can't go out the door without getting an upset stomach or an attack of vertigo, then we got to find some nice girl who's willing to support you. Otherwise, how am I ever going to get you out of this house and off my hands?

LAWRENCE: Why do you want to be rid of me, mama?

AMANDA: I suppose it's unmotherly of me, dear, but you really get on my nerves. Limping around the apartment, pretending to have asthma. If only some nice girl would marry you and I knew you were taken care of, then I'd feel free to start to live again. I'd join Parents Without Partners, I'd go to dinner dances, I'd have a life again.

Rather than just watch you mope about this stupid apartment. I'm not bitter, dear, it's just that I hate my life.

LAWRENCE: I understand, mama.

AMANDA: Do you, dear? Oh, you're cute. Oh listen, I think I hear them.

TOM (*from off-stage*): Mother, I forgot my key.

LAWRENCE: I'll be in the other room. (*Starts to limp away*)

AMANDA: I want you to let them in, Lawrence.

LAWRENCE: Oh, I couldn't mama. She'd see I limp.

AMANDA: Then don't limp, damn it.

TOM (*from off*): Mother, are you there?

AMANDA: Just a minute, Tom, honey. Now, Lawrence, you march over to that door or I'm going to break all your swizzle sticks.

LAWRENCE: Mama, I can't.

AMANDA: Lawrence, you're a grown boy. Now you answer that door like any normal person.

LAWRENCE: I can't.

TOM: Mother, I'm going to break the door down in a minute.

AMANDA: Just be patient, Tom. Now you're causing a scene, Lawrence. I want you to answer that door.

LAWRENCE: My eczema itches.

AMANDA: I'll itch it for you in a second, Lawrence.

TOM: Alright, I'm breaking it down.

(*Sound of door breaking down. Enter Tom and Ginny Bennett, a vivacious girl dressed in factory clothes*)

AMANDA: Oh, Tom, you got in.

TOM: Why must we go through this every night? You know the stupid fuck won't open the door, so why don't you let him alone about it? (*To Ginny*) My kid brother has a thing about answering doors. He thinks people will notice his limp and his asthma and his eczema.

LAWRENCE: Excuse me. I think I hear someone calling me in the other room. (*Limps off, calls to imaginary person*) Coming!

AMANDA: Now see what you've done. He's probably going to refuse to come to the table due to your insensitivity. Oh, was any woman as cursed as I? With one son who's too sensitive and another one who's this big ox. I'm sorry, how rude of me. I'm Amanda Wingvalley. You must be Virginia Bennett from the warehouse. Tom has spoken so much about you I feel you're almost one of the family, preferably a daughter-in-law. Welcome, Virginia.

GINNY (*speaking very loudly*): Call me Ginny or Gin. But just don't call me late for dinner! (*Roars with laughter*)

AMANDA: Oh, how amusing. (*Whispers to Tom*) Why is she shouting? Is she deaf?

GINNY: You're asking why I am speaking loudly. It's so that I can be heard! I am taking a course in public speaking, and so far we've covered organizing your thoughts and speaking good and loud so the people in the back of the room can hear you.

AMANDA: Public speaking. How impressive. You must be interested in improving yourself.

GINNY (*truly not having heard*): What?

AMANDA (*loudly*): YOU MUST BE INTERESTED IN IMPROVING YOURSELF.

GINNY (*loudly and happily*): YES I AM!

TOM: When's dinner? I want to get this over with fast if everyone's going to shout all evening.

GINNY: What?

AMANDA (*to Ginny*): Dinner is almost ready, Ginny.

GINNY: Who's Freddy?

AMANDA: Oh, Lord. No, dear. DINNER IS READY.

GINNY: Oh good. I'm as hungry as a bear! (*Growls enthusiastically*)

AMANDA: You must be very popular at the warehouse, Ginny.

GINNY: No popsicle for me, ma'am, although I will take you up on some gin.

AMANDA (*confused*): What?

GINNY (*loudly*): I WOULD LIKE SOME GIN.

AMANDA: Well, fine. I think I'd like to get drunk too. Tom, why don't you go and make two Southern ladies some nice summer gin and tonics? And see if your sister would like a lemonade.

TOM: Sister?

AMANDA: I'm sorry, did I say sister? I meant brother.

TOM (*calling as he exits*): Hey, four eyes, you wanna lemonade?

AMANDA: Tom's so amusing. He calls Lawrence four eyes even though he doesn't wear glasses.

GINNY: And does Lawrence wear glasses?

AMANDA (*confused*): What?

GINNY: You said Tom called Lawrence four eyes even though he doesn't wear glasses, and I wondered if Lawrence wore glasses. Because that would, you see, explain it.

AMANDA (*looks at her with despair*): Ah. I don't know. I'll have to ask Lawrence someday. Speaking of Lawrence, let me go check on the supper and see if I can convince him to come out here and make conversation with you.

GINNY: No, thank you, ma'am, I'll just have the gin.

AMANDA: What?

GINNY: What?

AMANDA: Never mind. I'll be back. Or with luck I won't.

(*Amanda exits. Ginny looks around uncomfortably, and crosses to the table with the collection of glass cocktail stirrers*)

GINNY: They must drink a lot here.

(*Enter Tom with a glass of gin for Ginny*)

TOM: Here's some gin for Ginny.

GINNY: What?

TOM: Here's your poison.

GINNY: No, thanks, I'll just wait here.

TOM: Have you ever thought all that loud machinery at the warehouse may be affecting your hearing?

GINNY: Scenery? You mean, like trees? Yeah, I like trees.

TOM: I like trees, too.

AMANDA (*from off-stage*): Now you get out of that bed this minute, Lawrence Wingvalley, or I'm going to give that overbearing girl your entire collection of glass gobbledygook—is that clear?

(*Amanda pushes in Lawrence, who is wearing a night shirt*)

AMANDA: I believe Lawrence would like to visit with you, Ginny.

GINNY (*shows her drink*): Tom brought me my drink already, thank you, Mrs. Wingvalley.

AMANDA: You know a hearing aid isn't really all that expensive, dear, you might look into that.

GINNY: No, if I have the gin, I don't really want any gator aid. Never liked the stuff anyway. But you feel free.

AMANDA: Thank you, dear. I will. Come, Tom, come to the kitchen and help me prepare the dinner. And we'll let the two young people converse. Remember, Lawrence. Charm and vivacity.

TOM: I hope this dinner won't take long, mother. I don't want to get to the movies too late.

AMANDA: Oh shut up about the movies.

(*Amanda and Tom exit. Lawrence stands still, uncomfortable. Ginny looks at him pleasantly. Silence for a while*)

GINNY: Hi.

LAWRENCE: Hi. (*Pause*) I'd gone to bed.

GINNY: I never eat bread. It's too fattening. I have to watch my figure if I want to get ahead in the world. Why are you wearing that nightshirt?

LAWRENCE: I'd gone to bed. I wasn't feeling well. My leg hurts and I have a headache, and I have palpitations of the heart.

GINNY: I don't know. Hum a few bars, and I'll see.

LAWRENCE: We've met before, you know.

GINNY: I've never seen snow. Is it exciting?

LAWRENCE: We were in high school together. You were voted Girl Most Likely To Succeed. We sat next to one another in glee club.

GINNY: I'm sorry, I really can't hear you. You're talking too softly.

LAWRENCE (*louder*): You used to call me BLUE ROSES.

GINNY: Blue Roses? Oh yes, I remember, sort of. Why did I do that?

LAWRENCE: I had been absent from school for several months, and when I came back, you asked me where I'd been, and I said I'd been sick with viral pneumonia, but you thought I said "blue roses."

GINNY: I didn't get much of that, but I remember you now. You used to make a spectacle of yourself every day in glee class, clumping up the aisle with this great big noisy leg brace on your leg. God, you made a racket.

LAWRENCE: I was always so afraid people were looking at me, and pointing. But then eventually mama wouldn't let me wear the leg brace anymore. She gave it to the Salvation Army.

GINNY: I've never been in the army. How long were you in for?

LAWRENCE: I've never been in the army. I have asthma.

GINNY: You do? May I see it?

LAWRENCE (*confused*): See it?

GINNY: Well, sure unless you don't want to.

LAWRENCE: Maybe you want to see my collection of glass cocktail stirrers. (*He limps to the table, and limps back to her, holding his collection*)

LAWRENCE (*holds up a stick*): I call this one Stringbean, because it's long and thin.

GINNY: Thank you. (*Puts it in her glass and stirs it*)

LAWRENCE (*fairly appalled*): They're not for use. (*Takes it back from her*) They're a collection.

GINNY: Well, I guess I stirred it enough.

LAWRENCE: They're my favorite thing in the world. (*Holds up another one*) I call this one Q-tip, because I realized it looks like a Q-tip, except it's made out of glass and doesn't have little cotton swabs at the end of it. (*She looks blank*) Q-TIPS.

GINNY: Really? (*She takes it and puts it in her ear*)

LAWRENCE: No! Don't put it in your ear. (*Takes it back*) Now it's disgusting.

GINNY: Well, I didn't think it was a Q-tip, but that's what you said it was.

LAWRENCE: I call it that. I think I'm going to throw it out now. (*Holds up another one*) I call this one Pinocchio because if you hold it perpendicular to your nose it makes your nose look long. (*He holds it to his nose*)

GINNY: Uh huh.

LAWRENCE: And I call this one Henry Kissinger, because he wears glasses and it's made of glass.

GINNY: Uh huh. (*Takes it and stirs her drink*)

LAWRENCE: No! They're just for looking, not for stirring. Mama, she's making a mess with my collection.

AMANDA (*from off*): Oh shut up about your collection, honey, you're probably driving the poor girl bananas.

GINNY: No bananas, thank you! My nutritionist says I should avoid potassium. You know what I take your trouble to be, Lawrence?

LAWRENCE: Mama says I'm retarded.

GINNY: I know you're tired, I figured that's why you put on the nightshirt, but this won't take long. I judge you to be lacking in self-confidence. Am I right?

LAWRENCE: Well, I am afraid of people and things, and I have a lot of ailments.

GINNY: But that makes you special, Lawrence.

LAWRENCE: What does?

GINNY: I don't know. Whatever you said. And that's why you should present yourself with more confidence. Throw back your shoulders, and say, "HI! HOW YA DOIN'?" Now you try it.

LAWRENCE (*unenthusiastically, softly*): Hello. How are you?

GINNY (*looking at watch, in response to his supposed question*): I don't know, it's about 8:30, but this won't take long and then you can go to bed. Alright, now try it. (*Booming*) "HI! HOW YA DOIN'?"

LAWRENCE: Hi. How ya doin'?

GINNY: Now swagger a bit. (*Kinda butch*) HI. HOW YA DOIN'?

LAWRENCE (*imitates her fairly successfully*): HI. HOW YA DOIN'?

GINNY: Good, Lawrence. That's much better. Again.

(*Amanda and Tom enter from behind them and watch this*)

GINNY (*continued*): HI! HOW YA DOIN'?

LAWRENCE: HI! HOW YA DOIN'?

GINNY: THE BRAVES PLAYED A HELLUVA GAME, DON'TCHA THINK?

LAWRENCE: THE BRAVES PLAYED A HELLUVA GAME, DON'TCHA THINK?

AMANDA: Oh God I feel sorry for their children. Is this the only girl who works at the warehouse, Tom?

GINNY: HI, MRS. WINGVALLEY. YOUR SON LAWRENCE AND I ARE GETTING ON JUST FINE. AREN'T WE, LAWRENCE?

AMANDA: Please, no need to shout, I'm not deaf, even if you are.

GINNY: What?

AMANDA: I'm glad you like Lawrence.

GINNY: What?

AMANDA: I'M GLAD YOU LIKE LAWRENCE.

GINNY: What?

AMANDA: WHY DON'T YOU MARRY LAWRENCE?

GINNY (*looks shocked; has heard this*): Oh.

LAWRENCE: Oh, mama.

GINNY: Oh dear, I see. So that's why Shakespeare asked me here.

AMANDA (*to Tom*): Shakespeare?

TOM: The first day of work she asked me my name, and I said Tom Wingvalley, and she thought I said Shakespeare.

GINNY: Oh dear. Mrs. Wingvalley, if I had a young brother as nice and as special as Lawrence is, I'd invite girls from the warehouse home to meet him too.

AMANDA: I'm sure I don't know what you mean.

GINNY: And you're probably hoping I'll say that I'll call again.

AMANDA: Really, we haven't even had dinner yet. Tom, shouldn't you be checkin' on the roast pigs feet?

TOM: I guess so. If anything interesting happens, call me. (*Exits*)

GINNY: But I'm afraid I won't be calling on Lawrence again.

LAWRENCE: This is so embarrassing. I told you I wanted to stay in my room.

AMANDA: Hush up, Lawrence.

GINNY: But, Lawrence, I don't want you to think that I won't be calling because I don't like you. I do like you.

LAWRENCE: You do?

GINNY: Sure. I like everybody. But I got two time clocks to punch, Mrs. Wingvalley. One at the warehouse, and one at night.

AMANDA: At night? You have a second job? That is ambitious.

GINNY: Not a second job, ma'am. Betty.

AMANDA: Pardon?

GINNY: Now who's deaf, eh what? Betty. I'm involved with a girl named Betty. We've been going together for about a year. We're saving money so that we can buy a farmhouse and a tractor together. So you (*to Lawrence*) can see why I can't visit your son, though I wish I could. No hard feelings, Lawrence. You're a good kid.

LAWRENCE (*offers her another swizzle stick*): I want you to keep this. It's my very favorite one. I call it Thermometer because it looks like a thermometer.

GINNY: You want me to have this?

LAWRENCE: Yes, as a souvenir.

GINNY (*offended*): Well, there's no need to call me a queer. Fuck you and your stupid swizzle sticks. (*Throws the offered gift upstage*)

LAWRENCE (*very upset*): You've broken it!

GINNY: What?

LAWRENCE: You've broken it. YOU'VE BROKEN IT.

GINNY: So I've broken it. Big fuckin' deal. You have twenty more of them here.

AMANDA: Well, I'm so sorry you have to be going.

GINNY: What?

AMANDA: Hadn't you better be going?

GINNY: What?

AMANDA: Go away!

GINNY: Well I guess I can tell when I'm not wanted. I guess I'll go now.

AMANDA: You and Betty must come over some evening. Preferably when we're out.

GINNY: I wasn't shouting. (*Calls off*) So long, Shakespeare. See you at the warehouse. (*To Lawrence*) So long, Lawrence. I hope your rash gets better.

LAWRENCE (*saddened, holding the broken swizzle stick*): You broke Thermometer.

GINNY: What?

LAWRENCE: YOU BROKE THERMOMETER!

GINNY: Well, what was a thermometer doing in with the swizzle sticks anyway?

LAWRENCE: Its name was Thermometer, you nitwit!

AMANDA: Let it go, Lawrence. There'll be other swizzle sticks. Goodbye, Virginia.

GINNY: I sure am hungry. Any chance I might be able to take a sandwich with me?

AMANDA: Certainly you can shake hands with me, if that will make you happy.

GINNY: I said I'm hungry.

AMANDA: Really, dear? What part of Hungary are you from?

GINNY: Oh never mind. I guess I'll go.

AMANDA: That's right. You have two time clocks. It must be getting near to when you punch in Betty.

GINNY: Well, so long, everybody. I had a nice time. (*Exits*)

AMANDA: Tom, come in here please. Lawrence, I don't believe I would play the victrola right now.

LAWRENCE: What victrola.

AMANDA: Any victrola.

(*Enter Tom*)

TOM: Yes, mother? Where's Ginny?

AMANDA: The feminine caller made a hasty departure.

TOM: Old four eyes bored her to death, huh?

LAWRENCE: Oh, drop dead.

TOM: We should have you institutionalized.

AMANDA: That's the first helpful thing you've said all evening, but first things first. You played a little joke on us, Tom.

TOM: What are you talking about?

AMANDA: You didn't mention that your friend is already spoken for.

TOM: Really? I didn't even think she liked men.

AMANDA: Yes, well. It seems odd that you know so little about a person you see everyday at the warehouse.

TOM: The warehouse is where I work, not where I know things about people.

AMANDA: The disgrace. The expense of the pigs feet, a new tie for Lawrence. And you—bringing a lesbian into this house. We haven't had a lesbian in this house since your grandmother died, and now you have the audacity to bring in that . . . that . . .

LAWRENCE: Dyke.

AMANDA: Thank you, Lawrence. That overbearing, booming-voiced bull dyke. Into a Christian home.

TOM: Oh look, who cares? No one in their right mind would marry four eyes here.

AMANDA: You have no Christian charity, or filial devotion, or fraternal affection.

TOM: I don't want to listen to this. I'm going to the movies.

AMANDA: You go to the movies to excess, Tom. It isn't healthy.

LAWRENCE: While you're out, could you stop at the liquor store and get me some more cocktail stirrers? She broke Thermometer, and she put Q-tip in her ear.

AMANDA: Listen to your brother, Tom. He's pathetic. How are we going to support ourselves once you go? And I know you want to leave. I've seen the brochure for the merchant marines in your underwear drawer. And the application to the Air Force. And your letter of inquiry to the Ballet Trockadero. So I'm not unaware of what you're thinking. But don't leave us until you fulfill your duties here, Tom. Help brother find a wife, or a job, or a doctor. Or consider euthanasia. But don't leave me here all alone, saddled with him.

LAWRENCE: Mama, don't you like me?

AMANDA: Of course, dear. I'm just making jokes.

LAWRENCE: Be careful of my asthma.

AMANDA: I'll try, dear. Now why don't you hold your breath in case you get a case of terminal hiccups?

LAWRENCE: Alright. (*Holds his breath*)

TOM: I'm leaving.

AMANDA: Where are you going?

TOM: I'm going to the movies.

AMANDA: I don't believe you go to the movies. What did you see last night?

TOM: Hyapatia Lee in "Beaver City."

AMANDA: And the night before that?

TOM: I don't remember. "Humpy Busboys" or something.

AMANDA: Humpy what?

TOM: Nothing. Leave me alone.

AMANDA: These are not mainstream movies, Tom. Why can't you see a normal movie like "The Philadelphia Story." Or "The Bitter Tea of General Yen"?

TOM: Those movies were made in the 1930s.

AMANDA: They're still good today.

TOM: I don't want to have this conversation. I'm going to the movies.

AMANDA: That's right, go to the movies! Don't think about us, a mother alone, an unmarried brother who thinks he's crippled and has no job. Stop holding your breath, Lawrence, mama was kidding. (*Back to Tom*) Don't let anything interfere with your selfish pleasure. Go see your pornographic trash that's worse than anything Mr. D.H. Lawrence ever envisioned. Just go, go, go—to the movies!

TOM: Alright, I will! And the more you shout about my selfishness and my taste in movies the quicker I'll go, and I won't just go to the movies!

AMANDA: Go then! Go to the moon—you selfish dreamer!

(*Tom exits*)

AMANDA (*continued*): Oh Lawrence, honey, what's to become of us?

LAWRENCE: Tom forgot his newspaper, mama.

AMANDA: He forgot a lot more than that, Lawrence honey. He forgot his mama and brother.

(*Amanda and Lawrence stay in place. Tom enters down right and stands apart from them in a spot. He speaks to the audience*)

TOM: I didn't go to the moon, I went to the movies. In Amsterdam. A long, lonely trip working my way on a freighter. They had good movies in Amsterdam. They weren't in English, but I didn't really care. And as for my mother and brother—well, I was adopted anyway. So I didn't miss them.

Or at least so I thought. For something pursued me. It always came upon me unawares, it always caught me by surprise. Sometimes it would be a swizzle stick in someone's vodka glass, or sometimes it would just be a jar of pigs feet. But then all of a sudden my brother touches my shoulder, and my mother puts her hands around my neck, and everywhere I look I am reminded of them. And in all the bars I go to there are those damn swizzle sticks everywhere. I find myself thinking of my brother Lawrence. And of his collection of glass. And of my mother. I begin to think that their story would maybe make a good novel, or even a play. A mother's hopes, a brother's dreams. Pathos, humor, even tragedy. But then I lose interest, I really haven't the energy. So I'll leave them both, dimly lit, in my memory. For nowadays the world is lit by lightning, and when we get those colored lights going, it feels like I'm on LSD. Or some other drug. Or maybe it's the trick of memory, and the fact that life is very, very sad. Play with your cocktail stirrers, Lawrence. And so, good-bye.

AMANDA (*calling over in Tom's direction*): Tom, I hear you out on the porch talking. Who are you talking to?

TOM: No one, mother. I'm just on my way to the movies.

AMANDA: Well, try not to be too late, you have to work early at the warehouse tomorrow. And please don't bring home any visitors from the movies, I'm not up to it after that awful girl. Besides, if some sailor misses his boat, that's no reason you have to put him up in your room. You're too big-hearted, son.

TOM: Yes, mother. See you later. (*Exits*)

LAWRENCE: Look at the light through the glass, mama. (*Looks through a swizzle stick*) Isn't it amazin'?

AMANDA: Yes, I guess it is, Lawrence. Oh, but both my children are weird. What have I done, O Lord, to deserve them?

LAWRENCE: Just lucky, mama.

AMANDA: Don't make jokes, Lawrence. Your asthma. Your eczema. My life.

LAWRENCE: Don't be sad, mama. We have each other for company and amusement.

AMANDA: That's right. It's always darkest before the dawn. Or right before a typhoon sweeps up and kills everybody.

LAWRENCE: Oh, poor mama, let me try to cheer you up with my collection. Is that a good idea?

AMANDA: It's just great, Lawrence. Thank you.

LAWRENCE: I call this one Daffodil, because it's yellow, and daffodils are yellow.

AMANDA: Uh huh.

LAWRENCE (*holds up another one*): And I call this one Curtain Rod because it reminds me of a curtain rod.

AMANDA: Uh huh.

LAWRENCE: And I call this one Ocean, because it's blue, and the ocean is . . .

AMANDA: I THOUGHT YOU CALLED THE BLUE ONE BLUE, YOU IDIOT CHILD! DO I HAVE TO LISTEN TO THIS PATHETIC PRATTLING THE REST OF MY LIFE??? CAN'T YOU AT LEAST BE CONSISTENT???

LAWRENCE (*pause; hurt*): No, I guess I can't.

AMANDA: Well, try, can't you? (*Silence*) I'm sorry, Lawrence. I'm a little short-tempered today.

LAWRENCE: That's alright.

(*Silence*)

AMANDA (*trying to make up*): Do you have any other swizzle sticks with names, Lawrence?

LAWRENCE: Yes, I do. (*Holds one up*) I call this one "Mama." (*He throws it over his shoulder onto the floor*)

AMANDA: Well, that's lovely, Lawrence, thank you.

LAWRENCE: I guess I can be a little short-tempered too.

AMANDA: Yes, well, whatever. I think we won't kill each other this evening, alright?

LAWRENCE: Alright.

AMANDA: I'll just distract myself from my rage and despair, and read about other people's rage and despair in the newspaper, shall I? (*Picks up Tom's newspaper*) Your brother has the worst reading and viewing taste of any living creature. This is just a piece of filth. (*Reads*) Man Has Sex With Chicken, Then Makes Casserole. (*Closes the paper*) Disgusting. Oh, Lawrence honey, look—it's the Evening Star. (*She holds the paper out in front of them*) Let's make a wish on it, honey, shall we?

LAWRENCE: Alright, mama.

(*Amanda holds up the newspaper, and she and Lawrence close their eyes and make a wish*)

AMANDA: What did you wish for, darlin'?

LAWRENCE: More swizzle sticks.

AMANDA: You're so predictable, Lawrence. It's part of your charm, I guess.

LAWRENCE: What did you wish for, mama?

AMANDA: The same thing, honey. Maybe just a little happiness, too, but mostly just some more swizzle sticks.

(*Sad music. Amanda and Lawrence look up at the Evening Star. Fade to black.*)

THE UNIVERSAL LANGUAGE

David Ives

David Ives

David Ives was born in Chicago and educated at Northwestern University and Yale Drama School. His first professional theatre production was presented when he was only twenty-two. Since then he has attracted attention with his full-length plays *Ancient History,* successfully produced in New York and Chicago, *The Red Address,* produced in San Francisco, and *Lives And Deaths Of The Great Harry Houdini,* which was performed at the Williamstown Theatre Festival when David was playwright in residence there.

Ives has had widespread success with his one-act comedies *Sure Thing, Words Words Words, The Universal Language, Variations On The Death Of Trotsky, Philip Glass Buys A Loaf Of Bread,* and *Speed The Play.* Under the title *All In The Timing,* these six plays premiered in 1993 to great acclaim in New York.

When several of these plays were produced at the New Hope Festival, *The Philadelphia Inquirer* hailed the evening as one of the best theatrical events of the year.

Ives also has numerous screenplays, including *The Enchanted* and *The Hunted,* to his credit, and television scripts for Fox's *Urban Anxiety.* An opera, *The Secret Garden,* with music by Greg Pliska, premiered at the Pennsylvania Opera Theatre in 1991. David Ives lives in New York City.

This play is for Robert Stanton, the first and perfect Don

Characters:

DAWN, *late 20's, plainly dressed, very shy, with a stutter*
DON, *about 30, charming and smooth; glasses*
YOUNG MAN, *as you will*

Setting:

A small rented office set up as a classroom. In the room are: a battered desk; a row of three old chairs; and a blackboard on which is written, in large letters, "HE, SHE, IT" and below that, "ARF." Around the top of the walls is a set of numerals, 1 to 8, but instead of being identified in English, ("ONE, TWO, THREE," etc.) we read: "WEN, YU, FRE, FAL, FYND, IFF, HEVEN, WAITZ."
There is a door to the outside at right, another door at left.
At lights up, no one is onstage. We hear a quiet knock at the door right, and it opens to reveal Dawn.

DAWN: H-h-h-h-hello . . . ?

(*She steps in quietly*)

Hello? Is anyb-b-b-ody here?

(*No response. She sees the blackboard, reads*)

"He. She. It. Arf."

(*She notices the numbers around the walls, and reads*)

"Wen—yu—fre—fal—fynd—iff—heven—waitz."

(*Noticing the empty chairs, she practices her greeting, as if there were people sitting in them*)

Hello, my name is Dawn. It's very nice to meet you. How do you do, my name is Dawn. A pleasure to meet you. Hello. My name is Dawn.

(*The door at left opens and Don appears*)

DON: Velcro!
["Welcome!"]

DAWN: Excuse me?

DON: Velcro! Belljar, Froyling! Harvardyu?
["Welcome. Good day, Miss. How are you?"]

DAWN: H-h-h-how do you d-d-d-do, my n-n-name is—

(*Breaks off*)

I'm sorry.

(*She turns to go*)

DON: Oop, oop, oop! Varta, Froyling! Varta! Varta!
["No, no, no! Wait, Miss! Wait!"]

DAWN: I'm v-very sorry to b-b-bother you.

DON: Mock—klahtoo boddam nikto! Ventrica! Ventrica, ventrica. Police!
["But—you're not bothering me at all! Enter. Please."]

DAWN: Really—I think I have the wrong place.

DON: Da rrrroongplatz? Oop da-doll! Du doppa da rektplatz! Dameetcha playzeer. Comintern. Police. Plop da chah.
["The wrong place? Not at all! You have the right place. Pleased to meet you. Come in. Please. Have a seat."]

DAWN: Well. J-just for a second.

DON (*cleaning up papers on the floor*): Squeegie la mezza. ["Excuse the mess"] (*He points to the chair*) Zitz?

DAWN: No thank you. (*She sits*)

DON: Argo.
["So."]
Belljar, Froyling. Harvardyu?

DAWN: "Belljar?"

DON: Belljar. Bell. Jar. Belljar!

DAWN: Is that "good day"—?

DON: Ding!
["Yes."]
"Bell jar" arf "good day." Epp—
["And—"]
Harvardyu?

DAWN: Harvard University?

DON: Oop!
["No."]
Harvard*yu*?

DAWN: Howard Hughes?

DON: Oop! Har*vard*yu?

DAWN: Oh! "How *are* you."

DON: Bleeny, bleeny! Bonanza bleeny!
["Good, good, very good."]

DAWN: Is this 30 East Seventh?

DON: Thirsty oyster heventh. Ding.
["30 East Seventh. Yes."]

DAWN: Suite 662?

DON: Iff-iff-yu. Anchor ding.
["Six-six-two. Right again."]

DAWN: Room B?

DON: Rimbeau.

DAWN: The School of Unamunda?

DON: Hets arf dada Unamunda Kaka-daymee. ["This is the School of Unamunda."] Epp vot kennedy doopferyu? ["And what can I do for you?"]

DAWN: Excuse me . . . ?

DON: Vot. Kennedy. Doopferyu?

DAWN: Well. I s-saw an ad in the n-newspaper.

DON: Video da klip enda peeper? Epp? Knish?

DAWN: Well it says—(*she takes a newspaper clipping out of her purse*) "Learn Unamunda, the universal language."

DON: "Lick Unamunda, da linkwa looniversahl!"

(*A banner unfurls which says just that. Accent on "sahl," by the way*)

DAWN: "The language that will unite all humankind."

DON: "Da linkwa het barf oonidevairsify alla da peepholes enda vooold!" (*Dawn raises her hand*) Quisling?

DAWN: Do you speak English?

DON: "English" . . . ?

DAWN: English.

DON: Ah! Johncleese!

DAWN: Yes. Johncleese.

DON: Johncleese. Squeegie, squeegie. Alaska, iago parladoop johncleese.
["Sorry. Unfortunately, I don't speak English."]

DAWN: No johncleese at all?

DON: One, two, three worlds. "Khello. Goombye. Rice Krispies. Chevrolet." Et cinema, et cinema. Mock—votsdy beesnest, bella Froyling?
["But—what brings you here?"]

DAWN: Well I wanted to be the first. Or among the first. To learn this universal language.

DON: Du arf entra di feersta di feersten. Corngranulations. Ya kooch di anda. (*He kisses her hand*) Epp! Voila-dimir da zamplification forum. (*Produces an application form*)

DAWN: Well I'm not sure I'm ready to apply just yet . . .

DON: Dy klink, pink dama?
["Your name?"]

DAWN: "Dy klink . . ."?

DON: Votsdy klink? Vee klinks du?

DAWN: Um. No nabisco. (*As if to say, I don't understand*)

DON: No nabisco. Klinks du Mary, klinks du Jane, orf Betsy, orf Barbara, orf Tina . . . ? Tessie? Fred?

DAWN: Oh. My name!

DON: Attackly! Mi klink. Echo mi. "Mi klink . . ."

DAWN: Mi klink.

DON: "Arf." Parla.

DAWN: Mi klink arf Dawn di-di-di-Vito.

DON: Dawn di-di-di-Vito! Vot'n harmonika klink doppa du!
["What a melodious name you have!"]

DAWN: Actually, just one d-d-"d."

DON: Ah. Dawn di Vito. Squeegie.

DAWN: I have a s-s-slight s-s-

DON: Stutter.

DAWN: Yes.

DON: Tonguestoppard. Problaymen mit da hoover.

DAWN: Da hoover?

DON: ["Mouth."] Da hoover. ["Face, nose, lips."] Da veasle, da nozzle, da volvos, da hoover. Et cinema, et cinema. Mock! Hets arf blizzardo. Hets arf molto blizzardo!
["This is very strange,"]

DAWN: Something's wrong?

DON: Dusa klinks "Dawn." Iago klink "Don." Badabba?
["Understand?"]

DAWN: Um. No.

DON: Dawn-Don. Don-Dawn.

DAWN: I'm Dawn and you're Don.

DON: Ding. Arf blizzardo, oop?

DAWN: Arf blizzardo, yes.

DON: Mock votdiss minsky? Dis para-Dons. Dis co-inki-dance.
["But what does this mean? This paradox. This coincidence."]

DAWN: Well. Life is very funny sometimes.

DON: Di anda di destiny, dinksdu?

DAWN: Di anda di destiny . . .

DON: Neekolas importantay. (*Back to the application form*) Argo. Da binformations. Edge?

DAWN: Twenty-eight.

DON: "Vont-wait." Slacks?

DAWN: Female.

DON: "Vittamin."

DAWN: How do you say "male"?

DON: "Aspirin." Oxipation?

DAWN: I'm a word processor.

DON: "Verboblender . . ."

DAWN: Is Unamunda very hard to learn?

DON: Eedgy. Egsovereedgy. (*He takes a book off a chair*) Da bop.

DAWN: Da bop?

DON: Da bop.

DAWN: Oh. Book.

DON: Da bop.
["The room"] Da rhoomba.
["The walls"] Da valtz.
["The door"] Isadora.
["The chair"] Da chah.
["Two chairs"] Da chah-chah.

DON & DAWN: ["Three chairs"] Da chah-chah-chah!

DON: Braga! Sonia braga! Iago trattoria Shakespeare enda Unamunda.

DAWN: You're translating Shakespeare into Unamunda?

DON: Forsoot!—Nintendo. ["Listen."] "Ah Romeo, Romeo, bilko arfst du Romeo?" (*Pointing to a rose on the desk*) "Na rosa polly-anna klink voop sent so pink!" Balloontiful, eh?

DAWN: Yes. Bonzo.

DON: Bonanza.

DAWN: Bonanza.

DON: "Mock visp! Vot loomen trip yondra fenstra sheint? Arf den oyster! Epp Juliet arf sonnnng!" Video, Froyling, Unamunda arf da linkwa supreemka di amamor!

DAWN: You know it's strange how much I understand.

DON: Mock natooraltissimississippimentay! Linkwa, pink dama, arf armoneea. Moozheek. Rintintintinnabulation! Epp Unamunda arf da melodeea looniversahl! Porky alla peepholes enda voooold—alla peepholes enda looniverse cargo a shlong enda hartz. Epp det shlong arf . . . Unamunda!
["Naturally! Language, sweet lady, is harmony. Music. And Unamunda is the universal melody. Because all the people in the world—all the people in the universe carry a song in their heart. And that song is . . . Unamunda!"]

DAWN: So "linkwa" is "language"?

DON: Perzacto. Wen linkwa. (*He holds up one finger*) Yew—(*Two fingers*)

DAWN: Two—

DON: Linkages. Free—(*Three fingers*)

DAWN: Three—

DON: Linguini.

DAWN: I see. And "is" is—?

DON: Arf.

DAWN: "Was" is—?

DON: Wharf.

DAWN: "Had been"—?

DON: Long wharf.

DAWN: And "will be"—?

DON: Barf. Arf, wharf, barf. Pasta, prison, furniture dances. ["Past, present, future tenses."] Clara?

DAWN: Clara.

DON: Schumann. (*He adds "WE, YOU, THEY" to the blackboard*)

DAWN: Well, Mr.—

DON: Finninneganegan. (*—like "Finnegan," slurred. "Finninn-again again."*)

DAWN: Mr. F-F-F—

DON: Finninneganegan.

DAWN: What kind of name is that?

DON: Fininnish.

DAWN: Mr. F-F-F-F—

DON: Police! Klink mi "Don."

DAWN: I'd love to learn Unamunda. I mean, if it isn't too expensive.

DON (*perfect English*): Five hundred dollars.

DAWN: Five hundred dollars?

DON: Cash.

DAWN: Five hundred dollars is a lot of money.

DON: Kalamari, Froyling! Kalamari! Da payola arf oopsissima importantay!
["Be calm, be calm! The money isn't important!"]

DAWN: I don't have much money.

DON: Oop doppa bonanza geld. Ya badabba.
["You don't have much money. I understand."]

DAWN: And the thing is, I do have this s-s-slight s-s-s-

DON: Stutter. Ya badabba.

DAWN: So it's always been a little hard for me to talk to people. In fact, m-most of my life has been a very l-l-long . . . (*pause*) . . . pause.

DON: Joe diMaggio. Mock no seperanto, Froyling!
["That's too bad. But don't despair!"]
Porky mit Unamunda—oop tonguestoppard.

DAWN: I wouldn't stutter?

DON: Oop.

DAWN: At all?

DON: Absaloopdiloop.

DAWN: The thing is, just because I'm quiet doesn't mean I have nothing to say.

DON: Off corset!

DAWN: I mean, a tuning fork is silent until you touch it. But then it gives off a perfect "A." Tap a single tuning fork and you can start up a whole orchestra. And if you tap it anywhere in the whole world, it's still a perfect "A"! Just this little piece of metal, and it's like there's all this beautiful sound trapped inside it.

DON: Froyling di Vito, das arf poultry! Du arf ein poultice!

DAWN: But you see, Mr. F-Finninn—

DON: —Eganegan.

DAWN: I don't think language is just music. I believe that language is the opposite of loneliness. And if everybody in the world spoke the same language, who would ever be lonely?

DON: Verismo.

DAWN: I just think English isn't my language. Since it only m-makes p-people laugh at me. And makes me . . .

DON: Lornly.

DAWN: Ding. Very lornly. So will you teach me Unamunda? I do have a little money saved up.

DON: Froyling di Vito . . .

DAWN: I'll pay. Yago pago.

DON: Froyling, arf mangey, mangey deep-feecountries.
["There are many difficulties."]

DAWN: I'll work very hard.

DON: Deep-feekal, Froyling.

DAWN: I understand. P-p-please?

DON: Eff du scoop.

DAWN: "Scoop" means "want"?

DON: Ding.

DAWN: Then I scoop. Moochko.

DON: Donutsayev deedeena vanya.
["Don't say I didn't warn you."] Dollripe-chus. Boggle da zitzbells. Arf raddly?
["All right. Buckle your seatbelts. Are you ready?"]

DAWN: Yes. I'm raddly.

DON: Raza la tabooli. Kontsentreeren. Lax da hoover, lax da hoover. Epp echo mi.
["Clear your mind. Concentrate. Relax your mouth, relax your mouth. And repeat after me."] (*Picks up a pointer*) Schtick.

DAWN: Schtick. (*Don puts the pointer down, and begins the pronouns*)

DON (*pointing to himself*): Ya.

DAWN: Ya.

DON (*points to her*): Du.

DAWN: Du.

DON (*points to "he" on the blackboard*): En.

DAWN: Du.

DON: Ogh!

DAWN: I'm sorry. Squeegies.

DON: Video da problayma?

DAWN: Let me begin again, Mr. Finninneganegan. You see? I said your name. I m-must be g-g-getting b-b-b-better.

DON: Okeefenoch-kee. Parla, prentice: Ya.

DAWN: Ya.

DON: Du.

DAWN: Du.

DON: En.

DAWN: En.

DON (*points to "She" on the blackboard*): Dee.

DAWN: Dee.

DON (*points to "It"*): Da.

DAWN: Da.

DON ["We"]: Wop.

DAWN: Wop.

DON ["You"]: Doobly.

DAWN: Doobly.

DON ["They"]: Day.

DAWN: Day.

DON: Du badabba?

DAWN: Ya badabba du.

DON: Testicle.
["Test."]

DAWN: Al dente?
["Already?"]

DON: Shmal testicle. Epp—alla togandhi.
["Small test. And—all together."]

DAWN (*as he points to "I, You, We, He, You, They"*): Ya du wop en doobly day.

DON & DAWN: (*Don points to her, then "it"*) Doo da! Doo da!

DAWN (*sings "Camptown ladies sing this song"*): Ya du wop en doobly day—

DON & DAWN: (*sing together*) Arf da doo-dah day!

DON: Bleeny, bleeny bonanza bleeny!

DAWN: Reedly-dee?

DON: Indeedly-dee. (*Dawn raises her hand*) Quisling?

DAWN: How do you say "how-do-you-say"?

DON: Howardjohnson.

DAWN: Howardjohnson "to have"?

DON: Doppa.

DAWN: So—(*indicating "he, you, she"*) En doppa, du doppa, dee doppa.

DON: Ding!

DAWN (*faster*): En doppa, du doppa, dee doppa.

DON: Ding!

DAWN (*faster still, swinging it*): En doppa, du doppa, dee doppa. ["They"] Day.

DON: Bleeny con cavyar! Scoop da gwan?

DAWN: Ya scoop if du do.

DON: Dopple scoop! (*Points left*) Eedon.

DAWN: Eedon.

DON (*pointing right*): Ged.

DAWN: Ged.

DON (*pointing up*): Enro.

DAWN: Enro.

DON (*pointing down*): Rok.

DAWN: Rok.

DON (*right*): Ged.

DAWN: Ged.

DON (*up*): Enro.

DAWN: Enro.

DON (*left*): EeDon.

DAWN: EeDon.

DON (*down*): Rok.

DAWN: Rok.

DON: Argo . . .

DON & DAWN: Ged eedon rok enro, ged eedon rok enro! ["Get it on, rock and roll, get it on, rock and roll!]

DON: Krakajak!

DAWN: Veroushka?

DON: Veroushka, baboushka.

DAWN: This is fun!

DON: Dinksdu diss is flan?
["You think this is fun?"]

DAWN: Flantastico!

DON: Ives-ing onda kick. (*Holds out hand*) Di anda.

DAWN: Di anda.

DON (*palm*): Da palma.

DAWN: Da palma.

DON (*index finger*): Da vinci.

DAWN: Da vinci.

DON (*middle finger*): Di niro.

DAWN: Di niro.

DON (*thumb*): Da bamba.

DAWN: Da bamba.

DON (*leg*): Da jamba.

DAWN: Da jamba.

DON & DAWN (*doing a two-step*): Da jambo-ree!

DON: Zoopa! Zoopa mit noodel!

DAWN: Minestrone, minestrone! ["Wait a second!"] Howardjohnson "little"?

DON: Diddly.

DAWN: Howardjohnson "big"?

DON: Da-wow.

DAWN: Argo . . .

DON: Doppa du a diddly anda?
["Do you have a small hand?"]

DAWN: Yago doppa diddly anda, dusa doopa doppa diddly anda.
["I have a small hand, you don't have a small hand."]

DON: Scoopa du da diddly bop?
["Do you want a little book?"]

DAWN: Oop scoopa diddly bop, iago scoopa bop da-wow!
["I don't want a little book, I want a big book."]

DON & DAWN: Oop scoopa diddly bop, iago scoopa bop da-wow, da-wow, da-wow!

DAWN: Ya video! Ya hackensack! Ya parla Unamunda!

(*a la scat*)

Ya stonda en da rhoomba
Epp du stonda mit mee.
Da deska doppa blooma . . .

DON: Arf da boaten onda see!

DAWN: Yadda libben onda erda

DON: Allda himda . . .

DAWN: . . . anda herda . . .

DON & DAWN: Douya heara sweeta birda?
Epp da libben's niceta bee!
Wop top oobly adda
Doop boopda flimma flomma
Scroop bop da beedly odda

DAWN (*really wailing now*): Arf da meeeeeee!
Arf da meeeeeee!
Arf da meeeeeeeeeeeeeee!

(*They collapse in a sort of post-coital exhaustion as the lesson ends*)

DON: A-plotz, Froyling. A-plotz! ["A-plus."] Wharf das gold for yu? ["Was that good for you?"]

DAWN: Gold formeeka? Das wharf gland! Wharf das gold for yu?

DON: Das wharf da skool da fortnox!

DAWN: Nevva evva wharfda bin so blintzful! Nevva evva felta socha feleet-zee-totsee-ohneeya! Da voonda! Da inspermation! Da cosmogrot-tifee-kotsee-ohneeya!
[I've never felt so blissful! Never felt such happiness! The wonder! The inspiration! The cosmic satisfaction!"]

DON (*doesn't understand*): Squeegie, squeegie. Cosmo . . . ?

DAWN: Grottifeekotseeohneeya.

DON: Off corset!

DAWN: Oh my galosh!

DON: Votsda mattress, babbly?

DAWN: No tonguestoppard! No problaymen mit da hoover!

DON: Voy diddle-eye tellya?

DAWN: GOOMBYE ENGLISH, BELLJAR UNAMUNDA! Oh, sordenly ya sensa socha frill da joy!
["Suddenly I feel such a thrill of joy!"]

DON: Uh-huh . . .

DAWN: Ein shoddra divina! Ein exztahz! Ein blintz orgasmico!
["A divine shudder! An ecstasy! An orgasmic bliss!"]

DON: Dawn . . .

DAWN: My slaveyard! (*She rushes to embrace him, but he slips aside*)

DON: Police! Froyling di Vito!

DAWN: Du gabriel mi a balloontiful grift, Don. A linkwa. Epp frontier ta deepternity, yago parlo osolomiento Unamunda!
["You gave me a beautiful gift, Don. A language. And from here to eternity I'm going to speak only Unamunda!"]

DON: Osolomiente?

DAWN: Epsomlootly! Angst tu yu.
["Absolutely! Thanks to you."]

DON: Um, Dawn . . . Dot kood bi oon pogo blizzardo.
["That could be a bit bizarre."]

DAWN (*suddenly remembering*): Mock . . . da payola!

DON: Da payola.

DAWN: Da geld. Fordham letsin.
["The money for the lesson."]

DON: Mooment, shantz . . .
["Just a second, honey . . ."]

DAWN: Lassmi getmi geld fonda handberger.
["Let me get my money from my purse."]

DON: Handberger?

DAWN (*holding up purse*): Handberger.

DON: Oh. Handberger.

DAWN (*as she digs in her purse*): "Ya stonda inda rhoomba epp du stonda mit mi . . ."

DON: Dawn . . .

DAWN (*holding out money*): Dots allada geld ya doppda mit mi. Cheer. ["That's all the money I have with me. Here."] Cheer! Melgibson da rest enda morgen. ["I'll give you the rest tomorrow."]

DON: I can't take your money, Dawn.

DAWN: Squeegie . . . ?

DON: I'm sorry, but I . . . I c-c-can't take your money.

DAWN: Du parla johncleese?

DON: Actually, yes, I do speak a little johncleese.

DAWN: Mock du parlit parfoom!

DON: I've been practicing a lot. Anyway, I-I-I-I don't think I mentioned that the first lesson is free.

DAWN: Mock ya vanta pago.
["But I want to pay."]

DON: But I don't want you to vanta pago.

DAWN: Votsda mattress? Cheer! Etsyuris!
["What's the matter? Here! It's yours!"]

DON: I can't take it.

DAWN: Porky?

DON: Because I can't.

DAWN: Mock porky?

DON: Because it's a fraud.

DAWN: Squeegie?

DON: Unamunda. It's a fraud.

DAWN: A froyd?

DON: A sigismundo froyd.

DAWN: Oop badabba.

DON: It's a con game. A swindle. A parla trick.

DAWN: No crayola.
["I don't believe you."]

DON: Believe it, Dawn! I should know—I invented it! Granted, it's not a very good con, since you're the only person who's ever knocked at that door, and I'm obviously not a very good con man, since I'm refusing to accept your very attractive and generous money, but I can't stand the thought of you walking out there saying "velcro belljar harvardyu" and having people laugh at you. I swear, Dawn, I swear, I didn't want to hurt you. How could I? How could anybody? Your beautiful heart . . . It shines out of you like a beacon. And then there's me. A total fraud. I wish I could lie in any language and say it wasn't so, but . . . I'm sorry, Dawn. I'm so, so . . . sorry.

DAWN: Vot forest?

DON: Will you stop?!

DAWN: Unamunda arf da linkwa looniversahl!

DON: But you and I are the only peepholes in da vooold who speak it!

DAWN: Dolby udders! Dolby udders!
["There'll be others!"]

DON: Who? What others?

DAWN: Don, if you and I can speak this linkwa supreemka, anybody can. Everybody will! This isn't just any language. This isn't just any room! This is the Garden of Eden. And you and I are finding names for a whole new world. I was so . . .

DON: Happy. I know. So was I.

DAWN: Perzakto.

DON: I was happy . . .

DAWN: And why?

DON: I don't know, I . . .

DAWN: Because du epp ya parla da dentrical linguini.

DON: Okay, maybe we speak the same language, but it's nonsense!

DAWN: Oop.

DON: Gibberish.

DAWN: Oop.

DON: Doubletalk.

DAWN: The linkwa you and I parla is amamor, Don.

DON: Amamor . . . ?

DAWN: Unamundamor. Yago arf amorphous mit du.

DON: Amorphous . . . ?

DAWN: Polymorphous.

DON: Verismo?

DAWN: Surrealismo.

DON: But how? I mean . . .

DAWN: Di anda di destiny, Don.

DON: Are you sure?

DAWN: Da pravdaz enda pudding. (*Points around the walls at the numbers*) "When you free fall . . ."

DON: "Find if . . ."

DAWN: "Heaven . . ."

DON: "Waits."

DAWN: Geronimo.

DON: So you forgive me?

DAWN: For making me happy? Yes, I forgive you.

DON: Yago arf . . . spinachless.

DAWN (*holds out her hand*): Di anda.

DON (*holds out his*): Di anda.

DAWN: Da palma.

DON: Da palma.

(*They join hands*)

DAWN: Da kooch.

(*They kiss*)

DON: Yago amorphous mit du tu.

(*They are about to kiss again when the door, right, opens and a Young Man looks in*)

YOUNG MAN: Excuse me. is this the school of Unamunda?

(*Don and Dawn look at each other, then*)

DON & DAWN: Velcro!

(*Blackout*)

THE MIDLIFE CRISIS OF DIONYSUS

Garrison Keillor

Garrison Keillor

Garrison Keillor was born in 1942 in Anoka, Minnesota. His career in radio began when he was an eighteen-year-old student at the University of Minnesota, from which he graduated in 1966. In 1974, while writing an article for *The New Yorker* about the Grand Ole Opry, Keillor was inspired to create a live variety show for radio. Thus, *A Prairie Home Companion* was born.

During its first eighteen years, the show and its creator received a George Foster Peabody Award, an Edward R. Murrow Award, and a medal from the American Academy of Arts and Letters. The show's listenership continues to grow and is currently heard by over 1.8 million listeners on over one hundred and eighty public radio stations.

Keillor also hosts *The Writer's Almanac,* a daily poetry program, distributed by Public Radio International. He is the author of *We Are Still Married, Happy To Be Here, Lake Wobegon Days,* and *The Book of Guys.* He has received a Grammy Award for his recording of *Lake Wobegon Days,* and two ACE Awards for television. Keillor was recently inducted into the Radio Hall of Fame at the Museum of Broadcast Communications, which called him, "contemporary radio's most inventive humorist."

Keillor has broken box-office records in performances with many symphony orchestras, and in *Lake Wobegon Tonight* at the Apollo Theatre in London. He has appeared at the Wolf Trap, Carnegie Hall, and other major concert halls as a member of the Hopeful Gospel Quartet and has also performed in one-man shows across the country.

Characters:

DIONYSUS, *the god of wine*

A NYMPH, *who also plays a hairstylist, an airline clerk, and narrator*

ARIADNE, *Dionysus's wife, who also plays a narrator*

GLADYS, *the muse of maturity, who also plays Theros and a narrator*

A GUY, *who plays a satyr, a doctor, an oil clerk, Zeus, and a narrator*

The curtain rises. A raised platform at center stage, with two bare backwalls, an open rear entrance and two open rectangular windows, suggests a building. Three Greek columns stand at the corners and two downstage. On the platform is a long padded table and an armchair. Dionysus and the Nymph enter from rear, and Ariadne enters from stage left. Dionysus lies down upon the table, holding a glass of wine, and the Nymph lies atop him. Ariadne comes downstage and speaks to the audience.

ARIADNE: Dionysus, the god of wine and of orgies, the bastard son of Zeus and Semele—Dionysus the god of great parties—to his complete surprise one sunny afternoon suddenly became fifty years of age. (*Off-stage sound: tin plates clatter to floor*) He was reclining beneath a beautiful young woman at the time, in his temple on Mount Cithaeron in Boeotia, enjoying a very fine 1925 B.C. Pinot Noir.

DIONYSUS: That orgy tonight—I donno. I've laid in six gallons of extra-virgin cold-pressed olive oil. You think that's too much or not enough? We'll have about fourteen nymphs and six satyrs and maybe a couple other gods, and some Macedonian guys—

NYMPH: I'd say you're going to need more, Di.

DIONYSUS: Really? Six gallons?

NYMPH: You're a guy who takes a lot of oil.

DIONYSUS: Have I gained weight?

NYMPH: No, no. You just need oil because—you create so much friction.

DIONYSUS: Oh. Well—I just hope nobody brings Roquefort salad dressing. It's such a mess when it gets in your ears.

NYMPH: I'll clean your ears, babes.

ARIADNE: Dionysus thought about this, and then he heard the sound of the sensible shoes of the Muse of Maturity, Gladys, coming up the steps and into his temple.

(*Gladys enters from the rear*)

GLADYS: Okay. Get out from under that girl, Gramps, and put down the beverage. I got news for you. You're fifty.

DIONYSUS: What? Fi—

GLADYS: That's right. Say it.

DIONYSUS: Fi-fi-fi-fi-fi-fi—

GLADYS: Fifty.

DIONYSUS: But—Fi—?

(*The Nymph carefully dismounts from on top of Dionysus*)

NYMPH: Listen. It's getting late. I gotta run. Okay? It was great. Call me. Okay? Call me next week.

DIONYSUS: Wait a minute. I'm immortal! Ageless! You can look it up in any mythology!

GLADYS: Everybody gets just so much immortality and then it's time to grow up. You were young for thousands of years, like everybody else, and now you're fifty. What's the problem?

DIONYSUS: But it's—it's not time for that yet. I'm divine!

GLADYS: That's your opinion.

NYMPH: Bye, babes. Listen. I'm sort of tied up next week, okay? Let's aim for the week after next. Okay? Listen, sorry I gotta miss your party tonight. Okay? You okay? Great. Bye. Love ya.

(*The Nymph carefully kisses Dionysus on the cheek and gathers herself up and departs*)

DIONYSUS: How can I be fifty? I'm Dionysus, the god of revels, the patron of satyrs, nymphs, Amazons, bull-roarers, madwomen in mink coats, I'm not just a wine kind of guy, I'm the guy who invented wine—I'm the god of wine, hey? I'm not ready to be fifty. I want more. Where'd she go? I'm not ready to be a geezer. I want more oysters! More wine in the wineskins! More women! Young women—slender—slim-hipped—long-legged—their bodies covered with a soft golden down. I'm not ready to sit in a sunny corner with a knitted comforter on my lap and chuckle. I want to get into trouble.

GLADYS: I got two words for you, mister. And that's grow up. Okay? Grow up. Happy birthday.

(*Gladys turns on her heel and comes downstage to stand alongside Ariadne*)

ARIADNE: Dionysus decided to forget everything she said, and he got himself ready for the orgy that night.

(*Dionysus picks up the armchair and brings it downstage and sits on it, looking gloomy*)

GLADYS: He went to the baths and sat in the steam and thought about naked young women and then he called for his hair stylist.

(*The Nymph enters, in modern dress, blue jeans and blouse, carrying a barbercloth and scissors. She drapes the cloth around Dionysus*)

NYMPH: Hi. How are we doing today? My name's Candy.

DIONYSUS: Hi, Candy. I'm Dionysus.

NYMPH: Oh sure! I'm sorry! I didn't recognize you! You—you look different. Tired or something.

DIONYSUS: Old?

NYMPH: No, no, no, no, no.

DIONYSUS: You're sure?

NYMPH: So how would we like our hair today, Mr. Dionysus?

DIONYSUS: I'd like my golden locks to tumble carelessly down around my ears.

NYMPH: Tumble? I don't know. Your hair is—it's sort of—

DIONYSUS: Old?

NYMPH: No, but maybe not quite as flowing as it used to. It maybe doesn't flow as fluidly. But let's see what we can do.

ARIADNE: And she took a handful of his hair and it felt like dead moss. It felt like a handful of hay.

GLADYS: He sat naked in the steambath, and his hands looked old, mottled, with big ropy veins, the skin wrinkly and rough, like a lizard's.

(*Dionysus rises from the chair, dismayed. The Nymph stands by the chair. Dionysus walks upstage, and stands, his back to the audience, looking down at the floor*)

ARIADNE: He looked into a pool and saw his reflection. Big tufts of hair poked from his ears, and his jawline looked very poorly defined —his chin seemed not so much to thrust forward as to be part of his neck. His neck looked poochy. His chest seemed to have descended about five inches.

DIONYSUS: Who did this to me?

NYMPH: Hey. You don't look that bad for fifty. Your back looks youthful. Sort of.

(*Dionysus groans and turns, he paces the back of the stage, agonized. The Nymph exits, and Gladys. Guy enters, dressed as a satyr, a man in hairy trunks, with paint daubed on his chest, wearing hooves on his feet, horns protruding from his head*)

GUY: What's the matter, Bubba?

DIONYSUS: I'm cancelling the orgy tonight.

GUY: What??? You can't!

(*The Guy stamps his feet rapidly in a childish fit of pique*)

DIONYSUS: It's off. Sorry. Another time.

GUY: Everybody's coming!

DIONYSUS: Tell them not to.

GUY: Why?

DIONYSUS: I'm just not feeling well.

GUY: C'mon. Good orgy be just what you need to get you back on your feet. (*He does some orgiastic grunts, to show Dionysus the healthfulness of it*)

DIONYSUS: I'm feeling sorta stiff and achy.

GUY: Hey—six or ten glasses of good wine, you strip naked, feel the oil trickle down your thighs, feel the heat of golden young women writhing around moaning and stuff—owooooooooooooooooooo.

DIONYSUS: No, thanks. I think I'll just stay home and have a quiet evening with my wife.

GUY: Ariadne? Hey, bring her along. I'll take her. She's a hot one.

(*The Guy grunts his orgiastic grunts*)

DIONYSUS: Get out of here.

(*The Guy exits, grunting, and Dionysus comes downstage, sits in the chair, facing the audience, and turns an invisible key in the ignition, makes a starter sound, and steers the invisible wheel*)

ARIADNE: So Dionysus drove home to the suburbs of Boeotia, listening to oldies on the radio, and thinking about the terrible fate that had befallen him, and on the way, he stopped at the olive-oil store to return the six gallons he had bought for the orgy that had been cancelled.

(*Dionysus climbs out of invisible car, as the Guy, now wearing a hat and jacket, enters*)

GUY: What's the problem? You didn't like it?

DIONYSUS: No.

GUY: What? It didn't feel right? Too slick? You want something with more texture, like a basil vinaigrette or honey mustard? Myself, I find that basil irritates the skin, but maybe you're looking for that, I don't know. One man's irritation is another man's stimulation. You interested in something sweet, like peach preserves? They're real popular at orgies now. Last night, I went to one where we—

DIONYSUS: No thanks. I just want my money back.

(*The Guy shrugs, and he exits. Dionysus turns toward Ariadne*)

ARIADNE: When he got home, I was there waiting for him. I'm his wife. (*To Dionysus*) Hi, honey.

(*They embrace and kiss lightly*)

DIONYSUS: Hi, honey.

ARIADNE: You tired?

DIONYSUS: Uh huh.

ARIADNE: You look beat.

DIONYSUS: Somebody else told me that too.

ARIADNE: I fixed you some poached grouper for supper, and a papyrus salad.

DIONYSUS: Papyrus! Bleaughhhh. It's so dry.

ARIADNE: High in fiber, honey. Time you started thinking about that sort of thing.

DIONYSUS: Where's the kids?

ARIADNE: Spending the weekend at Delphi. With Zeus. Remember?

DIONYSUS: Oh.

ARIADNE: Except Oenopion. She's spending the weekend with her boyfriend Marv.

DIONYSUS: Marv!

ARIADNE: He's nice. He's no god, but—

DIONYSUS: You let our daughter go with Marv???

ARIADNE: She's not a kid anymore, Dionysus. And neither are you. Honey, we need to talk.

DIONYSUS: Oh no.

(*He turns away and plops down in the chair*)

ARIADNE: We need to talk about your drinking, Dionysus.

DIONYSUS: Oh no.

ARIADNE: You're drinking way too much. I want you to stop. Give it up. Please. For me and for the kids but most of all for yourself.

DIONYSUS: Look, I'm Dionysus. Okay? I'm the god of wine, okay? I'm not the god of iced tea, babes.

(*He stands up, agitated, and walks away and turns*)

ARIADNE: I knew you were going to say that.

DIONYSUS: I am the god of revelry, and revelry is no idle thing, it is a crucial element of the whole fertility process. The dancing and the whirling and the drinking and the shouting and the ecstatic singing and whooping—that's what makes the wheat grow, babes. That's what gives us the corn crop. Why am I telling you this? You know this.

ARIADNE: I'm concerned about your health, Dionysus. I read an article that said most people drink to build up self-confidence and compensate for low self-esteem. Maybe you need to see someone.

DIONYSUS: I have no lack of self-esteem! I'm a god!

ARIADNE: Are you?

DIONYSUS: Of course I am. What do you mean, "are you?" What do you mean by that? Of course I'm a god.—Aren't I?

ARIADNE: You're fifty, Dionysus. To me, fifty means mortal.

DIONYSUS: C'mon. I'm the same beautiful guy with the same flowing locks, as when you married me. Look.

(*He takes a lock of his hair and stares at it, cross-eyed, and is disappointed*)

ARIADNE: Drinking all that wine is hard on your hair, honey. And it causes loss of memory. And it makes you flatulent.

DIONYSUS: Memory loss! What memory loss? I don't know what you're talking about.

(*He turns away and we hear a loud fart. He jumps slightly*)

ARIADNE: I love you, Dionysus. Go see a doctor. Please.

DIONYSUS: Okay.

(*She turns and exits, as Guy enters, wearing a stethoscope and white jacket. He walks up to Dionysus, pokes an invisible thermometer in his mouth, raps on his chest, listening with the stethoscope, looks quickly into both ears, takes out thermometer and reads it*)

GUY: Say Ah.

DIONYSUS (*as doctor pokes stick into his mouth*): Ahhhhhhhh-rghhhh-hhh-hhhhh.

GUY: Okay. Not bad. Not bad. Your prostate's a little enlarged but not bad for a guy your age. You should be able to get a few more years out of it. Brain function seems fairly sound, considering. Health's good, under the circumstances. You're no gem, but you're in good shape. I'd say you ought to live well into your senility and beyond.

(*The Guy exits, and Dionysus stands, his back to audience. Gladys enters and stands downstage, and addresses the audience, as the Guy returns, in his satyr garb*)

GLADYS: The next morning, the satyr knocked on Dionysus's door about nine o'clock. Dionysus had not slept well that night. He had dreamed terrible dreams about his mother and he had awakened four or five times to go downstairs and urinate.

GUY: Hey, hey, hey, hey—the orgy is going great! You never saw an orgy as orgiastic as this orgy, my man—yowsa, yowsa, yowsa. Owoooooooooooooo. We started at nine and we went straight through seven a.m. and now we're taking a little break for vomiting and baths and we'll resume at ten-thirty with more wine and a wild boar for breakfast. Hey, what do you say? Sixteen young virgins arriving in ten minutes from Phoenicia, guaranteed tender to the touch and lovely to the eye and tasty to the tongue. Take your pick! We'll pour basil vinaigrette dressing on them—some fresh cilantro—some croutons.

DIONYSUS: Look. I'd love to, but I've got a mortality problem I've got to deal with. Thanks. Have fun.

(*The Guy exits, as the Nymph enters, wearing a blazer over her outfit*)

GLADYS: He drove to the airport to fly to Mount Olympus to discuss the mortality problem with Zeus, his father, and to his great surprise, he got bumped off the first flight and put on stand-by.

(*Gladys exits*)

DIONYSUS: What's going on here? I'm a god. I'm supposed to get the automatic upgrade, go right into first class.

NYMPH: Sorry, sir. First class is full.

DIONYSUS: Well, kick somebody out. I'm a god!

NYMPH: I'm sorry, but your deity card has expired. Expired yesterday.

DIONYSUS: But I'm a god! Gods don't expire. It's an eternal thing.

NYMPH: I'm sorry, but this card is going to have to be renewed before we can upgrade you.

DIONYSUS: But you don't understand. I'm a god. I'm divine.

NYMPH: Believe me, if it were up to me, I'd do it, but I don't make the rules around here. Zeus does. You're going to have to talk to Zeus.

DIONYSUS: That's exactly what I'm trying to do.

NYMPH: I'll get you on the 4:15 if I can.

DIONYSUS: Please.

(*Dionysus turns away, pacing in frustration, as the Nymph comes downstage and addresses the audience*)

NYMPH: Dionysus got on the 4:15 flight, in tourist, a middle seat, between a man possessed of demons and a leper—it was the best we could do—and when he finally arrived at Olympus, Zeus kept him waiting another hour.

(*The Guy enters, wearing a crown, robe, golden slippers, and carrying a scepter*)

DIONYSUS: Hi, Dad. Good to see you. Dad—

GUY: Son, I've decided to make a change. Latromis is going to become the god of wine, and you're going to be the chairman of wine. He'll do the revels and orgies and lie around with the nubile young women and you can oversee the wine business. Form a wine board, organize wine programs, go to wine meetings, formulate wine goals, that sort of thing. Maximize wine. Whatever. And by the way, congratulations on turning fifty. I meant to send a card, but anyway, your birthday present is in there.

(*The Guy waves toward the wings. Dionysus exits and returns with a handful of ordinary things*)

DIONYSUS: A sack of apples, and a pound of cheese? And what's this?

GUY: It's a souvenir photograph of me. I autographed it for you. That's a real silver frame, by the way.

DIONYSUS: Dad—? Why am I fifty? Why did my deity card expire? I thought I was going to be a god forever. Why didn't you tell me this was going to happen?

GUY: What? You? Fifty? Gosh. You don't look that old. Listen. I'll look into it. I'll get back to you. Okay? Great. Happy birthday. Bye.

(*The Guy exits*)

NYMPH: It was a bad day for a guy who had up until then been a god.

DIONYSUS: I don't know what's going on. Doggone it. I'm just gonna go to that orgy. The heck with it.

(*Dionysus exits*)

NYMPH: So he did. He went to the orgy, which was down at the orgy center. (*SFX off-stage: orgy cries*) Everyone was there, three sheets to the wind, having a hell of a good time, ripping each other's clothes off, pouring oil on each other, and no sooner did Dionysus come through the front door than—

(*Dionysus enters*)

NYMPH: —a young virgin flung herself into his arms—

(*The Nymph strips off her garment and runs and leaps into Dionysus's arms*)

NYMPH: Wheeee!

DIONYSUS: Oh my god—

NYMPH: Take me. Ravish me. I'm supple, I'm pliant, I'm delicious, and I'm yours.

(*He kisses her soulfully*)

NYMPH: Oh wow!

(*He kisses her neck and her shoulders, as Ariadne enters and gives him a baleful look and addresses the audience*)

ARIADNE: And Dionysus felt a great surge of youth and strength in his fifty-year-old body—

NYMPH: Oh man. You are really something.

(*Dionysus carries the Nymph off, making deep throaty manly sounds, which continue offstage*)

ARIADNE: She was a wonderful lover, as virgins go, and after he had ravished her, and she had ravished him, they took a little break and they played ping-pong.

(*Off-stage SFX: ping-pong volley*)

ARIADNE: And she turned out to be, in addition to a wonderful lover, a very fine ping-pong player and she beat him the first game, 21–18—

DIONYSUS (*O.S.*): You're great!

NYMPH (*O.S.*): Thanks!

(*Off-stage SFX: ping-pong volley*)

ARIADNE: And he managed to win the second game, 22–20, but he won it by cheating when it was his serve and he was keeping score.

NYMPH (*O.S.*): You're really good.

DIONYSUS (*O.S.*): Oh, you're really better than me.

(*Off-stage SFX: long ping-pong volley, with improv reactions*)

ARIADNE: And they played a third game, and he gave it his all, but his legs were rubbery and his hand was shaky, and she beat him, 21–8, and in his despair, Dionysus reached for a bottle of what he thought was wine and he drank it all.

(*Dionysus enters, staggering, and falls onto the stage, clutching an empty Hilex bleach container. Ariadne turns and looks at him, and looks back at the audience*)

ARIADNE: And when he awoke, it was a long time later, the afternoon sun was blazing down, the virgin was nowhere around, he could hardly move.

(*Dionysus lifts his head, groans, and lays his head down again*)

ARIADNE: It hurt to open his eyes. It hurt just to blink them. His head felt like an immense lag bolt was screwed into the side of it. He could taste dirt in his mouth and something worse than dirt, a sour bitter taste. He was lying in a cornfield, and overhead, immense black buzzards slowly circled in the burning sky.

(*Off-stage SFX: loud shrill bird cries*)

ARIADNE: And something dangled from his mouth that felt like the tail of a small rodent.

(*Dionysus rolls over and spits something out of his mouth. He spits again and again*)

ARIADNE: And yet, he felt no regret. Pain, yes, but no regret. All he could remember was her saying—

NYMPH (*O.S.*): Oh wow.

(*Dionysus sits up and smiles wanly*)

ARIADNE: He sat in the dirt, his poor old body scratched and aching, his lips dry and crusty, his hemorrhoids burning, his ulcers smoking, the taste of laundry bleach in his mouth—and yet—

NYMPH (*O.S.*): Oh wow.

(*Dionysus stands up, a little unsteady*)

DIONYSUS: When I got home, I was hoping that my wife Ariadne would be asleep and I'd have a few hours to think up a story, but she wasn't. She opened the door and she looked at me and she said—

ARIADNE: Get help or get out.

DIONYSUS: What?

ARIADNE: Either you're sick or you're stupid. I prefer to think you're sick. So go to Theros and get help. Or else hit the road. I mean it.

(*Ariadne strides off, as Nymph enters. She continues narration*)

NYMPH: So Dionysus did what she wanted, and he went up to Mount Aesculapius where Theros, the muse of caring, ran a treatment program for gods, demigods, and ex-gods.

(*Gladys enters, wearing a clinical jacket*)

GLADYS: Lie down on the couch, Dionysus.

(*Gladys carries the chair over to the head of the platform where Dionysus has laid himself down*)

GLADYS: I assume you're insured.

DIONYSUS: I'm on a group deity program.

GLADYS: You have some sort of card?

DIONYSUS: I think I lost it. I was at an orgy last night—

GLADYS: Bring it next time then. I need it to fill in the claim forms. So —why don't we start from the beginning. Tell me about your parents.

DIONYSUS: You know about my parents. It's a famous story. It's in every mythology. My dad was Zeus, the Father of Heaven, the Head God, and he was fooling around with mortal women, and he fell in love with my Mom and then his wife Hera got jealous and—you know—

GLADYS: So Hera came to your mom in disguise and said, "Hey, congratulations, but if you want a really good time, tell him to bring his thunderbolts, it's a real charge"?

DIONYSUS: Right.

GLADYS: So your mom made him do it, and he brought his thunderbolts and while they were engaged in passionate embrace, she caught on fire, right?

DIONYSUS: Yes.

GLADYS: And your dad snatched you up from the ashes of her burning body and he sewed you up in his thigh and you spent most of your prenatal period there, in Zeus's left leg. Correct?

DIONYSUS: Right. Exactly.

GLADYS: And after you were born, your nurse was your mom's sister Ino, who tried to protect you, but Hera, your dad's wife, was still consumed with jealousy and she drove Ino mad so that Ino ran around in a wild frenzy with spit dripping from her lips and jumped off a cliff into the sea. I mean, we're talking dysfunctional family at this point, aren't we?

DIONYSUS: I guess so.

GLADYS: And then Hera had you torn into shreds and boiled in a steaming cauldron, and you were boiled to a white pulp—

DIONYSUS: Yes.

GLADYS: And you were rescued by your grandma, who put you back together, but you never forgot what happened, did you, Dionysus? You've never really come to terms with it, have you.

DIONYSUS: With being torn to shreds and boiled? No, I guess I haven't.

GLADYS: Maybe that's why you invented wine. Did you ever think of that? Maybe it was an escape from the terrible disapproval of your wicked stepmother. Do you ever have strange and frightening dreams?

DIONYSUS: Yes. I have dreams in which I have been locked in a chest with my mother and put out to sea and we drift for months, then she dies. I lie in the dark, starving, mad, next to her dead body, rolling on the ocean waves, and then I am found by kindly fisher folk and brought to a beautiful island paradise where I run naked in the woods.

GLADYS: I see.

DIONYSUS: And then, one day, wild swine with blood-stained tusks and tiny red eyes come charging at me through the tall booji grass and I run and run and run, panic-stricken, and fall off the edge of the mile-high cliff and wake up soaked with sweat, trembling, the sheet wound around my neck.

GLADYS: Interesting. What kind of chest?

DIONYSUS: Sort of a trunk.

GLADYS: With drawers?

DIONYSUS: I don't remember.

GLADYS: Like a cabinet? Or a dresser?

DIONYSUS: No. I don't think so. I don't know.

GLADYS: Did it have shelves? Or was it more like a trunk or a suitcase?

DIONYSUS: It's not important.

GLADYS: I think it is.

DIONYSUS: It was a chest, for crying out loud!! Okay? A chest!! Hear me? We were in it together, my dead mother and me! It was dark! Cabinetry was not my main concern at that point!

(*She watches him very coolly through this outburst and waits for him to say more, and when he does not, she writes in her notebook*)

GLADYS: How old are you?

DIONYSUS: What do you mean, "how old are you"? I'm a god. I'm immortal.

GLADYS: I see. How long have you considered yourself a god?

DIONYSUS: Theros—

GLADYS: Yes?

DIONYSUS: Being a god is not a matter of opinion. Whether one "considers" oneself a god or not is not as important as the fact of being a god. I don't "consider" myself a god. I am a god.

GLADYS: If you are a god, then why don't you consider yourself one?

DIONYSUS: Oh, for god's sake.

GLADYS: There seems to be a contradiction there.

DIONYSUS: Listen. I'm a god, okay? So get off my back.

GLADYS: You sound to me like the god of insecurity.

DIONYSUS: Oh shut up. Would you? Just shut your mouth. You're dumber than dirt. I don't know why I'm here.

GLADYS: I'd like to talk about your anger right now.

DIONYSUS: I'm not angry. You are. I'm actually having a very good life.

(*Dionysus stands and walks away*)

DIONYSUS: You know something? I am. My life is not that bad. Wine and love and laughter and a certain measure of tasteless excess and sensual adventure—I've got a darned good life. I just happened to get a bad bottle of bleach.

(*He turns to Theros*)

DIONYSUS: Life is a celebration. And I'm one of the celebrants.

GLADYS: Oh, that's priceless. That really is. (*She writes in her notebook*) You're not only the god of insecurity, you're the god of cliché.

DIONYSUS: It's only a cliché if you say it. If you don't say it and you just do it, it's true. Life is a celebration. Before we can create anything, we need to enjoy who we are now. Before you can get to tomorrow, you have to enjoy today. A person's most fundamental obligation in life is to enjoy it.

GLADYS (*writing rapidly*): Not so fast, I want to get this down.

DIONYSUS: The great killer isn't foolishness, it's sullen lethargy and depression, that's what kills off the corn crop, but if you can bring yourself to sing, have a little wine, fix a nice dinner, tell some jokes, have a good time, spend some of your treasure on happiness, get a little drunk, throw food at each other, it makes the fields fertile, and the wheat crop comes up, and we make more beer and whiskey, and life goes spinning on. Goodbye.

(*Gladys stands and comes downstage, now as narrator, as Dionysus strides toward the wings, running into Ariadne*)

GLADYS: Dionysus went home to Ariadne, and when he got there, he met her on her way out—

ARIADNE: I was going to look for you. I was worried. You done with your therapy?

DIONYSUS: Yes. Pretty much. For now.

ARIADNE: That's good. I missed you.

DIONYSUS: I missed you.

(*They embrace, and then Dionysus sits in the chair downstage, as Ariadne and Gladys take their places behind him and the Nymph and the Guy enter and stand beside them*)

GLADYS: Dionysus did not bother to renew his deity card. He waited for Zeus to do something about it, as he had promised, but months and months passed and there was no word from the Father of Heaven and finally Dionysus just forgot about the whole thing. The question of whether he was a real god or a demigod didn't interest him. He just went on being whatever he was.

NYMPH: His hair improved slightly, when he switched to a milder shampoo, one with some oil in it to make up for the oil he lost by not attending orgies anymore. He switched to a new brand of breakfast cereal made of flecks of birch boughs. He bought a Nautilus machine.

ARIADNE: He cut down on the wine, limiting himself to only the best varieties on special occasions, of which he tried to make as many as possible, but still there are limits to specialness—and he learned to enjoy the ordinary. He learned how to sit down, take a deep breath, look at the woods, and think his own long thoughts.

GUY: But he missed those wild orgies, those young Phoenician women, the dancing, the love-making. As the chairman of wine, he'd fly off to conferences on "Meeting the Wine Needs of the Nineties" and give a long boring speech on "Maximizing the Total Wine Experience," a real stink bomb, and it only made him remember how much fun those great orgies had been.

ARIADNE (*to Dionysus*): We're having the Snaffles over for dinner tonight. And Jim and Judy Woofle.

DIONYSUS: The Woofles?

ARIADNE: You met them at the Whipples'.

DIONYSUS: Oh.

GUY: He used to spend more time with nymphs and satyrs, singing dirty songs and chasing virgins through the tall grass, and now he spent more time with people who possessed the personal warmth of Lucite, people who sat and bored the shoes right off you, complaining about traffic congestion.

ARIADNE: They're nice people.

DIONYSUS: Well, that'll be fun. I'm looking forward to it.

ARIADNE: Good. What are you thinking about?

DIONYSUS: Nothing.

ARIADNE: You look like you're thinking about something.

DIONYSUS: No.

GUY: He was thinking about a swimming pool that lay surrounded by green grass in a forest—he had swum naked there at midnight surrounded by happy women who wanted to press their skin against his. There were some boring men in the pool too, men with loud ratchety voices, like handsaws, but they went away after awhile, went to the house to discuss trends in real estate and the advantages of aluminum siding, and all the women turned to him, Dionysus, their voices rose in song, they followed him dripping from the pool and lay with him on the grass as the great tide of pleasure rose higher and higher, carrying all of them with it.

ARIADNE: What is it?

DIONYSUS: What?

ARIADNE: What you're thinking.

DIONYSUS: I was thinking that here I am, and I've lived for thousands and thousands of years, and it's only now, since I turned fifty, that I start to get the hang of it.

ARIADNE: Good. I'm glad.

(*They freeze into a tableau, hold it for ten seconds, and then all exit. Curtain falls*)

THE MAGENTA SHIFT

Carol K. Mack

Carol K. Mack

Carol Mack's many plays include *Territorial Rites, Postcards, A Safe Place* and *Esther,* some of which received their premieres at the American Place Theatre, the Ensemble Studio Theatre, the White Barn Theatre Foundation, and the Berkshire Theatre Festival in association with the Kennedy Center. Her commendations include the Stanley Award, and the Julie Harris Award for *Borders.* A Rockefeller Foundation residency at Bellagio is to begin in the spring of 1995.

Ms. Mack's most recent play, *The Accident,* is a finalist for the Jane Chambers Award for 1994, and *The Magenta Shift,* which was commissioned by "The Difficult Women's Project," won a Playwright's Forum Award from Theatreworks at the University of Colorado. Other recent works include *Necessary Fictions* and *Variations In Ursa Major: The Last Case Of Franz Mesmer.*

Halftime At Halcyon Days was published in *The Best Short Plays of 1985,* and *Unprogrammed* in the 1990 edition. *Territorial Rites* was anthologized in the *Women's Project Anthology, Volume Two.*

Ms. Mack teaches fiction at NYU, from where she received her MA in Religious Studies in 1992.

Characters:

RHEA: *African-American. Great presence and comedic talent. Late 40s*
JANE: *Intense, anxious, intelligent & vulnerable, comedienne. Mid 30s*

Scene:

A subway station: a token booth, a bench, a pillar. The space is white tiled, lit cooly, black graffiti scrawls are like illegible code. The wall clock reads 2:07 and moves as the play progresses. When a [infrequent] train passes, the sound is distorted by a synthesizer, accompanied by flashes of strobe light. The token booth is somewhat oversized, the pillar at a slight angle, nothing representational gives the space a disorienting feel of an isolated empty outpost rather than a representational subway station. Precurtain: Lights flash by space with the sound of a passing train.

Lights up on Rhea who sits in a token booth behind glass. She speaks to an imaginary audience. Sometimes her audience is intimate and sometimes Las Vegas. She uses her booth microphone to create various effects, from game show M.C. to nightclub professional.

RHEA: Come on down! Come on down and step right up! I am ready for ya! (*Listens*) Nothin! . . . It's a hard day's night. It ain't only for the lonely. (*Hopefully*) Yeah, you got me right. Step on down here, you could be the lucky winner! YES. Come on down . . . somebody? . . . Hello? (*Stands*)
(*Defiantly*) I AM THE GREAT OZ!
(*Theatrically*) Yes I AM!
I am the Big Gypsy Oz. That's how come I got this gig! I can read your palm. I can tell your tea leaf. Man, I know all about your story before you do! I am all filled up with WON-ders. I am the Awesome and the Terrible so don't you mess with me . . . Hello?

(*Lights zap by. Distant train sound like distant thunder*)

RHEA:
(*Sudden mood swing. Sings, nonchalant supper club style*)
"It's quarter past three . . . there's no one in the place . . . 'cept you and me . . . Hey, set em up Joe . . ."
(*Conversationally, improvising*) I gotta secret. Every Oz gotta secret up the sleeve. God got the biggest secret but I found Him out. I tol His tea leaf allright!

(*Leans on elbow, points gun*)

I gotta gun. An that's my secret. My gun's name? It's Rory. Rory. I named it personal, like a pet. I don' have no pets cause I don' have no time to feed em. An one thing I hate it's a dead pet! I hate em all anyhow cause they can go crazy an turn on you. Even a goldfish! That's right!

(*Challengingly*)

Well it would if it could! Can't imagine how a goldfish turn mean? It'd giganticize itself up like the Hulk and suck you in like a Hoover! (*beat*) They all turn on you . . . KIDS do. My Boy, he turned crazy on me. I hadda take away his gun. I named it Rory . . . (*to gun*) didn't I, sweetheart? Now I got Rory hangin here on this string.

(*Swings gun gently, leaves booth, sings*)

"I got the world on a string . . . I'm sittin on a rainbow . . . Got the string around my FIN-ger . . ."

(*Stops abruptly*)

Oh I wish there was some kinda OUTside music down here! All I got in my head now is old tunes! . . . (*focus on gun again*) Rory, he's small but he can DO somethin! You get some dog an you feed it an you train it, an the time comes you say KILL an maybe that dog just looks at your shoes. You won't know till it's too late. Now Rory, he's clean, no feed. You say kill, he does the job. An if you wanna throw him outta the window, the ASPCA don't care none!

(*Suddenly struck by thought*)

My Boy's not gonna have no use for Rory in Heaven. There's a place!

(*Sings, sits on bench*)

"I'm in heaven . . . I'm in heaven" . . . heaven, yeah. The Lord named that place Hisself cause that's His main estate. It's got white pillars all round like Tara, like in the movies. It's all gold an He walks around barefoot on wall-to-wall Blue. My Boy's gonna do fine up there. He's gonna love Heaven like some kinda REsort hotel where they jus deal it out free from the clouds all day long. That's what clouds're made from anyhow . . . all that talk about acid rain? That's soooo UNscientific DUMB . . . They all so dumb!

(*Pause*)

It kills me. People so dumb. Don't know what's happenin. You gotta leave em clues. Yeah. I'm gonna leave that door WIDE open for em, YES. So they'll find his body right off . . . it'll only be a body is all. Like a walnut shell. Hisself, he's gonna be high up there floatin free, like an astronaut! No more pain, free at last!

(*She throws back her head as if she can see him. When she brings her gaze back her eyes are filled with tears. For a moment she seems lifeless, then, overwhelmed by the silence, she pulls herself together. Talks to Rory on bench quietly*)

RHEA (*cont'd*): Well, so Rory, tell me how you like it down here with me, huh? Not much? Me neither! Long time since I first come down here . . . long time. So how'd I think it was gonna be anyhow, DID I think? Nah, just take my thermos and they take out for the health an the rest I use up on the Boy. His Daddy, he never gave me nothin . . . Nobody ever gave me nothin, and the whole time I never did stop to ask why. (*A larger than life howl of pain*) WHHHHYYY!

(*Beat, then cool flat*) Whew! That question was cloggin my head. (*Sips coffee*) Well now I know, don't I? I got my answer now.

(*Train passes, drumlike sound accompanies lights and Rhea crosses back to booth*)

RHEA (*cont'd*): (*in her Oz persona in booth*) I know EVERYthing now! So just ask Oz now an you will get some illUMinatin information. Step on down!

(*Hears a sound, alert, tenses clutching gun*)

stepondown, stepondown . . . Who the hell is that?!

(*Footsteps, modified electronically now echo loudly and Rhea stares O.S. tense*)

(*Jane enters. She wears layers of clothing: parka, cap, muffler, mittens, large glasses, two cameras hang around her neck. She is nervous and very distracted by something O.S. so her focus is there, routinely*)

JANE: Hi! Uh, could I have a token please?

RHEA (*examining Jane carefully, then*): You say ONE?!

JANE (*reaches into her coat pockets*): Yeah, um . . . wait. Just . . . (*listens in direction of steps*) Wait a sec!

RHEA: LADY?!

JANE: SHHH! . . . (*Listens*) O.K. O.K. O.K., I think he's . . .

RHEA (*intently*): Lady you just won yourself a prize!

JANE (*doesn't hear, crossing to booth*): I think somebody was following me . . .

RHEA: You hear me?

JANE: Some kinda creep. Think I lost him.

RHEA: You won a Prize.

JANE: What?

RHEA (*with authority*): You are the One Millionth customer come down in the night shift.

JANE: What?!

RHEA: I can count can't I? All I do here is count, lady. I oughtta know what I'm talkin about.

JANE: Sure . . . right.

RHEA: One million is one million.

JANE (*lamely*): I didn't know they gave out . . .

RHEA: Why should you know?! You're an Ordinary Pedestrian.

JANE: Look, I gotta tell you something.

RHEA (*flatly*): I know Everything.

JANE: I wasn't really going anywhere, see.

RHEA (*immediately*): I knew that.

JANE (*turning out her pockets*): I'm disqualified. No money, see?

RHEA: You WON! Minute you come down here! You tryin to get out of it or what?!

JANE: But see I was only out shooting . . .

RHEA: Now you get three questions.

JANE: It's the only time I can get any work done.

RHEA: That's it.

JANE: What?

RHEA: That's it. That's the prize.

JANE: This prize is three questions?

RHEA: I won't count that one.

JANE (*a quizzical smile*): Oh, wow. That's, like a . . . Hey, am I on T.V. or what?

RHEA: Lady, I don't have all night. (*Closes her eyes. In persona*) Just ask Oz. She will answer.

JANE: I guess it must . . . it gets pretty uh, boring down here, huh? (*Confidentially*) You have any idea what it's like up there?

RHEA (*"Oz", quietly*): Is that your first question?

JANE (*"I'll play"*): Sure, tell me.

RHEA: You wanna know what it's like up on the street. I don't get it.

JANE: No, see, I was just trying to . . .

RHEA (*interrupts*): I give you three questions an you use the first one up askin bout where you just came from?

JANE: I want to tell you how it is. I'm trying to explain . . .

RHEA: But I al . . .

JANE: Listen, listen, it's like forty below, like the tundra. There's this sound-chill factor. You know the sound-chill factor?

RHEA: I know windchill.

JANE: Yeah, but tonight it's sound. It comes at you like icycles!

RHEA: Uh huh.

JANE: Everybody's awake, see? Everybody. But they're in their kitchens or their bathrooms and they're screaming at their walls. If they're sleeping, they're yelling in their dreams. And I'm out there on the street getting stabbed with all their stuff!

RHEA (*realizing*): You heard me yell, didn't you?

JANE: I don't know. Were you yelling?

RHEA: Is that your second question?

JANE: Yeah. Sure.

RHEA: Maybe I was. But I want to hear more bout up there, OUTside. I give you one extra question later.

JANE: O.K. . . . thanks.

RHEA (*solemnly*): But first, what I want to know is: you got some kinda special power or something?

JANE: Like ESP?

RHEA: Whatever.

JANE: Maybe. I'm like some kind of receptor, you know, I get human distress signals. They beam in on me. I keep trying to tune them out so I can just . . . get ON with my own life! I'm trying to get a show together, see?!

RHEA: So you heard me, huh?

JANE: It got so bad tonight I wanted to yell: Hey, come on out and we'll all sing and keep each other warm and . . . But if you start yelling on the street they put you away. You have to go home and scream in your own bathroom like everybody else . . . then I hear these footsteps? Heavy, flat, no heels, God, I really hate being followed! On top of everything else, being followed! Anyway that's why I had to come down here . . .

RHEA: No, that's not why you came. You heard me callin you, didn't you?

JANE (*backs off*): No, I don't know. Look, he's probably gone by now. I think I lost him. So . . . uh . . . goodnight, huh? Take care . . .

(*She backs towards stairs*)

RHEA: Maybe he's waitin. Holdin his breath. Waitin on the top of them stairs for you.

JANE (*caught, begins to pace*): Maybe he was only coincidentally walking behind me.

RHEA: That don't happen in real life.

JANE: Sure it happens! Like today? I followed somebody coincidentally, myself. This old lady with a cane? See I really hate to pass old ladies, it's like, if you flash by it's . . . you know? So today I'm behind this old lady, taking baby steps, I'm trying to make her think she's fast. So she turns around and bashes me with her cane. Lucky I've got all this padding.

(*Sudden inspiration*)

That's it. You know what I'm going to do next time? I'm just going to cross the street. Why didn't I think of that before?

RHEA: There's lotta people cross over to the other side of the street lotta them hearin screams and payin no mind.

JANE: Right. Maybe they should. I mean what can a person do anyway?

RHEA: Somethin. There's always something to do. Me, I know what I'm gonna do. Now give me your hand. I'm gonna read your hand now.

JANE (*torn, scared*): Forget it! I don't really want to count. I've gotta go now.

RHEA: Give me your hand.

JANE (*extends hand, reluctantly*): You really think he's still out there?

RHEA: Uh huh. I will now tell you your profession.

JANE: Can you really do this?!

RHEA (*professionally*): You are a surgeon by day and a fortune teller by night.

(*Immediately, looking at her*)

That is not the Truth.

JANE (*embarrassed for Rhea*): It's not. That's right. You're right.

RHEA: Then tell me the truth, goddamn it, cause your hand is lyin to my face!

JANE: I'm a photographer. I've got my M.F.A. and my uh . . . here's my card.

RHEA: Photographer. Sorry. It's the picture comes into my head, not the word. So I see a glint of somethin . . . but it wasn't no scalpel, it was a camera. And it wasn't X rays I see it was negatives. This happens.

JANE: Sure. Thanks anyway . . . mind if I take your picture before I go?

RHEA: As who?

JANE: As, uh . . . you.

RHEA: Yeah? Maybe when you see me. You gotta see somebody 'fore you take his picture. You probably think I don't have no power. Think I can't even read your hand?

JANE (*always polite, looks at her own palm*): No. No, I think it's probably murky. Lately I feel very . . . kind of in a fog, you know? Mostly from insomnia which I get from the ten o'clock news but . . . I'm under severe stress from all these . . . um global concerns. You know what I mean? Like who can really read the newspaper anymore and eat breakfast?

RHEA: Not me.

JANE: Right! If it isn't murder or famine it's toxic waste and if that isn't in your broccoli it's in your paint. Besides, one out of three people you're standing next to anywhere is criminally insane which leaves who? So what is going on anyway, like today? "Scout kills Mom". "Mom kills Tot". "Tot kills Dad."?

RHEA (*fascinated*): This is all in the same family?

JANE: It's everywhere, every day.

RHEA: You say a Boy Scout killed his Mama?

JANE: It was headlines. Don't you ever read the newspaper?

RHEA: I see em down here get carried round under the armpits.

JANE: Right! Thanks! You know I haven't slept in weeks? It's too cold for yoga. But I could just tune out! Cross the street and NOT read the newspaper! Get ON with my OWN life, huh! Thanks.

(*She crosses to steps*)

RHEA (*comes out of the booth*): Don't leave yet. Not before I tell you my story.

JANE (*nervously, surprised*): Are you supposed to be out here?

RHEA: Sit down, I'm gonna tell you . . .

JANE: Listen, first let me tell you something. I better tell you the problem. I mean the heart of the problem. O.K.? Did you . . . did you ever hear of the Magenta Shift?

RHEA: That like the night shift?

JANE (*shakes her head "no"*): It's . . . It's what's happening to all our photographs.

RHEA: Oh that shift, sure.

JANE: The problem started with the Kennedy photographs. The color?

RHEA: Uh huh. And?

JANE: See when all those photographs aged, the color started to shift. And then the first dominant color was magenta, which is how they named it the Magenta Shift and then . . . what happens is there's a slow fade. A fade to absolutely nothing!

RHEA: Nothing. And then?

JANE (*beat*): Nothing is the Problem.

RHEA: Nothing?! Nothing's no problem, girl.

JANE: Nothing's no problem?! Nothing's the problem! Everything's fading out! Soon there'll be no record at all. Of anything!

(*Jane sits on bench, overwhelmed with that*)

WHEW! (*beat*)

RHEA (*with energy to Jane*): O.K.! Now you ready for my story?

JANE: Wait! That was only the background. I can only tell this a piece at a time. It's too powerful.

RHEA: Oh.

JANE: O.K., about a month ago a woman calls my studio. She says her wedding pictures are turning pink. All the bridesmaids who'd been wearing blue are now wearing magenta. O.K., I say, calm down. Just take them out of your album and put them in the refrigerator.

RHEA: Yeah, why's that?

JANE: She's gotta put them in the refrigerator or else her wedding cake turns magenta, and then slowly the entire party would lose that color and fade out like it never even happened!

RHEA (*studies Jane like a moon rock*): So you tell this lady to stick it in the frigedaire?

JANE: It's guaranteed to keep in cold storage for more than five hundred years. Five. Hundred. Years! Get it?

RHEA: What was this lady's name?

JANE: Uh, Mrs. Sugarman.

RHEA: So this Mrs. Sugarman, she do what you say?

JANE (*intensely*): Don't you get it?! Five hundred years! Who's gonna look in Mrs. Sugarman's refrigerator?! Where is her refrigerator going to BE in five hundred years! (*Beat*)

RHEA: What's this story about anyhow?

JANE: That's from Columbus to now! That's from like Descartes to Derrida!

RHEA: And?

JANE: At the rate we're going? That refrigerator will be under some lifeless sea. ALL our photographs are turning mooncolor as we talk, and who cares? What are photographs but a collection of silver specks! Somebody's got to BE there to decode them! (*Beat*)

RHEA (*nods*): So we're talkin five hundred years from tonight?

JANE: All those photos are just dots. That's all. Just moments. They have absolutely no meaning without people to experience them! They're nothing.

RHEA: Oh boy oh boy oh boy. Lord, of all the customers to send me tonight!

JANE: And how about our books? Distintegrating? (*Claps her hands*) Now, this second, fifty million words just went. It's triage in the stacks. And all those bindings! They. They want to put it all on microfilm, send the books to Greenland and sink them under ice. Kids will grow up and not know what a page is! What's left? Frozen books! Who's going to defrost them! Who?

RHEA: This kinda stuff keeps you up nights, huh?

JANE: I can't stand it!

RHEA: You wander round all night with that camera on your neck?

JANE: Only since I started to really dwell on the Magenta Shift and everything disappearing. I close my eyes and imagine that refrigerator lying there like the Titanic in a silent sea! (*pause*)

RHEA: Look girl, alla this stuff is sometime else, and only maybe, huh? I mean who knows what's gonna be? There's big worries an little worries but yours, they're way out there! Don't you have no personal problems, now? Somebody home . . . ?

JANE: Who has time?! What I'm after is . . . I mean with all this fadeout, is what's the meaning of this reality now (*beat*) if there is an objective reality, I mean.

RHEA: The Meaning, huh? That's what you're tryin to get at?

JANE: Yes. Yes, exactly.

RHEA (*decisively*): You came to the right place. I have been told the Meaning. I'm gonna pass it on to you right now.

JANE (*looks fully at Rhea*): Yeah? Whew . . . how could I lay all this on you?! I mean this is exactly why all my friends turn their machines on. Sometimes I think they're voice-activated just for my voice? Maybe that's paranoid, but I think some of them? They just pretend to be tapes soon as they hear me? And here I am starting with a total stranger. I'm really sorry. I don't even know your name.

(*Squints at nametag*)

RHEA: "Oz".

JANE: But . . .

RHEA: Big Gypsy Oz. The name's been changed. The game's been played!

(*She hurls her I.D. tag across platform. Jane looks silently alarmed at the trajectory of the tag, very uncomfortable. Rhea watches her reaction. Beat*)

RHEA: Now we're gonna shift . . . You got somethin against my new name?

JANE: Wasn't that like your um official I.D. . . .

RHEA: Yeah. Well she was an ordinary token nobody, see. She couldn't tell you nothin cause she never asked! Big Gypsy Oz, she tells the Truth.

JANE: Would you mind if I took your picture right now? You have such a great face!

RHEA: Put that thing down. Stop changin the subject on me. I'm gettin dizzy from you! You out there wrigglin like a fish. Now can you take the Truth?

JANE: The truth . . . I'm not sure . . . I mean if it's relative I, well, no. No, actually I'm too stressed out for . . . uh . . . I can't.

RHEA: Where you come off say you're lookin for Meaning?

JANE: I . . .

RHEA: Get yourself some courage, girl. Listen good. I'm going to tell you my story.

JANE: I know too much. My head is a databank.

RHEA: The head's for countin small change. Readin the Walk sign. You after meaning, you don't lead with your head. Even a baby knows that. How'd you grow up anyway, girl? Now you listen. I'm going to tell you bout my pet, Rory.

JANE: Rory? Oh yeah? Who's . . .

RHEA: No bigger than a white rat, Rory is. I had one of them for a week once. That's when MY story starts. My Boy took it home from school when he was bout eight. I say to the teacher, I say: "We already got a lot of these type animal round here. Why stick this one in a cage? Why should it get itself served breakfast when the other ones is out in the garbage huntin for themselves?"

(*She regards Jane a beat*)

JANE: But who exactly is Rory? What kind of . . .

RHEA (*overrides intently*): SHE say, "This rat is an Albino Rat. This is our Class Rat." Well it was one ugly thing when you got close up. So one mornin while the Boy was gettin milk from the store, I just let it out. And that was the mornin the Boy shows off his potential for what he'd be when he growed up. He sees the cage door open and he knocks me right down and kicks me bloody in the head and the belly, and he was only in third grade at that time! . . . Well, the School Psychologist, she say the Boy tol her his Mama killed the White Rat but she knew "such a thing was not possible"! She knew it had to be an "accident" and it was all a matter of "CO-munication" but she didn't see I had iodine all over cause the Boy bit me too and maybe had the rabies from playin with that ALBINO rat!

JANE: Oh, this is gonna be one of those awful stories, isn't it, like the ten o'clock news. I can tell. But it's history, right? What I mean is I want to help, see? But I just don't want to get involved.

RHEA: I know you don't want to get involved, but you are involved.

JANE: . . . it's an accident I'm here. I only came . . .

RHEA: SO. I look at her and I ask does she want to con-tinue this dis-cus-sion bout co-munication in my cage? Cause I'd be there in the night shift makin my rent so the Boy don't have to eat outta the garbage and get hisself killed like the Class Rat.

(*She laughs suddenly*)

That's when she ask me . . . (*hoots*)
"What is your line of work?" WHAT IS YOUR LINE?

(*Hoots and her laugh is infectious. Jane joins in helplessly, reluctantly*)

They had this T.V. program back then they'd light up under your chin . . . you remember, no. See they'd get these people who looked like somethin they wasn't. And the job lights under the chin: This guy is a DISHWASHER! An everybody break up cause the guy next to him who LOOK like the dishwasher, he's really a banker. It gave me the idea!

(*Remembers clearly*)

I think I'm gonna say somethin to this Psychologist Lady an see if my light come on. I say: "I am a practicing surgeon by day, and by night I tell fortunes in a glass booth."

(*Jane watches Rhea intently as she recognizes wording, smile fades*)

RHEA (*cont'd*) (*cool, angry, remembering*): The Psychologist act like she don't hear. Jus writes in her book, an says the Boy is disruptin. I figure since she is not impressed by my two fabulous careers, I won't talk no more. Then she asks me direct bout the boy's Daddy and that's when I decide she looks like that Class Rat around the mouth.

(*Rhea stops. Pulls herself together and then looks at her nails*)

I say, "Funny you askin bout the Boy's Daddy, cause I do not know fer sure who that may be". NOW she's interested! I say, don't worry cause they tied up my tubes so the Boy won't ever have no "Sibling Rivalry" . . . (*bitter*) I could sound just like that fool if I wanted.

JANE (*touched by Rhea's pain*): Oh I'm so sorry that . . . (*She touches Rhea's arm*)

RHEA: Don't touch me. I didn't get to the sad part yet.

JANE: Oh, look I . . .

RHEA: SO. After that Rat there's LOTS of visitors. I always give em a cup of coffee and keep the kitchen real clean, but soon the Boy stop goin to school . . .

JANE (*very still*): What happened to your son?

RHEA: I'm tellin you about Rory.

JANE: Your pet? Rory is your pet, right?

RHEA: Better than a doberman and he don't eat nothin.

JANE: Oh? What, what do you mean he . . . ?

RHEA (*as storyteller*): I'm tellin you bout when they come to visit. See I used to fool them with little things like I had this one big bar of Visitor Soap. When they came I put it out on top of the sink and there it sit. The letters say I-V-O-R-Y, cut deep into the soap and not rubbed down none so you could see from across the room like this sign's blinkin: I-Vory, I-Vory, like saying this lady is a neat lady with a clean sink and no scum on her soap bar! Yeah. So you can't take her son away from her . . .

(*Looks hard at Jane*)

Little thing like that keep you outta trouble a long time. But the joke's on me . . . (*She reflects a beat*)

JANE (*direct, intense*): Please. What is it you want from me!?

RHEA: What do you know?! Columbus and the frigedaire? OBjective reality. Datahead! You're outta school now. I'm telling you a real story, OK.!

JANE: O.K.!

RHEA: I'm tellin you the real story behind the headline tomorrow mornin!

(*Rhea takes her gun out*)

JANE (*swallowing*): . . . what headline? What's that for?

RHEA (*standing, waving gun disparagingly*): This ain't some celebrity party where you talk bout what you don't know nothin bout, an you all ain't gonna do nothin bout it anyway! That's why you celebratin, and drinkin up, cause you don't have to feel nothin, do nothin, just TALK! Talk talk talk!

JANE: Tell me what you want me to do . . . please . . .

RHEA: Wearin that camera round your neck like a life jacket. What's it gonna do? Save you from drowning? From gettin in the picture, huh? That it? You know where you are, girl? This here's the frontline!

JANE: Look, whatever happened way back then, I can't UNdo it, can I? Some stupid school psychologist doesn't listen and . . .

RHEA: YOU. You're gonna witness tonight. That's what you came here for.

JANE: But . . . I'm just a photographer. I take pictures at night. That's all. Of all the empty places. (*Stops. Realizes*) You've seen so much. Your eyes . . .

RHEA: You don't click that thing at me! You don't read me like I'm some book, you just listen good.

JANE (*with total attention*): I AM listening. Really.

RHEA: Not good enough! Ya gotta feel what I'm telling you. Get in the booth. Now . . . That's right.

(*Jane enters booth reluctantly. Rhea locks her in*)

RHEA: O.K.! See without the booth you cannot be transformed. Remember Clark Kent? Remember Oz? But, on the other hand, you could work your lifetime in there and never realize your powers. That's the difference between a cage and a booth, what you make of it. Now remember that.

JANE: Uh huh. How . . . how long do you think I'll be in here?

RHEA: Don't know. Not a bad job for somebody like you . . . what with insomnia and all? You can bring alla those books with you, all the good they do you . . .

(*Beat, regards Jane, then posing formally*)

Now. When you see me clear, really see me, you take my picture.

JANE: That's what you want? That's what I do?

RHEA (*in her Oz persona*): I am the Big Gypsy Oz and I want that clear in my picture, Jane. I want it under my chin like a lit up sign.

JANE (*taking picture*): O.K. I've got it.

RHEA: Now, as a plain woman with her pet Rory.

(*Points gun*)

JANE: You have to point him at me?

RHEA: He's trained this way. Now you shoot. This time under the chin, you're gonna write: "Mom kills Boy".

JANE (*realizing*): Oh NO! Hey, no! Wait a minute . . .

RHEA: Got it? We're getting this down for five hundred years now. When it matters.

JANE: Oh, you can't . . . .

(*Seeing gun point at her*)

O.K. O.K. . . . I got it, but I . . .

RHEA (*points gun at her own head, action freezes Jane*): "Mom kills self".

JANE (*feels this, almost a whisper*): Oh . . . Noooo! Please, listen to me . . .

RHEA: Take it!

JANE: O.K., O.K., I've got it.

RHEA: Now you're gonna stay right in there till the police come. You're holdin tomorrow's headline in your hand. You got my thermos. Comfortable?

JANE (*begins to cry, wipes tears away*): Sure. Terrific. It's a great booth.

RHEA: Now, before I go, you read my hand.

JANE: I can't. You KNOW I can't do that!

RHEA (*holds her hand palm up to Jane*): What do you see?

JANE: I don't know how.

RHEA: Sure you do. You're in my booth now. You changed now.

JANE (*holding Rhea's hand, grasping it*): But . . . I don't see anything.

RHEA: But if you could, what would you see there?

JANE (*whispers, profoundly moved*): Nothing. Nothing's left . . .

RHEA: Not bad, first night on the job. I'm proud of you.

JANE (*grips the extended hand*): PLEASE, DON'T LEAVE ME! Let me help!

RHEA: You think that's an easy job?

JANE: No.

RHEA (*not letting go of Jane's hand*): But you meet interestin people. Stray people. Don't belong nowhere kindof people. I sit in there like you for years, go home, feed the Boy, keep the soap clean. But this stuff ate up his brain and ate up all his good and now people gettin killed for it. Only one right thing to do so nobody suffers no more. Nobody. After I'm gone, you tell my story for me.

(*Takes her hand away*)

JANE: WAIT. Let me go with you please and get help! PLEASE.

RHEA: What? You a dealer or a healer. You think I haven't tried all?

JANE: I'm telephoning for help. STOP! PLEASE DON'T GO.

RHEA: That thing ain't working for months but talk to the handle if you want.

JANE (*shakes booth*): I want to do something!

RHEA (*touched by Jane's emotion*): Look girl, I don't want them saying I cracked up. You tell em I hadda do what I hadda do. Got it now?

JANE (*smashes glass of booth with phone*): Damn it! You can't do this! DAMN IT! There's gotta be another way!

RHEA (*shocked, points gun at Jane*): You quit that! You stay where you are! Listen, life's ahead of you! You still got the negatives! Tell that to Mrs. Whatshername. Where there's negatives there's hope!

JANE (*starts climbing out of the booth*): You're gonna have to shoot me first!

RHEA (*alarmed, cajoling*): Look I gotta go while he's sleepin or it'll be too late!

JANE (*continuing out, cutting her hands*): NO, I am NOT gonna read about this tomorrow!

RHEA: I'm warning you, don't stall me now! I gotta do what I . . . .

JANE (*a torrent of feeling, unstoppable*): NO! GO ahead and shoot me! SHOOT me! Go ahead. I can't take it anymore. Listen! You wanta know what happened to me? I read this whole family burns up. I don't feel ANYTHING! The whole family burns up in some rotten shelter and I keep READING . . . it's all DOTS! . . . They're dying. Everybody's dying and they're turning into DOTS. You blow up the pictures till there's only dots, see, nothing but dots. I'm not gonna let you turn into nothing. You disappear, I disappear too, we'll be NOTHING. If I don't do something, we'll fade out to nothing! You understand me?! Now give me the gun!

(*She struggles with Rhea for the gun and with great energy wrests it from her. Rhea would not shoot Jane, but resists strongly. By end Rhea and Jane are panting heavily*)

RHEA (*crumples a bit, beat, sits. Evenly*): He's gonna wake up and know I took his gun away . . .

JANE (*panting, fierce*): So, let him come down. LET HIM! I got it now!

RHEA (*looking at Jane with surprise*): Must be that booth did it.

JANE: I'm in this story now, see!

RHEA (*beat*): All right, you win.

JANE (*takes off her glasses*): Damn right. I'm a prizewinning pedestrian!

RHEA: Yes . . . you may be . . . may be . . . (*sits, wondering*)

(*Jane suddenly hurls gun O.S. onto tracks. It goes off. Rhea looks at Jane, a beat*)

. . . now what?

JANE (*collapses on bench next to Rhea, beat*): . . . I get three questions and an extra.

(*A TRAIN PASSES. Jane and Rhea turn to look intently at each other, and then a strobe light flickers over them. Lights fade to black*)

MY LEFT BREAST

Susan Miller

In Memory of my Father,
who sent me to the dictionary for the words to say it,
who believed I could.

Susan Miller

Susan Miller is an Obie Award-winning playwright whose most recent work, *My Left Breast* (which she performed herself), premiered at the Actors Theatre of Louisville in the 1994 Humana Festival of New American Plays.

Her plays *Nasty Rumors And Final Remarks, For Dear Life* and *Flux* were produced by Joseph Papp and the New York Shakespeare Company; *Cross Country* and *Confessions Of A Female Disorder* were staged at the Mark Taper Forum in Los Angeles, where Ms. Miller held a Rockefeller Grant and served as playwright in residence. Her work has also been produced by the Second Stage and Naked Angels in New York.

She is a Yaddo fellow, a Eugene O'Neill playwright, and has twice been a finalist for the Susan Smith Blackburn prize. She serves as the director of the Legacy Project, a writing workshop, at the Public Theatre.

Ms. Miller's play, *It's Our Town, Too,* appeared in the Best American Short Plays 92–93. Other plays have been anthologized in *Gay Plays, Volume One,* edited by William Hoffman, *Monologues For Women By Women,* edited by Tori Haring-Smith, *Facing Forward,* and *Plays From The 1994 Humana Festival.*

AUTHOR'S NOTE: Although I have been, and continue to be, the sole performer of *My Left Breast,* it is my hope that eventually other actors will want to perform it.

Given the personal nature of the piece, it may be necessary for future productions to omit the "reveal" in the last stage direction, as well as the earlier line "I'm going to show you my scar. In a minute." I suggest and permit this script change in the belief that it in no way diminishes the strength of the play, but rather allows this story to be told in other voices long after mine, in places far from me.

Running time: approximately one hour and ten minutes.

Lights up

(*I COME OUT DANCING. Then, after a moment*)

The night before I went to the hospital, that's what I did. I danced.

(*Indicates breasts*)

One of these is not real. Can you tell which?

(*Beat*)

I was fourteen the first time a boy touched my breast. My left breast, in fact. I felt so guilty with pleasure I could hardly face my parents that night. It was exquisite. Well, you remember.

(*Beat*)

I always wonder in the movies when the female star has to appear topless in a love scene and the male star is caressing her nipples, how the actress is supposed to remain professional. See, I don't think this would be expected of a man whose penis was being fondled.

(*Beat*)

Anyhow, breast cancer.
The year it happened my son was eight. He looked at my chest, the day I told him. We had these matching Pep Boys tee shirts. You know—Manny, Mo, and Jack. He looked at my chest and said, "Which one was it? Manny or Jack?"
"Jack," I tell him.
"What did they do with it?"
"I don't know."
He starts to cry. "Well, I'm going to get it back for you!"
Now he is twenty and I am still his mother. I am still here. We are still arguing. He is twenty and I wear his oversized boxer shorts with a belt and he borrows my jackets and we wear white tee shirts and torn jeans and he says, "Why don't you get a tattoo."

"A tattoo?"
"Over your scar. It'd be cool."

* * *

Here's what I wear, sometimes, under my clothes.

(*Show BREAST PROSTHESIS to audience*)

Don't worry. It's a spare.

(*Beat*)

When you go for a fitting, you can hear the women in the other booths. Some of them have lost their hair and shop for wigs. Some are very young and their mothers are thinking: Why didn't this happen to me, instead? And there's the feeling you had when you got your first bra, and the saleswoman cupped you to fit. Cupped you and yanked at the straps. Fastened you into the rest of your life.

(*Beat*)

I miss it but it's not a hand. I miss it but it's not my mind. I miss it but it's not the roof over my head. I miss it but it's not a word I need. It's not a sentence I can't live without. I miss it, but it's not a conversation with my son. It's not my courage or my lack of faith.

(*Beat*)

I miss it—but it's not HER.

* * *

Skinnied on the left side like a girl, I summon my breast and you there where it was with your mouth sucking a phantom flutter from my viny scar.

* * *

We met at an artists' colony. One night at charades, (that's what people do there) when an outstanding short story writer was on all fours, being a horse, I sat on the floor and leaned against the sofa. I rubbed my back against what I thought was the hard edge of it. And realized after a minute that I was rubbing against Franny's knee.
"God, I'm sorry."

"Don't be."
"I thought you were the couch."
"It's the nicest thing that's happened to me all day," she said.
In town, one afternoon, we run into each other in the bookstore. It might as well be a hotel room. We might as well be pulling the bedspread off in a fever. We are in a heap. We are thinking the things you think when you are going to run away together. It is only a matter of time.
"You don't finish your sentences," she said.
"I've been told."
"I'm starting to get the drift, however. I know where you're headed."
I was headed toward tumult, headed toward breakage, headed toward her.
It's been a year since she left me and how do I tell someone new? Even though it will probably be a woman. See, a woman might be threatened. A woman might see her own odds. She might not want the reminder.

* * *

I threw on my ripped jeans and a pair of—I pulled on my black tights under a short black skirt—I threw on a white tee shirt and an oversized Armani Jacket—my hair was, well, this was not a bad hair day.
"I guess it's a date," I said to my therapist. "Two single gay women who don't know each other except through a mutual friend. I guess you'd call it a date."
"Do you realize you called yourself a gay woman? I've never heard you refer to yourself that way before."
"Well, it just doesn't seem to matter anymore. What I'm called."
"You mean, since Franny left. Interesting."
"You sound like a shrink."
"Why do you think it doesn't matter anymore," she says.
Because, I want to say, when you're a hurt and leaky thing, all definitions are off. What you were, who you told everyone you might be had a sheen, the spit of artifice. There was always something covert. But now, you've come apart. Like an accident victim in shock, you don't see who sees you and you don't care how you are seen. You are a creature, simply. You move or stop or lurch from side to side as you are able. You make a sound without will. Your former self, the husk of you, hovering near, looks on startled and concerned. But you are not. You are shorn of image. You are waiting to eat again and to speak in a language with meaning. You are not gay. You are not a woman. You are not. And by this, you are everything your former self defended

against, apologized for, explained away, took pride in. You are all of it. None of it. You want only to breathe in and out. And know what your limbs will do. You are at the beginning.

* * *

Hey want to meet for a cappucino at Cafe Franny? Gotta run, I'm off to the latest Franny film. Meet you at the corner of 83rd and Franny? How about Concerto in Franny at Carnegie Franny? Was anything ever called by any other name?

(*Beat*)

Oh, you play the piano? Franny plays the piano. You say words in English. Well, see so did Franny. Uh, huh, you have hair. That's interesting because you know, she also had hair.

(*Beat*)

Maybe I'm paying for the moment when I looked at her and thought I don't know if I love her anymore. Maybe she saw me look at her this way and believed what she saw, even though it was no more true than the first day when you looked at someone and thought, "She's the One." Thought, "I'm saved."

But, nothing can save you. Not your friends, not the best Fred Astaire musical you've ever seen—the grace of it, not your mother's beauty, not a line from a letter you find at the bottom of a drawer, not a magazine or the next day. Nothing can save you. And you stand in the moonlight and a sweetness comes off the top of the trees, and the fence around the yard seals you off from the dark and you can't breathe. It is all so familiar and possible. It is too simple that there is this much good and you don't know how to have it. And it makes you wonder when it was you lost your place. Then you catch a breeze, so warm and ripe, it makes you hope that someone will come who also cannot save you, but who will think you are worth saving.

* * *

A man I know said to me, Lesbians are the Chosen people these days. No AIDS. I said, Lesbians are women.

Women get AIDS. Women get ovarian cancer. Women get breast cancer. Women die. In great numbers. In the silent epidemic. He said, I see what you mean.

(*Beat*)

I miss it but I wouldn't have to if anyone paid attention to women's health care.

* * *

The surgeon in Los Angeles said it was a fibroadenoma. "Someday you might want to have it removed," he said. "But no rush. It's benign." I watched it grow. Then in New York, I saw another surgeon. He said, "What have you been told?"

"Fibroadenoma," I say.

"Well, I'm concerned," he said. "I want to biopsy it."

You know how when everything is going right, you figure it's only a matter of time until that bus swerves on to the sidewalk or you finally make it to the post office to buy stamps and that's the day a crazed postal worker fires his Uzi into the crowd.

Everything was going right for me. I had just won an Obie for a play at the Public Theatre. I had a contract for my first novel—I was in the beginning chapters. And a new relationship.

It was Jane who found the lump. The gynecologist said it was a gland. When it didn't go away, she sent me to the surgeon who said it was something it wasn't.

All of this happened at the beginning of a new decade. When we would all lose our innocence. It was 1980. In New York. I heard the Fourth of July fireworks from my hospital bed. I was thirty-six. I was too young. People were celebrating. And they were too young for the plague that was coming.

* * *

There were two positive nodes. I went through eleven months of chemotherapy and I had only one more month to go. But at my next to the last treatment, after they removed the IV, the oncologist and his nurse looked at me with what I distinctly recognized as menace. I thought, they're trying to kill me. If I come back again, they'll kill me. I never went back.

* * *

There are those who insist that certain types of people get cancer. So I wonder, are there certain types of people who get raped and tortured? Are there certain types who die young? Are there certain types of Bosnians, Somalians, Jews? Are there certain types of gay men? Are there certain types of children who are abused and caught in the crossfire? Is there a type of African American who is denied, excluded, lynched? Were the victims of the Killing Fields people who couldn't express themselves? And one out of eight women—count 'em folks—just holding on to their goddamed anger?

This is my body—where the past and the future collide. This is my body. All at once, timely. All at once, chic. My deviations. My battlescars. My idiosyncratic response to the physical realm. The past deprivations and the future howl.

I am a One Breasted, Menopausal, Jewish Bisexual Lesbian Mom and I am the topic of our times. I am the hot issue. I am the cover of Newsweek, the editorial in the paper. I am a best seller. And I am coming soon to a theatre near you. I am a One Breasted, Menopausal, Jewish Bisexual Lesbian Mom and I am in.

* * *

My son is having symptoms. His stomach hurts. He feels a tumor in his neck. He injures his toes in a game of basketball and suspects gangrene. He says, "My organs are failing." He stands in front of the refrigerator opening and closing the door. "Can I make you some breakfast?" I want to do something for him. I haven't done anything for him, it seems, in a while. I mean like my mother would do for me. But he isn't hungry. It's just a reflex, this refrigerator door thing. Some small comfort.

He walks into the living room and throws his leg over the arm of our formerly white chair. Sitting across from me, disheveled, morning dazed, he says, accusingly, "I think I'm dying."

"You're not dying."

"Maybe it won't happen for a year, but I'm dying."

"Honey, you're talking yourself into it. Why are you so worried about everything?"

"What if I have AIDS?"

That's something I didn't have to think about when I was twenty.

"Everybody's going to die. You'll see. All my friends. It's going to happen."

"Talk to me."

He's a dark thing. His eyes match my own. He'll see a child, overweight, wearing glasses maybe—he'll notice a child like this somewhere, trying to make his way against the odds and it will seem to Jeremy heroic. "Stud," he says. And means it.

"Maybe I have spinal meningitis."

I try not to laugh.

"I'm serious."

"I'm sorry."
Things are breaking down.

* * *

He is twirling a strand of hair around his finger. We're in the Brandeis parking area, waiting to take our children to their dorms. It's an oppressive August day. Everyone has gotten out of his car, but Jeremy won't move. He's in the back seat, regretting his decision. There are no pretty girls. The guys are losers. This was a big mistake.
Suddenly I'm in another August day. I've just put my eight year old on a bus to day camp. He looks out at me from the window. A pale reed, he is twirling his hair around his finger. I watch him do this until the bus pulls away. What have I done? I go home and fall onto my bed. I lie there and mourn all the lost Jeremys. My three year old. My infant boy. I lie on my bed and have grim notions. What if something happened to me and he came home from camp and I wasn't there to pick him up? What if I had an accident? Who would take care of him? What happens to the child of a single parent who is kidnapped by a madman? Then I imagine him lost. I see him twirling his hair, as it grows dark in some abandoned warehouse. He walks the streets of a strange neighborhood. I know that he is crying in the woods. He has gotten himself into an old refrigerator. He falls into a well. He is in the danger zone. He has wandered too far from me. I have cancer and what if I never see him grown. "I'll go and get it back for you, Mom." By the time I have to pick him up from camp, I'm frantic. Somehow, we survived. Until now.
We get to his dorm and unload. His room is in the basement. It is moldy and I feel homesick. This isn't right. Parents move toward their cars dazed and fighting every urge to run back and save their young from this new danger—independence. When I get home, the sound of Jeremy not in his room is deafening.

* * *

THE PHONE CALLS:
Mom, I'm all right. Don't get upset. Just listen, okay. I got arrested last night.
Mom, I'm all right. Don't get upset. Just listen, okay. I'm in the infirmary. The Doctor says it's pneumonia.
Mom, I'm all right. Don't get upset. I was playing rugby and I broke my nose. (That beautiful nose!)
"Mom," he calls from Los Angeles where he is visiting his girlfriend,

on the day there is an earthquake that measures 6.6. "Mom, I'm all right, but I think L.A. is gone."

He transfers to NYU and calls to tell me a car has driven into a crowd of people in Washington Square Park, but he's all right. He calls to say that the boy who was his catcher on the high school baseball team has jumped from a building. "I was walking down his street, Mom. I saw the ambulance. I saw his feet coming out from under a blanket. I can't stop seeing his feet."

* * *

Once after Franny and I had a fight, Jeremy and I were out to dinner. He was thirteen. I must've looked particularly hopeless. Maybe it was my inattention. Whatever shadowed my face, it was enough for him to say, "Are you going to die?" Did he worry himself orphaned every day since I had cancer?

"No, honey, no," I say, shocked into responsibility. "I'm sorry. Franny and I just had a fight. It's nothing. I'm fine. I'm not going to die."

"You looked so sad," he said.

I want to report myself to the nearest authorities. Take me now. I'm busted.

He was two and a half days old the day he came to us. My parents drove my husband and me to the lawyer's office. We handed over a sweater and cap we had brought with us and a blanket my sister made. And we waited. We waited for every known thing to change. Jeremy says he remembers the ride back. The Pennsylvania mountains. And how it was to be held in my arms. How it was to be carried home.

* * *

A woman is ironing her son's shirt. The palm tree shivers outside the window. Gardenia wafts through. Although she can't smell it. It's 4 A.M. She has laid out his button down oxford cloth shirt along with two lines of cocaine on the ironing board. She does them. After his sleeves.

Mothers have no business doing cocaine. Mothers have no business being tired all the time and sick from chemotherapy.

The surgeon said, "Don't join a cancer support group. It'll only depress you."

The drug of choice for most people undergoing chemo is marijuana. It's supposed to help the nausea. But, marijuana didn't work for me. I wanted something to keep me awake, to keep me going. Something I associated with good times, former times, something that assured me there was time.

Sleep, rest, these things were too close to the end of it all. I couldn't give in. If I stopped, the whole thing might stop.

The woman ironing her son's shirt was testing everyone. Who would stay after she'd pushed them away?

There were powerful drugs in her body. But the one she took through the nose kept her from knowing what she knew. Kept her from the ache of caring. In her dreams she could smell the truth. Cocaine—sharp, thrilling. The cancer drugs, acrid and sere. Terrifying. They were Proust's asparagus in her urine. A toxic taste in her mouth.

She had control over cocaine. She administered this to herself. In a breath. There were no needles, no invasion. It was a ritual of pleasure and retreat. It blotted out the anxiety of the waiting room.

And finally, it destroyed what was healthy and cured nothing at all.

The woman ironing her son's shirt felt ashamed. She was not the cancer heroine she'd hoped to be.

Some people would say, this woman is doing the best she can. And that's all anyone can do. But, I think that's just another moral loophole. She can do better. She will do better.

Morning broke. Her son came running down the hall. Her lover called to sing her show tunes.

"I might lose them," the woman thought. "But not while I can still have them." She vowed to stop. "This will be my last time." And it was. Her son was very pleased with his shirt.

* * *

I didn't lose my hair, I lost my period. Chemo knocks out your estrogen, which knocks out your period, which puts you, ready or not, into menopause. So, at thirty-seven I was having hot flashes and panic in the left hand turn lane.

(*Beat*)

It's like this. I'm driving and I'm in the left hand lane and the light turns red before I can make the turn. This isn't good. This for me is a life threatening situation. My heart races. My hands and feet tingle. I hyperventilate. I'm a lot of laughs.

Sometimes this happens if I walk too far from my house.

A lot of women take estrogen replacement therapy. But, you can't take estrogen if you've had breast cancer which is estrogen positive, and for most women under forty, that's the case. So years later, when the hot flashes are over and I can manage to sit in the left hand turn lane without calling the paramedics, Franny and I are visiting my par-

ents and I take a swing at a golf ball. Oh, don't misinterpret. This is my parents' golf course. Their idea. But it's a beautiful day. And I tee off quite nicely. I'm feeling proud of myself, so I take my second swing and I get this sudden, searing pain accompanied by a kind of pop in my side. I've fractured a rib. A year later. Same swing. Same thing.
Then, another time, I reach out my side of the car to remove a twig from the windshield. Pop. My friend Brock runs up behind me, lifts me into the air with his arms around my chest. Pop. I sit the wrong way on a theatre seat. I bend and reach awkwardly for something I've dropped. My trainer pushes my knees into my chest. Pop. Pop. Pop.
The bone scan is negative, but the bone densitometry shows a significant demineralization—or bone loss. Is the structure of everything dissolving? I can't count on whatever it was that held me up, supported my notions, my exertions. Osteoporosis. It's hard to say the word. It's an old person's disease. It's the antifeminine. It's the crone.
I go to see the doctor in Gerontology. The waiting room is full of old people. Naturally. They've come with their husbands. Or their grandchildren. With each other.
A few days after coming home from the hospital, after my mastectomy, I go to the movies in the middle of the afternoon. I notice two older women arm in arm, walking to their seats. And I know what I want. I want to get old and walk arm and arm with my old friend to a movie in the middle of the afternoon.
What movies are you seeing, Franny? Do you still walk out in the middle? On the street, do you take someone's arm? Will you grow old with her?
The gerontologist consults with my internist who consults with an oncologist, who probably consults with somebody else. The rib fractures seem consistent with chemotherapy and the resulting loss of estrogen. But she'd like to run more blood tests. I especially love the one they call a tumor marker. And why are these things always given on a Friday?
Excuse me, I need to scream now.

(*Screams*)

That was good. But what I really want to do is break a chair.

(*Beat*)

I have destroyed so much property in my mind. I have smashed so many plates against the wall, ripped so many books from cover to cover. In my mind, I have trashed apartments, taken all the guilty parties to court. Done damage for damage done. But I'm the accommodating patient. I move on. Get over it. Exercise restraint. I am appropriate.

(*Beat*)

Except for the day the doorman ate my pizza.
I was coming home from chemotherapy. With a pizza. Jane was trying to get me to eat right. Well, trying to get me to eat. So we had this pizza and then I got an urge for LiLac Chocolate which was right down the block from where we lived. I gave the doorman my pizza and asked him to hold it for a couple minutes. When I got back with my chocolate I asked him for my pizza. And he said, "I ate it."
You ate it? You fucking ate my pizza. You fucking murdered my child, you fucking destroyed my career, you fucking robbed me of my youth, you fucking betrayed me, you fucking know that? You fucking fucking idiot!
He offered to pay me for the pizza.

* * *

I walk home from Mt. Sinai, after the gerontologist, down Madison across the park. Trembling. The possibility that there is something else—
I walk around the reservoir. And I see a doorknob from my old house, hanging on the fence.
Then a remnant of a child's blanket worn down to a sad shred. My wedding band. And messages no one has picked up. "Come home. All is forgiven." Gifts that came too late. The opal ring I gave Franny at Christmas. A page torn from Chekhov.
There's a black and white photograph. It's a group of friends. When everything was fine. Before the bad news. I walk farther and I see people testifying. Telling their stories. Here at the wailing wall. And then I see my pink suitcase.
I have this pink suitcase. I don't know how I ended up with it really. It belonged to my sister. I was given the powder blue set for high school graduation. And she got the pink. Well, anyway, it's mine now.
My agent said, "I'm sorry. There's nothing more I can do. Maybe if you spoke to the publisher yourself." I had gotten a year's extension on my novel. It was up now. I called the publisher. I said, "Look, I need more time. I've had this thing happen to me and—"
"I know," she said. "That's unfortunate."

"I've been writing, though. I have about a hundred pages."
"I'm sure it's a wonderful book," she said, "Although I haven't read any of it, but we just can't give you any more time."
She asked for the return of my advance. The Author's League gave me half the money. I paid the rest, put my novel in the pink suitcase and turned the lock.
It is all that is incomplete in me. The waste. My fraud.

* * *

While I'm waiting for the results of this tumor marker, I go with an old college chum to a gay bar. We had gone to the Expo in Montreal together with our young husbands. We deposited our children at the same camp. She's divorced and seeing a woman now.
The first time it ever occurred to me that I might make love with a woman, I was in bed with my husband and I thought, I wonder what it feels like making love to me.
I don't understand the concept of this place. Everyone is cruising, but no one makes a move. All around me women are whispering, "Go on . . . Talk to her. Now's your chance." It ripples through the narrow, smoky, room. "Go on. Talk to her. Now's your chance."
Two women kiss nearby. I halt. I cave. To see this.

* * *

The gay bar in Paris, it was Franny's first. The women were fresh and attractive and we danced to a French hit. The lyrics translated meant the death of love, but we were far from dying. We were expressing ourselves in Paris.
A slave to love when she spoke French. A goner to her version of the Frenchman in America. The accent, the pout, the hands—she had them down. I was seduced. Sometimes after a rough patch, I'd say, all you have to do is speak in French and I'm yours. In the middle of a fight, switch to it, take me.
I had four years of college French, but I could say only, "Have you any stamps" and order grapefruit juice. "Vous avez jus de pamplemousse?"
She required me to say "pamplemousse" back in the United States, in our bed.
When will a French family struggling with directions on the subway fail to remind me?

* * *

We are mothers. We know the same thing. And sometimes it is too much to know. It drew me to her and it is the thing that would come between us.

She's a mother. I trusted she would take better care of things. A mother is a safe bet. A mother would not leave her children for someone else's children. A mother shows up. Stays put. She installs a light in the hall. Franny's a mother, I thought. She won't harm me.

* * *

It keeps coming back. What she said. The way she looked saying it. "We're not in the same place." WHAT DO YOU MEAN? "I don't think we'll ever live together." WAIT. DON'T. PLEASE. WAIT. "This is so hard," she says. OH MY GOD. HAVE YOU MET SOMEONE?

I can be standing in line for bagels. I can be punching in my secret code at the bank machine. It returns to me. A howl goes up.

* * *

"Well, you look fabulous."

"I'm a wreck."

"You'll see. People find that very attractive."

* * *

Every room. Every way the light fell. Every room we walked. Every way we combined there. Every room you moved into and out of. Every absence. Every room of our inclining. Every tender routine. Every room and way I learned you. Clings.

* * *

Just two and half months before Jeremy was born, my first baby died, and the doctor injected me with something so the milk in my breasts would dry up. My breasts became engorged. Hard and full to bursting. It's painful, this swelling of something that wants to come.

* * *

When I was pregnant, I took something called Provera. Later it was shown to cause birth defects.

So, when I got breast cancer I wondered, was it the time someone sprayed my apartment for roaches? Or too much fat in my diet? Was it the deodorant with aluminum, or my birth control pills? Or was it genetic?

"Here are your choices," the bone specialist in L.A. said. "Pick one. A shot every day of Calcitonin which costs a fortune. I wouldn't do it. Etidronate which can cause softening of the bones. Or Tamoxifan, an anitestrogen that acts like an estrogen."

I really hate this arrogant, out of touch son of a bitch specialist, you know? But my internist concurs, and him I love. So, I take the Tamoxifan.

Side effects: Increase in blood clots, endometrial cancer, liver changes.

Something interesting happens. My ovaries ache. I'm . . . well, how do I say this . . . the juices are flowing. But I'm in L.A. working on a television show and Franny's in New York. When I come home for good at Christmas, she tells me it's over. And I'm left to stew in my own juices.

* * *

I didn't call her the day I had a cold. I didn't call her on Friday because I wanted to talk to her so badly my throat closed up. I didn't call her the day before that around fifteen times because I was trying to make it until Friday. I didn't call her one day because I was at the bookstore waiting and hoping. I didn't call her on Wednesday because it would have been a failure, so I swallowed the history of it down. I didn't call just now to save my life, because the instrument of rescue was already in my hands.

* * *

I go back to Mt. Sinai to see the gerontologist. All my tests are normal. "There's really nothing to do. Increase the calcium in your diet. Maintain a consistent exercise program. Especially weight lifting."

Well, hey, I belong to a health club. With TV sets. And I was starting to see some nice rips in my shoulders. But, then over a period of five months, I had three separate rib fractures. They take four to six weeks to heal, so how do I maintain a consistent exercise program?

The doctor is a gracious woman and she sees my frustration. "All right, look, I know this sounds like I'm waffling, but I think I want to put you on Etidronate."

I don't think the names of these drugs are very friendly, do you?

"We'll follow you closely for a year," she says, and gives me a prescription.

I haven't filled it yet.

* * *

When my baby died, I felt I had no right to talk about childbirth or being pregnant. I had a baby. I was pregnant. I had morning sickness. I bought clothes and furniture. I had a son. He lived three hours. He was born to me. I finally understood what women were. And I wanted to talk about this, but it made people uncomfortable. In some ways losing Franny is like that.

I want to remember a Scrabble game where we made up words and meanings and laughed until we were in pain. I want to express my affection for her Miro bag, which held my glasses, a half stick of gum. I want to tell about the vegetable stand at the side of the road where we left our money in a bucket and the invisible proprietor trusted us to love his tomatoes and his sweet corn and his zucchini and we did. I want to talk about these things but I feel I don't have the right to tell the love story because it ended badly.

* * *

Okay, I'm in her kitchen and I grab wild for a knife and plunge it into my belly. She can't believe it. She says, "But I had to cut your bagels for you." I say, "Well that stopped, didn't it?" And I die. Better, I huddle against a wall outside of her apartment. All night long. In the morning when she leaves for work, she sees me there. Cold. Unattended. The drift that I am. Her detritus. She drops her books and bends to me. "Susan? Susan?" Who, I strain, is that? And the call. The call to say, oh this is from my friends, they call her. "Susan's dead." And they hang up.

* * *

My friends, these women with wild hair and good eyes, these women friends who engage my light and do not refuse me, dark as I am these days. These friends make room for disturbance. They have the wit to see it coming. This is who they are, these people who school themselves and event the city and construe fresh arguments and listen to the heart beat its woe. These friends are my history. What they know about me is in the record. Errors. Shifts. Defeats. Occasions of grace. They were there when I looked up from my hospital bed. They were there when I looked up after Franny left and couldn't see a thing. And these people, my friends, are taking out an ad. In the personals. "She's adorable. She's smart. And would you please take her off our hands? We can't stand it anymore!"

* * *

Maybe we're only given a certain amount of time with anyone. Or we can have the whole time if we remember on the days it is not going well, that these are not the days to measure by. The moment we marry is often so minor, so quotidian, that later we forget we've taken vows. When Franny walked to her study to write, I took my vows. When she asked me before sleep, if I wanted some magic cream on my cuticles and rubbed it into my fingers, I took vows. When I weeded her mother's garden, cleaned under her son's bed. Is it there in the beginning? The thing that finishes us?

* * *

Out in the country with my friends, I wake in the morning to the sound of a wasp in its death throes. A screen door shuts and the dog's paws sound like a hot drummer's brush across the floor. I walk outside to the buzz and the click and the hum. Suddenly, I feel bereft.

My favorite book in the Golden Book series was "The Happy Family". Imagine. Well, here's the picture. Beautiful clean cut boy and girl. Mother and Father. Crates arrive. Brand new bikes. They all go on a picnic. It was my touchstone.

* * *

He was dark and thin. She was dark and beautiful and not as thin. He introduced himself to her as Frank Lamonica. And she was Judy Grey, a singer with her own show on the radio. "I'll never smile again, until I smile at you." He said, "We're going to come back here next year, married."

Isaac Figlin and Thelma Freifelder. My model for romance.

(*Beat*)

There was a war. He went. She was a bride. They wrote letters. She sent him a lock of my hair.

Now she is seventy-four and he is eighty-three. My father says, "I've never been more in love with your mother than I am right now." On the night before my father has surgery to remove a kidney, my mother climbs up next to him in his hospital bed. We, my brother and sister and I turn our heads. Were they really ours?

Who might we have become without these two people who said yes one mad summer in the Poconos and taught us how to dance and spell and drive a car? Taught us what was good? They were good.

After I lost my baby, I was taken back to my room. And I saw my parents standing there, in the doorway, waiting for me.

(*Beat*)

So, I told them a funny story and made them laugh.
After my mastectomy, my father rubs my feet. My mother sings me a song. They do this for me and I let them.

* * *

House. It's a concept that cries out deconstruct. There is the universal notion of house and there is Susan's house. The house that longing built.
There was something important about Franny and me. I don't know. Maybe it was only that we tried.
We have children and we had to bring them up. We had to be their mothers. We would cry when we saw orphans arrive from Korea on television. But we had ours and they were still becoming and they had something to say about it. Now they are grown into that beauty of starting up.
The first time I went to Franny's house, I recognized the familiar aroma of boy's feet. Simon's sneakers were lurking under the coffee table. It reminded me of home.
Jody sang commercials and told me silly jokes. She is lovely, Franny's daughter. She is lovely and strong and difficult. She is Franny's daughter. Simon sits at the piano. "Hey, Susan, do you like this?" I do. I like what he plays. I like him. And so when I walk into the living room at the end, at Christmas and see him, I come apart.
They were ten, twelve, and fourteen, when we started out. Nearly eight years later, we'd lived through puberty and three sets of college applications.

* * *

"You bitch." "You're such a bitch." Our teenagers were not having a good day. My son punches his fist through a wall. Her daughter stops eating. The oldest weeps his lost structure. How much of this has to do with us, I can't say, but we blame ourselves, each other, and sometimes who we are.
"I can't do this," Franny would say. "I don't know how to be a mother and a lover. Can't we just wait until the children are grown and find each other again?"
A family is the faces you see and know you will see whenever you look up. When Franny is on the phone and Simon is reading a book, when Jody's watching her soaps, and Jeremy is in the kitchen complaining

there isn't anything to eat. When a person says, as casual as heartbreak, do you want a cup of coffee honey?

* * *

Here's what I did. I really did this. I rented a car and drove to the Howard Johnson's Motor Lodge outside of Woodstock. It was OUR place. We stayed there when we visited her parents. It seemed like every time we stayed at a cheap motel, there was child abuse going on in the next room. Perhaps it was only a haunting. Our own children tormenting us for the time we abandoned them at camp or wouldn't let them stay up late to watch some TV show or maybe they were just pissed off at us for having the bed to ourselves.

The motel is its orange self. Why do I weep? The air in the parking lot is hot and familiar. Somewhere close. Somewhere in the trees, around the bend, over the hill, she is. I can't breathe. It was in one of these rooms she asked me to make love to her. Her father had just died. And she needed this from me. I knew how to marry love with death. I knew if you kissed someone who needed you to live, you would live. The day after I came home from the hospital, still bandaged, half crazy from residual drugs and fear, Jane and I made love. I didn't care if my stitches came free. Let them rip. I shouldn't have been able to move in the ways I moved to her, but I was powerful. The possibility of death nearly broke our bed. In a few days I would start chemo but that night, I was not in possession of the facts. I was a body in disrepair and someone was healing me.

I wanted to heal Franny. I wanted to swoop her up, take her in my jaws, protect this love. She kissed me with her teeth. I swallowed her loss down whole. Everything was streaked with us. "My love." "Don't stop." "Darling." I placed myself at the source. So lovely. So known to me. Then she took me in her mouth. I shivered. We jammed our stuff against the bed. And for awhile at the Howard Johnsons outside of Woodstock, we kept chaos at bay.

(*Beat*)

I went to the town square. I didn't know where to walk exactly or where to set my sights.

I wondered if people could see me, or was I invisible because I didn't belong anymore? And if Franny actually came to town on this day, would she walk right past me? Turning a few feet away to look back as if there were something, a sensation she couldn't name, my scent more powerful than my substance, wafting through to catch her up short. I steadied myself against a store window and wished for a prop.

(*Beat*)

There she was. On the other side of the street, her hands in her pockets, singing Rodgers and Hart. Or thinking about semiotics. Going on about her life.

(*Beat*)

Just like I needed to go on about my own.

(*Beat*)

Goodbye Franny. Goodbye my friend. Goodbye my left breast. Goodbye my infant son. Goodbye my period. Goodbye thirty-five. Goodbye old neighborhood.

(*Beat*)

Your doctor says "It's Positive." Your lover says, "It's over." And you say goodbye to the person you thought you were.

(*Beat*)

I'm going to show you my scar. In a minute.

* * *

When you have a brush with death, you think, if I pull through this, I'm going to do it all differently. I'm going to say exactly what I think. I'll be a kind and generous citizen. I won't be impatient with my son. I won't shut down to my lover. I'll learn to play the trumpet. I'll never waste another minute.

(*Beat*)

Then you don't die. And it's God, I hate my hair! Would you please pick up your clothes! How long do we have to stand in this fucking line?

* * *

One day I'm sitting in a café and a man with ordinary difficulties is complaining. Our water heater is on the fritz. Just like that he says it. OUR something isn't working and WE are worrying about it.
I want to say, Cherish the day your car broke down, the water pump soured, the new bed didn't arrive on time. Celebrate the time you got lost and maps failed. On your knees to this domestic snafu, you blessed pair. While you can still feel the other's skin in the night, her foot caressing your calf, preoccupations catching on the damp sheets. You twist, haul an arm over. Remote kisses motor your dreams.

* * *

The people who made love to me, afterwards: There have been three. Jane, of course, who slept with me in the hospital, pretending to be my sister. David. And Franny. It's the way David said, "It's wildly sexy this body of yours that has given birth and given up a part." It's the way Franny loved me more for my lack of it, this symmetry that other women have.
How do I tell someone new?
Okay, help me out here. Say I've finally met someone I like. Do I tell her over the salad? Wait until dessert? Do I tell her when we're getting undressed? Does it matter? Would it matter to you?

(*Beat*)

I miss it but there is something growing in its place. And it is not a tougher skin.

(*Beat*)

The doctor says my heart is more exposed now. Closer to the air. You don't have any protective tissue, she says. I hardly need a stethoscope to hear it beat.

* * *

I cherish this scar. It's a mark of experience. It's the history of me. A permanent fix on the impermanence of it all. A line that suggests I take it seriously. Which I do. A line that suggests my beginning and my end. I have no other like it. I have no visible reminder of the baby I lost. Or the friend. No constant monument to the passing of my relationship. There is no other sign on my body that repeats the incongruity and dislocation, the alarm. A scar is a challenge to see ourselves as survivors, after all. Here is the evidence. The body repairs. And the human heart, even after it has broken into a million pieces, will make itself large again.

* * *

My son did get it back for me. In a way. Not the year it happened. But the year after that and the year and the year and the year after that.

(*Beat*)

It was little league that saved me. It was Jeremy up to the plate. It was Gabe Goldstein at second. It was Chris Chandler catching a pop fly. It was Jeremy stealing home. It was providing refreshments and washing his uniform. It was trying to get him to wear a jock strap. It was screaming, "Batter. Batter. Batter." It was Jeremy pitching the last out with the bases loaded. It was the Moms. The Moms and Dads and the coolers. It was the hats we wore and the blankets. It was driving him home from practice. It was his bloody knees. It was the sun going down on us, watching our sons and daughters play and be well.

(*Beat*)

This was the cure for cancer.

* * *

I miss it, but I want to tell all the women in the changing booths, that we are still beautiful, we are still powerful, we are still sexy, we are still here.

(*I unbutton my shirt to reveal my scar as the lights fade.*)

THE INTERVIEW

Joyce Carol Oates

Joyce Carol Oates

Joyce Carol Oates is the author of twenty novels, and many volumes of short stories, poems, essays and plays. Her 1992 novel *Black Water* was a Pulitzer finalist, and her short stories have twice won her the O. Henry Special Award for Continuing Achievement. Her 1970 novel, *them,* received a National Book Award, and in 1990 she was again nominated for that award for the novel *Because It Is Bitter, And Because It Is My Heart.*

In 1990, Oates received the Rea Award for the Short Story, given to honor a living U.S. writer who has made a significant contribution to the short story as an art form.

Her plays have been produced at the Actors Theatre of Louisville, and the Ensemble Studio Theatre and the American Place Theatre, both in New York City. Her newest play, *The Perfectionist,* premiered in October 1993 at the McCarter Theatre in Princeton.

A native of Lockport, NY, Ms. Oates was educated at Syracuse University and the University of Wisconsin. She is married and lives in Princeton where she is the Roger S. Berlind Distinguished Professor in the Humanities at Princeton University. Ms. Oates is a member of the American Academy and Institute of Arts and Letters.

Characters:

THE IMMORTAL: *an elderly, white-haired aristocratic gentleman*
THE INTERVIEWER: *a youngish man, in his 30's*
KIMBERLY: *a young woman, in her 20's*

Scene:

A contemporary hotel room with a suggestion of luxury. Minimal furnishings: a sofa, a table, a pitcher and a glass of water. Music is issuing from a cabinet.

Lights up. Lighting is subdued at the start of the play, then gradually increases in intensity. By the end, it is as bright and pitiless as possible. The Immortal is seated on an antique sofa, head high, hands clasped on his knees, in a posture of imperturbable dignity. His eyes are half shut as if he is contemplating a higher reality. He is dressed with Old World formality—a dark suit with a vest, a white flower in his lapel. Brilliantly polished black shoes. An elegant Mozart string quartet is playing. A rapping at the door. Immortal serenely ignores it.

INTERVIEWER (*voice*): Hello? Hello? Is anybody there? It's—me.

(*Frantic rapping. Immortal takes no heed*)

INTERVIEWER (*voice, desperate*): It's the 11:00 interviewer—am I late?

(*On the word "late" Interviewer pushes open the door, which is unexpectedly unlocked. He stumbles inside the room dropping his heavy duffel bag out of which spill a tape recorder, a camera, and several books. Interviewer is casually dressed in jeans, jacket, jogging shoes; hair in pony- or pigtail. He is breathless and apologetic*)

INTERVIEWER: Oh!—oh, my god! It's—you. (*Approaching Immortal reverently*) I—I'm—jeez, excuse me! (*Staring*) It is—you?

(*Immortal remains imperturbed. Music continues*)

INTERVIEWER (*nervous chattering as he fumblingly picks up his things*): I c-can't tell you, sir, what an honor this is. The honor of a lifetime. And here I am late! (*Angry, incredulous laughter at himself*) Held up in traffic for half an hour—plus my assistant Kimberly screwed up on the time—not that there's any excuse to be late for an interview with you, sir. I hope you will—forgive me? (*Craven*)

(*Immortal remains imperturbed. Music continues*)

INTERVIEWER (*awkward, nodding*): I, um—well, yes. Right. (*Fussing with tape recorder; drops a cassette, retrieves it*) That's right, sir. (*Nervous laugh*) That music—it's real high class. I—sort of thought—listening out in the hall—you might be playing it, yourself. You were trained as a classical musician, sir—in addition to your other talents—weren't you?

(*Immortal remains imperturbed. Music continues*)

INTERVIEWER (*first hint of his self-importance*): Your publisher explained who I am, sir, I hope? (*Pause*) I began with a modest Sunday books column for the Detroit News—within eighteen months was promoted to the editorial page—where my column HEAR THIS! ran the gamut from high culture to low controversy! (*Laughs*) No, seriously, I never shrank from any subject. I ran my own photos, interviewed both "big" and "little" folk, soon became syndicated in over 100 dailies—whiz bang zap zolly!—here I am: lead columnist for AMERICA TODAY, circulation 57 million daily. (*Breathless*) Interviewing, in depth, men and women of the stature, sir, of you.

(*Immortal remains imperturbed, unimpressed. Music continues*)

INTERVIEWER (*smiles, rubs hands, ebullient*): Well, now! The editors of AMERICA TODAY are asking 500 of the world's leading men and women in all the creative arts—at the cutting edge of science—politics—culture: What do you prophesize for the year 2000? (*Pause, jokes*) Will we make it? (*Laughs*)

(*Immortal remains as before*)

INTERVIEWER (*respectfully*): You, sir, having been born in 1798—Oops! (*Checks notes*)—1898—have lived through virtually the entire 20th century—so my first question will be—Will you make it? (*Laughs*)

(*Immortal remains as before, stiff and unresponsive; Interviewer ceases laughing, embarrassed*)

INTERVIEWER: Ummm—just a little joke. I'm known for my, um—sense of humor. (*Pause*) "Irreverent"—"refreshing"—"wacko in all the right ways"—(*Pause*) Bill Clinton said that, sir. About my column. (*Pause*) What Hilary said, I don't know. (*Awkward laugh*)

(*Immortal as before*)

INTERVIEWER (*slightly abashed, but taking a new tack*): Well, now! Here we go in earnest! (*With tape recorder*) You don't mind these, sir, I hope? (*Punching buttons*) Jeez if I tried to take notes the old, literate way, I'd really screw up. My handwriting's like Helen Keller's in an earthquake. (*Laughs*)

(*Immortal as before*)

INTERVIEWER (*slightly abashed, defensive*): Helen Keller was an old blind deaf dumb genius—I guess. You'd have gotten along real well together, sir.

(*Interviewer fusses with his recorder, muttering under his breath. Voices emerge squealing and squawking, unintelligible*)

FEMALE VOICE (*high-pitched squeal*): No no no no no you stop that!

INTERVIEWER: Oops! (*Punches a button, fast-forwarding*) That's an oldie —Barbara Bush.

INTERVIEWER'S VOICE (*on tape, volume loud*): —prophesize for the year 2000, sir?

MALE VOICE (*evangelical-sounding*): The Second Coming—the Resurrection of the Body—"And all ye shall rejoice, and see God"— (*Interviewer abruptly cuts off cassette, rewinds*)

INTERVIEWER: We'll just tape over that. (*Condescending*) One of those nuts—hitting all the TV talk shows last week—his book's a Number 1 bestseller—real lowbrow crapola, not highbrow, sir, like you. (*Kneeling at Immortal's feet, fussing with recorder*) You, sir—I reverence you. First time I read your work, sir, I was in sixth grade. Yeah, I was precocious! (*Chuckles*) That sure does bring problems, sir, doesn't it—precocity—peers get God-damned jealous. As you'd know, sir, eh?—your first book was published when you were 18? Wow. (*Pause*) Or am I thinking of—whosis—Rambo—(*Pause*) Hey, before we get going—(*Brings over a stack of books for Immortal to sign*) Would you sign these, please, sir? I know it's a nuisance—being so renowned—autograph seekers hounding you constantly—but I'd appreciate it so much, sir! Here's my card, sir, so you get the name right.

(*Immortal signs books in a pompous manner, his head still held stiffly high. Interviewer gives him a pen, opens books and positions them on his lap, chatting all the while*)

INTERVIEWER: Here, sir—please use this pen. It's a Mont Blanc—a little token from Samuel Beckett when I interviewed him. Last interview that great man gave. We really hit it off, Sam and me. I may be from Detroit but I can sure yuk it up with you immortals! (*Chuckles, then peers at books*) Um, sir—excuse me—would you date your signature, please? And, um—you might say "New York City" below, too—Thank you! Immensely! (*Checks the signatures, chuckles*) Your handwriting's like Helen Keller's in an earthquake, sir! (*Nudges Immortal in the ribs*)

(*The flower falls from Immortal's lapel. Immortal "comes alive" though retaining, at least intermittently, certain of his pompous mannerisms*)

IMMORTAL: Qu'est-ce que c'est? Qui êtes vous?

INTERVIEWER: Say what? (*Atrocious accent*) Non parlez-français here, sir. Nossir!

IMMORTAL (*stiff alarm, distaste*): Vous êtes—américain?

INTERVIEWER (*loudly, as if immortal is deaf*): Weewee! I zetes americain!

IMMORTAL (*elderly confusion*): Mais, pourquoi—

INTERVIEWER: Sir, parlez English, eh? (*Checks PR sheet*) It says here you're "septo-lingual"—speaks seven languages with equal fluency—so lets have it for English, eh? (*Joking*) I didn't know there were seven languages left in Europe.

IMMORTAL (*now in Italian, haltingly*): Non capisce . . . Chè cose? Mi sono perso . . . ? (*I don't understand. What is it? Am I Lost?*)

INTERVIEWER (*loudly*): Ing-lese, sir! ING-LESE! You know it, for sure. You're in the U.S. of A. now.

IMMORTAL: Per favore—aiuto! Mi sento male . . . (*Please help! I feel ill*)

INTERVIEWER: C'mon sir! ING-LESE! AMER-I-CAN!

IMMORTAL: Who are you? Have you come to help me?

INTERVIEWER: Terrifico!—English. (*Starts recorder*) You had me worried there for a minute, sir!

IMMORTAL (*dazed, tragic voice*): I want—to live again. (*Pause*) I want to die.

INTERVIEWER (*cheerfully, holding microphone*): Can't do both, sir! Not at the same time. Comment, sir: what do you prophesize for the upcoming millennium?

IMMORTAL: My beloved Marguerite, where are you—

INTERVIEWER (*rattling off choices*): "End of the world"—"things better than ever"—"more of the same"?

IMMORTAL (*wildly*): Marguerite! Help me—

INTERVIEWER (*as if humanly struck*): That's touching, sir. My goodness. Could you expand upon—

IMMORTAL (*squinting at Interviewer, tragic "classical" voice*): Please help me, have you been sent to help me? I am in pain. Where is the light?

INTERVIEWER: Light? Nah, there's plenty of light in here, it's pouring through the window. Plus I got a flash camera. (*Pause*) Enough of this, though—(*Strides over to a cabinet, switches off the Mozart abruptly*) That artsy stuff gets on your nerves after a while.

IMMORTAL: Marguerite, my dear one—

INTERVIEWER (*peering at PR sheet*): Um—"Marguerite"—"wife of"—"deceased, 1923"—"Christiane"—"wife of"—"deceased 1939"—

"Pilar"—"wife of"—"deceased 1961" "Claudia"—"wife of"—"deceased 1979"—"Chantal"—"wife of"—"deceased 1987"—Wow, sir! I mean—wow. I hate to tell you, though—you got some catching up to do.

IMMORTAL: Why am I—alone?

INTERVIEWER (*reading from sheet of paper*): Let's move on, sir, to more provocative issues. What's your frank opinion of American civilization, as viewed from your side of the Atlantic: are we a nation of coarse philistines, illiterates, and wannabee capitalist swine, or a "Brave New World"?

IMMORTAL (*confused*): "Brave New World?"

INTERVIEWER (*enthusiastically*): Right! I think so, too. One thing pisses me off it's that hypocritical bullshit, we Americans are crass and uncultured. Screw that! Every God-damn country in the world including your homeland, excuse me, sir, emulates us, and wants our dough. Any comment?

IMMORTAL: I feel such cold. Where is this terrible place?

INTERVIEWER (*consulting notes—briskly*): Um hum—moving right along now—Sir, in your Nobel Prize acceptance speech you stated—"As a youth I had wished to emulate—"

IMMORTAL (*overlapping with unexpected passion, clarity; hand gestures*): "As a youth I had wished to emulate Homer—Dante—Goethe—Balzac—setting myself the task of creating a great epic commensurate with the spirit of mankind. Immortalizing the heritage of the West. The tragedy of Nazism unleashed the terror that history and civilization could be annihilated—and so it remains for us to bear witness—unflinchingly."

INTERVIEWER (*clapping*): Wow! That's telling 'em, sir!

IMMORTAL (*continuing, gesturing*): "The future of humankind is legislated by its spiritual leaders—its artists—"

INTERVIEWER (*cutting right in*): Um-hum! Well, my editor's gonna make me cut all this back pretty much. AMERICA TODAY is reader-friendly—our paragraphs are never more than a single sentence. (*Briefest of pauses, no transition, abruptly and brightly*) Changing the subject somewhat, sir, moving from the lugubrious to the calumnious—is it true that you plagiarized your early dramas from Pirandello?

IMMORTAL (*shocked, agitated*): What! I! Plagiarize!

INTERVIEWER: AMERICA TODAY's readers just want the simple truth, sir: YES or NO?

IMMORTAL: H-He—stole from me—

INTERVIEWER (*checking notes*): One of you is the author of the immortal classic FIVE CHARACTERS IN SEARCH OF AN AUTHOR and the other is the author of the immortal classic SIX CHARACTERS IN SEARCH OF AN AUTHOR—so, which came first?

IMMORTAL (*spitting gesture*): Pirandello!—a shallow, meretricious talent! A mere mimicry of—

INTERVIEWER (*consulting notes*): You had a scandalous love affair with —Colette? Who threw you over publicly for—Franz Liszt? Wow!

IMMORTAL (*incensed*): How dare you! Whoever you are, how—

(*Immortal is so agitated, his hearing aid falls from his ear*)

INTERVIEWER: Uh-oh! We're getting a little hyper, sir, are we? (*Retrieves the hearing aid which has fallen to the floor*) What's it—oh, a hearing aid. Jeez, you scared me, I thought it was part of your brain falling out. (*Laughs*) That'd be weird, eh? Terrific story, but weird. Let me—(*Tries to fit the hearing aid into Immortal's ear, but it slips back out*) Damn! (*Tries again, jamming it in; Immortal flinches with pain, but the hearing aid slips out anyway*) Fuck it! These "miracles of modern technology"! (*Tries other ear*) Uh-oh! There's already one in this ear. (*Hearing aid falls to the floor and is apparently broken; Interviewer picks it up, chagrined*) Ooops! Looks like it's, um, a little cracked. Shit, I'm sorry!

(*Immortal reaches for the hearing aid, but Interviewer stuffs it into Immortal's pocket*)

INTERVIEWER: For safekeeping, sir! Wouldn't want you to lose the damn thing. (*Consulting notes*) Ummm, yes: how does it feel, sir, to be a great artist?—a "classic"?—the oldest living "immortal" of the French Academy and the oldest living Nobel Prize laureate since what's-his-name, that Bulgarian, croaked last year? Our audience yearns to know, sir: how does it feel to have "made it"?

IMMORTAL (*high, quavering voice*): So lonely. My loved ones, my friends—gone. My enemies—gone. (*Clutching at Interviewer's arm*) I had wanted to outlive my enemies—and I have.

INTERVIEWER: Terrific! That's sure candid stuff. (*Takes up camera*) Lemme take a few quick shots, and we can wrap this up. (*Blinding flash*) Little smile, sir? C'mon, little smile? You can do better than that, sir, come-on. (*Aggressively close, as Immortal flinches*)

IMMORTAL: What—place is this? Who are you?

INTERVIEWER (*taking photos*): Tell our audience about your friendship with the great Nabokov, sir. He plagiarized you—that's the scuttlebutt, eh?

IMMORTAL: Why am I—here?

INTERVIEWER (*chuckling*): You "Esthetes"—any truth to the rumor you and Nabokov, um, got it on together upon occasion?

IMMORTAL: Nabokov?

INTERVIEWER: Those were the days, eh? "Gay Nineties"—"Roaring Twenties"—"Lost Generation"—no "safe sex" for you, eh? (*Suddenly realizing, strikes forehead and consults notes*) Uh-oh! Shit! You are Nabokov!

IMMORTAL (*trying to escape but falling back weakly onto the sofa in terror*): I know you! I know you! Go away!

INTERVIEWER (*incensed*): What the hell, Mr. Nabokov, I'm slotted in for thirty minutes! That's bottomline rude.

IMMORTAL: I know your face—you are Death.

(*Pause. Interviewer is standing rigid, camera in hand*)

INTERVIEWER: Excuse me, Mr. Nabokov, but that's insulting.

IMMORTAL: Death! Come for me! But I am not ready! My soul is not ready! Go away!

(*Immortal lunges suddenly at Interviewer, trying to snatch his camera from him. The flash goes off*)

IMMORTAL: Oh!

(*As if the flashbulb has been a gunshot, Immortal collapses onto the sofa and lies limp. Interviewer's hair has come loose in the struggle, altering his appearance. He stands straight and tall and does indeed have the frightening aura of an agent of Death*)

INTERVIEWER: You Immortals—all alike. Guys like me, we got your number. (*Packs up his things into duffel bag, muttering to himself*) Where's he get off, calling me Death! Me with a syndicated readership of 57 million—second only to "Dear Abby."

(*Flurried knocking at the door. Kimberly runs in aghast*)

KIMBERLY (*biting thumbnail*): Oh! Oh God! Oh you're going to be mad at me, oh I just know it!

INTERVIEWER: What?

KIMBERLY (*little-girl, pleading*): Oh I just know you are! I know you are!

INTERVIEWER: Kimberly, what the hell—? I've had it up to here with fucking obfuscation this morning!

KIMBERLY: Promise you won't be mad at me . . .

INTERVIEWER (*shouting*): I promise! I won't be mad at you!

KIMBERLY: I, uh—um—this is the wrong hotel. This is the Plaza, and you're supposed to be at the St. Regis. Whoever he is—he's the wrong person.

INTERVIEWER (*louder*): What? Wrong hotel? Wrong person? What?

KIMBERLY (*little-girl manner, softly*): You promised you wouldn't be mad.

INTERVIEWER: You're responsible for me wasting my entire morning! And I'm not supposed to be mad?

KIMBERLY (*pleading*): It wasn't my fault—the FAX from the office is so smudged. See—(*She shows him the FAX which he snatches from her fingers*)

INTERVIEWER (*peering at it*): Holy shit! I am supposed to be at the St. Regis! I'm twenty minutes late already! (*In a fury, takes out his recorder, erases cassette*) There! ERASE! God damn.

(*As Interviewer moves to exit, Kimberly notices Immortal whom she approaches with concern*)

KIMBERLY: OH! This gentleman! Is he—

INTERVIEWER (*breezy, sarcastic*): He says he's Nabokov.

KIMBERLY (*impressed*): Oh! "Nab-o-kov"—that famous dancer? The one who deflected from the Soviet Union when it was still Communist?

INTERVIEWER (*exiting*): Defected.

(*Kimberly approaches Immortal. A strain of romantic music might be used here*)

KIMBERLY: Mr. Nabokov? Are you—alive? (*pause*) I never saw you dance, but—my grandmother did, I think. She said you were—(*pause*)—fantastic. Mr. Nabokov?

(*Immortal begins to stir, moaning. Kimberly helps him sit up; unbuttons his collar, loosens his tie, etc. She dips a handkerchief or scarf into the glass of water and presses it against his forehead*)

KIMBERLY: Mr. Nabokov, I guess you had a little fainting spell! I'd better call the hotel doctor.

IMMORTAL (*reviving slowly*): No—no, please.

KIMBERLY (*thumb to mouth*): You're sure? You look kind of—pale.

IMMORTAL: My dear one! Is it—you?

KIMBERLY: Who?

IMMORTAL (*hoarse whisper*): Not Marguerite, but—Chantal? returned to me?

KIMBERLY: "Chantal"—?

IMMORTAL (*with elderly eagerness*): My Dear! Darling! Don't ever leave me again!

KIMBERLY: Gosh, Mr. Nabokov, I'm afraid I—

IMMORTAL: I will die in this terrible place if you leave me. (*Takes her wrist*)

KIMBERLY: —afraid there's been some—

IMMORTAL: My darling, I'm so lonely. They call me a "living classic"—an "immortal"—but without you, I am nothing.

KIMBERLY: But you're so famous, Mr. Nabokov!

IMMORTAL: Chantal, please—don't leave me again, ever. I seem to have grown old, I know—but it's only an illusion.

KIMBERLY (*embarrassed*): Gee, I hate to say this but you're a little . . . confused, Mr. Nabokov. I'd better call the doctor . . .

IMMORTAL: You're still young, and I, in my heart, in my soul—I am unchanged.

KIMBERLY: You are? (*Pause, sees flower on floor*) Oh!—is this yours? (*Picks it up, restores it to his lapel*) There!

IMMORTAL: Chantal, my dear one—you won't leave me, will you? Say you won't!

KIMBERLY: I'm, uh, not Chantal but Kimberly. I'm the assistant of that man who just—

IMMORTAL (*pleading*): My "Chantal des fleurs"—my dear one? You won't abandon me in this terrible place?

KIMBERLY: I—don't know. How long do you want me to stay, Mr. Nabokov. (*Checks watch*) I guess I could skip lunch.

(*Immortal pulls at Kimberly's arm; she sits beside him on the sofa*)

IMMORTAL (*reverently*): You are—Life. Restored to me. My Chantal! The only woman I ever loved. (*Pause*) You can order up from room service anything you want, dear. This is America—all my expenses are being paid.

KIMBERLY (*a new idea*): Oh!—Mr. Nabokov, can I interview you? Nobody ever gives me a chance, but I know I'm a thousand times more emphatic—empathetic?—than he is.

IMMORTAL: Of course, my darling. Anything! Only don't ever leave me again.

(*Kimberly takes out her tape recorder, sets it going briskly*)

KIMBERLY: Oh, Mr. Nabokov, I sure won't. I promise. (*Sudden professional tone*) Mr. Nabokov, will you share with our readers your reflections on the imminent year 2000? When you deffected from the Soviet Union, did you ever guess all this would be coming to pass?

(*Lights very bright then fade rapidly*)
(*Lights out*)

TALL TALES
From: THE KENTUCKY CYCLE

Robert Schenkkan

"Some men rob you with a sixgun,
Some with a fountain pen."
Woody Guthrie

Robert Schenkkan

Robert Schenkkan won the 1992 Pulitzer Prize for Drama for his nine play, six hour epic *The Kentucky Cycle,* from which *Tall Tales* is extracted. This is the first time in the history of the Pulitzer that the prize was given to a play that had not yet been produced in New York. The *Cycle* was also awarded the largest grant ever given by the Fund for New American Plays.

The *Cycle* was developed in portions at the Mark Taper Forum in Los Angeles, the Ensemble Theatre Studio in L.A. and New York, and at Robert Redford's Sundance Institute. The complete play was premiered in 1991 at the Intiman Theatre in Seattle, and the pre-Broadway tryout was given at the Kennedy Center in Washington D.C. in August, 1993. The New York premiere was produced at the Royale Theatre.

Robert's other full-length plays are *Heaven On Earth,* which won a Julie Harris/Beverly Hills Theatre Guild Award in 1989; *Final Passages,* which premiered at the Studio Arena Theatre under the direction of A.J. Antoon; and *Tachinoki,* which was designated a Critic's Choice by the L.A. Weekly when it premiered at Ensemble Studio Theatre. His one-act play, *The Survivalist,* won the Best of the Fringe Award at the Edinburgh Festival.

Robert received his B.A. from the University of Texas, Austin, and his M.F.A. from Cornell. He resides in Seattle with his wife, Mary Anne, and their two children, Sarah and Joshua.

Characters:

MARY ANNE ROWEN: *age fourteen*
ADULT MARY ANNE: *age forty-nine*
JT WELLS: *a storyteller*
TOMMY JACKSON: *age fifteen, a neighbor*
JED ROWEN: *age fifty-two, Mary Anne's father*
LALLIE ROWEN: *age forty-seven, Mary Anne's mother*

Scene:

1885. Summer. The Prologue and Epilogue are approximately ten years later.

Prologue:

The hills of Eastern Kentucky, in Howsen County, near the Shilling Creek. A young girl, Mary Anne Rowen, kneels by a creek and arranges her hair. Standing off to one side is the woman she will become in thirty-five years. The Adult Woman watches her younger self and speaks directly to the audience.

ADULT MARY ANNE: Spring usta explode in these mountains like a two-pound charge of black powder hand-tamped down a rathole. After months of grey skies and that damp mountain cold what bores into your bones like termites in a truckload of wood, it's your dogwood trees that finally announce what everythin's been waitin' for.

First thing some morning, you might see a single blossom hangin' there, light pink, the color of a lover's promise . . . if lies had a color. And then later that afternoon, damned if that bud ain't been joined by a hunnert of his brothers and sisters all sittin' 'round, chattin' each other up, Sunday-go-to-meetin' style. 'Course, dogwood's just the beginnin'.

The spark what lights the fuse for spring, that's the azaleas. When they get to goin', you'd swear somebody'd scattered a whole handful of lit matches across those hills. Bible story is how old man Moses talked to a burnin' bush. But for my money, he was just conversin' with a scarlet azalea in full bloom. Story just got a little expanded in the retellin' . . . the way stories do.

Fella once told me a story, said these ain't no real mountains here at all—that if you stood high enough, you could see it was all just one big mound that had been crisscrossed and cut up into so many hills and valleys by the spring runoff, that it just looked like mountains. Leastways, that was his story.

Only, I don't put no truck in stories no more.

Scene 1

The light fades out on the Adult Mary Anne and comes up on the younger. A man, JT Wells, enters and stands quietly behind her. Smiling, he watches for a moment, and then picks up a pebble and tosses it over her shoulder and into the water. She turns, startled.

JT: Friend. I'm a friend.

MARY ANNE: Shouldn't sneak up on a body like that!

JT: No, you're quite right, young lady, I shouldn't have. And under any other circumstances, my rudeness would merit your harshest disapprobation.

MARY ANNE: Huh?

JT: You'd a right to be pissed off. But the fact of the matter is, if you hadn't been in mortal danger just now, I probably would've walked right on by, 'stead of saving your life.

MARY ANNE: My life?

JT: Well, your immortal soul at least.

MARY ANNE: How you figure that?

JT: Why, staring into that stream like that. I've heard it said from them that knows, that the devil himself hides his bleak heart in the muddy bottom of slow-movin' pools just like this.

MARY ANNE (*a little uncertain*): You're just foolin'.

JT: Would that I were, ma'am. But 'tis a widely known fact that the Father of Lies often assumes the shape of an *Ictalurus Punctatus* and . . .

MARY ANNE: A what?

JT: Channel catfish.

MARY ANNE: You use more twenty-five cent words when a nickel word would do that any man I ever met.

(*JT grimaces, mimes being shot by an arrow, pulls it out and hands it to Mary Anne*)

JT: I think this is yours. (*Laughs*) Where was I. Oh yeah, and thus disguised, he lies in wait for an innocent virgin to come along.

MARY ANNE: Devil hafta wait a might long time for one of those in these parts.

JT: Well, he's a mighty patient fella, the devil is. (*They both laugh*)

MARY ANNE: There is an old catfish in this crick.

JT: Oh yeah?

(*He moves down beside her. Both of them roll over onto their bellies and look into the stream. He is close to her, with just the slightest suggestion of sexuality*)

MARY ANNE: I ain't never seen him, but my daddy has. Almost caught him once. So's Tommy, but I think he wuz lyin'.

JT: That your brother?

MARY ANNE: Nah, he's my boyfriend. (*JT moves away slightly*) Leastways, he thinks he is.

(*JT moves back*)

JT: Mighty pretty here.

MARY ANNE: Yeah. (*Both are quiet for a moment*) I jist love them old trees. 'Specially that oak there? That's my favorite.

JT: That's a beaut all right.

MARY ANNE: Folks 'round here call it the "Treaty Oak" 'cause my great-great-grand-daddy, Michael Rowen, that's where he bought this land from the Injuns.

JT: That a fact?

MARY ANNE: That's what my daddy says. I don't think there's a tree in these hills comes close to touchin' it for size. Leastways, I ain't never seen one. When I was a kid, I used to think that tree was all that kept the sky off my head. And if that tree ever fell down, the whole thing, moon and stars and all, would just come crashin' down. I think sometimes how that tree was here way before I was born and how it'll be here way after I'm gone and that always makes me feel safe. I think this is just about my favoritest spot in the whole world. Not that I seen a lot of the world, but my daddy took me to Louisville onct when I was six. You ever been there?

JT: Well, it just so happens, I was in Louisville three weeks ago.

MARY ANNE: Yeah? I bet you been a whole heap of places, way you talk 'n' all.

JT: Oh, I been here and there.

MARY ANNE: Where?

JT: Well, places like . . . Atlanta.

MARY ANNE: You been to Atlanta, GEORGIA!?

JT: Hell, that ain't nothin'. I been to New York City!

MARY ANNE (*almost inarticulate with wonder and envy*): NOOOO.

JT: Yes ma'am, I have. And lived to tell the tale.

MARY ANNE: What's it like?

JT: Well, I tell you, it's . . . it's pert near indescribable. It's hundreds of buildings, each and every one taller'n that ole granddad oak of yours. "Skyscrapers." That's what they call 'em. Skyscrapers. Clawin' up at the very fabric of heaven, threatening to push old Jesus Christ himself off his golden throne! And not more'n two months ago, I's standin' in the top a one of them golden towers and John D. Rockefeller himself shook me by this hand.

MARY ANNE: No.

JT: Yes ma'am, he did. And me, just a poor boy outta Breathitt County. Said to me, he said, "JT, you've got a future here!" Imagine that—the richest man in the country—The "Standard Oil King" himself—standin' no further from me than you are now.

(*Beat*)

MARY ANNE (*shyly*): Is that your name?

JT (*still lost in reverie*): Huh?

MARY ANNE: JT. I was wonderin' what your name was.

JT: Oh Lord, isn't that just like me? Here I get to jawin' so much I clean forgot to introduce myself. JT Wells at your service. The JT stands for Just Terrific. And who do I have the honor of speaking to?

MARY ANNE (*mumbling, embarrassed*): Mary Anne Rowen.

JT: Say what?

MARY ANNE: Mary Anne Rowen. (*Quickly*) Most folks just call me Mare, though.

JT: "Mare?" Well, I don't know. That's not a proper name for a pretty thing like you. Let me see here. You know what your name is in Spanish?

MARY ANNE: No.

JT (*savoring it*): Marianna.

MARY ANNE (*delighted*): Yeah?

JT: Now that sounds about right, don't it? Got all the right colors in it and everything. Marianna.

MARY ANNE: Marianna. (*Giggles*)

(*Beat*)

JT: Marianna.

(*He moves closer to her. Begins to kiss her. A stick snaps underfoot. Both turn, startled, as a Teenage Boy steps out of the underbrush, cradling a shotgun loosely under one arm*)

MARY ANNE (*flustered*): Oh. Hi, Tommy. Umm . . . JT, this is Tommy Jackson. Tommy, this is . . .

TOMMY: "Just Terrific" Wells. Yeah, I heard.

JT: Ah, the boyfriend, yes? Well, it's a rare pleasure to make your acquaintance, young man. You're a very lucky fellow . . .

(*He starts towards Tommy, hand outstretched but stops when the boy shifts his gun*)

. . . but I guess you know that.

TOMMY (*laconically*): I been told.

JT: Yes, well.

MARY ANNE: Be nice, Tommy.

TOMMY: Like you were?

MARY ANNE: We weren't doin' nothin'.

TOMMY: Not yet, anyways.

JT: Now, Mr. Jackson, I think there's just a little misunderstanding here . . .

TOMMY: Take another step, Mr. "Just Terrific," and I'm gonna misunderstand a hole the size of a butternut squash in the middle of your chest.

(*Mary Anne moves between them*)

MARY ANNE: Now dammit, Tommy, you just put that gun up right now, you hear me? Right this minute. Or I ain't never gonna speak to you again, as long as I live! (*He grudgingly obeys*)

TOMMY: Well, what's he doin' here, huh? Answer me that!

MARY ANNE: Well, I'm sure I don't know, Mr. High and Mighty—why don't you just ask him yourself? You ever think of that? No, I guess not. I guess some people been up the creek and outta town so long that they plum forgot their manners. Mr. Wells, would you be good enough to tell this poor, ignorant hillbilly what you'd be doin' in these parts?

JT (*grinning*): Well, now, that'd be a real pleasure, Miss Rowen. Fact of the matter is, I'm here to see your daddy.

(*Stunned silence*)

MARY ANNE: My pa?

JT: Well, if your daddy's a Mr. Jed Rowen of Howsen County, Kentucky, currently living up on Shilling Creek, I guess I am. I'm a storyteller!

(*Blackout*)

(*Fast country music, violins and mandolin, fading up and then down into general laughter*)

Scene 2

Lights up to reveal the interior of the Rowen house. JT, Mary Anne, Tommy, Jed Rowen, and his wife, Lallie, are all seated around a wooden plank table, the remains of a country dinner in front of them.

JT: I tell you, Jed, there ain't nothing like a home-cooked meal. Now, you might think a traveling man like myself, eating at some fancy restaurant every day of the week, is a man to be envied. But there are moments, sir, when I'd trade it all, every green bean almondine and French this and French that, for a piece of cob-cured country ham and red-eyed gravy like I had tonight.

LALLIE: It was all right then?

JT: All right? Ma'am, the President doesn't eat better'n this in the White House!

LALLIE: Mare, I'll get the coffee, you clear the men's plates and then get yourself somethin' to eat.

MARY ANNE: I'm not hungry, Ma.

LALLIE: What's wrong with you, girl?

MARY ANNE: Nothin'. Just not hungry.

JED: Leave the child alone, Lallie. She's too busy feastin' her eyes and fillin' her ears to pay much attention to her belly.

(*Tommy laughs*)

Pity one can't say the same for you, Tommy Jackson.

(*Tommy shuts up. Both women bustle around*)

JT: You sure a mighty fortunate man, Jed.

JED: How you figure that, JT?

JT: Because, sir, you got the one thing a man needs to live a life worth livin'.

JED: That bein'?

JT: Your independence. You're not beholden to any man for anything on your . . . how many acres would you say you have?

JED: Oh . . . 'bout three, four hunnert acres.

JT: On your three-hundred-odd acres here in the middle of God's country, you're a virtual king. Republican nobility.

JED: Republican?

JT (*quickly correcting his error*): Figure of speech, Jed. What I mean to say is, you and the people like you, your neighbors, they're what makes this country great. I take it you served in the "Glorious Cause," sir?

MARY ANNE: My daddy was a hero—he fought with Quantrill!

JED (*warning*): Now, Mary Anne . . .

MARY ANNE: Well, you did!

JT: Is that a fact?

MARY ANNE: My daddy saved Quantrill's life!

JT: Isn't that somethin'!

MARY ANNE: That was in Lawrence, Kansas. Tell him, Daddy . . .

JED: It wasn't really all that much . . .

LALLIE: Go on, Jed . . .

TOMMY: Go on, Mr. Rowen . . .

MARY ANNE: See, they was trapped in this house in Lawrence and the Yankees had set it on fire and—

JED: MARY ANNE! (*Beat*) JT's the storyteller here; you gonna put the poor fella outta work.

JT: What was he like, Quantrill? I mean, you hear so many different things.

LALLIE: He was a real gentleman. That's what Jed always said—isn't that right, Jed?

JED: Well . . . I guess he was a lot of different things to different people, but . . . he always treated me square. Maybe, Mr. JT, you'd like a drop of somethin' a mite stronger than coffee, to settle your stomach?

JT: Well, sir, I'm not ordinarily a drinkin' man, you understand, but as this is a special occasion, I'd be honored to raise a glass with you.

JED: Mare, you get down that old mason jar and a couple of glasses.

LALLIE: Now, Jed, you promised . . .

JED: I know what I'm doin', Lallie . . .

LALLIE: But you know your stomach can't take it, Jed.

JED (*warning*): Lallie . . .

LALLIE: You go ahead, but don't you be wakin' me up in the middle of the night with them terrible dreams of yours!

JED: I said, I know what I'm doin', woman!

(*Lallie gives him a withering look as Mary Anne returns with mugs and the jar. Jed folds*)

Well, hell, get me a pitcher of buttermilk then.

(*Lallie smiles and exits, returning quickly with a pitcher. Jed pours a clear liquid out of the jar into two mugs. Then, sorrowfully, he pours buttermilk into one of the half-filled mugs*)

Terrible thing to do to good corn liquor. (*Looking at JT*) I don't suppose you'd care to . . .

JT (*straight-faced*): Ordinarily yes, but I'm trying to cut back on the buttermilk.

JED: So was I.

JT: To your health.

JED: Mud in your eye.

(*They drink*)

JT: Oh Lord, this is elixir of the gods. Pure liquid Kentucky.

JED: Heaven in a mason jar.

TOMMY: Mr. Rowen, you 'spect I might have some?

JED: Well, sure, Tommy—help yourself, boy . . . (*to JT with a wink as Tommy reaches over*) . . . to the buttermilk!

(*General laughter, to Tommy's embarrassment*)

JT: Well, I want to thank you good folks for havin' me in like this, but I know there's nothin' free in this life, so I reckon it's time to sing for my supper, as it were.

(*Murmurs of approval and enthusiasm*)

JED: Mr. JT, afore you get to spinnin' us a yarn, maybe you could say a word or two 'bout what's goin' on out in the world.

JT: Well, sir, we got us a new President, of course—fella named Grover Cleveland.

JED: Cleveland? Who's he?

JT: Democrat.

LALLIE: Praise be to God!

JED: A Democrat! Lord, we waited long enough for that! Lallie, pour us another round—this is cause for celebration!

TOMMY: Where's he from?

JT: New York.

JED: New York? New York?! Hell, I ain't drinkin' to no Yankee Democrat! What they gonna hand us next—Christian sodomites?

LALLIE: Jed!

TOMMY: What's a sodomite?

LALLIE: Never you mind!

JED: Read your Bible, boy.

TOMMY: Is that the fella who's so helpful and all?

MARY ANNE: That's Samaritan.

JED: Oh Lord, this is why us folk in the mountains don't miss the world out there: the news is always bad.

JT: Well, I got one piece of news I think you'll like.

JED: It ain't likely.

JT: Ulysses S. Grant died four weeks ago.

JED: Dead?

TOMMY: Hot damn!

LALLIE: Tommy Jackson, you watch your language in this house!

JED: Well, I'll be damned!

LALLIE: Very likely, Jed Rowen—you and Tommy Jackson both for your blasphemous ways!

JED: Oh, hush up, woman—it's just words. Way I always understood it, Lord don't care what you say, it's what you do. What'd he die of?

LALLIE: "Thou shalt not take the Lord's name in vain."

JED: Lallie, as much sin as there is in eastern Kentucky, I don't think the Lord'll notice some bad language.

LALLIE: "Not a sparrow shall fall but what He won't see it."

JED: ENOUGH! Tommy, pour everybody some corn liquor and I think we'll skip the buttermilk this round! Now, JT, maybe you'd favor us all with that story you promised.

JT: Well, sir, it'd be a privilege.

(*Throughout JT's story, the other characters feel free to comment and respond: Jed and Lallie with quiet pleasure, Mary Anne with enthusiasm, and Tommy with growing envy and resentment*)

I knew a feller once, luckiest man in the world! I remember him and me once went coon huntin'. Had a terrible time! Lost a dog, most of our shells, and when we finally did tree this old coon up a sycamore, couldn't get a decent shot at the critter. Well, by this time it was so dark you couldn't see your hand in front of your face.

TOMMY: Well, that was pretty dumb, goin' huntin' with no moon out.

MARY ANNE: Be quiet!

JED: Let the man finish his story.

JT: Anyway, we turned around to go home real dejected-like, when all of a sudden the clouds cleared the moon—which was full, of course—to reveal a sight that'd freeze your blood.

MARY ANNE: What?

JT: There in front of us was a big old mama grizzly bear and her cub! Now, my friend only had one shell left in his gun, and I had nothin' atall, so we turned to run, but there behind us was the biggest rattlesnake I ever seen! We was trapped! I fell to my knees sayin' a prayer, and as I looked up, I remember seein' this huge old flock of geese flyin' over us. Then my friend shot the grizzly bear.

Well sir, there was a terrible explosion as his gun blew up in his face! Anybody else'd be dead or blind at least. But my friend was so lucky, this is what happened: the bullet killed the she-bear dead; a piece of that stock kilt the rattlesnake and skinned him at the same time; and that old barrel flew up and knocked the lead goose so cold he fell in to the river. Well, course all the other geese followed him—must've been about a hunnert—right into the river and drowned themselves! Well, I commenced to skinnin' the bear while my friend waded the river to collect all the geese. Took him half an hour and when he stepped out of that creek, wouldn't you know it, he found about fifty pounds of fish stuck in his boots!

We gathered up the bear, the fish, the geese, and the rattlesnake and was just about to start off when that coon we'd been huntin' fell out of the tree stone dead at our feet. Seems in all the ruckus, that baby grizzly had climbed up the same tree to hide, scarin' that coon to death! You talk about luck—well, I guess that friend of mine was full of it!

(*General applause*)

TOMMY: Well, somebody was sure full of somethin'.

JED: Now, what's that supposed to mean?

TOMMY: What do you think?

JED: Keep a civil tongue in your head, boy.

JT: I'm sure the child don't mean any harm, Jed. You know how kids are at that age, liable to say all kinds of stupid things. Puts me in mind of a story I once heard about a couple of kids usta live over in Perry County. Seems there was these two families, the Montages and the Caplets, and they'd been a-feudin' as long as anyone could remember.

Now, the Caplets had a daughter name of Juliet, though everybody called her "Jewel," I guess 'cause she was so pretty. Anyway, she'd been promised to this Thomas fellow, about whom the nicest thing you could say was, he'd a few chairs missin' from his attic. Problem was, Jewel was in love with this other fellow she'd just met, a real nice-looking stranger, name of Jack. She'd made up her mind that she was goin' to marry him and live in New York City in a big old skyscraper. Unbeknownst to her, Jack was a Montage, and when she found out, it like to break her heart. But he said it didn't matter to him, her being a Caplet, so they planned to get married anyway, in secret, and then run off together.

Well, right after the weddin', Jack ran into a whole mess of Caplets, and afore you know it they drew on him and he had no choice but to defend himself. He dropped about five of 'em 'cause he was a crack shot, and then he lit out of town, leavin' a message for Jewel to join up with him in Louisville.

Well, she wanted to, but her daddy was real set on her marryin' this Thomas fellow, even if he was close to bein' an idiot. So Jewel went to see this old witch woman and get some help. This here witch, she give her some herbs which'd put her into a sleep like she was dead or somethin'. The plan was, this witch'd get word to Jack to come back and dig Jewel up after she been buried and then they could sneak off. So Juliet took them herbs and everybody thought she'd died and they buried her just like they'd planned. Only thing wrong was this old witch got a terrible arthritis which kicked up about then and slowed her up somethin' fierce. By the time she got to Louisville, Jack had already heard that Jewell was dead, and crazy with grief, he'd gone back home.

That night he snuck into the graveyard to say goodbye to his sweetheart and then kill himself. Well, who should he stumble into with a shovel in his hand but Thomas! Lord knows what he was doin' there, diggin' up dead bodies, but like I said, he was a strange sort of boy. Well, they started to fight, of course, kickin' and gougin' each other somethin' fierce. In the middle of this, Jewel wakes up and sees Thomas chokin' her Jack to death! She gotta lot of spunk, that girl, and afore you could blink, she picks up a shovel and bashes Tom's head in. Then she explained everything to Jack, who was real glad to hear she wasn't dead and all, and the two of them run off to New York City, where they was real happy!

(*Everyone applauds*)

MARY ANNE: I like that story!

TOMMY: You son of a bitch! I'LL KILL YOU!

(*He leaps across the table at JT and knocks him to the floor. Jed pulls Tommy off and then throws him across the room*)

JED: What the hell get into you, boy!

TOMMY: I ain't no fool!

JED: Well, you sure actin' like one!

TOMMY: I see what's going' on here! This stranger come dancin' in here with his smiles and his stories and everybody falls all over themselves offerin' him this and that, like he some kind of prodigous son, home from the wars!

MARY ANNE: Prodigal.

TOMMY: I seen you moonin' over him, makin' big cow eyes! "Oh, I like that story, I dooo!"

JED: I think you better get outta here, boy.

TOMMY: I'm goin'! Hell, you couldn't pay me to stay. Maybe I make a fool outta myself like you say, old man. But Mr. Silver Tongue stay here tonight with his stories and I bet Mary Anne make a bigger fool outta you by tomorrow mornin'!

(*Tommy starts to leave, and as he goes, he reaches for his gun by the door. Jed blocks his way*)

Gimme my gun!

JED: You cool off. Come back tomorrow, and we'll talk about it.

TOMMY: Gimme my gun, god damn it!

JED: You keep pushin' it, son, and I'm likely to do just that.

TOMMY (*near tears with humiliation*): Oh, come on, Jed, gimme my gun!

JED: Or what? You gonna cry, maybe? Stamp your feet and shout? Wet your pants? Don't know why your daddy let you carry a gun, boy—you ain't got the balls to use it or the sense to know when. Now get outta here, 'fore I turn you over my knee. Go on. Get!

TOMMY: I ain't forgettin' this. (*To JT*) I ain't forgettin' you.

(*He runs off. Jed empties the gun*)

JED: Damn fool kid.

JT: Mrs. Rowen, I surely wanta apologize for bringin' trouble into your home. I was just havin' a little fun. I didn't mean to hurt anybody.

LALLIE: Don't you worry your head about it, JT—I never did like that Jackson boy nohow.

JED: What she means is, she never thought he was good enough for our Mare.

MARY ANNE: Pa!

LALLIE: Well, he ain't.

JT: Well, you gotta problem there, ma'am, 'cause you gonna have to look far and wide to find the right somebody for this young lady. (*Beat*) Well, it's late, and I best be movin' on.

MARY ANNE: No!

LALLIE: Surely you're gonna spend the night here?

JT: I wish, but I got obligations . . . .

MARY ANNE: Couldn't you give us just one more story 'fore you go?

JED: There's an idea, one more story and another wet somethin' to go with it.

JT: Get thee behind me, Satan!

(*Everybody laughs*)

Well . . . all right!

(*General applause and bustle as everyone settles and Jed pours drinks*)

I'd like to dedicate this story to you, Jed and Lallie, for the warmth of your welcome and the graciousness of your hospitality. (*He drinks, laughs*) Lord, that's good!

Well, it seems a long time ago, Jesus Christ came down to Kentucky disguised as a poor traveler and walking from door to door askin' for hospitality. Well, sadly, things hadn't improved much since he'd shared Roman hospitality up on that lonely hill in Jerusalem, 'cause everywhere he went, people would curse him and shut their doors in his face.

LALLIE: Oh, Lord.

JT: Finally, at the end of the day he came to this little old shotgun shack belongin' to an old couple name of Baucis and Philomen. Well, they were tickled pink to have company, and they hustled the holy stranger inside and gave him the best seat by the fire. Then Philomen killed their only chicken and roasted him up real fine, while Baucis brought down the last of their 'shine and poured it out for the Lord. It was a simple meal, folks, spiced only with a little salt and that more complex and rarer seasoning, human kindness. Much like another simple meal on top of another hill, in Galilee.

LALLIE: Uh-huh.

JT: After the meal, our Lord revealed Himself in all His glory, and those two folks fell to their knees, their faces bathed in tears. He bade them get up and follow him outside. And then they saw the miracle. All the towns around them, full of inhospitable people, had been swallowed up by the earth.

LALLIE: Praise the Lord.

JT: The Lord said, "You alone, Baucis and Philomen, have shown kindness to the stranger, and as a reward, you may have one wish which I shall grant." Well, those two old people looked at each other, and right away they knew what they wanted. Baucis said, "Lord, if it wouldn't be too much trouble, Philomen and I have been sweethearts as long as we can remember, and we ain't never spent a night apart as long as we been married. If one of us were to die, it'd sure be hard on the other one. If you wouldn't mind, when the time comes, we'd both like to be called together."

And the Lord smiled and said he reckoned that'd be possible. Years went by, and then one day Baucis was workin' in the garden, he started to feel dizzy. He turned to Philomen and she saw him and smiled, 'cause she knew their time had come. They reached out to each other for one last hug, and as they did, their hands turned into twigs and they were changed into two big old oak trees standin' side by side for all eternity. And as the wind blows through their leaves, it says one thing over and over, throughout all eternity—and that is, "I love you."

LALLIE (*quiet*): I like that story.

JED: Amen.

(*They smile at each other*)

JT: You know, you folks been so kind to me 'n' all, I'd sure like to be able to do somethin' for you in return. I mean, when you see family like this one, so close, so full of love for each other 'n' all, it just makes you think: What if . . . ?

(*Beat*)

JED: What if?

JT: What if, God forbid, somethin' should happen to one of you? I mean, we can't all be as lucky as Baucis and Philomen and count on the Lord callin' us at the same time, can we? And in the unpleasant event of your absence, you'd sure want your wife and child looked after proper now, wouldn't you?

JED: Well, sure.

JT: Course you would. But how's a man to do that? You sure wouldn't want to rely on the Jacksons or the rest of your neighbors now, would you?

JED: No, sir.

JT: It's a problem for sure. But one for which, I'm happy to say, there is a solution.

JED: What's that?

JT: I have been empowered by certain parties to purchase the mineral rights from far-sighted Christian gentlemen like yourself.

(*Beat*)

JED: My mineral rights?

JT: Yes sir.

JED: Oh. Well . . . uh . . . what exactly are we talkin' about here, JT?

JT: Well, "mineral rights" is just a twenty-five cent word for rocks, actually.

JED: Rocks? You mean somebody wants to buy the rocks offa my land?

JT: That's it exactly. The people I represent will pay you fifty cents an acre for the right to haul off all mineral and metallic substances and combinations of the same. In your case, countin' your three-hundred-odd acres—

JED: Three hunnert and fifty-seven acres.

JT (*smiling*): That'd be about a hundred and seventy-nine dollars in cold, hard American cash.

(*Stunned silence*)

JED: Let me get this straight, JT—I been breakin' my back diggin' rocks outta my damn fields so I could plow for nigh onto forty years, and now there are people willin' to pay me money for the same privilege?

JT: What can I tell you, Jed, 'cept there's a fool born every day. Here, you read it for yourself, it's all down there in black and white.

(*He pulls out a contract from his jacket and hands it to Jed, who inspects it awkwardly, too embarrassed to admit he can't read*)

JT (*gently*): Light's kinda bad in here—maybe you'd like me to go over it for you.

JED: Can't do nothing with these old eyes of mine.

JT: Essentially, this says that for the sum in question, you, the owner, pass over the title to the mineral underlying your land with all the usual and ordinary mining rights. It says all that a lot longer, but that's what it boils down to.

JED: And that's all there is to it?

JT: That's all.

JED: Well, that sounds easy, don't it! Where am I supposed to sign?

JT: Right here.

(*Jed picks up the pen*)

LALLIE: Jed, I don't feel right about this.

JED: What don't you feel right about, Lallie?

LALLIE: This land been in your family back before anybody can remember, and I don't think you oughta be sellin' it.

JED: You heard him, Lallie—I ain't sellin' the land, I'm just sellin' the mineral rights.

LALLIE: I don't think you oughta be sellin' any part of it, even them rocks.

JED: Lallie, I know what I'm doin' here.

JT (*smiling*): I understand your feelings, ma'am, 'bout the land, and as a mountain boy I share 'em, but I don't think any of your family'd begrudge you makin' a livin' off your land. What's important is the land, that it stays in your family.

LALLIE: That's right, but . . .

JT: Now think about it. Everybody knows with corn, couple of bad seasons back to back and you might have to sell a piece of your land —all of it maybe—just to get by. But with all that money, folks, that one hundred and seventy-nine dollars, you're covered. You got somethin' to fall back on.

JED: Man's gotta point, Lallie.

JT: And why not make your life a little easier right now, Lallie? You know—get a new stove, maybe. A new dress for your daughter. A new—

LALLIE: We don't need things. We got everything we need.

JED: Lallie . . .

JT: I tell you what, I don't usually do this, but you folks been so nice to me 'n' all, maybe I could see my way to, say . . . sixty cents an acre.

(*Beat*)

JED (*smiling*): Seventy-five cents.

LALLIE: Jed!

MARY ANNE: Daddy!

JED: Hush up, now! JT and I are talkin' business now, and he knows as well's I do, you can't let your personal feelin's get in the way of business—can you, JT?

JT (*smiling evenly*): No sir, that's a fact. (*Beat*) Seventy-five, huh? Well . . . I reckon I might could see my way to seventy-five.

JED: Good enough for me.

LALLIE: It ain't right, Jed—ain't enough money in the world gonna—

JT: Jed, if your wife doesn't want you to do this, maybe we oughta just forget the whole thing . . .

JED: I make the decisions for this family, JT, and I say that's fine! (*Beat*) Now, where do I sign?

JT: Right here.

(*Jed picks up the pen and looks the document over again*)

JED: Just outta curiosity, JT, what exactly are those "usual and ordinary mining rights" you were talking about?

JT (*picking his way carefully*): That means they can excavate for the minerals . . . uh, build a road here and there, if necessary—long as they don't disturb you, of course. Use some of the local water . . .

JED: Hold it right there! You never said anything before about cuttin' across my land or taking my water!

LALLIE: Uh-huh.

JT: That was understood, Jed. I figured a man of your experience knew how these things worked.

JED: Nope! No way! Ain't no way anybody's gonna build a road over my land!

JT: Look, Jed, I promise you, I swear to God, you'll hardly know they're there! They gonna be real careful with your land.

JED: You want my mineral rights, that's one thing. But I just can't see my way to all that other stuff. Roads and water—no sir! (*Beat*) 'Less you're willin' to go a whole 'nother quarter an acre.

JT: What?!

JED: A dollar an acre and she's yours!

JT: Hell, Jed, you can practically buy land in these parts for that!

JED: Then you do it! 'Course I thought you wanted the mineral rights to a particular piece of land. Mine.

JT: You tryin' to cut my throat, Jed?

JED (*innocently*): Why no, JT—but you did start out by sayin' how you wanted to do me and mine a favor.

(*Beat. Both men are breathing a little hard. JT finally manages a smile*)

JT: Jed Rowen, I hope you won't take this the wrong way if I tell you I ain't never met anybody like you. You, sir, are one tough son of a bitch.

JED (*smiling*): I'd consider that a compliment. (*Beat*) We doin' business?

JT: Yeah, we're doin' business.

JED: Dollar an acre?

JT: Dollar an acre.

JED: Where do I sign?

(*Jed picks up the pen and then puts it down again*)

JT: I ain't goin' any higher, Jed!

JED (*embarrassed*): Ain't the money, JT. I don't know how to sign my name.

JT (*relieved*): All you do is touch the pen and make your mark. An X or whatever. (*Jed signs*) And here's a bank draft for . . .

JED: Three hundred and fifty-seven dollars.

JT: Now, you just take this draft to the bank—any bank, anywhere. That little paper's as good as gold.

(*Jed examines the paper with great respect. JT leans over the table*)

I'm gonna ask you a favor, Jed, man to man. I'd appreciate it if you wouldn't mention this price to your neighbors—least not till after I been around and had a crack at 'em. Make my job a little easier, you know?

JED: I understand, JT. (*With a wink*) When it come to business, everybody got his own lookout.

JT: Ain't that the truth. (*Beat*) Well, I sure want to thank you folks for your hospitality but I better be goin'.

MARY ANNE: Can't you stay the night, JT?

JED: Sure wouldn't be any trouble.

JT: No, I better be movin'.

JED: Suit yourself.

JT: Could use some direction gettin' back to the road, though.

MARY ANNE: I'll take him, Pa.

JED: All right, she'll see you down there. I'd do it myself, but I'd probably get us both lost! (*They laugh*)

JT: Thanks again for everything, Lallie. I'll dream of your red-eye gravy.

LALLIE: You're welcome.

JT: Jed? Take care of yourself, sir.

JED: Don't you worry 'bout me.

JT: No, sir, I guess I won't. (*JT and Jed laugh*)

JED: Mary Anne. It ain't all that far down there. Don't you be too long gettin' back.

MARY ANNE: I won't, Daddy.

(*Mary Anne and JT walk out of the scene and into the woods. Night sounds and shadows surround them*)

Scene 3

MARY ANNE: Where you goin' next?

JT: Oh, just down the road a piece.

MARY ANNE: You think you ever come back through here?

JT: Not likely.

MARY ANNE: Lucky you.

JT: Seems like a real pretty place to me, Mary Anne.

MARY ANNE: It's borin'. Its always the same. I'd love to do what you do —travel around, meet folks, see new places.

JT: Maybe my life isn't quite as glamorous as you might think.

MARY ANNE: No?

JT: No.

MARY ANNE: I don't know. (*She stops*) Wanta trade?

JT (*laughs*): No. (*Beat*) Come on, Mary Anne, let's get goin'.

MARY ANNE: Couldn't we just stop for a minute? Keep walkin' like this we get to that old road in no time.

JT: Well . . . maybe just a minute. (*They sit*)

MARY ANNE: Sure is a mighty fine moon tonight.

JT: Pretty.

MARY ANNE: Sometimes I get so restless on a night like this, I get up, sneak outta the house, and walk through the woods all by myself. Feels like I'm swimmin' through the moonlight, like a big old lake.

JT: Long time ago, all this was under water, you know.

MARY ANNE: When was that?

JT: Thousands and thousands of years ago.

MARY ANNE: What happened?

JT: Somebody pulled the plug.

MARY ANNE (*laughs*): No, really!

JT: Nobody knows. Things change, that's all. One time there was an ocean, now there isn't. One time there weren't any mountains here, now there are. (*Beat*) 'Course, these aren't really mountains, you know?

MARY ANNE: No?

JT: This is the Cumberland Plateau. Big, flat-topped rise of land. It's the water, year after year, thousands of years, cutting canyons and gulleys, just makes it seem like mountains.

MARY ANNE: Gosh.

JT: Ain't nothin' what it really seems. Not even mountains. (*Beat*) Let's get goin'. (*She doesn't move*) I can't take you with me, Mary Anne.

MARY ANNE: Why not?

JT: 'Cause . . . Because this is where you belong, swimming in this damn Kentucky moonlight, on these mountains that ain't mountains. Now let's go.

MARY ANNE: I ain't showin' you where the road is 'less you kiss me first.

JT: What?! You really are your father's daughter!

MARY ANNE: One kiss—what'd it hurt?

JT: Nothing. Except I couldn't promise you there'd be only the one.

MARY ANNE: That'd be all right too.

(*He kneels in front of her*)

JT: You sure this is what you want?

MARY ANNE: Just kiss me, JT. (*He does*)

JT: It won't change my mind.

MARY ANNE: I know.

(*She kisses him again and then slides down to the ground, pulling him with her. Tommy enters with a drawn knife. JT sees him and half gets up*)

TOMMY: I said I wouldn't forget you.

(*Tommy throws himself at JT, who flips him over. Tommy slashes at JT, cutting him on the shoulder. JT grabs him and they both go down. Tommy comes up on top. He kneels over JT and tries to push the knife into his face. JT holds him off but is clearly weakening*)

JT: Help me! Help me!

(*Mary Anne, who has watched the whole thing in mute horror, now comes to life. She kicks Tommy hard in the side. He rolls over and loses the knife. JT begins to kick and pummel the boy savagely. He winds up over Tommy, smashing the boy's head into the ground*)

MARY ANNE: Stop it! Stop it! You're gonna kill him! Stop it!

(*She pushes JT off Tommy, who is bloody and unconscious. JT holds his cut arm, somewhat in shock*)

JT: The son of a bitch cut me!

MARY ANNE: You coulda kilt him!

JT: He came at me with a goddamn knife! Ohh, the little son of a bitch cut me!

MARY ANNE: Lemme see.

JT: Son of a bitch!

MARY ANNE: It ain't bad.

(*He pulls away from her angrily*)

JT: Son of a bitch! (*Beat*) You saved my life.

MARY ANNE: I guess.

JT: How come?!

MARY ANNE: I need a reason?

JT: HOW COME?!

MARY ANNE (*simply*): I love you. (*Beat*)

JT: This doesn't change anything. I can't take you with me.

MARY ANNE: I know.

JT: Will you stop being so goddamn understanding about everything! Goddamn hillbillies! (*Getting hysterical*) I could cut your hearts out with a rusty razor but as long as I smiled and told another story, you'd just sit there happy as pigs in shit! Oh Lord, I can't do this no more. I can't do this.

(*He is sobbing now, his head in her lap*)

MARY ANNE: Can't do what?

JT: Everything I ever told you, it's all lies! All of it! (*Laughs*) Your poor old pa, thinking he's slick as goose shit—a dollar an acre! What a joke! There he is, sitting on top of maybe fifteen, twenty thousand tons of coal an acre!

MARY ANNE: What's coal?

JT: Oh, nothin' little hillbilly, just "rocks", that's all. Millions of dollars worth of "rocks" which your daddy just sold me for a lousy buck! Millions! Oh, he's slick, he is, the poor dumb son of a bitch!

MARY ANNE: You're lyin'!

JT: That ain't even the worst of it! You ain't seen what they do. "I swear, Jed, I promise they be real careful with your land." Oh yes sir, they careful—careful not to miss a trick. First they come in here and cut down all your trees . . .

MARY ANNE: No!

JT: Listen to me, god damn it! First they cut down all your trees. Then they cut into the land, deep—start huntin' those deep veins, diggin' 'em out in their deep mines, dumping the crap they can't use in your streams, your wells, your fields, whatever! And when they finished, after they squeezed out every nickel, they just move on. Leaving your land colder and deader'n that moon up there.

MARY ANNE: It ain't so!

JT: The hell it ain't!

MARY ANNE: If that's true, how can you do it? How can you do that to your own people? You a hillbilly just like my daddy, just like me!

JT: I ain't no hillbilly!

MARY ANNE: You said you was a boy off the creek, just like . . .

JT: That was a long time ago! Now I'm whoever I say I am. I'm JT Wells and I invent myself new every day, just like the stories I tell!

MARY ANNE: Don't matter what you call yourself—you still one of us, that's the truth!

JT: Truth? Hell, woman, there ain't no such thing. All there is, is stories!

MARY ANNE (*frightened and unsure why*): What're you sayin'?

JT: Sure. Everybody got his stories! Your daddy got his stories. Civil War hero, right? Rode with that "gentleman" Quantrill, right? Shit! Quantrill was a thief and a murderer, and when he died folks danced in the streets!

MARY ANNE: My daddy was a hero!

JT: 'Course he was! And he's the son of heroes, right? Pioneer stock! That ain't the truth! He's the son of thieves, who came here and slaughtered the Indians and took their land!

MARY ANNE: We bought this land from the Indians under that oak tree fair and square!

JT: Well, sure you did! And the people I work for, those Standard Oil people, they bought this land "fair and square" too. And you think they'll sleep any worse at night than your pa does? When they come in here, maybe they'll cut the heart out of that old oak you love so much . . .

MARY ANNE: NO!

JT: . . . and they'll ship it off to New York, where somebody'll cut it into a fine banker's desk and swivel-back chair for Mr. Rockefeller himself! You think when he sits his skinny ass down on that polished surface he gonna be thinkin' about some poor hillbilly girl whose heart got broke in the process?! You won't be part of his story, Mary Anne! And when I finish my job for him, I won't be part of his story either. See, he'll give some money to a school or something, and grateful people will call him a hero, a great man, a Real Christian! And that story is the one that'll survive—he'll see to that. While the other story, the one where he's just a thief, that'll fade away. That's your "Truth."

MARY ANNE: That ain't . . . you're wrong . . . it ain't just stories . . . !

JT: That's how somebody like me can do what he does! I just tell people the stories they want to hear. I say what people want me to say and I am wherever they want me to be.

MARY ANNE: Then what's left?

JT: Of what?

MARY ANNE: At the end of the day, when you're by yourself—who are you? (*He shrugs*) Why'd you kiss me back there?

(*Beat. And then right in her face*)

JT: Tell me what you want to hear, and I'll tell you why I kissed you.

(*She slaps him. Beat. Tommy moans and moves slightly*)

Take your boyfriend home, little hillbilly. At least he fights for what he believes in . . . thinks he believes in. At least he thinks he believes in something. Take him home and marry him and live happily ever after.

(*JT staggers up. He pulls Jed's contract out of his pocket and puts it in her hand*)

Here, I owe you one. Tear it up. Tell Jed to tear his bank note up, too.

(*JT exits. Mary Anne sobs and moves to Tommy. The lights fade down on her while they come up in a single spot on the adult Mary Anne. Again, she contemplates her younger self while she speaks to the audience*)

MARY ANNE: I told my pa what JT said . . . and Pa said it was a lie. That JT was lyin'. That he'd beat JT in the deal and that JT was just tryin' to get out of it now, tryin' to get his money back. I asked Pa about Quantrill and Kansas and he said I'd just have to make my own mind up about that. That I could believe him, believe my own daddy, or I could believe this stranger. And if I chose JT—well, here was the contract and I could tear that up too.

I didn't tear it up. I didn't want to believe JT, and so I chose not to. Like he said I guess, people believe what they want to believe. And he was right, of course. Probably the only time in his life, JT Wells told the truth and he wasn't believed. And people say God ain't got a sense of humor.

They came a couple of years later, just like he said they would, and they cut down all of the trees, includin' my oak. I was right about it holdin' up the sky 'cause when they chopped it down, everythin' fell in: moon and stars 'n' all. Spring's different now. Without the trees, you get no color; no green explosion. And you got nothin' to hold the land down neither. What you get is just a whole lotta rain, moving a whole lotta mud. I try to tell my boy, Joshua, what it was like, so he'll know, so it won't be forgotten, but he just looks at me and laughs. "Mama's tellin' stories again," he says.

(*Pause*)

Maybe I am.

(*Lights fade slowly out*)

BLUE STARS

Stuart Spencer

Stuart Spencer

Stuart Spencer is the author of numerous plays, many of which have been performed at the Ensemble Studio Theatre where he is currently a member and was formerly the Literary Manager. In that capacity he supervised the Playwrights Unit, helping to discover and cultivate new American writers. He served as dramaturg for an ongoing series of readings, workshops, and productions which featured such notable writers as Eduardo Machado and John Patrick Shanley.

Mr. Spencer teaches playwriting and dramaturgy, both privately and at Sarah Lawrence College and the Playwrights Horizons Theatre School at NYU. He helps to bring theatre to the inner city through the Young Playwrights Festival program.

Formerly a story editor at CBS Films, Mr. Spencer now edits the film and theatre section of the quarterly *Bomb Magazine,* interviewing such luminaries as Joyce Carol Oates, Campbell Scott, Horton Foote, John Ford Noonan and Robert Schenkkan.

Blue Stars was originally produced in the Ensemble Studio Theatre Marathon '92. It was directed by Jane Hoffman and performed by Cecilia DeWolfe, Kevin O'Keefe, and Eric Conger.

Mr. Spencer is a member of the Dramatists Guild and is a fellow of the Edward Albee Foundation.

Characters:

EMMA

HORACE

FREDDY

Scene:

Morning.

A white kitchen. An old style refrigerator, black wall phone, coffee percolator. A small breakfast table.

(*The set for the original production was an abstracted naturalistic kitchen. Only the furniture and props essential to the play were present. It had a skewed, off-center look that made it clear to the audience from the opening that this would not be a kitchen-sink drama.*)

Horace sits sipping coffee, eating a piece of toast and reading the paper. He is dressed in a suit and tie. A small briefcase on the floor next to him. Emma enters.

EMMA: You're up.

HORACE: Hm?

EMMA: You're already up and dressed.

HORACE: I couldn't sleep.

EMMA: Nightmares?

HORACE: No, I just couldn't sleep.

EMMA (*moves into the kitchen*): I had nightmares.

HORACE: Did you? I'm sorry.

EMMA: Terrible nightmares. I couldn't wake up. What do you think of that. You had pleasant dreams and you couldn't sleep. I had nightmares and I couldn't wake up. (*Beat*) You made the coffee.

HORACE: Yes.

EMMA (*pours some*): I would have made it.

HORACE: I didn't know when you'd be up.

EMMA (*sips*): It's fine.

HORACE: I thought it was pretty good.

EMMA: It is. It's very good. Did you want breakfast?

HORACE: Toast is fine.

EMMA: I'd be glad to make you something.

HORACE: You don't need to, really.

EMMA: Pancakes, maybe. With blueberries. We still have a lot of blueberries from the bunch I picked up at the cottage. They'd be wonderful in some pancakes. They'll only go bad, sitting in the refrigerator. Would you like some? Some blueberry pancakes?

HORACE: Emma, please, sit down and have your coffee. (*Pause*)

EMMA: Have you been outside today?

HORACE: Outside?

EMMA: To get the paper, I mean. Did you go out in front?

HORACE: Yes.

EMMA: Did you see anything out in the front of the house? Anything unusual?

HORACE: Like what, for instance?

EMMA: You'll laugh at me.

HORACE: Emma, I would never laugh at you.

EMMA (*slight pause*): An airplane.

HORACE: Did I see an airplane out in front of the house.

EMMA: Yes.

HORACE: On the front lawn.

EMMA: Not on the lawn—on the street. At the curb. Pulled up to the curb, like an automobile, only it's a plane. A little plane, with a little stubby nose. Cute, almost. Just big enough for one person, or maybe two if you squeeze. The pilot and a passenger. And the pilot is there, dressed like a . . . well, like a pilot. A leather jacket with the fleece lining and a scarf and a cap. He's standing next to his plane. Young man. Nice looking. He wanted me to go with him. He wanted me to get into his airplane.

HORACE: And did you?

EMMA: No, I wouldn't.

HORACE: You refused.

EMMA: I told him I didn't like to fly. I told him I was afraid of going up in airplanes.

HORACE: So you didn't go.

EMMA: No. Heavens, no.

HORACE: Then why was it a nightmare?

EMMA: It just was. It felt like a nightmare.

HORACE: Emma, if you had gone in the airplane against your will, if he had tricked you, or forced you somehow, and then if you had taken off and you were actually in flight and something terrible happened, like you crashed, or he threw you out of the plane—that might have been a nightmare. What you had was a dream. A strange dream, that's all. People have them all the time. Some people enjoy them.

EMMA: It was very real.

HORACE: The stranger they are, the more real they seem. Don't you know that?

EMMA: I guess not.

HORACE: Have your coffee, dear.

EMMA (*takes her coffee to the window*): I suppose it was the prospect of something bad. The potential for it. The potential for something really dreadful happening.

HORACE: You might have gone with an attractive young man in his airplane. You might have done something very exciting that you have never done before and in all likelihood will never do again. I do not see that as particularly dreadful.

EMMA: That never occurred to me.

HORACE: Of course it didn't. Now please, Emma, dear—relax. Please.

EMMA (*pours more coffee*): Your coffee's really very nice.

HORACE: Thank you.

EMMA: I didn't know you could make such good coffee.

HORACE: There are many things I am capable of.

EMMA: Would you like some more?

HORACE: I'm not quite ready, thanks.

(*She unplugs the percolator and puts it on the table*)

HORACE (*cont'd*): I'd prefer it back where it belongs, please, and plugged in.

(*She puts the percolator back on the counter and plugs it in*)

EMMA: Horace.

HORACE: Yes?

EMMA: Do you think we'll go up to the cottage this weekend?

HORACE: The cottage?

EMMA: Yes.

HORACE: Again?

EMMA: Yes.

HORACE: Well, I'll have to see if I can get away.

EMMA: I do hope we can.

HORACE: You're free to go alone, you know. You don't have to have me with you.

EMMA: You mean, me go up and leave you here?

HORACE: Yes.

EMMA (*astonished*): Are you serious?

HORACE: If you want to, why not?

EMMA: Me? Go up to the cottage by myself?

HORACE: Yes.

EMMA: What would make you think I would do such a thing?

HORACE: I thought you might want to, that's all.

EMMA: I can't imagine it.

HORACE: It was only an idea.

EMMA: I'd like to pick more blueberries.

HORACE: I thought you said we had plenty of blueberries.

EMMA: We do, but . . .

HORACE: They were going to go bad, you said.

EMMA: Yes, they will, but . . .

HORACE: We have a basket of blueberries going bad in the refrigerator, and you want to pick more.

EMMA: I like to pick them, that's all. I like to go out with the basket, picking. I could do it for hours. Out in that enormous meadow, all afternoon, nothing to do but pick berries.

HORACE: All by yourself.

EMMA: Yes.

HORACE: Out by yourself all afternoon, picking berries.

EMMA: Yes.

HORACE: But when I say, why not go up to the cottage by yourself, you say you can't imagine it.

EMMA: That would be different.

HORACE: Different how? What's different about it?

EMMA: The one way you're there, and the other way you're not.

HORACE: Either way, I'm not there.

EMMA: Well, that's true.

HORACE: I still exist, dear. It's not as if I have ceased to exist.

EMMA: It's not the same, that's all. I don't want to go up to the cottage without you. If you don't go, I'm not going.

HORACE: You do make it awfully difficult, do you know that? You make things very, very difficult.

EMMA: If you want to go to the cottage, we'll go. If you don't want to go, we won't. And that's that. (*He gets up*) Where are you going?

HORACE: To work.

EMMA: Already?

HORACE: I like to allow ample time.

EMMA: But it's so early.

HORACE: It's not early. You got up late, remember?

EMMA (*beat*): When will you be home?

HORACE: I don't know.

EMMA: Call me, will you?

HORACE: If I have time.

EMMA: I want to know about dinner, is all.

HORACE: What about dinner?

EMMA: I want to know what time.

HORACE: I'll call you when I know something.

EMMA: I think that's reasonable, isn't it?

HORACE: I'll call you.

EMMA: I have to plan a little bit, don't I?

HORACE: I said I'd call. Don't worry about it. (*He takes a last sip of his coffee*) That's good. (*Beat*) Will you stop looking at me like that? I'll call you. Don't worry. Please, please don't worry.

EMMA: I'm sorry.

HORACE: I'll call you.

EMMA: All right.

HORACE: Kiss?

(*They kiss*)

HORACE (*cont'd*): You promise not to worry?

EMMA: I promise.

HORACE: I'll see about this weekend.

EMMA: Thank you.

(*He begins to exit*)

EMMA (*cont'd*): Don't work too hard.

(*He exits. She goes to the window, waits a minute, waves*)

EMMA (*cont'd*): Good bye!

(*He is gone. She looks a moment longer. Then she turns from the window, goes to the refrigerator, gets a basket of blueberries out. She puts them on the table, sits down. She eats a berry. A ring at the door. She goes to it and opens it. A young man is there, dressed casually, cap in his hand*)

FREDDY: Good morning.

EMMA: Good morning.

FREDDY: Are you ready, ma'am? (*Beat*) Are you ready to go? (*Beat*) I'm Freddy. The driver. I'm here to pick you up. You wanted someone to pick you up, didn't you?

EMMA: Pick me up?

FREDDY (*consulting a slip of paper*): This is 122 North Maple, isn't it?

EMMA: Yes.

FREDDY: And you are Emma Thorn?

EMMA: Yes.

FREDDY: Mrs. Emma Thorn? 122 North Maple? You called to have someone pick you up this morning at eight thirty.

EMMA: No, not me.

FREDDY: I've got the order right here, ma'am.

(*He shows it to her*)

EMMA: But I didn't call anyone.

FREDDY: I see. (*Beat*) Maybe you could let me use your phone. Would that be all right?

EMMA: Yes, yes. Come in. (*He enters*) It's right over there.

FREDDY: Thank you ma'am. (*He goes to the phone*) Frank, it's Freddy. I'm over at 122 North Maple, a Mrs. Emma Thorn. She um . . . she says she didn't order any car. (*Pause*) That's right. (*Pause*) Yeah, I know Frank. Uh-huh. Hold on. (*To Emma*) You mind if I wait here for a few minutes? They've got to check things out down there and call me back.

EMMA: I don't mind.

FREDDY (*into the phone*): Yeah, it's all right. (*Reading off the phone*) Five—four six oh three. (*Pause*) Right. (*Pause*) Okay, Frank. (*Pause*) Yes, I know Frank. (*Hangs up*) He's going to call back in a minute.

EMMA: Would you like some coffee?

FREDDY: Thank you. I could use some.

EMMA: My husband made it. Cream and sugar?

FREDDY: Black for me.

EMMA: Was that your boss?

FREDDY: That was Frank. The dispatcher.

EMMA: I'm sorry about the mix up.

FREDDY: It's not your fault, I'm sure. Don't worry about it.

EMMA: You sound like my husband.

FREDDY: How's that?

EMMA: Telling me not to worry. My husband is forever telling me not to worry.

FREDDY: Good advice, I guess.

EMMA: Very good advice. Very sound advice. (*Slight pause*) Sit down, won't you . . . Freddy? Is that it?

FREDDY: That's right.

EMMA: Please, sit down.

FREDDY: Good coffee.

EMMA: My husband made it.

FREDDY: I like a good, strong cup of coffee. I like the taste of coffee, the actual taste of the coffee. I make it myself at home but it comes out weak. (*Pause*) You've been out picking berries, I see.

EMMA: Oh yes. This past weekend. We have a cottage up north. It's just surrounded by blueberry bushes. Acres and acres of them. You could pick blueberries all day and never run out of them. There'd always be more to pick.

FREDDY: Like stars. In the sky.

EMMA: Yes, exactly.

FREDDY: You'd think you could count them all, but there's always one you missed.

EMMA: That's right.

FREDDY: A little cottage up in the woods, surrounded by a sky full of blue stars wherever you look.

EMMA: That's exactly it. I never thought of it like that before, but that's it exactly.

FREDDY (*pause*): I guess this means you're not going anywhere today.

EMMA: What means I'm not going anywhere?

FREDDY: That you didn't order a car.

EMMA: Oh that. Yes—no, I'm not going anywhere.

FREDDY: Too bad. I was jealous of you going away like that.

EMMA: Were you?

FREDDY: Oh sure, going away like that? I'd like to go away places.

EMMA: You're young. I'm sure you could go anywhere you liked.

FREDDY: No, ma'am, I don't think I could.

EMMA: Why not?

FREDDY: Where would I go?

EMMA: I don't know. Where would I go? Where would anybody go? Where were you going to take me?

FREDDY: I don't know.

EMMA: What does it say on your slip there?

FREDDY: It doesn't say anything. That part's not filled in. See? "Destination." It's blank.

EMMA: I see.

FREDDY: Just says Mrs. Emma Thorn. 122 North Maple. 8:30 a.m.

EMMA: Isn't that strange.

FREDDY: Strange, ma'am?

EMMA: That the destination isn't filled in.

FREDDY: No, ma'am. It's often blank like that.

EMMA: Is that right.

FREDDY: Yes ma'am.

EMMA: But then, I could tell you I wanted to go somewhere that you didn't go. Somewhere far away. Another town, maybe.

FREDDY: That'd be fine, ma'am.

EMMA: You go as far away as another town?

FREDDY: Yes ma'am.

EMMA: To Cherryville even? Or Oshotowoc?

FREDDY: Yes ma'am, anywhere you wanted.

EMMA (*pause*): Are you a pilot?

FREDDY: A pilot, ma'am?

EMMA: Are you a pilot? Do you fly an airplane?

FREDDY: Why do you ask that?

EMMA: You see, I just had this . . . this thought. I could see you out in the front of this house, standing in front of an airplane. You don't have an airplane parked outside this house, do you? (*Pause*) Do you?

FREDDY (*pause*): I'm afraid I don't. (*She goes to the window*) I have my car. The company's car. That's the only thing I have parked out front.

EMMA (*beat*): More coffee?

FREDDY: Thanks.

EMMA: Just black, is that right?

FREDDY: That's right.

EMMA: My husband made it. He got up before me this morning and he made it. Normally I'm up before my husband and I make the coffee. But I woke up late—I was having the strangest dream—and he was up and dressed already. It was odd not to have him there next to me. He's always there beside me when I wake up and . . . I'm sorry. I do go on.

FREDDY (*pause*): But where do you think you might have been going? If you had been going somewhere? Where do you think that could have been? It's like a game. (*Slight pause*) Downtown, maybe?

EMMA: Maybe.

FREDDY: Or over to the island? Visit a friend?

EMMA: Possibly.

FREDDY: Up to Cherryville, maybe?

EMMA: Yes.

FREDDY: Or Oshotowoc.

EMMA: I suppose, any of those places.

FREDDY: What about Johnson Mills?

EMMA: I don't know—that far?

FREDDY: Or Minneapolis. Or Chicago.

EMMA: Oh, I don't think you could possibly go that far.

FREDDY: I don't see why not.

EMMA: But I don't see how.

FREDDY: Maybe I was going to take you to the bus stop, or the train station. From there, you get off one train, you get on another. You take it to the coast and you get on a ship, or an airplane. You fly over the polar cap and places you thought were far away aren't really so far. I could get you anywhere you wanted, if you thought of it like that.

EMMA: The polar cap . . . !

FREDDY: Sure. You could be in Hong Kong before you know it, or Singapore, or Bangkok, or Oahu, or Guam, or Sydney, Australia.

EMMA: Stop . . . stop . . . !

FREDDY: What's the matter?

EMMA: The thought of all those . . . places . . . ! And the polar cap! Really! Chicago, maybe. Or Milwaukee. I might have been going to Milwaukee, but I don't think the polar cap.

FREDDY: Where do you want to go?

EMMA: I don't want to go anywhere.

FREDDY: Nowhere at all?

EMMA: I want to stay right here.

FREDDY: Not me. I'd love to get away.

EMMA: Get away from what?

FREDDY (*beat*): Have you ever been up in a plane?

EMMA: No, I haven't.

FREDDY: When you're up in a plane, the sky is always blue, because you're up above the clouds, see? The clouds are all among you, or below you. You're flying through them, in and out of them—beautiful white clouds. And down below, it's a perfect little world when you're in a plane. There's nothing you couldn't make better by just reaching down and making it right. And above you, when it's night, there are stars. Thousands of stars. You could be in among the stars, for all you know. You could be one of them. I can remember being up at night, looking out around me and thinking, here I am among the stars. I've left the earth behind me altogether.

EMMA (*beat*): When were you ever up in a plane?

FREDDY: Navy Air Corps, ma'am. In the war.

EMMA: You flew a plane?

FREDDY: Yes ma'am.

EMMA: Then you're a pilot. You said you weren't a pilot.

FREDDY: Not any more, ma'am. The war's over.

EMMA: But you were—you were a pilot. That's what I meant. You lied to me. (*She stands up*)

FREDDY: Ma'am?

EMMA: You lied! You said you weren't a pilot!

FREDDY: No, I didn't—!

EMMA: Oh my goodness . . .

FREDDY: What did I do?

EMMA: You said you weren't a pilot and you are!

FREDDY: I was—but not anymore!

(*She goes to the window and looks out*)

EMMA: Is that your car?

FREDDY (*goes to the window*): Yes, ma'am.

EMMA: Is that how you got here?

FREDDY: Yes ma'am, that's the company car.

EMMA: Well, I wish you'd get in it and drive away.

FREDDY: They haven't called from the office yet.

EMMA: I'd like you to go!

FREDDY: I could lose my job, ma'am! (*Pause*) I need this job. It was the only thing I could get and hold onto. There's competition for this kind of job, believe it or not. They'd fire me in a second if they had any trouble with me. They've told me so. There's plenty more where I came from—that's what they say. I'm not what you'd call highly employable. The only other thing I know is how to fly a plane and they won't let me do that anymore on account of my injury.

EMMA: What injury?

FREDDY: I had a bad landing there at the end. I'd lost my right flap and I came in at an angle. I flipped over, got jammed up against my left side here. I got out okay, but I lost most of the strength on my left side. It was the last time I ever flew. I can drive a car all right. It's not the same, but sometimes I use my imagination and it almost seems like I'm flying again. Driving the car, see? In my mind, while I'm driving down East Main with the sunlight coming through the trees, I imagine I'm back in my little baby. And the treetops, the branches hanging down covered in leaves, they're the clouds. With the sunlight flickering through them. And the sky over me. And if I squint a little bit, I can imagine it's the whole earth below me, not just East Main Street. (*Looks out the window*) You'd never think that I could do that, would you. Looking at that old Ford. You'd never think I could imagine such a thing. But that's one thing about me—ever since I was a kid, I had a powerful imagination. I guess I never lost it. (*Pause*) Maybe I should call them again.

EMMA: Maybe you should.

FREDDY (*goes to the phone and dials*): Frank? It's Freddy. (*Pause*) Yeah, uh-huh. Right. No, I'm still here. (*Pause*) She says no, Frank. (*Pause*) Okay. (*Pause*) Okay, I'll see what I can do. (*Hangs up*) He says there's no mistake. They definitely got an order in for a car for Mrs. Emma Thorn, 122 North Maple.

EMMA: Freddy, would you sit down?

FREDDY: What's the matter?

EMMA: Please. (*He sits*)

FREDDY: You're going to cancel the order.

EMMA: I never placed the order. Don't you see? I have nowhere to go. There's no place I want to go. If there were a place I needed to get to, my husband could take me. We have a car, you see. A brand new Chevrolet. It's sitting out in the garage. If I needed to go somewhere . . . well, I don't drive myself, but my husband would take me.

FREDDY: It's not the money, is it?

EMMA: The money?

FREDDY: Because the ride is already paid for.

EMMA: It is?

FREDDY: Pre-paid. In full. It says so on the slip.

EMMA: Who paid for it?

FREDDY: Whoever placed the order, I guess.

EMMA: Of course.

FREDDY: I'll tell you what. How about if I take you out for a spin, wherever you want. It doesn't matter where. And we'll call it even. What do you say?

EMMA: You're very nice . . . but I . . . I can't. I just can't.

FREDDY: I don't know what it is. People do this. They say, "No, not me. I never ordered a car. I don't know what you're talking about. I'm not going anywhere." It doesn't seem to happen to the other drivers, just to me. They said they were going to fire me if it kept up.

EMMA: But that's not fair. It's not your fault.

FREDDY: To them, though—to them it looks that way.

EMMA: Yes of course, but it's not.

FREDDY: But to them . . .

EMMA: I can't imagine anyone refusing to ride in your car because of you. You're certainly not the problem. If there were any reason not to get into that car and drive away, drive anywhere at all, it would certainly not be you.

FREDDY: Isn't there anyplace you'd want to go? Anyplace at all?

EMMA: I'm sorry, no.

FREDDY: Some shopping you might want to do?

EMMA: My shopping is all done.

FREDDY: Someone you want to visit?

EMMA: No, no one.

FREDDY: Just a drive then, around town.

EMMA: I don't think so.

FREDDY: Or out of town. A drive into the country. We could go take a ride into the countryside.

EMMA: No, no, Freddy, I . . .

FREDDY: Find a patch of blueberries. (*Pause*) A patch of blueberries, as wide as the sky, blueberries wherever you look, like a green sky of blue stars, waiting for you to bring them down, put them in your basket.

EMMA: I only know one patch of blueberries. We'd never find a patch like that.

FREDDY: Have you ever looked? (*Pause*) You never really looked, I bet.

EMMA: No, I suppose I haven't.

FREDDY: We could go for a look.

EMMA: For a patch of blueberries.

FREDDY: There's bound to be one, out there.

EMMA: I suppose there must be, but . . .

FREDDY: But what?

EMMA: It might be hours.

FREDDY: Are you on a schedule?

EMMA: Me? No, no schedule.

FREDDY: Then we both have time.

EMMA: It's not a question of time. I just don't know if I . . . if I can.

FREDDY: You mean, are you able?

EMMA: Yes, exactly.

FREDDY: I think you are certainly able.

EMMA: I wouldn't be so sure.

FREDDY: Mrs. Thorn, I think you're very able, if you don't mind my saying so. (*He goes to her*) I think you are able, and willing, and I think you can imagine it. Isn't it true? Isn't it true that you imagine a sky full of blue stars, waiting to be gathered into your basket? (*He takes her by the elbows*) Mrs. Thorn.

(*Horace appears at the door*)

HORACE: Is that your car out there?

FREDDY: Yes sir.

HORACE: I wish you wouldn't park it at the curb like that. They're cleaning the street this morning and they'll have to go around you if you leave it there.

FREDDY: Sorry, sir. I was just going to move it.

HORACE: They only come by once a week, and I hate to be the only fellow on the street with a dirty curb. (*Pause*) I was almost to the office before I realized I didn't have my briefcase. I reached for the door of my building with my right hand, which is the hand I normally use to carry my briefcase. When I reached for the door with that hand, I knew right then, something was missing. That's the value of having a routine, you see. The second the routine is broken, you know something is wrong. You identify the problem, solve it, and get on. (*He picks up the briefcase*) Fortunately, I allow plenty of time to get to work. I can still walk back and be there in good time.

FREDDY: You walk to work?

HORACE: Walking is healthful, isn't it. It wouldn't make sense to drive the car to work. It only uses gas and oil, and the wear and tear—well, it adds up.

EMMA: My husband likes to walk.

HORACE: Indeed I do.

FREDDY: If you like to walk, that's fine.

HORACE: And who are you, may I ask.

FREDDY: I'm from the taxi service, sir.

HORACE: Oh?

FREDDY: There was some kind of mix-up. We thought Mrs. Thorn ordered a car.

HORACE: I don't understand. You people must not have a routine down there.

FREDDY: That must be it, sir.

HORACE: I'd have that business of yours straightened out in no time if I were running it.

FREDDY: Yes sir.

EMMA: It was pre-paid and everything.

HORACE: Is that so?

FREDDY: Yes sir.

HORACE: Well someone is out a sum of money, aren't they.

FREDDY: Yes sir, they are.

HORACE: Someone, somewhere along the line wasn't thinking.

FREDDY: It looks that way.

HORACE: Are you enjoying the coffee?

FREDDY: Yes sir.

HORACE: Black, I see.

FREDDY: Yes sir.

HORACE: Cream and sugar myself.

FREDDY: I like the actual taste of the coffee.

HORACE: I made it, you know. I just got up and made it—didn't seem to require any help at all.

EMMA: I told him, dear.

HORACE: I think it turned out pretty well.

FREDDY: Yes, sir, it did.

HORACE: Well I have to be off. Don't want to come in late—lower management begins to resent you. You take care of Mrs. Thorn, young man. Mistake or no mistake, you're here now. It wouldn't do to leave a woman in distress.

EMMA: I'm not in distress.

HORACE: I thought you were.

EMMA: I don't know why you thought that.

HORACE (*to Freddy*): Are you married?

FREDDY: No sir.

HORACE: Well, there's no use explaining then. (*They kiss and he begins to exit*) And don't forget to move your car. Street cleaners.

(*He exits. She goes to the window*)

EMMA: He's going now.

FREDDY: Yes?

EMMA: He's just turned the corner and now he's . . . he's gone.

FREDDY: I knew a man like that in the war.

EMMA: Oh?

FREDDY: He was in our outfit. No one disliked him, really, but at the same time we hardly knew him. Even now, I can't remember his name. (*Pause*) You all right, ma'am?

EMMA: Yes, I'm all right.

FREDDY: I better be going now. If Frank calls, you let him know I'm on my way, could you ma'am?

EMMA: Freddy?

FREDDY: Ma'am?

EMMA: I believe I'll be going with you.

FREDDY: That'd be fine, ma'am.

EMMA: It does seem to be what he wanted also, isn't it. That isn't why I . . . but I feel it makes it somehow, somehow more . . .

FREDDY: I understand.

EMMA: I am right, aren't I?

FREDDY: You're very right.

EMMA: I'm very right. I'm very right. (*Smiles*) Where shall we go?

FREDDY: We'll drive out of town.

EMMA: Yes?

FREDDY: I know some places.

EMMA: Blueberry patches.

FREDDY: Places there are likely to be blueberries.

EMMA: And if there aren't?

FREDDY: That's no way to think, is it Mrs. Thorn?

EMMA (*looking around*): Well . . . do I need anything?

FREDDY: Not that I can think.

EMMA: Just you and I and your car.

FREDDY: That's right. (*He goes to the door*) Coming?

(*She goes to the door*)

EMMA: Wait. I know.

(*She goes to the basket of blueberries, picks them up, hesitates a moment, then dumps them. They spill across the table and onto the floor*)

Something to put them in. (*She smiles at him*) All those blueberries.

(*He withdraws a light, thin scarf from his jacket pocket and tosses it around his neck*)

FREDDY: After you.

(*She exits. He follows, closing the door. End*)

AN ACT OF DEVOTION

Deborah Tannen

Deborah Tannen

An Act Of Devotion, was commissioned by the McCarter Theater in Princeton and produced by Horizons Theater in Washington, DC. It is Deborah Tannen's first play, but she is well known for fifteen books which have been published worldwide. Her most recent book, *You Just Don't Understand: Women And Men In Conversation,* was on the New York Times best-seller list for four years, and was number one on the paperback list for eight months. It has been translated into eighteen languages and has sold over a million and a half copies.

A new book, *Talking from 9 to 5,* has recently been published by Morrow. Tannen has also published short stories, poetry, and over seventy articles which have appeared in major magazines and newspapers throughout the world.

Dr. Tannen is one of only three University Professors at Georgetown, where she is on the faculty of the Linguistics Department, and she has lectured to schools and universities all around the globe. She has appeared on many national television and radio shows, and has been a public speaker to civic, professional and government organizations.

Dr. Tannen was born in Brooklyn and educated in New York and Michigan. She received her doctorate from the University of California, Berkeley. She is married and lives in Washington, DC.

Characters:

FATHER: *a man of eighty-five*
DAUGHTER: *a woman in her late forties*

Scene:

A hotel room in Warsaw in August, late afternoon. Father and Daughter enter. He is unsteady on his feet. Trying not to be too obvious about it, she keeps an eye on him, ready to catch him if he falls. She throws down packages.

DAUGHTER: Boy, I'm tired.

FATHER: Are you really? I thought you only came back here because you don't think I can get anywhere by myself anymore. Wouldn't you rather have kept shopping with Mother and David?

DAUGHTER: No, I wanted to come back, too. I can't shop that long.

FATHER: What about David? Does he really like it or was he just keeping Mother company?

DAUGHTER: I don't think he minds but I guess he was mostly keeping her company.

FATHER: What a nice guy, your David. I never have the patience to shop as long as Mother wants.

DAUGHTER: Neither do I. And he probably also wanted to give me some time alone with you.

FATHER: How kind of you to say that. Most daughters can't wait to get away from their old fathers.

DAUGHTER: Not when their fathers are like you. We wouldn't have come on this trip if I didn't like being with you. Are you going to lie down on the bed and rest?

FATHER: No, I'll just sit here and read.

(He sits in an upholstered chair, after picking up a newspaper that had been left on it)

Would you like the paper?

DAUGHTER: No thanks. If you read, I'm going to write. I've been wanting to write some things down since our first day. The trip's almost over, and I haven't had a chance to write anything.

(*She sits on the bed, her back against the headboard, and picks up a notebook in which she begins to write. As she writes, her voice is heard reciting what she is writing; very quickly her voice changes to a speaking rather than a "dictating" voice, but the understanding is that the audience is still hearing what she is writing. As she speaks, Father falls asleep, and the newspaper drops onto his lap. By the time Daughter's first speech ends, Father is asleep. With the lights dim, he gets up from his chair, no longer moving like an old man, and speaks in the voice of his memory, a younger version of himself. The tone of both Daughter's and Father's dialogue is understatement and subtle irony, not stereotypically or exaggeratedly Jewish cadences*)

DAUGHTER: The first thing we did after checking into our hotel in Warsaw was to take a taxi to where my father had lived as a child. The street was still there, with its street sign, Twarda (*pronounced "tvarda"*), but in place of the apartment house he had lived in was a grim gray building with a cement wall covered with obscene spray-painted graffiti—a big mouse with a huge phallus that he was gleefully inserting into the rear end of a smaller mouse. I was overwhelmed with the thought that I was standing on the street I had heard my father talk about all my life.

FATHER: We stood under the sign, Twarda Ulica (*pronounced "tvarda ooleetsa"*). How dull and quiet it was, how faceless and bland the buildings that had been put up since the war. When I was a child, the neighborhood was always in commotion and crowded with life. Both sides of the street were lined with stores, and the sidewalks were teeming with people—Hasidim with their long beards, black boots, and the ritual fringes of their prayer shawls peeking out from under their vests. Working men, women shopping, men going to and from the synagogue. There were "tragers"—carriers—men hired by people too poor to hire a wagon, carrying amazing loads on their backs—a desk, a bed. Epileptics would fall down and have convulsions in the street. No one stopped to watch, because it was common. And beggars, everywhere beggars in torn clothes. Some wore garments sewn from sacks, some had rags on their feet instead of shoes. Many of the beggars were cripples. When I came to America, I always wondered: where were the cripples?

DAUGHTER: On the second day, we went to the National History museum where we'd heard there was a film about the destruction of Warsaw during World War II. The narrator told how the inhabitants of the city were deported to another part of the country as the Germans systematically demolished their city. When the war ended, the city's inhabitants returned. There was inspiring documentary footage of the Poles handing stones from man to man as they rebuilt Warsaw—but nothing about the killing of thirty per cent of the population of the city—the entire Jewish population. There were a few fleeting shots of Jews being deported, as the narrator's voice said, "The Jews were the first to go." He neglected to mention that they didn't come back.

FATHER: In the street were droshkis (*pronounced "DROSHkeez"*)—horse-drawn carriages that took passengers, and open wagons for trade. The drivers were beating and yelling at their horses, and yelling at pedestrians to get out of the way. Occasionally a "kareta" drove by—a fancy carriage that rich people rode in. That caused a stir, as people wondered whether a rich person might get out, and what he might be after. Streetcars ran in both directions, their bells clanging. The streetcar tracks ran down the middle of the street, so people waited at the curb and walked out to the streetcar when it stopped. One day an old Hasid stepped off the curb just as an automobile came rushing into the space between the streetcar and the curb, and its wheel ran over the old man's foot. As the man shrieked in pain, the driver stopped his car, got out, rushed over to the old man, and began loudly berating him for getting in his way. Soon after I arrived in America, I saw a cab driver and his passenger standing by the cab, arguing with each other. I couldn't get over the contrast. In Poland, if you were rich enough to drive an automobile, you had the right to yell at anyone. In America, a cab driver, in his worker's cap, was shouting at a rich man in a silk top hat.

DAUGHTER: We went to the Jewish cemetery where my father's grandmother was buried. He told us about attending her funeral when he was eleven, shortly before he left for America. He had walked behind the horse-drawn hearse with his grandfather and his uncles Joshua and Boruch Zishe (*pronounced quickly, it sounds like*

"Bookhzeesha"), as the other mourners rode in carriages behind. He was proud to be walking with the men, until his mother sent her friend to fetch him and make him sit in the carriage with her. When they arrived at the cemetery, he clung to the side of his uncle Boruch Zishe, following him to the room where the body was ritually cleansed before burial. He said his grandmother's funeral was so vivid in his mind, he felt as if he could walk right to her grave, but he couldn't walk to it, because the cemetery he'd visited as a child had been destroyed during the war. Headstones had been smashed by vandals or uprooted by trees that sprouted up; paths had been obliterated by undergrowth. This was the first time I heard my father use the Yiddish name, Boruch Zishe, for the quiet, homely man I had always known as Uncle Bob.

FATHER: Our apartment building was built around a cobblestone courtyard. You entered through a huge archway with wooden doors that were locked at night. There were storefronts facing the courtyard, at ground level. One was a small factory that made frankfurters and delicatessen. We couldn't afford to buy from them, but I always loved the smell. During the day vendors came in, shouting about what they had to sell. Beggars came in and went from door to door, asking for a kopek or a piece of bread, which they'd put into a sack. Singers and fiddlers came into the courtyard. Some people wrapped coins in pieces of newspaper and threw them down. There was a joke that you couldn't tell if the coins were alms or payment to stop the dreadful music.

DAUGHTER: We went to the memorial to the Warsaw ghetto uprising. There's a long approach to the monument, leading up to a dynamic statue hurtling out of a stone wall: muscular young men brandishing arms, who chose to die fighting rather than follow orders for deportation. On another day, a Polish woman, a friend of a friend, took David and me back to see the other side of the monument: a frieze of a throng of people streaming to their deaths—a rabbi carrying a torah, families with children dwarfed by the legs around them. This, she told us, was the truer representation. There were sixty thousand people left in the ghetto at the time of the uprising. Three hundred thousand of the ghetto's inhabitants had been killed in Treblinka in the months before. We had missed this part of the monument on our first visit. We hadn't thought to walk around and look at the back.

FATHER: Vendors came into the courtyard, shouting about what they had to sell. One man had a grinding wheel; people brought him knives and scissors to sharpen. Another man would push a wheelbarrow into the courtyard and set up shop. He took iron pots blackened from cooking and returned them sparkling and shiny. One time my grandmother sent her youngest son, my uncle Boruch Zishe down with some pots, but when he brought them back, one was only half done, so she sent him down again, and he got into a loud argument with the man. An audience gathered to witness his victory, but I was stuck in the house because I was sick. I had to strain to see what I could from the tiny balcony. I couldn't get over the injustice—all my friends got to enjoy the show, and I missed—and it was my uncle!

DAUGHTER: At the ghetto monument, my father got into a conversation with a young Danish woman holding a guidebook. As he walked away, I told her that he had grown up in Warsaw, that his grandfather had died in the ghetto, and that other family members and people he'd grown up with had died there, or lived there and died in the camps. I brandished this information as a badge of honor, as if it gave me a greater right to be visiting the memorial. I also figured it would make her visit more memorable. I've always had this impulse to be helpful to strangers.

FATHER: Our third-floor apartment was my grandfather's home. I was born there, and so was my mother. I lived there until I was seven. My mother was one of the oldest of sixteen brothers and sisters. The youngest was only six years older than I, so I was like the youngest brother, and my grandfather was the closest I ever came to having a father.

DAUGHTER: On the approach to the monument, vendors had set up tables selling trinkets and books. David bought a book about the Warsaw ghetto.

FATHER: For years I thought my grandfather's name was "zahzogit" because that's what my grandmother called him: "Zahzogit, would you pull out that chair?", "Zahzogit, may I have money to shop for food?" Then I found out that "zahzogit" meant "be so good." When she spoke to him, she began that way to be properly deferential to her husband. His children feared him, because he was stern and authoritarian with them, but he was always kind and gentle to me. He once took me by the hand to the "mikvah," the ritual bath. As we walked, I asked him why paper money had value but other paper didn't. At the mikvah, he patiently instructed me on how he covered his facial openings while immersing himself in the water: thumbs on the ears, index fingers on the eyes, middle fingers on the nostrils, and ring fingers on the mouth. I guess the pinkies rested on the chin. (*As he speaks, he places these fingers on his face*) I remember because I was amazed to see him naked!

DAUGHTER: When I was seven or eight, I wrote my first story. It was about my father when he was a child. The story took place in the stairwell outside his apartment in Warsaw. It was a story he'd told me: when he was very little, his mother dressed him in his older sister's outgrown dresses, rather than spend money buying boy's clothes for him. He was too ashamed to go out and play dressed as a girl, so he sat in the stairwell all day and cried.

FATHER: One year I decided to fast on Yom Kippur (*pronounced "yum KIPper"*), because that's what grown ups did. When my mother couldn't get me to eat, she enlisted her father's help in persuading me. He explained that I didn't have to fast because I wasn't bar-mitzvahed yet. If I fasted, it wouldn't please God, but it would displease my mother.

DAUGHTER: I had no idea what the building my father had lived in as a child looked like, so I pictured him in the vestibule of the apartment house across the street from our house in Brooklyn, with its white marble steps, wrought iron railing, and tiny black and white tile floor. I pictured him as the age I was when I wrote my story, but he was probably only three.

FATHER: My mother was married at eighteen to a man she'd never met, and she never liked him. She threw him out when I was two. She never told me directly that I was ugly, but whenever she spoke of my father, she'd say how she hated his looks, especially his long hooked nose. And whenever she spoke about me, she'd say I looked exactly like him. When I did something she didn't like, which was just about anything I ever did, she'd say, "Just like your father." If I slept late, "Just like your father"; if I stayed up late, "Just like your father." The way I ate, what I ate, the time I ate, how I dressed, if I spent money, how much I spent, what I spent it on—it was all the wrong thing, all the wrong way, and all "just like your father." It wasn't until I was an adult and talked to people who knew him that I found out my father had been a wonderful man. They said he was kind, gentle, intelligent, and generous. Everyone loved him, except my mother.

DAUGHTER: My father talked so much about his childhood that I felt it as if it had happened to me. But it hadn't happened to me. I believed that nothing that happened to me could be as significant as what he had suffered. What right did I have to be miserable—which I was.

FATHER: My father wasn't a good business man, and he wasn't practical. He opened a leather goods store with my mother's dowry, and lost it all. She used to tell with disgust how she'd bring him the wholesome lunch she'd prepared for him and find him eating lox and chocolate. Somehow that captured for her what she scorned in him.

DAUGHTER: In my memory, my childhood is an endless train of days spent with my mother, missing my father. He left the house before I woke up in the morning, and he often worked late, so he came home after I had gone to sleep. My favorite object in the house was an old black typewriter with yellow keys rimmed in silver. I'd spend hours typing letters to my father, telling him what had happened to me during the day and laying out my grievances against my mother. I couldn't have any grievances against him, because he wasn't there.

FATHER: My father had tuberculosis. My mother told people that was why she threw him out—so he wouldn't infect my sister and me. And she said she never remarried because she didn't want her children to grow up with a stepfather. Maybe it was true. But I always believed she preferred to live on her own. She wasn't the kind of woman who wanted to spend her life waiting on a man.

DAUGHTER: When I was a child, my father used to say, "We're so lucky we have your mother. If it was up to me, I'd just ride around the country on a motorcycle. Thanks to your mother, we live in this nice, clean house and have regular meals." But I thought riding around the country on a motorcycle with my father sounded fabulous!

FATHER: My mother and sister and I shared a room in my grandfather's house. One night my mother woke me out of a sound sleep, and I saw that my father was there; he must have come by to discuss something with her. She had cooked frankfurters for him, and she woke me up to give me a bite. (She knew I loved them, and they were so rare during the war.) I guess I was still sleepy, because when I tried to swallow the frankfurter chunk, it got stuck in my throat. I don't know if I remember this because it was one of the few times in my life I saw my father, or because I nearly choked.

DAUGHTER: On the days he was coming home in time for dinner, I'd wait for my father to return from work. My sister and I would watch for him in the direction of the subway station. When we spotted him, we'd run to him, and he'd lift us up and enfold us in his arms. Then he'd put us down and walk with us back to the house, holding our hands. I loved the feel of his huge callused hand engulfing mine.

FATHER: In two more memories I have of my father, he is talking to my mother. In the earliest one, I am standing with my mother, holding her hand, at the enormous arch that led into our courtyard. My father is on the other side of her—a tall, reddish man, saying things I can't understand. In the other memory, he is sick in bed in a small room, and my mother is talking to him at his bedside. I was in the room with them, but I couldn't get near. Because of his illness, my mother made me stand at the door.

DAUGHTER: Sometimes when he was home at our bedtime, my father told us stories that he made up himself—long elaborate tales of dragons and eagles in which we were the heroes. We especially begged for "stories with action." As we lay in our beds, he'd move around the room, acting out all the parts, suddenly rushing right up to our delighted, mock-scared, laughing faces. And then, when it was time to sleep, he'd lie down with us, and we'd snuggle up to him with our heads on his shoulder. That way I could always fall asleep.

FATHER: The only other time I remember seeing my father is also the only memory in which he spoke to me. I was walking with him in the country, and we came to a brook. He wanted me to cross it with him, but I was afraid. I was convinced the bottom was quicksand and would suck me in. He picked up a large green pine cone and threw it into the water, to show me that it didn't sink. For some reason, that reassured me, and I crossed the brook with him. Later we came to a field of wheat. I still recall it as one the most beautiful sights I've ever seen: the yellow wheat curved in the breeze as far as I could see. I asked my father if the wheat field went to the end of the world.

DAUGHTER: When I was a teenager, I prided myself on my irreverence. I liked to shock people by saying, "If my father had stayed in Poland, he'd be a lamp shade."

FATHER: When I was six, my father died. He was twenty-seven years old. Since I didn't know him, I wasn't sad; I thought it was an interesting piece of news. When I ran into a neighbor on the staircase, I boasted excitedly that I knew something she didn't. "What is it?" she asked. "That your father died?" I saw from her manner that my excitement wasn't the right emotion to have. "No," I lied. "That isn't it." But I wouldn't tell her what it was.

DAUGHTER: When I call home, I talk to my mother. It's always been that way. When I was younger, she was the one who called me. A few times, after I'd talked to my mother for a long time, she said my father wanted to talk to me. I got a rush of excitement, feeling suddenly important—my father wanted to talk to me! It was like a boy you had a crush on finally calling. But when he got on the phone, he said, "Well, it was nice talking to you." "Wait a minute," I said, "You haven't talked to me yet." "We'll talk when we see each other," he said. "We don't have to make the phone company rich." He had gotten on the phone just to get me off.

FATHER: Though I never knew my father, I certainly knew my grandfather. There was no question in my mind that he was the most powerful, most dignified man in the world, and I was sure everyone else knew this too. But one day, after World War I finally ended, he took me with him on an expedition to the home of someone who owed him money. I was shocked to see the manner he assumed in this house, as he doffed his cap in deference. I couldn't believe my eyes: my grandfather, taking his hat off to someone!

DAUGHTER: Years ago I had a dream. I'm having a birthday party. My father is there, but he's suspended about two feet off the ground, with his head near the ceiling. I don't know what he's doing up there; he doesn't seem to be doing anything, just floating in his own world. I can't reach him, and he doesn't hear me or see me. I desperately try to make contact with him, but he's stuck up there and I can't get him to come down.

FATHER: When we were about to leave for America, my grandfather called me to him and took me on his lap. Tears streamed from beneath his gold-rimmed glasses, down his cheeks, and into his beard. He knew he would never see me again. With his arm around my shoulders, he said, "Never forget that you are a Jew."

DAUGHTER: I'd always known that my father's grandfather died in the Warsaw ghetto, but somehow I'd assumed he died of old age, and the ghetto happened to be where he lived when his time came. In my mind, "the ghetto" was just a dilapidated section of town where Jews were forced to live. But when I read the book David had bought, I realized how much I didn't know—that Jews had been crammed into the ghetto from all over the city and the country; that 100,000 people died there from starvation, and from epidemics that broke out, caused by the overcrowding and unsanitary conditions. Naked corpses lay in the streets—corpses in the street because people had to pay a fee to bury their dead and they had no money; naked because every shred of cloth had to be salvaged and used. Women nursed infants in the street, but they had no breasts, no nourishment to give their dying babies. German soldiers strolled through the ghetto on their way to somewhere else and shot people for fun. I thought I knew about the Warsaw ghetto, but I really didn't know anything about it at all.

FATHER: Those were my grandfather's last words to me: "Never forget you are a Jew." He believed that when Jews went to America, they ceased to be Jews, because they stopped being Hasidic. Have I betrayed him? What do my daughters know of their Jewish heritage? What can being Jewish mean to them, having grown up in America? Only one of them married a Jew—and she doesn't have children, so what difference does it make?

DAUGHTER: We went to the Unschlagplatz, where each day thousands of Jews gathered to be shipped to Treblinka, where they'd be gassed. Today it's a green park with a monument, a series of stone walls. One wall is a glittering white stone slab with Jewish names, meant to represent the three hundred thousand people who had been sent to be killed from this square. Mordechai, Moishe, Shmuel, Abraham, Rachel, Rebecca, Naomi, Leah, Sarah, Miriam,

Deborah. Another stone slab bore the words of a poem. We all lined up facing this wall, and asked my father to translate the Polish text etched into the stone. (*As she speaks these lines, Daughter walks over to Father and stands beside him on his left, as they both enact the scene she describes*) He began to read the words, but his voice faltered, and he stopped. I turned to see that his body was shaking. He put his right hand up to his left cheek, palm out, making a barrier between our eyes, so I couldn't see his face as he sobbed. I put my arm around him. He gathered himself up and started to read again. But again, he stopped. Again, he held his hand to the side of his face, like a shield against my gaze. On the third try he read:

FATHER: "Earth, do not cover my blood; wind, do not silence my screams . . ."

DAUGHTER: As we walked away, my mother whispered to me that in the sixty years of their marriage, she had never seen him break down before. Days later, he told David that what overcame him was a picture in his mind of his grandfather and his uncle Joshua, the only son who had stayed behind with the old man, and Joshua's wife and five children. They had all almost certainly been shipped to their deaths from the spot on which we stood. And he kept thinking, "What had they done to deserve their fate? They had never done anything to hurt anyone." I was envious that my father had confided this to David and not to me.

FATHER: I stood under the street sign, Twarda Ulica. Inside my head, it was all still there: the busy courtyards, the people calling out of the windows, the streetcars clanging, the drivers yelling, my grandfather going to shul. But outside, there was nothing. No trace of the world I grew up in. In place of the three-story apartment house with its courtyard was a gray utilitarian building covered with obscene graffiti. After I'm gone, who will remember? If no one remembers, what will remain?

DAUGHTER: My father wanted to take pictures of the Jewish cemetery, but he hates to waste pictures with no one in them, so he asked David and me to stand in front of a wall that had been built of the broken prices of tombstones that had been smashed during the war. David posed for the photos, but I hung back. I couldn't figure out if it was a desecration to pose for pictures, like tourists, in a place like that, or if it was an act of devotion, to try to remember.

(*During Daughter's last speech, Father has taken his place in the chair, asleep, the newspaper in his lap. The telephone rings; they both jump. Daughter picks up the receiver, which is on a night table on the side of the bed where she has been sitting up*)

DAUGHTER: Oh, hi Mom. We're fine. Daddy fell asleep, and I'm writing. No problem, take your time. See you soon.

(*She hangs up the phone*)

FATHER: What were you writing about?

DAUGHTER: I was writing about you.

FATHER: About me? I'm flattered, but what could you write about me? I'm not interesting.

DAUGHTER: I was trying to write down the stories you've told me, but I could only remember a few. I want to get them all.

FATHER: I'll be happy to tell you more, if you have time. But you're busy and I don't know how much longer I'll be around.

(*She gets up and walks to where he is sitting across the room, and kisses him*)

DAUGHTER: Daddy, you can't die before I write it all down. Promise you won't.

FATHER (*he laughs*): I'm not planning to go yet. I always regretted missing the turn of the century. I was born eight years too late. I plan to stick around to see the year 2000. I'd hate to miss it a second time.

(*Curtain*)

ZIPLESS

Ernest Thompson

Ernest Thompson

Zipless had its premiere production at Alice's Fourth Floor in New York City on February 11, 1994. It is the second part of a trilogy called *Valentines For Two.* Part one, *The Valentine Fairy,* was included in *Best American Short Plays 1992–93.* The final installment will be produced in 1995.

The cast for *Zipless* was the author and Julie Hagerty, and was directed by Susann Brinkley.

Thompson's other plays include *On Golden Pond* (Best Play, Broadway Drama Guild), *The West Side Waltz* (starring Katharine Hepburn), and *A Sense of Humor* (with Jack Lemmon). He has also written *The One About The Guy In The Bar, Human Beings, The Playwright's Dog, Amazons In August* and *Murdering Mother.*

On Golden Pond won Thompson an Academy Award for Best Screenplay Adaptation. He wrote the screenplays for *Sweet Hearts Dance* and *1969,* which he also directed, and wrote and performed in the NBC Movie of the Week, *The Lies Boys Tell.* A television film of *The West Side Waltz,* two feature films, *The Love Line* and *The Red Rovers,* and a new play, *Rip Your Heart Out,* are forthcoming.

Ernest Thompson resides in New Hampshire with his wife Kristie, an architect, and their three children, Heather, Danielle and August.

A play that defies the standard restriction imposed in the theatre. Time and place are only suggested. Whole chunks of life elapse without notice and the audience comes along because we invite them. The set need be only a few chairs or boxes and all props, with one exception, are indicated. At lights up, a woman sits at a bar, jotting on a napkin, having a one-way dialogue.

DORA: I'm waiting for someone. Very large and menacing. (*As if answering*) Leo, Virgo rising, my moon is in the seventh house. Advertising, I write jingles. I can't think of any offhand.

(*A man saunters in and sits by her*)

DICK: Hi, how ya doin, nice night, nice crowd, good mix, you alone?

DORA: Chicago. Well, actually just outside, in Rockford County.

DICK: Uh. I hate to have to ask this, but what sign are you?

DORA (*not looking at him*): Dora.

DICK: Oh. I'm a Dick myself. On the cusp of scrotum. (*He smiles*) What sort of work do you do, Dora? I don't mean to pry.

DORA: East 80s, it's a sublet. I'm not really an East Side person.

DICK: Are you picking up static on the line? Whatcha writin here?

DORA (*covering it*): June 15th. I hate June, because you have to make plans for the summer. I never have plans. Everyone else has plans, but not me. It's very sad.

DICK: Well. I was just working out at the gym, I usually stop in and try to counterbalance whatever possible good I've done to myself on the Nautilus. Have fun in Bellevue.

(*He wanders to another part of the stage. She continues, oblivious*)

DORA: Available? No. Except Wednesdays. And sometimes Tuesdays and Thursdays if they don't need me on the Suicide Hotline. And weekends. Mondays I have my Coexisting in Society class, and then Cooking for One. (*She looks about. Dick has his jacket off, working out, grunting. Dora steps to him shyly, watching*) What's that prepare you for? Some of these machines, I notice, lend themselves to practical application. Are you a fireman?

DICK: Mountain climber.

DORA: Oh. What mountains have you climbed, anything I would know?

DICK: Vernon. Mt. Vernon, Mt. Cisco. Several of the Royal Canadian Mounties. You're from the bar. What'd you, track me down?

DORA: No. It's just a coincidence. (*He nods skeptically, he flexes*) Yes, so? Is that supposed to turn me on?
(*He nods, licks his biceps*) It doesn't. I'm not interested in how strong a person's muscles are. I like to know the strength of someone's heart, and head.

DICK: Yeah? Look at this. (*He pounds his head on the "machine"*)

DORA: You're not a mountain climber. You just said that because you're a man and you feel duty bound to impress me, not to mention your rampant insecurity.

DICK: Really? I guess you know what I'm going to say next then, too.

DORA: Probably a swear word.

DICK: Nah. I was just going to comment on my lack of judgment in getting out of bed this morning, going to work, eating shit for lunch, then running into a shrivel-twat ball-breaker like you.

DORA (*she smiles*): Those are wild words. The mating call! I accept. (*He scowls. Puts on his jacket, holds a car door for her. Sits*) You learn so much about a person by the car he drives. You, I'm happy to see, are clean, moderately well-off, and not a smoker.

DICK (*pulling out a cigarette, the real prop*): It's my brother's car.

DORA (*she takes the cigarette and breaks it*): So? Dick.

DICK: Yes? Cunt.

DORA: Your name is Dick, isn't it? Or was that a lie, too? Because that would seem like an unsuccessful direction to go in.

DICK: My name is Dick. Said trippingly on the tongue. Not Diiicckk.

DORA: You're sensitive, I like that. My name is Dora, said any way you like. Dick and Dora. What do you know, like the movie.

DICK: All we need is a dog named Asshole.

DORA: Conversely, I don't like profanity. I don't feel it serves any useful purpose other than to alienate. Can we agree on that?

DICK: I don't see why the fuck not. (*He speeds*) This is like the movies. You ever notice that, how people steer in movies? (*He mimes absurdly*) You would throw up riding with them. (*He slams on the brakes, Dora is thrown about. He stares at her*)

DORA: You have the look of love in your eyes. Or are you stigmatic? I have a cousin who sees triple, lives his life in a crowd. (*He kisses her*) Oh. You kissed me. Have I already contracted something, do you think? I'm not a jump-into-it girl.

DICK: No shit.

DORA: I try to be open-minded. But there are certain aspects of life and love, in spite of my best efforts, I still find repellent.

DICK: So we probably won't be butt-fucking on the first date then?

DORA (*she cries*): I'm sorry. I'm such a brick. I would love to be free and easy, I would, just the way Jong said it should be.

DICK: Jong?

DORA: Jong.

DICK: Erica or Carl?

DORA: I want it to be zipless, Dick, I really do. I just need to get to know the person first. (*He nods, discouraged. She puts her arms around him, sweet*) I have a joke for you.

DICK: You have a joke? Now? This is not a joking time.

DORA: It's a knock knock joke. Say it, say knock knock.

DICK: But I don't know the joke. (*Giving in*) Knock knock.

DORA (*a mischievous grin*): Dora's open, come on in. (*She kisses him meaningfully. They stand, holding hands*)

DICK: To love, honor and . . . to agree with occasionally, to fuck with gusto, to share the covers with and always put the seat down.

DORA: And obey. You didn't say obey.

DICK: To tolerate your mother, to not punch your father in his fascist mouth. To watch football sparingly. And to never fart.

DORA: And to obey. Excuse me, he didn't say obey. This doesn't count.

DICK: It's your turn.

DORA: I wanted it to be traditional. We should have done it in Latin, then no one would've known what the hell we were saying.

DICK: There's no point in my being married if you're not.

DORA: I promise to obey. But not you. I'll obey myself. I'll be pliant but not acquiescent, I'll menstruate unnoticeably, I'll cook sensible meals and forgive you for not appreciating them. And I'll keep my crippling sense of disappointment to myself. (*She unfolds a paper*) Please join me in a brief wedding song I personally composed, when I was eleven. It's to the tune of the German, Mein Dachshund, Mein Dunkelheit. (*And also, as a point of departure, the Lennon-Ono "Happy Christmas" song*) The Valentine bride . . . (*She glares at him*)

DICK (*singing faltering*): And the Valentine groom . . .

DORA AND DICK (*sort of*): With hearts open wide, rose up from the gloom, of life, and said, I love you so gravely, it's a love beyond blame. I was hoping you'd save me, so I could do the same. (*They kiss*)

DORA: This is the new part: (*She sings*) I've rewritten my policy, you're now my beneficiary, I hardly can wait till I die. (*She elbows him*)

DICK (*he sings*): No, I will obstruct you, because now I can deduct you, I'm seeing my dependents multiply . . . (*End of song, he stares at her*) So. You actually wrote that.

DORA: Yes. And thank you for not sodomizing my humble effort.

DICK: No, it's lovely, in a trapezoidal sort of way.

DORA: You missed the point. Two minutes into our marriage and you're already dumb as toast.

DICK: What is the point?

DORA: Forget it, stupid. (*Relenting*) OK. I'm pregnant. (*She grins*)

DICK (*in French*): Pardon? That's not possible. We haven't been to Club Med yet and had a ménage à trois and mutually masturbated.

DORA: Well. Who needs a tan when you can have a glow?

DICK: I do! I have fantasies that I wanted to realize. I wanted to wear costumes and pretend we were astronauts alone in the space shuttle except they're watching us in Houston ground control.

DORA: This is a fantasy, Dick. It is. (*She lies back, hips up*) Look, we're creating life! (*She screams*) Acch! Isn't it beautiful?

DICK: Um. Well . . . from my particular vantage point . . . I never want to eat turkey again, I'll tell you that.

DORA: I'm breathing—in, out, IN, GODDAM OUT! I'll forget the pain, that's what they say. It had to be a man who thought that one up. I'd like to turn his pecker inside out! It's coming! Acch! (*Dick catches "the baby", holding it awkwardly*) My god, Dick! Now I understand! Why we're married, why we were born, why we put up with all the miserable crap of life.

DICK: Why? (*He lies with her and the baby*)

DORA: Hmm? He has your looks. But my brains, thank God. (*To it*) Who painted all the little Polynesian people in Tahiti? (*Cooing*) Gauguin. Yes! He's a genius!

DICK (*watching, troubled*): I guess you probably don't want to put him to sleep and walk out in the moonlight and blow me or anything.

DORA: Silly. (*To it*) You're daddy's a big silly. Mommy's going to teach you to be sensitive at all times and to pick your spots. And learn German folk songs. Loi dee doi, dee doi dee doi . . .

DICK (*turning away, to the audience*): Today's lecture is on the Pythagorean Theorem and how it impacts modern man, when his wife has no time for him. Some of you may want to move closer. Not you. You, in the spandex. It might be reassuring if you were to sit by me, it could help your GPA.

DORA (*from a distance, holding the baby*): You're not cheating on me. You're not that low class, are you?

DICK (*to an imagined coed*): A square plus B square equals C square. This is very sophisticated stuff. Very sexy.

DORA: You broke the sacred trust. You big fat prick. Diiicckk.

DICK (*to the coed*): E, on the other hand, equals mc^2, which only proves that when you get right down to it, everything in life, every transgression and grievance and heartache, is relative.

DORA: What do you want to do now, now that you've taken the fragile sand castle of our love and pissed all over it?

DICK: Let me make it clearer: a train leaves Chicago, heading west at ninety m.p.h. Another heads east from Detroit, also doing ninety. On the same track. You know what happens? (*He claps*) This is the true theory of relativity: love hurts, life sucks, train wrecks are not good for you. (*He turns sadly away, back to Dora*) Are you OK?

DORA (*to the baby*): Tell him my general health and well-being are none of his business.

DICK: I miss you. Tell her I miss her.

DORA: Tell him I'm glad and that I can only hope his prostate turns to concrete.

DICK: Tell her I'm lonely. Tell her I'm losing sleep, I'm losing confidence, tell her I'm losing my mind.

DORA: Tell him how happy that makes me. But don't tell him I miss him, too. Don't tell him I'm sad. Don't tell him to come home. (*She makes room for him, he sits*) It's embarrassing to discover we are nothing more than clichés. The misunderstood husband, the lonely wife. The fucked up child. We're so Geraldo.

DICK: Shh. (*Watching the baby on the floor*) What's he doing?

DORA: Growing up. He's walking already. (*To it*) What's the hurry?

DICK: That's walking? Is he drunk? He's running. Where's he going?

DORA: He's running away. He doesn't like us. You scared him. No, he's coming back. He has something in his hand, what is it?

DICK: It's a gun, get down.

DORA: It's not a gun, he's four years old. It's flowers, for his mommy. What a smart boy to bring mommy flowers. Oh, and Daddy, too.

DICK (*taking them*): Um, thanks. You little fag. What's he doing?

DORA: He wants to play with you, he wants to play ball.

DICK: I'm not going to play ball with an eight-year-old, I'll kill him. (*Holding his crotch, where the boy has planted the ball*) Ow! OK, go out for a pass. Go on, keep going, keep going, go to another town. (*He throws that ball, watching, pleased*) Look at that, he caught it, the kid's a jock, just like me.

DORA: Go, sweetie! That's my baby! Tackle those buggers, hurt them!

DICK: Maybe he'll get a scholarship to Penn State and quit and join the NFL and buy us a condo. And be everything I wanted to be.

DORA: Mmm. He looks handsome, doesn't he, in tights? Go, sweetie.

DICK: He's a fairy. Why would a boy want to be a modern dancer? What does that even mean?

DORA: It means he can have a life of beauty and pain and expression and starvation. The lucky kid. We should be so proud of him.

DICK: Yes. I guess so. Go, son! Tour jêté, plié! Wear a condom. (*They look off in the direction he went, wistful. Look at each other*)

DORA: That was fast. What are we going to do now?

DICK: I don't know. Have a drink. (*He does*) I thought I might learn to tie flies. You know, for fishing. Some of the other professors seem to get pleasure out of it. (*He ties one*)

DORA: But you don't fish.

DICK: No. But I tie. Look. This look like a ring winged gypsy moth?

DORA: The spitting image. I just question how one benefits from spending one's time doing something he doesn't do.

DICK: Look a dragon fly. A may fly, a house fly. A humming bird.

DORA: I was thinking of going back to work, possibly. Would you mind, would you notice? (*No response. She turns away, sitting for an interview with an imagined executive*) Years ago, when I was unbelievably young, I wrote jingles. You're familiar with the Löwenbrau song? I didn't write it, but I liked it. How about Mercedes-Benz? (*She sings*) When you drive a Benz, you make lots of friends, interesting men and ladies. When you own a Mercedes. They almost went with it. I like German folk songs, they're my inspiration. Though I understand that may not immediately qualify me for the Come To Israel account. (*She steps back to Dick, shyly proud*) Well. We're a two income family.

DICK (*drunk, still tying*): A butterfly, an octopus, a small monkey.

DORA: I suppose I should be grateful they hired me at all. I just feel that even working in payroll gets me close to the action.

DICK: An alligator, a submarine, an old shoe.

DORA: I figure I can write at home, in my spare time, which you certainly are allowing me plenty of, for which I'm grateful.

DICK: A cement block, a pirate's chest, my dreams . . .

DORA (*singing*): The Valentine bride got married and died . . .

DICK: My youth, my enthusiasm—a fish would eat this shit right up.

DORA (*singing*): And the Valentine groom sat in his room and tied. Flies, we don't know why. It makes one cry. (*She does*)

DICK (*noticing at last*): You're . . . very beautiful when you cry.

DORA: And you're very perverse. You like runny noses? Where were you when we had a child? He occasionally had caca, we kept it secret so as not to upset you.

DICK: I like your juice. I like the emollient of your passion. I like your sadness. (*He tries to kiss her*)

DORA: Good thing, I've got lots of it. What are you doing? It's the middle of the afternoon.

DICK: Yes. Undo my pajamas.

DORA: No! Stop it! Who do you think you are?

DICK: Fuck me, please, before it's too late . . . Please! You angel, you saint, you bitch! (*He rapes her, sags by her on the floor*)

DORA (*she pulls herself up, moves away, to another bar. She sits, chatting with someone*): Leo, Virgo rising, my moon is in the seventh house. Advertising, I write jingles. I write pay checks. I write police complaints and divorce papers, who are you?

DICK (*he stands stiffly, facing his students tiredly*): Today's lecture is on the subject of mission bells. If nine bells chime in the village of Anna Capri and a fisherman hears them, as he rows solo past the Blue Grotto, what—sort of fly would he use? Yes? Can't hear, sorry. What relevance does it bear? It bears no relevance. Thank you. (*He walks away, to the bar*)

DORA: Oh, what are you doing here?

DICK: Was in the neighborhood, nice neighborhood, lots of queers. Lot of women in here. I could have a good time in a place like this.

DORA: I don't think so. (*To someone else*) He's OK, he used to be my husband, he's been altered. See ya later.

DICK (*watching curiously*): Wasn't that intimate? The sort of thing that could turn an insecure man's thoughts to lesbianism and other threats to his flimsy masculinity.

DORA: I'm glad you're secure. It's very attractive. She's my lover.

DICK: Ah. I'm from Pluto, I ever mention that? Tell her to come the fuck over here, I wanna punch her out! Hey, you! Rug muncher!

DORA: Dick. They'll kill you in here, they really will. You don't have to go any further to prove what a fool you are.

DICK: (*he calls, trying to sound contrite*): Sorry. Les-be friends. (*To Dora*) I hate to have to ask you this, but what does she have that I don't have?

DORA: It's the other way around. We write songs together. How's the fishing?

DICK: OK. Was just in Alaska, fishing for salmon. (*Facetiously*) With my boyfriend, Bruno. (*Unexpectedly sincere*) I miss you now and then, thought you'd like to know.

DORA: You miss raping me or you miss avoiding me or you don't want to grow old gracelessly alone or what?

DICK: I saw the baby.

DORA: What baby is that?

DICK: Our son. The machine welder.

DORA: Our son is a sculptor. And he's thirty-one.

DICK: Ah, well. His nose still runs. He told me you were happy.

DORA: And what, you've come to fix that?

DICK: I've come to find out how that could be. Maybe you could lend me some. Happiness.

DORA: Are you familiar with the theory of relativity?

DICK: No. Not since I took early retirement.

DORA: Every hiding place is heaven till you get found out. You OK?

DICK: Oh, yes. Probably. You? (*She nods. Shrugs*) Well, OK. Bye. (*He turns away, sits on a pier, fishing*) There are seven signs of advancing dementia. One, you know the seven signs. Two through five are the obvious ones, you talk to yourself. Worse than this, you find yourself interesting. You take careful stock of everything you've ever discarded. You rack your brain to think of the simplest things, like number five. Number six is phantom pain, such as amputees feel, pain that has no cause but hurts like a bastard anyway. Number seven is hearing voices, the sad laughter of children you once knew or gave birth to or were, the boring humdrum of teachers and parents and garage mechanics, everything they ever said comes back to you, with accents "You got da broken carboorater, why you no change de oil, you stupid?" And lovers, people you loved and lost and who lost you, too, sing songs to you in the wind.

DORA (*singing from a distance*): The Valentine bride . . .

DICK: You look, but there's no one there. Just your stubbornness, just your expectations and disillusion, written on the clouds. It's enough to drive you fuckin' bonkers.

DORA (*singing*): And the Valentine groom rose up from the gloom and said I love you so gravely. Dick? Can you hear me? (*Singing*) It's a love beyond blame. (*She stands by him*) She left me for an older woman. With no teeth presumably.

DICK: Ah. No comment.

DORA: Guess where I've been staying? With our little boy. Of forty.

DICK: Oh, good. He still have the junkyard?

DORA: Sculpture garden. He's still waiting for you to approve of him.

DICK: Oh that. I'll, um, I'll try to drop by and see him. I bought a little boat, it doesn't run, maybe he could fix it.

DORA: Sounds artistic, I'm sure he could. How's your health?

DICK: Fine, good. A minimum of agony. Don't ask about my mind.

DORA: What's wrong with it?

DICK: With what? (*Staring at her*) What's wrong with you?

DORA: Nothing, that a little death wouldn't cure. My doctor has this theory that I'm dying. I can't seem to talk him out of it. You'd be amazed how much it doesn't help to be stared at.

DICK: I'm sorry. (*He looks away*)

DORA: Me, too. (*She sings*) I've rewritten my policy, you're gonna win the lottery. (*A wistful smile*) Sorry we never quite made it to Club Med. Think they'd still have us?

DICK: Sure. They welcome people with saggy flesh, it looks so good in the brochure. You could sit here with me, by the dank and fetid waters, and we could pretend. We could fantasize. (*She smiles, sits painfully*) How long do you have?

DORA: Oh. A few minutes. To illustrate that he's a better man than us, Junior has very generously imposed no curfew on me.

DICK: That's not what I meant.

DORA: I know what you meant. I'm proud to say I didn't ask. (*Pause*) This is not the way I'd imagined it. Damn it, fuck it! (*Dick nods. Puts his hand on her shoulder. They sit in silence*) You would seem an odd sort of person to have as a friend. I'm a Leo, did I mention that? My moon is in the seventh house. Maybe we could stay there, over the summer. You seem mellow, what's wrong with you? It's very attractive.

DICK: Thanks. It's amazing what having one's nuts removed will do for a person.

DORA: I didn't do that to you, did I, Dick?

DICK: Yes, but I had them surgically restored. And enhanced. (*He mimes how big they are*) So thank you. (*He checks his line*)

DORA (*watching him wistfully*): You seem peaceful. Can you give me some? Can you give me a piece?

DICK: Sure. (*He whistles*) Didn't see my dog, did you? (*Calling*) Asshole! (*She sings quietly*) I was hoping you'd save me, so I could do the same.

DORA (*she nods, touched*): Merry Christmas, by the way. For all the ones we missed. And the ones . . . we missed.

DICK: Right. Happy birthday.

DORA: Fuck you. Happy New Year. Never mind, too depressing.

DICK: Happy Halloween, that's a safe one.

DORA: Yes. And Armistice Day.

DICK: Happy Martin Luther King. To show our admirable PC-ness. Happy Flag Day. (*She seems to be asleep. He looks at her, worried. She looks up, smiling faintly but comforted*)

DORA: Happy Valentine's. (*She rests her head against him*)

DICK: Same to ya. (*He cuddles her*)

(*Curtain*)

DATE WITH A STRANGER

Cherie Vogelstein

Cherie Vogelstein

Cherie Vogelstein's career was launched in the sixth grade when she wrote *My Kingdom For A Hammentaschen* for the Purim festival. She has received the Hobson Award for excellence in playwriting from Johns Hopkins University, a Rhodes Scholarship nomination, and an MFA from Columbia University's School of Playwriting. Her plays have been successfully produced in New York, Baltimore and Los Angeles.

Ms. Vogelstein won the 1991 Warner Bros. Comedy Writing Talent Search, and co-founded Aural Stage, a New York-based theatrical alliance of playwrights, actors and directors. She chaired the playwriting department for the National Handicapped Theatre Workshop, created a line of greeting cards (Noah's Art, Microsoft), and was playwright-in-residence for the New York Teen Theatre. Her musical *Lost And Found* is currently touring the East Coast. In the summer of 1993, her play *Misconceptions* had a sold-out off-Broadway run.

Ms. Vogelstein is presently working on her first screenplay. She lives in New York City with her husband Eric and their newborn son, Zachary Tov.

Scene:

A typical Manhattan diner. Paula, 29, nibbles at a muffin as she furtively glances over at Clark, 31, seated two stools away. Clark self-consciously reads MY MOTHER, MY SELF, steals a look at Paula whenever he can. At the end of the counter, a business man, early 40's, impassively reads THE WALL STREET JOURNAL throughout the action of the play. Note: Paula and Clark must swing furiously from emotion to emotion without missing a beat. They experience life as it is: fast, big, and uncensored.

PAULA (*reaches across Clark for sugar*): Sorry.

CLARK (*smiles graciously, slides it to her*): No, no, please.

PAULA (*giggles, pours sugar steadily into cup*): I really, really like sugar in my coffee.

CLARK (*explodes in laughter*): HAHAHAHA! Hello!

PAULA (*also laughs nervously as she continues to pour*): And now I'm ruining it!

CLARK (*this is even funnier*): OH WOW . . .

PAULA: Anyway . . .

CLARK: Hmm . . . yeah . . . (*Beat. He reluctantly returns to book*)

PAULA (*plunges back in*): You know, I was watching you turn those pages. And I was wondering to myself, "Is he really reading the words of that book?" I was wondering that so much.

CLARK: Oh, well, what I always say is, when you're reading . . . why fake it, right?

PAULA (*nodding contemplatively*): Hmm, that's what they say about orgasms, but . . .

CLARK (*moves quickly to stool next to her*): But?!

PAULA: Oh my God! How did that . . . I'm so embarrassed . . . I can't say another word!

CLARK: Yes you can . . . come on . . . who am I? A stranger, nobody, nothing. (*Urgently*) TELL ME!

PAULA: Okay but what if we went out to dinner or something, you know, say to Ernie's where we'd get salad, bread, spinach pasta with almonds and—

CLARK: Whoa, whoa, whoa! I'm allergic to almonds.

PAULA: Really?! I'm lactose intolerant! That is so funny! Anyway, there we'd be, taking a cab home, waltzing into the apartment, French kissing like teenagers, maybe you'd have a tough time getting my bra undone—

CLARK (*amazed*): How did you know that?!

PAULA (*nods, points knowingly to her head*): Anyway, if we, you know, DID it, and I had told you now that I, you know, fake my orgasms, you'd be worrying I was faking it the whole time.

CLARK: No way! What would I care?

PAULA (*upset*): You don't care?

CLARK (*confidentially*): Well no, I care. I care A LOT, but see, if I told you I cared, it would inhibit you from faking it and I want you to feel free to fake it, I want you to have a really good time faking it, see?

PAULA (*touched*): Yes. I do. (*Almost touches his hand*) You're not bisexual, are you?

CLARK: Who, me? (*Macho*) Come on, do I seem it? Ha . . .

PAULA: No, it's just—

CLARK (*tense*): Because I'm not—

PAULA: It's just . . . you're so sensitive—

CLARK: Well, I really like the way you took the initiative with me—

PAULA (*horrified*): What?! Is that what you thought I was doing?

CLARK: Oh well I uh . . . isn't that what you meant to be doing? (*Nervous laugh*)

PAULA: Not so that it would seem like I was doing it—

CLARK: Oh, well it didn't. That was just my women's intuition talking.

PAULA (*suspicious*): What are you doing with women's intuition, Mister?

CLARK (*quickly*): Nothing. I just meant . . . I have a strong feminine side to my personality.

PAULA (*relieved and happy*): Hey! So do I!

CLARK: Which is not to say I'm not all man which I am (*flexes muscle*) but I still read books like MY MOTHER, MY SELF (*beat*) because I care.

PAULA (*staring deep into his eyes*): Are you . . . are you attracted to me?

CLARK: Why? Are you attracted to me?

PAULA: I asked you first.

CLARK: But I asked you right after, very quickly.

PAULA: Yes but it's very important for you to perceive yourself as the pursuer, otherwise—puh, puh, puh—God I love P's and things that begin with P. Can you think of some? Porch, ping-pong, penis, pumpkin—I'm stalling—I feel vulnerable because of the attractive issue you didn't answer me you don't want to answer me—police, pigeon, PUTZ—

CLARK: Look, I do want to answer you, and believe me, I will, but before I do, I first want to say, and I'll say it now—there are a lot of things I perceive myself as, but not being the pursuer is definitely not one of them, okay?

PAULA (*great sigh of relief*): Thanks, that really helped. (*She swallows some pills, smiles*)

CLARK: You look pretty when you smile.

PAULA (*unsmiling*): And when I don't smile?

CLARK: You still look pretty.

PAULA (*sweet smile*): How pretty?

CLARK: Very pretty.

PAULA (*still playful*): Prettier than say, your last girlfriend?

CLARK: Hmm, yeah, I'd say that.

PAULA (*dead serious*): Say it.

CLARK: Uh, you're prettier than my last girlfriend.

PAULA (*playful again*): Oh, you're just saying that. (*Bashful beat*) Anyway, it's not like I think my looks are the most important thing in the world, you know.

CLARK: Good for you!

PAULA: How so?

CLARK: Well, beauty is only skin deep.

PAULA: Bullshit, Mister. Swear on your mother's life I'm prettier.

CLARK: Gladly. I hate my mother.

PAULA: Just what the hell are you trying to say?

CLARK: That she really knows how to get me mad—you know, in a funny way, you kind of remind me of her.

PAULA (*horrified*): Your mother?

CLARK (*thinking he's off the hook*): No, no, my ex-girlfriend.

PAULA (*with relief*): Oh! (*Ferocious*) That's even worse!

CLARK: Wh-why?

PAULA: Well I mean did you want to marry this woman? I don't get it—

CLARK: Not really.

PAULA (*shaking with fury*): Not really?

CLARK: Well . . .

PAULA: Look: did you break up with her or did she break up with you?

CLARK: I don't know how to put it really—

PAULA: How about she dumped you like a plate of hot, steaming shit?

CLARK: Yeah! That's it exactly!

PAULA (*starts eating ferociously*): Terrific. Just terrific.

CLARK: What—I don't understand!

PAULA (*starts to sob*): How am I supposed to feel here? You're still carrying this torch, for Christ's sake—

CLARK: No, no, no—

PAULA (*devouring food*): I hate feeling like second best. Like if she had wanted you, you'd still be with her instead of me. I mean, THIS IS ALL I NEED!

CLARK: Listen, please, don't worry about that, really—I was dying to break up with her myself, I mean . . . her rates were going through the roof!

PAULA: Her rates?

CLARK (*nods*): She was my therapist.

PAULA: You had sex with your therapist?

CLARK: Well sure. I mean, eventually you run out of things to say, right?

PAULA (*turning indignantly away*): I'm certain I don't know.

CLARK (*trying to recover*): Oh, oh of course not, how could you? Because the truth is, you're really not like her at all—you're . . . you're much prettier and . . . you never look at your watch, and you're realiy special! I promise!

PAULA (*mollified*): And when you first saw me, you got the jolt?

CLARK: The jolt?

PAULA: You know. That feeling of all your energies dropping right into your underpanties—you . . . you got that with me?

CLARK: Oh yeah, I got that. I'm still getting it. (*Beat, moves in closer*) Hi, I'm Clark.

PAULA: (*sipping coffee*): That's your name? Clark? I LOVE IT—"Clark." I never met a Clark before. That's so wild. (*Sips*) "Clark." I love saying it: "Clark, Clark." It's like wearing dentures in a beautiful kind of way. "Clark." I could just go on saying it all day. "Clark, Clark, Clark, Clark, Clark, Clark—"

CLARK: Yeah, you've really got it down—but listen, can I be frank with you for a second?

PAULA: Oh God, I was so enjoying you as Clark—

CLARK: No, no I mean about the coffee—you . . . you've got to give it up.

PAULA (*wide-eyed*): I do? (*He nods, she makes a decision*) Alright. (*She throws cup over her shoulder*)

BUSINESS MAN (*momentarily looking up*): What the hell—?

CLARK (*shakes his fist in victory*): Now that's what it's all about—sacrifice!

PAULA (*intensely*): Yes! Are you Jewish?

CLARK: Now you ask? No. Are you?

PAULA (*haughty*): As a matter of fact, I am. And a pretty committed one at that.

CLARK (*happy*): Oh! How committed are you?

PAULA: Well, I'm so committed that I would never marry out of the faith.

CLARK (*deeply disappointed*): Really? That's too bad.

PAULA: Alright look. Maybe I would. I'm not a fanatic, you know.

CLARK: Good for you!

PAULA: Oh Clark, wouldn't it be great if we could just skip all the formalities and automatically be living in the same apartment, really committed to making it work?

CLARK: Yes, but you never told me your name.

PAULA: Guess.

CLARK: Hmm. I like it. It's different.

PAULA: No, I mean guess my name.

CLARK: Oh okay. (*Thinks hard*) Debbie?

PAULA: Right!

CLARK: Really? That's right? I can't believe I guessed it on the first guess, that's amazing! But I knew it, you know? (*She nods*) You look like a Debbie, I just knew you had to be a Debbie.

PAULA: That's funny because I'm not. I was just testing you. My name's Paula.

CLARK: Wow. You're a very complicated person, aren't you Paula?

PAULA: Michelle, and it's funny you should say I'm complicated since all my life, people have gone on and on about how incredibly shallow I am.

CLARK (*laughs*): That is funny but I guess I meant that you're so deeply shallow that that's something I find complicated because I'm very complicated myself in a way.

PAULA: Are you? Or are you just a big buffoon with delusions of grandeur?

CLARK: Gee, wow—

PAULA: Stop it Annette! I'm so mad at myself. I mean this is how I destroy all of my relationships—why? Why do I have to protect myself at your expense, Ken?

CLARK: Clark.

PAULA: Exactly! Why am I so terrified of commitment, you know? I mean, why can't I just let my hair down with you and get naked with you and love you my God, body and soul?

CLARK (*thinks*): You're asking some good questions.

PAULA: Sometimes I dream I'm in a shtetl in Warsaw and life is so simple: I know my place, I know my chickens, I'm at peace. (*Scared*) Until of course the Cossacks come and knock my father into a ditch, raping my sisters over and over and over—(*she's spent*)—Yes! That felt good.

CLARK: Wow, you're really real, aren't you? You're all out there.

PAULA: Where?

CLARK: Here. You're really here.

PAULA: God, you really know where I am.

CLARK: Okay, look: I sell health club memberships at the Paris. That's what I do.

PAULA: Oh.

CLARK: That turned you off.

PAULA: Oh, now you're going to say we Jewish girls only care about money and success, aren't you? It's just like my mother warned, that's always what it comes down to in the end, isn't it? The Goy always ends up calling the Yid a dirty Jew.

CLARK: Believe me, there are alot of repulsive, heinous, disgusting, putrid, ugly, gross things I'm going to call you, but dirty Jew is not one of them.

PAULA: Oh Clark, tell me all of your faults.

CLARK: Why?

PAULA: So I can feel superior to you.

CLARK (*angry*): Is that really what you want?

CLARK: I shouldn't have said— PAULA: More than anything, darling—

CLARK: Sorry I accused you, I— PAULA: I'm sorry I said that, I—

(*They laugh*)

CLARK: Our first fight! It was inevitable!

PAULA: I enjoyed it!

CLARK (*he moves in close*): It brought us closer together.

PAULA (*she moves back*): You have something in your nose.

CLARK (*shaking his finger at her*): Unh uh uh, you're trying to distance yourself—you're not being who you are, Michelle—

PAULA: Annette.

CLARK: Susan.

PAULA: Janet.

CLARK: Paula.

PAULA: Yes! God, you know me like a piano.

CLARK: A book.

PAULA: A piano book—Clark! New York is so scary! Here we are, intimate as two poppyseed humentaschen and you might be plotting my murder as we speak.

CLARK: Believe me, that's not what I'm plotting.

PAULA: Really? What are you plotting?

CLARK: You don't want to know.

PAULA: Yes I do.

CLARK: I've been fantasizing crazy things.

PAULA: Sick things?

CLARK: Stupid things.

PAULA: Dirty things?

CLARK: Unrealistic things.

PAULA: Does it involve animals?

CLARK: No.

PAULA: Then tell me.

CLARK: I've been fantasizing about you in this soft, billowing white gown.

PAULA (*worried*): A hospital gown?

CLARK: No, it's a . . . a wedding gown.

PAULA: Oh, Clarky, yes!

CLARK: And I'm wearing a black, fur hat and those long, curly sideburns the Hassidim wear, what are they called?

PAULA: CHassidim.

CLARK: What?

PAULA: Not HAssidim, CHassidim.

CLARK: No, I mean the sideburns, what are they called?

PAULA: Look, I'm not a mind reader.

CLARK: I'm not a Jew.

PAULA: I'm not a therapist.

CLARK: I'm not a kleptomaniac!

PAULA: Touché. (*She removes salt-shaker from her purse, returns it to counter*) Go on.

CLARK: That's as far as I got.

PAULA: Okay: I was just thinking of mine while you were talking.

CLARK: That's alright, I thought of mine while you were talking.

PAULA: Oh well please try not to do that anymore, it really hurts my feelings. (*Pouting*) I mean, here we are on the threshold of marriage and—Clark, wait! Are you circumcized?

CLARK (*embarrassed smile*): Well . . .

PAULA (*horrified*): You mean you still have your foreskin?!

CLARK: Not with me.

PAULA: Then convert! Convert for me!

CLARK: Wow. That's a big step.

PAULA: Then do it for the baby.

CLARK: The baby?

PAULA: I'm pregnant.

CLARK (*whispers*): Really?

PAULA (*also whispers*): In the fantasy.

CLARK (*whispers*): Is it my child?

PAULA (*indignant, loud*): Of course, my God, what do you think I am?

CLARK: Look. I'm not good with children. You might as well know that.

PAULA: I don't believe you.

CLARK: Believe me.

PAULA: How do you know?

CLARK: I know.

PAULA: How do you know?

CLARK (*angry*): I just know, Paula, I don't want to discuss it!

PAULA: Hey! I think this merits a little conversation, don't you? I mean it's not some insignificant, little matter you just brought up, Clark, you dropped a bombshell on me—I think I have a right to know!

CLARK: O.K., O.K., O.K., O.K., I'm not good at hiding things. Ten years of therapy, seven days a week, including holidays, has destroyed my capacity to hide things. I can't hide it from you. It seems

I can't hide anything from you. I'm sterile, Paula. I'm half a man. Not even. Three sevenths.

PAULA: Oh my God, Clark. I'm shocked. I'm so sorry. I didn't mean to—

CLARK (*a pressure cooker*): To what? To get turned off? To look at me differently? To stop loving me? Is that what you're trying to say? Then just say it. Let's not play games. Let's not beat around the bush. Let's not NOT tell it like it is, Paula, shall we not? You just lost your jolt, now didn't you? Didn't you? (*He leans close to her face*) DIDN'T YOU? (*He pulls back with a disgusted sneer*)

PAULA (*quickly covers her mouth*): Is my breath bad?

CLARK (*also covers his*): Why? Is mine?

PAULA (*shaking her head, sympathetically*): Listen, I'm sorry about your . . . impotency.

CLARK (*shouts*): I'm not impotent, I'm sterile!

(*Man With Newspaper looks up with interest, turns page*)

CLARK (*deeply morose*): And I'm not really sterile . . . I was just kidding.

PAULA (*reaches out to him*): Oh Clark—

CLARK (*grabs her hand*): Oh Paula! Most people are so bitter—but not me, I can't be. I sit here listening to so many sob stories, I can't help but feel my life is better than it really is. Much better. (*Beat*) God! I wish it was half that good. (*Beat*) Because it stinks, my life stinks! Oh, it's not so bad, it's really—

PAULA: —I know how you feel. My husband treats alot of people like you.

CLARK: Your husband?! You're married?

PAULA: To a doctor!

CLARK: My God . . . well . . . good for you.

PAULA: What's so good about it?

CLARK: If you're happy then it's good. It's great—

PAULA: Do I seem happy?

CLARK: I've discovered that people are not always what they seem, Annette. For instance, you seemed single.

PAULA: Now what the hell does that mean?

CLARK: Why did you go on and on about what I thought of your looks if you're married?

PAULA: I still treasure your opinion, Clark. You're a very important person in my life.

CLARK: Why did you let me go on and on about our marriage? Why did you tell me you were pregnant with our child?

PAULA: I was making small talk.

CLARK: My God, I thought . . . I thought . . .

PAULA: I know.

CLARK: I feel used. I feel foolish.

PAULA: I feel bad, I feel rotten.

CLARK: Do you?

PAULA: Not really. I feel powerful, I feel sexy. I feel like I got you to love me so fast.

CLARK: Fast? You call three hundred and ten years fast?! Why, I was just remembering how we drew water from the old town well together. I saw us crossing Iowa in a covered, shitty wagon. One of our horses broke his leg and we had to shoot him.

PAULA: Oh Clark—

CLARK (*choked up*): I loved that horse—(*notices her hand*)—hey! If you're married, where's your ring?!

PAULA: I'm not married.

CLARK: Oh thank God!

PAULA: I only said that because I thought it would be less painful for you than being rejected for your sterility.

CLARK: Paula, I lied.

PAULA (*hopeful*): You mean . . . you're really not sterile?

CLARK: No I lied when I said I was kidding. I am sterile.

(*Man With Newspaper looks up again, he screams*)

THAT'S RIGHT, ALRIGHT?—I'M STERILE! I'M STERILE, I'M STERILE, I'M STERILE!

(*Man shakes his head, turns back to paper*)

PAULA (*tries to quiet Clark*): Well don't brag about it. Look: I need children. I can't live my life with a man who . . . (*warming to him*) . . . but then I look into your dilated pupils and bulging member and I think . . . he deserves more.

CLARK: So then maybe you could live with a sterile man?

PAULA: No. But at least I think you deserve more. (*She hangs her head*)

CLARK (*in agony*): My God, my God, I feel like I'm seeing you for the first time.

PAULA: And what do you see?

CLARK: I see that your nose is big—

PAULA: Clark! (*She rises, he rises with her*)

CLARK: —and you're overweight—

PAULA (*big gasp*)

CLARK: —and you're a cheap, sadisitic, manipulating whore!

PAULA (*calmly*): That's true. (*Sits*)

CLARK (*begins circling her*): There she sits so high and mighty downing the sugar from her muffin and the fat from her cheesecake and the cholesterol from her butter my God! I thought I had problems, but I'm a model of health compared to you!

PAULA (*indignant*): Name somebody who isn't.

CLARK: And to think . . . I thought . . .

PAULA: It was just the jolt.

CLARK (*bangs fist on table*): NO! I thought it was MORE than the jolt! Much more!

PAULA: What could be more than the jolt?

CLARK: The mighty, mighty jolt!

PAULA (*relenting*): Alright, there's that, but still—

CLARK: No, no I'll do the but-stilling, lady, because I've learned a lot about myself through you. I've learned that I don't need women who only need children, and I don't need children who only need those kind of women and I don't need Prozac but most of all, Margaret, I don't need you!

PAULA: I'm sensing a little hostility here, Mister.

CLARK: That's the way things usually end, you spread-eagled slut.

PAULA: Oh! So you're telling me it's over?

CLARK (*venomously*): Don't be stupid. We never had anything to begin with but your fake orgasms.

PAULA (*thrilled by the memory*): Ahh, they were something else, weren't they? (*Goes to him*) Oh Clark, we had some good times, didn't we?

CLARK (*nods, sits broken-hearted*): It just goes to show you. You never know somebody till . . .

PAULA: Till what?

CLARK: Till after you meet 'em. (*He holds his head in his hands*)

PAULA (*softly, painfully*): I . . . I can't believe this is happening to us.

CLARK (*agonized*): I know. (*Beat*) I know.

PAULA: We're like . . . strangers—(*Clark looks up at her with desperate love*)

CLARK (*reaching out to her*): Oh Paula—

PAULA (*completely recovered, she turns to man with newspaper*): Excuse me, are you reading that paper?

MAN: You mean the one in my hand?

CLARK (*to Paula, shocked*): What are you doing?

PAULA (*to Man*): Yes, I was wondering if—

CLARK (*approaches*): What are you trying to pull here?

PAULA (*through clenched teeth*): Do you mind? (*To Man*) I was won—

CLARK: You're acting like you don't even know me.

PAULA (*to Man*): —if I might borrow a section of—

CLARK (*incredulous*): In front of me? You do this right in front of me?

PAULA (*hisses to Clark*): I'm trying to get on with my life! (*To Man, adorably*) Could you please pass the salt?

CLARK (*muttering to himself*): That's the same way we—(*to Man*) Don't do it, man, don't do it! She'll take your heart and—

PAULA (*to Clark, furious*): STAY OUT OF MY LIFE!

MAN: I'm not reading the Metro section. You want that?

CLARK (*staggering about*): I can't take this! I won't, I can't, I won't.

(*He takes his soda and book and goes to stool at end of counter. The Man then moves to Clark's original seat*)

PAULA (*to Man*): I used to just read the News Summary but . . .

MAN: But? (*He moves closer as the lights fade to black*)